BLAZING STAR, SETTING SUN

OSPREY
PUBLISHING

JEFFREY R. COX

THE GUADALCANAL-SOLOMONS CAMPAIGN
NOVEMBER 1942–MARCH 1943

BLAZING STAR, SETTING SUN

OSPREY PUBLISHING
Bloomsbury Publishing Plc

Kemp House, Chawley Park, Oxford OX2 9PH, UK
29 Earlsfort Terrace, Dublin 2, Ireland
1385 Broadway, 5th Floor, New York, NY 10018, USA
Email: info@ospreypublishing.com
www.ospreypublishing.com

OSPREY is a trademark of Osprey Publishing Ltd

First published in Great Britain in 2020
This paperback edition was first published in 2021
by Osprey Publishing Ltd

Hardback ISBN: 978 1 4728 4046 2
Paperback: 978 1 4728 4047 9
ePub: 978 1 4728 4045 5
ePDF: 978 1 4728 4044 8
XML: 978 1 4728 4048 6

Maps by www.bounford.com
Index by Angela Hall
Typeset by Deanta Global Publishing Services,
Chennai, India
Printed and bound in Great Britain by CPI (Group)
UK Ltd, Croydon CR0 4YY

23 24 25 26 27   10 9 8 7 6 5 4 3 2

Editor's note
Throughout the book particular names, places, terms or measurements might be presented more than one way, depending on how the US or the Japanese respectively referred to them. For example, where the story is being told from the Japanese viewpoint, kilometers are usually used, and from the US perspective miles are used. Aircraft names are presented as the Japanese designation (e.g. "G4M" or "Type 1") and also as the Allied reporting name (e.g. "Betty"). The Japanese called a certain airbase "Buin" but the Allies called it "Kahili". Unit names would sometimes change over time as well.

About the author
Jeffrey R. Cox is a litigation attorney and an independent military historian specializing in World War II, Ancient Greece, and Ancient Rome. His first interest was in the Pacific War, which he has studied for more than 30 years. A student of history, international affairs, and defense policy for most of his life, Cox holds a degree in National Security Policy Studies from The Ohio State University and a doctorate of jurisprudence from Indiana University School of Law. He is a contributor to Military History Online (www.militaryhistoryonline.com) and resides in Indianapolis.

The Woodland Trust
Osprey Publishing supports the Woodland Trust, the UK's leading woodland conservation charity.

www.ospreypublishing.com
To find out more about our authors and books visit our website. Here you will find extracts, author interviews, details of forthcoming events and the option to sign-up for our newsletter.

CONTENTS

LIST OF MAPS

PROLOGUE:

RUMBLINGS

As May 9, 1883, turned into May 10, 1883, the lighthouse keeper at the southeastern entrance to the Soenda Strait – a place sailors called Java Head – had felt a slight rumbling: an earthquake, it seemed. Not a large one; it was barely noticeable, especially in the East Indies, where earthquakes big and small were, and still are, common. This one seemed different, though. Unlike the normal instances when two tectonic plates collide, this tremor seemed to reverberate through the air, not the ground. Like a whisper. The lighthouse seemed to shift on its foundations. And the water ...

For an instant, the water seemed to freeze and turn white.

Five days later there was another rumbling, stronger, more widely felt.

This strange phenomenon continued for almost two weeks. Then even stranger things – ominous things – started happening.

On the morning of May 20, the people of Batavia (as Jakarta was then known) felt these weird tremors, but they also heard a distant booming sound, like artillery – from where, they could not tell. The next day the tremors continued and reports filtered in of smoke rising miles into the air from an old volcano in the Soenda Strait thought long extinct.

Known in the language of the Dutch rulers of the East Indies as "Perboewatan," the volcano was not a visually impressive one. It was one of three volcanic cones that formed what sailors referred to as "The Island With The Pointed Mountain," an uninhabited island that looked something like an old boot with a tapered shaft. Perboewatan was the northernmost and shortest volcano, perched on top of the toe of the boot.

The rumblings continued into mid-June. Then several loud explosions caused a thick black cloud to cover the island, seemingly ending the commotion, at least for the most part.

August 22 found Captain W.J. Watson and the crew of the commercial sailing ship the *Charles Bal* sailing from Belfast to Hong Kong. As it approached the Soenda Strait from the west, Watson noticed the water looked unusual and had a strange white appearance.

As they got closer to the strait, thick black clouds formed and frequent lightning struck. The morning of August 26, 1883, the *Charles Bal* passed Java Head and entered the Soenda Strait itself.

Captain Watson took note of the many islands ahead in the strait. One of them, The Island With The Pointed Mountain, was almost completely hidden by more thick black clouds. As the *Charles Bal* headed across the strait toward the Java coast, the crew watched aghast as a giant ash column shot up from the island, followed by a thunderous boom, which later became an almost continuous roar. The crew found themselves facing a dark squall, which was, in fact, an ash cloud – one so thick that day immediately turned into night. Complete blackness engulfed the *Charles Bal*, illumination provided only by the constant if uneven strikes of lightning. Ash and large chunks of pumice rained down on the ship, choking and blinding the crewmen trying to shovel it overboard, before it could make the ship top-heavy and capsize it. The thunder of what sounded like a thousand cannons echoed through the heavy, sulfur-soaked air.

"[F]earful" and "truly awful," was how Captain Watson described it. But not fearful or truly awful enough to turn around and head away from it, it would seem. The skipper doesn't appear to have asked if getting his cargo to Hong Kong on time was worth sailing through *this*. The *Charles Bal* groped her way along, all alone, in the darkness, passing The Island With The Pointed Mountain somewhere to port, glimpsing maybe the lighthouse near the town of Anjer (Anyer) on the Java coast ahead. Only then did Captain Watson order the ship to turn around.

And head straight for The Island With The Pointed Mountain.

Exactly why, Captain Watson never really explained, which suggests that he and his crew simply wanted to see the volcano. Around 11:00 pm, Watson and the crew of the *Charles Bal* were rewarded by finally being able to see through the ash and lightning, dead ahead of them, The Island With The Pointed Mountain, now some 11 miles away. In the midst of her titanic tectonic convulsions: "Chains of fire appeared to ascend and descend between it and the sky," apparently on the northern part of the island between Perboewatan and the middle volcanic cone, a series of peaks known as Danan, "while on the [southwestern] end there seemed to be a continued roll of balls of white fire," which were probably coming from the "Pointed Mountain" itself, the tapered shaft of the boot, the southernmost and by far the tallest cone, called Rakata.

Having satiated her curiosity, the *Charles Bal* and her crew turned back toward the north to head out.

As dawn of August 27 approached, Captain Watson was able to make out the lighthouse at the coastal town of Anjer and later the town itself. But his hails brought no response. As far as he and his crew could tell, normally friendly Anjer was deserted. The *Charles Bal* moved on.

The atmosphere seemed to clear up, for a time. Around midmorning Watson and his crew heard a "fearful explosion" from the direction of The Island With The Pointed Mountain, now some 30 miles away. Then the darkness quickly returned. With utter blackness overhead, like a blanket blocking all sunlight, the *Charles Bal* endured a pelting of hot mud that continued for most of the rest of the day. The darkness would not clear for another two days.

Captain Watson and the crew of the *Charles Bal* escaped as the only people to see firsthand even part of this cataclysmic phase of the volcano's eruption and live. They did not see the "fearful explosion"; no one could have witnessed it and survived. "Fearful explosion" was something of an understatement. It was heard 3,000 miles away off Africa. Though the *Charles Bal* was lucky enough to have been shielded somewhat by a land mass, ships 40 miles away from the explosion suffered entire crews with ruptured ear drums. Anyone near the explosion would have been liquefied by the shockwave.

If all this was not bad enough, the blasts caused tsunamis to roll into the Soenda Strait. Anjer itself was wiped out, leveled to its building foundations. Hundreds of villages were decimated. Countless corpses, of man and beast, were washed through the Soenda Strait and into the Indian Ocean, visible for weeks afterward.

After the tsunamis had subsided the next morning, a coastal steamer poked its way through a Soenda Strait that was almost unrecognizable from just 24 hours earlier. The strait was now filled with new ash islands, some more permanent than others. Other, older islands were nowhere to be seen, including The Island With The Pointed Mountain. All that remained was a sliver of The Pointed Mountain, Rakata, looking like half a pyramid, sheared roughly down the middle.

No one knows exactly why the island disappeared – was it blown apart or did it collapse into a caldera? – only that what sailors called The Island With The Pointed Mountain was just … gone. But the locals' name for the island – "Krakatau" – though misspelled in a news telegram announcing the catastrophe, became instantly immortal, infamous, a symbol of death, destruction, and disaster on a biblical scale: Krakatoa.

Quietly, surreptitiously, through the hundreds of years of unchanging landscape, geological pressure of a barely imaginable magnitude had been building, creating a pressure cooker under Krakatoa, until the earth itself could no longer contain it. The world changed as a result of Krakatoa. The map changed. The people changed. Indigenous Indonesians seethed at what they considered to be the sluggish and indifferent rescue efforts by the Dutch colonial government, leading to a death toll that they claimed was more than 100,000. The Dutch colonial administration made some reforms, but they were too little and far too late. The damage had been done. The fire had started and would continue growing, slowly but inexorably.

Something else was growing, too. In the Soenda Strait, in a spot roughly between where Danan and Perboewatan had been, a lava dome was trying to break through the water and stay there. In 1930, it finally succeeded. A baby volcano. The Indonesians christened it *Anak Krakatau* – "Child of Krakatoa."

Anak Krakatau was growing – at the rate of five inches per week, at least until almost all of it slid into the Soenda Strait in December of 2018, at which point it promptly started growing again. Growing with it was the anger in the East Indies. While indigenous peoples across the world chafed at colonial rule in varying degrees, relations between government and governed in the Netherlands East Indies veered toward the worse end of that spectrum. By the early 1940s, the native Indonesians regarded the Dutch with feelings ranging from indifference to hostility, an attitude that did not go unnoticed in Japan. Having gobbled up pretty much everything worthwhile in mainland China, Japan was turning its covetous eyes toward what its Emperor Hirohito and ruling clique, led by Prime Minister General Tojo Hideki, called the "Southern Resources Area" – Malaya and the Netherlands East Indies – whose conquest they considered essential for Japan to become self-sufficient.[*]

Even before Pearl Harbor and the events of December 7, 1941, the Dutch knew their East Indies were a primary target of the Japanese offensive. But the Dutch had to defend the Indies without the support of its native population, a split that was skillfully exploited by the Japanese, and without the support of the mother country, now under Nazi occupation. Though there was some assistance from the US, Britain, and Australia, Dutch colonial efforts against the Japanese in the East Indies were akin to trying to defend Hadrian's Wall from both sides.

Even the preparations the Dutch had made for the inevitable turned out wrong. Although they had had the foresight to build a network of airfields across the Indies to aid in its defense, they had failed to properly defend those airfields from Japanese ground attacks. And on those rare occasions when they had set up a proper defense, the local troops often fled without firing a shot. The Japanese conquered the airfields and turned them against their former owners, creating an impenetrable protective umbrella of Japanese air superiority.

Not surprisingly, by the end of March 1942 the entire Netherlands East Indies had fallen to the Japanese. As the Japanese swept across Java and the Pacific, the local indigenous population mostly greeted the Japanese as liberating heroes while Anak Krakatau watched silently.

At sea some 3,700 miles from Anak Krakatau, 59 years after the disappearance of Krakatoa, and eight months since the Japanese conquest of the East Indies, in the early morning darkness of November 10, 1942, Lieutenant Commander John Tennent was watching the effects of the first depth charge just dropped on a Japanese submarine by his ship, the USS *Southard*. Lieutenant Commander Tennent was not looking to be a liberating hero. Nor was his ship. Indeed, the *Southard* would not normally be at the tip of the spear. She

---

[*] The emperor's given name of Hirohito is used here because of its familiarity to readers, but it should be noted that in Japan its use is considered improper. According to Japanese tradition, the name of the emperor was not referenced during his rule or after. Only in the West was the emperor called by his given name, Hirohito. In Japan, he is properly called by his posthumous name, Showa, the name the emperor gave to the era of his rule. "Showa" means "enlightened peace." Hirohito would use this period of enlightened peace to start two wars.

had been a *Clemson*-class destroyer, a kind of destroyer built too late for World War I yet too early for World War II.

But though old and obsolete by any standard, the *Clemson*s remained very useful ships. They were still excellent antisubmarine platforms; they still had large banks of torpedoes, and they were almost infinitely modifiable. The US Navy often converted remaining *Clemson*s into minesweepers, minelayers, seaplane tenders, fast transports, and basically anything needed – in the *Southard*'s case, a minesweeper.

And though the *Southard* had not been at the tip of the spear, she had been pretty damn close. She was there the morning of August 7, 1942, bombarding suspected Japanese positions before clearing the way for the landing craft carrying US Marines to Guadalcanal and Tulagi in the deceptively bleak southeast corner of the Solomon Islands in the South Pacific.

That was how, on August 7, 1942, the *Southard* had been witness to the beginning of a new phase of the Pacific War, Operation *Watchtower*. Ever since Pearl Harbor, and especially since the destruction of the US Army's Far East Air Force on December 8, the sinking of the British battleship *Prince of Wales* and battlecruiser *Repulse*, and the destruction of the US Navy's Cavite Navy Yard on December 10 – all by air attack – Japan had been on the offensive. Like a kraken, the Japanese had methodically, voraciously, and viciously grabbed one strategic objective after another, in some cases even grabbing them simultaneously: Guam, Hong Kong, Wake, Malaya, Singapore, Rabaul; which quickly became Japan's major fortress in the South Pacific; Lae, Salamaua, the Netherlands East Indies, the Philippines.

This is why *Watchtower* was more than a military operation; it was the changing of a mindset, from desperate hunted to opportunistic hunter and, for the enemy, vice versa. It was a mindset Fleet Admiral Ernest J. King, Commander-in-Chief of the US Fleet and Chief of Naval Operations, had been trying to instill since he took command in December 1941. Being outnumbered and outgunned was no excuse for inaction. "Make the best of what you have" was his philosophy. *Watchtower* was that philosophy manifested.

As a general rule, to have the best chance of success, a military operation requires meticulous planning, thorough intelligence gathering, careful logistical arrangements, massive husbanding of resources, comprehensive organization, and exhaustive preparation before that first shot is fired. Naturally, *Watchtower* had none of the above.

Admiral King was brilliant, determined, arrogant, and in some instances actively disliked.* Well aware that he was far more respected than liked, King strove to have the US Navy maintain an aggressive posture. Even in the midst of the dark days after Pearl Harbor during the Japanese offensive across East Asia and the Pacific, King would needle his subordinates, including Admiral Chester Nimitz, the new commander-in-chief of the

---

* General Dwight Eisenhower once said of Admiral King, "One thing that might help win this war is to get someone to shoot King. He's the antithesis of cooperation, a deliberately rude person, which means he's a mental bully."

Pacific Fleet, to not just wait for the next Japanese attack, but to take the war to the Japanese, to attack at every opportunity. It was left to Admiral Nimitz, mild-mannered and tactful but no less brilliant or aggressive, to translate Admiral King's directives to his subordinates in the Pacific Fleet – not always an easy job, especially in the midst of the Japanese offensive.

It was on December 31, 1941, that Admiral King, at the Arcadia Conference between President Roosevelt and Prime Minister Churchill, issued his first substantive orders to Admiral Nimitz. The Pacific Fleet was, first, to hold the line at Hawaii-Midway and protect the lines of communication with the West Coast. Second, and "only in small degree less important," the fleet was to protect the lines of communication with Australia.[1] Because the Arcadia agreement was very clearly "Europe First" for resources and efforts, the declaration did state that efforts in the Pacific would involve "Maintaining only such positions in the [Pacific] theatre as will safeguard vital interests and deny to Japan access to raw materials vital to her continuous war effort while we are concentrating on the defeat of Germany."[2] "Vital interests" was left undefined. Moreover, "points of vantage from which an offensive against Japan can eventually be developed [were to] be secured."[3]

And Admiral King had a plan for securing those "points of vantage." As Vice Admiral George Dyer pointed out, while Australia was some 7,000 miles from San Francisco:

A straight line on a mercator chart from San Francisco in California to Townsville [...] passes just south of the island of Hawaii and just south of Guadalcanal Island in the Solomons. In Admiral King's belief, the Japanese should not be permitted to impinge on this line, if the line of communications from Hawaii to Australia through Samoa, Fiji, and the New Hebrides was to be secure.[4]

The Solomon Islands were an archipelago of volcanic islands some 1,100 miles northeast of Townsville, the principal Allied airbase in northern Australia, and about 1,100 miles east of New Guinea, across the Coral Sea. The very tropical islands of the Solomons were a jumble of names granted by European explorers – Guadalcanal, Bougainville, New Georgia, New Florida, Shortland, and others, comprising a double chain of islands running northwest, where Bougainville acted as a plug on the double chain, to southeast, where the chain ended at the island of San Cristobal. Largely forgotten since the 19th century due to a hostile climate, even more hostile native inhabitants, and the lack of natural resources, the Solomon Islands were about to get very popular, very quickly.

It was on March 2 at a meeting of the newly formed Joint Chiefs of Staff – with Admiral King, Army General George Marshall, and Army Air Force General Henry "Hap" Arnold – that King passed out his proposal. It was summarized in nine words: "Hold Hawaii; Support Australasia; Drive northwestward from New Hebrides."[5] "The general scheme or concept of operations is not only to protect the lines of communication with Australia," he wrote, "but in so doing to set up 'strong points' from which a step-by-step general advance can be made through the New Hebrides (southeast of the Solomons), Solomons, and Bismarck Archipelago (northwest of the Solomons)."[6]

Admiral King's Army counterparts, Generals Marshall and Arnold, were completely uninterested in the Pacific War – that is, until General Douglas MacArthur was rescued from the fall of the Philippines in March 1942. Douglas MacArthur was a national hero with a formidable public relations machine that made him a domestic political threat to President Roosevelt. Keeping him on the sidelines was out of the question, a reality that was well known to everyone. For the first time, General Marshall became open to reinforcing the Pacific for offensive action – if that offensive was led by MacArthur. It also brought up the question of whether the Pacific needed to be like Europe under General Eisenhower and have one theater commander. Douglas MacArthur was the obvious choice – to the Army, at any rate.

But Douglas MacArthur had his ... quirks. When the Japanese first attacked the Philippines on December 8, 1941, MacArthur "demonstrated his unique leadership style: when he was good, he was very, very good[;] when he was bad, he was horrid."[7] After long predicting the Japanese could not attack until spring of 1942, MacArthur had refused to consider evidence that a Japanese attack was, in fact, imminent. Then, after being informed of the Pearl Harbor attack, MacArthur disappeared for several hours – the first hours of the war – apparently shell-shocked that his predictions had been proved wrong. Disastrously, he allowed his aircraft to be destroyed on the ground at the Clark Field base complex. The result was an inability to even contest Japanese control of the air over the Philippines, and, later, the Netherlands East Indies. MacArthur refused to position supplies on the Bataan Peninsula for a protracted campaign because the idea of withdrawing there was "defeatist," so that when MacArthur ultimately did withdraw to Bataan, his troops had neither the ammunition nor the food for prolonged resistance. After the situation in the Philippines went south, Roosevelt ordered MacArthur to go south, too, all the way to Australia, leaving the troops he had so poorly served behind, to spend the rest of the war in Japanese prisoner-of-war camps.

The Navy was well aware of Douglas MacArthur's quirks. During his time in the Philippines, MacArthur had constantly berated the Asiatic Fleet and its commander Admiral Thomas C. Hart as not being worthy of the name. The destruction of MacArthur's air force gave the Japanese air superiority that they used to destroy the Asiatic Fleet's main base at Cavite. To top it off, MacArthur blamed the collapsing situation in the Philippines entirely on the Navy. Unsurprisingly Admiral King, with the full backing of the Navy leadership, vowed that MacArthur would never have operational command of the Pacific Fleet.[8]

As a result, on March 9, the Joint Chiefs created two command areas of the Pacific theater. One, the "Southwest Pacific Command," comprised the Philippines, the Netherlands East Indies, Australia, the Solomon Islands, and the adjoining ocean areas under General MacArthur. At his new headquarters in Melbourne, MacArthur told a reporter, "[T]he best navy in the world is the Japanese navy. A first-class navy. Then comes the British navy. The US Navy is a fourth-class navy, not even as good as the Italian navy."[9] Admiral Nimitz got the rest as part of a "Pacific Ocean Area," with him, like General MacArthur, reporting to his respective service chiefs on the Joint Chiefs of Staff, who would be conducting this Pacific War by committee. Nimitz's Pacific Ocean Area was further divided into three regions – North, Central, and South – with boundaries at 40 degrees north latitude and the equator. Admiral Nimitz could directly command the first two, but the new South Pacific Command for the area south of the equator would have to be handed off to a subordinate, with Vice Admiral Robert L. Ghormley eventually selected.[10]

Admiral Ghormley, 59, had served in destroyers and battleships, followed by multiple staff assignments culminating in a stint as chief of the War Plans Division in 1938–39, in which he earned a reputation as "a brilliant strategist."[11] Considered by King to be "a very able man," Ghormley was highly respected for his intelligence and well liked by his subordinates.[12] Even so, many shared the opinion of Lieutenant Colonel Samuel Griffith of the 1st Marine Raider Battalion, who later wrote, "It is not entirely clear what prompted King to this appointment."[13] While one cannot rise to flag rank without some sense of politics, and, indeed, there has been some suggestion that Roosevelt, a fan of Ghormley's, may have interceded on his behalf, Ghormley seems to have been shy and introverted, especially among peers.[14] An outgoing personality is not needed to be an outstanding commander or a capable administrator, but Ghormley's previous positions had never required the proactivity he would need in the South Pacific.

On April 16, King's assistant chief of staff for planning, Rear Admiral Richmond Kelly Turner, presented a four-phase "Pacific Ocean Campaign Plan," which would become the basic plan for the US Navy in the Pacific. Phase One was the buildup of forces and bases in the South Pacific to secure the area and position for an offensive against the Japanese. Phase Two was an offensive through the Solomons and New Guinea to seize the Bismarck and Admiralty islands. Phase Three would extend that offensive to the central Pacific, such as the Marshall and especially the Caroline islands. Phase Four would involve a drive into the Philippines or the Netherlands East Indies, "whichever offers the more promising and enduring results."[15]

Admiral Turner had also recommended the establishment of an amphibious assault force in the South Pacific. King agreed and ordered Admiral Nimitz to create it. Orders were passed to Admiral Ghormley to "prepare to launch a major amphibious offensive against positions held by the Japanese." The Pacific Fleet staff conducted studies that examined the Santa Cruz and lower Solomon islands. King made Turner commander of this new amphibious force. Turner, very uncharacteristically, admitted that he knew little of the subject. Calling Turner by his nickname, King responded, "Kelly, you will learn."[16] Turner, like most in this new war, would have to learn on the fly, something that American officers would later call "makee learnee."[17]

Like King and Nimitz, Admiral Turner would leave his sizable and controversial imprint on the Pacific War, starting with *Watchtower*. At 57 years old, he looked like a college professor, with the intellect, the vision, and the patronizing manner to match. A trained aviator, Turner would be described by eminent naval aviation historian John Lundstrom in strident terms: "A tough, bright, even brilliant officer, 'Terrible Turner' was also arrogant, abrasive, irascible, and domineering, grasping for power where he had no business. Only strong-willed commanders kept him in check."[18] Nimitz remarked that Turner was like King in that he was "brilliant, caustic, arrogant, and tactless – just the man for the job."[19]

While Admiral Turner got to work building the "South Pacific Amphibious Force" from scratch, Marine Major General Alexander Archer Vandegrift was busy training the 1st Marine Division in New Zealand. They were to form the new Landing Force of the South Pacific Amphibious Force. Since they were expected to be seeing combat soon, the general was now to get his division – at that time consisting of the 1st, 5th, and 11th Marine regiments, all green – ready for combat very, very quickly.[20]

Meanwhile, the Japanese were pushing ahead with their next offensive, seizing Tulagi in the Solomons and moving on to Port Moresby, the only remaining position of value in Allied hands in New Guinea. Always keeping his eye out for opportunities to attack, Nimitz believed the Tulagi position was exposed and proposed raiding it using the 1st Marine Raider Battalion. This proposal started another tug of war between General MacArthur; who, though he would shortly field slightly more than three divisions, admitted he did not have the forces to take Tulagi; and Admiral King, who thought Tulagi was too small and wanted something more.[21]

There things sat while carrier battles took place in the Coral Sea, in which the Japanese invasion force directed at Port Moresby was turned back; and near Midway, in which four of the six carriers of Vice Admiral Nagumo Chuichi's Japanese Carrier Striking Force *Kido Butai* that had attacked Pearl Harbor were sunk. Despite the losses of the carriers *Lexington* and *Yorktown*, destroyers *Sims* and *Hammann*, and oiler *Neosho*, the positive effects of both actions, especially Midway, on sagging American morale cannot be overstated. The Japanese kraken had reached out with its tentacles, only to be slapped down at Coral Sea and then reduced to a bloody stump after Midway. But the American strategic victory at Coral Sea and the total victory at Midway would not have been possible without "Magic."

Magic was a subset of what is more commonly and famously known as "Ultra," the term adopted by the Allies to reference signals intelligence obtained by breaking encrypted enemy radio and wireless telegraph communications. While *Ultra* covered all such intelligence, the US adopted the term *Magic* for its decrypts specifically from Japanese sources. In the case of Coral Sea and Midway, a breakthrough had come in the Japanese naval high-level command and control communications code the Allies called "JN-25."* With the Japanese both unaware of the breach and refusing to consider evidence that there had been a breach, *Magic* and signals intelligence would be the gift that kept on giving.

---

* In the designation "JN-25," "JN" means "Japanese Navy" and "25" references this being the 25th such code identified.

But *Magic* was not perfect. It only gave glimpses into Japanese communications and organization. And occasionally the Japanese would switch to a new version of the same code, which would effectively blind Allied intelligence, usually at the most inconvenient times, until the new version could be broken.

With the victory at Midway and *Magic* still effective, the question for US strategic planners became how to take advantage of the current situation. By his March plan for a South Pacific counteroffensive and his orders for the development of a South Pacific amphibious force, Admiral King was well down the road to answering that question. But Douglas MacArthur interjected with his own plan for a counteroffensive.

The disagreement produced another interservice standoff that was resolved only in the last two days of June 1942. General Marshall and Admiral King hammered out the "Joint Directive for Offensive Operations in the Southwest Pacific Area Agreed on by the United States Chiefs of Staff" that consisted of three phases. Phase One, already given its own code name of *Watchtower*, would involve the seizure of Tulagi and the Santa Cruz Islands. This task would be completed by the Pacific Fleet. Phase Two would be the capture of Lae, Salamaua, and the rest of the northeast coast of New Guinea, and the central Solomons. Phase Three would involve the reduction and capture of Rabaul. Phases Two and Three would be under the command of General MacArthur. This three-part plan in its entirety was given the cheerful name of "Pestilence."

Admiral King started putting into motion *Pestilence* and especially its component *Watchtower*, involving the capture of the Santa Cruz Islands, Tulagi, and "adjacent positions," scheduled to begin August 1. On June 27, the planned attack on Tulagi was expanded to include the capture of an unspecified airfield site, if not a finished airfield.[22] Admiral Turner also intended to capture various islands to create a web of mutually supporting airfields. His first target would be Ndeni in the Santa Cruz Islands, some 250 miles north of Espiritu Santo in the New Hebrides, where Admiral Nimitz had already authorized development of a base, and 350 miles southeast of Tulagi.[23] Turner had originally thought Ndeni would make a great airbase to guard the eastern flank of the Solomons, but Ndeni was too far away. So Turner suggested they look at Guadalcanal, an island some 18 miles south of Tulagi.[24]

For a little-known corner of the primitive Solomon Islands, Guadalcanal was attracting a lot of attention. Some of that attention was from a group known as "Ferdinand." Named after the children's story *Ferdinand the Bull*, whose title character preferred smelling flowers to fighting, *Ferdinand* was the brainchild of Australian naval reservist Lieutenant Commander Eric A. Feldt, a veteran of the British Grand Fleet in World War I. Feldt had been local affairs administrator on New Guinea, where he became familiar with the talented, temperamental, and fiercely independent Melanesian natives. When Feldt was recalled to service, he came up with the idea of enrolling plantation managers, government administrators, missionaries, and anyone who wanted to serve, but not to fight, not to be noticed, not to cause any trouble for the Japanese, except to watch and warn of Japanese movements, actions, and other developments. By December 1939, *Ferdinand* had 800 members, located everywhere in New Guinea, the Bismarcks, and the Solomons, and including chief observers trained to communicate by radio.[25] They would become known as "coastwatchers."

It was one of these coastwatchers, former district officer Martin Clemens, who first noticed Japanese activity on the north coast of Guadalcanal in the area of Lunga Point. When a convoy carrying construction workers arrived, Clemens and the other coastwatchers deduced the Japanese were building an airfield. Construction on the base progressed under the watchful and thoroughly enraged eyes of Clemens.

As a result of the work of Clemens and friends, *Ferdinand* reported work at the Lunga site on July 1.[26] *Ferdinand* was joined the next day by *Magic*, which concluded the Japanese had landed construction troops on Guadalcanal.[27] Admiral Nimitz had wanted to seize an airfield site. Now he had one. King and Nimitz agreed to replace Ndeni in Phase One with Guadalcanal for the time being. But that airfield construction was an hourglass, so as it inched closer to completion, the sand was running out.

Meanwhile, Admiral Ghormley was struggling to set up a South Pacific Command that was little more than a cabin on the command ship *Argonne* with a tiny staff headed by Rear Admiral Daniel J. Callaghan, former skipper of the cruiser *San Francisco* and formerly President Roosevelt's naval aide.[28] Ghormley was "flabbergasted" by the June 25 order to arrange the capture of "Tulagi and adjacent positions."[29] His "immediate mental estimate of the situation was that [they] were far from ready to start any offensive."[30] And they weren't, a situation he discussed with General Vandegrift.

But while Vandegrift set out to get the 1st Marine Division as ready for *Watchtower* as it could be, Ghormley set out to tell everyone that they simply could not be made ready for *Watchtower* and thus the operation was not viable. He worked with General MacArthur to make his case, which earned him no favors with Admiral King.

As such, *Watchtower* continued to move forward in fits and starts. General Vandegrift was faced with massive supply entanglements in the port of Wellington that compelled him to request a one-week delay in *Watchtower* to August 7. It was granted, but any longer and it further risked the Japanese completing the Guadalcanal airfield.

That same day, July 16, Admiral Ghormley formally issued his simple 174-page operational plan for *Watchtower*. Under his South Pacific Command were two task forces. Task Force 63, under Rear Admiral John S. McCain, consisted of all the land- and water-based aircraft. Everything else he placed in what he called Task Force 61, "The Expeditionary Force," under the command of the newly promoted Vice Admiral Frank Jack Fletcher.

Generally speaking, the Pacific Fleet in 1942 had two experienced carrier admirals: Frank Jack Fletcher and William F. Halsey. Halsey normally commanded the task force centered on the aircraft carrier *Enterprise*, while Fletcher normally commanded the force centered on the *Yorktown*, to which the *Lexington* had been added for the Coral Sea action. The aggressive and popular Halsey had commanded the *Enterprise* group, to which the *Hornet* had been added to conduct Lieutenant Colonel Jimmy Doolittle's April bombing attack on Japan, until just before Midway, when he was diagnosed with dermatitis and forced into a hospital at Pearl Harbor. Upon Halsey's recommendation, Rear Admiral Raymond Spruance took his place, serving under the more senior Fletcher.

In July 1942, Admiral Halsey was still down with dermatitis and unavailable for combat deployment. Admiral Spruance had done so well at Midway that Admiral Nimitz plucked him for his chief of staff, so he was unavailable as well. That left Admiral Fletcher to command the *Watchtower* operation.

There was a lot to recommend Fletcher. He was the US Navy's most experienced carrier task force commander, known for being thoughtful and careful. He was also the US Navy's most successful carrier task force commander, having turned back the Japanese Port Moresby invasion force and sunk the light carrier *Shoho* in the Coral Sea, then turned back the Japanese Midway invasion force, in the process sinking four of the six carriers of the Japanese Carrier Striking Force *Kido Butai* that had attacked Pearl Harbor. Fletcher had thus earned two strategic victories.

But ... Admiral Fletcher's victories always came with a *but*. Yes, Fletcher turned back the Japanese Port Moresby invasion force in the Coral Sea and sank the light carrier *Shoho*, *but* he lost the fleet carrier *Lexington* to battle-damage-induced fuel vapor explosions. Yes, Fletcher turned back the Japanese Midway invasion force, in the process sinking four of the six carriers of *Kido Butai*, *but* he lost the fleet carrier *Yorktown* to submarine torpedoes while she was under tow. Never known as an aggressive commander and ordered by Admiral Nimitz before Midway to use his carriers based on the principle of "calculated risk," Fletcher may have become more inclined to caution by the losses of the *Lexington* and *Yorktown* – which, some would argue, made him the perfect commander for the expedition.

It all added up to a rendezvous of 72 of the 76 Allied ships involved in the *Watchtower* landings, including the aforementioned *Southard*, on July 26 southeast of the Fiji Islands, where, it was hoped, they would be safe from prying Japanese eyes. It was there that a conference between Admiral Fletcher and the various senior commanders in *Watchtower* devolved into a shouting match between Fletcher, who declared the operation would fail, and Admiral Turner, who insisted they had to try their best to make it succeed.

The conference, such as it was, concluded when Fletcher, the veteran carrier admiral, announced: "Gentlemen, in view of the risks of exposure to land-based air, I cannot keep the carriers in the area for more than 48 hours after the [initial] landing."[31] General Vandegrift and Admiral Turner were stunned, but there was no changing Fletcher's mind.

There was no time to dwell on it, because after a dress rehearsal for the invasion of Guadalcanal and Tulagi that was variously described as "a complete fiasco" and "a complete bust," the Allied armada, including the little *Southard*, left the Fijis on July 31, heading for Guadalcanal – codenamed "Cactus" – and Tulagi – codenamed "Ringbolt."[32]

Historians and military analysts would comment, not always favorably, on "the sheer audacity of taking the strategic offensive" here. "Seldom has an operation been begun under more disadvantageous circumstances," General Vandegrift would later say.[33] Operations officer Lieutenant Colonel Merrill Twining feared, "The stage was rapidly being set with all the props needed for a first class disaster."[34]

Historian John Prados described the operation in less than complimentary terms:

> This resulted from one of the most gigantic improvisations imaginable – makee learnee on a grand scale [...] Rather the 'Canal – or "Operation *Watchtower*," to give it its proper code name – became the first major American amphibious landing of the war, an application of doctrines hitherto extant only on paper, practiced in small-scale exercises with rudimentary techniques and novel, unproven equipment. The landing boats, cross-shipping, and fire-support arrangements [...] was mostly experimental at Guadalcanal. Moreover, *Watchtower* would be carried out by an untried area command, viewed with some suspicion by another theater boss quite zealous in protecting his own prerogatives. All of this amounted to something far less than a formula for success.[35]

Maybe. Maybe it really was the Athenians heading to catastrophe in Sicily with the hesitant, indecisive Nicias at its head, this time sitting in the aircraft carrier *Saratoga*. But there was no time and no benefit for the troops to have such disquieting thoughts. "I felt like the Greeks going to Troy or something," said Marine Captain Paul Moore[36] – a more comforting thought, perhaps: a ten-year siege followed by domestic upheaval was far preferable to the salt mines of Sicily.

At 76 ships and 19,000 Marines, it was the largest armada yet assembled by the US Navy in the Pacific. It included three aircraft carriers, one brand-new battleship, and two brand-new light cruisers intended for antiaircraft work. The impressive picture was misleading as to just how desperate the circumstances in the Pacific remained for the Allies – the Japanese still held the advantage in aircraft carriers, battleships, cruisers, destroyers, and aircraft – but it was a start.

But it was complicated. Admiral King saw a Japanese airfield under construction, the completion of which would hinder Allied efforts in the Pacific. Others, like Admirals Ghormley and Fletcher, saw obstacles, the forces under their command outnumbered, outgunned, and outsupplied.

Admiral Turner's ships trudged along. The three aircraft carrier task forces – the *Saratoga* task force under Vice Admiral Fletcher's direct command; a task force built around the carrier *Enterprise* under Rear Admiral Thomas Kinkaid; and a task force built around the carrier *Wasp* under Rear Admiral Leigh Noyes – hung back off the coast of Guadalcanal while the rest of the ships, including the *Southard*, kept going.

The invasion force split up, as planned. One force, with the *Southard*, headed toward Tulagi. The remainder headed for Lunga Point on Guadalcanal.

As the light improved and the ships got closer to the invasion beaches, Guadalcanal came into view. One Marine war correspondent recorded his first impressions:

> … Guadalcanal is an island of striking beauty. Blue-green mountains, towering into a brilliant tropical sky or crowned with cloud masses, dominate the island. The dark green of jungle growth blends into the softer greens and browns of coconut groves and grassy plains and ridges.[37]

Admiral Turner described Guadalcanal as "A truly beautiful sight that morning."[38] The Marines who would have to live there had other ideas. Some remembered simply that "it gave you the creeps." Others remembered all the palm trees, beaches, lush jungle – and the stench of something rotten beneath it all.[39]

The ships of the invasion force moved to their respective positions and targets. The *Southard*, then under the command of Lieutenant Commander Joe Brice Cochran, and fellow minesweeper *Zane* headed for Bungana Island, just off the southern tip of the eastern arm of Florida Island, which hugs around Tulagi. Intelligence suspected there was a Japanese artillery emplacement on Bungana or on the peninsula of Florida just to its north. After the bombardment revealed no evidence of the alleged gun, the *Southard* moved off to start sweeping the area for mines.

Meanwhile, the respective US Navy invasion forces for Tulagi and Guadalcanal moved toward their respective invasion areas. They were bracing themselves for the expected bitter defense of this remote corner of the "Greater East Asia Co-prosperity Sphere" (which was neither in Asia nor prosperous) by so-called "Japanese Marines" – actually the naval infantry of the Imperial Japanese Navy's Special Naval Landing Force, troops that had a reputation for not surrendering.

Indeed, after a large pre-invasion bombardment that wiped out several Japanese flying boats moored around Tulagi, the 1st Marine Raider Battalion landed on and around Tulagi and the 1st Marine Regiment landed on Guadalcanal near Lunga Point. The Special Naval Landing Force troops on Tulagi and several satellite islands had to be violently and viciously dug out over two days and killed to a man. The Special Naval Landing Force troops on Guadalcanal ran away into the jungle, leaving the defense of the beaches to a bunch of wild pigs.

While the US Marines were digging out recalcitrant Japanese troops and boisterous boars, the *Southard* was continuing to sweep parts of Savo Sound for mines. While she was hard at work, she saw the approach of the first Japanese counterattack, 27 of the bombers the Japanese called the "Mitsubishi G4M Type 1 Attack Bomber." The Allies would develop a simpler reporting name system for Japanese aircraft and gave the G4M the name "Betty." The Allies were much more familiar with the Betty than they cared to be, but they were more familiar still with the bombers' escorts on this day: 18 fighters the Japanese called the "Mitsubishi A6M2 Type 0 Carrier Fighter." The Allies would give this fighter the reporting name "Zeke," but it would be immortalized by friend and foe alike by one simple word: "Zero."

The *Southard* could not see the results of this counterattack, but she didn't miss much, as on this August 7 the Betty did not live up to the fearsome reputation it established in Asia. They just strolled in and dropped their bombs among Admiral Turner's transports. All at once. And they all missed. A later attack by nine "Aichi Type 99 Carrier Bombers" – named "Val" by the Allies – got one bomb hit on the destroyer *Mugford* and a near miss on the destroyer *Dewey*. That was the only damage of the day to Allied ships. Not one Allied ship or landing craft had hit a mine. The *Southard* and her fellow minesweepers *Zane*, *Hopkins*, *Trever*, and *Hovey* did their job well, aided to some extent by the fact that the Japanese had not laid any mines.

With her *raison d'etre* complete, Lieutenant Commander Cochran had his ship settle in to screening for enemy submarines. But this was where the concept of "makee learnee" made itself felt. The transports and especially the cargo ships had not been what is known as "combat loaded" – that is, weapons, ammunition, and supplies needed by the first units to disembark were not stowed correctly so they could be offloaded first. Moreover, there were not enough stevedores to unload the supplies. The result was a logjam of ships trying to unload on the beach and a logjam of supplies on the beach, so much so that the offloading of supplies had to be halted for a time so part of the beach could be cleared by moving some of the supplies inland. This jam would prove critical.

The next day, while the 1st Marine Raider Battalion continued the vicious fight on Tulagi and satellite islands Gavutu and Tanambogo, the 1st Marine Regiment captured the Guadalcanal airfield. Originally, they were also supposed to capture a "grassy knoll" 4 miles further south. But General Vandegrift saw that the grassy knoll was actually the 1,514-foot Mount Austen. Called Mambula by the locals – "rotting body," for reasons that would soon become apparent – it was too far away and far too big to be taken initially. He ordered them to halt at the airfield and to stay off the grassy knoll, hoping they would not later regret it.[40]

By then, Admiral Fletcher was regretting keeping his carriers around for even this limited period. The Japanese returned with their Bettys, now armed with torpedoes, the same configuration in which they sank the *Prince of Wales* and *Repulse*. Once again, the Betty did not live up to its fearsome reputation, as the attacking bombers were cut to pieces by antiaircraft fire, including that of the *Southard*. Their only concrete accomplishment was a single torpedo hit on the destroyer *Jarvis*.

The *Southard* would be very busy on August 8, thanks to Admiral Fletcher. Fletcher announced he was withdrawing his carriers, meaning Admiral Turner and his transports and cargo ships would have no air cover to continue to not shoot down the attacking Japanese, just as they had not done for the past two days. Turner felt compelled to consult with General Vandegrift about withdrawing his ships before they were fully unloaded.

Turner had the *Southard* stand by to serve as the general's transportation to take him to Tulagi and assess the situation there, which she proceeded to do.

But while she was waiting for General Vandegrift to finish, she saw aircraft flares south of Tulagi. Then she saw a different kind of flare. A fire had flared up and continued to burn. Two more appeared in short order, all in the vicinity of Savo Island to the west. The *Southard* took them to be burning ships. She returned with General Vandegrift to Admiral Turner's flagship, the transport *McCawley*, around dawn.

The *Southard* saw how right she had been about those "burning ships." Savo Sound was a mess of oil, debris, and bodies. The flare-ups she had witnessed during the night were floatplanes on US Navy cruisers catching fire and taking the rest of their ships with them, the result of gunfire from a sweep by Japanese ships around Savo Island. The full brunt of the Japanese attack fell on the 8-inch-armed heavy cruisers and their screening destroyers guarding the western approaches to the invasion beachheads. It was a disaster, the worst defeat in US Navy history. Cruisers *Vincennes* and *Quincy* were sunk during the night, the *Astoria* was fatally damaged, and the Australian cruiser *Canberra* was disabled, possibly by an errant American torpedo, and, in Admiral Turner's rather questionable estimation, had to be scuttled. American cruiser *Chicago* had an unhealthy chunk of her bow bitten off, earning the scorn of the Marines ashore on Guadalcanal who assumed – rightly, according to US Navy investigators – that her performance had been underwhelming. Destroyer *Ralph Talbot* was damaged, and destroyer *Jarvis* simply disappeared; it was later determined she just passed through the battle and was sunk by those fearsome Betty bombers. The Japanese left the virtually defenseless transports and cargo ships untouched. No one has ever quite figured out why.

So ended what the US Navy called "the Battle of Savo Island" but what the Marines on Guadalcanal disgustedly called "the Battle of the Four (or Five) Sitting Ducks," and which earned Savo Sound the new name "Ironbottom Sound." The Marines had even more reason to be disgusted when, after bravely continuing to offload the transports and cargo ships all day despite the lack of air cover and the danger of a Japanese air attack that never came, Admiral Turner followed Admiral Fletcher's carriers out of the combat zone.

With that, *Watchtower* got off to a rumbling, stumbling start. The 1st Marine Division was left feeling marooned, even cheekily being renamed the "1st Maroon Division" by Lieutenant Colonel Twining.[41] Having all of their transports and cargo ships up anchor and leave, carrying most of their supplies, with no definite timeframe as to when they would be back, can leave one with that feeling. The Marines were shocked, a feeling intensified by news of the disaster at Savo Island.

Almost all of the Marines' heavy equipment had been on the cargo ships at whose defense Admiral Fletcher had balked. The Marines had enough food for perhaps 37 days and enough ammunition for just four days of combat.

Lieutenant Colonel Twining described their predicament:

We were left without exterior communications or support of any kind and with no assurance that help would be forthcoming. We had no source of information or observation except what we could derive from a twenty-four foot observation tower constructed of palm logs inherited from the emperor. We were on half rations, had little ammunition and no construction equipment or defensive materials whatsoever, and no one would talk to us when we improvised a long-distance transmitter from captured Japanese radio equipment. Outside of that we were in great shape.[42]

The Marines got to work, lugging the dropped-off supplies to hidden caches, finishing the airfield, and establishing a defense perimeter around it. Said perimeter started west of the Lunga River, encompassed the village of Kukum, then crossed the river into jungle the Marines considered "impenetrable" before reaching the coast again to the east of the airfield at a body of water the Marines called "Alligator Creek," though it had no alligators and was not a creek. It was known as the Ilu River, though it was not actually a river, but a tidal lagoon. Nothing on Guadalcanal was as it seemed.

It was once they were established at this Lunga roadstead that the Marines really got to know Guadalcanal. And, as one Marine said, "what a putrefying shithole it really was."[43]

Many English speakers not versed in history find it shocking that Guadalcanal does not have an actual canal. The very name suggests a fundamental dishonesty about the island – an island that, as many a writer has opined, looks like paradise but is more like *Paradise Lost*. Marines quickly picked up on the dishonesty, seeing that Guadalcanal was a lie. The Marine, and later historian, William Manchester called it "a vision of beauty, but of evil beauty,"[44] like Pandaemonium, Milton's capital of Hell. And just like Hell, the first thing one notices about Guadalcanal is the heat. And it's not even a dry heat. Public affairs officer Major Frank O. Hough described it, saying, "No air stirs here and the hot humidity is beyond the imagination of anyone who has not lived in it."[45]

With the humidity comes the rain. Technically, the Solomons have two seasons, "wet" and "dry," though to the Marines the seasons were more like "wet" and "really wet." In the *New York Times*, F. Tillman Durdin wrote, "It rains almost every night – weepy tropical rain that soaks into the bed rolls and seeps through the tarpaulin. The nights are passed in wet chill and discomfort and the days in mud and filth."[46] Marine Captain Joe Foss said the foxholes where most of each night was spent "never dried out" and "smelled like an owl's nest."[47]

Everything started with the rain. It rained so much that standing water and drainage issues were constant. And with standing water came Guadalcanal's most numerous resident: the mosquito. The mosquitos brought malaria but this was not the only jungle disease: yellow fever, typhus, typhoid fever, dengue fever, dysentery, and a variety of fungal infections also abounded. The island was rife with poisonous and dangerous animals and reptiles. Even the plants were hostile, with the stiff, serrated kunai grass, which could grow to 10 feet, slashing and cutting uniforms and skin. It was like walking through a field of swords.

Oh, and on top of all this, the Marines had to fight the Japanese, too, which is why, as aged and small as she was, the old destroyer-turned-minesweeper *Southard* was important. But she was busy working between Espiritu Santo and Nouméa and did not return to Guadalcanal until September 8. By then, things had changed, a bit, on Guadalcanal.

First, the Marines had – using captured Japanese equipment and supplies, which sustained them during this early period – completed the airfield. Inspired by Major Lofton Henderson, who had led 16 green Marine dive-bomber pilots in a futile, fatal attack on the Japanese carrier *Hiryu* at Midway, the airstrip was named "Henderson Field." It would have helped if it had some aircraft, but it was not until the afternoon of August 20, almost two weeks after the capture of the airfield, and almost one week after the airfield was declared operational, that it finally got some actual aircraft: 19 Marine Grumman F4F Wildcat fighters from Marine Fighter Squadron 223 and 12 Douglas SBD Dauntless dive bombers of Marine Scout Bombing Squadron 232 from Marine Air Group 23, 1st Marine Air Wing. With their arrival on Guadalcanal the "Cactus Air Force" was born.

Soon after the first wave of aircraft arrived, some 900 Imperial Japanese Army troops, under the command of Colonel Ichiki Kiyonao, landed at Taivu Point, east of the Marine perimeter. Their presence, though not their numbers, was revealed by coastwatcher Martin Clemens.[48] Just after midnight on August 21 they launched a "banzai charge" with bayonets fixed, into the teeth of American machine guns and artillery; three times they were driven back with horrendous losses. Of the 800 or so troops who attacked, about 770 were killed, including Ichiki.

The confidence and morale of the formerly green Marines soared – just in time for the Japanese to make another push to send reinforcements to the island with support from their aircraft carriers *Shokaku* and *Zuikaku*, the only two carriers remaining out of the six members of the Japanese Carrier Striking Force *Kido Butai* that had attacked Pearl Harbor. Admiral Fletcher chose to show up with his aircraft carriers *Saratoga*, *Enterprise*, and *Wasp* to give the Americans an overwhelming advantage. Then he proceeded to throw that advantage away by sending the *Wasp* off to refuel. Even so, the Americans managed to sink the light carrier *Ryujo* while Marine and *Enterprise* dive bombers drove back the Japanese reinforcement convoy, sinking one transport, while B-17s from the 11th Heavy Bombardment Group out of Espiritu Santo sank a rescue destroyer that was strangely stationary – all at the cost of damage to the *Enterprise* that necessitated her return to Pearl Harbor. Fletcher never did find the *Shokaku* or the *Zuikaku*, but *Kido Butai* lost a good number of its aircrews this day. It was called, in US Navy circles, the Battle of the Eastern Solomons.

From there the Guadalcanal campaign settled down into a monotonous routine. The Japanese would send down raids from their land-based air arm, the 11th Air Fleet, which the Japanese called "Base Air Force." The Marines would receive an early warning from the coastwatchers, then, from around the beginning of September, from radar too, allowing

MAP 1: THE SOLOMON ISLANDS, AUGUST 1942–JANUARY 1943

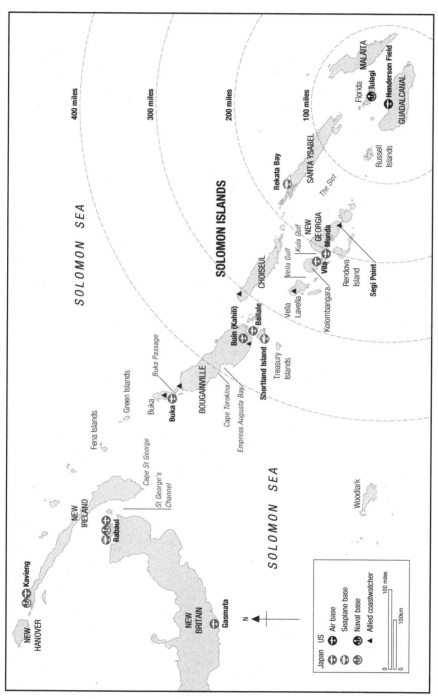

them to scramble fighters and send their vulnerable Dauntlesses out of harm's way. Arriving at Guadalcanal around the same time every day, which the Marines called "Tojo Time," the bombers would be driven to high altitude by the heavy antiaircraft guns of the 3rd Defense Battalion. Their bombing would cause some damage but would be largely ineffective. Wildcats would tangle with Zeros and Bettys, the Japanese and Marines would each suffer losses, and the Japanese would return to their bases around Rabaul.

It was on August 28 that another Japanese reinforcement attempt attracted the attention of the Cactus Air Force. This one involved four destroyers packed with troops trying to make it to Guadalcanal. Just before dusk, Marine and *Enterprise* Dauntlesses found the little convoy off Santa Ysabel, only some 60 miles north-northwest of Savo Island. The *Enterprise*'s Ensign Christian Fink dropped a bomb on the torpedo tubes of one destroyer, later identified as the *Asagiri*. The bomb detonated the torpedoes, resulting in a spectacular explosion that blew the destroyer in two. Another *Enterprise* pilot, Lieutenant Turner Caldwell, planted a bomb on the quarterdeck of a second destroyer, the *Shirakumo*, leaving her disabled. A Marine pilot also hit the bridge of a third destroyer with a bomb. The lone relatively undamaged destroyer took the *Shirakumo* in tow as the three destroyers skulked toward Shortland, the largest of an eponymous island group off the southeastern coast of Bougainville.

This small air attack evidently had a big impact. Afterwards, starting at the end of August, the Japanese stopped trying to land troops and supplies on Guadalcanal during the daytime out of fear of air attack, usually restricting such efforts to the night. These efforts ran with a regularity that the Marines found infuriating, yet the US Navy, especially after the disaster at Savo Island, seemed powerless to stop.

The nighttime runs evinced a very curious and unique changing of the control of the seas around Guadalcanal every time the sun crossed the horizon. When the sun rose, the aircraft of the Cactus Air Force would control the skies over Guadalcanal. The Japanese bases at Rabaul were so far away that their Zeros and Bettys, even when they had numerical superiority, were very limited in when they could appear and for how long they could stay over Guadalcanal. Even so, they were still extremely dangerous to ships when they arrived; the *Colhoun*, a former sister of the *Southard* who had been converted to a high-speed transport, was bombed and sunk off Kukum on August 30. Conversely, close to their Henderson Field base, the Cactus Air Force could operate throughout daylight, and any Japanese ship it caught in its range was vulnerable – ask the *Asagiri*. During the day, Allied ships would discharge supplies, move between Guadalcanal and Tulagi, and generally run errands. Every morning, the Stars and Stripes controlled the seas around Guadalcanal.

But when the sun went below the horizon, the situation reversed. Allied ships left Ironbottom Sound, and in the midnight air the Rising Sun assumed control. Typically, a convoy of Japanese destroyers would sail from their anchorage off Shortland Island. The destroyers would sail down the New Georgia Sound – the area between the double line of the Solomons that the Allies nicknamed "The Slot." But they would not enter the range of Henderson Field until after dark. Then they would dash in and land their troops and supplies. Often they would be accompanied by a cruiser floatplane, operating from a seaplane base the Japanese established in Rekata Bay, Santa Ysabel.* The floatplane would drop flares to light the landing areas and to illuminate the airfield so the destroyers could bombard it. The floatplane would also drop a few bombs, just to keep the Marines awake. It was nicknamed, "Louie the Louse." Another nocturnal visitor to Henderson Field was a twin-engine Betty – badly tuned, to make the engines loud and annoying, it would seem – that also dropped bombs and flares, just to keep the Marines awake. The Betty was nicknamed "Washing Machine Charlie."

In any event, the Japanese destroyers, sometimes accompanied by a light cruiser, would go into Ironbottom Sound. Here any Allied ship they caught was vulnerable. Destroyer *Blue* was torpedoed on August 22; the disabled destroyer was scuttled the next day. The night of September 5, the *Gregory* and the *Little*, other former sisters of the *Southard* who had been converted to high-speed transports, were caught by Japanese destroyers and sunk. Consequently, Allied ships and boats generally stayed out of Ironbottom Sound once the sun was down.

After the Japanese destroyers had landed their troops and supplies, perhaps lobbed a few shells into Henderson Field, and maybe even sunk an Allied ship, they would scooch back up The Slot to be out of range of the Cactus Air Force by daylight. The Marines had a nickname – war typically involves a lot of nicknames – for these convoys: "The Cactus Express." But "Cactus" was a code name, so a different nickname got past the censors to the news media and the public, with whom it would become famous: "The Tokyo Express."

The frustrated Marines could not respond at all. Not until September 1, when 5-inch coastal defense guns – the same guns that were on US destroyers and the same guns that had been left on the cargo ships on August 9 – of the 3rd Defense Battalion arrived. Even then, it was difficult to pick out their targets in the darkness of Ironbottom Sound.

Every day involved a combination of some or all of these elements: warning from coastwatchers or radar of approaching Japanese aircraft; scrambling fighters; air attack by Base Air Force between 11:00 am and 3:00 pm; air battle over Henderson Field and Ironbottom Sound; Tokyo Express, Louie the Louse, Washing Machine Charlie. Every single day: lather, rinse, repeat.

And the Guadalcanal campaign started taking on its deceptive, desperate character. What seemed like victories could in fact be defeats, and vice versa, Savo Island being a case in point. Just when one side had the upper hand and thought it had turned the corner, 24 hours later the situation would be reversed. It was a veritable tug of war between the Japanese, with their main South Pacific fortress at Rabaul, the excellent harbor just northwest of the Solomons on New Britain, and their forward base in the Shortlands off Bougainville, and the Allies, with their main base at Nouméa, French New Caledonia, and their forward base at Espiritu Santo in the New Hebrides. One side would pull the rope toward them, but could not get the traction to hold it or pull it further, and so the other

---

* Rekata Bay should not be confused with and has no relation to the Rakata peak of Krakatoa.

side would pull it back, not get the traction to hold it or pull it further, and so the struggle went on.

All the while each side was suffering casualties – air, land, and sea – and not necessarily replacing those casualties quickly. To pull and get that traction, each side would need reinforcements.

For the Marines two batches were already en route. One was the Army Air Force's 67th Fighter Squadron. Having arrived in New Zealand, they had expected to be equipped with the Army's front-line fighter, the Curtiss P-40 Warhawk. But when their mechanics opened the crates in which their disassembled aircraft were shipped, they found not the Warhawk, but the Bell P-39 Airacobra and its foreign export equivalent, the P-400, a weird fighter (its engine was behind the cockpit) with which the pilots of the 67th were almost entirely unfamiliar. There weren't even any instructions for its assembly. But after trial and error (and probably more than a few parts left over), the Airacobras of the 67th under Captain Dale Brannon were put together and, starting on August 22, staged to Henderson Field. The only problem was the Airacobras were unable to reach high altitude, where most fighter interception took place, and proved worse than useless against the Japanese Zeros. By the end of August, the Airacobras were restricted to low-level interception and ground attack. Another subsequent reinforcement came from 19 Wildcats of Marine Fighter Squadron 224 and 12 Dauntlesses from Marine Scout Bombing Squadron 231. They staged into Henderson on August 30.

Two days later, a unique reinforcement arrived in the form of the 6th Construction Battalion. The men of the construction battalions were skilled tradesmen – carpenters, electricians, metalworkers, machinists, demolition experts, and the like – who had volunteered to put their skills to work in the war effort. The construction battalion was a US innovation, and the 6th was the first such unit to be deployed to a combat area. Despite being relative noncombatants in a combat area, these "Seabees," as they became known, quickly proved their value, from building a new runway out of a poorly drained pasture, dubbed "Fighter 1," to repairing bomb damage to the existing runway.

Other reinforcements, while badly needed – before the arrival of Marine Fighter Squadron 224 and Marine Scout Bombing Squadron 231, the Cactus Air Force had been down to just five operational Wildcats – came from rather unfortunate circumstances. When the *Enterprise* headed back to Pearl Harbor for repairs, she left behind 11 of her dive bombers, some of which had taken a hand in driving back the Japanese convoy. Now designated "Flight 300," they were incorporated into the Cactus Air Force. The carrier *Hornet*, under Rear Admiral George Murray, came down from Pearl Harbor to replace the *Enterprise* in theater, just in time for the *Saratoga*, Admiral Fletcher's flagship, to take a torpedo from a Japanese submarine later identified as *I-26*. Before the *Saratoga* headed back to Pearl for repairs, she launched off her attack aircraft to Espiritu Santo. With Fletcher's flagship out of action, Admiral King took this opportunity to remove Fletcher himself. Fletcher had simply lost King's confidence. Admiral Ghormley was also rapidly losing King's confidence. But for now, the commander of US Navy carriers in the South

Pacific was Rear Admiral Leigh Noyes in the *Wasp*. Despite Fletcher's desire to protect the carriers in limiting their exposure off Guadalcanal, in less than a month, the US Navy had gone from four operational aircraft carriers (three active in theater and one in reserve) to two operational carriers (both in theater). Nevertheless, the Marines on Guadalcanal were benefiting from the US Navy troubles in a perverse way: the *Saratoga's* aircraft, like those of the departed *Enterprise* before her, would stage into Henderson Field. It established the pattern that when a carrier was knocked out, its surviving aircraft – F4F Wildcat fighters, SBD Dauntless dive bombers, even new Grumman TBF Avenger torpedo bombers – would reinforce the Cactus Air Force.

So, after a botched start, by the time the *Southard* returned on September 8, the Marines were at least on their feet, which was a good thing, because the Japanese had landed more troops. The *Southard* arrived that morning with destroyers *Hull*, *Hughes*, *Zane*, and *Hopkins*, escorting the cargo ships *Fuller* and *Bellatrix* with supplies for the Marines. Inadvertently, the *Southard* and the accompanying ships had pulled into Ironbottom Sound right behind a successful raid by Colonel Merritt Edson's 1st Marine Raider Battalion on a Japanese supply cache for an imminent Japanese attack near Taivu Point. Edson's Raiders captured critical intelligence information, took as many of the supplies as they could – including the white dress uniform of Major General Kawaguchi Kiyotake, commander of the appropriately named Kawaguchi Detachment – and destroyed the rest.

Colonel Edson and his men returned to the Henderson Field perimeter to prepare for the Japanese attack. The *Southard* went back to her business and later that day she was anchored in Tulagi when a pair of Japanese aircraft, likely floatplanes, bombed her without effect. The next day, she watched the usual Japanese air attack on Henderson Field, and fished a downed Marine fighter pilot, 2nd Lieutenant Clayton Canfield, out of Ironbottom Sound. The *Southard* investigated a report from the *Bellatrix* of a submarine, but found none before returning Canfield to Guadalcanal that afternoon.[49]

The *Southard* and her friends sorted themselves and headed out for Espiritu Santo, but during the night the minesweeper got separated from her convoy. A little before 4:00 am, she sighted what she thought was a ship of the convoy, but quickly changed the identification to that of a surfaced submarine some 800 yards to port. Lieutenant Commander Cochran had his guns trained on it, but the submarine dove before he could open fire. His sound gear could not establish contact, so the minesweeper dropped an "embarrassing" barrage of two depth charges with no observed results.[50] The *Southard* kept hunting and at around 5:30 made a sound contact, presumably with the same submarine. She attacked with eight depth charges, but saw no evidence of damage. Contact would not be re-established after the attack, and she abandoned the search a little before 7:00 am.[51] She did not find her convoy until the following day, September 11, when she was in sight of Espiritu Santo.[52]

While the *Southard* was making her way back to base – alone – Colonel Edson was left trying to figure out where and when the Japanese would attack the Henderson Field perimeter. Edson deduced most of the Kawaguchi Detachment had tunneled into the jungle and would thus attack from over a ridge just south of the runway that pointed at the base like a dagger.

This was a problem. Even though the Marines had some 15,000 troops on Guadalcanal, they did not have enough to maintain a continuous defense line around Henderson Field and its new satellite airfield, Fighter 1. Despite evidence that the Kawaguchi Detachment had gone into the jungle surrounding the perimeter, General Vandegrift, in one of his few misjudgments of the war, decided the Japanese would attack along or even from the coast, where he had deployed most of his troops, and would not authorize a redeployment. In a bit of bureaucratic subterfuge, the operations officer Colonel Gerald Thomas suggested having Edson's Marines, who had just completed multiple missions, bivouac on the ridge in what he called a "rest area." Edson agreed.

There was an effort to remedy that relative lack of troops, however. That same day Admiral Turner and Admiral McCain arrived to meet General Vandegrift. They bore a message from Admiral Ghormley that revealed an imminent Japanese offensive, as close as ten days away. But Ghormley was willing to release the 7th Marine Regiment for transport to Guadalcanal – if Turner could get them there. Turner believed that he could. They began making arrangements to get the 7th to Guadalcanal.

As they did 24 F4F Wildcats from the *Saratoga* arrived for operations from Henderson Field. The *Saratoga* had left her aircraft behind when she left for repairs to her torpedo-damaged hull. A dozen of the *Saratoga*'s SBDs had arrived on September 6. But it was these 24 fighters that were desperately needed. Before their arrival, the Cactus Air Force was down to just 11 Wildcats.

The morning of September 10, Colonel Edson announced to his Raiders and Parachutists that they were moving to a quieter spot on the ridge. Once there he had his troops deploy facing south, toward the supposedly impenetrable jungle. Then he had the bemused Marines dig foxholes, string barbed wire, and clear fields of fire.

The position on the ridge was indeed a quiet spot until the Kawaguchi Detachment launched their nighttime attack on September 12. Over the course of two nights the Japanese would launch banzai charge after banzai charge. Repeatedly cut down by machine-gun fire, grenades, and artillery, they would fall back and reform.

Like with the Ichiki Detachment, the Japanese suffered frightful casualties over the course of September 12 and 13. But the Kawaguchi Detachment was attacking with some 3,000 men, outnumbering the defending Marines on the ridge almost 4-to-1. There were simply too many Japanese and not enough Marines. "There were so many of them that came over the ridge compared to what we had strung out there," remembered one Marine. "You could shoot two and there would be six more."[53]

Colonel Edson's presence was critical. One officer later commented, "[I]f there is such a thing as one man holding a battalion (plus the paratroopers) together, Edson did it that night. He stood just behind the front lines – stood, when most of us hugged the ground."[54]

Nevertheless, the crush of Japanese numbers was having an effect. Edson had been pushed to his final defense position, the northernmost part of the ridge, within 1,000 yards of Henderson Field. His communication line to the division headquarters had been cut. After a new wire had been run at around 2:30 am, Edson called Colonel Thomas. "My losses have been heavy. I need more men."[55]

General Vandegrift got on the line. "Can you hold?"

"We can hold," Edson replied, but he needed more ammunition and more men. Thomas started feeding in the companies of the reserve 5th Marines.[56]

Dawn brought an end to the main attacks, the back of the Japanese offensive broken. Total Japanese losses are difficult to determine, but by one estimate more than 800 Imperial Japanese Army officers and men were killed, with 505 wounded. It was a major victory by the US Marines and cause for celebration.

It lasted barely 24 hours.

Dawn on September 15 saw Admiral Turner leading a convoy carrying the 7th Marine Regiment to Guadalcanal. The direct escort of this convoy included, once again, the *Southard*. Despite weather conditions that made antisubmarine operations difficult, the *Southard* and her cohorts did an effective job, and none of the convoy or the escorting ships was attacked by a submarine.

Other ships were not so fortunate, however. Providing air cover for the convoy were the carriers *Wasp* and *Hornet*, operating in two separate task forces under Rear Admiral Noyes. So important was getting the 7th Marines to Guadalcanal that their protection was entrusted to these, the only two operational US Navy carriers in the Pacific.

That quickly became one. The *Wasp* was just concluding flight operations when she was stung by two, maybe three, torpedoes shortly before 3:00 pm. The torpedoes ruptured her aviation fuel tanks, releasing fuel vapors throughout the ship and sending flaming fuel through her fueling system. The hangar deck and much of the interior of the ship was turned into an absolute inferno and, for reasons that remain undetermined, the fire suppression system failed to work. Like Hercules wearing the Shirt of Nessus, the *Wasp* burned from the inside out. Surrounded by burning gasoline, rent by volcanic explosions, the *Wasp* had to be scuttled. Admiral King took the opportunity to relieve Noyes, yet another commander in whom he had lost confidence.

While the *Wasp* was in her mortal agony, another torpedo gashed the new battleship *North Carolina*, and yet another hit the bow of the destroyer *O'Brien*, both escorting the carrier *Hornet*, whose task force was about 10 miles from the *Wasp*. The battleship was compelled to return to Pearl Harbor for repairs, while the *O'Brien*'s injuries proved fatal when she sank on the way back to the West Coast. It was much later determined that all this mayhem was the result of one spectacular spread of torpedoes from the Japanese submarine *I-19*. US Navy investigators could only tip their hats to the submarine's skipper, Lieutenant Commander Kinashi Takakazu.

Now stripped of much of his air support and well aware that he was in a zone infested by enemy submarines – this area of water between Guadalcanal and Espiritu Santo had been nicknamed "Torpedo Junction" – Admiral Turner turned the convoy around. But whatever else Kelly Turner was, he was also undeniably courageous. At 3:00 pm on September 16, he turned the convoy back toward Guadalcanal,[57] risking yet further Japanese attacks.

Just before dawn on September 18, Admiral Turner and the convoy arrived safely in Lunga Roads and, with the *Southard* proudly standing guard, began unloading the 4,262 men of the 7th Marine Regiment and their supporting artillery, putting to good use the hard-earned lessons of unloading cargo from the initial *Watchtower* landings – more of that "makee learnee." They were joined by the destroyer-seaplane tender *McFarland*, destroyer-minelayer *Tracy*, and cargo ship *Bellatrix* bringing in aviation fuel.[58]

The arrival of the 7th brought the number of US Marines on Guadalcanal to a little more than 19,000. Meanwhile, the number of operational US Navy carriers was now down to just one – Admiral Murray's *Hornet*. She would have to hold the line in the South Pacific until at least mid-October, when, hopefully, a freshly repaired *Enterprise* would come back with a recovered Admiral Halsey leading her task force.

The apparent dichotomy between the troop strength of the Marines on Guadalcanal and the carrier strength of the Pacific Fleet was reflected in a dichotomy in their relative assessments of the campaign, as was soon discovered by *New York Times*' military affairs correspondent Hanson Baldwin.

Baldwin met General Vandegrift and gave him some rather disconcerting news. The reporter told the general that the American public were under the false impression that the Marines held most of Guadalcanal. The public was completely unaware of the conditions under which the troops were living and fighting. Washington was aware of those conditions, and "top officials" were deeply concerned about the situation and seemed ready to give up.[59] The attitude was even worse in the Allies' main base of Nouméa, where the harbor was packed with supply ships waiting to be unloaded because of the disorganization of Admiral Ghormley's headquarters, where defeatism had clearly taken hold.

Vandegrift bristled at the idea that his troops were on the verge of defeat. He pointed out that they had finally stopped the Japanese advance across the Pacific, during which the Japanese had suffered heavy naval and air losses, from which they might not quickly recover. In fact, the American offensive on Guadalcanal seemed to have taken them by surprise.[60]

Baldwin cut to the chase. "Are you going to hold this beachhead, General? Are you going to stay here?"

"Hell yes. Why not?"[61]

It would become General Vandegrift's most famous quote. It wasn't much of a battle cry – American troops were not going to storm enemy positions hollering "Why not?" But it was a message of optimism, of hope, in the face of a vicious enemy and weak-kneed or ambivalent superiors.

But those weak-kneed superiors were a major problem in this campaign, none bigger than Admiral Ghormley. Baldwin went to Pearl Harbor, where he told a similar story to

Admiral Nimitz. The poor results of the South Pacific campaign so far had come from "overcaution and the defensive complex."[62] Indeed, Ghormley had never visited Guadalcanal; he had never even left his flagship *Argonne* in Nouméa.[63]

Baldwin was not the only journalist with the impression that Ghormley and his staff were timid and defeatist. According to Associated Press correspondent Clark Lee, "It seemed to me some officers thought only of NOT losing more ships, and it was in that mood that we undertook our early operations in the Solomons."[64]

In light of these worrying reports, Admiral Nimitz decided he had to go to the South Pacific himself and personally check on his South Pacific commander. En route, he crossed paths with Admiral McCain, who was going to Washington to work for Admiral King. The highly respected McCain had been among the first to notice a significant drop off in the combat performance of Japanese aircrews. Once, while speaking with staffers at Pearl Harbor, McCain described what was unthinkable just six months earlier. "The Japs are afraid of our F4F and will not attack it," he said. "It seems reasonable to suppose that we have now destroyed the cream of [the enemy's] naval air pilots."[65] Now Nimitz asked McCain for a short briefing on what to look for in the South Pacific.

"The first thing is to get as many reserve planes to [Espiritu Santo] as possible. Cactus cannot handle any more planes right now, but you have to be ready to feed them in all the time. Aviation gasoline supply at Cactus is the present most critical question." Admiral McCain later added, "The Marines are not worried about holding what they have on Cactus but you have got to stop the Japs coming in."[66]

Admiral Nimitz was about to see just how right McCain was. The commander-in-chief of the Pacific Fleet arrived in Nouméa on September 28 and headed for Admiral Ghormley's flagship *Argonne*. On the way, Nimitz saw 80 cargo ships and freighters carrying badly needed supplies simply sitting in the harbor, with the ships themselves desperately needed elsewhere. They could not be sent to the front because they had not been combat loaded. This was evidence of the disorganization in Ghormley's command. It was more of that makee learnee, but they were almost two months into the Guadalcanal campaign; some of these issues should have been remedied by now.

Nimitz's mood was not improved when he got to the *Argonne*. There he went to a conference with his South Pacific commander Admiral Ghormley, Ghormley's chief of staff Admiral Callaghan, and Admiral Turner. Also present were General Arnold, head of the Army Air Force, who was on his own fact-finding tour of the South Pacific; General MacArthur's chief of staff Major General Richard K. Sutherland; MacArthur's 5th Air Force head Major General George Kenney, and Major General Millard Harmon, commander of Army Air in the South Pacific.

Admiral Ghormley's performance at the conference did little to assuage the Pacific Fleet commander's concerns – quite the opposite, in fact. Admiral Nimitz first noted with some unease that Ghormley looked exhausted, nervous, and overwhelmed. Ghormley seemed to have large substantive gaps in his understanding of the situation on Guadalcanal. Around the beginning of September Ghormley had formed a cruiser-destroyer force designated Task Force 64 – "about a month late," in the opinion of Admiral King.[67] That force could be useful in stopping the incessant Tokyo Express runs, but Ghormley kept the task force too far from Guadalcanal "to do much about visiting enemy ships."[68] It was not so much "playing not to lose" as it was "playing as if already lost." Ghormley had opposed *Watchtower*, did not think it would succeed, and was husbanding his resources so when it did fail, and Guadalcanal did fall to the Japanese, he would have those resources with which to act.

Perhaps what concerned Admiral Nimitz most was how Admiral Ghormley handled bad news, or at least news that Ghormley considered bad. Twice during the conference, staffers intruded to deliver urgent messages from Guadalcanal for the South Pacific commander. Both times he exclaimed, "My God! What are we going to do about this?"[69] It was if he had no idea what to do and didn't necessarily want to find out. It made a big impression on those present, especially Nimitz.

A privately seething Admiral Nimitz headed for Guadalcanal in a B-17 that struggled to find the island in one of the Solomons' typical storms. Despite the pouring rain, which secretly pleased General Vandegrift since it showed the issues of the muddy runway, Admiral Nimitz inspected the flight operations, the newly named Edson's Ridge, on which Colonel Edson had defeated the Japanese; and parts of the defense perimeter. That evening Nimitz dined with Vandegrift and the senior officers, then spoke with the general alone to get his real thoughts. It was not the gloom and doom that Admiral Ghormley seemed to believe it was, and optimism seemed to increase the closer one got to the front. Vandegrift and his troops were confident they could hold Guadalcanal. The general said what he needed most were more troops to hold the perimeter and more aircraft to beat back the constant Japanese air attacks.[70]

It was a common refrain. By this time, most of the Marine pilots had been at Henderson Field for over a month. It was a unique situation for pilots inasmuch as, though serving as pilots, they basically lived as infantry. The aircrews were housed in tents in a coconut grove between Henderson Field and the beach. A shortage of cots meant most of them slept on captured Japanese straw mats in the dirt that served as the floors of their tents. And when it rained, the dirt became Guadalcanal's trademark: stinking black mud that could swallow cots and men whole.

The black mud was the curse of Henderson Field. There was not enough Marston matting – perforated steel planks that could be hooked together to create a temporary runway – to cover the runway. So pilots taking off and landing had to deal with the dirt strip, which the official Marine Corps aviation history described in not-entirely complimentary terms: "Henderson Field was a bowl of black dust which fouled airplane engines or it was a quagmire of black mud which made the take-off resemble nothing more than a fly trying to rise from a runway of molasses."[71] All in all, the Cactus Air Force pilots had to endure circumstances that were "probably the worst any American airmen faced for a prolonged period during the war."[72] Admiral Nimitz saw it firsthand on his visit.

MAP 2: MARINE FACILITIES AT GUADALCANAL, LATE SEPTEMBER 1942

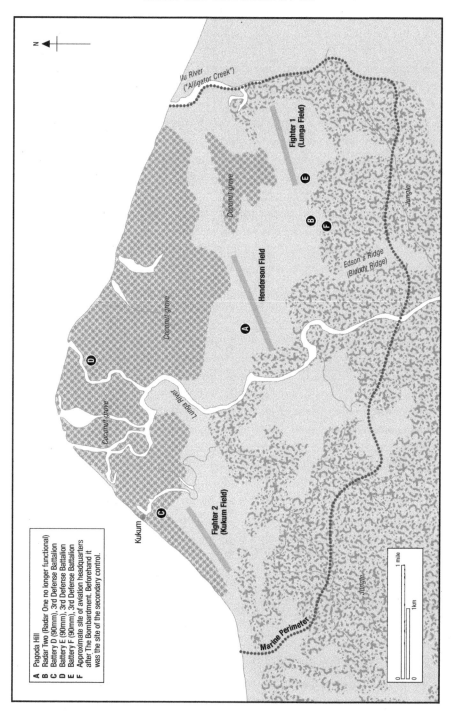

A Pagoda Hill
B Radar Two (Radar One no longer functional)
C Battery D (90mm), 3rd Defense Battalion
D Battery E (90mm), 3rd Defense Battalion
E Battery F (90mm), 3rd Defense Battalion
F Approximate site of aviation headquarters
   after The Bombardment. Beforehand it
   was the site of the secondary control.

The next morning, after handing out merit citations, the admiral promised General Vandegrift "support to the maximum of our resources."[73] Nimitz and his staff headed back to Nouméa, where he met Admiral Ghormley again on October 2.

This time, Admiral Nimitz gave very definite and forceful instructions that left no doubt what he wanted from his South Pacific commander. In general, he wanted support for Guadalcanal – more support than Admiral Ghormley had been willing to give. Ghormley had so far refused to commit the Army's Americal Division, then being trained in New Caledonia, because he believed it would be lost when Guadalcanal inevitably fell to the Japanese. The division's commander Major General Alexander M. Patch disagreed. So did Nimitz, who ordered it sent to Guadalcanal.

Among the Pacific Fleet commander's other directives to Admiral Ghormley were that he provide Guadalcanal with equipment to allow construction of all-weather airfields and roads, which meant a lot of that Marston matting; better storage facilities for aviation fuel; better cargo facilities; better repair facilities for aircraft; and better housing, specifically Quonset huts, for pilots so they did not have to fight like pilots and then sleep like infantry in the black mud of Guadalcanal. Perhaps most importantly, Nimitz added, "I want you to go up and see conditions for yourself. Callaghan can take care of things here while you are away."[74]

The Pacific Fleet commander left for Pearl Harbor, hoping his instructions and admonitions to Admiral Ghormley would be enough to enable the South Pacific commander to pull himself together. But the Japanese had other plans, with the tempo of Base Air Force's attacks markedly increasing. The Japanese had completed a new airfield at a place the Americans called Kahili on the southeastern tip of Bougainville, so Base Air Force could attack twice a day. And a new kind of fighter started appearing, which was, in theory, a modified version of the original Zero: the "Mitsubishi A6M3 Model 32 Type 0 Carrier Fighter."

The increased pace of Japanese air attacks put even more pressure on the Marine, Navy, and Army pilots of the Cactus Air Force, many of whom had been on Guadalcanal for over a month and were at or beyond the limits of their endurance. In addition to the terrible living conditions, they had limited rations and were continuously sleep deprived thanks to Louie the Louse and Washing Machine Charlie. Unsurprisingly, more operational accidents began to occur. One pilot lamented, "At this rate we can whip ourselves without any help from the Japs."[75]

Other problems appeared as well. All aviators, but especially fighter pilots, make mistakes in combat. Those mistakes were now happening with increasing frequency. Dauntless pilots and radiomen on reconnaissance missions can make basic errors of identification and navigation. The Marine Dauntless pilots had not gotten a direct hit on a Japanese ship with a bomb since they hit the *Asagiri* on August 28.

And they needed to get direct hits, and soon, because the Tokyo Express was ramping up. The convoys were running more often and, ominously, some were centered on one of the Imperial Navy's unusual seaplane carriers, the *Nisshin*. This was a problem, because the

Nisshin could carry more than seaplanes. Unlike the destroyers that normally comprised the Tokyo Express, she could carry tanks and artillery. If she was in the Tokyo Express, that could only mean the Japanese were running tanks and artillery to Guadalcanal to use against the defenders of Henderson Field.

But, try as they might, the Dauntless, Avenger, and Fortress pilots were unable to get a damaging direct hit on her. On October 3, the Japanese seaplane carrier made a run to Tassafaronga, the area on the northwest coast of Guadalcanal west of Henderson Field that had become a new landing point for Japanese troops and supplies. Here she managed to drop off General Maruyama Masao and elements of his 2nd Sendai Division.[76] She made another run the night of October 8–9 and escaped an air attack without damage. The *Nisshin* would prove to be a thorn in the American side.

On her next run on October 11, the *Nisshin* was joined by fellow seaplane carrier *Chitose* and six destroyers, all carrying reinforcements and supplies.[77] They would be covered by a bombardment of Henderson Field by 8-inch-armed heavy cruisers *Aoba*, *Furutaka*, and *Kinugasa* with destroyers *Fubuki* and *Hatsuyuki*.

This was one of those rare times when both sides attempted to reinforce Guadalcanal at the same time. Admiral Ghormley was finally sending the US Army's Americal Division. The 164th Infantry Regiment was to be sent to Guadalcanal as the vanguard of the Americal, the name a contraction of "America" and "Caledonia" as the only US Army division formed outside US territory, in this case New Caledonia.

The regiment, along with 210 men of the 1st Marine Air Wing and supplies for the 1st Marine Division, was loaded onto the transport *Zeilin* and Admiral Turner's flagship transport *McCawley* on October 8. The next day they sailed from Nouméa, with a close escort of destroyers *Gwin*, *Nicholas*, and *Sterett*, and three mine layers. Providing air cover was the only operational American carrier left in the Pacific, the *Hornet*, while protecting the right flank was a task force centered on the only operational American battleship left in the Pacific, the *Washington*.

Covering their left flank was that cruiser force that Admiral Ghormley had formed "about a month late," in the opinion of Admiral King.[78] It consisted of the 8-inch-armed heavy cruisers *San Francisco*, his flagship, and *Salt Lake City*; 6-inch-armed light cruisers *Boise* and *Helena*; and destroyers *Farenholt*, *Buchanan*, *Laffey*, *Duncan*, and *McCalla*. The force was commanded by Rear Admiral Norman Scott.

Norman Scott was a survivor of the Battle of Savo Island. He had been on board his flagship light antiaircraft cruiser *San Juan* that horrid August night, commanding a group on the opposite end of Savo Sound, uninvolved in the combat. But he had studied all the information that could be gleaned from the battle. Scott was determined that no such disaster would happen again, not on his watch. And Scott now had a chance to put his studies into practice.

Norman Scott had been "one of the best-liked men in the class" of 1911 at the Naval Academy.[79] He had done a tour of duty in the office of the Chief of Naval Operations, but had made everyone's life miserable because he wanted to be at sea. He got his wish.

As commander of this still-new task force, Admiral Scott had established a reputation as "kind of like a junior Halsey."[80] The popular Scott was ready for battle. Were his men? "We would talk about it constantly," said radio officer C.G. "Chick" Morris of the light cruiser *Helena*. "The talk was always of the impending clash with the enemy's warships. Were we good enough? None of us knew. We had never been through the real thing."[81] Scott aimed to make them good enough.

Whenever they had a free moment, during those last few weeks of September and the first week of October, Scott made sure his crews got in a lot of gunnery practice and a lot of practice in what Marine gunner Private Clifford Spencer on the heavy cruiser *San Francisco* called "Night Fighting Course 101." "For the next two weeks we held daily gunnery practice and high speed night tactical maneuvers, every night, all night," recalled Spencer. "We were at general quarters every night and had mock battles with opposing ships, all moving at flank speed. Some fun!"[82]

But Spencer was not complaining:

The object of the practice was to have everyone sharpen their night vision and spot the enemy before he saw you. With training, helmsmen were able to maintain ship intervals with more expertise and direct more energy to finding the enemy ships, allowing you to get off those very important first salvos.[83]

There is no substitute for combat experience, but relentless training can help one survive that first combat experience, replacing fear with procedure, instinct, and muscle memory. "Admiral Scott had to instill behavior into his ships and crews that the Japanese had perfected over many years. The Admiral had days or at best a few weeks. We bitched and probably whined a lot, but by God, we learned!"[84]

This was how Admiral Scott earned the respect and the love of the men under his command. It was exhausting, it was dangerous, but his men knew Scott was preparing them for survival. "In Texas the battle cry had been 'Remember the Alamo!' Here the battle cry was 'Remember Savo Island!'" Spencer later recalled. It was better than "Why not?"

Admiral Scott's orders were to go to a spot about 150 miles south of Guadalcanal near Rennell Island and wait. When air reconnaissance showed Japanese ships moving toward Guadalcanal, Scott would take his ships to the Savo Island area to intercept them. Scott's specific mission was to "search for and destroy enemy ships and landing craft." That was fine with the aggressive, confident Scott. Ever conscious of the disaster of Savo Island, he held one last night battle practice on October 8. The next day Scott issued his preliminary battle plan. It incorporated many of the lessons of Savo.

For starters, Scott decided to keep a simple column formation, the cruisers in the center with the destroyers in front and back. It was hoped this formation would improve communications and identification. The destroyers were to illuminate targets as soon as possible after radar contacts, launch torpedoes at large ships, and fire their guns at enemy destroyers. The destroyers in the lead were reminded to be alert for turn signals by voice radio or blinker, and to watch for turns if the voice radio failed. The heavy cruisers were to use continuous fire against small ships at short range, rather than full gun salvos with long intervals; this was standard operating procedure for the US Navy. The cruisers were also to open fire without orders from Admiral Scott.

Admiral Scott had tried to think of everything. It was as complete a plan as was possible, and was certainly reasonable under the circumstances. Naturally, when the Japanese showed up, the plan fell apart.

Having assumed a position between Savo Island and Cape Esperance, blocking entrance to the Lunga roadstead, Admiral Scott's ships were reaching the northern terminus of their patrol run shortly before midnight on October 11. Scott ordered his ships to reverse course in a column turn to maintain the blocking position. But the turn went awry. Some of his destroyers got separated and Scott did not know where they were.

This was, of course, when the Japanese, under their commander, Rear Admiral Goto Aritomo, were detected on radar, although they displayed no awareness of the presence of the Americans. Admiral Scott's flagship *San Francisco* did not have the most advanced radar, the SG-type that produced what was basically an overhead picture on a screen. Scott could not tell which ships were Japanese and which were his own. The *Helena*'s skipper, Captain Gilbert C. Hoover, among others, could, as he did have the new SG radar. Not wishing to let the chance to ambush the Japanese slip away due to Scott's confusion, Hoover seems to have engineered a "miscommunication" that served as an order to open fire.

The first salvos seem to have been decisive: the Japanese flagship *Aoba*'s bridge was smashed, Goto was mortally wounded, and the cruiser's guns disabled. Her sister ship *Furutaka* was hit by a torpedo, the first enemy ship hit by a US Navy surface torpedo since the previous January, and set afire. Destroyer *Fubuki* was quickly overwhelmed – all while Admiral Scott was desperately trying to get his crews to stop firing because he feared he was firing at his own ships. This was partially true. One of the wayward destroyers, the *Duncan*, had bravely charged the Japanese all by herself and had taken a beating from both sides, leaving her fatally damaged. By the time Scott had determined where his ships were and fully authorized opening fire, the element of surprise was lost. The *Kinugasa* recovered from the shock of the ambush by heavily damaging the *Boise* with her guns and causing lighter damage to the *Salt Lake City*. The *Aoba*, *Furutaka*, *Kinugasa*, and *Hatsuyuki* sped northward for the safety of the Shortlands, but *Furutaka* lost power, staggered to a halt, and sank.

The Japanese sent down several destroyers to pick up the *Furutaka*'s survivors and assist the *Kinugasa* in escaping. The Cactus Air Force, in the form of Dauntlesses and Avengers from the *Wasp* and *Saratoga*, paid them a few visits, sinking the *Natsugumo* and putting a torpedo into the *Murakumo*, forcing her to be scuttled.

The US Navy annals would call it the Battle of Cape Esperance. It was the US Navy's first victory in a surface engagement since the previous January's action off Balikpapan, Borneo, in the East Indies. Hardly a perfect action – Admiral Scott's indecision caused by his wayward destroyers prevented a perfect ambush – but it was a victory nonetheless; certainly a victory made possible by Admiral Scott's energetic efforts to learn the lessons of Savo Island and impart these lessons to those under his command.

It would have important, if rather nebulous, ramifications further down the road. But it was only a tactical victory, because that Japanese reinforcement convoy with the *Chitose* and the *Nisshin* managed to offload their troops and cargo without so much as a mild inconvenience. And for that oversight, General Vandegrift and his men would pay dearly – sooner than anyone expected.

For now, however, came the promise of the Americal Division's 164th Regiment. Its roughly 2,200 men began disembarking in the Lunga roadstead on October 13. Their arrival would bring the number of American troops on Guadalcanal up to some 23,000. The Cactus Air Force now had 90 operational aircraft: 39 Dauntlesses, 41 Wildcats, four P-400s, and six P-39s.

The Japanese countered with two airstrikes on this day. And, curiously, they began bombarding with Imperial Army artillery. Several 150mm shells splashed near the offloading transports *Zeilin* and *McCawley*, Admiral Turner's flagship. Their escorting destroyers *Gwin*, *Nicholas*, and *Sterett* moved into position for counterbattery fire.

Joining them was the old destroyer-turned-minesweeper *Southard*. The *Southard* had undergone a short refit at the beginning of October and her skipper Lieutenant Commander Cochran stepped aside for Lieutenant Commander Tennent. She and fellow old destroyer-turned-minesweeper *Hovey* had just towed four of the new "patrol torpedo" ("PT") boats to a point 300 miles south of Tulagi; from then on the PT boats proceeded under their own power in the company of the *Southard* and *Hovey* to Tulagi, where they arrived on October 12. There the two minesweepers offloaded some 250 drums of aviation gasoline. The aviation gasoline and, for that matter, the PT boats would end up being far more critical than anyone had imagined.

The *Southard* joined the *Gwin*, *Nicholas*, and *Sterett* in bombarding the area from which the Japanese shelling was thought to have originated, the Point Cruz area west of the Matanikau River. Worrying to General Vandegrift and his staff was that the shelling was close to the Henderson Field runway itself. General Roy Geiger, commander of the 1st Marine Air Wing, was concerned enough to move many of the Cactus Air Force fighters southeast to Fighter 1.

That night, Louie the Louse made his customary irritating appearance,[85] dropping flares for a naval bombardment. But there was something different about these flares. They were much more colorful: red over the western edge of the Henderson Field runway, white in the center over the Pagoda, green over the east.[86] And well-spaced, like they were bracketing the Marine positions.

Meanwhile, Corporal Frank Blakely, at the 1st Marines message center near the beach, thought he heard "a sound from the channel like a cork being pulled from a champagne bottle, a gentle *pop*."[87]

And then the world exploded.

"Outside, a thousand rockets burst in the sky," recalled Lieutenant Karl Thayer Soule, a photographer and officer of the Marine intelligence unit. "The blast blew me from my bunk."[88]

The warning sirens of the headquarters wailed, calling Marines, soldiers, and aviators to find cover immediately – if they could. Inside the command bunker, Colonel Thomas understood almost immediately. This wasn't the normal bombardment by destroyers: "My God, those aren't 5-inchers they're throwing at us!"[89]

The talented writer Corporal C. Grady Gallant was with one of the coastal defense gun crews on the beach when "[W]ithout warning of any kind, the sound of a heavy freight train filled the air, the earth shook, there was a series of great explosions and the ground shook again […]"

"It's one of their damn battleships … That's what it is," shouted a gunner. "No doubt about it, by God … A damn battleship … The bastards are trying to kill us with a stinking battleship!"[90] It was in fact two battleships: the *Kongo* and her sister ship *Haruna*, hurling 14-inch shells – incendiary, high explosive, and, oddly, armor-piercing – at the Henderson Field complex.

The immediate result within the American perimeter was pandemonium. According to Lieutenant Colonel Twining, "[T]he earth seemed to turn into the consistency of Jell-O, making it difficult to move or even remain upright."[91] For coastwatcher Martin Clemens:

The ground shook with the most awful of convulsions, and there was dust and smoke everywhere. Our tent was in confusion, as a jagged piece of red-hot steel snapped off the tent pole above our heads […] The top of the tent collapsed over us, together with a few tons of earth that had been blown out of the immense shell craters.[92]

To fighter pilot Captain Joe Foss, "It seemed as if all the props had been kicked from under the sky and we were crushed underneath."[93] The Marines had never been through anything like this. The psychological toll was crushing, Private Robert Leckie described:

[T]he Americans were passing through an agony not to be repeated in World War II. It was a terror of the soul. It was as though the roar of colliding planets was exploding in their ears. Self-control was shattered, strong faces went flabby with fear, men sobbed aloud or whimpered, others put their pistols to their heads. It was not possible to pray.[94]

The Marines could only respond with their 5-inch coastal defense guns, which lacked the range to reach the battleships. The battleships were screened by a full destroyer flotilla and its flagship light cruiser *Isuzu*, who shelled the Marine gun positions to suppress the guns, and shone their searchlights to blind the Marine gunners.[95]

"At the height of the bombardment the express train roar of the bursting salvos was so loud that it overloaded the capacity of the human ear," remembered Captain Foss. "Those two hours were simply indescribable. Nothing like them can be imagined."[96]

Writing later, General Vandegrift agreed. "Unless the reader has experienced naval or artillery shelling or aerial bombing he cannot easily grasp a sensation compounded of frustration, helplessness, fear and, in case of close hits, shock."[97]

But in the midst of this enemy naval bombardment, some Marines wondered, *Where on earth is the US Navy?* "It was the hopelessness, the feeling that nobody gave a curse whether we lived or died," said Lieutenant Commander John E. Lawrence, Cactus Air Force air information officer.[98]

The US Navy was there – just not in the form of warships or even submarines. Enter the four PT boats the *Southard* and *Hovey* had helped lug to Tulagi. They were the *PT-38*, *PT-46*, *PT-48*, and *PT-60*, comprising one section of Motor Torpedo Boat Squadron 3 under Lieutenant Commander Allen Montgomery. The PT boats were basically wooden yachts with torpedo tubes and machine guns bolted on. With the devastating power of the battleships apparent and no other US Navy units available to try to stop them, Montgomery led his four PT boats out to the attack. They were easily brushed aside by the escorting destroyer flotilla. *PT-38* targeted the light cruiser with four torpedoes, three of which malfunctioned. *PT-60* was driven aground trying to escape a destroyer.[99]

At 2:56 am, after firing 973 shells, the *Kongo* and *Haruna* and their companions glided out of Ironbottom Sound. They were replaced by two Mitsubishi G4Ms who harassed the beleaguered Americans by circling the Lunga perimeter loudly and dropping the occasional bomb, relieved by two more G4Ms who kept it up until dawn, at which point the 150mm guns took over. The guns were now dubbed "Millimeter Mike," or, more popularly for those averse to the metric system, "Pistol Pete."[100]

When dawn finally came the Americans emerged from their dugouts, foxholes, and trenches, only to find a shocking, demoralizing scene of abject devastation. The optimism of just 24 hours before was gone. Palm trees were leveled; palm fronds littered the ground, along with shrapnel, splinters, baseplates, and incendiary tubes. Tents were perforated, if they stood at all. Half the headquarters was reduced to rubble. The radio station was knocked out. Henderson Field had 13 craters, 13 holes in the Marston matting. There were burning, wrecked aircraft. Of the 39 SBD Dauntless dive bombers present the day before, only seven were operational, which was seven more than there were operational Avengers.

At Fighter 1, General Geiger's move of the fighters now seemed prescient. The runway was far less damaged than Henderson's. Only six Airacobras remained but 18 of 30 Marine Wildcats were operational.[101] Most fortunate for the Americans on Guadalcanal and surprising considering the severity of the bombardment, only 41 were killed.

Most unfortunate for the Americans on Guadalcanal, almost the entire supply of aviation fuel was torched. Lieutenant Colonel Walter L.J. Bayler, the Cactus Air Force communications officer, saw a "ghastly blaze of light."[102] Burning aviation gasoline was all over the base.

To the Americans on Guadalcanal, this night became immortalized as "The Bombardment," or "All Hell's Eve" – or quite simply, "The Night of the Battleships."

By superhuman effort, two Dauntlesses took off from Henderson Field for the dawn search on October 13. They found yet another Japanese convoy, a so-called "High-Speed Convoy" of six transports carrying some 4,500 troops, plus artillery, tanks, and supplies. It was escorted by a full flotilla of Japanese destroyers. And it was only 140 miles away.

Inside the Lunga perimeter, sleep-deprived Marine engineers and mechanics and Seabees got to work. It took three hours to get the radio repaired and moved into a bunker for General Vandegrift to get off an urgent message to Admiral Ghormley: "Urgently necessary that this force receive maximum support of air and surface units."[103] He added, "absolutely essential aviation gas be flown here continuously."[104] The Cactus Air Force pilots called it a "virtual SOS."[105]

US Navy surface units were in no position to help, however. Admiral Scott's task force was resupplying and could not get to Lunga before dawn on October 15. The lone operational US carrier in the Pacific, the *Hornet*, was refueling. Admiral Nimitz's assessment was "our position is not favorable to prevent a major enemy landing."[106]

To his credit, Admiral Ghormley already had a convoy en route carrying aviation fuel. The convoy consisted of cargo ships *Alchiba* and *Bellatrix* towing two gasoline barges, with motor torpedo boat tender *Jamestown* and fleet tug *Vireo*, escorted by destroyers *Meredith* and *Nicholas*. Unfortunately, this convoy would not make it to Guadalcanal, instead suffering various fates that varied from lucky to tragic to just plain weird.

In a bizarre series of events, the *Meredith* was sunk by Japanese carrier bombers from the *Zuikaku*, while the *Vireo* and her tow were abandoned. But before she could become the *Mary Celeste* of the Pacific, on October 21 the destroyer *Grayson*, sent to find the *Vireo*, ran into her – literally. The resulting damage apparently light, the *Grayson* dropped off a salvage crew who successfully brought the *Vireo* and her tow back to Espiritu Santo.[107]

The sacrifice of the *Meredith* and *Vireo* did bring one critical benefit: the *Zuikaku's* airstrike was so focused on them it missed the *Alchiba*, *Bellatrix*, *Jamestown*, and *Nicholas* heading back to Espiritu Santo. A later airstrike of five Vals managed to get only a few near misses on the *Bellatrix*.[108] Nevertheless, the air attack compelled the *Bellatrix* to cut her tow and leave it adrift. The *Southard* was directed to find the gasoline barge, which she did and began towing it herself, only to be ordered later that day to release it.[109] Somehow, one of the gasoline barges ended up in Tulagi.

Back in Espiritu Santo, Admiral McCain's replacement as commander of all land-based aircraft in the South Pacific area, Rear Admiral Aubrey Fitch, highly respected and a good mix of aggression and caution, recognized the danger of the situation. He did not have a lot to offer, but what he did have he sent – 17 SBD Dauntlesses (six of which were from the *Enterprise*) and 20 Wildcats of Marine Fighting 212 under Lieutenant Colonel Harold F. "Joe" Bauer.

It was now that the Marines began to pay for their inability to capture the "grassy knoll" – Mount Austen, the mountain south of Henderson Field – in *Watchtower's* first days. Now Japanese artillery spotters and lookouts had a beautiful panoramic view of Henderson Field.

Nor were the Japanese about to let up the pressure. Base Air Force mounted two air attacks that day. The Seabees were able to repair enough of Henderson Field and ground crews were able to cobble together some flyable fighter aircraft (even utilizing pieces of partially destroyed aircraft) to resist the air attacks with little additional loss. Working feverishly throughout the day despite the virtually continuous Japanese air attacks, fires, and Pistol Pete, the mechanics managed to slap together enough aircraft for a few airstrikes at the approaching reinforcement group, but, again, none of the American attacks were effective.

The situation on Guadalcanal had gone from hopeful to desperate. The aviators of the Cactus Air Force were warned that once the aviation gasoline ran out, they would have to join the infantry.[110] As it was, the *Saratoga* pilots, with no serviceable Avengers, had already taken up arms to fight alongside the infantry.[111]

Even though eight Dauntlesses of the *Enterprise's* Fighting 6 arrived just before dark, the night of October 13 promised to be another difficult one for the Americans on Guadalcanal. Under the cover of dark the seaplane carrier *Nisshin*, two light cruisers, and three destroyers landed some 1,200 troops on Cape Esperance. Guarding them were two heavy cruisers and two destroyers. The cruisers spent a half-hour lobbing 752 8-inch shells into the Lunga perimeter. This was nothing compared with the night before. The Marines shrugged it off.

What they could not shrug off was the view that greeted them the next morning. "Brazen and bold," in full view of the Marines inside the Lunga perimeter, the transports were anchored and offloading troops, guns, and supplies.[112] The Japanese had assumed that the bombardments by the battleships and cruisers and army artillery would keep the flyers at the Lunga airfield grounded. But just in case, they had about 30 aircraft overhead.

General Geiger's men were scrounging parts to make aircraft flyable and scrounging aviation gasoline to fuel them. As they pieced individual aircraft together, they sent them up in individual attacks. This accomplished little except to put the men in danger. Just as the Cactus Air Force was approaching its last drop of aviation gas, one of General Geiger's staff officers remembered that former chief of staff Colonel Louis Woods had managed to assemble hidden emergency stashes of gas. Geiger bellowed, "By God, find some!"[113]

And they did. Stashed away in swamps and thickets, couch cushions and desk drawers were a total of 465 barrels, enough for two days of operations.[114] Admiral Fitch had arranged for an airlift of R4Ds and C-47s to run a dozen drums apiece to Henderson Field, braving the fire of Pistol Pete to land. Fitch had also arranged for the old four-piper *McFarland*, now a seaplane tender, to bring in 40,000 gallons along with a dozen torpedoes. Another 200 drums were being run from Tulagi. And coming up from Efate in the New Hebrides south of Espiritu Santo was the *Southard*, who would discharge 175 50-gallon drums of aviation fuel, but she would not arrive until October 19.[115]

General Geiger stopped the pinprick attacks and at 10:15 started sending up larger, repeated attacks, including Marine and Navy Dauntlesses, Army Air Force Airacobras, and a single PBY-5A Catalina flying boat, Geiger's personal plane flown by his personal pilot, with a Mark 13 torpedo slung under each wing. Between them, the transport ship *Sasago Maru* was hit, starting a large fire. She had to be beached to prevent her sinking, a total loss, but her troops, tanks, and guns were landed successfully. Another strike of SBDs placed a bomb on the bridge of the transport *Kyushu Maru*, starting a major fire. With no one at the helm and her engines running at full speed, the *Kyushu Maru* drove herself high onto the beach at Bunina Point near Kokumbona.[116] Her troops, tanks, and guns were landed successfully, but the tank fuel and ammunition she carried were lost when the ship burned herself out.[117] A separate strike by 11th Bombardment Group B-17s got at least one bomb on the transport *Azumasan Maru*, igniting a fatal fire that forced her to be beached to prevent her sinking. Her troops, tanks, and guns were landed successfully, but the tank fuel and ammunition she carried were also lost.[118]

With Base Air Force unable to suppress the repeated attacks by the Cactus Air Force, the Japanese were forced to abort their unloading. All 4,500 troops had been landed, but only about two-thirds of the supplies, at a cost of three transports. The Cactus Air Force still lived, but it was on the ropes – and still unable to suppress the nighttime Japanese naval bombardments. In the early hours of October 16, it was two heavy cruisers and a destroyer flotilla doing the honors. The cruisers tossed up 912 8-inch shells, while two of the escorting destroyers added 253 rounds of 5-inch ammunition.[119]

At dawn on October 16, the Cactus Air Force had only nine Wildcats, 11 Dauntlesses, and seven Airacobras operational. Speaking for many within the Lunga perimeter, General Geiger snarled, "I don't think we have a goddamn Navy." With the bombardments becoming too much even for Admiral Ghormley, the *Hornet* was allowed off her leash to finally help the Marines on Guadalcanal, her aircraft joining Marine and Army pilots in some of their seven attacks on the Japanese landing zones and supply drops near Kokumbona.[120] The Cactus Air Force needed the help, because the strain was showing. On one mission involving four P-400 Airacobras, one had a bomb, but only one .30-cal machine gun functioning; the second had a bomb but no functioning guns; the third and fourth had most of their guns functional, but no bombs. The 67th Fighter Squadron's history does not describe it in glowing terms. "The day … was a weary succession of taking off, bombing and strafing, landing to refuel and rearm, and taking off again."[121]

Ongoing runs of aviation fuel took a hit when some Vals from Base Air Force found the *McFarland*, anchored off Lunga with 40,000 gallons of aviation fuel. One bomb landed on the *McFarland*'s stern, detonating the depth charges, blowing off the stern, and sending white-hot fragments into 20,000 desperately needed gallons of aviation fuel that had been offloaded onto a barge, which went up in flames. A vengeful Lieutenant Colonel Bauer, with the fuel tanks of his Wildcat almost dry and in full view of those at Lunga, roared after the Vals at full speed and, coming from the back of the column, proceeded to shoot down three, one by one by one. Bauer later grumbled that if he had had the gas he would have shot down all eight of them.

It was a gruesome end to the day, but October 16 ended far better than had the previous three nights. Before the attack, the *McFarland* had landed the remaining 20,000 gallons of precious aviation fuel. Moreover, once Joe Bauer landed, he gave a rousing speech that provided a desperately needed morale boost, which carried on into the next day, October 17. Dawn found destroyers *Aaron Ward* and *Lardner* shelling Japanese supply dumps near Kokumbona. A rare raid on Guadalcanal by Japanese carrier aircraft, these from the carriers *Junyo* and *Hiyo*, turned into an ineffective and costly attack on the destroyers. It was followed by a warning at 10:30 that the standard air attack by Base Air Force was incoming.[122] A half-hour later, Colonel Bauer, affectionately known as "Coach," called in his pilots for a briefing. But it was more than a briefing; it was a motivational speech – one that would turn the tried and true conventional wisdom on its head: "Be an aggressor. You're out there to shoot down enemy planes. Have complete faith in your armor and confidence in your ability to shoot down the enemy when you have him in your sights … When you see Zeros, dogfight 'em!"[123]

Up until this point, the conventional wisdom, learned from painful, bitter experience, was "Never, *ever* dogfight a Zero." A Zero could and did outperform American fighters, such as the F4F Wildcat or the P-40 Warhawk, in such facets as range and maneuverability. The Americans were forced to use the tactic of "Boom and Zoom" – take one pass at a Zero and speed away, then try again. But not anymore. Now, for the most part, they were no longer facing the Japanese pilots who attacked Pearl Harbor, sank the *Prince of Wales* and *Repulse*, and rampaged through the Indian Ocean. The skill level of Japanese pilots had decreased markedly. Admiral McCain had noticed it, and now Colonel Bauer had, too. A full day of air battles using Joe Bauer's new philosophy cost the Japanese four Zeros and three Bettys at a cost of two Wildcats shot down, with both pilots rescued, and a third lost due to accident, the pilot killed. The airfield was not touched.[124]

By General Vandegrift's estimate, the Japanese now had some 15,000 troops on Guadalcanal, enough to make a land attack on the Lunga perimeter. That same day, he sent a message to Admirals Nimitz, Ghormley, and Turner:

Our force exceeds that number but more than half of it is in no condition to undertake a protracted land campaign due to incessant hostile operations … The situation demands two urgent and immediate steps: A. Take and maintain control of sea areas adjacent to CACTUS to prevent further enemy landings and enemy bombardment such as this force has taken for the last three nights; B. reinforcement of ground forces by at least one division in order that extensive operations may be initiated to destroy hostile force now on CACTUS.[125]

Admiral Ghormley quickly responded with a message to Admirals Nimitz and King – and all the ships under his command:

Urgently need this area one additional army infantry division. Present forces … insufficient to garrison present bases and therefore obviously inadequate [to] support offensive operations. Have neither on hand nor in sight sufficient forces to render CACTUS secure against present infiltration tactics.[126]

In other words, even in this crisis Admiral Ghormley was still unwilling to take forces from the rear bases in order to support the Marines on Guadalcanal. It went back to his original belief that the Guadalcanal offensive would fail and those rear bases would then need to be defended.

Moreover, despite the emergency on Guadalcanal, Ghormley yanked the *Hornet* away from supporting the Marines and sent her to the southeast, out of range of the Japanese, where she would hopefully meet the *Enterprise* soon. After receiving reports from Canberra that a Japanese carrier force was west of the Santa Cruz Islands, at 4:00 pm on October 16, Admiral Ghormley sent another dispatch to Admirals Nimitz and King: "This appears to be all out enemy effort against CACTUS, possibly other positions also. My forces totally inadequate [to] meet situation. Urgently request all available reinforcements possible."[127]

For Admiral Nimitz, it was the last straw. That same night, he met with his staff members who had accompanied him on his South Pacific tour. Nimitz opened the meeting with a short lecture. Apparently referring to Ghormley's message, he stated, "I don't want to hear, or see, such pessimism. Remember, the enemy is hurting too."[128]

After a sleepless night, the next morning Admiral Nimitz sent a message to Admiral King: "In view Ghormley's [latest dispatch] and other indications including some noted during my visit I have under consideration his relief by Halsey at earliest practicable time. Request your comment." King's response was prompt, succinct, and brutal: "Affirmative."[129]

When Vice Admiral Halsey had arrived in Nouméa to take command of the task force centered on the newly repaired carrier *Enterprise*, he found a lieutenant waiting for him with an envelope. Inside that envelope was another envelope, marked "SECRET." Halsey opened the envelope: "CINCPAC: You will take command of the South Pacific area and South Pacific forces immediately." Admiral Halsey had to read it twice. "Jesus Christ and General Jackson! This is the hottest potato they ever handed me!"[130]

The news of Admiral Halsey's appointment spread like the proverbial wildfire across the South Pacific. The effect was electric, with cheers ringing out among the officers and sailors of the fleet. "We were absolutely elated when we heard the news," said Assistant Gunnery Officer Ed Hooper of the battleship *Washington*. "It was a shot of adrenalin for the whole command; things had been getting pretty wishy-washy down there."[131] The light antiaircraft cruiser *Atlanta*'s Robert Graff took a slightly different angle:

> During wartime it's important how the leadership, starting with the Chief of Naval Operations, gets a message across to everybody in every ship, submarine, airplane, and shore station. You need to hear it said that this is an extraordinary moment in your life and in the life of the country, and that you're not going to let it down. Until that day, we had received no such message.[132]

If the effect on the fleet was electric, the effect on Guadalcanal was nuclear. Lieutenant Commander Roger Kent, an air information officer there, described the atmosphere upon hearing the news: "One minute we were too limp with malaria to crawl out of our foxholes; the next we were running around whooping like kids."[133] Two Marines embarked on a scientific discussion of the true value of "The Old Man," as they knew Admiral Halsey. One claimed Halsey was worth two battleships and two carriers; the other insisted Halsey was worth two battleships and three carriers. This largely theoretical disagreement was settled only with increasing volume and, ultimately, some physical debate.[134]

Admiral Halsey went straight to work. By word-of-mouth and even by posted signs he made everyone aware of his wartime credo: "Kill Japs! Kill Japs! Kill more Japs!" He almost immediately officially ended the plan from the original *Watchtower* operation to build an airbase in the Santa Cruz Islands. The forces for that operation were needed on Guadalcanal, and the seaplane tenders that had temporarily based in the Santa Cruz had discovered the islands were home to a unique and vicious strain of malaria. He told Pearl Harbor he would need his best staffers sent down to serve at his headquarters; Admiral Ghormley's old staffers had absorbed his defeatism, which Halsey did not want on his staff.

Admiral Halsey moved the official fleet base from distant Auckland to more convenient Nouméa, where he already was anyway. He demanded 1 million square feet of covered storage space for supplies. Halsey himself came ashore with a contingent of Marines and seized the local headquarters of the High Commissioner For Free France in the Pacific for his own. He worked hard to eliminate distinctions, and thus rivalries, between the services. People would not be of the Navy or the Army anymore, just warriors of the South Pacific Fighting Forces. He would pull in Army technicians to service the fleet and bases, and he wanted their cooperation publicized. "I would like to see it widely advertised that the army is helping us here. I have never seen anything like the spirit here in this neck of the woods. It is a real United States service."[135]

Since the centerpiece of the South Pacific was Guadalcanal, Admiral Halsey wanted to know everything about the island and its environs, as he wrote:

> I began my new job under the crippling handicap of never having seen Guadalcanal, the keystone of the area I was defending. My information about it was not even second-hand, since Bob Ghormley and his Chief of Staff, Rear Admiral Daniel J. Callaghan, had never had an opportunity to see it either.[136]

Halsey did the next best thing: asked the men in command in and around Guadalcanal to fly to Nouméa and brief him.

So, on the night of October 20, Admiral Halsey met with General Vandegrift; General Patch; General Harmon, the senior army officer in the South Pacific; Lieutenant General Thomas Holcomb, the Commandant of the Marine Corps, who was in Nouméa on an inspection tour; Major General C. Barney Vogel, who had just arrived as commander of I Marine Amphibious Corps; Admiral Turner and Ghormley's other subordinate commanders; and Halsey's staff, such as it was.

Generals Vandegrift and Harmon told their stories to Admiral Halsey. Vandegrift said his troops were "practically worn out," with not nearly enough sleep or food but more than enough combat for the past two months.[137] He said his troops needed material support and eventual relief, emphasizing that General Patch's Americal Division be sent in as well as the remainder of the 2nd Marine Division.[138] It was necessarily a very, very long briefing. When they finished, Halsey cut to the chase: "Are we going to evacuate or hold?"

Vandegrift replied, "I can hold, but I've got to get more active support than I've been getting."

Halsey was decisive. He nodded. "All right. Go on back. I'll promise you everything I've got."[139]

Halsey started sending everything he had. This involved crossing the infamous Torpedo Junction. The *Southard* would make a submarine contact in this area the evening of October 21. Lieutenant Commander Tennent dropped two depth charges in an "embarrassing" barrage. This time, the barrage was embarrassing inasmuch as both depth charges failed to detonate, just sinking to the ocean floor like kegs of beer. The *Southard* could not further develop the contact and abandoned the search at 10:15 pm.[140]

Nevertheless, the most serious issues in the South Pacific command continued to be air power. As of October 18, the 1st Marine Air Wing had only 74 aircraft available – 32 Wildcats, 27 Dauntlesses, a measly four Avengers, and 11 Airacobras.[141] By comparison, Base Air Force had 55 Zeros, 49 Bettys, 13 Vals, one land reconnaissance plane, and five flying boats.[142] To support Guadalcanal, all the nearby bases had been stripped to the point at which they barely had enough to defend themselves. Espiritu Santo, for example, had only 16 fighters left to protect it.[143]

The only replacements en route to Guadalcanal were eight Dauntlesses and two Avengers being shipped on the carrier *Enterprise*, but no one knew when they would arrive. General Geiger reported a "critical shortage of fighters" to Fleet Air West Coast at San Diego, who were loading the escort carrier *Altamaha* for shipment to the South Pacific. When she left port, she would be carrying, among other things, 50 Wildcats. But she would not leave until November 3 and would take three weeks to get there.[144] So, in terms of air power, Admiral Halsey would be on his own until mid-November.

Specifically, this meant that Admiral Halsey would be on his own for responding to the Japanese combined arms offensive that Pacific Fleet intelligence knew was coming. With some 20,000 troops on Guadalcanal, the Japanese launched the short-awaited attack on the evening of October 24. It was, in concept, a replay of the Battle for Edson's Ridge, with a diversionary attack on the Matanikau River while the main attack took place from the jungle to the south along the ridge that had been renamed in honor of Colonel Edson.

This time, however, the Marines were very much ready for an attack from the jungle to the south and had fortified their positions on top of the ridge. The Japanese attacked with half their intended force, as the right prong of the two-pronged attack got lost in the jungle and ended up moving tangentially to the Marine line, with very few of the Japanese troops seeing any action. The left prong drove straight into the fortified positions of the 1st Battalion, 7th Marine Regiment – that Marine regiment that had been brought in at such tremendous cost. It proved its value. Once again, the Japanese made their banzai charges: bayonets into machine guns, mortars, and heavy artillery fire. They managed to carve a salient in the middle of the Marine line at a cost, once again, of horrendous casualties. The Marines eliminated the salient the next day.

The Combined Fleet was positioning itself in support of the Imperial Army's attack on the Henderson Field perimeter. That morning, the search Dauntlesses out of Henderson found three Japanese destroyers just 35 miles northwest of Cape Esperance and closing in fast. About 90 minutes later, they spotted a second Japanese force centered on a light cruiser that morning some 100 miles from Cape Esperance.[145]

At about the same time, those three Japanese destroyers had arrived off Lunga and were making merry mischief. They chased off two old destroyers-turned-minesweepers, *Trever* and *Zane*, and sank the tug *Seminole* and the patrol boat *YP-284*. Submarine *Amberjack*, off Tulagi delivering another emergency cargo of aviation fuel, tried to position herself for a torpedo attack but was unable to do so.

The terrible trio of Japanese destroyers was not done yet. They started to bombard American positions with 5-inch shells. But the Marine 3rd Defense Battalion, with several 5-inch coastal defense guns, scored one hit on the destroyer *Akatsuki*, setting fire to the magazine for the Number 3 mount, killing four and severely injuring one.[146] The destroyers retreated behind a smoke screen.[147]

That left the light cruiser and her friends headed for Lunga. Five Dauntlesses from the *Wasp*, commanded by Lieutenant Commander John Eldridge, found the cruiser *Yura* and four destroyers in the northern entrance to Indispensable Strait some 30 miles northeast of Florida Island.[148]

Lieutenant Commander Eldridge himself led off, dropping a 1,000lb bomb from 3,000 feet that exploded in the *Yura*'s engine room. One of his pilots got a near miss on the cruiser as well. The *Yura* coasted to a stop, settling by the stern.[149] The large antiaircraft destroyer *Akizuki* took a hit from a small bomb amidships and two near misses that ruptured hull plating and flooded her after engine room. The starboard propeller stopped and her speed was cut to 23 knots.[150] The Japanese ships started heading back to Shortland.[151] But the damaged *Yura*, subject to multiple attacks throughout the day, would never make it and had to be scuttled that evening.[152]

Yet this was a "combined arms" offensive, and that meant *Kido Butai*: the carriers *Shokaku* and *Zuikaku* in its current iteration. But Admiral Halsey was ready for them – or at least he thought he was ready. On October 24, mere hours before the Japanese attacked Henderson Field, the newly repaired *Enterprise* and her escort group, still under the command of Admiral Kinkaid, had met the *Hornet* group northeast of the New Hebrides, forming Task Force 61 under Rear Admiral Thomas C. Kinkaid.[153] Task Force 61 had two component parts. One was Task Force 16 under Kinkaid's personal direction, featuring the *Enterprise* screened by the new battleship *South Dakota*, heavy cruiser *Portland*, light antiaircraft cruiser *San Juan*, and seven destroyers. Task Force 17, still under Admiral Murray, had the *Hornet* screened by the heavy cruisers *Northampton* and *Pensacola*; light antiaircraft cruisers *San Diego* and *Juneau*; and six destroyers. In Halsey's words, "Until the *Enterprise* arrived, our plight had been almost hopeless. Now we had a fighting chance."[154]

The reason? Admiral Halsey believed "Carrier power varies as the square – two carriers are four times as powerful as one."[155] Halsey's mathematical proof of this formula was somewhat lacking. So, too, was his intelligence information. Pearl Harbor thought Halsey's ships would only face the *Shokaku* and *Zuikaku*, two fleet carriers. In fact, they were also facing one light carrier, the *Zuiho*, as well as the *Junyo*, the latter larger than a light carrier if not quite a fleet carrier, which could be counted as three or even four aircraft carriers, with the power, under Halsey's bizarre formula, of nine or even 16 carriers. Nevertheless, as he told Admiral Nimitz a few weeks later, Admiral Halsey knew, "I had to begin throwing punches almost immediately. As a consequence quick decisions had to be made."[156]

And Admiral Halsey made them, sending out orders to Admiral Kinkaid: "[M]ake a sweep around north Santa Cruz Islands thence southwesterly east of San Cristobal to area in Coral Sea in position to intercept enemy forces approaching [Guadalcanal-Tulagi]."[157] It was a bold, aggressive move, unlike anything seen out of Admiral Ghormley, going outside the air cover, such as it was, of Espiritu Santo, into waters visited by no American carrier in two months. The idea was to place the *Enterprise* and *Hornet* outside the range of Japanese air power on Rabaul, but able to strike from the east at the flank of, and hopefully ambush, the Japanese carriers.[158]

In short, it was to be another Midway. These were the same maneuvers that had enabled the badly outnumbered US Navy to win at Midway. But past performance is no guarantee of future results.

And this Midway II was already not going nearly as smoothly as Midway I, due to Admiral Halsey himself. Halsey's plan for another Midway by having the carriers "[M]ake a sweep around north Santa Cruz Islands" had, as he explained to Admiral Nimitz about a week later, one caveat: the carriers were to sweep past Santa Cruz only "if no enemy comes down" – in other words, if no large enemy force appeared north of the Solomons. Somehow, that particular aspect of the plan did not make it into Halsey's orders to Admiral Kinkaid.[159] It's always the little things.

As Admiral Kinkaid sped northward – too far northward – they received a report of Japanese carriers launching within striking distance of Henderson Field.[160] Monitoring all the sighting reports from Nouméa, Halsey dispatched an order to Admiral Kinkaid that would encapsulate the new attitude emanating out of Nouméa and electrify the men fighting in the South Pacific. The order read simply, "Strike, Repeat, Strike."[161]

They would, but so would the Japanese. October 26 started out with a pair of scouts putting two bombs into the aft flight deck of the Japanese carrier *Zuiho*, wrecking her arrester gear and rendering her useless for the remainder of the battle. Then it turned into an exchange of airstrikes between the *Enterprise* and *Hornet* on one side and *Kido Butai* on the other. But the *Enterprise* and *Hornet* struggled to launch their airstrikes. Ultimately, they launched three groups of attack aircraft with each acting independently and making no effort to coordinate with the others. The eminent Guadalcanal historian Eric Hammel pointed out, "[T]here was no US doctrine allowing the subordination of one air-group commander to another, nor the meshing of squadrons of one air group with like squadrons of another."[162] Not yet, anyway. Hammel went on to comment:

> [T]he US strike groups went off as a stream of separate mixed units, each one composed of whatever aircraft happened to be available at the time of the launch. Indeed, each of the three strike groups lacked internal cohesion; each was itself strung out over distances of several miles.[163]

In other words, the American airstrikes had been sent up in driblets, stayed aloft in driblets, and broke up into even smaller driblets. One group could not find the Japanese carriers and ineffectually attacked a vanguard force of battleships and cruisers. Another group attacked the same vanguard force, heavily damaging the heavy cruiser-seaplane carrier *Chikuma*. The *Hornet*'s Dauntless dive bombers commanded by Lieutenant Commander William J. "Gus" Widhelm were the only ones that actually reached *Kido Butai*. Defending Zeros hacked mercilessly at them, shooting down two, including Widhelm, who was later rescued. But the "hell divers," as the Japanese called the SBD Dauntlesses, made their attack all the same. In a very impressive performance, they got anywhere from four to six or more hits on the *Shokaku*. The *Shokaku*'s flight deck amidships was pummeled. The

1,000lb bombs left it an inferno, so shattered it "looked like an earthquake fault zone."[164] The center elevator was trashed. Beneath the flight deck, the nearly empty hangar deck was devastated. But this was not Midway, the *Shokaku* was not the *Kaga*, and the Japanese had learned a thing or two about preparing for an air attack. While the damage to the carrier was heavy, her watertight integrity was not impacted, and her engines remained functional. She would make it back home for repairs.

The first hint the American aviators got that the day was not going according to plan was when the *Hornet*'s Dauntlesses passed a large group of Japanese carrier aircraft flying in the opposite direction heading for the US carriers. This would not be an ambush like Midway. The *Hornet* had been found. The pilots wondered if the *Hornet* would still be there upon their return.

The bad luck that was not present at Midway would continue. The warning of incoming aircraft from the *Hornet*'s strike was garbled, though both Admirals Kinkaid and Murray were able to deduce that a Japanese airstrike was coming. Kinkaid guessed that the *Enterprise* was in the path of this strike and told Murray that the *Enterprise* would handle fighter direction for this incoming attack.[165]

Admiral Kinkaid had guessed wrongly. The Japanese target was actually the *Hornet*. Moreover, in taking over fighter direction Kinkaid had trusted the defense of the *Hornet* to an inexperienced officer instead of the *Hornet*'s veteran and very capable Fighter Director Officer Lieutenant Allan Foster Fleming. Worse yet, for reasons that have never been fully established, the radars of both the *Enterprise* and the *Hornet* did not detect the incoming Japanese aircraft. The radars of some of the escorting warships did, but that information was not passed on because they assumed the carriers had it. To compound matters, the *Enterprise* entered a rain squall. Most of the Japanese aircraft were able to attack the *Hornet* without interference from US Navy Wildcats.

The result was disastrous. Sixteen Val dive bombers and 20 "Nakajima B5N Type 97 Carrier Attack Planes" – "Kate," the Allies would call this aircraft – attacked the *Hornet* in the face of extremely heavy antiaircraft fire, especially from the escorting light antiaircraft cruisers *San Diego* and *Juneau*. The carrier suffered three bomb hits. But far worse was the damage from the torpedo attack by those 20 Kates: two torpedo hits, which disabled the *Hornet*'s engines. And to add injury to injury, two proto-kamikazes plowed into the carrier as well. One burning Val dove straight into the carrier's stack, then bounced off the island superstructure and embedded itself into the flight deck, where it exploded, spewing flaming gasoline on the signal bridge, the island, the flight deck, and into the ready room for Scouting 8 one deck below – all, ironically, without its 250kg bomb exploding.[166] Seven men on the signal bridge were incinerated. A second Val whose bomb had missed flew into the port gallery walkway just forward of the 5-inch antiaircraft battery. The burning fuselage penetrated the hull as far as the Number 1 elevator pit, spewing burning metal on the hangar deck and leaving yet another serious fire in its wake.[167]

The *Hornet* was left dead in the water and burning, with no power to move or fight the fires. As the Japanese pilots returned to their carriers – far fewer in number than had launched – one of them saw the *Enterprise*, the last operational US Navy carrier in the Pacific. They reported its location to *Kido Butai*.[168]

Admiral Kinkaid radioed Admiral Halsey with two words: "*Hornet* hurt."[169] The reply from the commander of American forces in the South Pacific suggests he was a little slow on the uptake: "Operate from and in positions from which you can strike quickly and effectively. We must use everything we have to the limit."[170]

The *Enterprise* now had to juggle her own aircraft and those from the *Hornet*. The carrier struggled trying to recover her aircraft, put up a strike, and put up and keep up air cover. A traffic jam resulted, both on and over the flight deck. She tried to keep the air cover by landing a few Wildcats, refueling and reloading them right on the flight deck, then spotting and launching them immediately, like a pit stop in auto racing.

Some aircraft had to ditch because of a lack of fuel. One damaged TBF ditched; the destroyer *Porter* was directed to recover the aircrew. While she did so, she was hit by a torpedo that was initially thought to have come from a Japanese submarine but is now believed to have come from the Avenger itself, with the entry into the water unjamming its damaged torpedo release mechanism. The *Porter* had to be scuttled.

As another Japanese airstrike approached, the *Enterprise*'s radar was still performing poorly, and the fighter direction was even worse. But the antiaircraft response was not. Admiral Kinkaid positioned his assets to meet the incoming strike, including the light antiaircraft cruiser *San Juan* and the battleship *South Dakota*, and her powerful antiaircraft battery was positioned in the path of the incoming Japanese. When the battleship opened fire, it was so voluminous she was described as a "volcano" and a "ring of fire" by the destroyer *Maury* off the starboard bow.[171]

And while under repair at Pearl Harbor, the *Enterprise* had 16 of the powerful 40mm Bofors antiaircraft gun in four quadruple mounts added to her. On top of that, the *Enterprise* had received fire direction radar for her eight 5-inch guns and an increase in the number of 20mm Oerlikon guns. In the *Enterprise*'s sky control, Lieutenant Commander Elias B. "Benny" Mott II, the assistant gunnery officer, would later say, "As each plane came down, a veritable cone of tracer shells enveloped it. You could see it being hit and bounced by exploding shells."[172] Gunnery officer Lieutenant Commander Orlin Livdahl was with Mott in sky forward, the position from which the antiaircraft guns were directed. He was sure that "the amount of gunfire put out by the fleet far surpassed the prodigious volume at Eastern Solomons[.]"[173]

The result was a typhoon of white-hot steel directed at the incoming Japanese. In the face of this typhoon, the Japanese still managed two bomb hits. The first pierced the flight deck 20 feet from the forward edge, passed through the forecastle deck, and exploded in midair just off the port bow.[174] About a minute later, a second bomb hit the flight deck almost on the center line 10 feet aft the forward elevator, piercing the deck to strike a girder and break in two, causing two distinct explosions.[175] One part blasted through the hangar deck; the other exploded on the third deck, devastating officers' quarters, wiping out a repair party almost totally, and starting a fire in the pit to elevator Number 1.[176]

The Vals also managed a very damaging near miss – about 10 feet from the starboard quarter. It opened a seam in the side plating 3 inches wide for a length of 50 feet. As the ship shuddered from top to bottom, the main turbine bearing was damaged; three fuel tanks, one of them full, ruptured; and the mast was rotated half an inch, knocking out of alignment a suite of antennae mounted there.[177]

The Japanese attack had damaged the *Enterprise* and killed 44 of her crew, but the carrier was not crippled and was still operational, though her ability to juggle her aircraft in the air was hampered by the jammed Number 1 elevator.

Coming in on the Vals' tail fins were 16 Kates with torpedoes escorted by four Zeros. This time, the attacking Kates ran into a buzzsaw of Wildcats as well as a typhoon of hot steel. No torpedoes hit the carrier, though three did hit the heavy cruiser *Portland*, but all at the end of their runs, without enough momentum to detonate the warheads. One Kate crashed into the destroyer *Smith*, causing a large fire and throwing clear the bodies of the pilot and his radioman, one of whom carried a copy of the current Japanese aircraft code.

Next were 17 Vals from the carrier *Junyo*. They got another damaging near miss, a bomb that glanced off the port bow near the waterline and detonated less than 10 feet from the *Enterprise*'s hull, the concussion denting and rupturing hull plating. They managed one bomb hit each on the *South Dakota* and *San Juan*, causing moderate damage to both ships.

The carrier resumed flight operations, but she was in desperate shape. Her forward elevator was out, which slowed striking aircraft below. As of 11:40 am, in the air were no fewer than 73 aircraft: 28 Wildcats (9 *Hornet*, 19 *Enterprise*); 24 Dauntlesses (21 *Hornet*, 3 *Enterprise*), none of which had folding wings; and 21 Avengers (15 *Hornet*, 6 *Enterprise*). All were critically low on fuel.

This was the entirety of US Navy carrier striking power in the Pacific. The *Enterprise* had to recover as many planes as possible. Commander John Crommelin, the *Enterprise*'s air officer, had promised his pilots, "If you get back to the ship and into the groove [basically the final approach for landing on the carrier], we'll get you aboard." And they did. In 43 minutes Crommelin and landing signal officers Lieutenants James Daniels and Robin Lindsey landed 47 planes – 23 Wildcats and 24 Dauntlesses – without an accident. In so doing, they saved American naval air power in the South Pacific. Five Wildcats had to ditch, but no Dauntlesses did.

Admiral Kinkaid knew they were lucky. The *Enterprise* was still – barely – operational. He believed, correctly, there was still one or two undamaged Japanese carriers out there, plus Japanese surface forces were approaching as well. Kinkaid had to make a very difficult and painful decision, but he did so "without hesitation." He had to get the *Enterprise* out of danger. He signaled Admiral Halsey and Admiral Murray: "I am proceeding southeastward toward [Efate]. When ready proceed in the same direction."[178] He could provide no air cover for the *Hornet*.

As damage reports continued coming in, Kinkaid was forced to report to Admiral Halsey that the *Enterprise* was damaged far worse than previously thought. Halsey understood the danger and ordered all forces to "retire to southward."[179] They had attacked, but they had bitten off more than they could chew. It was now a question of whether the *Hornet* could be saved.

The *Hornet*'s crew was outraged. They believed the *Enterprise* had botched her aerial defense, for which she paid the price, and now the *Enterprise* was abandoning her. They were right, but in the cold light of military logic it didn't matter. The *Enterprise* was the last operational US Navy carrier in the Pacific. She had to be protected.

With help from escorting destroyers, the *Hornet*'s crew had put out all the fires. Her engineers had managed to get one boiler lit and were in the process of building up enough steam pressure to the still functional after engine room to get the *Hornet* moving. In the meantime, the heavy cruiser *Northampton* was trying to tow the carrier.

But all that came to naught when an attack by seven Kates from the *Junyo* arrived. The tow line had to be cut. With an almost stationary carrier and with reduced antiaircraft defenses and no fighter opposition, it was almost impossible to miss. But miss the Japanese did. The torpedo bombers managed only two hits, more testimony as to the declining skill of Japanese pilots. And only one of those torpedo hits detonated. But it was enough. It flooded the after engine room. Now there was no way to get the *Hornet* moving on her own.

With Japanese surface forces approaching, there was no choice but to abandon and scuttle the *Hornet* to eliminate the possibility of the Japanese salvaging her. The carrier was evacuated efficiently through three more Japanese attacks by a total of 12 dive bombers that resulted in two hits and one near miss.

Though the *Hornet* could not move, despite the three torpedo hits she was not exactly sinking. While the rest of the *Hornet*'s task group headed southeast to join the *Enterprise*'s group in their flight toward Nouméa, destroyers *Mustin* and *Anderson* were ordered to finish off the *Hornet*. But the torpedoes they launched, if they hit at all, were not enough to sink the derelict, nor were their 5-inch guns. With Japanese ships on the radar, the destroyers withdrew with the hulk still burning fiercely. The Japanese were unable to salvage the burning *Hornet* and sank her themselves.

But the danger was not over. The US retreat took the *Enterprise* and her cohort through Torpedo Junction. While trying to avoid a Japanese submarine, the *South Dakota* collided with the destroyer *Mahan*. But other than this collision the other US Navy ships made it through unscathed.

So ended the carrier engagement the US Navy would call the Battle of the Santa Cruz Islands.

The Japanese had suffered severe damage to the *Shokaku* and serious damage to the *Zuiho* and *Chikuma*, which would keep them out for extended periods of time. Aside from the loss of the *Hornet*, the Americans had suffered heavy damage to the *San Juan* and *Smith*, relatively light damage to the *South Dakota*, and heavy damage to the *Enterprise*, the last remaining operational American carrier in the Pacific. By any measure, it was a Japanese tactical victory.

Whether it was a strategic victory for Japan is not nearly as clear. After the battle the Japanese had the only two fully operational aircraft carriers in the Pacific, the *Zuikaku* and the *Junyo*, both of whom had come out of Santa Cruz unscathed.

The Americans did still have one carrier left in the South Pacific – the *Enterprise*, although badly damaged and hampered in air operations because the Number 1 (forward) elevator was jammed, fortunately in the "up" position so at least aircraft could still take off. While the *Enterprise* was still en route to the relative safety of New Caledonia, Admiral Halsey called the senior officers of all branches in Nouméa and told them to pool their mechanics to get ready for the repairs to the *Enterprise* and other ships and aircraft.[180]

But not having seen the *Enterprise* yet, Admiral Halsey had to assume the worst about the carrier's condition. He went so far as to ask Admiral Nimitz to get one or more British aircraft carriers sent to the South Pacific. Nimitz forwarded the request to Admiral King.[181] In turn, Nimitz ordered Halsey to prepare a coordinated defense plan for the rear bases.[182] They were bracing for the worst.

The *Enterprise* limped into Nouméa, where it was estimated it would take three weeks to be repaired, leaving the Japanese dominant in the seas in the meantime.

As such, it can be (and has been) argued that the battle was a Japanese strategic victory.[183] But this hinges on whether "fully operational" means "effective." The effectiveness of a carrier force depends on its aircraft and especially its aviators. Since September, Americans such as Admiral McCain and Lieutenant Colonel Bauer had been commenting on the declining skill level of Japanese pilots. The attacks on the *Hornet* at the end of Santa Cruz, while fatal, were not nearly as effective as they perhaps should have been. This reflected the heavy casualties suffered by the "Sea Eagles" of the Japanese Naval Air Force since the beginning of the war. The Americans were aware that the casualties had been heavy, but not how heavy.

Admiral Halsey was defiant in the face of the adversity brought on by Santa Cruz. In an October 31 letter to Admiral Nimitz, Halsey vowed to "patch up what we have and go with them." He went on to say, "I will not send any ship back to Pearl Harbor unless it is absolutely necessary. This may mean operating the *Enterprise* with a slightly reduced complement of planes and under difficulties, but under the present circumstances, a half a loaf is better than none."[184]

Here was the big difference between the Japanese two fully operational aircraft carriers and the US Navy's: the latter had veteran, skilled pilots. What to do with these highly skilled and battle-hardened aviators would be a question for Admiral Halsey as he pondered his next move.

The Japanese still had a numerical advantage in every major warship category in the Pacific – more aircraft carriers, more battleships, more cruisers, more destroyers. They had a numerical advantage in aircraft, as well. And they had more of those major warships and aircraft close to the South Pacific theater than the Allies did. They remained poised to move on Guadalcanal, with a crushing bombardment of the airfield by battleships, followed by Imperial Army troops landing to overwhelm the Marine defenders. But their most powerful striking arm, the Sea Eagles, had been shattered.

The Americans could oppose this collection of forces with one beaten-up aircraft carrier, albeit one who now had the best carrier air group in the Pacific; two new battleships, one of which was damaged; and an unsinkable airfield on Guadalcanal that had resisted all Japanese attempts to capture or reduce it. Both the carrier and the airfield were home to experienced, battle-hardened aviators; the airfield could house more. On these battered but tough aviator shoulders rested the fate of Guadalcanal.

That was a very long list of advantages for the Japanese, a very short one for the Americans. But as Admiral Nimitz explained, "While our situation in the Southern Solomons is far from satisfactory, it is far from hopeless."[185]

Into this "far from satisfactory, far from hopeless" situation sailed the little, infinitely expendable, old destroyer-turned-minesweeper the *Southard*. She had had a busy time, mostly making runs to deliver aviation fuel to Guadalcanal, though she did also escort the destroyer *Conyngham* back to Espiritu Santo after it had collided with the destroyer *Fuller* on November 2.[186] The next morning, the destroyer *McCalla*, escorting another supply convoy to Guadalcanal, took a surface radar contact from the *Helena*'s SG radar and chased it down, forcing the contact, a surfaced submarine, to dive.

The *McCalla* at 5:37 am started dropping depth charges …

For an instant, the water seemed to freeze and turn white.

Eleven times. Then her sound gear picked up a series of three underwater explosions. She could no longer pick up the submarine on her sonar and there was a thick stench of oil. The submarine, the *I-172*, with a crew of 91 under Lieutenant Commander Ota Takeshi and carrying Captain Okamoto Yoshisuke, commander of Submarine Division 12, was never seen again. The entire exchange had taken maybe a half-hour.[187]

Now it was the *Southard*'s turn. She had turned around and left Espiritu Santo for Guadalcanal on November 8 with a load of aviation fuel. That night, the freighter *Edgar Allen Poe* had taken one torpedo from a Japanese submarine. The offending boat, the *I-21*, tried to finish off the freighter, but after a few surprising shots from the *Poe*'s deck gun, discretion got the better part of valor for skipper Commander Matsumura Kanji and he ordered a dive to end the fight. The *Poe* was towed to Nouméa, where it was determined she would sail nevermore.[188]

The *Southard* no longer carried torpedoes, but the minesweeper remained a first-class antisubmarine platform. During her long trips taking supplies to Guadalcanal and bringing wounded back to Espiritu Santo, her crew would listen for Japanese submarines. During their long voyages between Guadalcanal and points south, they had spent hundreds of hours listening for Japanese submarines, becoming very good at it.

And so the *Southard*, under Lieutenant Commander Tennent, was heading for Guadalcanal on November 10 when, at around 2:30 am, she detected a submarine off

Cape Recherche, on the northwestern coast of San Cristobal, in the dark heart of Torpedo Junction. She did not need her sonar equipment to pick it up, though; it was on the surface, recharging its batteries, its crew getting a breath of fresh night air after being cramped all day in the hot, stuffy submarine. This particular boat was a picket, stationed as a set of eyes for the Japanese to warn of Allied traffic and, if possible, attack it.

The *Southard* crept to within gun range and opened up with her 4.5-inch guns. These were old guns, manually aimed, and apparently the minesweeper's first shots missed. The shocked Japanese crew quickly dove for the open hatches so the submarine could dive herself. Amazingly, the submarine got off two torpedoes – they missed – and she disappeared beneath the surface.

Disappointed but undeterred, the *Southard* now began a hunt in the dark. It took her sound crews ten minutes to pick up the submarine. At 2:42 am, Lieutenant Commander Tennent ordered that first attack with depth charges.

For an instant, the water seemed to freeze and turn white.

At least a small patch of it. That's what depth charges usually did, before sending up a big bubble to break through the surface with a rumble – not a big bang or a giant plume of water, like they show in the movies.

The hope was that the shockwave from the underwater detonations, known as the bubble pulse, would cause the submarine's hull to crack. But all it did was cause the sound guys to lose their target. Again, they were disappointed but undeterred.

And that determination paid off. At 6:07 am, just after daybreak, they picked up their prey once again. And now came another depth charge attack. But their target submarine was proving very hard to pin down precisely. It clearly had a savvy, veteran skipper.

On came six more depth charge attacks.

For an instant, the water seemed to freeze and turn white.

It was not followed by any debris, however, but instead, at 10:03 am, the submarine's conning tower. The *Southard*'s gunners mercilessly blasted it. A 4.5-inch salvo hit the tower. Submarines are unarmored, so any shell hit can be devastating. And this one was. The submarine's stern rose out of the water and she slid beneath the waves. The *Southard* kept looking for her, as did her sister ship *Hovey* and a Consolidated PBY Catalina flying boat out of Espiritu Santo, but the submarine was never seen again.[189]

There is a dispute as to the identity of the *Southard*'s target. Some credit the *Southard* with sinking the *I-172*, though that submarine was actually sunk by the *McCalla*.[190] But US Navy records credit the *Southard* with sinking the *I-17*, with a crew of 91 under the command of Lieutenant Commander Harada Hakue. Making a fairly persuasive case against the US Navy's identification is the *I-17*'s appearance at the Japanese naval base at Truk a few weeks later. The Japanese identify the sunken submarine as the *I-15*, with a crew of 91 under the command of veteran Commander Ishikawa Nobuo. Indeed, the *I-17* was patrolling in the same area as the *I-15* (along with the *I-26*) and heard the *Southard*'s depth charge attacks. Thus, the target here was the *I-15*.[191]

It was perhaps a small thing, blinding one pair of Japanese eyes watching the route between Espiritu Santo and Guadalcanal, but it was also the first rumbling of the cataclysm about to permanently change the Guadalcanal campaign. The pressure had been building for months, yet nothing had changed. The Americans still controlled Henderson Field; the Japanese were still in position to capture it. The Americans still controlled the skies over Guadalcanal; the Japanese could still challenge it. The Americans still controlled the waters around Guadalcanal during the day; the Japanese still controlled those waters at night. And if the Japanese made a total commitment of their forces in the South Pacific, they could still cut off Guadalcanal and capture it.

The pressure was too much. Something had to change. And change it would.

CHAPTER 1

THE STORMS BEFORE THE STORM

The admiral read his orders with anger and no small measure of disgust. His superiors had not listened to him – again. He had a central role in an operation with which he did not agree – again.

Rear Admiral Tanaka Raizo was a veteran of the Combined Fleet, the ocean-going portion of the Imperial Japanese Navy. A 1913 graduate of the Japanese naval academy at Etajima, Tanaka had been at the forefront of Japanese operations to establish the Greater East Asia Co-prosperity Sphere since almost the very beginning of that effort in China.

The Japanese started their full invasion of China in August 1938 by landing troops near Shanghai. Emperor Hirohito had been promised that the Chinese capital of Nanking would be captured and the Nationalist government of Chiang Kai-shek would be forced to capitulate within a month of the invasion.

One month into this one-month war the Japanese still had not cleared Shanghai. Five months in the Imperial Japanese Army reached Nanking, the Nationalist government's capital, although Chiang and his government had fled. Out of frustration, celebration, malice, or any combination thereof, the Imperial Japanese Army committed what became known as the "Rape of Nanking," with some 20,000 women raped, upwards of 300,000 civilians killed, and everything of value shipped back to Japan.

As brutal as the Rape of Nanking was, it was only of limited military value, because Chiang's government was now in Chunking, on the upper Yangtze, well out of reach of the Japanese. So the Japanese focused on conquering everything of value in China – ports, industrial areas, arable land, population centers, transportation routes. It was 14 months into this one-month war that the Imperial Japanese Army seized Canton and its valuable port. In support of this operation was an Imperial Japanese Navy force that included the light cruiser *Jintsu*, commanded by one Tanaka Raizo.

Even so, 48 months into this one-month war, the Japanese had indeed conquered everything of value in mainland China and expanded outward, seizing French Indochina as well. They had used their new wonder aircraft, the Zero, to literally chase the Chinese Air Force from the skies. Yet China had become a quagmire for Japan with Chiang's government refusing to surrender. Worse, the barbaric conduct of the Imperial Japanese Army in China and the aggressive geostrategic moves by Japan had alienated most of the trading partners on whom Japan depended for raw materials. With British-held Malaya and Singapore clearly threatened, as well as the Netherlands East Indies and the American-held Philippines, unsurprisingly, the United States, quickly followed by Britain and the Dutch government-in-exile, implemented a trade embargo.

This was a problem. The embargo would cripple Japan's war effort, and force a withdrawal from China. That would mean a humiliating loss of "face," that abstract Asian concept so imperfectly understood in the West. The embargo would throttle supplies of tin, rubber, and, especially, oil – all the crucial resources necessary to wage war. So 52 months into this one-month war, the Japanese sought to secure victory by starting a second war. Well, it made sense to them.

And so began what has been called the "Centrifugal Offensive." Vice Admiral Nagumo Chuichi and his Japanese Carrier Striking Force, officially the 1st Air Fleet, unofficially *Kido Butai* ("Striking Force"), with the carriers *Akagi*, *Kaga*, *Hiryu*, *Soryu*, *Shokaku*, and *Zuikaku*, left for Pearl Harbor and a date with infamy on December 7, 1941. The Pearl Harbor attack, the most powerful and spectacular of the Japanese offensive operations, the brainchild of Combined Fleet head Admiral Yamamoto Isoroku, was well away from the center, the actual objectives, of the Centrifugal Offensive – the "Southern Resources Area," consisting of the aforementioned British-held Malaya and Singapore, and, especially, the Netherlands East Indies. Seizure of the American-held Philippines was essential to secure the supply line from the Southern Resources Area back to Japan. All in the hope of building up a self-sufficient "Co-prosperity Sphere" before the Americans had built up their navy.

And Tanaka Raizo, now a rear admiral in his flagship, the familiar light cruiser *Jintsu*, commanding the 2nd Destroyer Flotilla, found himself at the center of the Centrifugal Offensive.[1] While the Imperial Japanese Naval Air Force's land-based 11th Air Fleet under Vice Admiral Tsukahara Nizhizo kneecapped Allied resistance efforts by destroying the US Far East Air Force on the ground at Clark Field, destroying the US Asiatic Fleet's main base at Cavite, both in the Philippines, and sinking the British battleship *Prince of Wales* and battlecruiser *Repulse* off Malaya, Admiral Tanaka was escorting and supporting transports in the capture of Legaspi in the Philippines.

The 2nd Destroyer Flotilla quickly followed the capture of Legaspi by supporting the successful amphibious invasions of Davao and Jolo, also in the Philippines. The New Year 1942 opened with Admiral Tanaka supporting the seizure of northern Celebes, in the Netherlands East Indies, quickly followed by Ambon and Timor.

All of which led up to the main event – the invasion of Java, the capital island of the Netherlands East Indies and the last of the primary objectives of the Centrifugal Offensive.

At the end of February, Tanaka and his 2nd Destroyer Flotilla were given the honor of escorting the very large convoy carrying Imperial Japanese Army troops to land near the eastern end of Java. Since combat was expected, Rear Admiral Takagi Takeo's 5th Cruiser Division and the 4th Destroyer Flotilla under Rear Admiral Nishimura Shoji were assigned to escort the convoy as well.

It was Admiral Takagi who at this time pioneered the unique Japanese tactic of escorting troopships by positioning warships well behind them. It made sense, in a way. If the enemy showed up, the thin-skinned, slow, defenseless transports would be sunk and thousands of troops lost along with their supplies, but the troops could at least die secure in the knowledge that the warships would be all right. Takagi had his cruisers approximately 200 miles behind the invasion convoy. Admiral Tanaka and his destroyers were left in the middle of the Java Sea guarding the convoy by themselves. When informed that an Allied striking force was approaching the transports, Takagi angrily ordered the cruisers to speed up to catch up to the convoy. Tanaka spent a very uncomfortable period wondering if his light cruiser *Jintsu* and his destroyers would have to face the five cruisers and nine destroyers of the Allied Combined Striking Force by themselves. Takagi's cruisers appeared on the horizon behind him just as the Allied cruisers appeared on the horizon ahead of him. The Allies suffered a crushing defeat that effectively ended their already crippled defense of the Indies. It was another example of the bad luck that followed the Allies throughout the Java Sea Campaign.

So by the time the Japanese completed their conquest of the Netherlands East Indies, Admiral Tanaka was considered an expert on amphibious operations. Admiral Takagi, fresh off his victory in the Java Sea, was kicked upstairs and told to command an operation to land Japanese troops at Port Moresby in the hope of capturing Papua New Guinea and isolating Australia. Tanaka was not in on this and it showed. It became the Battle of the Coral Sea. The Japanese managed to capture Tulagi, costing the Japanese the destroyer *Kikuzuki*, but the convoy to Port Moresby was turned back, with the effort costing the Japanese the light carrier *Shoho* and, temporarily, the services of the carriers *Shokaku* and *Zuikaku*.

This would prove to be a disaster because Admiral Yamamoto was focused on a decisive battle – that Holy Grail of Japanese naval strategy since their victory over the Russians at Tsushima in 1905 – against the Americans at Midway. It was a plan that was simple on paper. The Japanese would send almost every ship in the Combined Fleet, including Admiral Tanaka's 2nd Destroyer Flotilla and four carriers of Admiral Nagumo's *Kido Butai* – *Akagi*, *Kaga*, *Hiryu*, and *Soryu* – to attack and capture Midway atoll, the furthest west of the Hawaiian Islands. That would compel the Pacific Fleet to come out and fight, at which point the Japanese would destroy them. What could go wrong?

Neither Admiral Yamamoto nor Admiral Nagumo nor any of the other Japanese senior officers stopped to consider what they should do if the Americans showed up first. That is, before the Japanese had captured Midway. This is exactly what happened. To complicate matters, the Imperial Japanese Navy was not a maven for individual initiative, flexibility, and adaptability to changing situations. Their lack of adaptability ended up costing the

Japanese the *Akagi*, *Kaga*, *Soryu*, and, last but not least, the *Hiryu* – two thirds of the *Kido Butai* that had attacked Pearl Harbor. The Japanese were compelled to retreat, during which they lost an additional heavy cruiser, the *Mikuma*.

Midway was a disaster for the Japanese. But not, they felt, so much of a disaster that it stopped their offensive ambitions. They were still looking to cut off Australia. The Imperial Japanese Army thought the solution still involved capturing Port Moresby, this time by crossing Papua New Guinea's Owen Stanley Mountains. Their attempts to do so had failed so far because the Owen Stanleys could only be crossed by using the Kokoda Trail, which was the width of one man and was thus easily defended. To General Hyakutake Harukichi, commander of the Japanese 17th Army, the solution was simple: send more men.

Meanwhile, the Imperial Japanese Navy was also considering how to cut off Australia, and also looking to strengthen their defenses against the inevitable Allied counterattack. This ended up having the same solution: building airfields in the lower Solomons and beyond. When the Japanese found a suitable site for an airfield at Lunga Point on Guadalcanal, they started construction. Using only hand tools, they completed the airfield in a little more than a month.

At which point, the Americans swooped in and evicted the Japanese from their newly constructed airfield.

The August 7 Allied landing on Guadalcanal caught the Japanese completely by surprise. Starting that same day, the 11th Air Fleet – an air force that flew from land bases and thus, under Japan's dual naming system, was given the creative title "Base Air Force" – launched two days of air attacks against the invasion fleet, mostly with twin-engine Mitsubishi G4M Type 1 Attack Bombers – the same aircraft that helped sink the *Prince of Wales* and *Repulse*. But the G4Ms were largely ineffective.

Meanwhile, Japanese naval forces were also scrambling to respond to the invasion of Guadalcanal. Vice Admiral Mikawa Gunichi, head of the 8th Fleet, slapped together an attack force with his designated fleet flagship, the luxurious heavy cruiser *Chokai*, four old heavy cruisers of the 6th Cruiser Division (*Aoba*, *Kako*, *Furutaka*, and *Kinugasa*) under Rear Admiral Goto Aritomo; two old light cruisers of the 18th Cruiser Division (*Tenryu* and *Yubari*) under Rear Admiral Matsuyama Mitsuharu; and all of one destroyer, *Yunagi*. His goal was to sail to Guadalcanal and destroy the invasion transports in a night attack.

Through some incredible good luck on Admiral Mikawa's part and some even more incredible incompetence on the Allies' part, the Japanese squadron was able to gain complete surprise, sinking four heavy cruisers and blowing the bow off a fifth, all without loss. Then, after accomplishing pretty much everything except his objective, he turned around and went home, leaving the defenseless invasion transports and cargo ships alone. He wanted to get away before sunrise allowed the American carriers, whose location he did not know, to attack him. Mikawa had no way of knowing the American carriers had been withdrawn, an action that helped create the environment that led to his victory. This First Battle of the Solomon Sea, as the Japanese called it, or the Battle of the Savo Island, as it was known to the Allies, was a missed opportunity, or at least an enraged Admiral Yamamoto thought so.

As if to emphasize that missed opportunity, the 6th Cruiser Division was ambushed by a submarine off Kavieng, New Ireland, and lost the *Kako* to its torpedoes.

This was where Admiral Tanaka came in.

With his presumed amphibious command abilities Admiral Tanaka was made "Commander Reinforcement Group," and his 2nd Destroyer Flotilla was given the job of transporting reinforcements to Guadalcanal. His would be the centerpiece of what the Japanese called Operation *Ka*, after the first syllable of Guadalcanal – *Gadarukanaru* – as pronounced in Japanese.

But just because Tanaka Raizo was considered an expert on amphibious warfare did not mean that his superiors would seek his input with regard to the strategy or planning. It simply meant that virtually every time the Japanese needed something done amphibiously, they would order Tanaka to do it. If Tanaka succeeded, that's what he was supposed to do. If Tanaka failed, it was his fault.

Back in August, Admiral Tanaka had read his orders from the 8th Fleet with shock and extreme consternation. He would later write:

> With no regard for my opinion, as commander of the reinforcement force, this order called for the most difficult operation in war – landing in the face of the enemy – to be carried out by mixed units that had no opportunity for rehearsal or even preliminary study. It must be clear to anyone with knowledge of military operations that such an undertaking could never succeed. In military strategy expedience sometimes takes precedence over prudence, but this order was utterly unreasonable.[2]

But like a good samurai, Tanaka tried to follow his orders to the best of his ability. First order of business had been to transport the first echelon, 916 men, of the Imperial Japanese Army's 28th Regiment under Colonel Ichiki Kiyonao.* His "Ichiki Detachment," as it was known, was dropped off by Tanaka's destroyers after midnight on August 19, east of the American-held airfield. Tanaka held up his end of the bargain, but Ichiki did not. In the wee hours of August 20, the cries of "Banzai!" and "Totsugeki!" ("Charge!") went up and, like an Asian version of the Greek phalanx, the Ichiki Detachment, with bayonets and swords, charged the Americans. And were slaughtered by the Americans.

While "[t]he attack of the Ichiki Detachment was not entirely successful," as General Hyakutake reported to Tokyo, the far worse news was that earlier that day, August 20, the Americans had finally deployed combat aircraft to the Japanese-built airfield.[3] Now, just as the Japanese had done to the British in Malaya and the Dutch in the East Indies, the Americans were turning Japan's own airfields against them.

But Operation *Ka* would go forward. Admiral Yamamoto had the idea of throwing *Kido Butai* – the *Shokaku* and *Zuikaku* were all that was left of the original *Kido Butai* – and a bunch of ships into the South Pacific while Admiral Tanaka transported the second

---

* Ichiki is sometimes rendered as Ikki.

echelon of the Ichiki Detachment (renamed the Kuma Detachment) and members of the 5th Yokosuka Naval Landing Force – often called Japanese Marines, though a more accurate description would be "naval infantry." While Tanaka's objective was to get the troops to Guadalcanal, Yamamoto had a different objective: enticing the American carriers to come out to play.

This was not consistent with Admiral Tanaka's mission of getting the troops to Guadalcanal. The light carrier *Ryujo* was split off from *Kido Butai* and moved forward, but with no clear orders. Maybe she was somehow supposed to provide Tanaka with air cover, but she got herself sunk.

This was a price worth paying for Yamamoto as the Americans had indeed come out to play, in what became known to the Allies as the Battle of the Eastern Solomons and to the Japanese as the "Battle of the Stewart Islands" or the "Second Battle of the Solomon Sea." In which, by Yamamoto's estimation, *Kido Butai* had sunk or heavily damaged three carriers, a battleship, five heavy cruisers, and four destroyers.

Even so, Admiral Tanaka was still left trying to transport those troops to Guadalcanal – on slow troopships and with no fighter protection – heading directly for an enemy airfield that had just been reinforced with fighters and dive bombers. Tanaka knew it was a dangerous combination, but even he was not ready when a US Marine dive bomber planted a 1,000lb bomb between the Number 1 and 2 5.5-inch guns of his trusted flagship *Jintsu*, killing 24 and knocking Tanaka unconscious.[4] The large transport *Kinryu Maru*, carrying members of the 5th Yokosuka Special Naval Landing Force, was sunk. Destroyer *Mutsuki* stayed motionless to help rescue the troops and crew, in the process becoming the first Japanese warship sunk by B-17s bombing from high altitude.

All of which convinced Admiral Tanaka that using slow transports to transport troops to Guadalcanal would not work. He would find another way.

And he did. It was a method he had used before the ill-fated Colonel Ichiki: run reinforcements in to Guadalcanal on destroyers. Now Admiral Tanaka would basically systemize this idea. Fast destroyers would leave the Japanese anchorage in the Shortland Islands off the southeastern coast of Bougainville, but remain outside the range of American air power until nightfall, at which time they would dash in and land their troops safely, maybe bombard the airfield if they had time, then quickly depart to be outside the range of American air power on Guadalcanal by dawn.

And so he did. The Allies would dub these destroyer runs of troops and supplies – really any Japanese run of troops and supplies – the "Tokyo Express." But at the start the destroyers had a little trouble getting the timing right, and one early destroyer convoy was caught just before dusk by US Marine dive bombers, who sank the *Asagiri*, disabled the *Shirakumo*, and blasted the bridge of the *Yugiri*, killing the destroyer division commander. Admiral Tanaka and his superiors were frustrated when other batches of destroyers were scared off by the presence of American dive bombers.

Beginning the last week of August, Base Air Force began attacking the Guadalcanal airfield every day, weather permitting (and it frequently did not). A typical air attack would consist of a mixture of 18 or 27 Mitsubishi G4M Type 1 bombers, escorted by maybe 12 to 18 Zeros, flying all the way from Rabaul to Guadalcanal – 560 nautical miles – and back. The airstrikes became as predictable as clockwork. They would normally take off on or after sunrise and return no later than sunset. With a four-hour flight to Guadalcanal, that left a window of only, at its widest, four hours around midday for them to be over the target. The Americans on Guadacanal christened it "Tojo Time." To add to the lack of surprise, the Australians had seeded the Solomon Islands with operatives known as "coastwatchers" who would report on movements on Japanese ships and aircraft, including incoming Japanese airstrikes. The coastwatchers defied any and all Japanese efforts to wipe them out. To top it off, in early September, an air warning radar came online at the Lunga airfield.

Those were just the beginning of the issues facing Base Air Force as it tried to suppress the Lunga airfield. Rabaul may have had the top-rated anchorage in the South Pacific in Simpson Harbor, but it also had an annoying habit of getting itself buried in volcanic ash. It was home to numerous active volcanoes, two of which were particularly problematic. The primary airfield for bombers was Vunakanau ("Rabaul Upper Airstrip" or "Rabaul West," as the Japanese pilots would call it), 11 miles south-southwest of Rabaul near Keravia Bay and way too close to the active volcano Vulcan. The primary air strip for fighters was located at Lakunai (or "Rabaul Lower Airstrip" or "Rabaul East"), 2 miles southeast of Rabaul between Simpson Harbor and Matupit Harbor and yet closer to Tavurvur and other vociferous volcanoes on what was called the Crater Peninsula. The ash and noxious gases spewing from Vulcan and, especially, Tavurvur, created maintenance problems for aircraft and runways, and left Rabaul at constant risk for becoming a Pacific Pompeii.

Some of these problems were unavoidable, but more than a few were self-inflicted. The Japanese could not reduce the 560-mile distance between Rabaul and Guadalcanal, but they could have built some airbases on the many Solomon Islands in between. They didn't. Base Air Force was an air force without a base between Rabaul and Guadalcanal. After the Americans had taken the Lunga airfield, the Japanese readied an old Australian airfield on Buka, just northwest of Bougainville, for use in emergencies. They began construction on another airfield at Buin, at the southeast tip of Bougainville, near the critical Japanese base in the Shortland Islands just off Bougainville and some 300 miles from Guadalcanal.

Until Buin was operational, that 560-mile distance created numerous headaches, quite literally if the pilots did not have their own oxygen supply. Base Air Force had two types of Zero fighters, the A6M2 Model 21 and the A6M3 Model 32. From Lakunai, Guadalcanal was at the very end of the A6M2's range. Though the A6M3 was the newer model with squared wings and a heavier engine, its range was much shorter than that of the A6M2 – about 600 miles less. Thus, the A6M3 could not make the trip and was relegated to defending Rabaul for the time being while the A6M2 could only stay on site for maybe 15 minutes or so before being compelled to head back. Guadalcanal was easily within range of the G4M bombers, which had a relatively puny payload, but that range was a double-edged sword, thanks to another conscious decision by the Japanese Naval Air Force.

That decision was to emphasize speed, maneuverability, and range in its aircraft designs over an armored cockpit, shatterproof glass, or self-sealing fuel tanks, all of which added weight to the aircraft. It was an expression of confidence in the pilot, but it also meant that the pilot had to be near perfect or he would soon be dead. Both the Zero and the G4M bomber had a tendency to catch fire and explode when hit by gunfire or even when you just looked at them the wrong way. That was where the 560-mile distance came up again. At Guadalcanal, the Americans had home field advantage, so to speak. Allied pilots that were shot down in the area could be recovered and return to duty while damaged Allied aircraft had a decent chance to land at the Lunga airfield. Damaged Japanese aircraft had to travel that 560 miles back to Rabaul or maybe the 400-mile distance to the emergency facility at Buka, all that time hoping the aircraft could hold on for that distance and that any wounds would not overcome the pilot during that time. More often than not, it could not. A Japanese pilot shot down was likely to never return to duty.

In their quest to emphasize speed, maneuverability, and range at the expense of everything else, the Japanese Naval Air Force made another conscious sacrifice: they took the radios out of all but a few of their fighters. The Japanese believed the radios were too short-ranged and too unreliable to be effective, and removing the radios saved almost 40lb in weight. Presumably the pilots would simply have to communicate with each other by hand signals or waggling wings.

Admiral Mikawa had a different solution to the problem of that 560-mile distance. Mikawa reorganized all of 8th Fleet's seaplanes and their parent tenders into something cryptically titled the "R-Area Air Force," under the command of Rear Admiral Jojima Takatsugu. Jojima operated his air force from his seaplane carrier *Chitose* at anchor in Shortland Harbor while rotating his other tenders through Santa Ysabel's Rekata Bay, only 135 miles north of the Lunga airfield. From there, they would harass the Americans, especially with the annoying floatplane "Louie the Louse." For its part, at night Base Air Force liked to send a "Washing Machine Charlie" bomber or two.

None of which made Admiral Tanaka feel any more confident in reinforcement operations. Still, he did manage to get most of the Imperial Army's 35th Brigade under Major General Kawaguchi Kiyotake to Guadalcanal. Once ashore, the general put his carefully crafted plan for taking the airfield, based on just one hydrographic map of the north coast of Guadalcanal, into motion. Kawaguchi would hack his way into the jungle until he was south of the airfield. Then he, like Colonel Ichiki had done, would launch a banzai charge.

General Kawaguchi and his troops started battling their way inland through the jungle, which proved to be much more difficult and time consuming than the general had anticipated. The Japanese troops shed supplies, weapons, weight, and clothes as they zigzagged through the thick underbrush, tangling vines, stinking mud, tripping roots, rotted trees, slicing kunai, putrid water, and malarial mosquitos of the island. Eventually, they arrived at their attack position south of the airfield; where they found a ridge between them and said airfield that did not appear on his hydrographic map of the north coast of Guadalcanal. Nor did his attack position. An incensed Kawaguchi attacked anyway. After a false start on the night of September 12, he launched his major attack the night of September 13 on what would become known as "Edson's Ridge," in honor of the US Marine commander. Not, tellingly, "Kawaguchi's Ridge." The Marines were backed up almost to the airfield, and one small Japanese unit did break through to a satellite airfield. But the cost in personnel had been horrific. Far too great. Kawaguchi had to order a retreat. Like Colonel Ichiki's attack, Kawaguchi's attack had been a disaster.

Back in Rabaul at 17th Army headquarters, General Hyakutake determined that he would need to travel to Guadalcanal himself and lead a renewed Operation *Ka*. But this led to a major disagreement at Imperial General Headquarters, that organization whose title made it sound much more formal than it actually was, whose job it was more to coordinate the activities of the Imperial Army and Navy than to command them.

The Army complained that the Navy had delivered too many troops and not enough supplies, which was true. Army troops on Guadalcanal had even taken to calling it "Starvation Island," which is a pun derived from the first phoneme in the Japanese name for the island – *Ga* – which means, in one inflection, "hunger."[5] The Army also complained that the Navy had not adequately supported the Army. The Navy countered that it had deployed almost all its land-based aircraft and most of its seagoing warships to support the Army, which was true, and that the Army simply took too long to make its attacks.

It was left to one Colonel Tsuji Masanobu, Army operations officer at Imperial General Headquarters, to negotiate a resolution to the dispute. The highly intelligent Tsuji was a brilliant tactician who was known as the "god of operations," and had developed the plan for the conquest of Malaya and Singapore. In the words of Pacific War historian H.P. Willmott, "[T]here was no disputing [Tsuji's] industriousness, and equally there was no denying the fact that he achieved results."[6]

However, "Tsuji's unendearing traits combined extreme rudeness with irritability," Willmott also states.[7] He possessed unmeasurable arrogance with extreme racism and misogyny. In an army with more than its fair share of sadists, rapists, and thugs, Tsuji was in a class all by himself. He had ties to the massacre of some 50,000 Malayan Chinese after the fall of Singapore, the brutal abuse and murder of American prisoners in the Bataan Death March, and the execution of captured Philippine government officials. Tsuji was a master of political intrigue and was seen as a stooge of the prime minister, General Tojo Hideki. In the words of Willmott again, Tsuji "enjoyed an extremely unsavory reputation even in an Army hardly noted for its exacting standards of personal behavior."[8]

Colonel Tsuji was arrogant enough to go to the Combined Fleet flagship *Yamato*, then sitting comfortably in Truk Harbor, where he found the architect of the attack on Pearl Harbor Admiral Yamamoto sitting on the floor of his stateroom engrossed in writing *haiku*. Tsuji used his considerable rhetorical skills to convince the admiral to give complete support to the renewed Operation *Ka*, even promising to bring the *Yamato*, the biggest battleship ever built with the biggest guns (18.1 inch) ever deployed on a warship, alongside Guadalcanal if necessary.

But it wasn't necessary. Not yet, anyway. This was a new, improved Operation *Ka* that would involve sending a lot more troops to Guadalcanal, with heavy artillery and armor support. First came increased efforts to build up the troops and supplies on Guadalcanal, mainly using Admiral Tanaka's system of destroyer reinforcement, though during this time he wasn't in charge of it. These were larger reinforcements. Many centered on the seaplane carrier *Nisshin*, which could carry heavier weapons such as tanks and 150mm howitzers.

These bigger convoys needed air cover, but Admiral Tsukahara's Base Air Force was hard pressed to provide that air cover, in part because Tsukahara was hard pressed to provide much of anything. With Rabaul's climate not much different from Guadalcanal's and its health effects not much better, Tsukahara had managed to contract dengue fever, malaria, and dysentery – at the same time. So in early October he was sent home, to be replaced as Base Air Force and area commander by Vice Admiral Kusaka Jinichi, cousin to Admiral Nagumo's infamously cautious chief of staff.[9] Kusaka was promptly stricken with chronic diarrhea.[10] Welcome to Rabaul.

At about the same time, the Japanese finally completed their new airbase at Buin; the Allies would call it "Kahili." Vice Admiral Kusaka staged the A6M3 Zeros into Buin and began a program of attacking the Lunga airfield twice a day. He also sent Lieutenant Commander Mitsui Kenji, former air officer of the 4th Air Group, and ten communications personnel to Mount Austen on Guadalcanal to enjoy its view of the Lunga airfield and the Lunga roadstead beyond. And to report on anything of interest, such as air operations at the airfield, the coming, going, and presence of ships in the roadstead, and the weather.

To carry out the plan, the 17th Army got serious reinforcements, including the 2nd Sendai Division under Lieutenant General Maruyama Masao; the 38th Kanoya Division under Major General Ito Takeo, with a proud history of conquering Hong Kong, Sumatra, and Timor, and an equally sad history of war crimes; and the 8th Tank Regiment. General Hyakutake, though, wanted to save most of the Kanoya Division for that all-important New Guinea offensive that he had to mothball for *Ka*.

Hyakutake also took receipt of the *Nisshin* and *Chitose* on October 11. The *Chitose* was the flagship of Admiral Jojima, who commanded both the 11th Seaplane Tender Division and that cryptically named R-Area Air Force. So Jojima was placed in charge of the more obviously named Reinforcement Group. It was said that Jojima "could navigate a warship even on dry land."[11] A skill that might very well be needed before this campaign was over.

Admiral Jojima led his Reinforcement Group down The Slot in that considerable peculiar Japanese way of escorting transports. Speeding well behind the Reinforcement Group was Admiral Goto and his 6th Cruiser Division, last seen off Savo Island shooting up Allied warships, but not invasion transports. His remaining heavy cruisers *Aoba*, *Furutaka*, and *Kinugasa* were screened by the destroyers *Fubuki* and *Hatsuyuki*. The Americans had never contested by sea a transport mission at night; there was no consideration that they would do so this night.

So it was a surprise when a storm of shells battered Admiral Goto's flagship *Aoba*. At least one cut through cruiser's bridge without exploding, but it created enough shrapnel to cut down most of the bridge crew and mortally wound Admiral Goto. As he was carried below decks for treatment and comfort, Goto Aritomo growled at the Japanese who he thought had ended his life, "Bakayaro!" Which might be most politely translated as "Stupid bastards!"[12]

But Admiral Goto was wrong. He never understood that he was not the victim of a friendly fire incident, but was instead the victim of an imperfectly executed ambush by the US Navy. Unlike the admiral, his flagship *Aoba* survived, but was so heavily damaged she had to return to Japan for repairs for an extended period. Cruiser *Furutaka* and destroyer *Fubuki* were not so lucky, as they were sunk. So were the destroyers *Murakumo* and *Natsugumo*, sunk as they tried to cover the Japanese withdrawal and rescue survivors from the *Furutaka* and the *Fubuki*.

So ended what the Japanese would call the Sea Battle of Savo Island and what the Allies would call the Battle of Cape Esperance. Admiral Tanaka later called it "a crushing defeat for the Japanese Navy."[13] In terms of ego, it was. They took a lot of pride in their night-fighting ability. They could not believe the US Navy had bested them.

Throughout the night battle off Savo Island, Providence abandoned us and our losses mounted. Especially since the enemy used radar which enabled them to fire effectively from the first round without the use of searchlights, the future looked black for our surface forces, whose forte was night warfare.[14]

Even so, Admiral Jojima had completed his reinforcement mission unscathed, so while it was a tactical defeat and a loss of "face" for Japan, it was a strategic victory, the bitter fruits of which the Americans would reap in short order. Enough troops and supplies had been built up on Guadalcanal to now try to retake the Lunga airfield in a combined arms operation.

It started with the Combined Fleet's 3rd Battleship Division, under the command of Rear Admiral Kurita Takeo, with two battleships: the *Kongo* and her sister ship *Haruna*. Screening the battleships was Rear Admiral Tanaka, back on the front line with his 2nd Destroyer Flotilla.

Converted from battlecruisers, the *Kongo* class were lightly armored for battleships but were fast, rated for 30 knots. The battleships' magazines carried a new munition designated the Type 3 shell. This shell had a casing that would burst and spread 470 individual incendiary sub-munitions over a wide area. It was originally designed for an antiaircraft role, but the Japanese decided it could work well for bombardment of aircraft on the ground, fuel and ammunition dumps, and other land targets. They would try this new shell on the Lunga airfield.

With four seaplanes for illumination and a gunnery officer from the *Yamato*, Lieutenant Funashi Masatomi, on Mount Austen for spotting, the flagship *Kongo* opened fire at 1:33 am on October 14, followed at 1:35 by the *Haruna*.[15]

The result, from the Japanese literal view, was a "lake of fire" where the airfield was supposed to be.[16] US Navy motor torpedo boats attempted to attack the battleships, but were driven off by Admiral Tanaka's ships without too much effort. Admiral Kurita saw the gunflashes from the destroyers brushing off the PTs and concluded the destroyers were engaging a submarine. Kurita wanted none of that. Since the shelling was almost complete anyway, the admiral decided to end it five minutes early. At 2:56 am, after firing 973 shells, Kurita handled the withdrawal of the *Kongo* and *Haruna*. What the battleships left behind was a scene of devastation around the Lunga airfield.

At 5:00 am, Admiral Yamamoto issued an order stating American air power on Guadalcanal was "suppressed" and thus the 2nd and 3rd Fleets – the battleships under Vice Admiral Kondo Nobutake and *Kido Butai* under Admiral Nagumo, respectively – were to head south and destroy the US fleet.[17] So it was quite an unpleasant surprise to Lieutenant Commander Mitsui Kenji and his comrades on Mount Austen when at 5:40 am two SBD Dauntlesses took off from Henderson Field for the dawn search and two Marine Wildcats took off for the dawn patrol.[18]

Even if the Lunga airfield was "suppressed," Base Air Force's Admiral Kusaka wanted to keep it that way by continuing his air attacks. They would cover a so-called "High Speed Convoy" of six transports carrying some 4,500 troops, escorted by Rear Admiral Takama Tamotsu's 4th Destroyer Flotilla with the big new antiaircraft destroyer *Akizuki* serving as his flagship and destroyers *Yudachi*, *Harusame*, *Samidare*, *Murasame*, *Shigure*, *Shiratsuyu*, and *Ariake*.

The "High Speed Convoy" highlighted one of the drawbacks of the use of destroyers as pioneered by Admiral Tanaka to run troops and supplies to Guadalcanal at night to avoid air attacks. While the Allies called it the "Tokyo Express," the Japanese gave it the less flattering nickname "rat transportation." Destroyers simply cannot carry a whole lot of troops and supplies, meaning Japanese forces on Guadalcanal could only be reinforced in driblets, never really enough to develop a critical mass of forces to overwhelm the Marine defenders of Henderson Field.* That was why the *Nisshin* and the *Chitose* had been called in to deliver heavy weapons and tanks that the destroyers could not. But the *Nisshin* and *Chitose* were just two ships – warships that were fast, or at least faster than transports. They could not deliver all the necessary weapons and supplies by themselves.

Moreover, while they were the smallest of the men-of-war, destroyers were the biggest fuel hogs in any navy. With small fuel tanks, destroyers were always thirsty for fuel, a commodity in short supply for the Japanese, and moreover running at high speed had an unfortunate side effect of reducing their estimated miles per gallon. The destroyer runs were taking a toll. The *Murakumo*, and the *Natsugumo* had just been sunk, while the *Mutsuki* and *Asagiri* had been sunk early in the campaign. That's not even counting all the

---

* The Japanese Army had to overwhelm the defenders of Henderson Field because their generals were simply not good enough to be able to succeed at anything else.

destroyers damaged in American attacks, and all the time they had to spend getting repairs afterwards. The costs were adding up.

In short, in running not quite enough troops and supplies to Guadalcanal to retake the Lunga airfield, the Japanese were not only suffering combat losses, but were seriously chugging up their fuel supplies, which defeated the purpose of the war. The rat transportation was barely enough to maintain the status quo. To hope to win, the Japanese needed those slow, fat transports, and they needed those slow, fat transports like the ones Admiral Takama was guarding to run the gauntlet of American air power in the Solomons. And to protect those slow, fat transports, the Japanese needed to suppress American air power at the Lunga airfield.

But still the rat transportation ran. That night light cruisers *Yura* and *Sendai*; seaplane carrier *Nisshin* – again – and destroyers *Asagumo*, *Akatsuki*, *Shirayuki*, and *Ikazuchi* landed 1,129 troops, four field guns, four rapid-fire guns, ammunitions, and provisions on Cape Esperance. Guarding them was Admiral Mikawa himself with his flagship heavy cruiser *Chokai*, heavy cruiser *Kinugasa*, and destroyers *Amagiri* and *Mochizuki*. When that was done and while the destroyers stood guard, the cruisers spent a half-hour lobbing 752 8-inch shells into the Lunga perimeter.

Between the failed American air attack and the series of bombardments of the airstrip, Admiral Takama felt comfortable anchoring the transports off Tassafaronga on October 15 to offload troops, guns, and supplies in full view of the Lunga base. But just in case, Takama had six Type 0 observation seaplanes from the R-Area Air Force, 12 Zeros from Base Air Force, and 11 Zeros from the carrier *Junyo* to protect them.

It was a wise precaution. Even though the airfield had been "suppressed," the Americans still managed several attacks on his transports. Wondering just how "suppressed" the airfield really was, Admiral Takama aborted the operation after all 4,500 troops had been landed, but maybe two-thirds of the supplies. At a cost of three transports, six Zeros, and one Type 0 observation seaplane.

Now it was the turn of the Imperial Army. General Hyakutake's plan to finally take the Lunga airfield was overly complicated, as Japanese plans tended to be. Colonel Matsumoto Hiroshi, the operations officer for the 2nd Sendai Division, wanted to attack near the coast. The politically powerful Lieutenant Colonel Tsuji of the 17th Army wanted to attack from heights several miles inland to the south of the American perimeter. Hyakutake decided on both.

So began the most recent Imperial Japanese Army operation to capture the airfield. The plan was to have one regiment of the Sendai, supported by tanks and artillery, attack Marine positions along the Matanikau River near the coast to the west, complete with a flanking move. Meanwhile, two more regiments of the Sendai and one regiment of the 38th Nagoya Division, would have worked their way through the jungle around the American perimeter to perform the real attack – a two-pronged assault from the south. In other words, very similar to General Kawaguchi's attack in September. Imperial General Headquarters set the night of October 21 for the attack.

The tricky part of this plan was the "through the jungle" part. Not surprisingly, the march took longer than anticipated. On October 20, General Maruyama radioed that the attack would have to be delayed by one day, to October 22. When October 22 came, however, Maruyama radioed again, delaying the "time of the decisive battle between Japan and the United States" to October 23. October 23 saw the decisive battle pushed back yet again to October 24.

During that time, the perfidious Lieutenant Colonel Tsuji connived to get the veteran General Kawaguchi, the most experienced senior Imperial Army officer on Guadalcanal, leading the right flank of the attack, removed and replaced with Colonel Shoji Toshinaro, who let it be known he did not actually want the job on the eve of battle.[19]

But though the attack had been postponed – again – no one had bothered to tell the units attacking along the coast of the latest postponement. They attacked on schedule at around 6:00 pm on October 23 and were easily repulsed. The 1st Marine Division lost 25 killed and 14 wounded. The Japanese had lost some 600 troops and gained no ground whatsoever.

It was – finally – the night of October 24 that the great pincer attack on the south side of the Marine perimeter took place. Except that Colonel Shoji's pincer got lost in the rain and the jungle and missed the battle entirely. That can happen when you change commanders on the eve of battle, which is exactly why Shoji had not wanted the job. Nevertheless, after midnight, a phone call came in to General Maruyama's headquarters. It was Colonel Matsumoto, his operations officer acting as a liaison with Colonel Shoji's troops.

"The right flank attacked the airfield!" Colonel Matsumoto shouted. "The night attack is a success!"

"Banzai!" replied General Maruyama.[20]

And so, 50 minutes after midnight on October 25, 17th Army sent the victory message: "2300 Banzai! – A little before 2300 right wing captured the airfield."[21] Finally, the long national nightmare was over.

North of the Solomons, the ships of the Imperial Japanese Navy had been waiting impatiently. Admiral Yamamoto had committed a lot of ships to this operation, and a lot of ships at sea meant using a lot of fuel. The 17th Army had been told its naval support could remain at sea for only two weeks or so because of fuel limitations; whether the 17th actually appreciated this is unclear. As General Maruyama's march to attack position had dragged on, fuel issues started to manifest themselves. Oilers had to be sent back to Truk to siphon fuel from the *Yamato* and battleship *Mutsu* to keep the fleet operating. Some ships had already been forced to withdraw once to refuel.

Just before they did so, the carriers *Junyo* and *Hiyo* under Rear Admiral Kakuta Kakuji, had attempted an air raid on Guadalcanal on October 17, with disastrous results. Four days later, the *Hiyo* suffered a fire in her starboard generator room that disabled her starboard engines. Taking two destroyers with her as escorts, the *Hiyo* limped back to

Truk. She left her aircraft behind, split between the *Junyo* and Base Air Force. The price for the Army's delay in launching its attack now included the services of an aircraft carrier. Two, actually. Because by this time Combined Fleet was aware the US carrier *Enterprise* had left Pearl Harbor heading for the South Pacific.[22]

With the Lunga airfield now in Japanese hands, Admiral Yamamoto ordered the various elements of his fleet to head south to meet the Pacific Fleet, who were expected to come up and challenge the Japanese. Already the area around Guadalcanal was crawling with Japanese naval units, mostly from Admiral Mikawa's 8th Fleet.

But doubts started to arise when an Imperial Army Air Force Mitsubishi Ki-46 twin-engine "Type 100 command reconnaissance plane" – called "Dinah" by the Allies – from the 76th Independent Air Squadron flew over the airfield to confirm that it was held by the Japanese and was promptly shot down.[23] Finally, some six hours after announcing the airfield had been captured, Colonel Matsumoto called again: "I was mistaken about the success of the right flank. They crossed a large open field and thought it was the airfield. It was a mistake."[24]

The reaction of the Imperial Navy officers who were privy to this revelation is not recorded, but the Imperial Navy ships off Guadalcanal were the first to pay the price. An air attack damaged the destroyer *Ikazuchi* and Marine shore batteries damaged the destroyer *Akatsuki*. Other air attacks damaged the *Akizuki* and the light cruiser *Yura*, the latter mortally.

Nevertheless, Admiral Yamamoto went ahead with his offensive. The objective in his mind all along had been destruction of the American carriers, hopefully bringing about that Imperial Japanese Navy holy grail of the "decisive battle" that would decide the war in the Pacific in Japan's favor. He saw no reason to call off that offensive because the Imperial Army could not tell an open field from an airfield, at least not without some six hours of consideration.

Exercising direct control of the fleet from the *Yamato* sitting comfortably in Truk, Admiral Yamamoto arranged the fleet according to the Japanese principle of divide and conquer, once again preferring not to divide the enemy's forces, but to divide their own into bite-sized pieces. It had not worked at Coral Sea. It had not worked at Midway. It had not worked at Eastern Solomons. But Yamamoto was confident it had to work eventually. So confident, in fact, that he even divided *Kido Butai*.

In an arrangement that had been tried earlier at Eastern Solomons, the fleet was arranged in three major groups to form a triangle. They were collectively called the "Support Force" and were nominally commanded by Vice Admiral Kondo Nobutake, commander of the 2nd Fleet, operationally called the "Advance Force," which was positioned to the west with the carrier *Junyo* under Admiral Kakuta; the 3rd Battleship Division with *Kongo* and *Haruna* under Admiral Kurita; heavy cruisers *Myoko* and *Maya* under Admiral Takagi; two more heavy cruisers, the flagship *Atago* and her sister ship *Takao* under the direct command of Kondo; and the 2nd Destroyer Flotilla under Admiral Tanaka, back in action, with flagship light cruiser *Isuzu* and twelve destroyers.

About 100 miles east of the Advance Force was the "Main Body," consisting of the reconstituted Japanese Carrier Striking Force *Kido Butai*, with Admiral Nagumo leading fleet carriers *Shokaku* and *Zuikaku*, now with new light carrier *Zuiho* and a minimal escort of heavy cruiser *Kumano* and eight destroyers.

The carriers' escort was so small because most of it was about 100 miles to the south. Again using an organizational breakdown similar to that used at Eastern Solomons, this group under Rear Admiral Abe Hiroaki was called the "Vanguard Force," which should not be confused with the "Advance Force." It featured the 11th Battleship Division with the *Hiei* and *Kirishima* under Abe's direct command; one member of the 7th Cruiser Division, *Suzuya*, under Rear Admiral Nishimura Shoji; the traditional escorts of *Kido Butai* of the 8th Cruiser Division, the heavy cruiser-seaplane carrier hybrids the *Tone* and *Chikuma* under Rear Admiral Hara Chuichi; and the 10th Destroyer Flotilla under Rear Admiral Kimura Susumu with flagship light cruiser *Nagara* and seven destroyers.

With memories of Midway still fresh in his mind, Admiral Nagumo was hesitant to advance with his carriers. Admiral Yamamoto and Yamamoto's Chief of Staff Vice Admiral Ugaki Matome had to repeatedly prod him, including a deliberately insulting dispatch from Yamamoto "urging" Nagumo to attack "with vigor."[25]

Midway came to mind with quite a few officers when, early on October 26, a Japanese scout plane found a US Navy aircraft carrier to the southeast. Not where the Japanese had expected one to be. In a position to ambush *Kido Butai* – as had happened at Midway.

That would not happen now. Admiral Nagumo needed no prodding to immediately launch the airstrike he had already prepared and to immediately prepare a second strike for launch. But as he did so, he was surprised by a pair of US Navy dive bombers, who planted two bombs into the *Zuiho*, wrecking her arresting gear so she could not land aircraft.

But the admiral's spirits brightened when he received a message sent by an unidentified Japanese radioman "… one *Saratoga*-class carrier is on fire."[26] Then American dive bombers showed up. The combat air patrol of Zeros could not turn them away, and the hell divers planted potentially six bombs into the midships flight deck of Admiral Nagumo's flagship *Shokaku*. The 1,000lb bombs left the flight deck an inferno, so shattered it "looked like an earthquake fault zone."[27] The center elevator was trashed. Beneath the flight deck, the hangar deck was devastated. Memories of Midway flashed through the minds of every witness, including and especially Nagumo.

But this was not Midway. The *Shokaku*'s devastated hangar deck was almost empty. Neither the hangar nor the flight deck was full of fully armed and fueled aircraft. The fueling system was not active. The water-tight integrity and the engines were not affected. The damage was severe, but the *Shokaku* could be repaired. She headed for home with the *Zuiho* and destroyers *Arashi*, *Maikaze*, and *Hatsukaze*, who had been detached from the *Zuikaku*'s group.

By that time, this Battle of the Santa Cruz Islands was over. To the *Zuikaku* initially fell the job of recovering the returning strike craft and fighters from the *Shokaku* and *Zuiho* as well as her own. Both the *Zuikaku* and the *Junyo* launched follow up attacks with a mixture of aircraft from the four carriers, whichever aircraft happened to be available and usable. It wasn't a lot.

But it was enough. Late that night, they had the pleasure of coming across a burning, listing derelict with a number "8" on her hull. The number identified her as the aircraft carrier USS *Hornet*. Japanese floatplanes had watched with amusement as two US destroyers tried to scuttle the carrier, obviously without success. The destroyers had fled just ahead of the Japanese. Admiral Kondo considered the carrier's salvage "hopeless" and ordered Admiral Abe to sink her.[28] With that, the destroyers *Akigumo* and *Makigumo* each launched two Type 93 torpedoes – the famous "Long Lance" torpedo – at the wreck, ending the *Hornet*'s misery once and for all.

The Japanese eventually concluded that at Santa Cruz they had faced three US Navy carriers, one battleship, eight cruisers, and 18 to 20 destroyers, of which all three carriers, the battleship, two heavy cruisers, and one destroyer went down. Two of the enemy carriers were definitely the *Hornet* and the *Enterprise*, but the third remained unidentified.[29] That meant the US Navy had no aircraft carriers in the Pacific. The Japanese had lost no ships, only heavy damage to the carriers *Shokaku* and *Zuiho* and the heavy cruiser-seaplane carrier hybrid vessel *Chikuma*, who had absorbed a nasty bombing attack from US Navy pilots who could not find the Japanese carriers.

In response to this "Battle of the South Pacific," as the Japanese would call the Battle of the Santa Cruz Islands, Emperor Hirohito issued an imperial rescript: "The Combined Fleet is at present striking heavy blows at the enemy Fleet in the South Pacific Ocean. We are deeply gratified. I charge each of you to exert yourselves to the utmost in all things toward this critical turning point in the war."[30]

But just because a carrier force is "operational" does not mean it is effective. The effectiveness of a carrier force depends on its aircraft and especially its aviators. Toward the end of the Santa Cruz action, the *Junyo* sent six Type 97 torpedo planes against the *Hornet*. Of those six torpedoes, two hit, but only one exploded. Then came two Type 99s from the *Zuikaku*, six *Zuikaku* Type 97s armed with bombs, and, lastly, four Type 99s from the *Junyo*. Together, they got a total of two hits and one near miss, all against a carrier that was disabled and stationary, with no air cover and reduced antiaircraft protection. Such a performance does not speak well of their effectiveness.

It was the result of Japanese carrier aircraft losses in the Santa Cruz action that might be best described as devastating to Japanese naval aviation. In the face of a poorly coordinated American air defense, the Sea Eagles had been sitting ducks. On the morning of October 26, the four Japanese carriers had 203 carrier aircraft available – 82 fighters, 63 bombers, 57 attack planes, and one reconnaissance plane. By the evening of October 26, they were down to 104 – 55 fighters, 22 bombers, and 27 attack planes. One day of action had cost them almost half their carrier planes – 67 shot down, 28 more ditched, usually the result of battle damage; and four were destroyed on the carriers.[31]

The Japanese had not lost just quantity, but quality as well: three carrier attack plane squadron leaders; two of three carrier bomber squadron leaders, and 18 section leaders.[32] The consequence of these losses could be seen in the sloppy and undisciplined, albeit still fatal, late attacks on the *Hornet*.

It was a problem that had now caught up to the Imperial Japanese Navy and especially *Kido Butai*. Of the 765 elite carrier aviators from *Kido Butai* who had attacked Pearl Harbor, 409 were now dead. At the beginning of the war, the Japanese Naval Air Force had 3,500 Sea Eagles. They had anticipated needing as many as 15,000 new pilots for the war, but they only trained "several hundred" per year.[33]

Nagumo would later call Santa Cruz "a tactical win but a shattering strategic loss for Japan."[34]

But to Admiral Yamamoto, with no American carriers to oppose them, it was an unqualified victory. Guadalcanal now lay at Japan's feet – though the Japanese had thought Guadalcanal was theirs for the taking since the August 7 invasion, and had completely failed to take it. In almost three months, nothing had changed. The only real change was a lot of people that had been alive at the beginning were now dead. The key to the conundrum was, of course, the Lunga airfield. Whoever controlled the field controlled the air over Guadalcanal. The Combined Fleet had superiority over the Pacific Fleet. But as long as the Americans controlled the airfield, the Americans had local air superiority over the Japanese, and Japanese ships could not operate with any guarantee of safety during daylight hours within range of the airfield. It was a classic "Catch-22." The Japanese needed to capture the airfield to gain air superiority; but unless they gained air superiority they could not capture the airfield, because the necessity of using fast destroyers to run troops and supplies in at night meant the Imperial Army could never develop the critical mass of force to capture the airstrip. From a practical standpoint, Guadalcanal had become a vortex, sucking in men and materiel, from which the Japanese (and, for that matter, the Allies) could not extricate themselves without a final denouement.

It was a dilemma without an obvious solution. So, the Imperial Japanese Navy, the Imperial Japanese Army, and Imperial General Headquarters simply did what any self-respecting bureaucratic organization would do when faced with such a quandary – they kept doing what they were doing, hoping the next time would be successful. Now, with seemingly no American carriers to worry about, all they had to worry about in terms of American air power was the Lunga airfield. Could they neutralize it? They thought they could.

The Japanese had a plan, in this case one developed by Vice Admiral Kondo Nobutake, commander of the 2nd Fleet. In preparation, part of the 38th Nagoya Division, including its commander, Lieutenant General Sano Tadayoshi, was landed in a piecemeal fashion on Guadalcanal via nighttime destroyer runs made on November 2, 7, 8, and 10, bringing the total number of Japanese troops on Guadalcanal to about 30,000.[35] But these rat runs had demonstrated the dangers of this method of transportation. On the November 7 run, aircraft from the Lunga airfield damaged the destroyers *Takanami* and *Naganami*, while on November 8, PT boats from Tulagi had plunked a torpedo into the destroyer *Mochizuki*, a torpedo that did not explode but did leave a large, unsightly dent, a visual reminder of the threat the US forces still posed.

But it was still safer than relying on slow transports which were far, far easier for American pilots to target. Yet this is exactly what the Japanese now turned to for the rest of the reinforcements – some 12,000 men, and some 10,000 tons of supplies, in a convoy of 11 transports and cargo ships.[36] This was where Admiral Tanaka, the amphibious expert, again in command of the 2nd Destroyer Flotilla, would come in.

To offer some means of protection the convoy was to be escorted by 11 destroyers of a reinforced 2nd Destroyer Flotilla. Tanaka was not happy with this new assignment. He had invented rat transportation, after all. He invented it specifically to avoid the issue of American air power. He had been knocked to the floor by that air power – literally – on August 26 during the end of the Battle of the Eastern Solomons, when US aviators had attacked a convoy similar to, if smaller than, the one he was asked to command now.

How then to deal with the threat of American air power? Admiral Kondo had two methods. First, some limited air cover would be provided over the transports by the *Junyo*, commanded by the fiery Rear Admiral Kakuta Kakuji, who had watched with satisfaction the glow of the fires from the stricken *Hornet* just a few short weeks earlier. The *Junyo* class of carriers were, in fact, too slow to be classed as fleet carriers and too large to be classed as light carriers. But, still, the *Junyo* itself was a carrier, and that was one carrier more than the US Pacific Fleet had at its disposal – or so the Japanese Navy believed.

The *Junyo* was part of Admiral Kondo's "Advance Force," the operational name for the 2nd Fleet, which consisted of the four *Kongo*-class battleships, two heavy cruisers, one heavy cruiser-seaplane carrier hybrid, two light cruisers, and some 20 destroyers. In theory, Kondo could simply have had this armada advance on Henderson Field and the Americans would be hard-pressed to stop them, but that was just not the Japanese way. As already noted the Japanese way was to divide their forces into bite-sized pieces. It had not worked at Coral Sea. It had not worked at Midway. It had not worked at Eastern Solomons or Santa Cruz. But the Japanese figured it had to work eventually.

So the Advance Force was once again divided up. The *Junyo* was the centerpiece of the "Air Striking Unit," with an escort of the battleships *Kongo* and *Haruna* and an additional four to eight destroyers. Kondo also had an "Eastern Reconnaissance Unit" with the heavy cruiser-seaplane hybrid *Tone*, light cruiser *Sendai*, and destroyer *Ayanami*. Kondo chose to define the "Main Body" of this "Advance Force" as exactly two heavy cruisers; the admiral's flagship *Atago* and her sister ship *Takao*.

In addition, Admiral Kondo planned to deal with US air power by suppressing Henderson Field with shore bombardments. In October, the aforementioned *Kongo* and

Haruna had performed "The Bombardment" of Henderson Field that singlehandedly almost destroyed American aspirations for Guadalcanal. Unfortunately for the Japanese, the 17th Army on Guadalcanal could not follow up on that success quickly enough, and the damage and losses were largely rectified. The Japanese now needed a repeat performance.

Curiously, though, despite the clear determination to retake Henderson Field and turn the tide of the war, it was not deemed quite significant enough to get the head of the Combined Fleet, Admiral Yamamoto Isoroku, to fulfill his alleged promise to bring his massive flagship battleship *Yamato* and her 18.1-inch guns alongside Guadalcanal if necessary.[37] So, while the largest, most powerful battleship ever built sat in Truk Harbor, where the head of the Combined Fleet sat on the floor of his stateroom writing *haiku*, Admiral Kondo planned to use the other two battleships of the *Kongo* class, *Hiei* and *Kirishima*, as part of a "Vanguard Force" to deliver the bombardment on the night of November 12–13. The Vanguard Force would also have light cruiser *Nagara* and 14 destroyers.

This main bombardment was to be followed up by a smaller bombardment by Admiral Mikawa's cruisers of the 8th Fleet, technically not part of Admiral Kondo's fleet, on the night of November 13–14. Mikawa would have his "Main Force" of the heavy cruisers *Chokai* and *Kinugasa* and destroyers *Arashio* and *Asashio* escort a "Support Force" under veteran Rear Admiral Nishimura Shoji of heavy cruisers *Suzuya* and *Maya*, light cruiser *Tenryu*, and four destroyers that would perform the actual bombardment.[38] If the bombardments were successful, the transports of the Nagoya Division would not have to face American air power at all and would even be able to follow up on the bombardments' success.

That was the plan to land the troops. But, as usual, Admiral Yamamoto also had another agenda. He believed that the large troop convoy would draw the Americans out to battle. With no aircraft carriers in the Pacific, as far as the Japanese knew, the Americans would have to commit surface units, hopefully even their battleships. This was exactly what Yamamoto wanted. Admiral Kondo's massive surface force could engage the Americans in night combat, for which the Japanese had planned and trained for decades, giving them a decided advantage throughout the war so far. They fully expected to win a night engagement, which had the potential to cost the US Navy so many ships as to drive it from active operations in the Pacific for a year or more.[39]

More careful than others about what he wished for, Admiral Tanaka actually started out hopeful about this assignment. "Unlike some previous assignments, this mission would be successful, I believed," Admiral Tanaka later wrote, "because the force was adequate and my subordinates were all experienced."[40]

That opinion quickly changed after those nighttime destroyer runs of November 2, 7, 8, and 10 that had landed part of the Nagoya Division, but left the destroyers *Takanami*, *Naganami*, and *Mochizuki* damaged, there were also two Allied air attacks on the Shortland anchorage where Tanaka's transports were loading on November 11 and 12. Tanaka's optimism vanished:

> It was evident that the enemy was aware of our plan and was making an all-out effort to disrupt it by concentrating his sea and air forces around Guadalcanal. Consequently, we had good reason to expect that the landing of the Thirty-eighth Division main body at Guadalcanal would be extremely difficult.[41]

As Admiral Tanaka led his ships out of the Shortlands anchorage at 6:00 pm on November 12, he had a sense of foreboding. "In the flagship *Hayashio* I led the formation," Tanaka would later write, "and wondered how many of our ships would survive this operation."[42]

Back in October, Admiral Halsey had told General Vandegrift, "I'll promise you everything I've got." Now it was time for Halsey to pay up.

And pay up Admiral Halsey would. In fact, he had already started. On October 30, the light antiaircraft cruiser *Atlanta* and destroyers *Aaron Ward*, *Benham*, *Fletcher*, and *Lardner* escorted transports carrying 155mm artillery to Guadalcanal. The escorts went on to shell Japanese positions near Point Cruz in support of a Marine offensive. On November 2, destroyers *Shaw* and *Conyngham* also provided artillery support to this offensive. That night, 1,500 Japanese army troops and some artillery managed to land near Koli Point, east of Henderson Field. This new Japanese position was blasted by the heavy cruiser *San Francisco*, light cruiser *Helena*, and destroyer *Sterett*. The Marines followed up and, within a week, the Japanese at Koli Point were largely wiped out.[43]

Meanwhile, on November 7, while the destroyer *Lansdowne* was offloading supplies to the Marines in Lunga Roads, the anchored Navy cargo ship *Majaba* took a single torpedo hit from a Japanese submarine at 9:29 am. The *Lansdowne* and fellow destroyer *Lardner* launched depth charge attacks but could not locate the perpetrator, which was the *Ha.11*, a Japanese midget submarine, yet another example of the puzzling Japanese fixation with weapons that were marginally useful and borderline suicidal. In this case, though, it paid off, to a degree. The *Ha.11* had been launched from submarine *I-20* earlier that morning off Lunga Point. Her mission completed, the *Ha.11* was scuttled, and her crew escaped ashore on Guadalcanal, to join the Imperial Army troops already on starvation rations. The *I-20* herself escaped to Truk and reported a sinking, but the *Majaba* was not sunk; it was beached and eventually salvaged.[44]

Yet these were simply the preliminaries. Admiral Halsey and General Vandegrift were well aware of the Japanese reinforcements brought in by destroyers in the first ten days of November. And they knew a lot more were coming. The Japanese had switched to new code books on November 1, which temporarily flummoxed *Magic*, but there were clues.

By November 4, Pacific Fleet intelligence was noting renewed indications of an upcoming Japanese offensive, far larger than the numerous Tokyo Express runs of late. On November 6, the fleet intelligence summary commented, "All indications ... point to continued preparations for offensive action." Three days later Admiral Nimitz's summary said, "Predict an enemy all out attempt upon Guadalcanal soon." That wasn't exactly specific, but word came on November 11 that the attack would begin the next day or the day after.[45]

At Pearl Harbor, the cryptographers managed to again break the new codes. Admiral Yamamoto's operations order for the new offensive ended up at Pearl Harbor.[46] Admiral Halsey had been on a visit to Henderson Field, where, concerned for General Geiger's health after two months on Guadalcanal, he replaced him with the former chief of staff, Louis Woods, now a brigadier general.[47] When Halsey returned to Nouméa on November 9, "[Chief of Staff] Miles Browning was waiting for me, with news that another enemy offensive was brewing, one that would employ a vast number of ships and planes."[48] Intelligence estimated the Japanese would launch heavy aircraft attacks on November 11, a naval bombardment the night of November 12, and carrier air raids on November 13, to be followed by the landing of troops. Thanks to the intelligence reports, Halsey understood what they were up against:

> First reports credited this combined assault and invasion fleet with two carriers, four battleships, five heavy cruisers, about thirty destroyers, and possibly twenty transports and cargo vessels. To intercept it, I had a fleet that would have been inferior even if two of its heaviest units were not crippled; moreover, not only was it dispersed, but it was already committed, in part, to delivering the support I had promised Archie Vandegrift.[49]

But Admiral Halsey could make it work – mostly. He scheduled Admiral Turner's transports to make supply runs from Espiritu Santo to Guadalcanal on November 12. They would go in two separate groups. A force designated Task Group 62.4 with the light antiaircraft cruiser *Atlanta* and three destroyers under Admiral Scott would escort three "attack cargo ships" – a euphemism only the military could concoct – carrying the 1st Marine Aviation Engineer Regiment and supplies from Espiritu Santo to Guadalcanal. A second force designated Task Group 67.4, with the heavy cruisers *Pensacola*, *Portland*, and *San Francisco*; light cruiser *Helena*; light antiaircraft cruiser *Juneau*; and nine destroyers would escort four transports carrying the US Army American Division's 182nd Infantry Regiment of the Massachusetts National Guard, and even more supplies from Nouméa.[50] Admiral Turner would command this force personally, but the escorts would be commanded by Rear Admiral Daniel J. Callaghan.

Also at Nouméa was the carrier *Enterprise*, still being repaired from her close call at Santa Cruz. When her repairs would be complete was not known. With her as part of Task Force 16 under Admiral Kinkaid were the battleships *Washington* and *South Dakota*, whose Number 1 turret was damaged and offline; heavy cruiser *Northampton*; light antiaircraft cruiser *San Diego*; and eight destroyers. They would set sail for Guadalcanal. If the *Enterprise* group could not get there in time, the battleships and four destroyers would be detached into their own task force, Task Force 64 under Rear Admiral Willis Augustus Lee, and sent on ahead.

Supporting these efforts were Admiral Fitch's air assets, designated Task Force 63, at Espiritu Santo; the Cactus Air Force at Henderson Field; and 24 submarines in the Solomons, though, for reasons known only to the US Navy, not necessarily in The Slot, the most obvious and probable route of advance for the Japanese.

This, then, represented the commitment of practically all the operational surface assets of the US Pacific Fleet to the reinforcement of Guadalcanal and the defense thereof. Nevertheless, the US Pacific Fleet in this last, most important operation, was still badly outnumbered by the Imperial Japanese Navy. The US did have three important advantages, however. The first and inarguably most important was the aforementioned ability to read Japanese communications through the magic of *Magic*, which had given Admiral Nimitz and Admiral Halsey the warning they needed. The second was Henderson Field itself, which effectively lengthened the distance the Japanese had to travel to attack it, while protecting American efforts to reinforce it. The third was the relative simplicity of the US operation: just send transports to Guadalcanal and defend them. The operation was divided into three forces, but the idea was to merge them as much as possible before engaging the enemy.

For the Pacific Fleet, the operation got off to a less than ideal start. The *Southard's* sinking of the Japanese submarine worried Admiral Turner. The submarine had been on the direct route to Guadalcanal from Espiritu Santo, but it was also very close to the alternate route Turner had chosen for his transport units, which was around the east and north coasts of San Cristobal, for the very purpose of avoiding Japanese submarines. Admiral Scott's task group was using this route and was too far along to change course, but if Japanese submarines were scoping the alternate route anyway, what was the point of using it? In light of the submarine threat it made more sense to use the shorter, more direct route, which is what Turner proceeded to do. As it was, Scott's group was indeed spotted by a Japanese floatplane launched from a submarine.

In the early morning of November 11, Admiral Turner sent out a warning from his flagship at sea:

> It is expected that Task Force 67 while unloading will be subjected to heavy air attack from both carrier-based and land-based aircraft … in view of expected air attacks on November 12, and since a heavy landing attack will probably be made by the enemy on November 13, it becomes highly essential to get troops, organizational weapons, ammunition, and food ashore at the earliest possible moment.[51]

Admiral Scott's Task Group 62.4 successfully reached Lunga Roadstead and immediately began offloading as fast as possible. They knew as well as Admiral Turner that a Japanese air attack would come soon. But not this soon. Normally the Japanese arrived around noon in the form of Mitsubishi G4M medium bombers, the infamous Bettys. However, at 9:05 coastwatchers reported that a dozen (actually 18) Zeros and nine Aichi D3A Val dive bombers were approaching, which not only posed an immediate threat but raised a worrying concern regarding where they had come from. Japanese aircraft carriers were known to be operating north of the Solomons. Had these aircraft come from them? The aircraft were mostly from the carrier *Hiyo* (with the fighters led by Lieutenant Commander Kaneko Tadashi and the bombers by Lieutenant Abe Zenji, both of the *Hiyo*), but had staged into Buin so they could be used while the *Hiyo* was tending to her blown engine at Truk.[52]

Unloading was immediately suspended, and the ships got under way. The *Atlanta* formed a column with the three "attack cargo ships" *Betelgeuse*, *Libra*, and *Zeilin* behind her. The destroyers *Aaron Ward*, *McCalla*, *Fletcher*, and *Lardner* paired up to screen each side of the column. Eight Marine Wildcats were scrambled from Henderson Field's satellite fighter airstrip, Fighter 1. They were joined by 13 others, taking positions at 18,000 feet over the ships now moving at 14 knots.[53]

The Wildcats were under strict orders to only go after the Vals, but the escorting Zeros had a vote in whether that order could be followed. The Japanese strike first appeared over Cape Esperance at 9:36. The Wildcats were hampered by cloud cover, which allowed the Zeros to ambush them, shooting down six and killing four pilots, at a cost of two Zeros.[54] At 9:40 the Vals reached their pushover points at 8,000 feet for a glide bombing attack.[55] It is worth noting that a glide bombing attack requires less skill than the more difficult dive bombing attack. Whether this was a direct result of losses sustained by the Imperial Japanese Naval Air Force at Midway, Eastern Solomons, and Santa Cruz is not known.

In their glide dives, the Japanese pilots had to deal with the *Atlanta*, which had 16 5-inch twin-mount dual-purpose rapid-fire guns. The combination was brutal for the Vals. Four were shot down and a fifth forced to land. They only achieved three near misses on the *Zeilin*, which suffered from flooding and temporarily lost rudder control as a result, nearly colliding with the *Betelgeuse*.[56]

The "attack cargo ships" went back to work unloading, only to receive at 11:00 am the helpful warning that "an indeterminate number of unidentified warplanes was in the area."[57] Once again, unloading was halted and the ships got under way into an antiaircraft formation.

This time the intruders were 25 Betty bombers led by Lieutenant Watanabe Kazuo of the 703 Air Group, escorted by 26 Zeros led by Lieutenant Ito Toshitaka of the 253 Air Group.[58] Fortunately for the ships, the bombers operated at high altitude and were targeting Henderson Field, though the ships did send up a few antiaircraft bursts to discourage the Bettys further. The six Marine Wildcats on combat air patrol over the field were joined by 11 more that were scrambled.[59] The Japanese bombers managed to miss Henderson Field completely, cratering Fighter 1 instead, but the aerial combat showed just how vicious the Pacific War had become. Fighter pilot 1st Lieutenant Roger "Uncle"

Hagerman, wounded by gunfire from the waist gun of a damaged Betty and with his guns jammed, tried to shear off the Betty's right aileron with his left wing, after which he hoped to be able to parachute to safety. The bomber dodged the maneuver, and the wounded Hagerman gave up and headed back to safely land at Fighter 1. As he left, Hagerman saw the Betty's gunners looking back at him with huge, frightened eyes.[60] Four Bettys were destroyed, at the cost of two Wildcats and one pilot lost in a collision.[61]

Offloading was resumed at around noon and continued until midafternoon. The damaged *Zeilin* was given four captured Japanese pilots to transport back to the rear areas. At 4:00 pm, she departed Lunga, escorted by the destroyer *Lardner*. Later that night, *Atlanta*, *Aaron Ward*, *McCalla*, and *Fletcher* escorted the *Betelgeuse* and *Libra* eastward through Sealark Channel, where the transports would mark time for the night. The warships then returned to Lunga Roads to patrol and await Admiral Callaghan's forces.

The first of Callaghan's forces arrived around 11:00 pm: four cruisers and four destroyers. They joined Admiral Scott's group in patrolling for Japanese surface forces. None were expected but it paid to be cautious. At 1:15 am on November 12, the destroyer *O'Bannon* thought she had spotted a surfaced midget submarine off her starboard beam and fired off a few shots, while destroyer *Shaw* tried a depth charge attack. There was no surfaced submarine.[62] In the hot, humid atmosphere of the Solomons tensions were simply running high.

At 5:31 am, Admiral Turner's four transports *McCawley*, *President Adams*, *President Jackson*, and *Crescent City* arrived off Kukum and anchored to begin unloading the 182nd Infantry Regiment and supplies. The *Betelgeuse* and *Libra* returned from Sealark Channel to enjoy the protection of Turner's surface forces. However, although Japanese surface forces were expected off Guadalcanal that night, the 8-inch-armed heavy cruiser *Pensacola* and destroyers *Gwin* and *Preston* would be sent away from this scene of imminent surface action to, eventually, escort the carrier *Enterprise*.

But that was later. The Japanese had a response now. Lieutenant Commander Emura Kusao, the Japanese lookout on Mount Austen, reported to Rabaul three battleships, three cruisers, 11 destroyers, and five transports off Lunga.[63] At 6:42, "Pistol Pete" near Kokumbona began firing on Admiral Turner's flagship *McCawley* although not very accurately. A Marine artillery battery began counterbattery fire and was soon joined by the *Helena* and destroyers *Monssen* and *Shaw*. Destroyers *Cushing* and *Buchanan* were then sent to bombard Japanese positions west of Kokumbona. After apparently destroying a Japanese ammunition dump, they were later joined by *Helena*, *Monssen*, and *Shaw* in destroying some 30 landing boats the Japanese had pulled onto the beach.[64] Imperial Japanese Army troops would now not be able to outflank Henderson Field by sea.

The artillery duel at least gave an outlet to the inescapable tension. The US Navy was still convinced that a Japanese submarine was lurking off Lunga, but no one could find it. The *Southard* and *Hovey* had been called over from Tulagi to begin antisubmarine patrols. Unidentified aircraft were spotted approaching the transports at 10:05 am. Every 5-inch gun that could bear was opened up on the interlopers, who were found to be a Marine transport plane and five fighters coming up from Espiritu Santo. Antiaircraft fire was stopped before any hits were scored.[65]

Soon, however, new interlopers would not be as friendly. Lieutenant Commander Emura's report had gotten a response in Rabaul. At 1:17 pm, Henderson Field passed a report from Australian coastwatcher Paul Mason, hiding near Buin, of a Japanese airstrike inbound, expected to arrive at 1:30.[66] Unloading was suspended and the ships got under way, the transports forming two columns of four each, heading roughly north-northwest.[67] The escorts, now including two antiaircraft cruisers in the *Atlanta* and the *Juneau*, formed a protective circle around the transports in the middle of Sealark Channel. Eight Wildcats under Marine Major Paul Fontana were scrambled to join a combat air patrol of eight Wildcats and eight Army Airacobras, which were at 29,000 feet ready for action.[68]

But the Japanese did not come at 1:30 as predicted, nor at 2:15, a revised prediction, but at 2:10. Then, the 16 Betty bombers (a 17th had aborted) under Lieutenant Commander Nakamura Toomoo of the 705 Air Group, escorted by 30 Zeros under Lieutenant Suganami Masaji of the 252 Air Group, swung around the north side of Florida Island, out of view. When they reappeared, they were descending past 500 feet, Suganami's fighters on the right wing of Nakamura's bombers with the bombers carrying aerial torpedoes.

Marine Captain Joe Foss, leader of the combat air patrol, saw that they had been fooled into defending against a high-level bombing attack and were now too high to engage the Bettys. Shouting "They're coming in low. Let's go get 'em, boys!" he put his fighters into a dive straight down, diving so fast from the freezing upper atmosphere into the hot and humid Solomons air that many of their windshields frosted over, forcing the pilots to scratch the ice off. One, Army Air Force 2nd Lieutenant Frank Clark, piloting a P-39 Airacobra, apparently could not clear the ice in time, and ended his dive by plunging at full speed straight into the water.[69]

With the Japanese attackers coming in two groups low to the water, one coming from the north, one swinging to the east, Admiral Turner understandably assumed they were attempting an anvil attack – attacking the transports from two different vectors so that whichever way the ships turned, they would be exposing their broad side to the torpedoes; this is what the Japanese had done to the battleship *Prince of Wales* and battlecruiser *Repulse* off Malaya in the first days of the Pacific War. The Mitsubishis came line abreast, blazing fast, so close to the water that their propellers kicked up spray.[70]

Admiral Turner ordered an emergency turn to port to offer his transports' broadsides to the nearer attacking Japanese, which were Lieutenant Suganami's fighters. In so doing, he presented the narrow stern profile of his ships to the torpedo-carrying Bettys who now had little chance of getting a hit.

The Bettys flew directly into lines of 20mm tracers, the almost continuous thunder of 5-inch shellbursts, especially from the *Atlanta* and *Juneau*, and even shell splashes from the 8-inch guns of the *Portland* and *San Francisco*, used in an attempt to literally splash the attackers (it didn't work; it never did).[71] And above and behind the blazing Bettys were the

Wildcats and Airacobras of Captain Foss, as well as the Wildcats of Major Fontana, pouncing on the bombers at altitudes of 50 feet or even less.

This was no repeat of the Java Sea Campaign's *Prince of Wales* and *Repulse* ambush; this was a slaughter. Of Lieutenant Commander Nakamura's 16 Mitsubishi G4Ms, 11 were shot down or crash landed. The five that managed to return to a Japanese base of some sort were so badly damaged as to be considered total losses. Only a few of the Bettys were able to drop their torpedoes, and some of those were not dropped cleanly, but simply tumbled into the water.[72] Though the *San Francisco* had to maneuver adroitly to avoid a torpedo meant for her, none hit.[73] The damage inflicted by the Japanese was not even remotely commensurate with the losses they suffered.

Three Wildcats were shot down but their pilots survived. The only American pilot lost was Lieutenant Clark. The destroyer *Buchanan* was hit by friendly fire, a 5-inch antiaircraft round in the after stack, killing five men, wounding seven others, destroying a 20mm antiaircraft mount, and disabling her torpedo tubes.[74] One Betty, set afire by the guns of the *McCawley*, flew in the wake of the *San Francisco* and crashed into her after control station, bounced off the superstructure, and landed in the water. Flaming gasoline from the Betty's ruptured fuel tanks was splashed over the secondary command post Battle II, the after 5-inch director, and the after fire-control radar. The crews of three 20mm antiaircraft mounts around the director were incinerated. Altogether 23 men were killed and 45 were wounded, including badly burned Commander Mark Crouter, who refused medical treatment until everyone else had been treated. When 28 injured were later transferred to the *President Jackson* for treatment and evacuation to Nouméa, Crouter again refused.[75]

The viciousness that had taken hold in the Pacific War, due largely to Japanese atrocities, was again evident. The destroyer *Cushing* came upon the wreck of a Betty floating in the water and a Japanese pilot standing on a wing. As the destroyer slowed to rescue him, the pilot pulled out a pistol and fired at the destroyer. A 20mm gunner high on the deckhouse received permission to return fire. He had to depress the gun almost vertically to target the pilot. The gun then misfired, shrapnel from the 20mm round badly cutting the arm of loader Seaman Ed Shively. A cook manning the 20mm mount near the *Cushing*'s bow had watched the entire proceeding, and immediately fired a burst of his own, cutting the pilot in half.[76]

There was a mood of celebration at Henderson Field. The head of Cactus Fighter Command Lieutenant Colonel Bauer exclaimed, "We did fine! Had one of the best days we've had."[77] And it was going to get better. Admiral Turner's transports anchored at the Lunga Roadstead once again and by 6:30 pm had landed approximately 90 percent of the personnel and much of the cargo.[78] And more reinforcements were coming: air reinforcements. The escort carrier USS *Nassau* had put in at Espiritu Santo on November 11, and some of her gifts were being ferried to Henderson Field – ten Marine SBD Dauntless dive bombers, six Marine TBF Avenger torpedo bombers, and six Marine F4F Wildcat fighters. Even better were eight of the new long-range twin-engine P-38F Lightning fighters from the Army Air Force's 339th Fighter Squadron.[79] Total air strength at the Henderson Field complex was now 20 Wildcats, eight Lightnings, 18 Airacobras, 23 Dauntlesses, and eight Avengers. Espiritu Santo now had the 69th and 70th Bomber Squadrons of the Army Air Force, armed with B-26 Marauders, the only American land-based bombers equipped to carry torpedoes.[80]

But this newly expanded air force was threatened almost immediately. At 10:35 that morning, a B-17 had reported through General MacArthur's headquarters in New Guinea two battleships or heavy cruisers, one cruiser, and six destroyers 270 miles north of Santa Ysabel or about 335 miles north of Guadalcanal, heading 180 degrees True (due south) at, later reported, 25 knots.[81] Ten minutes later, another B-17 reported five destroyers 110 miles north of Santa Ysabel.[82] At 2:50 pm, Admiral Turner received a report that two Japanese aircraft carriers and two destroyers were sighted in heavy weather 265 miles west of Henderson Field, in other words, south of New Georgia.[83]

Separating the wheat from the chaff in intelligence analysis can be frustrating – akin to trying to piece together a puzzle when you don't know what it is supposed to look like, a puzzle that is likely missing pieces and even has extra pieces that don't belong. Admiral Turner had been burned at Savo Island. He would not be burned again.

Turner knew from wire intercepts and *Magic* the broad outline of the Japanese plan. A major offensive to retake Henderson Field was evidently in motion. Turner was already aware that a large surface battle group had left the Japanese fortress at Truk headed for the Solomons while simultaneously a large surface force was to clear the way for the transports carrying infantry and supplies for Guadalcanal. How did the sighting reports fit into that? The report of the carriers clearly did not, so Turner dismissed it. He estimated enemy strength as two battleships, two to four heavy cruisers, two light cruisers, and 10 to 12 destroyers.[84] And they were coming for him.

What Turner didn't know was whether they intended to focus their attacks on the transports, Henderson Field, or both. It didn't actually matter. His transports had to be gone before they arrived, and the Japanese attack on the airfield had to be stopped.

But who would stop them? Who could stop them?

Admiral Tanaka entered this latest incarnation of Operation *Ka* with a glum foreboding. Even worse was the opinion of Admiral Abe, who was to command the battleships.*

Promoted to vice admiral less than two weeks earlier, in the words of destroyer skipper Commander Hara Tameichi, "[Admiral Abe] was known for his extreme caution,

---

* Admiral Abe must not be confused with the other Japanese admiral of the same name in the same war, who ordered US Marine prisoners taken at Makin to be executed. Nor with two other Admiral Abes. According to Morison (*Struggle*, 258 n. 33), there were "at least" four admirals named "Abe" in the Imperial Japanese Navy in World War II.

which his critics claim often amounted to timidity."[85] His already foul mood was made worse by the death of his longtime friend Goto Aritomo off Cape Esperance on October 11. Abe was well aware of "The Bombardment" by the *Kongo* and *Haruna* in October. He didn't think the Americans would be so stupid as to fall for that again.[86] As a result, he fully expected to face US Navy surface opposition to his mission, a prospect he did not relish.[87]

Regardless of the trepidation felt by some of the senior commanders, on November 9 the light cruiser *Nagara* led the six destroyers, *Akatsuki, Ikazuchi, Inazuma, Teruzuki, Yukikaze,* and Hara Tameichi's *Amatsukaze,* of the 10th Destroyer Flotilla under the command of Rear Admiral Kimura Susumu, out of Truk Harbor. In the early morning hours of November 12 near the Shortlands they linked up with Admiral Abe's flagship *Hiei,* her sister *Kirishima,* and the five destroyers *Asagumo, Harusame, Murasame, Samidare,* and *Yudachi* of the 4th Destroyer Flotilla under the command of Rear Admiral Takama Tamotsu. Together, the "Vanguard Force of the Advance Force" then started toward Guadalcanal in a column formation. At 6:00 pm that same day, Admiral Tanaka's transports left the Shortland anchorage.[88] Three destroyers, technically part of Abe's force, were sent out from Shortland to act as pickets between Guadalcanal and the Russell Islands.

Early that same morning, the new Japanese naval observer on Mount Austen, Lieutenant Commander Emura, reported the Americans had three battleships, 11 destroyers, and five transports off Lunga.[89] The report was noticed by Admiral Ugaki at Combined Fleet Headquarters. Believing the US Navy ships would try to disrupt the Japanese reinforcement, Ugaki considered ordering Admiral Mikawa to join Admiral Abe's force and ordering Admiral Kondo to follow up with the rest of the Advance Force. But when he suggested it to the staff, the senior staff officer predicted the Americans would "go away as usual," while others predicted Mikawa's 8th Fleet would "galvanize itself." So Ugaki dropped the idea.[90]

But the report had also reached Admiral Abe. It was at about 10:30 am that day when a B-17 out of New Guinea flew over Admiral Abe's force. It was chased off by some Zeros from the *Junyo,* the carrier herself hiding north of the Solomons, but Abe was certain the bomber had reported his approach. The report and the incident did nothing to lighten his dark mood. If anything, it made him more cautious.

At approximately 3:30 pm, Admiral Abe acted on that caution. He ordered a drastic change in formation that left his skippers baffled and more than a little nervous. Commander Hara would call it a "double-half-ring formation."[91] The five destroyers of the 4th Destroyer Flotilla were arrayed in a half-circle 8,000 yards ahead of the *Nagara.* The six destroyers of the 10th Destroyer Flotilla were arrayed in a half arc inside that of the 4th around the *Nagara.* The *Hiei* was 2,000 meters behind the *Nagara,* the *Kirishima* 2,000 meters behind the *Hiei.* "I thought the aim of this formation was to prevent surprise attack by submarines or aircraft during our approach to the target area," Hara would later say.[92] It was a complicated formation, drawn in tight, to complicate it still further, but Abe thought they could handle it because Admiral Kimura in the *Nagara* was a well-respected navigator.[93]

The change in formation was completed by 4:00 pm, and the force continued its journey to the southeast at 18 knots. Shortly thereafter, the *Hiei* catapulted her Mitsubishi F1M Type 0 Observation Seaplane to check out the Allied dispositions near Lunga.* About an hour later, a storm boiled up and enveloped Admiral Abe's ships. Commander Hara described it as "a tremendous driving downpour which covered everything in darkness. It became difficult to see the nearest vessel."[94]

"In peacetime, a force commander would never take his ships through a blinding storm at such speed and in such a complex formation. Anything could happen," related Hara.[95] But despite pleas from his staff that he cut the force's speed, Admiral Abe was resolute. "We must maintain this speed to reach the target area in good time," he responded.[96] The situation frayed the nerves of the destroyer skippers. Tens of thousands of tons of steel, carrying thousands of explosive munitions and thousands of gallons of fuel, speeding in a close, complicated formation with other ships that can't be seen through the blinding rainstorm buffeting them: what could go wrong? But surprisingly the storm seemed to buoy the admiral's spirits. "This blessed squall is moving at the same speed and on the same course as we are," Abe said.[97]

The *Hiei*'s floatplane sent in its first and last report: "More than a dozen enemy warships seen off Lunga." Admiral Abe laughed. "If Heaven continues to side with us like this, we may not even have to do business with them."[98]

To the skippers and helmsmen of the Vanguard Force, if this was Heaven siding with them, they'd hate to see when it didn't. Trying to maintain station in these conditions was draining, especially as the storm dragged on, as Hara recalled:

> The squadron pressed on. Hours passed, but the rain squall did not abate. If anything, it got stronger. In all the years of my career I have never experienced such a rain. It was completely enervating. My officers were bored and expressed their boredom. Ensign Shoji said "Phew! This rain is killing me. Let us fight the Americans, not this rain."[99]

At midnight, as the Vanguard closed on Savo Island the Imperial Japanese Army's observation post on Guadalcanal reported, "Weather now very bad here."[100] So bad that the *Hiei*'s floatplane broke off its mission and headed to Bougainville rather than attempt to find the battleship in the storm.

It occurred to Admiral Abe that if he could not see the ships around him because of the storm, he probably could not see the targets of his planned bombardment on Guadalcanal, either. Nor could any forward observers on shore. The storm was now threatening his mission. Hoping to clear the storm, the *Hiei* radioed, "All ships stand by for a simultaneous 180-degree turn."[101]

---

* The Type 0 Observation Seaplane must not be confused with the Type 0 Reconnaissance Seaplane.

But he could not complete the maneuver because the *Yudachi* and *Harusame*, on the right flank of the 4th Destroyer Flotilla sweeping ahead, had not acknowledged the order. They were too busy swerving to avoid running aground.[102] To Hara Tameichi's horror, the *Hiei* switched to a medium-wave frequency – one that could be picked up by the enemy – to reach the two wayward destroyers.[103]

Eventually, they reached the destroyers and executed the immediate course reversal at 12:05 am November 13 without it resulting in any major problems. Admiral Abe ordered speed slowed to 12 knots, in theory to give his now disorganized force a chance to re-form. Some 30 minutes later, the squall had finally passed, and at 12:38 am Abe ordered another reversal of course – 225 degrees True, or southwest – to clear Savo Island and, by 1:00 am, had his force on a course due south headed back toward Guadalcanal.[104]

But to the horror of Commander Hara on the *Amatsukaze*, the admiral kept the complicated, tight double-half-ring formation:

> I was sure he would now form the force into a single column. Our complex formation was good for opposing attacks by small torpedo boats, but we would be stymied if an enemy stormed us in strength. For the first time, I began to doubt his wisdom. In battle it is bad to doubt one's leader.[105]

As Admiral Abe's large flagship was steaming into danger, with enemy contact imminent in one form or another, the admiral's mood darkened once again. He buried himself in reports. The Japanese observers on Guadalcanal radioed that the rain had stopped and there were no enemy ships in sight off Lunga. Good, but somehow not good enough; Abe was still nervous. At 1:25, the lookouts spotted navigation lights placed by the Japanese on Cape Esperance, and Abe ordered a course change to 140 degrees True – southeast – to make the final run toward Lunga.[106] By 1:30 am, the force was just 12 miles from shore and closing.[107]

This was perhaps not the best time for the admiral's staff to start arguing about whether they were so far behind schedule that they should scrub the mission. Admiral Abe's chief of staff Commander Suzuki Masakane wanted to abort, to which Admiral Abe's operations officer Commander Chihaya Masataka responded with words to the effect of "Our bombardment was the start of a general offensive of the Combined Fleet, which would last about three days. If we did not make the bombardment, all the offensive plan would be ruined."[108]

Admiral Abe settled it. "Tell *Hiei* and *Kirishima* to ready main batteries for Type-3 shelling," came the order.[109] The Type 3 was a new kind of incendiary shell, first tried during "The Bombardment" with great success, and the gun crews were eager to use them again.

The crews worked quickly, readying the magazines to send the new Type 3 shells to the guns as quickly as possible. It is worth noting that because this was supposed to be only a bombardment mission, they had hardly any armor-piercing shells and furthermore the

14-inch guns were trained upward for the long-range bombardment. They were ready. One more minute and Commander Chihaya would give the order ...

The signal came at 1:42 am from the destroyer *Yudachi*: "Enemy sighted."[110]

Admiral Abe's US Navy counterpart was staring at the flag plot, a large map of the battle area on which staff members marked the locations of reported contacts. Also marked in some cases were the times of the reported contacts and, if available, the course, speed, and composition of those contacts. In theory, it should not be much different from looking at the plan position indicator of a radar.

The problem was that the markings on the flag plot could give you all the available information, but it could not provide you with a definitive vision of the actual situation. For example, say you have six contacts marked on the plot, all from different times. Are they six groups of ships? Or are they one group of ships detected six times? Or two groups of ships detected three times? How that question is answered would largely determine how the battle would be conducted. But, with the enemy clearly nearby, the admiral was struggling to answer that question. More precisely, he did not know in what formation were the enemy ships he was facing. He did know, however, what the enemy was.

Admiral Turner had already done the calculations and briefed him thoroughly. A large enemy surface force was en route to clear the way for the transports carrying infantry and supplies for Guadalcanal. He estimated enemy strength as two battleships, two to four heavy cruisers, two light cruisers, and 10 to 12 destroyers.[111] The only things standing between the approaching Japanese on one end and Henderson Field and Turner's transports on the other end were the warships of Admiral Callaghan and Admiral Scott: cruisers and destroyers attempting to stop battleships or, more accurately, cruisers and destroyers whose guns could not normally penetrate the hull armor of battleships attempting to stop battleships. Not a hopeful prospect nor something for which they trained at the Naval Academy. But Turner saw no alternative.

In one of the personally boldest decisions of the war, Admiral Turner chose to strip his transports of almost all their escorting warships. His transports would leave at sunset and be escorted only as far as Sealark Channel and, except for the minesweepers *Southard* and *Hovey*, the damaged destroyer *Buchanan*, and the destroyers *Shaw* and *McCalla*, who were low on fuel, all of the warships would return to protect Henderson Field. Five cruisers and eight destroyers – *San Francisco*, *Portland*, *Helena*, *Atlanta*, *Juneau*, *Cushing*, *Laffey*, *Sterett*, *O'Bannon*, *Aaron Ward*, *Barton*, *Monssen*, and *Fletcher* – would, as darkness fell, "return to Cactus tonight and strike enemy ships present."[112]

The final question for Admiral Turner was, who was to command this collection of warships? Turner was tempted to take charge himself but he had a responsibility to the overall situation, to protect the transports and get them out of harm's way.[113]

Rear Admiral Norman Scott, the victor of the Battle of Cape Esperance, was an obvious candidate. He by no means had fought a perfect battle, but he had conducted it well enough to gain a US victory, a rare feat in surface actions since the beginning of the war. Furthermore, he had subsequently studied the battle, and especially the performance of SG surface search radar, and was willing to learn from his mistakes. He had resolutely drilled his crews in night combat and was comfortable fighting at night. In short, Admiral Scott was the perfect officer to command this force. Naturally, Turner did not choose him.[114]

Instead, in another one of Admiral Turner's vague decisions, he chose Rear Admiral Callaghan. Daniel Judson Callaghan had been Admiral Ghormley's chief of staff, "a task in which he had escaped distinction," to borrow Guadalcanal historian Richard Frank's description.[115] When Admiral Halsey had taken over from Ghormley, he had sacked Ghormley's entire staff and brought his own, so Admiral Turner scooped up Callaghan. But Callaghan had not been at sea in months. His only combat experience had been the air attack that very afternoon.

Seemingly, what made Admiral Callaghan better suited than Admiral Scott to command this force was the fact that he had been promoted to rear admiral two weeks before Scott, and thus, in the Navy's rigid system, had seniority. Callaghan's seniority was selected over Scott's experience and training. Turner had a history of going by seniority more than anything else, including at the aforementioned Battle of Savo Island. In fact, there is little evidence that Turner even considered going outside Navy seniority in designating the officer in tactical command.[116]

A naval aide to President Roosevelt for three years, the President had released Callaghan for wartime duty as captain of the cruiser *San Francisco*, though he spent most of his time as skipper in drydock with the *San Francisco* being overhauled. Nonetheless, he was hard-working, conscientious, devoutly Roman Catholic, and well respected by his colleagues and men under his command. Callaghan was the first wartime skipper of the *San Francisco*, to whose crew he became so loved that he was called "Uncle Dan," though not to his face. He had left the ship when he was promoted to rear admiral in August when he became Ghormley's chief of staff. He had almost no combat experience, and he knew it. But he was not at liberty to turn down an order from a superior officer to take charge, especially when Admiral Turner was said to have believed Admiral Halsey had "practically hand-picked" Callaghan for this command.[117]

Unsurprisingly, Admiral Callaghan chose the *San Francisco* as his flagship for this engagement. The 8-inch-armed heavy cruiser was the largest and most powerful of the ships then available. It was also within then-Navy rules pertaining to the ship of senior officer afloat. *Atlanta* and *Juneau* were considered too light (though not too light for Admiral Scott).[118] With combat on the immediate horizon, Callaghan felt he needed to be among friends, like the crew of the *San Francisco*, which was also the namesake of his home city. He knew the capabilities of the cruiser and her crew, and, in any case, he had very little time to choose.[119]

But the crew was struck by the change in his demeanor from his days as skipper. On the *San Francisco*'s flag bridge, Radioman 3rd Class Bill Potwin saw Admiral Callaghan endlessly pacing, muttering that he was reluctant to carry out his orders, expressing his desire to talk things over directly with Admiral Halsey, admitting there was no time to do so, and telling the rattled officers and men around him that they were in for a rough night.[120] His old boss Admiral Ghormley had clearly not had a good effect on him. Admiral Callaghan's cook, Eugene Tarrant, asked the admiral if he really thought the mission was hopeless. Callaghan responded, "Yes, it may be that. But we are going in."[121]

Lieutenant Jack Bennett, who had duty on the bridge, overheard Admiral Callaghan discussing the situation on the starboard wing with Captain Cassin Young, the *San Francisco*'s new skipper of all of three days. "They were discussing the unannounced fact that there were battleships in the Tokyo Express," Bennett would later write. Young, who had won the Congressional Medal of Honor for bravery at Pearl Harbor in the repair ship *Vestal*, "was in an understandably agitated state, sometimes waving his arms, as he remarked: 'But this is suicide.' Admiral Dan Callaghan replied, 'Yes, I know, but we have to do it.' He was calm, unemotional, resolute, and perhaps resigned to his fate."[122]

The rumors that they were going to fight battleships – and, Uncle Dan believed, lose – rapidly spread through the cruiser. "We were all prepared to die," recalled Joseph Whitt, a seaman 1st class whose battle station was in Turret 1. "We could not survive against those battleships."[123] Not with guns; they could with torpedoes, but the US Navy had stupidly stripped the torpedo tubes off almost all its cruisers.

At around 10:00 pm, the transports were safely away in Sealark Channel. An hour later, Admiral Callaghan hailed Admiral Turner one last time in what seems to have been the former's moment in the Garden of Gethsemane. He asked if Turner was aware that three separate Japanese forces were coming down. In other words, "Do you *really* want us to do this?" Turner answered that yes, he was aware, and it simply had to be done since the Japanese still had to be stopped.[124]

Admiral Callaghan's ships turned around and, unseen by the Japanese lookouts on Mount Austen, headed back toward Lunga. Callaghan was now on his own, essentially his first combat command, outgunned and outnumbered. He set about arranging his ships for battle.

Most of these ships had not worked together before and now they were facing a nighttime battle. Admiral Callaghan sought to keep things simple. He seems to have studied Admiral Scott's performance at Cape Esperance and sought to copy it as much as he could.

So, like Admiral Scott, Admiral Callaghan placed his ships in a column, or line ahead, formation called "Baker One."[125] In the lead, or van, were four destroyers at 500-yard intervals: *Cushing*, *Laffey*, *Sterett*, and *O'Bannon*. Then, after an 800-yard gap would come the cruisers at 700-yard intervals: Admiral Scott's flagship light antiaircraft cruiser *Atlanta*, Admiral Callaghan's flagship heavy cruiser *San Francisco*, heavy cruiser *Portland*, light cruiser *Helena*, and light antiaircraft cruiser *Juneau*. Finally, after another 800-yard gap would come the rear destroyers, also at 500-yard intervals: *Aaron Ward, Barton, Monssen,* and *Fletcher.*

About the best that could be said for this formation is that it had a certain symmetry to it – it started with four destroyers and a light antiaircraft cruiser and it ended with a mirror image.[126] But as military analysts and historians have pointed out *ad infinitum,* there is much to criticize about this formation. Admiral Callaghan seems to have studied Admiral Scott's performance at Cape Esperance and learned the wrong lessons. The column formation is simple and, because these ships had not worked together before, it was arguably necessary, but it made massed destroyer attacks with torpedoes problematic, especially with the destroyers in the rear. In fairness to Callaghan, it should be noted that he was concerned about the treacherous waters of the narrow Lengo Channel, through which his force would have to pass. A column formation reduced the chances of running aground. Additionally, Callaghan was rightfully concerned about misidentification and friendly fire, and a simple column formation reduced that danger, although it had clearly not worked at Cape Esperance. And while the positioning of his destroyers front and back made a fully coordinated torpedo attack practically impossible, Callaghan believed this formation meant at least some of his destroyers could launch torpedoes no matter from which direction the Japanese came.[127]

But American torpedoes had issues. For some time, US Navy submarines had strongly suspected there were serious mechanical problems with their torpedo, the Mark 14. The Bureau of Ordnance denied any such problems. Then Admiral King got involved. Shortly thereafter in late August, a notice was sent that tests had proven the torpedoes were running some 10 feet deeper than set.[128] Because the Navy had been too cash-strapped to test the torpedoes with actual warheads and instead used dummy warheads, which were lighter than real warheads, the torpedoes' depth setting had been calibrated incorrectly. Once the depth issue was identified, this particular problem was relatively easy to fix.[129]

Unfortunately, the problems did not end there. The Mark 14 would be detonated by the Mark 6 exploder, which included a contact exploder and a magnetic influence feature. This feature was intended to cause the torpedo to detonate when it entered a ship's magnetic field. So, if the torpedo went under the ship, it would enter the magnetic field beneath the ship and detonate, fracturing the unarmored bottom of the ship, snapping the keel, and causing the ship to break in half. This was the theory, at least – except the size of the magnetic field varied depending on where one was on the earth, so the magnetic field of a ship off, say, Newport, Rhode Island, home of the US Navy's Newport Torpedo Station, was of a different size and shape than the magnetic field of a ship off, for instance, Guadalcanal.

Since the beginning of the war, the submariners had reported a never-ending stream of premature explosions and non-explosions from their torpedoes. They were suspicious something was wrong with the Mark 6, especially that magnetic influence exploder, but the Navy Bureau of Ordnance and the Newport Torpedo Station refused to even consider the matter and blamed the malfunctions entirely on user error.

The Navy's destroyers did not usually launch their torpedoes under the slow and carefully documented conditions that submarines did, so they could not know for sure. But they had achieved little success with their torpedo, the Mark 15, which also used the Mark 6. And in those rare cases when destroyers could launch torpedoes slowly and in the perfect conditions, problems still appeared. In one instance, the skipper of the destroyer *Lansdowne*, Lieutenant Commander Smedberg, had to deactivate the magnetic influence feature in order to get his Mark 15 torpedoes to actually sink the blazing carrier *Wasp*.

The crown jewel of US Navy torpedo performance, if you could call it that, was the attempted scuttling of the disabled carrier *Hornet* by the destroyers *Mustin* and *Anderson* after the Santa Cruz battle. The *Mustin* had fired eight Mark 15 Model 1 torpedoes, each with the Mark 6 Model 1 exploder, at the *Hornet*'s port side.[130] Commander Arnold E. True, who commanded the carrier's screening destroyers, and his crew, as well as survivors of the *Hornet*, watched the torpedo wakes, "running hot, straight, and normal," disappear in the encroaching dark. They waited for the expected explosions.

What they got was the second Mark 15 torpedo reappearing, leaping into the air like a dolphin about 300 yards off the *Mustin*'s starboard quarter, at which point it exploded, showering the ship with fragments. The third Mark 15 also reappeared – astern of the carrier, running on a course about right angles to the angle at which it was fired. The fourth apparently exploded, though no one could tell where. What happened to the first and eighth torpedoes is anybody's guess. The fifth, sixth, and seventh torpedoes did actually hit the *Hornet* and exploded like they were supposed to – but the badly listing carrier still did not sink and showed no signs she would do so anytime soon.

After these "most discouraging results" according to Commander True, the *Mustin* was now out of torpedoes.[131] So the *Anderson* came over and launched eight Mark 15 torpedoes at a range of less than 2,000 yards. Soon after launch, one of the torpedoes turned about 3 degrees to the right and disappeared. A second torpedo detonated prematurely. Six of the torpedoes hit the carrier and exploded, but the effect was described as "negligible."[132] Now the *Anderson* was out of torpedoes. The destroyers resorted to gunfire, which still did not sink the carrier but instead "[left] the hulk burning fiercely from end to end."[133] Eventually, Japanese destroyers sank the derelict with one of the crown jewels of the Imperial Japanese Navy, the deadly oxygen-powered Type 93 torpedo, whose effectiveness earned it, from Navy historian Samuel Eliot Morison, the immortal nickname "Long Lance."

The Mark 6 was supposed to be a wonder weapon; so far, its users were only left wondering, an unhealthy activity on the eve of battle. Wondering about your weapons is bad enough. Wondering about your leader is even worse. But questions about Admiral Callaghan started appearing. Exactly how Admiral Callaghan planned to use this "Baker One" column formation remains somewhat ambiguous. It is generally believed that he wanted to have the formation perform a column turn to starboard to attempt to "cross the T" of the approaching enemy force; that is, have his column ahead of and perpendicular to the approaching enemy, thus allowing Callaghan's ships to use their forward and after guns while limiting the Japanese ships, at best, to using only their forward guns, and quite possibly limiting the Japanese to using only the forward guns of their leading ship. Nevertheless, there is also some belief that Callaghan intended the column to run straight through the Japanese formation and hit them with everything he had at close range. The column would then continue on the other side – seaward – of the Japanese, going northwest of Savo to gain maneuvering room to fight a more traditional battle while the Japanese were pinned against the Guadalcanal coast and thus limited in their maneuvering ability. Callaghan would have hoped to accomplish all this before the Japanese realized what exactly was going on.[134]

Another issue with Admiral Callaghan's chosen formation was radar, still a new apparatus at this time, especially the SG surface search radar, which had the plan position indicator (PPI) display that gave an overhead view of the area and radar contacts positioned therein. Four ships in Admiral Callaghan's force had the new SG radar: *Helena*, *Juneau*, *O'Bannon*, and *Fletcher*. The *Helena*, with a battle-tested skipper in Captain Hoover and 15 rapid-fire 6-inch guns, would have made an ideal flagship – except Navy regulations considered her "too light" when 8-inch-armed cruisers were available. Callaghan did not choose her for his flagship, nor did Admiral Scott. Callaghan was in the *San Francisco*, Scott in the *Atlanta*, neither of which had SG radar.[135]

Moreover, of all the SG-equipped ships, only the *O'Bannon* was placed anywhere near the front of the formation, and she was fourth. The *Helena* was eighth, *Juneau* ninth, and *Fletcher* thirteenth. Because they were so far back in the formation, their radar ranges (especially that of the *Helena*, which was positioned higher on the mast than the other sets) could not extend as far in front of the force as they could have – and thus they could not provide as much warning – had they been positioned properly. Callaghan seems to have not even considered the SG radar in the arrangement of his ships. He had not had good experiences with previous iterations of radar such as the SC type, a user-unfriendly model made infamous by its poor performance in the Savo Island debacle the previous August. As naval aide and staff officer, Callaghan was simply unaware of advances in radar since that time, including the effectiveness of the SG radar.[136]

There were more issues to the positioning of the warships, especially regarding the light antiaircraft cruiser *Atlanta*. There was no reason why the 5-inch-armed *Atlanta* should have even been in this force instead of the 8-inch-armed *Pensacola*. That is not the fault of Admiral Callaghan, but of Admiral Halsey and Admiral Turner for sending the *Pensacola* back to escort the *Enterprise*.

Yet Admiral Callaghan was responsible for the positioning of the *Atlanta* and her sister ship *Juneau* within the formation. The *Atlanta*-class antiaircraft cruisers were little more than floating magazines, lightly armored, and thus could not take a lot of punishment in combat. The *Atlanta*s had 16 dual-purpose 5-inch guns in eight dual mounts, but likely had very little ammunition for piercing the armor of warships. Unlike most US cruisers, they did carry torpedoes, a holdover from the earlier intent for these ships to serve as destroyer squadron leaders, as Japanese light cruisers frequently did. In fairness, the *Atlanta* was positioned to make a massed torpedo attack with the destroyers in the lead, and the

Juneau with those in the rear. But there is no indication that their participation in massed torpedo attacks was a consideration for Callaghan.

Moreover, since the *Atlanta* had Admiral Scott on board, positioning her just ahead of the *San Francisco* in the column formation had the effect of making Scott not so much a second-in-command to Admiral Callaghan as superfluous – while exposing him to at least as much if not more enemy fire as Callaghan. On a warship in combat, the skipper and executive officer always separate themselves so both will not be killed at once. The same consideration applied here. At the very least, Callaghan should have had the *Atlanta* and *Juneau* switch places, so the *Juneau* could have better used her SG surface search radar.

But switch them Admiral Callaghan did not. Exhausted, discouraged, believing the mission was suicide, he evidently had no real plan for facing the enemy or even for controlling his own ships in what was sure to be a chaotic night action.

By no means was Admiral Callaghan alone in his belief that this mission was suicide. On the cruiser *Portland*, at around 10:30 pm, executive officer Commander Turk Wirth came to the bridge to receive an update from skipper Captain Laurence DuBose. Dubose handed Wirth a report formalizing a conference Callaghan had had earlier with Admiral Turner. The report indicated the Japanese were sending in "big fellows" – battleships.*

"This is suicide, you know," the skipper said.

"Oh, I don't know," replied Wirth.

"You are an incorrigible optimist," retorted the captain.[137]

Elsewhere, the feeling was not quite that dark. Captain Lyman Swenson of the *Juneau* did what all good captains do: gave a rousing speech to his crew to bolster their morale and confidence. "We'll see action tonight, but we'll get through it. We can either run or stay and fight," Swenson said to the men assembled on deck. "If we run, we lose Guadalcanal. So we're going to stay and fight!" The crew cheered. As he returned to the bridge, however, Swenson revealed that he was not nearly as confident in their prospects as his speech would suggest.[138]

The column continued in a westerly direction, 280 degrees True, at a speed of 15 knots.[139] The night was unusually dark with no moon, low cloud cover, and a few squalls. The result was a darkness that seemed to suck in all light, revealing nothing. The lookouts were essentially staring into a black hole.

Seaman 1st Class Walt Brandt, a lookout on the *Helena*'s bridge, amused himself by holding one hand in front of his face and trying to find it with the other hand. Brandt could see nothing, not even the wake of the ship ahead. Gunner's Mate 2nd Class Jim Tooker on the *Cushing*'s Number 1 mount – essentially the most forward lookout in the entire force, the point man on its point ship – stared and strained into the blackness all evening and saw absolutely nothing.[140] Gunnery Officer Lieutenant C. Raymond "Cal" Calhoun didn't have it quite that bad in the gun director of the *Sterett*; he could at least see

---

* It probably did not actually say "big fellows" but instead "big f***ers" – a word that many would consider inappropriate for family viewing.

the dim silhouettes of the *Cushing* and *Laffey* ahead of him, and "the almost indiscernible forms of the long column astern."[141] With Calhoun in the director was Lieutenant (jg) Joseph D. "J.D." Jeffrey, who marveled at how difficult it was to keep station in this formation.[142]

The air was humid and warm, although not quite as warm as it had been in recent weeks. A slight breeze from the southeast brought in the smell of tropical flowers, a smell that started out as sweet but soon became sickening.[143] It at least gave the crews something to think about aside from the horror they knew was coming. "We were mindful of the fact that the Tokyo Express had comprised a battleship or two during recent bombardments, but we had not been told what kind of enemy force we might expect on this run. Although our adrenaline was flowing, there was no particular apprehension about what lay ahead," said Calhoun.[144]

But with others there certainly was. On the whole the sailors were bored, fearful, and tired. Some sailors tried to pass the time by doing mundane duties or other tasks – cleaning weapons (yet again), laying out medical supplies, sorting signal flags.

Some of the sailors, a superstitious lot from time immemorial, became obsessed with the number 13. On the *Monssen*, a sailor in the gun director pointed out that there were 13 ships in this task force, tomorrow was Friday the 13th, and the destroyer's hull number – 436 – added up to 13.[145] Seaman 1st Class Gene Oliver in the *Monssen*'s Number 3 mount thought he was a "dumb bastard" for mentioning it.[146] But there were a lot of dumb bastards talking about the number 13 this night. Captain DuBose of the *Portland* had graduated from the Naval Academy in 1913 and considered it a lucky number. "If we can get across midnight into tomorrow, we might make it," he told Commander Wirth.[147]

They did get into tomorrow as midnight passed uneventfully. It was now Friday, November 13, 1942.

At approximately 1:00 am the destroyer *O'Bannon* spotted a bright light on the port bow, in the Japanese sector on Guadalcanal itself. The *San Francisco* spotted two white lights, with the eastern one sending long flashes: navigation signals to aid the approaching enemy.[148]

Concerned about his formation, Admiral Callaghan sent out some navigation signals of his own. "Keep well closed up. Report any contacts immediately. Do not answer." As historian C.W. Kilpatrick acidly points out, "The Admiral, whose job is to lead, expects that other ships will make radar contact first, and he wants to be kept informed."[149]

As the enemy got closer, or at least was perceived as closer, the tension rose. "We had the feeling that we were being watched," wrote Seaman 2nd Class Joseph Hartney of the *Juneau*, "that out there in the mantled sea, eyes peered at us, full of malevolence and hatred, waiting to pounce on us. Little pinpricks ran across our scalps."[150]

Guadalcanal sent out an air warning. Lookouts thought they saw an unidentified aircraft overhead with its running lights on.[151] Was this Savo Island all over again? No. There was no relaxation. They expected the enemy to come. And come hard.

"Radar contact. Bearing 312 True. Distance 27,100 yards."[152]

The report came at 1:24 am over the voice radio from Captain Hoover of the *Helena*, using her SG surface search radar from astern of the flagship to spot the enemy ahead of the flagship. The Americans were just past Lunga Point.

This first real contact with the enemy seemed to cause everything to freeze, including Admiral Callaghan. Silence enveloped all the ships.[153]

"Radar contact. Bearing 310 True. Distance 31,900 yards." This second report from the *Helena* came a minute after the first.[154] There were two groups of ships. This second group was behind the first.

Admiral Callaghan was having issues taking these reports of radar contacts and visualizing what they meant. The communications officer, Lieutenant Commander Bruce McCandless, said that when these reports came in:

> This and subsequent information was sent via TBS ["Talk Between Ships"] voice radio to Admiral Callaghan in the *San Francisco*, which was not equipped with SG radar.
>
> Additional reports followed; the staff tried to reproduce on a chart what officers in SG-equipped ships could see on their radar scopes, but had to convert into terms of bearing and distance for transmission to the flagship. And the Admiral had to use this same TBS circuit, over which information was coming in, to give orders to his group.[155]

At 1:28 am, a full four minutes after the first contact, Admiral Callaghan ordered a column turn to 310 degrees True, that is, northwest. As a column turn, more properly a column movement, it required each ship to turn as it passed the same spot one at a time.

This caused some consternation among the other skippers in the force, who were perhaps visualizing the rapidly developing situation better than the admiral was.[156] Admiral Callaghan should be trying to cross the enemy's T. Instead, he was heading straight for the enemy, straight for that first radar contact. In fairness, it must be pointed out that neither of these first reports gave Callaghan information on the course or speed of the contacts, though perhaps the course could have been deduced from the positioning of the two contacts relative to each other.

At 1:31, the *Helena* reported, "Now three targets. Bearing 312. Distance 26,000." She rapidly followed it with, "Their course 107. Speed possibly 23."[157] This was the first real course and speed information Admiral Callaghan received. The admiral reacted by ordering the *Cushing* to turn to starboard to lead the column on a new heading of 0 degrees True – due north. He raised the speed to 18 knots. The new heading placed one of the three Japanese groups directly ahead of the *Cushing*, the other two to port.[158] The skippers were baffled. What was the admiral doing?

They couldn't ask him. This voice radio circuit, called "Talk Between Ships" or "TBS," was limited to one frequency (one to which the Japanese were not listening, fortunately), so all the ship-to-ship communication – sightings, confirmation, positioning, clarifications, repeats, all legitimately necessary communications – had to be handled on this one frequency. To request or receive information, Admiral Callaghan had to compete with all this other chatter on the voice radio. His rank did not necessarily afford him priority and it made his control of his ships and of this action slip further and further out of his grasp.

Certainly, Callaghan seems to have been conflicted as to what to do. Evidently not happy heading due north, he reversed his earlier order and had the force turn back to port and course 310 degrees True – back to the northwest. But at 1:37, he reversed his reversal and ordered it back to due north.[159]

At 1:39, the *Helena* reported four ships in line "in fan like cruising formation" off her port bow, but did not give a bearing or range.[160] Admiral Callaghan asked for the distance, and the *Helena* sent it – 3,400 yards – but he likely did not receive it.[161] Events were starting to take over from the admiral, and his control of his force slipped a few notches further.

At 1:40 am the *O'Bannon* crowded Admiral Callaghan off the voice radio by reporting three contacts with her SG radar: one group bearing 287 degrees True, distance 11,000 yards, and containing three or more units; a second group bearing 318 degrees True, distance 8,500 yards, and composed of two or three units; and a third group bearing 42 degrees True, distance 6,000 yards, and containing three units.[162] This was the clearest picture yet of the positioning of the Japanese ships. But the admiral was still struggling to visualize it.

For Lieutenant Commander Edward Nelson "Butch" Parker, skipper of the *Cushing*, visualizing the Japanese ships was not a problem. He could actually see the Japanese ships.[163] "There is a ship crossing bow from port to starboard, range 4,000 yards, maximum," he reported, a near-collision in nautical terms, as it happened at 1:41.[164] The ship was the *Yudachi*. The lookouts on the *Cushing* saw a second ship, the *Harusame*, then a third, larger ship cross their bow, apparently the *Nagara*.[165] On the *Laffey*, torpedo officer Lieutenant (jg) Tom Evins saw the wakes of the two destroyers crossing in front of the *Cushing*. Even from his spot some 500 yards behind the *Cushing*, he thought the Japanese ships were "right on top of us."[166]

Butch Parker, a winner of two Navy Crosses as the aggressive, energetic skipper of the four-piper destroyer *Parrott* in the Java Sea Campaign, was used to long odds. As the range closed to 2,000 yards, he threw the *Cushing* into a hard port turn, to 330 degrees True, both to avoid colliding with the *Yudachi* and to unmask his torpedo batteries to launch at the Japanese. While Parker was at work, Commander Murray Stokes, the commander of 10th Destroyer Division who was also in the *Cushing*, radioed Admiral Callaghan, "Shall I let them have a couple of fish?"[167]

"Stop using the TBS!" snarled Admiral Callaghan, angrily adding that Commander Stokes would be told when to open fire.[168] Both were having problems getting through on the TBS voice radio. It was now swamped with requests. For information. For clarification. For permission to fire at the now visible Japanese. Captain Hoover on the *Helena* radioed, "We have a total of about ten targets. Appear to be in cruising disposition."[169] Two minutes after the report, Admiral Callaghan finally and rather more politely gave permission for the *Cushing* to launch torpedoes, but he was too late. The *Yudachi* and *Harusame* had passed the *Cushing* and were speeding away, ruining the firing solution.[170]

Back aboard the *Cushing*, Yeoman 2nd Class Tom Foreman was on duty in the gun director, watching the fire control radar. He was astonished when the radar scope lit up, showing targets everywhere. *That can't be right*, he thought. Radar must be malfunctioning, reflecting off the land nearby. He duly reported it to his gunnery officer. Then, to make absolutely sure it was a malfunction, Foreman decided to stick his head out of the open-topped director to see for himself. He did. The radar was not malfunctioning.[171]

Right behind the *Cushing*, aboard the *Laffey*, the two Japanese destroyers had just sped away when Lieutenant Evins spotted a larger target. He turned to his director operator. "Have you got the third ship? The one with the big silhouette? She looks like a cruiser." This would have been the *Nagara*. Evins turned to his skipper, Lieutenant Commander Bill Hank, and proudly said, "I have an enemy cruiser to starboard. I request permission to fire torpedoes."

"Permission not granted," Hank responded. Admiral Callaghan had not yet given permission to open fire.[172]

Aboard the *Sterett*, third in the column, Jack Shelton, manning the rangefinder, had a great view of the Japanese as they appeared out of the dark. For the crews who had not been told what they were facing, Shelton made a chilling discovery. "Two large targets in that formation," he reported to his shipmates. "They look like battleships."

"Battleships!" Lieutenant Calhoun thought. "And we had two heavy cruisers to match them. Fortunately, there was no time for that sort of thinking."[173]

No, there was not, as the skippers and gunners and lookouts and radar operators of the force had mostly another thought in mind:

We can see the Japanese. All around us. Right on top of us. Shouldn't we be shooting at them?

———————————— ⊙ ————————————

Admiral Abe's worst fears were being realized. "What is the range and bearing?" he thundered at his flag signal officer. "And where is *Yudachi*?"[174]

Immediately, frantic shouts came from a lookout on the top of *Hiei*'s towering pagoda foremast: "Four black objects ahead ... look like warships. Five degrees to starboard. Eight thousand meters ... unsure yet. Visibility bad." Abe did not know where the *Yudachi* was. Unfortunately, neither did the *Yudachi*. Her skipper, Commander Kikkawa Kiyoshi, a veteran of the Java Sea Campaign, was shaken by his near-collision with an enemy ship that had unexpectedly appeared out of the black. "I was flabbergasted to see an enemy destroyer suddenly emerging from the darkness, and bearing down to strike us amidship. [...] We frantically turned around, radioing our discovery to *Hiei*, but we could not give positions because we did not know where we were relative to our own forces," Kikkawa would later say.[175]

Commander Kikkawa knew that *Yudachi* was out of position, having gone astray during the first course reversal during the storm, and was headed roughly east somewhere ahead of the *Harusame*. But Kikkawa had no idea exactly where he was or, for that matter, where Abe was. The admiral was furious, but he was just as shaken as Kikkawa.

It was left to Admiral Abe's chief of staff, Commander Suzuki, to debrief the lookout. He shouted, "Is eight thousand meters correct? Confirm."

"It may be nine thousand, sir."[176] Closer to the flagship than the *Yudachi*?

The *Hiei* flashed to the other ships of the Vanguard Force, "Probable enemy ships in sight, bearing 136 degrees."[177]

Admiral Abe had never liked this mission, never supported it. Now his worst fears were realized. Far from a simple bombardment mission, he was facing enemy ships, and doing so with the wrong kind of ammunition – ammunition designed to destroy land targets, not armored enemy warships. The *Hiei*'s skipper Captain Nishida Masao and his gunnery officer started arguing over whether they had time to replace the incendiaries with Type 1 armor-piercing shells, an argument cut short by Commander Chihaya.

"The 11th Battleship Division change the firing target!" Chihaya boomed, without waiting for orders from Admiral Abe. "New target is enemy ships starboard ahead. Start firing with searchlights on!"[178]

At exactly this point Admiral Abe weighed in. "Tell *Hiei* and *Kirishima* to replace all those incendiaries with armor piercing, and set turrets for firing forward," the admiral commanding two battleships, a light cruiser, and 11 destroyers said in a weak, faltering voice.[179] The replacement would come after five salvos, so the turrets would be able to fire while the ammunition was being rearranged to allow access to the Type 1 armor-piercing shells.[180] Should they turn around while they rearmed? No, the admiral decided. Abe was in shock – strange for someone who had originally expected to face enemy ships during this mission – and it showed. He staggered back to his command chair. According to Hara, the admiral was "in agony."[181] It could not have had a good effect on the crews.

Admiral Abe's order threw both the *Hiei* and *Kirishima* into chaos. The few armor-piercing shells the battleships currently carried were buried in the very depths of the magazines. They had to get the Type 3s out of the way just to get at the Type 1s. Hara Tameichi recalled the scene:

On the decks of the two battleships there was pandemonium. Almost every hand had left his battle station to help cart away the Type-3 shells. There was a stampede in the magazines, men pushing and kicking to reach the armor-piercing shells stored deep inside. At a range of 9,000 meters capital ships can fire with deadly accuracy. Just one shell landing on the deck of either of those battleships, stacked high with mountains of incendiary shells, could ignite it like a mammoth match box.[182]

All it would take would be one enemy shell. Not even a big hit, or even a lucky hit – simply if it landed on the deck, then both battleships would become virtual firestorms.

The big question was, could they get all those incendiary shells off the decks before that one shell hit?

At 1:43 am, Admiral Callaghan finally gave the order – sort of. "Enemy to port and on starboard bow. Stand by to open fire."[183] It was not quite what the exasperated skippers and gunners were hoping for.

They knew that the side that opened fire first could usually count on getting the first hit, and the side that got the first hit had a major tactical advantage. Savo Island was one such example of that. But until the admiral authorized them to open fire, they could do nothing except maintain the target locks from their gunnery radars and aim the torpedo tubes and guns. And worry. How much longer would the Japanese let them wait?

Meanwhile, Admiral Callaghan seems to have been less focused on opening fire as maintaining his column, control of which was slipping further and further out of his grasp. A frustrated Seaman 1st Class Lester Zook on the *Juneau*, like Hara Tameichi, reached the dangerous conclusion that his admiral "didn't know what the hell he was doing."[184]

When the *Cushing* had swerved to avoid the *Yudachi* and bring her torpedo tubes to bear on the Japanese destroyer, she had turned to course 330 degrees True, toward the north-northwest. The *Laffey* had apparently followed the *Cushing* in this course change. Then the *Sterett* made the same turn.

Admiral Callaghan ordered the ships to return to course 000 degrees True – due north – at 1:47.[185] The multiple course changes caused the destroyers at the head of the column to bunch up, throwing the entire column into confusion with a sort of domino effect. After the *Sterett*, third in the column, turned to port, the destroyer *O'Bannon*, fourth in the column, had to turn to port inside the *Sterett* to avoid hitting her, which placed the *O'Bannon* square in the path of the *Atlanta* behind her. The *Atlanta's* skipper Captain Samuel P. Jenkins was forced to order an even more radical turn to port inside the *O'Bannon* and a temporary cut in speed to avoid plowing into the destroyer's port quarter.[186] At the helm of the flagship *San Francisco*, just astern of the *Atlanta*, Lieutenant Commander McCandless called to the flag bridge: "The *Atlanta's* turning left! Shall I follow her?" The response was immediate and firm – "No! Hold your course!" – as was the countermand a few seconds later: "Follow the *Atlanta!*"[187]

With enemy ships all around him at close range and a clock of unknown duration ticking away, instead of giving the very belated order to open fire, Admiral Callaghan called out Captain Jenkins on the voice radio. "What are you doing, Sam?"

"Avoiding our own destroyers," came the calm, matter-of-fact reply from Captain Jenkins.

The admiral turned to Commander Parker on the *Cushing*. "What have you got now? Have you come back on course?"

"Coming back," replied Parker.[188] Callaghan turned back to Captain Jenkins on the *Atlanta*.

"Come back to your course as soon as you can. You are throwing the whole column into disorder."[189]

As the minutes, the seconds ticked away, the *Cushing*'s Lieutenant Commander Parker, however, had more pressing matters on his mind than the admiral's formation. As he was trying to bring the destroyer back to the all-important course of 000 degrees True, the *Cushing*'s lookouts shouted, "Ships to port!" Parker turned his head left. Against the dark he saw several black shapes, of which one very much stood out: one huge shape, headed straight for him, only 20 degrees off the port bow.[190]

The American sailors, most of whom had not been told what they would be facing, were now coming face to face with it, and were momentarily stunned. In the *Cushing*'s Number 1 5-inch mount, the talk was that a huge warship was bearing down from the port bow and looked like it planned to run them down. The shell loader, Seaman 2nd Class Felton Maillot, was preparing ready shells when he heard someone shout, "Dead ahead!" Maillot looked up. For a few seconds he could see only blackness. Then his eyes adjusted and he realized that the blackness was actually the bows of the largest warship he had ever seen towering directly over them. Maillot looked down at his ready shells and went back to work.[191] The 5-inch mounts were trained on the large target – for all the good those guns could do against something so large and so well armored.

On the *Sterett*, Lieutenant Calhoun popped his head out of the director to see if he could make out the enemy. When the range closed to 4,000 yards, Calhoun was finally able to see the Japanese warships – and the giant among them. As the range closed to 3,000 yards, "I recognized the gigantic superstructure of a *Kongo*-class battleship. She looked like the Empire State Building to me. We had chosen this ship [*Hiei*] as our target right from the start and had a perfect solution on her. The tension in the gun director grew as we waited for orders." And waited. "She was now clearly visible to the naked eye, and it seemed that at any moment she could blow us right out of the water."[192]

On the *Atlanta*, Boatswain's Mate 1st Class Leighton Spadone was captain of a 1.1-inch mount on the cruiser's starboard side, but he had experience with 5-inch guns. On the battle phone, he listened to his division officer, Lieutenant (jg) David Hall, describe the approach of the massive ship out to port. "I can see them now," Hall said. "Range three-oh-double-oh."

Spadone thought to himself, *Boy, that's close.* But it got closer. Hall gave the warning, "Stand by. Action to port," followed by "Range two-three-double-oh." In Spadone's experience, it would be impossible for the 5-inch guns on the *Atlanta* to miss a target only 2,000 yards away.[193] An exasperated plotting room officer in the *Helena* spoke for everyone when he shouted, "For Christ's sake, what are we going to do? Throw potatoes at them? We're so close!" [194]

Just astern of the *Atlanta* and two ships ahead of the *Helena*, Lieutenant Commander McCandless had to swing the *San Francisco* slightly right to clear the *Atlanta*, then hard to port.

The flagship ended up paralleling the *Atlanta* on a northwesterly course, with the cruiser slightly on the flagship's port bow.[195] On the *San Francisco*'s well deck, Seaman 1st Class Willie Boyce, after coming off watch at midnight, had staked out a spot to sleep; he quickly awakened, certain something "big" was about to happen.[196]

As the *San Francisco* settled in astern of the *Atlanta* once again, from somewhere to the west, a bright, blinding light stabbed out of the dark. Searchlights.

Crewmen on the *Juneau* were frozen with shock; some crewmen cried, or vomited, or just hit the deck. One colorfully described it as feeling "like I was naked on the stage at Radio City Music Hall, with a giant spotlight on me, and everyone in the audience had a gun."[197] Ensign Deale Binion "Bin" Cochran of the *Helena* failed to suppress a chuckle when he saw every senior officer on the bridge duck behind cover or hide in a shadow. But he spoke for pretty much every American sailor who was topside:

> There was a shocking moment when, staring into that light, all seemed completely silent. Everything in the night was quiet and black and here we were standing out for all to see. [...] There was a feeling, one that you knew was without logic, that there was protection in getting out of the direct glare of that light. Everybody I could see crouched into a shadow.[198]

The bright white beam slowly swept the column and then settled with an ominous finality on the ship with the tallest superstructure, the *Atlanta*.

With the port wing of the bridge illuminated by an icy light as bright as a sunny winter day, the *Atlanta*'s bridge crew was stunned. The light was so close, so intense, that Admiral Scott's operations officer Lieutenant Stew Moredock thought he could almost feel the heat coming from it.[199] Everyone crouched. On the cruiser's starboard side, Leighton Spadone heard the call to take cover.[200]

It was 1:50 am. Time had run out.

CHAPTER 2

BARFIGHT IN THE DARK

Eight minutes: that's how long it took the crews of the *Hiei* and the *Kirishima* to switch from the Type 3 incendiary ammunition to the Type 1 armor-piercing ammunition, and get the incendiaries safely stowed away in the protective magazines.

During those eight minutes the American ships had not fired a shot, a shell, a bullet, or even a potato at the Japanese – not one shot that could have turned both battleships into firestorms. Hara Tameichi on the *Amatsukaze* was flabbergasted at the inaction of the enemy.

But Admiral Abe was not about to question the divine providence he and his ships had been given. With the period of most extreme danger over, he could now turn to the battle at hand. The first order of business was training the searchlights. One Japanese report of the engagement stated, "Visibility allowed shelling without the use of searchlights, but Abe ordered *Hiei* to use her searchlight so the whole fleet would know enemy targets and to screen the Japanese fleet."[1] The idea of the use of searchlights actually came from Commander Chihaya, who had lobbied hard with Admiral Abe for their use ever since leaving Truk.[2]

The *Hiei* followed Commander Chihaya's order. But Admiral Abe could not have been happy with what the light from his flagship revealed.

Aboard the *Nagara*, apparently Admiral Kimura's vaunted navigation could not overcome Admiral Abe's complicated formation, sailing through a blinding storm and two reversals of course. The *Nagara* was supposed to be some 2,000 meters ahead of the battleship, but she was more than twice that, and was now shifting to port to lead the destroyers *Yukikaze*, *Amatsukaze*, and *Teruzuki* in column to port of the flagship. Five destroyers of the 4th Destroyer Flotilla – *Asagumo*, *Harusame*, *Murasame*, *Samidare*, and *Yudachi* – were supposed to be in an arc more than 4 miles ahead. They were not, to put

MAP 3: THE FIRST NAVAL BATTLE OF GUADALCANAL, NOVEMBER 13, 1942

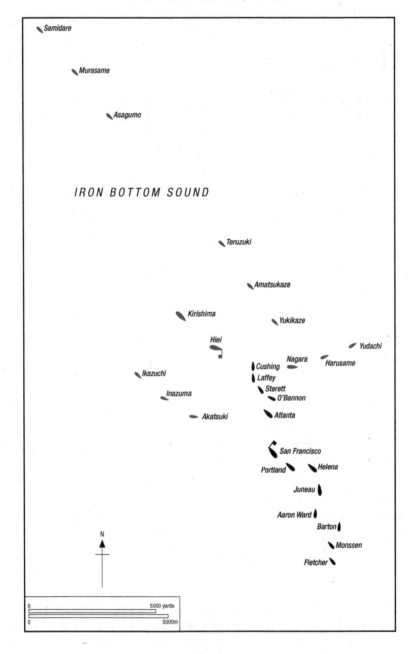

IRON BOTTOM SOUND

it mildly. The 4th had split off during the first reversal of course and was never able to correct it.[3] The *Yudachi* and *Harusame* were not even 2 miles ahead, and instead of being off the port bow, they were off the starboard bow – but at least they were still ahead of the battleships. The other three destroyers of the 4th – *Asagumo*, *Samidare*, and *Murasame* – nowhere to be seen, were actually behind the *Kirishima*, off her starboard quarter.

Admiral Abe had had no idea until now that the arc that was supposed to be sweeping 4 miles ahead of him had entirely disintegrated; that almost all of his screen had disintegrated. The *Nagara* was too far ahead to screen his battleships. The destroyers of the 4th had no idea where they were or where everyone else was. In short, the *Hiei* was dangerously exposed.

To starboard of the Japanese flagship, the destroyers *Akatsuki*, *Ikazuchi*, and *Inazuma* were not in a column, but in a sort of blob. The *Akatsuki* quickly snapped on her searchlights, followed a few moments later by the *Nagara*. Commander Chihaya's impeccable logic in ordering the use of searchlights was that if you use searchlights in the dark, you can see things. The problem with that, of course, is that things can see you too.

The searchlights were the last straw for some of Admiral Callaghan's skippers. Commander Stokes on the *Cushing* decided it was now too dangerous to wait any longer. He calmly ordered Lieutenant Commander Parker to open fire.[4] Crouching on the *Helena*'s open bridge, gunnery officer Commander Rodman Smith, an expert gunner, went over to his captain and asked, "Permission to open fire, Captain?"

Ducking out of the light, Captain Hoover nodded emphatically and shouted back, "Open fire!"[5]

Meanwhile, on the bridge of the *Atlanta*, now in the spotlights of a show in which she wanted no part, Captain Jenkins barked a word seldom used in the English language: "Counter-illuminate!" His gunnery officer Lieutenant Commander William R.D. Nickelson was more direct: "F**k that! Open fire!"[6]

Nickelson's assistant Lieutenant Lloyd Mustin called out the official order to the gun captains: "Action port. Illuminating ship is target!"[7] The *Atlanta*'s four 36-inch searchlights snapped on.[8] Mustin took control of the aft guns, the four dual 5-inch mounts which swiveled, targeting the source of the menacing searchlights to port, the flagship *Hiei*. The first shots of Friday the 13th flashed in the night.

Disappointingly, and rather anticlimactically, they missed, splashing short of their target. After a quick correction to a range of some 2,000 yards, the 5-inch shells started hitting the *Hiei*. The shells could do little against the battleship's hull armor, but they could wreak havoc topside. And they did. Seaman Boyce on the *San Francisco*, struggling to stay on his feet from the ship's violent maneuvers, watched the bright white light turn to dull red then disappear completely.[9]

The *Atlanta* also used her 1.1-inch antiaircraft guns against the *Hiei*. They seem to have mostly missed, going over the battleship to splash on the opposite side – in the neighborhood of the destroyer *Amatsukaze*. Commander Hara was dazzled by the falling shells for a few minutes, then shouted, "Gain speed! Let's get the hell out of here to starboard!"

The *Amatsukaze* sped forward and, with the *Yukikaze* on her tail, raced past the starboard side of the *Nagara*.[10]

A group of destroyers had been seen crossing the *Hiei*'s searchlight beam. The *Atlanta* tried her hand at multitasking, keeping her aft guns on the battleship, but redirecting her forward guns to one of these new targets, which turned out to be the *Akatsuki*, still using searchlights of her own.

On the *San Francisco*'s bridge, Admiral Callaghan was losing the last threads of control over his ships. He shouted over the voice radio an order that would become famous – or infamous: "Odd ships commence fire to starboard, even ships to port!"[11] Callaghan's intent was to avoid needless concentration of fire on one target, but in adding that condition to the long-overdue order to open fire, he created confusion that was ultimately counterproductive.

The *San Francisco*'s gunnery officer Lieutenant Commander William Wilbourne had ordered the main guns to train on the nearest target, which was the *Akatsuki*. Because of the cruiser's violent maneuvering behind the *Atlanta*, the *Akatsuki* was actually to starboard. Sixth in the column, the flagship should have been firing to port under Admiral Callaghan's order. But Captain Young ignored it, and the flagship fired the first of nine full 8-inch salvos at the Japanese destroyer. Destroyers *Laffey* and *O'Bannon*, second and fourth in the American column, respectively, looked for targets to port to comply with the admiral's order. Both settled on the *Akatsuki*. Astern of the flagship, the *Helena*, eighth in the column, her guns almost horizontal, also joined in on the Japanese destroyer. So much for avoiding an overconcentration of fire on one target; Callaghan's order had in this case actually caused it.

On the Japanese destroyer's bridge, Lieutenant Shinya Michiharu attempted to line up a target through his torpedo director when one of her searchlights picked out what looked like a destroyer, the *Atlanta*. In using her searchlight to illuminate the *Atlanta*, the *Akatsuki* turned herself into the target. Shinya's world exploded, as an avalanche of explosives from no fewer than seven ships, including seven of the nine salvos fired by the *San Francisco* and half of the approximately 40 shells fired by the *Atlanta*, smacked the hapless destroyer.

"You couldn't help but see our projectiles were just tearing into it," the *Atlanta*'s Lieutenant Mustin later said. "Shooting into a destroyer-sized hull from six hundred yards, you just don't miss. You just don't miss."[12] The *Laffey* watched the searchlights go out, come back on, then go out again.

In addition to the searchlights, the first hits also smashed the *Akatsuki*'s bridge. Lieutenant Shinya was flattened, with a head wound and shrapnel in his cheek. His hat and shoes blown off, he struggled to his feet on a bridge deck slippery with the blood of almost all the bridge crew, whom he saw lying dead. In this emergency Captain Yamada Yusuke, commanding 6th Destroyer Division, ordered a port turn away from the American column, but when Shinya grabbed the wheel it did not respond. The skipper, Commander Takasuka Osamu, called out to the gunnery officer with no reply.[13]

Lieutenant Shinya left the bridge to go to manual steering aft, but he never made it. Another hit had disabled the starboard engine room. Shinya got to the wardroom, found that power was out, and saw that the fire room was itself on fire. The port engine room was hit and wrecked, depriving the *Akatsuki* of her last source of propulsion. Disabled, burning from the bridge aft, listing to port, settling by the stern, the *Akatsuki* was finished. Exploding, she sank a few minutes later, having not fired a shot, her deadly Type 93 torpedoes still in their tubes.[14]

The *Akatsuki*'s two destroyer mates in the former starboard column, the *Inazuma* and the *Ikazuchi*, understandably wanted no part of her fate, so they did not use their searchlights and tried to stay out of the glare of her fires. Commander Terauchi Masamichi, skipper of the *Inazuma*, had no orders from Admiral Abe; the only message he had received from the flagship was a request for information. So, Terauchi and Commander Maeda Saneo of the *Ikazuchi* fell back on that ancient Japanese credo: "When in doubt, launch torpedoes." Each destroyer fired six of the deadly Long Lances at the American column. The *Inazuma* added 54 5-inch rounds to the munitions she hurled at the Americans. The trailing *Ikazuchi* also gunned for the US ships, but she was smacked by at least three 8-inch shells from the *Portland*, behind the bridge, at the base of the superstructure, and on the Number 1 5-inch mount.[15] The mount was disabled and a dangerous fire was burning in its handling room. She turned away to tend her wounds, hoping to avoid joining the *Akatsuki*.

The *Akatsuki* had been the first blood drawn by the *Atlanta*, but the antiaircraft cruiser had no time to celebrate. She had been pinned in the Japanese searchlights long enough for them to get a visual fix on her position. And now she paid the price. At least three Japanese ships opened fire on the *Atlanta*: the *Hiei*, *Nagara*, and either or both of the destroyers *Inazuma* and *Ikazuchi*.

Captain Jenkins had ordered the torpedoes on the port side to be launched. One of the first hits, from the *Hiei*, was on the bridge splinter shield of the port torpedo director. The director was damaged and rendered unusable. The torpedo officer Lieutenant (jg) Henry P. Jenks, the entire director crew, and a number of signalmen were killed. Without the director, the port torpedo tubes could only be trained manually, too slow for use against the fast-moving enemy ships. Jenkins was moving to check on the director when another blast from the *Hiei*, probably a 14-inch incendiary shell, exploded just below the bridge.

The hit was devastating. Fragments ignited 20mm ammunition near Turret 2 and in the forward 20mm handling room. It started a fire that exploding ammunition turned into an inferno, spreading to the wardroom two decks below.

Fragments also smashed against the bridge. Captain Jenkins looked back toward the starboard wing of the bridge to see no starboard wing of the bridge.[16] Lieutenant Moredock, watching the action form the port wing of the bridge, was struck in the arm by shrapnel. He didn't know he was wounded until he tried to move his arm, when intense pain convinced him it was not a good idea; it turned out his right hand was broken. He looked over toward Admiral Scott on the opposite wing of the bridge. The admiral was in the process of taking a step forward when he collapsed to the deck, never to rise again. Scott's entire staff except for Moredock died with him. Jenkins determined that the admiral was dead, then stepped over him in returning to the bridge to resume fighting.[17]

The hits just kept coming, nonstop, straight to the top. A 5-inch shell from the *Inazuma* or *Ikazuchi* struck the foremast, toppling it to port. Another 5-inch shell struck the mainmast. Still another hit Turret 1, partially exploding, killing four men and disabling the turret. As the crew exited the turret, another 5-inch shell exploded in the upper handling room of the already-battered Turret 2, spreading debris and shrapnel, killing three, and jamming the turret against the manual train.[18] A shell from either the *Hiei* or *Nagara* started a major fire in the forward director, killing the lookouts and forcing the crew to jump into the water 40 feet below; they later reboarded the ship.[19] Another hit wiped out a fire director and crew for the 1.1-inch guns, and started yet another ammunition fire. Altogether, the *Atlanta* suffered some 30 hits during this one or two minutes of Hell.

And then, in the words of one historian, "things deteriorated."[20]

On the bridge, Signal Officer Robert Graff felt "a tremendous *piiing*. The ship lurched like when you hit a heavy pothole."[21] It was a large underwater explosion. "A monstrous column of water and oil rose on our port side and cascaded down all over the ship, drenching all of the topside. People were thrown to their knees, including me, by the shock of the explosion," recalled Lloyd Mustin.[22] Eleven-hundred pounds of explosives, the warhead of a Type 93 torpedo believed to have been launched by the *Ikazuchi*, had just detonated in the forward engine room.

The plotting officer Lieutenant James C. Shaw was thrown against a bulkhead, smashing his right hand. When Shaw saw the deck flooding, he called the gunnery officer, Commander Nickelson, to inform him of the situation and ask for direction. Nickelson's solution? "Stick a pillow in it." Then the line went dead.[23]

But Lieutenant Shaw would need a very big pillow. The *Atlanta* was literally blown out of the water, lifted up to come crashing back down with another large splash. Everyone in the forward engine room was killed, along with almost everyone manning a damage control station a deck above in the mess hall. The forward engine room was flooded, and, worse, the bulkheads to both fire rooms were cracked, causing both to flood. All at once the *Atlanta* was without power. Reduced to using only emergency diesel generators, she was unable to fight or even move – powerless, helpless, adrift.

On the cruiser's starboard side, Boatswain Leighton Spadone had felt the concussions and the severe jolt from the torpedo, but was not overly concerned. Then he noticed the *Atlanta*'s guns were no longer firing. But the enemy's were.

Spadone softly muttered a prayer: "Please, God, stop them from firing, stop them from firing, stop them from firing …"[24]

It is at this point that the battle – with American and Japanese ships "mingled like minnows in a bucket," to use Samuel Eliot Morison's phrase – descended into general chaos, "a no-holds-barred barroom brawl, in which someone turned out the lights and everyone started swinging in every direction – only this was ten thousand times worse," in the famous words of Cal Calhoun.[25] The battle has challenged historians trying to explain it ever since, like trying to describe the path of each noodle in a plate of spaghetti and its relation to all the other noodles.[26]

But the chaos of the action can be more easily understood, at least in the narrative sense, if it is accepted that the focus of the combat was the battleship *Hiei*. The various almost simultaneous ship-to-ship actions that comprise this First Naval Battle of Guadalcanal can then be broken down into two categories: the combat involving the *Hiei* and everything else. Because she was the lead battleship, literally towering over the US Navy ships, with most of the Japanese ships behind her, and using her searchlights, the *Hiei* was bound to gain attention. Like the *Akatsuki*, she attracted the enemy's fire, although much more able than the destroyer to take it. But Admiral Abe's complicated formation and the two turnabouts had, far from protecting the flagship, actually left it exposed and vulnerable. And Abe was about to find out just how exposed and vulnerable his powerful flagship was. For just after the *Hiei* had finished blasting the *Atlanta*, she found herself besieged and caught in something of a crossfire between the *San Francisco* and, much to Admiral Abe's surprise, the destroyers leading the American column.

Admiral Callaghan's "Odd ships fire to starboard, even ships to port" order had thrown the entire American column into confusion, but especially the forward destroyers, two of whom had this massive, black monstrosity bearing down on them from port, but under Callaghan's order had to switch targets to starboard. Due to the admiral's delay, Commander Parker on the lead destroyer *Cushing* had lost his targets in the *Yudachi* and the *Harusame*. But he caught a target speeding past in the opposite direction, the *Amatsukaze*. He got off a few shots, which missed, but the concussions knocked out the *Cushing*'s voice radio.[27]

On the *Sterett*, third in the column, Lieutenant Calhoun was frustrated by Admiral Callaghan's order. "Oh, Christ!" he muttered as he abandoned a perfect firing solution they had worked out on the battleship to search for a target to starboard. The gunners found one – the light cruiser *Nagara*. The plan had been for the *Sterett* to illuminate targets with starshells while the other ships did the actual damage to the targets. But Calhoun fired the guns all the same at a range of 4,000 yards. The shells landed on the cruiser's forecastle and around her forward 5.5-inch mount, where they ignited, giving a nice light show that looked like a fire but in reality did little damage. The next 12 salvos from the *Sterett* were all armor-piercing, tracking the *Nagara* as she passed on the opposite course, but all missed.[28] In the middle of this exchange, the *Sterett* took a hit from off the port quarter that disabled her steering, but skipper Commander Jesse B. Coward switched to steering with the engines and the destroyer barely missed a beat.[29]

Just astern of the *Sterett*, the *O'Bannon* had been among the first to open fire. When the *Akatsuki*'s searchlight snapped on, skipper Commander Edwin Wilkinson roared, "Action port! Get that searchlight!" And her guns roared as well, just as a starshell burst behind the Japanese column, revealing a behemoth closing in on them.

With the *Sterett* now being steered by engine, she lost speed. The *O'Bannon* quickly came onto her stern and only by a "hard right" then a "hard left" was she able to avoid the *Sterett*[30] – by 30 feet.[31]

In passing the *Sterett* to starboard, the *O'Bannon* had fouled the *Sterett*'s range to the *Nagara*. The *Sterett* was actually about to switch fire from the *Nagara* to the *O'Bannon* until, at the last second, she recognized the *O'Bannon* as an American destroyer – albeit, oddly, the *Aaron Ward*.[32] In turn, the *Sterett* had fouled the *O'Bannon*'s range to the *Akatsuki*. The chaos in the American column from Admiral Callaghan's orders was having serious combat consequences.

But on this night, the star of one of the most extraordinary encounters of the war was second in the US column, the destroyer *Laffey*. Interestingly, the *Laffey* had her attention directed to starboard, particularly the *Nagara*, when Admiral Callaghan's order came in. Amidst more grumbling, the guns were trained to port, where they locked onto a searchlight from a "light cruiser," actually the *Akatsuki*, which was then subjected to a few more American shells. Curiously, though, no one had noticed that the three white vertical battle recognition lights were on, which could serve as much of a point of aim as a searchlight.[33] Even more curiously, up to this point no one on the *Laffey* had noticed the massive black object on the port side, headed straight for them.

Until now. Torpedo Officer Lieutenant (jg) Tom Evins saw the eyes of his talker* get very large. The talker then shouted, "Fire torpedoes to port!" Evins turned his head and saw it for the first time: "There, bearing down on us on a collision course from the port side, was what seemed to be the biggest manmade object ever created."[34] The forward destroyers *Cushing*, *Laffey*, *Sterett*, and *O'Bannon* all saw it – the object of their dread, towering over the destroyers and the sea like an ancient colossus, topped with what looked like a pagoda, and about to barrel through the American formation like a bull running through Pamplona, smashing, trampling all in its path. It was Admiral Abe's flagship, the battleship *Hiei*.

The *Cushing* had been headed straight north looking for targets, when lookouts had reported a battleship. Commander Parker, one of the best in the business, calmly examined it and decided he was indeed looking at a battleship. With that pressing question settled, the torpedo crews, not so calmly, now trained their tubes to port, as did the gunners for the 20mm battery.[35]

In turn, the *Hiei*'s lookouts shouted out the presence of the *Cushing*. The battleship's 14-inch main guns were occupied with the *San Francisco* to starboard, so Captain Nishida decided to try multitasking by having the 6-inch secondary battery target the destroyer.[36] The *Cushing* was quickly surrounded by shell splashes and a few began scoring. Hits near the port-side torpedo mount and on 5-inch Mount 3, which killed the mount's crew, disrupted the destroyer's efforts to fire torpedoes. Only one was launched from the port

---

* An officer's assistant who stands nearby repeating the officer's orders or reports over the phone, and also repeating the responses.

tubes at a range of 1,000 yards before the tubes had to be abandoned due to the fire in Mount 3.[37] That one torpedo vanished in the water, never to be heard from again. The topside crew watched in awe and disbelief as the *Hiei* passed within 500 feet of the *Cushing's* port side.[38] Nishida's guns had done their job, like swatting at flies.

But *Cushing* wasn't the only fly; there were three others. On the *Laffey*, Lieutenant Evins and his crew were frantically trying to aim torpedoes at the approaching behemoth. "She was only about a thousand yards away, and there clearly was not a second to lose," he said.[39] The tubes had to be trained – rotated – from starboard all the way over to port. "It seemed like an eternity before I was able to launch our single spread of five gas-operated fish. Meanwhile the great battleship came relentlessly on, as if to crush us."[40] Those seconds added up to one minute, one crucial minute. With no time to change the depth or speed settings, they let the first torpedo loose – only to have Commander Hank order Evins to cease fire. Then, perhaps realizing that this was not a time to hold back, Hank ordered Evins to resume. The remaining four torpedoes were launched at 3-degree intervals.

As Lieutenant Evins let loose with his torpedoes, with the battleship now a mere 1,000 yards away, Gunnery Officer Lieutenant Ratliff unloaded with everything the *Laffey* had: the 5-inch main armament, the 20mm battery, and the port side 1.1-inch mount.

Behind *Laffey*, the *O'Bannon* had just passed the hobbling *Sterett* and was training her 5-inch mounts on the *Hiei* at a range of 1,800 yards. Limping but full of fight, the *Sterett* trained her guns on the *Hiei* as well, at a range of 2,000 yards.[41]

On the battleship, the range to the *Laffey* was so close that her main battery, already committed to the *San Francisco*, could not depress enough to hit her; nor could the *Hiei's* secondary battery. Only some of the 25mm guns could target the destroyer. Watching the *Laffey* through binoculars on the starboard wing of the bridge, Commander Chihaya thought, "We missed the antiquated rams very badly."[42]

Lookouts warned Captain Nishida of the *Laffey's* approaching torpedoes. They had been launched from a bad angle for the *Laffey*, the battleship in a bow profile, almost a down-the-throat shot. Nishida swerved slightly to cause one to miss. Two more bounced off the side of the battleship; they had not traveled far enough to arm themselves, but they did leave unsightly dents. The last two missed astern.

They weren't particularly concerned about the destroyers on the *Hiei*, though, as a destroyer's guns could not penetrate the hull armor of a battleship. But Japanese battleships were peculiar creatures, with the tripod foremast modified by so many gunnery directors, range finders, lookout posts, searchlights, and the bridge that it now resembled a pagoda. The *Kongo* class of battleships, of which the *Hiei* and *Kirishima* were members, were in fact ancient ships, built before World War I as battlecruisers. The general rule of warships is: firepower, speed, armor – pick any two. As battlecruisers, the *Kongo*s had speed and firepower. In their conversion to battleships they were heavily modernized, but they were still lacking in armor and were still quirky, perhaps none more so than the *Hiei*. Her 6-inch secondary armament was still in casemates like an artillery bunker at sea. Unlike her sister ships, she didn't have the traditional pagoda foremast, but instead had a prototype bridge tower that nevertheless looked virtually identical to the other pagodas. And like the other pagodas, it presented a very, very big – and relatively unarmored – target.

Sterett's Lieutenant Calhoun shouted to his gunners, "Get on that goddamned pagoda!"[43]

And so, as Commander Chihaya watched, the *Laffey* let loose with all her 5-inch guns, then moments later was joined by all the 20mm guns that could bear and the 1.1-inch port side mount – all aiming for the *Hiei's* pagoda. From a range of 1,000 yards that was rapidly getting shorter and shorter, the gunners shot frantically, angrily, defiantly, at the nerve center of the Japanese flagship.

"It was so close we could throw hand grenades and hit it," said Richard Hale, a pointer in the *Laffey's* 5-inch Mount 2. "The flight of our shells to the target was instantaneous," he added. "We saw them penetrate their bulkheads and explode inside."[44] The *Laffey* was soon joined by 5-inch gunfire from the *O'Bannon* and *Sterett* astern and later 20mm gunfire from the *Cushing*, whose gunners opened fire without orders,[45] firing so close their shots couldn't miss. They couldn't sink the *Hiei* with gunfire, but they could certainly hurt her.

On the bridge of the battleship, Admiral Abe was stunned at the defiance of the destroyers directly in front of him, shooting at him with their little guns. This was certainly not in the rulebook. *A battleship was not designed for close combat like this*, he thought, as a typhoon of tracers, steel, and shrapnel all came directly at the bridge, directly at him.

The little tin cans were relentless, chipping away at the pagoda. Shells smashed the superstructure, sending debris – and people – plunging to the main deck below, and starting fires on several levels. Lieutenant Evins was amazed by the flare of bursting shells behind the battleship's portholes.[46] No one on the pagoda was safe; no one on deck was safe. Lieutenant Calhoun saw Japanese sailors dive overboard with their clothes on fire.[47]

But the battleship kept coming, responding rather feebly with her own 25mm guns, her bow still knifing through the water – and about to slice the *Laffey* in two. On the destroyer, the collision alarm sounded. Her sailors thought the *Hiei* was trying to ram her. Skipper Lieutenant Commander Hank was known as one of the worst ship handlers in the Navy. As one historian put it, "[H]e had a marked propensity for running *Laffey* into solid objects, particularly when trying to dock her."[48] With yet another collision imminent, machine gun officer Ensign David Sterrett thought their much larger, more powerful foe couldn't possibly know more about collisions than Hank.[49]

Still they kept lashing away at the *Hiei's* pagoda. Seaman John Jenkins heard his 20mm gun go silent. He looked up and saw the gunner was dead, his body hanging by the straps binding him to the gun's shoulder harness. Jenkins jumped behind the gunner's body and, using it as a shield, fired the remainder of the 20mm gun's magazine into one of the *Hiei's* portholes. As he finished, a large section of burning debris cascaded down the pagoda, landing on and around Main Turret 2; Jenkins thought the pagoda had collapsed.[50] Another 20mm gunner, Bill Davis, took a 25mm shell in his gunshield. Yet another 20mm gunner, Bill Sims, took a fatal 25mm hit. The Japanese cannons were taking a toll.

The battleship continued her relentless advance, straight at the *Laffey*, seemingly uninterested in the damage being done to her nerve center. With her size, the *Hiei* didn't need Commander Chihaya's ram; she could run over little *Laffey* like a speed bump. Officers and crew topside and on the bridge of the *Laffey* could only watch in horror as now the battleship's bow towered over them.

Perhaps because of his extensive experience with collisions, Lieutenant Commander Hank remained remarkably cool under pressure. "Emergency back," he ordered the helmsman, followed a few seconds later by, "Emergency full ahead." The former was a sort of windup, or a spring contracting; the latter was the release of the force in the windup. Indeed, the *Laffey* seemed to leap forward – just enough to clear the bow of the *Hiei*. The battleship passed astern of the destroyer, missing her, Ensign Sterrett thought, by barely 20 feet.[51]

The *Hiei* had missed the *Laffey*, but the *Laffey* was not going to miss the *Hiei*. The maelstrom of white-hot steel directed at the pagoda continued. Three shells from the *Laffey* smashed the *Hiei*'s combat bridge from the port side, shattering glass and spreading shrapnel and debris that cut down most of the bridge crew. One killed Commander Suzuki instantly, his lifeless body falling on operations officer Commander Chihaya behind him. Another blast sent shrapnel bouncing off Chihaya's binoculars into his hands, breaking both thumbs. That same blast sent splinters into Admiral Abe's face. Captain Nishida called for a corpsman for the admiral and went to help him, only to be floored by another blast that caused shrapnel to lacerate his calf. Nishida refused aid and bound his wound with a sailor's neckerchief.[52] The dead included the assistant gunnery officer, searchlight control officer, and paymaster; the wounded included executive officer Commander Tamura Raizo, who had to go to sick bay. So did Abe, who seems to have suffered a concussion. He would be described as "dazed," and would mostly disappear from the surface engagement at this point, remembering nothing of the battle following his wound.[53]

Not that Admiral Abe had done much worth remembering. Since the moment the Japanese snapped their searchlights on, he had issued almost no orders, leaving his ships to fend for themselves. Destroyers *Yudachi* and *Harusame*, which had started the domino effect on the American column, had largely split up. Having lost sight of *Yudachi* among the shell splashes at 1:51 am, *Harusame* was trying to follow the *Nagara*, flagship of Admiral Kimura, who also issued no orders because Abe had not given him that authority.[54] Meanwhile, the encounter with the *Cushing* left skipper Commander Kikkawa in a panic, his ship racing east away from the American column. "We ran for a few minutes and I saw gunfire. I was covered with confusion and shame," Kikkawa later admitted. "I ordered *Yudachi* about to head back toward the American column. By that time, every man in my ship was boiling mad – at our failure to hit the enemy."[55]

The *Amatsukaze*'s Commander Hara was proving to be far more aggressive. Racing away from the shells directed at the *Hiei*, Hara had crossed in front of the American column and was looking for targets. The *Nagara* obliged by firing flares that backlit "five or six" American ships. Hara picked the closest one, 5,000 meters away, 30 degrees off the starboard bow, approaching on a roughly parallel course. He ordered the *Amatsukaze* to turn to starboard, approach the target, and follow a hyperbola, a combat maneuver all of Hara's own making. When the range was down to 3,000 meters, and an adjusted firing angle of 15 degrees, the *Amatsukaze* launched eight torpedoes and turned away on the hyperbolic course.[56]

Meanwhile, the *San Francisco* had by this point fired maybe nine salvos at the *Akatsuki*. Seeing other ships take the hapless destroyer under fire, she switched to another target, a "small cruiser or large destroyer."[57] After firing two salvos at this target, Lieutenant Commander Wilbourne spotted the *Hiei* 20 degrees off the starboard bow at a range of 2,200 yards.[58] The American flagship now trained her forward turrets on the Japanese flagship while turning 90 degrees to port – due west – to unmask her aft turret. The *Portland* followed, passing the upturned hull of the *Akatsuki* as she did so.[59] Behind *Portland*, the *Helena* tried to follow as well.

In the *San Francisco*'s Turret 2, Boatswain's Mate 2nd Class Vance Carter, superfluous for the time being since the forward turrets were trained by the main battery director, kept peeking through the sight port to see what was going on – that is, until he saw, for the first time ever, a huge Japanese battleship with a towering pagoda. It was the *Hiei*, at what looked like point-blank range. It stopped the veteran Carter cold. He thought there was no way a cruiser could beat a battleship. He pulled himself from the sight port and vowed to look no more.[60]

But the *San Francisco* would fight nonetheless. Lieutenant Commander Wilbourne gave the order, and all nine 8-inch guns of the American flagship let loose at the Japanese flagship. Naturally, all but one of them missed, falling short, the shell splashes colored green by dye the gunners had added to mark her shots.

The *Hiei* held up her end in one the few flagship-to-flagship confrontations of the war. Her two aft turrets masked by her superstructure, she fired a four-gun 14-inch salvo from her two forward turrets. They all fell short. On impact, the shells burst with a greenish flash. Not from dye, though; the flash identified these shells as incendiary.

Lieutenant Commander Wilbourne adjusted his aim and ordered the forward two turrets to go to automatic fire; the aft turret had to stay in local control because the aft fire director was still disabled from the afternoon air attack. The second salvo struck the battleship's hull at the waterline, as did the third, knocking off hull plates, chipping away at the hull armor. The *Hiei* fired another four-shot salvo, which again fell short. Wilbourne noticed her pagoda was burning brightly, taking a pounding from the forward American destroyers.[61]

It was apparently one of these two 8-inch salvos from which two shells struck the *Hiei* on the starboard side near the stern.[62] One shell was a dud, but the other exploded in the steering room, blowing a two-meter hole in the hull below the waterline and rupturing a ventilation duct.[63] Water gushed into the room, shorting out the generators for the steering gear. Captain Nishida realized what had happened and quickly switched to steering by engine, which required the crew in the flooded steering room to physically keep the rudder centered, nothing the big battleship couldn't handle.[64]

It was around this time – 2:00 am – that Admiral Abe issued his last order, a course change to the north, running east of Savo Island. Exactly why he did so is unclear; it has been assumed that he wanted to reassess the situation. The *Hiei* was seriously damaged. Her pagoda had suffered no fewer than 25 shell hits. Internal communications were almost gone; the only operable line left from the pagoda was to the engine room. The main battery director and searchlight control had been destroyed; the wiring rooms had been hit, which cut power to, among other things, the secondary battery directors; the radio rooms, the antiaircraft control positions, and the compass bridge – the battleship had one bridge for navigation and a second bridge for the conduct of battle – had been heavily hit. Moreover, the battle bridge was mostly destroyed by the *Laffey*'s shells and was now burning brightly. The passageways for escape were cut off by flames and smoke. The men had to climb out the smashed bridge windows by use of knotted ropes to the main deck almost 100 feet below, except for Commander Chihaya, his hands rendered useless from his wounds, and two others, who pushed Chihaya out the window to half-fall, half-slide to the weather deck below before they themselves climbed down.[65]

Theoretically, the battleships could still have carried out the bombardment; the *Kirishima* was basically undamaged and the *Hiei*'s engineering spaces, magazines, and turrets were all protected with armor and were operational, though the turrets had to go to local control since the fire directors were offline. But with his bridge destroyed, with enemy ships intermixed with his own, and suffering a probable concussion, Admiral Abe could not get a good sense of what he was facing and seems to have believed he was facing superior enemy forces. Yet even if he had wanted to disengage only to reassess the situation, his order effectively ended all chances of bombarding Henderson Field that night. Moreover, just after Abe issued the order, the *Hiei*'s external communications went dead.[66]

Meanwhile, American communications were far from dead, which may not have been entirely a good thing. The voice radios – most of them, anyway – barked, "Cease firing, our ships." The voice was Admiral Callaghan's.[67] The order went out to all US ships, though many either didn't receive it or didn't hear it over the roar of gunfire. Those who did get the order were left baffled and frustrated.

Captain DuBose of the *Portland* was one of those skippers. "What's the dope?" he asked over the voice radio. "Did you want us to cease fire? Authenticate that."

"Affirmative," came the reply from Admiral Callaghan.[68] Captain DuBose and the other skippers were left confused. But they couldn't have known.

Watching from the bridge of the *San Francisco*, Admiral Callaghan and Captain Young had seen the two salvos Lieutenant Commander Wilbourne had earlier directed at the "small cruiser or large destroyer" smash through a ship's superstructure and set it afire. The results were so devastating they may have been the most effective gun salvos of the battle. Then an explosion, apparently from the *Akatsuki* as she sank, backlit the burning ship. To the horror of everyone on the flagship's bridge, it revealed the silhouette of an American ship, the USS *Atlanta*.

How this incident occurred remains disputed. There is some belief that the ship identified as the "small cruiser or large destroyer" in the first place actually was the *Atlanta*, which would fit the description. A more likely theory, one supported by Lieutenant Commander McCandless, is that Lieutenant Commander Wilbourne was aiming for a target beyond the *Atlanta*, the destroyer *Harusame*, and the disabled light cruiser just drifted into the line of direct, almost perfectly horizontal fire.[69] Wilbourne, high in the director, would not necessarily have seen the *Atlanta* enter the line of fire because of the director's high and narrow view; the crippled cruiser could have drifted in below that view as the *Atlanta*'s foremast, which could have been tall enough for the director to catch it, had toppled over.

However it happened, the results on the *Atlanta* were indeed devastating and deadly. Four 8-inch armor-piercing shells passed through the bridge area – three through the flag plot and nearby passageways just above deck level; one through the after starboard corner of the pilothouse. None of these shells actually detonated, but flying debris cut down almost all of the bridge crew and set another fire in the bridge area. Some believe it was actually this hit from the *San Francisco* that killed Admiral Scott.

Another 8-inch shell passed through the radio room and the coding room, killing several with flying splinters. Two more destroyed Turret 4, killing all but one of its crew. Two more passed through the superstructure and exploded in Turret 5 on the starboard side, again killing all but one. The barrage was so devastating that Captain Jenkins, who survived the attack, thought these were radar-directed shells. By the estimates of Jenkins and his crew, 19 8-inch shells struck the *Atlanta*.[70] When the *San Francisco* was done with her, the *Atlanta*'s superstructure was an inferno.

Even as it was happening, the crew of the *Atlanta* knew they were being hit by friendly fire. Captain Jenkins stated it in his After Action Report. Not just the silhouette of the *San Francisco*, but the size of the shells – 8 inches ("You could measure them [the holes] with a ruler," Mustin would later say) – and the green dye all over the superstructure were the big giveaways.[71] Indeed, the 8-inch holes were all over the bridge area, which was almost completely destroyed and now useless as a command center. Captain Jenkins told Lieutenant Moredock, now the only surviving staff officer of Admiral Scott, "Let's get below. There's nothing we can do up here."[72] They separated to look for an intact ladder to climb down. Failing to find one, Moredock decided to climb over the railing and lower himself to the deck below. With his right hand broken, he had to do so using only his left hand. But in the awkward position of trying to lower himself, his left wrist, unable to support all of his weight, snapped. Moredock plummeted some 20 feet to the deck below, near the ruins of Turret 3, with a landing far softer than it should have been. "I hit, I'm pretty certain, a bunch of dead bodies on that gun emplacement," Moredock later recalled. "I heard the noise of their, you know, lungs. It was a shattering kind of feeling."[73] Afraid to look, the lieutenant just lay there among the corpses, trying to compose himself.

Undoubtedly, it must have been shocking for Admiral Callaghan and Captain Young to witness the near-destruction of the *Atlanta* and know they were at least partially responsible. But it does not justify the admiral's order to "Cease firing, our ships!" however reflexive it was under the circumstances. For a starter, it was completely unnecessary, since by the time of the order Lieutenant Commander Wilbourne had already switched targets. It has been suggested that Callaghan yelled "Cease firing, our ships!" into the open voice radio microphone by mistake.[74] But his response of "Affirmative" to Captain DuBose's query as to whether he meant to cease fire belies that theory. Even if it was an accident, it was a reckless one that threw most of the US ships into confusion at a critical moment.

For while the *San Francisco* and several other US ships had stopped shooting, the Japanese had not. Leading the rear group of destroyers in the American column, the *Aaron Ward* had received the admiral's cease fire order and had stopped shooting. She had gotten some salvos off against the *Hiei*, with indeterminate results. But the *Ward* was having issues. She was using her main battery director for navigation instead of gunnery. Now, in the light of a fresh and very bright Japanese starshell from the *Nagara*, her lookouts saw a dark silhouette coming from off the starboard bow very, very fast on a collision course. When the fire control radar had the mysterious ship's range down to 1,200 yards, skipper Commander Orville Gregor ordered full stop, then backed with both engines at full emergency power. He was desperate to avoid a collision with the ship, which turned out to be the destroyer *Yudachi*. Commander Kikkawa was continuing his efforts to make up for his earlier panic by sailing directly into the American column with his guns blazing like a kamikaze.* However, Gregor did succeed in avoiding a collision with the destroyer, which passed directly across the *Ward*'s bow.

Once again, the *Yudachi* had thrown the American formation into confusion and Kamikaze Kikkawa wasn't done yet. He spied a US cruiser that was distracted by the *Hiei* and let loose with a brace of Long Lances.

Meanwhile, the new destroyer *Barton*, just astern of the *Aaron Ward*, had launched five torpedoes at the *Hiei*; naturally, being American Mark 15 torpedoes, none of them hit. Now the *Barton* was coming up very quickly on the *Aaron Ward*, who was starting to move again after her stop. To avoid a collision, the *Barton*'s skipper Lieutenant Commander Douglas Fox ordered all engines stopped.

Stopping your ship in the middle of a shooting battle is generally not recommended, for reasons that were now brutally demonstrated. As the *Barton* slowed to a stop, she simply exploded into a towering pillar of fire courtesy of two torpedoes from the *Amatsukaze*, one that struck the forward fire room, the second that struck the forward engine room. Some ten seconds later, the *Barton* was gone. Commander Hara had feared if the *Barton* turned to avoid the *Aaron Ward*, his torpedoes would miss.[75] But she didn't. She stopped. Her combat career had lasted exactly seven minutes. The torpedoes that hit

---

* The Imperial Japanese Navy did have a destroyer named the *Kamikaze*. Ironically, she survived the war.

the *Barton* had passed beneath and in front of the destroyer *Monssen* behind her. Hara let loose with another brace of torpedoes at a cruiser, then took his hyperbola and scurried back toward the *Hiei*.[76]

The water was still boiling from where the *Barton* went down when the *Monssen* spotted the *Hiei* 4,000 yards off her starboard bow. Skipper Lieutenant Commander Charles E. McCombs had told his torpedo officer Ensign Robert Lassen to fire at his discretion. So five were released from the aft mount, depth set at 10 feet with a 2.5-degree spread. Lassen thought he had gotten two hits on the battleship, others thought three, the *Hiei* thought zero. The remaining five torpedoes were loosed from the forward mount at a "cruiser or destroyer" – probably the *Nagara* – 2 or 3 miles away off the starboard beam with probably no hits.[77]

If the target was indeed the *Nagara*, the cruiser would soon use her new lease on life to cancel that lease for the destroyer *Cushing*. With her voice radio out, the *Cushing* had not gotten Admiral Callaghan's "Cease fire, our ships" order. After the *Hiei* had passed astern of the *Laffey*, Lieutenant Commander Parker ordered a hard turn to starboard to unmask the *Cushing*'s torpedo tubes for a strike at the battleship. "Torpedo action! Starboard!" Parker shouted, and the torpedo officer launched six torpedoes at the *Hiei*.[78] Naturally, being American Mark 15 torpedoes, none of them hit.

Then the *Cushing* started taking heavy fire. The *Hiei*'s secondary battery continued hammering away at the American destroyer. Additionally, a sort of battle group of the destroyers *Yukikaze* and *Teruzuki* had started to form around the *Nagara*, now off the *Cushing*'s port bow. They started taking the destroyer under fire, heavier and more accurate fire than the *Hiei* was doing.

Lieutenant Commander Parker ordered a hard port turn to bring the *Cushing*'s after mounts to bear on this new threat. They were being trained out when a shell struck the face of the gun director, disabling it, killing two instantly, and blowing the gunnery officer over the top of the director to land on the bridge at Butch Parker's feet; he died on the way to surgery.[79]

A Japanese shell, apparently from the *Nagara* group, detonated in the upper handling room of Mount 1, killing its entire crew and starting a serious fire. Efforts to fight the fire were hamstrung by additional hits, most likely from the *Hiei*'s secondary battery, knocking out the machinery. One round started a fire in, curiously enough, the forward fire room. A hit to the base of the after stack caused the after fire room to fill with soot, forcing the engineers to don gas masks. Lieutenant Commander Parker ordered the room abandoned when he was incorrectly told the room was flooding. The men tried to reoccupy it, but by that time the feed water to one of the boilers had failed, causing the boiler to melt down into slag. So there was no power, and, soon thereafter, no engines when the engine room tank providing lubricating oil was hit.[80] The *Cushing* drifted to a stop, unable to move, with her few remaining guns reduced to firing off their ready ammunition.

The Japanese were starting to make their firepower advantage felt, in part because of the arrival of three relatively fresh destroyers – *Asagumo*, *Murasame*, and *Samidare* – the advance destroyers who had actually been trailing the *Kirishima* but had looped around to port and were now entering the battle on the northern side of the Japanese formation.

Among the first to notice was the light antiaircraft cruiser *Juneau*. The stars may not have been out, but the *Juneau* had been having a star-crossed night nonetheless. Originally at the back of the cruiser section of the American column, the mess of entangled ships in front of her had been such that the *Juneau* ended up to port of *San Francisco*, who ordered her to move so the flagship could fire at the *Hiei*. So the *Juneau* sped across the *San Francisco*'s bow and got back toward her starboard side.

Anxious to make herself useful, she opened fire on the first target she saw: *Yudachi*, which had just crossed the American column behind her and ahead of the *Aaron Ward*. Commander Kikkawa saw the *Juneau* on a parallel course to starboard and launched eight torpedoes. All missed. As Kikkawa later explained to Commander Hara, "The cruiser answered with a powerful salvo, to which I could only respond with guns. That was bad. I felt I was pinned at last. A destroyer cannot outgun a cruiser. Then all of a sudden, a burst of flames rose from the cruiser. It stopped firing [.]"[81]

The source of the torpedo that caused the "burst of flames" on the *Juneau*'s port side has never been conclusively determined. Both Commanders Hara and Kikkawa thought it was from the *Amatsukaze*,[82] but much more likely it was from the *Murasame*. The *Murasame* along with the *Samidare* were being led by the *Asagumo*, flying the flag of Rear Admiral Takama Tamotsu (since his old flagship light cruiser *Yura* had been sunk) when all three destroyers spotted a large target. The *Asagumo* turned to port and, unbeknownst to her followers, launched torpedoes at the *Helena*.[83] The destroyer saw a "great fire" on the target that resulted in a "sinking," which was news to the *Helena*. But seeing the *Helena* appear to sink convinced the *Murasame* to fire eight torpedoes, not at the *Helena* but instead at the *Juneau*, while firing her guns at the cruiser as well. In return, she took a hit in the forward fire room that limited her speed to 27.5 knots.[84] The torpedo officer Senior Lieutenant Ishizuka Sakae claimed three torpedo hits and believed the *Juneau* had sunk.[85] She had not, but it might have been better if she had.

The torpedo struck the *Juneau* below the armor belt in the forward fire room, killing 17. Like her sister ship *Atlanta*, the *Juneau* was lifted from the water, twisting and shaking, and then settled deeper with a slight list to port. She lost fire-control for her turrets and much of her electrical power for the forward part of the ship. Initially it didn't seem too bad, but there were a few ominous signs. The propellers jammed, causing the bridge to lose helm control, and she lost almost all of her speed.[86] Most disconcerting of all, her deck was buckled, which can be the sign of a catastrophic injury. Sure enough, the chief engineer Lieutenant Commander Thomas Oberrender reported that "in his opinion" her keel had been broken.[87]

A keel is generally the bottom of a ship, but specifically it is the bottom longitudinal girder on which the entire weight of the ship rests. A broken keel is often called a "broken back," as if it is like a human spine, but the analogy is imperfect. The keel helps keep the ship together; there is no redundant structural system to the keel. If the keel is broken, then the ship is held together only by its hull and its internal bulkheads, which are not designed to take all the weight or resist the stresses that can normally be handled with the keel.

Once skipper Captain Lyman Swenson received this news, he knew the *Juneau* was in grave danger of simply falling apart, breaking in two in the middle of the battle. The point was hammered home by several Japanese shells from the *Murasame* that hit the bridge area.[88] Swenson had no choice but to immediately steer the *Juneau* out of the battle, after only some 25 rounds from her main guns. He hoped to find a cove where they could hole up and make emergency repairs before gingerly heading to Espiritu Santo.[89] As a parting gesture, Swenson ordered a few torpedoes loosed at the *Hiei*. Naturally, being American Mark 15s, none hit.[90]

Meanwhile, Admiral Takama's three newcomers continued with their errand of mayhem. Next to face their wrath was the destroyer *Laffey*. After her all-too-close encounter with the *Hiei*, she had sped away toward Savo Island, trying to clear the fracas and camouflage herself in the blackness of the island behind her. She spotted the *Kirishima* approximately 10,000 yards off her port beam, with an entourage of some destroyers. But Lieutenant Commander Hank concluded that, with no more torpedoes, she had pushed her luck enough with battleships for one night. He moved on.

Hank was shocked to see two shadows materialize out of the dark, crossing from port to starboard maybe 3,000 yards out. The 5-inch gun director trained on the lead one, then the second, without firing. The torpedo officer Lieutenant (jg) Tom Evins was heading back to the bridge from the main deck when the night all of a sudden turned into day. The two shadows had passed the *Laffey*'s bow, but the destroyer's lookouts had missed a third shadow behind them, the *Samidare*, which now snapped its searchlight on and pinned the *Laffey* before shooting some starshells over the American destroyer. Evins heard a voice nearby say "Oh-oh."[91]

The voice was right. The *Samidare* and the other two shadows, the *Asagumo* and the *Murasame*, unloaded on the *Laffey* – 16 5-inch guns, all at once. Three against one: it was no contest. It seemed at least a dozen of the 5-inch shells were on target. The *Laffey* was smothered in gunfire. One 5-inch round detonated on the bridge, killing the communications officer and wounding others. Another one wrecked 5-inch Mount 3. Yet another detonated a ready powder charge in 5-inch Mount 2, killing all but two of the mount's crew. A fatal explosion was averted only when Gunner's Mate 3rd Class Roy Myers flooded the upper handling room. Still another shell disabled the gun director, forcing the remaining guns to local control.[92]

The *Laffey* tried to respond. She sped up – chief engineer Lieutenant Eugene Barham said she was rated for 37.5 knots but he was sure that about now she was going in excess of 40.[93] Gunnery officer Lieutenant Ratliff illuminated the *Samidare* and had the 5-inch Mount 1 fire on the Japanese destroyer. He was sure he got a hit forward of the *Samidare*'s bridge. The *Samidare* disagreed, but her searchlight did go out. The Japanese destroyers moved off to the east,[94] only to be replaced by something much worse. As a few parting

5-inch shells struck near the bridge, massive shell splashes erupted on both sides of the *Laffey*. Lieutenant Evins recalled:

> The next second I was hanging onto a stanchion, trying to keep myself from being thrown from the ship. She seemed to pitch herself into the air and then nosedive for the bottom. Tons of water poured down over our superstructure; it was difficult to stand under the weight of it and every man topside was drenched to the skin.[95]

The *Laffey* had been straddled by a salvo of 14-inch shells from the battleship *Kirishima*, passing astern. The splashes drenched the destroyer; at one point the water on the bridge was knee deep.[96] A 14-inch shell from a second salvo passed through the superstructure, through the electrical workshop amidships and the after fire room, carrying away an electrical junction box that flew right in front of Lieutenant Evins' face before the entire sparking conglomerate disappeared off the port side. The shell passed through the ship without exploding, suggesting it was an armor-piercing shell.[97] If so, the *Kirishima*, at least, had completed the changeover from incendiaries.

Then *Laffey* suffered a massive underwater explosion near her stern. A torpedo hit, from whom has never been conclusively determined. It may even have been an American Mark 15 torpedo from one of the rear destroyers – *Aaron Ward*, *Barton*, or *Monssen*. When the *Monssen* launched at the "cruiser or destroyer" that was most likely the *Nagara*, her torpedoes were roughly on a track to the area of the *Laffey*. If it was American, it would have been a remarkable if ignominious feat for the Mark 15 to have struck multiple hulls this night, yet detonated only on the one occasion when it struck a friendly hull. However, due to, if nothing else, the Mark 15's reliability in being unreliable, more likely the culprit was a Japanese destroyer. Candidates include the *Asagumo* in her earlier launch, though that would give her the curious achievement of having passed her target before her torpedo hit, or the *Teruzuki*, whose actions at this time are rather vague but who was sort of following the *Nagara* and launched at a target going away from her.[98]

The nature of the hit suggests it was a Japanese torpedo, because the hit was indeed devastating. It blew 50 feet of the deck on the fantail up at an almost vertical angle against and over Mount 4 and started a fire in one of the fuel tanks. Because of the damage to the deck, damage control could not reach the fire. Worse, the fire was dangerously close to the magazine. "I could see that a fire of that magnitude meant the magazine could blow at any time. I went back up to the bow to get as far away from that fire as I could," said Signalman Richard Hale.[99]

Nor was that all. Chief Engineer Lieutenant Barham noticed the ship was slowing down while the turbines were spinning faster and faster. That meant one thing: the propellers had been blown off; for that matter, so had the rudder. The starboard propeller shaft was bouncing up and down, further proof that the propeller was gone. The port propeller shaft had shredded the glands securing it against the bulkhead, so the engine room was flooding. Pressure was building in the boilers and the steam lines were about to burst, so Barham ordered the engine rooms evacuated.[100]

After he got to the main deck, Lieutenant Barham did a quick inspection. He noticed a two-foot bulge in the main deck just forward of the torpedo hit, which suggested the *Laffey*, like the *Juneau*, had a broken keel.[101]

With the power out, Ensign Sterrett mobilized members of the crew to fight the inferno aft of Mount 4 with a bucket brigade – without actual buckets, but instead with mostly empty shell casings and empty powder cans. Once he got that started, he began tossing filled powder cans overboard. Against a conflagration of this magnitude, it was a pitiful effort. They could not get rid of enough powder cans before the fire reached the magazine.[102] Meanwhile, Lieutenant Evins joined a group trying to free a gunner trapped in the wreckage of Mount 4 and in danger of being burned alive.[103]

Because the steel ladder to the bridge had been destroyed, Lieutenant Barham had to climb up a rope ladder to report the bad news to Lieutenant Commander Hank and to recommend the *Laffey* be abandoned. Hank adamantly declined. "I'm not going to abandon my ship. You get us underway and I will get us out of here."

"Captain," Barham replied, "we don't have any propellers." That would seem to complicate things. "May I have permission to put the boats and rafts in the water in case?"

Hank told him to do so just in case. Barham left for the boats while the skipper presumably pondered over a way to get his ship moving out of an active combat zone with no propellers. He didn't ponder too long, however; Barham had barely gotten back to the main deck when Hank gave the order to abandon ship.[104]

Barham then went to his abandon-ship station. Hank came out and told him to immediately go over the side. Barham yelled back, "You are coming, aren't you?"

"I'll be right behind you, Chief, as soon as everyone has abandoned."[105]

While the blazing *Laffey* was being abandoned, the destroyer *Monssen* was also feeling the effects of the new arrivals. Lieutenant Commander McCombs noticed a ship off his port quarter fire up starshells that burst ahead of him. He was certain they had come from an American ship. McCombs ordered the *Monssen* to turn on her recognition lights to establish his ship's identity.

And indeed it did. But flashing your recognition lights was often a recipe for disaster in these parts. Lieutenant Commander McCombs was experienced, but still new as a skipper. He would learn. When two searchlights snapped on and pinned the *Monssen*, he learned the starshells had come from the Japanese – specifically destroyers *Asagumo*, *Murasame*, and *Samidare*, having just finished with the *Laffey*.[106] Flashing the recognition lights had revealed the *Monssen* to yet another trio of attackers, the *Nagara* and *Yukikaze* – both of which were pinning the destroyer – and *Teruzuki*, all some 2,500 yards away to starboard.[107]

The starboard 20mm guns fired at the offending searchlights, which went out, but it was too late. The recognition lights now attracted an avalanche of gunfire. The 5-inch Mount 1 was hit immediately through the gunshield, its crew killed. Another shell started a fire in the handling room of Mount 2, taking it offline as a third passed through the mount without exploding.

The bridge and the gun director were hit, forcing the aft 5-inch mounts to go to local control. A lookout spotted a pair of approaching torpedoes, which Lieutenant Commander McCombs deftly avoided with a right full rudder. He then ordered flank speed, course 50 degrees True, to try to get clear of their tormentors, but a hit to the forward fire room severed the steam line, another hit ruptured the throttle manifold in the after engine room, and the *Monssen* drifted to a stop – just in time to see two further torpedoes approaching before passing beneath her.

By then the torpedoes were superfluous. The *Monssen* was simply pummeled, taking an estimated 37 hits, ten of which were immediately below the superstructure. Two were 14-inch armor-piercing shells, evidently from the *Kirishima*, that passed through the superstructure without exploding. Both after mounts were quickly disabled. The rudder jammed 26 degrees to starboard. A hit to the captain's cabin started a fire that eventually cut off the bridge and engulfed the entire superstructure. Both fire rooms and both engine rooms were hit. With no power to the fire mains, which were ruptured anyway, and the inferno about to reach the magazines, damage control officer Lieutenant (jg) George S. Hamm recommended they abandon ship.[108] Cut off on the bridge by the flames, Lieutenant Commander McCombs carefully laid down his binoculars and jumped off the bridge into the water below, breaking both shoulders.[109]

The *Sterett* and the *O'Bannon* had obeyed the "Cease firing, our ships!" order from Admiral Callaghan. Commander Coward kept the *Sterett*'s guns silent just for a moment, in the words of one respected historian, "to consider the sanity of the order against the backdrop of objective reality," then resumed firing, once again at the *Hiei*.[110] By this time, the Japanese flagship had slowed down to a crawl, approximately 5 knots, probably in part because she was steering by engine but also because Captain Nishida had ordered a cut in speed to slow down flooding as a result of the hit from the *San Francisco* that, due to the absurdly close range, penetrated her steering room.[111] With the range less than 1,000 yards, Lieutenant Calhoun had his gunners further punish the already severely damaged pagoda with nine four-gun salvos, all of which hit. The *Sterett* also launched four torpedoes at the *Hiei*. Calhoun saw two explosions on the battleship's starboard side and took these to be torpedo hits in the engineering spaces. Fires on her main deck seemed to flare up, and more crewmen were seen jumping off the *Hiei*'s deck into the water. The *Sterett* crossed the *Hiei*'s bow less than 500 yards ahead of the battleship, once again too close for the *Hiei*'s guns to depress enough to hit the destroyer.[112]

Meanwhile, the *O'Bannon*'s Commander Wilkinson kept his guns silent for only a matter of seconds. Then they resumed firing at the *Hiei*, at a range of 1,800 yards, once again so close that the guns could hardly miss. Gunnery officer Lieutenant George Philip, working from the fire director, kept calling to the plotting room to order the range to the battleship decreased. After several instances of this, the gunnery computer operator, clearly irritated, shouted back to his superior that he was already at minimum range and could reduce it no further.[113] Philip muttered, "God! This is murder!"[114] Once again, the *Hiei's* upper works took a pounding, witnesses describing how each hit sliced away a piece of the battleship like "a knife cutting through a block of butter."[115]

But the battleship *Hiei* was one really big block of butter. Slicing away pieces of it with 5-inch shell hits simply wasn't going to get the job done in the time at hand. Commander Wilkinson understood he would need to use torpedoes to punch holes into the side of the *Hiei* and he knew he needed to do so quickly before the situation deteriorated. The *Nagara* was back on the starboard quarter and starting to find the range on the destroyer with her guns. Wilkinson ordered his torpedo officer Ensign John Tazewell to prepare for torpedo action to starboard to first take care of *Nagara*. Moreover, although the battleship's gunfire was getting increasingly sporadic, she was now starting to return the destroyer's fire. But, once again, the *Hiei's* target was so close that the battleship's 14-inch and 6-inch guns could not depress sufficiently to hit the *O'Bannon*, merely whistling over the destroyer to splash on the opposite side.[116]

While redirecting his guns to target the *Nagara*, Commander Wilkinson shouted at Ensign Tazewell, "Torpedo action to port! Torpedo action to port!" Likely wishing his superior officer could make up his mind, Tazewell, believing that the *Hiei* was dead in the water, sent two torpedoes churning toward the battleship. Then he ordered a third launched. As he did so, the battleship was rocked by an explosion that sent sheets of flame across the *Hiei's* main deck. Thinking – wrongly – that the Japanese flagship was finished, Wilkinson ordered a cease fire.[117] But whatever blasts on the *Hiei* the *Sterett* and *O'Bannon* witnessed, they were not torpedo hits. There has been some speculation that the torpedoes detonated prematurely as they entered the battleship's magnetic field, another fine moment for the Mark 6 exploder and its magnetic influence detonator on the Mark 15 torpedoes.

As the *O'Bannon's* guns drove off the *Nagara* by, it appeared, hitting the light cruiser near her after mounts, Commander Wilkinson determined to find out why the *Cushing* and *Laffey* were no longer in view. In so doing, he left executive officer Lieutenant Commander Donald MacDonald to conn the ship. MacDonald ordered full speed ahead and turned hard to starboard to pass in front of the *Hiei's* bow. The *Hiei* had ideas of her own, turning toward the *O'Bannon* in an effort to comb the torpedoes, thus putting herself in the destroyer's path. MacDonald shouted, "Hard right!" Then, "Emergency full astern!" hoping to milk enough from the *O'Bannon's* forward momentum to avoid the *Hiei*. The little destroyer virtually skidded toward the big battleship's hull, like a speeding car screeching its tires in a tight turn, but slowed down just enough to avoid sideswiping or even touching her much bigger rival. MacDonald then ordered full speed ahead on a course due east away from the *Hiei* and the battle area in general, as the destroyer was surrounded by near misses from the battleship's guns as the range increased.[118]

Unfortunately, speeding away from the battle area meant speeding through another area full of ships that were damaged, burning or sinking. Lieutenant Commander MacDonald could barely make out the disembodied bow of a sinking ship with what he thought was the number "459," the numeric designation of the *Laffey*. In fact, the number was "599," that of the *Barton*. MacDonald ordered a hard turn to port, to avoid it. Sailors on the *O'Bannon* tossed life jackets overboard and shouted encouragement to the *Barton's* survivors in the water as the speeding destroyer unavoidably ran some of them down. More were run down when MacDonald ordered another hard port turn to avoid some approaching torpedoes, their source unclear.[119]

At that point, Admiral Callaghan had the US ships resume firing, though he did not so much order them to do so, as forget that he ever ordered them to stop firing in the first place. In an example of an order that would have been better given early in the battle – or better yet before it – Callaghan barked over the voice radio, "We want the big ones! Get the big ones first!"[120]

Unfortunately, the Japanese shared that thinking. During the lull in shooting from the American flagship, the *Hiei* had snapped on a set of three searchlights – two lights over one in an upside down triangle – and trained them on the *San Francisco*.[121] From the starboard quarter, another set of searchlights came from the ever-annoying *Nagara*, which opened up from about 3,000 yards on the flagship, knocking out the two aft 1.1-inch mounts.[122] More worrisome still, the *San Francisco's* lookouts noticed a new set of very large shell splashes – from a battleship, clearly, but not the *Hiei*. They could only be from the *Kirishima*. Her skipper Captain Iwabuchi Sanji had kept her lurking somewhere in the dark behind the *Hiei* and was quite content to stay there. Now, she was about to make her appearance from off the American flagship's port bow.

The American flagship had no choice but to start multitasking. The aft 8-inch turret and the starboard 5-inch battery were coming to bear on the *Nagara*, while both forward 8-inch turrets stayed trained on the *Hiei*. Admiral Callaghan and his staff went to the starboard side of the flag bridge. The *Hiei* was turning to port, away from the *San Francisco*, passing in the opposite direction. Eventually, the *Hiei* moved out of the American flagship's forward firing arcs and the forward turrets had to stop shooting.[123]

Still under the glare of enemy spotlights, Admiral Callaghan over the intercom said to the navigation bridge, "Tell the navigator to get us out of here."[124]

The navigator was Commander Rae Arison, who was also serving as Admiral Callaghan's operations officer because no one on the admiral's staff was qualified for the position; no one else was qualified to be navigator, either. As a result, Arison had spent most of the night running between two, sometimes three places – the charthouse, the flag bridge, and the navigation bridge. He was in the doorway from the chartroom to the navigation bridge, watching Captain Young and Lieutenant Commander McCandless, when a 1,400lb 14-inch shell from the *Hiei* made its uninvited entry into the chartroom.

The Type 3 shell demolished the charthouse and killed a radioman sitting to the commander's right. Arison himself suffered a fractured elbow and a full break in his arm. He was shuffling over toward the navigation bridge to report to Captain Young when a second Type 3 shell blew him out of the charthouse and head-first into the port wing of the bridge. The blast killed most of the bridge crew outright. The only ones left standing on the bridge were Lieutenant Commander McCandless, whose life vest was peppered with fragments, and Quartermaster 3rd Class Harry Higdon, the helmsman. McCandless was still dazed, his ears ringing, when Higdon shouted, "I've lost steering control!" and spun the useless wheel for dramatic effect. Out of control, the *San Francisco* started swinging to port at 18 knots.

The acting executive officer Commander Joseph C. Hubbard had watched the smashing of the bridge from his position high up in a partially repaired and restaffed Battle II. Unable to reach the bridge by phone, he ordered Central Station to transfer control of the ship to Battle II. As soon as that was completed, a 14-inch Type 3 shell from the *Kirishima* crashed through the roof of Battle II, hitting it for the second time in 12 hours, this time completely destroying it and killing everyone there.[125]

At this point Quartermaster 3rd Class Floyd A. Rogers, waiting alone in the armored conning tower directly below the navigation bridge, shouted, "I have control!" McCandless and Higdon left the bridge to join Rogers.[126] Fortunate for them they did, too, as immediately after they left, another Japanese shell, probably a 6-inch from the *Hiei*'s secondary battery, struck the bridge. Lying in a crumpled heap on the bridge's port wing, Commander Arison had just rousted himself up when the explosion blew him over the railing. Arison did two complete turns in the air before landing feet-first on a 5-inch mount two decks below. The impact broke both of his legs, and he collapsed into the arms of the gun captain. But Rae Arison was not finished being a human missile just yet. The gun captain, who was firing the weapon, thought Arison was dead, so he "unceremoniously threw him off," through a break in the deck. Arison landed with what had to be a very painful thud on the main deck. Hot shell casings were tossed through the break after him. When Arison looked above him, everything seemed to be on fire.[127] Arison himself was in a puddle, in which he lost consciousness and would have drowned had not Mess Attendant 1st Class Leonard Roy Harmon pulled him out.[128]

In the armored conning tower, Lieutenant Commander McCandless peered through a view slit. The *San Francisco*'s starboard secondary battery of 5-inch guns had been in a duel with the *Hiei*'s starboard secondary battery of 6-inch guns. The *San Francisco* lost. All four of the 5-inch guns were smashed, but they had scored hits on the battleship's deck; according to McCandless, "a shower of luminous snowflakes rose above her masthead and fell like a waterfall," suggesting the *Hiei*'s pyrotechnics locker had been hit or one of her own incendiary shells had detonated.[129] McCandless ordered Quartermaster Rogers to head between Savo Island and Cape Esperance to get out of the fight for the moment. He left Quartermaster Higdon to act as Rogers' eyes through the view slit.

Then Lieutenant Commander McCandless went back to the remnants of the navigation bridge to ascertain the condition and whereabouts of Captain Young. It was a ghoulish scene:

> The navigation bridge was a weird place indeed in the intermittent light of gunfire. It had been hit several times more during my brief absence. Bodies, helmeted and life-jacketed, limbs and gear littered the deck. The siren was moaning and water was raining down

through holes in the deck above from the ruptured water-cooling system of the forward 1.1-inch "quads." I could not identify Captain Young in my hasty search of the navigation bridge, but left convinced that neither he nor anyone else up there would take further part in this action.[130]

They would not, but the *San Francisco* would, against her will because now the destroyer *Amatsukaze* crossed the flagship's bow from starboard to port. Commander Hara had been surprised and even struck senseless by the *San Francisco*'s sudden appearance:

I screamed as a big ship suddenly appeared out of the darkness just in front of us … I wondered what ship it could be. We passed so close I could not see its whole shape. There was no apparent activity on board. It had no turrets, but it was not a merchant ship. It was familiar and yet I could not place it. This disturbed me as I knew every kind of ship and decided that this must be *Jingei*! She was a submarine tender, and had no turrets. But what was she doing here? The next moment I realized she could not be *Jingei*, and knew this must be an enemy ship. I jumped up and yelled "Gunners! Torpedomen! Stand ready to port!"[131]

Hara ordered searchlights directed at the ship. Only then did Hara realize, "Our target appeared unmistakably to be an enemy cruiser."[132] He ordered the *Amatsukaze* to unload everything on the cruiser.

The Japanese destroyer was on a course opposite that of the *San Francisco*, passing her to port. For the first time in this battle, the *Amatsukaze*'s gunnery officer Lieutenant Shimizu Kazue was allowed to use his six 5-inch guns.[133] At a distance of only a few hundred yards guns could not miss. And they did not, hitting the forward part of the already-smashed bridge while Lieutenant Commander McCandless was in the back.

At the same time, the destroyer launched its last four torpedoes at the *San Francisco*.[134] An excited Commander Hara listened for the hits and the explosions that would surely sink the American flagship. He heard the hits – THUNK! THUNK! THUNK! THUNK! – but there was no earth-shattering explosion.

Then, in Hara's words, "I realized my stupid mistake."[135] It took Japanese torpedoes about 500 meters to arm themselves for detonation. The range to the *San Francisco* was maybe half that. In his haste to sink the *San Francisco*, Hara, who had literally written the book on torpedo tactics in the Imperial Japanese Navy, had launched his last torpedoes too close to the target. The cruiser never even realized it had been hit by Hara's torpedoes; apparently, they didn't even leave unsightly dents. "I cursed my stupidity. Through haste I had lost the chance to make a certain sinking."[136]

While Hara was cursing himself for his stupid mistake, he made a second one. The *San Francisco*'s port secondary battery of 5-inch guns was now responding to the *Amatsukaze*'s attack, forcing the destroyer to switch targets from the superstructure to the unruly guns. One 5-inch shell apparently hit the *Amatsukaze*'s stern. The destroyer was surrounded by shell splashes.

Angry at this resistance, angry that a simple sinking had gone so wrong, but mostly angry at himself, Commander Hara snarled, "Gunners, don't budge an inch! Finish it off!"[137] One of the cruiser's four 5-inch port side guns was destroyed by a direct hit; the remaining three were wrecked by shrapnel.[138] So furious were Hara and his gunners that they didn't notice those shell splashes were coming from a new direction.

But lookout Warrant Officer Iwata Shigeru did. He shouted to Hara, "Another cruiser is sniping at us from 70 degrees to port!"[139] Hara turned in that direction and saw another cruiser – and immediately realized he had made yet a third mistake: so focused was he on sinking the *San Francisco* that he had forgotten that the *Amatsukaze*'s searchlights were on, still trained on the *San Francisco*. As they had done for the *Akatsuki* and the *Hiei*, those searchlights attracted gunfire, this time from the monster light cruiser *Helena*.

The *Helena* had been having a frustrating night. She had the best radar in the force, but that radar wasn't much use when friendly and enemy ships were so intermixed. All the radar operators could do was tell Captain Hoover where concentrations of ships were located; they still had to rely on visual sighting to determine if a potential target was American or Japanese.

All the while, Captain Hoover was doing his best to stay in Admiral Callaghan's original column designation, right behind the *Portland*. Maintaining his position was not all that hard until the heavy cruiser started making a strange turn to starboard and kept turning, for no apparent reason. Realizing the *Portland* was having rudder issues, the *Helena* swerved around her to continue following the *San Francisco*, only to see that the flagship was having issues of her own from a ship shining a searchlight on it. That was visual identification enough for Hoover, who ordered his monster light cruiser to open fire on the impudent, imprudent *Amatsukaze*.

A horrified Hara Tameichi shouted, "Douse searchlight, stop shelling, spread smokescreen!" The words were not even out of his mouth when the *Helena*'s third salvo smashed into the *Amatsukaze*.[140]

One shell destroyed the fire director over the bridge. A second detonated just below the bridge in the radio room. Commander Hara had to hunch over and cling to the railing to keep from being blown off the bridge. Deafened and dazed for a few moments, Hara checked himself for wounds, found none, and then found everyone on the bridge was okay.[141]

Elsewhere, though, this was not the case. Commander Hara called out to Iwata, but found him doubled over the range finder, lifeless, with a piece of shrapnel lodged in his brain. He called to gunnery officer Lieutenant Shimizu. Silence. He called to the radio room. Silence. The helm was not responding and the *Amatsukaze* was starting to circle to starboard.[142]

Fires were flaring up under and around the bridge. Commander Hara was flaring up as well. "Damn it! Let's return fire!"

A wounded gunner staggered onto the bridge. "Sir, the turrets won't move. The hydraulic system has failed." An orderly from the engine room joined this impromptu confab. "The rudder mechanism no longer works, sir. The hydraulics have failed!"

Commander Hara questioned both. "What happened to Shimizu? How's the engine? Any fuel fires?"

"Lieutenant Shimizu was blasted from the ship, sir, leaving only one of his legs."

"The engine works unimpaired, sir. The fuel has not caught fire."

The skipper ordered the gunner to get medical attention and set about stopping the ship so the rudder could be operated manually; that is, by hand, or, more accurately, hands – 20 of them, to be precise.[143] With 43 dead, the *Amatsukaze*'s fighting night was over, and the arrogant Commander Hara was chastened.

After firing 125 6-inch rounds at the *Amatsukaze*, the *Helena* stopped firing only because the *San Francisco* drifted into her line of fire. Lieutenant Commander McCandless was still trying to sort out the chain of command amidst the ruins of the flagship. He realized Admiral Callaghan had been oddly silent for some time and headed to the flag bridge. There he found a trail of cigarettes leading from the admiral's cabin to the starboard wing of the bridge, where Daniel J. Callaghan, holding an open pack of Philip Morrises, and his four-person staff were lying in a grisly, motionless heap.[144] A 6-inch shell from the *Hiei*'s secondary battery had detonated on a beam just above them.[145] McCandless headed back to the armored conning tower. He could not see that one of Callaghan's staff, Lieutenant Commander Emmet O'Beirne, was still alive, badly injured, and buried at the bottom of the mound of corpses. O'Beirne would have to wait an hour for his rescue.

Once back in the conning tower, McCandless took stock of who among the senior officers was both still alive and able to exercise command; Captain Young was badly wounded and Commander Crouter had been killed. He concluded that Lieutenant Commander Herbert E. "Rocky" Schonland was the senior officer able to take command. Schonland was currently running damage control efforts out of Central Station. McCandless contacted Schonland to ask him for orders. But Schonland, a veteran who was intimately familiar with the *San Francisco*, was the best person for the job he had, the job that was most urgent now: damage control. And he knew it. Schonland told McCandless that they would sort out the command arrangements at a more convenient time, but for now he should continue to conn the ship while Schonland tried to save the ship.

Lieutenant Commander McCandless turned back to trying to get the *San Francisco* out of danger. He could not just turn the ship around; not knowing Admiral Callaghan was dead, the other American ships might interpret it as a general retreat. McCandless reiterated his earlier order to the helmsman to get the cruiser out of battle, and went to the vision slit to peer out through his binoculars – just in time for a 14-inch incendiary from the *Hiei* to strike the top of the conning tower, two feet over their heads. It was the last hit from this battleship, who was targeting the *San Francisco* with her aft turrets while her forward turrets had switched targets to the *Portland*.

Still trying to follow the *San Francisco*, Captain DuBose in the *Portland* decided he had had enough of what was to him and most everyone else in the force an inexplicable order from Admiral Callaghan. She started railing at the *Hiei* again, only to see two destroyers passing close to starboard. The *Portland*'s forward starboard 5-inch mounts fired starshells to try to identify the unknown ships. But the starshells revealed something far worse – a torpedo rapidly closing in on the starboard quarter. Gene Howard, an ammunition handler on one of the 5-inch mounts, shouted, "Torpedo!" But it was too late.[146]

The underwater explosion, just forward of Turret 3, sent up tons of seawater, which crashed back down onto the *Portland*. Part of the main deck was now curled up around the base of Turret 3, which had been knocked right off its track and jammed at about 15 degrees to starboard and the guns at about 30 degrees in elevation.[147]

But that was not the worst of the damage. The Long Lance had created a 45-foot gash in the hull, maybe 6 feet below the waterline, with damage some 25 feet inside the hull. Both inboard propeller shafts had been destroyed, the steering engine disabled, and the rudder jammed 5 degrees to starboard. Worst of all, the hull plating had been blown in 45 degrees to the centerline.[148] The interaction of the twisted hull with the rules of fluid dynamics meant the *Portland* was now damned to an eternal hard starboard turn.[149]

As bad as the damage was, the *Portland* was lucky – the torpedo had missed the compartment storing bombs for the seaplanes by a mere 10 feet. If the torpedo had hit there, the resulting explosion would have destroyed the ship.[150] As it was, the explosion was so big that the destroyer *O'Bannon* thought the torpedo had hit her.[151] Nevertheless, the US Navy has always prided itself on crack damage control, and the *Portland* was no exception. Chief Petty Officer J.E. Jones and his assistant Water Tender 2nd Class Hubert Johnson shifted oil and water from various tanks on the damaged starboard side to various tanks on the port side to keep the hole in the starboard side as high out of the water as possible to minimize flooding. Meanwhile, Machinist's Mate 1st Class Pete Cole prevented the steam lines from rupturing by shutting down their supply to turbines for the shafts whose propellers had been blown off.[152] Both of these actions contributed significantly to saving the ship and what remained of her crew. An official Navy report on the *Portland*'s damage control concluded her performance was "impressive and ... a tribute to the skill of her personnel as well as the ruggedness of her design and construction."[153]

But now the relatively lightly armored *Portland* was heavily damaged and steaming in circles in the middle of a shooting battle. This did not faze her veteran crew one bit. Gunnery officer Lieutenant Commander Elliott Shanklin found that he had the two forward 8-inch turrets and six of the eight 5-inch mounts still operational. The aft fire-control radar – the only main-battery radar still functioning – and the two starboard 5-inch directors, along with multiple lookouts had picked out a large, slow-moving target to starboard that was already burning: the *Hiei*. Despite his damaged cruiser, Shanklin was determined to tackle the battleship. The equally aggressive Captain DuBose agreed, telling Shanklin, "Commence firing when on the target." As the *Portland* began her second involuntary turn to starboard, when the Japanese flagship was dead ahead, the cruiser let loose with a six-gun salvo.[154]

So began what Executive Officer Commander Wirth called "rodeo gunnery" – firing only when the involuntary starboard turn unmasked her guns. Before the turn masked her guns again, the *Portland* fired four six-gun salvos of 8-inch ammunition. Shanklin claimed ten to 14 hits on the *Hiei*'s already-mangled superstructure.[155] Admiral Nimitz would later call this "one of the highlights of the action."[156] In return, she took one 14-inch incendiary shell from the battleship, which did little damage, before the *Hiei* disappeared into the dark to the north.

But the *Hiei*'s last hit knocked Lieutenant Commander McCandless out of the conning tower, rendering him unconscious for a few minutes. When he came to, he had a shrapnel wound in his head. His ruined binoculars had saved at least his eyes and probably his life. Quartermaster 3rd Class Rogers announced, "We've lost steering and engine control!" Left unsaid was the word "again."[157]

This time it was due to a convoluted series of factors. Shrapnel had struck the diesel oil tank just above the after engine room and shattered the ventilation shaft. Diesel oil flowed down the shaft and onto the after generators, where it produced smoke and threatened to catch fire. In some quick thinking, Lieutenant (jg) Herschel Chipp, in charge of the room, shut down the generators. This act prevented a fire that could have destroyed the generators, but it also cut power to the aft turret, power steering, and engine-control systems until power could be rerouted. Steering and engine commands from Lieutenant Commander McCandless had to be verbally passed through Central Station until power was restored.[158] But it could have been worse.

And it soon was. All Lieutenant Commander McCandless was trying to do was sail his battered, decapitated *San Francisco* out of danger. But the fates were not through chewing up the ship just yet. McCandless' chosen course to the northwest brought the smoking wreck of a flagship across the other Japanese battleship, *Kirishima*, who had already sent a few shells into the cruiser. She herself was trying to exit the battle northeast in accordance with Admiral Abe's orders. But now she had a clear target, and she was not nearly as damaged or distracted as her sister ship.

So began a rather bizarre exchange. At a range of 2,500 yards – point-blank, again – the *Kirishima* unloaded a 14-inch salvo. It went down the *San Francisco*'s starboard side and splashed, drenching the cruiser, which immediately responded with her two forward turrets, which missed. On the battleship's next salvo, one incendiary shell hit the main deck outside Turret 2 and exploded. As repair crews were trying to deal with that, another incendiary hit Turret 2's barbette. The turret itself was not penetrated, but shrapnel cut down most of the forward repair crews, further impairing damage control efforts. As a safety measure, they tried to flood the lower magazines of Turret 2, but the electrical panel responsible for controlling the flooding was damaged, so when the flooding was started, there was no way to stop it. The entire magazine for the turret was flooded, taking it out of action.[159]

Lieutenant Commander McCandless realized Turret 2 had stopped firing; he had no idea why. Since the *San Francisco* was on a collision course with the *Kirishima*, McCandless ordered a wide loop to port, which allowed Turret 3 to bear on the battleship. The cruiser fired; her salvo fell short. The battleship responded; her salvo fell short. Despite the point-blank range at which it was impossible to miss, both the *Kirishima* and the

San Francisco found ways to not only miss, but not even reach the target. The *Kirishima* managed only her freak hit off the *San Francisco*'s Turret 2; the cruiser managed only a grazing 8-inch hit in return. The last shots fired at the battered flagship came from the battleship's aft turrets over her stern as she sailed away to the north. They splashed short.[160]

Seeing her flagship in some difficulty with a battleship, the *Helena* trained her guns on the retreating *Kirishima*, firing ten salvos in two minutes. They all splashed short. Lieutenant Commander Smith got a new firing solution and asked Captain Hoover for permission to fire. "Hell, no, not with 6-inch guns! Let's get away and then you can shoot!"[161] But if not 6-inch guns, how about 40mm guns? The *Helena* sprayed the *Kirishima*'s pagoda with 40mm rounds. The battleship responded with a 14-inch shell that detonated against Turret 4, but did minimal damage. At that point, Hoover decided discretion was the better part of valor and ordered his 40mm guns to cease fire.

But the *Kirishima* was not the biggest threat to the *Helena* at this time. She had a stalker who at 2:22 launched ten torpedoes, all toward the light cruiser.[162] *Helena* doesn't seem to have even been aware of them or her stalker, the US destroyer *Fletcher*. Skipper Commander William R. Cole, frustrated at the inability of his SG radar to tell friend from foe, decided to eyeball it and launched over the objections of his executive officer Lieutenant Commander Joseph C. Wylie, who was watching the radar screen and believed the target was American. Compounding the embarrassing attack was that all ten torpedoes missed, which was mighty fortunate for the *Helena*. Cole thought he had gotten hits on "a large cruiser or a battleship ... her general outline was somewhat comparable to our *Augusta* class. She could have been a *Kongo* battleship or a *Maya* cruiser."[163] The *Fletcher* headed out, took no further part in combat, and took no more damage.

Not heading out just yet was the *Aaron Ward*, who had managed to save herself from a collision with the *Yudachi* and now tried to find a way to get back into the fight, surrounded by potential targets she could not identify. A frustrated Commander Gregor decided to punt by changing course to due north at a speed of 18 knots, in compliance with the last order from Admiral Callaghan that anyone could remember. At 2:03, she sighted a very large object to port heading away from the destroyer toward the east. Gregor had her quintuple torpedo tubes train on the target, *Kirishima*, only to have the firing track fouled by a burning ship, immediately identified as the *San Francisco*, crossing it some 1,500 yards away. It would have been on a difficult receding stern profile, but it would have been a shot on a battleship. Gregor had to let the *Kirishima* go.[164]

Since those were the only ships she could identify, the *Aaron Ward* was forced for some four minutes to simply observe the shooting going on around her until she could sort out some of these dark shapes shooting at each other. The torpedo officer Lieutenant (j.g.) John Drew was working on that when he thought he saw one of those dark shapes rapidly closing on a collision course from port, the destroyer's disengaged side.

In such situations, the chain of command can be optional. Right in front of his startled skipper, Lieutenant Drew roared, "Left full rudder! Come left! Come left!" Commander Gregor swiveled his head to port and saw the silhouette coming right at them, shouting,

"Left full rudder!" as the helmsman spun the wheel to the left. The other ship, the US destroyer *Sterett*, had to go to full reverse, and both ships barely avoided a collision.

After unwittingly nearly bashing each other in, the *Sterett* and the *Aaron Ward* would next unwittingly collaborate to bash someone else in. The *Aaron Ward* had spotted what she thought was a *Katori*-class light cruiser destroyer 10 degrees off her starboard bow, showing her recognition lights of green over white over red, a common mistake off Guadalcanal.[165] Spooked by the near collision with a friendly ship, Commander Gregor had to doublecheck with Chief Signalman Fred Hart as to the ship's identity.

"Is that one of our ships, Hart?"

"No, Captain."

"Are you sure?"

"Yes, Captain, I'm sure."[166]

The *Aaron Ward* sent 25 salvos toward the target, actually the destroyer *Yudachi*. The result was a hit to the Japanese destroyer's forward fire room that caused her to slow down and a second hit that started a fire on the forecastle. In return, two Japanese shells knocked the US destroyer's main battery director offline. A third plowed into the foremast and brought the radar antenna down across the whistle line, causing a deafening whistling noise that continued until Lieutenant Drew shot the line in two, at which point the foremast came crashing down.[167]

Licking her wounds and reloading her torpedo tubes, Commander Kikkawa's destroyer steamed away slowly toward the northwest, her guns trained fore and aft.[168] Kikkawa believed he had adequately made up for his panicking in the early moments of battle, and therefore the *Yudachi* was finished making mayhem for the night.

But the night was not finished making mayhem for the *Yudachi*. At 2:26 am, the destroyer's bridge exploded under the force of four 5-inch shells from the *Sterett*. Lieutenant Calhoun had caught Commander Kikkawa unawares in "nearly a perfect setup."[169] Two torpedoes left the *Sterett*'s tubes and were never heard from again. A second salvo from the American guns detonated in the *Yudachi*'s after gun mounts, and a massive explosion sent a fireball hundreds of feet into the night sky and lifted Kikkawa's command from the water to come crashing down again, the after part of her hull cherry red, hissing, and throwing off steam.

"Oh, you poor son of a bitch!" sneered Lieutenant Calhoun.[170] The gunners came out on deck to see their handiwork and cheered as the *Sterett* passed the smashed *Yudachi* some 200 feet away to starboard. The *Yudachi* lost power and staggered to a halt, her well deck awash, her main director, forward engine room, Number 3 fire room, and communications room all destroyed. The *Sterett* thought she had sunk, but the *Yudachi* had not. Not yet.

Even so, the *Yudachi* got some revenge, as her fires backlit the *Sterett* for another Japanese ship, and the American destroyer was shocked to find a hailstorm of shells engulfing her after section from a ship that materialized out of the dark on her port beam: the destroyer *Teruzuki*. The salvo started powder fires in the handling rooms of Mounts 3 and 4; an electrical fire knocked both mounts offline. The next salvo hit the quarterdeck, knocking out the starboard torpedo mount, detonating in the 20mm clipping room, and causing flooding in the forward fire room's cooling system. The *Teruzuki* was a very new ship, a member of the new *Akizuki* class of destroyers designed specifically for antiaircraft purposes, and thus had a main battery intended for both antiaircraft and antisurface action with eight rapid-fire 3.9-inch guns in four dual mounts. And she certainly knew how to use them.

With only two mounts functional, the torpedo supply effectively depleted, a jury rig for steering, and a serious fire that both revealed her position and her nationality, the *Sterett* had done her bit for president and country. Commander Coward turned to his executive officer Frank Gould and said, "OK, Frank, let's get out of here."[171]

The destroyer sped off, settling on a high-speed course through Lengo Channel at around 2:30. They succeeded in dousing the fire in Mount 3, but the fire in Mount 4 proved more stubborn, forcing Commander Coward to keep juggling several balls in the air. After avoiding what she thought was a torpedo, the *Sterett* increased speed to 23 knots, only to have to take the forward fire room offline at around 3:00 am because of the damaged coolant system. Then at 3:27 the jury-rigged steering system failed and the rudder jammed hard to starboard; Coward had to back both engines at full power to keep from grounding on Guadalcanal.[172] Coward apparently used some sort of black magic to keep his ship moving forward.

The *Aaron Ward* was also damaged and her guns were operating on local control, but she was still full of fight. Commander Gregor chose as his next target a searchlight that snapped on some 3,000 yards off the port bow. The light was obviously Japanese – so blinding that no one could identify its source. Gregor had his destroyer perform some fancy footwork to try to stay out of the beam while bringing all his guns to bear, but the mysterious ship foiled his best efforts. After a fashion, the main battery director was able to lock on to the searchlight and all four guns fired away.

The other ship fired back, sending a 6-inch shell into the emergency radio room, killing one and badly wounding another. The *Aaron Ward* got off three more four-gun salvos, only to have a 6-inch shell shatter the radar dish atop the main battery director. Seconds later another 6-inch shell disabled the director itself, killing one and mortally wounding another. Then she took two 14-inch incendiaries in succession in the area of the galley.[173] She had apparently picked a fight with the battleship *Kirishima*.

Another searchlight from the starboard quarter pinned the *Aaron Ward*. Mounts 2 and 4 trained out on this target, which was believed to be a destroyer that has not been identified. But at this time, the *Aaron Ward* took two critical hits: one hit on the weather deck disabled the torpedo tubes; the other wrecked the quadruple 1.1-inch antiaircraft mount.[174] These hits were estimated to have been caused by 8-inch ammunition, meaning either the *San Francisco* or the *Portland* was the culprit.[175]

Her assailants stopped shooting, but several starshells bursting and a searchlight from the port quarter attracted shell splashes from 14-inch and 6-inch rounds. One 6-inch shell tore through the canvas windscreen at the after end of the bridge, passed between the legs of torpedo officer Lieutenant (jg) John Drew, and broke one of the legs supporting the gun director.[176] With that, Commander Gregor decided it was time to get out and headed north.

The *Aaron Ward* managed to escape the gunfire, but at around 2:20 a torpedo was spotted crossing about 50 feet ahead from port to starboard. Five minutes later, helm control was lost, and Commander Gregor started steering by engine, heading east to clear the battle area, where the shooting seemed to have stopped.

At about 2:40, so did the *Aaron Ward*. Without warning, she lost all power and went dead in the water. A few moments later, the engineer called through the voice tube saying, "Captain, we have trouble in the firerooms."[177]

Executive Officer Lieutenant Commander Frederick Julian Becton volunteered to check it out. When he reached the main deck, the engineering officer told him, "We're out of feed water." The distilled fresh water used to make steam and run the turbines was simply gone. Without it, the destroyer had no power. Becton went to work figuring out what to do about it.

The *Aaron Ward* may have been pinned in the persistent searchlight of the *Nagara*, who all night long had been a constant threat. At around this time, Admiral Kimura's flagship was playing the role of a maritime vulture. She crept up off the starboard quarter of the *Cushing*, snapped on her searchlight to illuminate the disabled destroyer, and at a range of 2,000 to 4,000 yards began circling the *Cushing*, using her seven 5.5-inch guns to mercilessly blast her helpless target the entire time.[178]

Next the *Nagara* interrupted the abandonment of the *Laffey*. Appearing about 2,000 yards off the starboard beam, she slowed to a near-crawl, trained out her guns, and examined the stricken destroyer. Then the Japanese light cruiser moved on. The *Laffey* was obviously finished and not worth the ammunition.[179]

On the *Laffey*, everybody resumed bailing out, hoping to get as far away as possible from the time bomb that was the burning aft magazine. Seaman 1st Class Rod Lambert had fainted from fright, but had come to, still in something of a daze. A sailor he knew raced past him toward the bow. "Rod," the sailor shouted, "she's going to blow!" Shocked into consciousness, Lambert followed him into the water. One poor soul in the Mount 3 magazine had panicked when the torpedo hit and had clamped himself to a stanchion. No one was able to talk him or even pry him off, and he had to be left behind. As the order to abandon ship arrived, the gunner trapped in Mount 4 was somehow freed and transferred to a litter. But could he and his saviors get far enough away from the ship?[180]

Ensign Sterrett was finally preparing to leave, having left it dangerously late, when a large flashlight shone in his face. "Who's that? Oh, Sterrett," came the voice of Lieutenant Commander Hank. With that, the skipper then walked away around a corner …

And then the aft magazine exploded.

This was a massive detonation, almost volcanic, sending up a mushroom cloud and massive pieces of what had once been the *Laffey*. Only 50 yards or so from the ship, Lieutenant Barham saw that the entire stern had been blown off. Lieutenant Evins was injured by flying debris and overwhelmed by hot water, his life jacket saving him. Ensign Sterrett huddled in a corner to shield himself from the missiles, then made a beeline for the bow and jumped off the ship. Probably the last man off, Sterrett was barely in the water when he turned around and watched the bow of the *Laffey* slide backward into its final grave in Ironbottom Sound. The poor gunner and his saviors were killed. Lieutenant Commander Hank, the man who took on a battleship, was never seen again.[181] He was posthumously awarded the Navy Cross.

By this time, the shooting was over – for now – but not the danger. On the *Helena*, a black shape approached on a collision course from off the starboard bow. It was a ship, obviously, although its front half and back half didn't quite connect. It was identified as the *Juneau*, staggering out of control from her broken keel. A collision was barely averted.

Led by their biggest ship *Kirishima*, but otherwise in no particular order or grouping, the Japanese were now heading north, away from the battle – well, most of the Japanese. The *Amatsukaze*, her power steering disabled, was wobbling northward. Destroyers *Akatsuki* and *Yudachi* were heading nowhere, the former now at the bottom of Ironbottom Sound, the latter disabled. Commander Kikkawa had tried to rig a sail to get the *Yudachi* moving toward a Japanese-held shore on Guadalcanal, but it was impossible. At around 3:00 am, Admiral Takama came by in the *Asagumo* with the *Marusame* tagging along and looked over the *Yudachi*. Takama left two boats and instructions for survivors to head for Cape Esperance 3 miles away, then he took off toward the north.[182]

Very conspicuous by her absence was the flagship *Hiei*.

Some 800 American survivors would make it out of Ironbottom Sound, some washing up, staggering onto shore and others fished out – all soaked, covered in oil, retching, bloody, exhausted. The wounded totaled 250, the treatment of whom would further tax the Marines' slender medical resources until they could be sent to hospitals in the rear. As the survivors stepped onto dry land, they had one universal comment, one borne of bitterness and exhaustion, with no hint of the irony it deserved.

"You can't fight battleships with tin cans."[183]

CHAPTER 3
THE MORNING AFTER

As the sun rose on that Friday, November 13, 1942, south of Guadalcanal, a small flotilla of ships was sailing off to war. One of the biggest was the *Washington*, a brand-new, state-of-the-art battleship. She boasted nine brand-new 16-inch, 45-cal Mark 6 guns; 20 5-inch, 38-cal dual purpose guns in ten dual mounts, five to a side; the most modern radars – FC (fire-control), FD (fire-direction), and SG (surface search); and the flag of relatively new admiral, Rear Admiral Willis Augustus Lee.

With the *Washington* was another relatively new battleship, though this one looked a little less pristine. She was the *South Dakota*, who had already suffered a bomb hit on her Number 1 main turret during the Battle of the Santa Cruz Islands. The turret was so well armored that the gunners inside did not even realize their turret had been hit by a bomb, but the superfiring Number 2 turret behind them certainly did. Shrapnel had gouged the barrels of the center and left guns of the three-gun turret. One of the gunners, Lieutenant (jg) Paul H. Backus, later recalled:

> As you can imagine, we made all kinds of measurements and sent messages back to the Bureau of Ordnance in Washington, describing these gouges, their depth, their length, and asked the question, "Can we shoot [with] these barrels?" We never did get an answer that we could live with.[1]

No doubt the bureau was too busy denying the defects in their torpedoes to give proper consideration to the gun barrels. Eventually, it was settled that the two guns were not to be fired.

Also damaged at Santa Cruz was the *South Dakota*'s skipper, Captain Thomas L. Gatch. Radioman 2nd Class Henry Stewart described Captain Gatch at Santa Cruz:

> Capt. Gatch refused to take cover. He said he wouldn't "duck for any damned bomber" and was seriously injured from shrapnel wounds.
>
> [...]

The captain's jugular vein was severed and if it hadn't been for the immediate availability of a corpsman who stopped the bleeding he would have lost his life. After the bleeding was stopped Capt. Gatch went back on duty with his arm and neck immobilized. His arm had to be positioned over his head due to the nature of the neck wound. Even with this injury, Capt. Gatch personally continued to steer the ship during the remainder of the battle and also during the Battle of Guadalcanal which followed. For the next two years, he didn't have the use of his left arm.[2]

But the third ship, the one at the center of the formation, the most important ship present, was in far worse shape. She was trailing an oil slick, a shimmering rainbow in the sunshine and a trail for anyone who saw it to find her. She was shipping water – not seriously, but annoyingly. Seventy sets of officers' quarters were still wrecked and there was a rather prominent and even more unsettling bulge in her main deck.[3] Perhaps worst of all, one of her three elevators could not be used.

She was the aircraft carrier USS *Enterprise*. And she was a survivor.

The *Enterprise* was a survivor of every carrier battle of the Pacific War except the Coral Sea, and she had missed that battle only because she was returning with the *Hornet* from the Doolittle Raid. Most significantly she was a survivor of the Battle of the Santa Cruz Islands. After the *Hornet* had been disabled, the *Enterprise* had been the target of attack after attack. She took two direct bomb hits and two near misses. Dancing like a ballerina while still juggling returning aircraft, both her own and those of the *Hornet*, the *Enterprise* had evaded nine torpedoes launched with her name on them. But she had escaped.

Not unscathed, however. The bomb hits had wrought havoc with her flight deck elevators, jamming the Number 1 (forward) and Number 2 (midships) elevators at different times. The midships elevator was cleared, but the forward elevator was stuck, fortunately in the up position; anything else and the *Enterprise* would have had a large hole in her flight deck rendering her useless for flight operations. One near miss, about 10 feet from the starboard quarter, opened a seam in the side plating 3 inches wide for a length of 50 feet. The concussion damaged the main turbine bearing; ruptured three fuel tanks, one of them full; and knocked out of alignment a suite of antennae on the mast, including the radar. A second near miss glanced off the port bow near the waterline and detonated less than 10 feet from the hull, the concussion denting and rupturing hull plating, leaving her down 4 feet at the bow. Admiral Kinkaid had to break off Santa Cruz and retreat, leaving the *Hornet* to her fate.

While the *Enterprise* was still en route to the relative safety of New Caledonia, Admiral Halsey called the senior officers of all branches in Nouméa and told them to pool their mechanics for the repairs to the *Enterprise* and other ships and aircraft.[4] Not having seen the *Enterprise* yet, he assumed the worst about the carrier's condition. He went so far as to ask Admiral Nimitz to get one or more British aircraft carriers sent to the South Pacific. Nimitz forwarded the request to Admiral King.[5] In turn, Nimitz ordered Halsey to prepare a coordinated defense plan for the rear bases.[6] They were bracing for the worst.

After the *Enterprise* limped into Nouméa, the repair ship *Vulcan*'s men swarmed the battered flattop. They estimated it would take three weeks to repair the carrier.[7]

There doesn't seem to have been any question of not sending the *Enterprise* back out, especially after *Magic* had forwarded the deciphered Combined Fleet operations order on November 10. By then, Admiral Halsey, unlike his predecessor defiant in the face of adversity, had placed the *Enterprise* and her air group on a precautionary 24-hour sailing notice. In the words of Halsey in a letter to Nimitz sent on October 31: "… operating the *Enterprise* with a slightly reduced complement of planes and under difficulties, but under the present circumstances, a half a loaf is better than none."[8]

That night, Halsey informed the *Enterprise* task force they would be on one-hour sailing notice starting at 9:00 am the next day. As it was, their sailing orders came just after 8:00 am, to leave at 11:00 on November 11 and to be 200 miles south of San Cristobal and prepared to strike targets near Guadalcanal by 8:00 am on November 13.[9]

Some 60 officers and men from the *Vulcan*'s battalion of Seabees, Construction and Repair Department, had done their country proud. She was back at sea in just 11 days[10] – but not in tip-top shape, obviously. The biggest of her problems now was that only two of her three elevators could be used to transport aircraft between the hangar and flight decks because her forward elevator was declared offline. The crews thought they had fixed it, but they dared not test it out of fear it could jam in something other than the up position. This meant that the flight operations of the *Enterprise* would be slowed significantly; perhaps slowed to the extent that she might be forced to stage some of her aircraft, especially the heavy TBF Avengers, to Henderson Field. But only slowed. Not stopped.

In her hangar hung a message of defiance: "*Enterprise* versus Japan."[11] The angry aviators of the *Enterprise* and the *Hornet* would not dream of missing this chance to strike back at their Japanese tormentors, to make up for Santa Cruz.

Ideally, the *Enterprise* would have launched airstrikes against the Japanese force of battleships before the enemy force had arrived off Guadalcanal. The problem was that the *Enterprise* had only just left Nouméa on November 11 and was too far away. So were the battleships *Washington* and *South Dakota*, and the *Enterprise* wanted them and their powerful antiaircraft batteries with her during daylight hours. In general, Admiral Halsey had not given the *Enterprise* group its orders to sortie early enough to help Admirals Callaghan and Scott. There has been speculation that the delay was because of poor staff work or because Halsey wanted to give the repair crews at Nouméa more time to repair the carrier.[12] However, the *Enterprise* task force sailed roughly 24 hours after Halsey was informed on November 10 of the imminent Japanese offensive.[13] It may not have been possible for her to be ready any earlier.

But she was ready now. Pearl Harbor estimated the *Enterprise* operated at 70 percent effectiveness.[14] So she was more than Admiral Halsey's half a loaf; she was 70 percent of a loaf, which was 70 percent of a loaf more than the Japanese were expecting.

Morning dawned at Lunga Point — hot, sticky and oppressive, before the sun had even completely risen over the sea. But there was something different in the atmosphere the morning of November 13. Intermittent rainstorms, to be sure, but there was more than that. Excitement? Apprehension? Dread? All of the above?

Overnight the Marines at Lunga Point had seen the light show some 15 miles off shore, near Savo Island; a "gigantic ping-pong game using fireballs," in the words of one Marine.[15] It had been a veritable cornucopia of color — red tracers, white searchlights, blue flares, green explosions, orange fires — and a cacophony of sound — guns firing, shells exploding, torpedoes striking. Awakened around 1:30 am by the wailing of the air raid siren, Marines trekked from Henderson Field to Lunga to watch in complete silence.[16] They knew what it heralded. It was a battle for their future, the future of Henderson Field, and the future of the war itself. They had no idea who was winning or losing, just that there was not a damn thing they could do about it now. Only later would they realize they had played a critical role.

With the rising sun they saw the aftermath. Ironbottom Sound was littered with wrecked ships, some of them still burning. One column of smoke, its source a mystery, was hiding behind Savo Island.[17] The Marines set out in the little boats of their small "navy" to try to pick up as many survivors — and prisoners — as they could. Meanwhile, in the pre-dawn storm, Henderson Field sent up seven Marine SBD Dauntlesses to search north and west of Guadalcanal.[18] They had to find the status of the Japanese transport convoy they knew was coming. And those Japanese carriers were still out there — somewhere.

Shortly after dawn, Major Joe Sailer, commander of Marine Scout Bombing 132, led three Dauntlesses on a "tracking mission" toward Savo Island, surveying the area in the aftermath of the night battle, looking for crippled ships.[19] Major Sailer and his pilots and gunners looked with tremendous interest at the spectacle unfolding below them. Oil, easily identifiable by its dulled rainbow colors, covered much of the water, shimmering in the light. Patches of it were still burning. Small boats, rafts, survivors, and debris were floating everywhere — and so were bodies. Lots of bodies, and parts thereof.

There were ships still in Ironbottom Sound, though how much longer until they left or became permanent residents the airmen could not say. Major Sailer and his pilots made low passes over each to determine their condition.[20] Closest to shore was one mangled, twisted, gutted antiaircraft cruiser dead in the water — *Atlanta*. East of her was a heavy cruiser slowly circling in the water — *Portland*. West and northwest were three small ships — destroyers — all burning. As the Marines watched, one of the destroyers took a salvo from the *Portland*, exploded, and sank.

Furthest to the north was another destroyer, dead in the water, with something that looked like a tug. Some smaller craft were seen coming out of Tulagi to assist the US Navy ships and pick up survivors. Further out, still more ships were reported. A few of the scout planes sent up before dawn unsuccessfully attacked a destroyer. One other scout, that of 2nd Lieutenant George Herlihy, reported a battleship.[21]

That mysterious smoke column behind Savo Island drew Major Sailer's attention, and he led his charges toward it. Just north of Savo, out of view of the Marines at Lunga Point, sat a pair of ships. One of them was big, very big, and smoldering. Major Sailer wasn't sure whether these ships were friendly or not. His gunner, Howard Stanley, took their signal gun and flashed the recognition signal, a simple single letter of the alphabet, at the big ship. The ship responded by taking its antiaircraft guns and firing a simple burst at the Dauntlesses. *Probably not friendly*, Sailer guessed.

Ignoring any and all warnings about the dangers of distracted flying, Major Sailer took out his enemy ship identification book and compared it with the behemoth below. The ship had four big gun turrets, although they didn't look in very good condition. The forward part of the battleship was blackened and smoldering. Some of the aft secondary guns looked askew, as though they might fall out of their casemates into the water. The ship also had what appeared to be a pagoda foremast. It certainly looked like a Japanese battleship. Major Sailer matched it to a silhouette in his identification book – the *Kongo* class.

This *Kongo*-class ship was certainly badly damaged; in Major Sailer's words, "forward turrrets smoking, rear turrets dangling, proceeding at five knots." But it was just 8 miles from the crippled US ships in Ironbottom Sound. Worse, it was less than 30 miles from Henderson Field. Just outside the battleship's gun range. The Marines at Henderson Field had learned the hard way what Japanese battleships, especially the *Kongo* class, were capable of doing. Even damaged, one so close was simply too dangerous. Sailer called it in.[22]

The report started major buzzing at Henderson Field. Captain Joe Foss of Marine Fighting 121 was sent up in an F4F to inspect the battleship and determine its condition.[23] As he did so, staying safely out of the range of Japanese antiaircraft guns, airstrikes were hastily prepared.[24] Sailer had later seen four destroyers moving to join the battleship, with another battleship and three destroyers 20 miles north of Savo, so the clock was ticking.[25]

The Marine, Navy, and Army fliers had been on the receiving end of a pair of Japanese battleships a month earlier during "The Bombardment." The US Navy had not had the chance to knock out any of Japan's battleships – until now. This was their chance to get some revenge for that October blasting by the behemoths, to start evening up the lopsided battleship score since Pearl Harbor. "We've got to sink it!" became the order of the day.

They were going to enjoy this.

If the view from above Ironbottom Sound was not pleasant, then the view from inside Ironbottom Sound was certainly no more so. All ships able to leave had left. In a testimony to American skill at damage control, even a few ships that initially could not do so on their own – the staggering *Sterett*, the jointed *Juneau* – had managed to find a way to leave as well.

But nothing was simple around Guadalcanal, not even leaving it. Between 2:07 and 2:12 am, the *Helena*'s Captain Hoover had asked twice for a course from Admiral Callaghan and received no response. He then asked the *Portland*'s Captain DuBose, the senior skipper, but again, Hoover received no answer to his inquiry, although the *Portland* did in fact respond – by asking the *Helena* for a tow. Hoover refused, much to the annoyance of the *Portland*. Then Hoover radioed, "Any ship from *Helena*: Can you hear me?"[26]

In the *San Francisco*, a 15-degree differential between the compass in the conning tower and the one in emergency steering aft was not immediately detected. Worse, the cruiser was suffering from major flooding from an unusual source. Turret 2 had been forced offline when its magazines and handling rooms were flooded after a 6-inch shell from the *Kirishima* struck and short-circuited the flood control panel. The damage control team responsible for fixing it had all been killed, so the sprinklers kept spewing water and flooding the ship, especially the second deck, where there were no drains.

This water was making the cruiser top-heavy, sloshing inside the ship with every turn: it was an example of a well-known mechanism called the "free surface effect." At one point, when Lieutenant Bennett ordered "Right full rudder" to avoid grounding on Malaita Island, the cruiser heeled over 40 degrees in the process.[27] The risk of capsizing was a serious one until Ensign Robert Dusch waded his way through darkened, flooded corridors to shut off the sprinkler valves. Then Dusch and Lieutenant Commander Schonland managed to find a way to shunt the water into the lower decks, where it could be pumped out.[28]

Having dished out friendly fire, the flagship almost became a recipient of it as well. Around 2:40 am a dark shape pulled up on the starboard side, about 2,000 yards away. Lieutenant Commander McCandless could make out two stacks and five turrets – trained on the *San Francisco*. That wasn't good. Then the ship flashed a coded challenge "H-I-S H-I-S."[29] It was the *Helena*.

At 2:26 Captain Hoover, unable to reach Admirals Callaghan or Scott, had ordered all ships to rendezvous on the *Helena* and take an easterly course.* At 2:35 Hoover ordered all ships to turn on their fighting lights briefly.[30] But the *San Francisco*'s lights had been shot away. So, the *Helena* challenged what, to her, was an unidentified ship.

As Lieutenant Commander McCandless later explained:

[T]he carefully memorized reply had been driven from my mind by the events of the last hour, and when I looked around for the challenges and replies that had been written in

---

* Among the many deficiencies of Admiral Callaghan's plan for the battle, such as it was, was the failure to establish in advance a meeting point for after the battle.

chalk on the bulkhead of the flag plot enclosure, I found only holes and burned paintwork. In seconds, unless the correct reply were given, fifteen 6-inch and four 5-inch would fire into us.[31]

Lieutenant Commander McCandless had a lone signalman with a blinker gun flash "C38 ... C38 ...," which was close enough to the *San Francisco*'s hull identification number for Captain Hoover, and the *Helena* stood down. "Thank God the *Helena* accepted that," Jack Bennett later said. "Captain Hoover, may he live forever, took a second look before letting us have it."[32]

McCandless then had signaled in plain English: "C50 V C38 BT Admiral Callaghan and Captain Young killed X Ship badly damaged X Take charge."[33] At around that time Lieutenant Commander Schonland took command on what remained of the bridge.

The *Fletcher* joined the two cruisers, and together the three ships left through Sealark Channel. One by one, like the *San Francisco* and the *Fletcher*, the American ships that were able to joined the *Helena*. After reporting in at 3:22, the *Sterett* retired through the strait, joining with Captain Hoover at 6:00. She was struggling with fires, the loss of two boilers due to ventilation problems, and a balky rudder, which jammed at 3:27, nearly causing her to run aground on Guadalcanal.[34] The *O'Bannon* left on a parallel course through Lengo Channel, detecting the *Juneau* on radar and picking her up, after which they both joined the *Helena*, and headed toward Espiritu Santo.[35]

Only the unnavigable remained. Among the Japanese, the destroyer *Yudachi* was burning and adrift without power. The *Asagumo* and the *Murasame* had been standing by her, but at 3:35 Admiral Kimura ordered them both to join the *Kirishima*. 2nd Destroyer Division head Captain Tachibana Masao, who flew his flag in the *Murasame*, was not happy about leaving the *Yudachi* behind, so he ordered the *Samidare* to assist her.[36]

When the *Samidare* arrived about 17 minutes later, skipper Commander Nakamura Noburu saw no way to tow the destroyer, as she was trailing burning oil and paint. Commander Kikkawa gave the order to abandon ship, and 167 officers and men, led by 35 wounded, climbed over to the *Samidare*. Kikkawa went to the destroyer's bridge and asked Nakamura to scuttle the ruined ship.[37] He ordered two torpedoes fired at her but somehow neither hit. Gunfire was ineffective as well, and with the sun coming up he was compelled to head off to Shortland and leave the burning hulk to her fate.[38]

Among the Americans, destroyer *Cushing*'s skipper, Commander Parker, ordered her abandoned sometime between 2:30 and 2:45. The fires on the destroyer made salvage impossible.[39] *Monssen* was an inferno as well, and with fears the fires would reach her magazines, she too was abandoned. They both sank that afternoon.

The destroyer *Aaron Ward* was stuck, with a bizarre problem: she was out of feed water for her boilers. No one could figure out how that had happened, but she couldn't distill more because her electrical system had been hit, forcing her to shut down her evaporators. In other words, she could not generate power without fresh water, and she could not distill fresh water without power. Lieutenant Commander Becton was forced to use saltwater as a temporary substitute, not normally advisable because it would leave residue in the boilers and tubes. But Becton felt he had no choice; the crew started filling the 2,000-gallon tank in the forward engine room, which was also flooding from what the best engineering minds on the ship could identify only as "something."[40]

To make matters worse, the *Aaron Ward* also had a steering breakdown. There was only one person on the ship who knew the "secret solution" that would fix it: 12th Destroyer Division communications officer Lieutenant Bob Weatherup. And, of course, no one could find him. After a long time spent tracking him down, Weatherup determined the connecting cables could not be repaired easily, so he proceeded to decouple the rudder from the power drive.[41] The crew would have to use manpower, like Hara's *Amatsukaze* was doing, to move the rudder.

By 5:00 am, the tank was finally full, and the *Aaron Ward* got moving. Ten minutes later, it was passed by some PT boats returning from the Savo Island area. The destroyer asked them to relay a request to Tulagi for a tug. At 5:30 the boilers and their tubes clogged with salt, and the destroyer again went dead in the water. They hoped they could get moving again toward the dubious safety of Tulagi before the Japanese noticed them.[42]

During the night the *Portland* continued her involuntary circling, but since she was still buoyant, she took on as many survivors as she could – 38, to be precise. At one point, the sound of splashing in the water was reported to Captain DuBose. He asked if they were American or Japanese. "American, Captain," was the reply.

DuBose turned to the men in the dark water below and shouted, "I'm bringing the ship to a stop. Paddle your life raft over here. We have no steering control."

"Roger, Captain. We have no life raft, either."[43]

When it was light enough to see, around 5:30 am, the *Portland*'s lookouts identified all the visible ships – a Japanese battleship, *Atlanta*, *Aaron Ward*, *Cushing*, and *Monssen* – except for one derelict destroyer burning south of Savo Island. The *Portland* requested the *Atlanta*'s help in identifying the ship, but the *Atlanta*, who was busy aiming torpedoes at the *Portland*, demanded she identify herself.[44] Once that was addressed, the destroyer was identified as Japanese.

Over the intercom, Captain DuBose invited anyone not manning the main battery to watch. Crewmen in the *Atlanta* stopped work. "We stood, frozen at the life-lines, spectators to a kind of action rarely witnessed," wrote Electrician's Mate 3rd Class Bill McKinney.[45]

Because of the *Portland*'s unwilling circling, the cruiser's gunners struggled to get a target lock on the destroyer from the aft fire-director. The first four salvos missed the stationary ship. Then gunnery officer Lieutenant Commander Shanklin reported that the target was flying a white flag.

Even so, the fiery Captain DuBose was livid at the damage his ship had taken and the casualties his crew had suffered. Determined to get his pound of steel, he asked Lieutenant Commander Shanklin what nationality the flag was. "It's not in my registry," Shanklin deadpanned.

"Sink the SOB," DuBose growled.[46]

The next salvo blew up the destroyer.

On the disabled *Atlanta*, "We raised a cheer," McKinney wrote. "A sentimentalist near me croaked, 'Don't cheer fellows. The poor guys are dead. It could have been you.' All shared his observation, few his recommendation."[47]

A tug, the *Bobolink*, had steamed out of Tulagi and approached the *Portland* at about 9:30 am, but Captain DuBose waved her off and directed her to the *Atlanta*, which was in far, far worse shape.[48] The light antiaircraft cruiser had managed to extinguish her fires, but not without drama. There were smoking guns, not just in her turrets, but in the form of green dye on the port side of the superstructure. A panicked lieutenant commander was running around telling everyone to abandon ship. Captain Jenkins had to hobble around the ship on a wounded foot telling everyone to stay, after which he tracked down the officer and gave him the chewing out of his life. Then the skipper got his wounds treated.[49]

The *Atlanta* was in desperate shape. The message sent to Captain DuBose in the *Portland* regarding her condition makes for grim reading:

> Damage as result night action X Six turrets out of commission, both firerooms and forward engine room flooded, after engine room gradually flooding, have only diesel auxiliary power, steering gear inoperative, foremast gone X Ship received many 8 inch hits and one or more torpedo hits, latter in vicinity of number one engine room port, bridge structure completely gutted X Have requested assistance from Cactus intend to send wounded and others there retaining nucleus crew aboard in case facilities available for towing X If not available condition of ship warrants sinking X Request instructions regarding.[50]

Listing to port and down by the bow, she jettisoned her port anchor and chain to try to remove weight from the port side. That left her with the starboard anchor, which had to be dropped to try to end her drift toward a Japanese-held beach. Small arms were issued to the crew to defend the ship from boarders if necessary.

That was the first order of business when the *Bobolink* arrived. While the crew was busy rigging the auxiliary diesel generator to provide some power, the tug pulled the *Atlanta* away from hostile territory, though not hostile aircraft. A Japanese Betty flew low over the ship, but the newly powered aft 5-inch mount drove her off before she could attack. The tow continued until around 2:00 pm, when the starboard anchor caught on the seabed. The *Bobolink* stopped the tow and headed off to help the *Portland*.

Although the damage to the *Atlanta* was severe, the possibility of salvage was promising. The crew tried to pump out the aft fire room so the boilers could make steam again, enabling the *Atlanta* to limp near Tulagi for repairs. Boats from Guadalcanal came to take off the wounded. To try to ease the weight on the port side, the crew cut away the port whaleboat and davits and dumped the 5-inch ammunition from Turrets 4 and 5, along with the smoke generators and almost all the depth charges. Four torpedoes were fired from the port side as well.[51] But Captain Jenkins and his crew were fighting a losing battle.

The flooding continued inexorably, so much so that efforts to pump out the aft fire room proved futile. The ship would have no power except that from the emergency generator.

Efforts continued throughout the day, but the pumps could not keep up with the flooding. When reports indicated Japanese warships could arrive that night, November 13–14, the possibility of the *Atlanta* being captured by the Japanese sealed her fate. Captain Jenkins reported her status to Captain DuBose, who in turn reported it to Admiral Halsey, who authorized them to act at their discretion.

The crew was evacuated except for Captain Jenkins and a few others, and the *Bobolink* was given the sad duty of towing the *Atlanta* to her final resting place as chosen by Captain Jenkins. A bucket of explosives was lowered into the after steering room, wired to a plunger on the forecastle. Jenkins was the last of the survivors to leave the ship. As he stepped off into a boat at 6:30 pm, he pushed the plunger.

Weirdly, although the *Atlanta* was already sinking, the scuttling charge seems to have had no effect. It was almost two hours before the cruiser rolled over and started slipping beneath the waters of Ironbottom Sound.[52] In the process, she revealed just how bad the torpedo hit had been. Unbeknownst to her crew, like the *Juneau*, the *Atlanta*'s back had been broken. The hole was massive, stretching from just below the waterline on the port side across the keel to the starboard bottom. "If we had tried to steam that ship, she might have opened in half," Lieutenant Mustin said.[53] Captain Jenkins agreed, saying that even if salvage facilities had been available, they "would have been of doubtful value."[54] The location and extent of the damage was such that Admiral Halsey suspected it was the result of a magnetic influence exploder detonating under the keel.[55]

The *Bobolink* returned to help the *Portland* once again, who still kept turning in circles. Nothing anyone did made the slightest difference. At 1:00 pm, the patrol boat *YP-239* arrived to try to tow the cruiser, to be joined by the *Bobolink* at 2:30. The tug tried pushing against the starboard side under the bridge while the "Yippie" boat, as the YP boats were nicknamed, pulled the bow to port. Still, the cruiser turned. Then the tug moved starboard aft. But still the cruiser turned. Finally, the *Bobolink* moved to the starboard bow and, with the Yippie, pushed against that while the *Portland* had her port propeller in reverse and her starboard propeller in forward. It was this bizarre combination that finally worked, and the *Portland* crawled toward Tulagi on a course of 35 degrees True at a speed of no more than 3 knots.[56]

This slow, tedious inching toward dubious safety continued throughout the day. That afternoon, when an air attack was reportedly imminent, Captain DuBose advised the *Bobolink* to cast off so she could maneuver. The tug's popular and respected skipper, Lieutenant James L. Foley, called DuBose back: "Hell no. It took all day to hook up and I'm not about to cut loose." Day turned into night, only to become all too exciting. As they approached Tulagi, Captain DuBose heard a voice on the radio say, "Here comes a bear. Give him two fish."[57] The voice came from American PT boats. The "fish" was a torpedo. The "bear" was a target. But who was this bear? The skipper listened for a bit longer, only to come to the disconcerting conclusion that *he* was the bear.[58]

Captain DuBose immediately sent out a message: "This is the American cruiser Portland X This is Captain DuBose speaking X There is a tug standing out from Tulagi to assist us X The name of her captain is Lieutenant Foley X We are not repeat not a Japanese."[59] It didn't work.

Captain DuBose called the *Bobolink* for help. Her executive officer, Ensign Charlie Ziegler, knew some of the PT boat skippers. But this didn't work, either. *PT-48*, under the command of Lieutenant (jg) Tom Kendall, actually launched four torpedoes at the helpless cruiser. It is unclear which is more embarrassing: that the US Navy PT boat fired four torpedoes at a helpless US Navy ship or that, having overestimated the helpless US Navy ship's speed, all the torpedoes missed. Angry *Portland* gunners fired back at the PTs, who didn't appreciate being the target of a shot by the US Navy ship at whom they had just taken a shot.[60]

But no harm, no foul. At 12:12 am a harbor pilot came aboard the *Portland* to guide her into Tulagi, where she tied up to a palm tree at 1:18 am. The crew ran a gangway to the shore and covered the ship with camouflage netting. "Then we all dropped in our tracks and fell asleep," said Harold L. Johnson. We had been at general quarters over 50 hours by this time."[61]

About one hour later, they would be at general quarters again.

In 279 BC, the Greek mercenary general Pyrrhos defeated the Romans near Asculum in southern Italy. It was his second very costly victory, a victory that was anything but decisive. Pyrrhos is believed to have said words to the effect of "One more victory like that over the Romans will destroy us completely." It is from here that the term "Pyrrhic victory" originates.

At dawn on November 13, 1942, the men of the remaining operational ships of what was officially called Task Group 67.4 off Guadalcanal, sailing southeastward at the painfully slow speed of 18 knots toward the relative safety of Espiritu Santo, could have sympathized with Pyrrhos – if they knew they had been victorious at all.[62] If this was how victory felt, then defeat must be an unimaginable horror.

The remnants formed around a column of two ships. The acting flagship, light cruiser *Helena*, was in the lead, her skipper Captain Gil Hoover now burdened with not just commanding his own ship but trying to command the task force as well. Fortunately, the *Helena* had suffered only superficial damage.

Not so superficial was the damage to the other ships. Destroyer *Fletcher*, on the cruiser's starboard bow, suffered no damage, but the *Sterett*, on the port bow, had damaged sonar circuits and during the fight had needed to dump some depth charges that were about to be cooked off. The *O'Bannon* had lost her sound gear and was thus useless in detecting lurking submarines, so she had been sent out some 50 miles to radio a message to Admiral Halsey, reporting their status and requesting "maximum air coverage."[63]

Even worse was the ship right behind the *Helena*, the heavy cruiser *San Francisco*. The *Sterett*'s Lieutenant Calhoun counted 26 shell holes in her port side.[64] Her bridge was smashed and gutted. Battle II was a blackened ruin. Evidence of fire was everywhere. The talk on the bridge of the *Helena* was the charred, twisted thing that had once been the flagship. George A. DeLong, the *Helena*'s helmsman, thought the *San Francisco* would be lucky to reach Espiritu Santo.[65] McCandless, who put his ship's fighting efficiency at 25 percent, with almost all of his communications out, had a message semaphored to the *Helena*: "Admiral and all of staff except one killed captain seriously wounded hundreds of casualties can use two turrets six five inch and make twenty eight knots steering from conn urgently need all medical assistance you can spare."[66]

At 8:00 am, Captain Hoover had the force stop dead in the water to deal with this request. He ordered the *Helena* and *Juneau* to send their junior doctors and several corpsmen to help the *San Francisco*. They immediately complied.[67] Medical officer Lieutenant Roger W. O'Neil and three pharmacist's mates of the *Juneau* arrived, although O'Neill let it be known he was not happy about it. "I don't know why they sent us over here," he growled. "You people are going to sink, and we are needed back on the *Juneau*."[68]

The light antiaircraft cruiser the *Juneau* was about 1,000 yards off the *San Francisco*'s starboard beam. As bad as the *San Francisco* looked, at least she had taken very few underwater hits, all of which had been promptly addressed. Although the *Juneau* appeared to be in fairly decent order – down by the bow 10 to 12 feet, with an approximately 2-degree list to port – if the sailors looked closely, they could see the biggest reason for that limit in speed: the bow half of the *Juneau* was twisted ever so slightly in the opposite direction from the stern half.[69] With her keel broken, she was being held together – barely – by her bulkheads and damaged hull. The pressure on those bulkheads and hull could easily become too much and thus snap the ship in two if she moved too fast or turned too quickly. She had to avoid that at all costs; as it was she could not steer from the bridge and could only steer from some jury-rigging at Battle II. She could not turn quickly except, potentially, to starboard.[70] If a torpedo approached, in her condition, evasive maneuvers would be just too dangerous and close to impossible.[71] So *Juneau* shuffled along and Captain Swenson's uncertainty about her ability to hold course caused him to request to be offset from the rest of the cruiser column, by about 1,500 yards, to minimize the risk of a collision.[72]

The damage control parties on the *Juneau* determined that the keel was in fact broken and requested that Captain Swenson ask the other ships for both welders and welding tools to try to fuse the keel back together. Swenson flashed a message to this effect. So many volunteers responded that Captain Hoover had to slow the force down to facilitate this second set of transfers.[73]

Slowing down – or stopping, as they had done earlier – was necessary but extremely dangerous in this situation. They were now entering the infamous Torpedo Junction southeast of Guadalcanal. And it quickly made its presence felt: at 9:50 am, the *Sterett* made a sound contact with her damaged gear. She dropped five depth charges, but the results were inconclusive.[74]

The force continued on. To a man they were dead tired but there would be no rest. Bad news came in at 10:35 as the *Helena*'s radar picked up a bogey and lookouts reported a large aircraft intermittently visible in the clouds to starboard. San Cristobal, where the Japanese were rumored to have set up a seaplane base, was about 20 miles to port. Captain Hoover ordered the formation to close in tight for antiaircraft protection.[75]

The good news was, after a few tense moments, the unidentified plane turned out to be a US Army Air Force B-17. The bad news was that its bomb bay doors were open. Nothing was ever easy around Guadalcanal. The Flying Fortress finally recognized the ships as American and veered off. With that done, Captain Hoover ordered the wide antisubmarine formation resumed as quickly as possible, and the destroyers moved out at high speed. A sensible precaution, this did, however, reduce the effectiveness of their sound gear.[76]

While the ships were spreading out again, Commander Charles L. Carpenter, the *Helena*'s navigator and officer of the deck, walked out to the port wing of the bridge to get some fresh air. Sitting, almost collapsing, into a chair, Carpenter started to clean his sunglasses.

And saw a white streak in the water to port, speeding toward the *Helena*.

"Hard right rudder, DeLong!" he shouted. "Torpedo to port!"[77]

Normally calm, cool, almost contemptuous of danger in a crisis, Captain Hoover simply stood there, frozen.[78] And the *Helena* started an emergency turn to starboard.

On the *San Francisco*, Seaman 2nd Class Victor Gibson was serving as a lookout when he saw two white streaks in the water, racing toward the port bow from the northwest. Speechless with terror, he grabbed Schonland and pointed at them. Schonland barked, "Full right rudder, emergency full ahead."[79] The loudspeakers blared with the message: "Stand by for an attack!"[80]

The former American flagship basically slammed on her brakes, and the torpedoes passed between her and the *Helena*, about 100 to 200 yards from the *San Francisco*'s bow.[81]

Upon hearing the alarm, McCandless raced to the bridge. He joined Schonland in the ruins of the flag bridge just in time to see the two torpedoes racing away off the starboard bow. One disappeared in the distance; the other headed straight for the *Juneau*.

Time plays games in war. There are those instances where time seems to stop and there are those moments when time slows down, just enough to get a sense that there is not enough of it. This was one of those moments for Schonland, McCandless, and everyone on the bridge of the *San Francisco*. Their minds raced, then slowly stopped with the chilling realization as the torpedo streaked closer and closer to the helpless *Juneau* that there was not a damn thing anyone could do about it. But even with that chilling realization, with the events of the past 12 hours, nothing could have prepared them for what happened next.

Joseph Whitt on the *San Francisco* heard a "loud crrrrrack, like a lightning strike nearby."[82] It wasn't a crack as much as a Krakatoa, for in the words of McCandless, "The *Juneau* didn't sink – she blew up with all the fury of an erupting volcano":

> There was a terrific thunderclap and a plume of white water that was blotted out by a huge brown hemisphere a thousand yards across, from within which came the sounds of more explosions. Lieutenant (j.g.) Bennett saw a whole 5-inch 38 cal. twin mount rise above this ugly thunderhead, hang there an instant as though supported by some invisible hand, then drop back out of sight. When the dark cloud lifted from the water a minute or so later, we could see nothing of this fine 6,000-ton cruiser or the 700 men she carried. Those who witnessed it called this terrible end of a gallant ship the most awesome spectacle of the battle.[83]

Calhoun, who was watching the *Juneau* and appreciating her beauty, said she simply "disintegrated."[84]

As best as could be determined, the *Juneau* was hit "on the port side very close to the location of the first torpedo hit[.]"[85]Even the limited protection offered by her thin armor would have been negated by the torpedo detonating where that armor was already breached. The torpedo could have and probably did go straight into the magazine that housed thousands of 5-inch shells. Only a magazine explosion could explain the size of the blast and the secondary explosions that followed.

The explosion was so devastating that it spewed flying bits of ship, oil, and body parts everywhere. On the *San Francisco*, Lieutenant Commander Schonland, Lieutenant Commander Wilbourne, and Lieutenant Commander McCandless were standing in a group on the starboard side of the flag bridge when they witnessed it. The officer-of-the-deck Jack Bennett shouted "Scatter!" and everyone did – just in time to avoid a large piece of plating about the size of a door from the *Juneau*.[86] It smashed into the side of the bridge only a few feet from where they had been standing. Other, smaller pieces also crashed back to earth. Farther aft, an enlisted man had both legs broken by one.[87] A twin 5-inch mount splashed less than 100 yards astern of the *Fletcher*.[88]

The torpedo had come from a Japanese submarine that was rapidly becoming a US Navy nemesis, the *I-26*, under the command of Commander Yokota Minoru, who had already collected the scalp of the carrier *Saratoga* by torpedoing her and forcing her to drydock almost three months earlier. The *I-26* escaped without incident.

"No words, then or now," Calhoun would later say, "could possibly express the shock and despair that we felt over the loss of the gallant *Juneau*. It was the most horrendous tragedy I have ever witnessed."[89]

On the *San Fancisco*, Lieutenant O'Neil, then starting surgery on Captain Young, heard "the most terrific explosion I shall ever hear." He looked out the porthole and saw only "tremendous clouds of gray and black smoke."

"What was that?" O'Neil asked an assistant.

"That was the *Juneau*, doctor," the man answered. "She's gone."

O'Neil froze. With his eyes watering, O'Neil went back to trying to save the life of Captain Young. As it was, one of the pharmacist's mates who had come over from the *Juneau* with Lieutenant O'Neil could only mumble over and over, "Oh, no! Oh, no!" Captain Young's wounds proved mortal and he died on the operating table.[90]

McCandless admitted, "This disaster – unexpected and cataclysmic – affected us all[.]"[91] The reaction aboard the other ships was dead silence. Witnesses were struck speechless by the blast; some even went into shock. From the *Helena*'s radio room, Chick Morris observed:

> No one moved or spoke … A man needs some kind of mental and physical reserve to accept such a disaster when not prepared for it, and we had exhausted our reserve during the night. … Many a man aboard *Helena* walked the decks for the following few hours in a kind of trance, brooding and frightened. The man who felt it most, perhaps, was Captain Hoover himself.[92]

In shock, wide-eyed, and open-mouthed, Captain Hoover turned to an officer beside him and gasped, "My God, I can't believe it!"[93] It was "the most awesome explosion he had ever seen."[94]

Captain Hoover was left with a gut-wrenching decision. He could stay and try to rescue the few, if any, survivors. To do this, however, would put his remaining ships at risk, while he had only one fully functioning destroyer, the *Fletcher*, to attempt to find the enemy submarine.

But how could he just leave those sailors, brothers-in-arms – even his longtime friend Lyman Swenson – without even trying?

On instinct, the *Fletcher* approached the site of the *Juneau*'s death, but Captain Hoover ordered the destroyer to resume station. Captain Hoover had made a quick, agonizing decision: he would have to leave them behind. However, he would use another option, one presented by that B-17. He would ask the B-17 to relay a message about the *Juneau*'s fate. The message read: "*Juneau* torpedoed and disappeared lat. 10 degrees 32 minutes S. long. 161.2 degrees 2 minutes E at 1109 x Survivors in water x Report ComSoPac."[95]

Few believed there would in fact be any survivors, but someone had to look. In fact, there were about 120 survivors of the *Juneau* in the water, most of them wounded.

The Army Air Force B-17 struggled to translate the Morse code message flashed to it by frantic Navy signalmen. On a mission for Army Intelligence to locate the cruiser *Portland* and any Japanese ships still in Ironbottom Sound, pilot 1st Lieutenant Robert Gill of the 198th Bombardment Squadron decided his orders did not allow him to break radio silence to report this sinking. But he would do it as soon as he got back to Espiritu Santo – at 5:30, some seven hours later.

And indeed, when he got back, he dutifully submitted a verbal and a written report. Which was buried beneath a stack of paperwork on his superior's desk.[96]

During the night, after the battleship *Hiei*'s bridge pagoda was smashed by shell and machine-gun fire, the *Aaron Ward*'s Lieutenant Commander Becton said the Americans had "blinded the Cyclops."[97] As the sun rose over Ironbottom Sound, another analogy from the Trojan War, perhaps more common, even cliché, came to mind: the Americans had shot the arrow into Achilles' heel.

In the *Nagara*, Admiral Kimura had taken tactical command of the Vanguard Force because Admiral Abe's communications were completely down. Kimura had watched the *Kirishima* head northward along the east side of Savo, followed by all the other Japanese ships that were able, though not necessarily in any semblance of organization. Kimura saw that the flagship *Hiei* was not among them, nor had he heard anything from Abe since the withdrawal order. At around 3:00 am, the *Kirishima*'s skipper, Captain Iwabuchi, reported to Truk about a "severe mixed battle," saying that both sides suffered "considerable damage," and that consequently the bombardment had been cancelled.[98] Stunned by this report of American resistance, Admiral Yamamoto responded at 3:44 am by postponing the landing on Guadalcanal by one day, until November 14. He then ordered Admiral Tanaka's transports to head back toward the Shortlands and vectored several submarines toward the route between Guadalcanal and Espiritu Santo to try to intercept any fleeing American ships.[99] Meanwhile, Kimura broke away in the *Nagara* from the fleeing Japanese to search for his admiral.

After steering around the south side of Savo Island, Admiral Kimura finally found the *Hiei* on the west side of Savo.[100] During the night battle, the flagship had protected her consorts by drawing much of the enemy fire upon herself with her searchlights and her leading position in the Vanguard Force.[101] Now, those consorts were not returning the favor. The flagship, slowly shuffling northward, had fires burning in her pagoda and on her main deck. She was very obviously hurt – and all alone.[102]

With the *Hiei*'s steering engine disabled, Captain Nishida had drastically cut the *Hiei*'s speed to try to slow down the flooding in the steering compartment. At the same time, he quickly switched to steering by engine, which required both a cut in speed and the crew in the steering compartment, led by Petty Officer Kurabawa Minoru, to physically keep the rudder centered so the battleship could maneuver by varying the speed of her propellers. It was tricky to keep the heavy rudder in place against heavy hydrodynamic pressures, but thanks to some burly sailors, just about workable.[103]

The hurricane of gunfire from the US destroyers had cost the flagship not just her bridge – Captain Nishida was now overseeing the firefighters trying to put out the fires in the lower levels of the pagoda – but almost all of her internal and external communications as well. The last order Petty Officer Kurabawa received was "Right rudder," probably to avoid the torpedoes from the *Laffey*; then communications with the bridge went dead. After that order, Kurabawa and his men centered the rudder to keep the ship from going in circles.[104]

This combination – an abandoned, shattered bridge; a distracted skipper; no communications; steering by engine; and crewmen holding the rudder in place in a flooding compartment, all at night – resulted in confusion regarding the *Hiei*'s intended course and how the engine room could power the propellers to get her onto that course.[105] Instead of heading north with the other Japanese ships, she ended up heading west; whether that was a result of the confusion or an attempt to avoid adverse currents east of Savo Island and take advantage of favorable currents south and west of Savo is unclear.

Admiral Kimura seems to have found the *Hiei* around 2:30 am. He pulled the *Nagara* alongside to assist the stricken flagship and to act as a communications link. Combined Fleet at Truk was made aware of the *Hiei*'s plight. Their solution? "Have *Kirishima* tow *Hiei* out of combat area."[106] The problem was that they were about 30 miles from an active enemy airbase. Admiral Abe thought the idea of trying to rescue his one battleship that was vulnerable to air attack by making his other battleship vulnerable to air attack was preposterous and did not act on it.

After a fashion, the fire in the lower areas of the pagoda was finally put out, and Captain Nishida and Admiral Abe returned to the gutted bridge. Each man was just as battered as the flagship. Nishida was hobbling around on his slashed leg. Abe seemed shell-shocked, likely a result of his concussion, and had returned from sick bay with his head wound so bandaged up that it, together with his bloody, tattered white uniform, gave him more than passing resemblance to a South Pacific mummy.[107] The atmosphere was something out of Dante: burning ships were everywhere, their identities mostly obscured by low-hanging smoke; the bridge was blackened and bloody, wet and windowless; the smell, a combination of burned paint, oil, blood, human waste, and charred flesh, is probably better imagined than experienced.

Captain Nishida took a formal damage report from his damage control officer Commander Onishi Kenji. Main battery control was destroyed and all four 14-inch turrets had been hit, but the turrets and guns remained operable. The 6-inch battery control station and three 6-inch guns were hit; there was no power to the 6-inch directors; and there was a serious ammunition fire amidships. Three of the 5-inch antiaircraft guns were also hit, as were two of their handling rooms, which were ablaze as well. Several of the 25mm guns were also out. There were six 8-inch hits that penetrated the hull armor, causing some minor flooding in places and a slight list to starboard, which was difficult to correct because several of the pumping stations were damaged. The superstructure was gutted by fire; radio communication was out; and nine more fires were burning in various parts of the ship as a result of about 102 hits, of which about one-third were duds.[108]

This certainly comprised a lengthy damage report, but the good news was the *Hiei* was in no danger of sinking, her engines were fully functional, and her main armament was still operable. She could still fight if she had to. Nishida rightly determined that the steering issues were the most serious problem and kept the battleship's speed very slow, basically going with the current, to try to limit flooding in the steering compartment.

The wounded battleship continued slinking northward on the west side of Savo. Commander Hara reported that his *Amatsukaze* passed the *Hiei* to port at about 5:00 am. The flagship presented a sad sight. She was still smoldering, though most of her fires appeared to be out. The *Hiei* appeared to Hara to be all alone, but he was probably blocked by the bulk of the battleship from seeing *Nagara* on the other side. With *Amatsukaze* having her own rudder issues, weaving and wobbling like a drunken sailor as she headed north, Hara could offer no help to the stricken flagship.[109]

As dawn broke, Captain Nishida went below to try to encourage his crew as they braced for air attacks.[110] But the air attacks were hardly the only – and arguably not even the biggest – problem the battleship was facing, because while the *Hiei*'s painfully slow speed may have delayed the flooding in the steering compartment, it by no means stopped it. When the oily water in the compartment had reached the crew's necks – while they were standing on their toes – Petty Officer Kurabawa decided that dying by holding a rudder in place was not the heroic death for the Emperor he or his men had envisioned. They let go of the rudder, swam forward two compartments to an access hatch, and climbed up to the main deck to await orders.

At around 6:00 am, as the battleship was rounding the north side of Savo on a slight starboard turn, the *Hiei* started swinging hard to starboard uncontrollably. Damage control determined that since the rudder was no longer held in place by Petty Officer Kurabawa and his men it had swung all the way to the right and jammed.* The suffering *Hiei*, desperate to get as far away from Henderson Field as possible, was now doomed to doing donuts north of Savo – only 30 miles from Henderson Field.

Some reinforcements started trickling toward the beleaguered behemoth. Combined Fleet told Admiral Kimura that the *Shigure*, *Shiratsuyu*, and *Yugure*, the three destroyers of 27th Destroyer Division that had been patrolling off Cape Esperance, were en route. Kimura ordered the destroyers *Yukikaze*, *Harusame*, *Samidare*, and *Teruzuki* to join him. The *Samidare* politely declined the invitation, on account of her fuel running low and being packed with survivors from the *Yudachi*. Kimura approved, and the *Samidare* continued into The Slot – to be rewarded by an attack by two Dauntless bombers which did no damage to either side.[111]

The *Samidare* was not the only Japanese destroyer to face air attack all alone. Commander Hara's wobbling *Amatsukaze* was the target of three bombers herself. With exactly one remaining fully functioning antiaircraft gun, the *Amatsukaze* scored a lucky break when the bombers overestimated her speed and released their bombs too early, the closest some 300 meters in front of the destroyer. Heading north toward the relative safety of Admiral Kondo's forces, the *Amatsukaze* next passed the *Yukikaze*, heading in the opposite direction to help the *Hiei*. Hara gave the insightful advice to expect air attacks.[112]

The Japanese were well aware of the danger of air attacks. Admiral Kakuta's aircraft carrier *Junyo* was ordered to provide air cover for the *Hiei*, and at 5:30 am launched eight Zeros led by Lieutenant Shigematsu Yasuhiro. Two B5N carrier attack planes were also launched to guide them to the battleship, supposedly because of the bad weather, but

---

* It is an unwritten but immutable law of the sea that when a rudder jams, it will almost always be all the way to port or all the way to starboard.

sending up guide planes was becoming increasingly common in the Japanese Naval Air Force, symptomatic of the declining skill level of its pilots after almost a year of casualties.[113]

At around this time, someone in the *Hiei*'s damage control came up with the brilliant idea that they should plug the hole in the steering compartment, pump the water out, reoccupy it, and center the rudder. This would have had a better chance to work if it had been tried during the night, when the chances of air attack were minimal, or before the compartment had completely flooded, or before the rudder had jammed all the way to the right. Better late than never was Captain Nishida's only hope.

Meanwhile, Captain Nishida returned to the *Hiei*'s bridge to hear the faint rumble of distant gunfire. He grabbed his binoculars and spotted the destroyer *Yudachi*, burning and surrounded by shell splashes. Enraged, Nishida shouted through a megaphone an order for the main guns to fire on what he thought was a *Honolulu*-class light cruiser, and at 6:07 am the aft 14-inch turrets swung out and unloaded with a two-gun armor-piercing salvo.[114]

The target of Captain Nishida's anger was not a cruiser, but the disabled destroyer *Aaron Ward*, currently being towed by the *Bobolink*. Lieutenant Commander Julian Becton, standing on the bridge, saw the flash of the *Hiei*'s guns, then heard the double "CRACK," and passively watched the two shells splash 1,000 yards west of the destroyer. Captain Robert Tobin, commander of 12th Destroyer Division, leaned over and whispered, "Julie, I think she's firing at us."[115]

Becton was calm and matter-of-fact. "I agree, Commodore, but our gunnery officer reports that she's 13 miles away," he replied. "We can't reach her with our guns or torpedoes." Another two 14-inch shells splashed in the water, over the *Aaron Ward* but closer than the first two. Then two more shells landed ahead of her.[116]

The *Hiei* fired again. One shell fell short of the destroyer, the other beyond – a straddle. The next salvo was surely going to be a smashing hit on the little *Aaron Ward* from two big 14-inch shells. In desperation, Commander Gregor cast off the *Bobolink*'s tow and got the destroyer moving, well aware that the saltwater would foul his boilers. Everyone on the destroyer cringed.[117]

But on the *Hiei*, everyone cheered. From their perspective in the aft turrets, the gunners had seen their target disappear among the shell splashes, so they had reported a sinking.[118] If they had kept watching, they would have seen the *Aaron Ward*, still very much afloat, go dead in the water again at about 6:35. The "yacht-patrol" *YP-236*, a commandeered California tuna boat, picked up the *Aaron Ward*'s tow. They arrived in Tulagi Harbor at about 8:30, where the destroyer tied up to a coconut tree on Makombo Island and went to work cleaning her boilers.[119]

But the *Hiei*'s gunners could not keep watching as they had more pressing issues. Six brand-new SBD Dauntlesses of Marine Scout Bombing 142 under Major Robert H. Richard, all of whom had arrived the day before during the Japanese air attacks, had taken off from Henderson Field at around 6:15 and were now making their final approaches to the *Hiei*, preparing to attack with 1,000lb bombs.[120] Major Richard's would not be one of them, as when he tried to arm his bomb, he accidentally dumped it into the water. His squadron mates were more effective. Master Technical Sergeant Donald V. Thornbury planted one 1,000lb bomb in the battleship's already-smashed superstructure; the rest got four near misses along the port side.[121] They all returned safely to Henderson.

As soon as the attack was over, the *Hiei* stopped dead in the water and ten "divers" – a grandiose term for strong swimmers stripped to their underwear – jumped over the side and stuffed rolled-up blankets into the offending hole. They also found one of the 8-inch shells responsible, which had not exploded, and the divers preferred to keep it that way. A temporary rudder was being built to be lowered over the stern, but it could not compensate for the ship's rudder's hard right position. That rudder had to be centered first, which meant the flooded steering compartment had to be pumped out.[122]

At about 6:20, the *Yukikaze* arrived. She was the command ship of Captain Shoji Kiichiro, commander of 16th Destroyer Division, and thus had ample communications facilities. While the *Hiei*'s crew started pumping out the steering compartment, Abe's staff tried to convince him to leave the gutted flagship and move to the *Yukikaze*, but he demurred.[123]

Admiral Abe started to reconsider when four TBF Avenger torpedo bombers under Captain George E. Dooley appeared around 7:15 am. Lieutenant Shigematsu's Zeros, following their guiding B5Ns, had spotted Savo Island around 7:00 am, but somehow missed the *Hiei*. Over Savo they ran into three Marine Wildcats under 2nd Lieutenant Archie G. Donahue from Fighter Squadron 112. They had been patrolling over Henderson Field when Shigematsu's fighters were picked up on radar, and were vectored in to intercept. Five of Shigematsu's eight Zeros decided to harangue the Wildcats, costing them two Zeros, including veteran pilot Chief Petty Officer Mukai Tasuke, on detached duty from the carrier *Zuiho*.[124]

Meanwhile, having now located the *Hiei*, three A6Ms under Warrant Officer Ono Zenji moved to intercept the attacking Avengers. They managed to shoot up – but not down – one TBF with 20mm cannon fire before they themselves were ambushed by seven Marine Wildcats under Major William R. Campbell.

Captain Dooley used the cover of the dogfight to make his approach on the battleship. Captain Nishida ordered work stopped in the steering compartment and got the *Hiei* under way, ready to use the only evasive maneuvers now available to him – varying his speed and turning to starboard. The gunners manned the remaining 25mm guns and put up as fierce a fusillade of fire as they could, but that wasn't their best weapon – or so they thought.

Captain Dooley had survived a midair collision during training, the accident leaving him horribly scarred over most of his body. Multiple skin grafts later, he fought his way back to earn his wings, to now make the first-ever Marine torpedo attack. Dooley was not a man easily daunted. But even Dooley was probably awestruck when he saw the battleship's four very large main turrets with a total of eight 14-inch guns swivel to aim directly at him and all fire at once.

For all the talk of the Type 3 incendiaries intended for use against Henderson Field, the Japanese had originally designed the Type 3s for an antiaircraft role. The Type 3 was supposed to turn each 14-inch gun into a giant shotgun to blast enemy planes out of the sky. This was the first use of the antiaircraft weapon that would gain some notoriety by its vaguely menacing and ominous-sounding Japanese name – *Sanshikidan* – which translates literally as "Type 3 shell."[125]

All eight *Sanshikidan* exploded in front of Captain Dooley and his horrified pilots. Webbed bursts raised a wall of water in front of them, and left a film of saltwater on their windshields. The webbed burst of the *Sanshikidan* looked spectacular. It didn't actually shoot down any planes, but it looked spectacular and that had to count for something.[126]

Captain Dooley and his crews persevered in the face of shot and spume to have the usual American luck with torpedoes. One Avenger, its hydraulics damaged by a Zero, was unable to drop its torpedo; upon return the aircraft was declared a total loss. The remaining TBFs dropped their fish, but one porpoised when it hit the water and circled harmlessly. The remaining two were last seen approaching the battleship's port side. One explosion was seen; on that basis, Dooley was credited with a hit. In reality, at least one torpedo detonated some 100 meters from the ship, possibly as a result of fire from the *Hiei*'s lone remaining dual 5-inch mount. The other one either missed altogether or hit but did not detonate.[127] Admiral Abe was impressed by Captain Nishida's skill. The battleship's crew cheered. Then Commander Onishi revealed that due to the increase in the battleship's speed the rolled-up blankets used to plug the hole causing the flooding in the steering compartment had been yanked out, and the flooding had resumed.[128] They stopped cheering.

Captain Nishida and his crew were now trapped in a relentless cycle. The *Hiei* would stop so the hole could be patched and steering compartment pumped out; progress would be made in those endeavors; another airstrike would show up; the *Hiei* would have to get moving, which invariably ripped out the patch and caused the steering compartment to flood yet again.

These developments also had to be very discouraging to Admiral Abe. Both he and Captain Nishida had been witnesses to the destruction of most of *Kido Butai* by American air power at Midway. More pertinently, they had been witnesses by wireless and voice radio of the plight of the cruisers *Mikuma* and *Mogami* after Midway. Both cruisers had been slowed by damage caused in a collision while trying to evade a US submarine in pre-dawn fog. Abe and Nishida had to listen to their pleas for air cover that was no longer available while they were subjected to a day-long pummeling by American carrier planes. A bomb had detonated the *Mikuma*'s torpedo stowage, sinking her immediately. The *Mogami* was so smashed up that she was out of action for a year, and when she returned she was literally no longer the same ship. Midway had changed everything.

Moreover, by this time, Admiral Abe, exhausted and injured, seems to have been very dispirited, possibly to the point of depression. This may have affected his judgment. The admiral's staff again pleaded with him to transfer to the *Yukikaze* and its better communications and, by now, more comfortable accommodations. Abe relented, and boarded the destroyer at around 7:00 am.[129] With that, he had Admiral Kimura take the *Nagara* to rendezvous with the other remnants of the Vanguard Force and Admiral Kondo to the north near Ontong Java atoll. The destroyers *Shigure*, *Shiratsuyu*, and *Yugure* of the 27th Destroyer Division and the antiaircraft destroyer *Teruzuki* finally arrived. The *Hiei* stopped again to try to pump out the flooded steering compartment. Abe deployed the destroyers in a defensive perimeter some 3,000 meters around the battleship. Air cover in the form of six Zeros from the *Junyo* under Lieutenant (jg) Watanabe Torio, who had to fight his way past a B-17 on a scouting mission, arrived as a further defensive measure.[130]

It was becoming clear that the *Hiei* was going to need a tow. Reluctantly, Admiral Abe ordered the *Kirishima* to return and prepare to tow the *Hiei* to Shortland that night. He didn't like the idea any more than when Combined Fleet had suggested it some four hours earlier. He liked it even less when he received a report that, while the *Kirishima* was en route, at the northern entrance to Indispensable Strait she took at least one torpedo from the US submarine *Trout*.[131] By now, the US had vectored submarines in to the routes of approach and retreat. The Mark 14 torpedo did not explode – again – but Admiral Kondo stepped in and used the attack as reason to abort her mission of mercy and send her scurrying back to the north and her rendezvous with his Advance Force.[132]

But if the *Kirishima* couldn't tow her, how could the *Hiei* escape? The *Nagara* could tow her, except Admiral Abe had just sent her away. None of the destroyers had the engine power. Combined Fleet suggested the biggest of the destroyers, the *Teruzuki*, act as rudder for the *Hiei*. However, *Teruzuki* was not only the biggest of the destroyers; she was also the most powerful of the available antiaircraft platforms, and Abe needed her to have maximum maneuverability to protect his unnavigable battleship, so he refused.[133]

Captain Nishida had developed an idea for, if worse came to worse, running the *Hiei* aground on Guadalcanal. The battleship could then shell Henderson Field and her food stocks could feed the starving army troops. Admiral Abe approved the idea and ordered the battleship to be beached near Kokumbona, some 14 miles from Lunga, behind Japanese lines but within gun range of the airfield. Nishida got together with his navigator Commander Shiwa Takeshi to ponder how a ship that could only steam in circles was to get from north of Savo Island to Guadalcanal.[134] Where was Admiral Jojima when you needed him?

In the meantime, after Lieutenant Watanabe's fighters had left, Major Joe Sailer returned with nine SBDs to make bombing runs on the battleship. They scored no hits, however. Then, at around 10:15, Captain Dooley returned with three Avengers (a fourth had aborted) covered by Marine fighter ace Captain Joe Foss, and six Wildcats arrived in the skies above.[135] Seeing no Zeros about, Foss and his fighters harassed the escorting destroyers before roaring low over the *Hiei*, making strafing runs on the beleaguered antiaircraft gunners to suppress their fire. Foss's fighters couldn't do much about the 14-inch turrets, though, which trained out again to face Dooley's TBFs. The webbed bursts of the *Sanshikidan* were once again spectacular. And once again they didn't shoot down anyone.

Captain Dooley would later say the *Hiei* was "a sorry sight," perhaps showing a twinge of sympathy for the besieged battleship – a triumph of human engineering now being systematically reduced to a smoking ruin.[136] Dooley and his crews successfully dropped their torpedoes, and 1st Lieutenant William W. Dean received credit for a possible hit on the battleship's port side, though apparently this was yet another premature detonation.[137]

As Captain Dooley and his charges cleared the area, Captain Foss returned to the fight in a different way. Right in front of the *Hiei*'s blackened bridge tower, Foss brilliantly executed a right pylon turn in spectacular fashion, while his arm was extended toward the Japanese spectators with his middle finger raised.[138]

But the hard-pressed Japanese had little time to ponder the meaning of this gesture. At 10:20 they noticed yet more torpedo bombers coming from ahead. Four were closing in from each bow at an altitude of 150 feet – an anvil attack.

Nine TBF Avengers of Torpedo 10, the "Buzzards Brigade," under Lieutenant Albert R. Coffin, were covered by six F4F Wildcats under Lieutenant John F. "Jock" Sutherland, all of the USS *Enterprise*. By 5:00 am, the *Enterprise* had reached a point some 270 miles south-southeast of Henderson. Still concerned about the aircraft carrier reported the previous afternoon, Admiral Kinkaid had sent up ten Dauntlesses as scouts, launched eight Grumman Wildcats as air cover, and prepared a possible airstrike on the flight deck, just in case. By 7:00 am, he was reasonably certain that the search results would be negative, so Kinkaid implemented a contingency plan to reinforce Henderson Field with nine Avengers (eight armed with torpedoes and one with 500lb bombs) and six Wildcats fitted with wing tanks. Taking off at 7:22, they were to round Cape Esperance and get a peek into The Slot before landing at Henderson.[139]

It was while getting that peek that Lieutenant Coffin's flight found the *Hiei* and her escorts, seemingly on their way to bombard Henderson Field, albeit at a ludicrously slow speed. Improvising an attack on the fly, Coffin set up his anvil attack on both bows. Once again, the battleship got under way. Once again, the Japanese gunners were forced to go to ground because of strafing from low-flying Wildcats. Once again, the Avenger pilots watched in awe as the forward turrets trained out, aiming directly at Coffin's flight coming from port, all four guns booming in defiance. This time, though, there was no spectacular webbed blast from the *Sanshikidan*. The pilots watched the shells zip past and the gunners watched them create spectacular splashes several miles astern.

The fighter pilots were impressed at the antiaircraft fire, Hank Carey commenting, "My God what a wall of fire they put up as we made our attack over those torpedo planes."[140] At higher altitude than the torpedo bombers, the Wildcats were likely taking fire from the escorting destroyers as well, because the Avenger pilots were not impressed at all. Lieutenant Coffin was very much surprised by what he believed was the weak antiaircraft fire from the battleship.[141] Lieutenant James W. McConnaughhay noticed that the battleship did not appear damaged, but she was moving slowly and sluggishly in the face of the aerial torpedo attack. They dropped their fish at a range of 1,000 yards, then roared down the sides of the *Hiei*, strafing the stunned, struggling Japanese gunners yet again. It was now that they saw why the battleship was moving so slowly and sluggishly, why her antiaircraft fire was so light. Her topsides were burned, blackened, holed, still smoldering. Many of her guns were warped or not firing. They had no idea what had happened, only that she had been in a scuffle of some sort.[142]

Lieutenant Coffin and his fliers saw three geysers erupt around the *Hiei* – one starboard amidships, two to port near the bow and stern. But Lieutenant (jg) George Welles thought the splashes were too small, as if they were from small detonations and not the torpedo warheads. Welles said, "Anyhow after the attack she was sailing along just as majestically as before. We must not have even damaged her paint job."[143] Indeed, the Japanese recorded no hits to the *Hiei* at this time. The solo bombing run, by Lieutenant (jg) John Boudreaux, also registered no hits. As the carrier planes cleared the area and made for Henderson Field, unidentified aircraft were spotted in the distance at high altitude. They were six Zeros of Base Air Force's 204 Air Group under Lieutenant (jg) Morisaki Takeshi, sent all the way from Buin to provide air cover. But they arrived too late – again – to stop Coffin's attack.[144]

However, Lieutenant Coffin's flight arrived just in time at Henderson Field, landing before shocked onlookers, including General Woods, who had no idea of the *Enterprise*'s approach or the planned reinforcement.[145] The general told them, "Boys, I don't know where you came from, but you look like angels dropping out of heaven to us."[146]

For Admiral Abe aboard the *Yukikaze*, the air attacks were even more of a headache than the one he already had. It was not that each attack was big – they were all relatively small – or that each attack was dangerous, although they were. It was that there were so damn many of them. There was no time for the crews to even rest, let alone make the critical repairs to the *Hiei*. This was *Mikuma* at Midway all over again. It did not help that the promised air cover had displayed an annoying propensity to show up just after one attack and leave just before the next attack.

At 10:34, Admiral Abe signaled from the *Yukikaze*: "Hiei must be disposed of X All hands evacuate X Each destroyer is to send a launch."[147] The battleship's crew could see the message displayed in flags from the destroyer's yardarm. The reaction was dead silence. Captain Nishida thought the order was absurd. Despite some minor flooding caused by the 8-inch hits and bombing near misses, the *Hiei* was in no danger of sinking and her engines were still functional. They just needed to get that jammed rudder straightened and everything would be okay. The skipper refused to obey the order. In no shape to be fighting his flag captain as well as the Americans, Abe yielded.

Soon the next attack began. At around 11:00, three Grumman Avengers under Captain Dooley came roaring in. Again they thought they scored two torpedo hits but yet again they had in fact failed. This attack was not recorded in the Henderson Field records. Dooley saw Lieutenant Morisaki's Zeros circling high above them, but the Zeros did not pursue them.[148]

About ten minutes later came 14 B-17 Flying Fortresses of the 72nd Bombardment Squadron out of Espiritu Santo under the direction of Major Donald E. Ridings. Flying in two flights at 14,000 feet, they dropped a total of 56 500lb bombs on the *Hiei*. They thought they had gotten five or six hits. But the Army Air Force, unlike their Betty-flying counterparts in the Japanese Naval Air Force, had not mastered the art of dropping bombs on ships at sea. They did get some photographs of the *Hiei* – which showed her desperately circling below while trailing an oil slick – that verified only one hit. The protective umbrella of Lieutenant Morisaki's Zeros managed to miss this attack as well.[149]

But they quickly got another chance. At around 11:20, Major Joe Sailer came back with six Dauntlesses armed with 1,000lb bombs. Screaming out of the sky, his group planted three bombs on the *Hiei*. The bombs heavily damaged more of the pumping control equipment and Fire Rooms 2, 3, and 4. Near misses along the port side ruptured hull plating and caused minor flooding, which nevertheless robbed the battleship of the ability to counterflood to correct the 7-degree list to starboard.[150]

Just as Major Sailer's SBDs pulled out of their dives, Torpedo 8, formerly of the *Saratoga*, formerly of the *Hornet*, painfully reconstituted after its near-total destruction at Midway, and now under the command of Lieutenant Harold H. "Swede" Larsen, came in with six Avengers. Two of their torpedoes missed, two failed to drop, and two were reported hits on the port side bow and amidships. Again, the Japanese reported no torpedo hits. This time Lieutenant Morisaki's Zeros did see the attacking Americans – on their way out. A brief scrum with 12 escorting Wildcats under Major Campbell resulted in no losses to either side.[151]

Lieutenant Morisaki's less-than-observant fighters departed, to be replaced at about 12:30 by six Zeros from Base Air Force's 252 Air Group under Lieutenant Yamamoto Shighasa, coming all the way from Rabaul.[152] For Admiral Abe and his aching head, the air attacks had now crossed into the realm of the ridiculous. With no sign of the incessant attacks abating anytime soon, Abe again ordered the *Hiei* scuttled.

Like Admiral Abe, Captain Nishida was also frustrated, and not just with the Americans. It seemed Abe wanted the *Hiei* sunk almost as much as the Americans did. She had survived (by Japanese count) 60 American sorties. They had caused significant damage – those three fire rooms were damaged, and two pumping control stations on the starboard side and the aft pumping control station were flooded – but the battleship was still in no danger of sinking. It was a standoff – the *Hiei* could not escape and the Americans with their malfunctioning torpedoes could not sink her. The American frustration was summed up by Torpedo 10's Lieutenant Coffin with the quip, "We've got to sink it or else the admirals will stop building carriers and start building battleships again!"[153]

With this standoff, Captain Nishida liked his chances of saving his ship. All he had to do was hold on until dark, when the air attacks would stop. Then he could complete repairs and get the *Hiei* going again. To placate Admiral Abe, Nishida sent Senior Lieutenant Ogura Masatoshi to the *Yukikaze* in a launch with the emperor's portrait, various papers and mementos, and a plea for more time. Abe gave him one hour.[154]

And so did the Americans. The aircrews needed rest, the search missions needed supplementing, the aircraft needed maintenance. Captain Nishida made the most of this brief respite. The *Hiei* stopped, damage control went to work – again – and within an hour, divers reported work to pump out the steering compartment was 70 percent complete. Admiral Abe logged that "manual steering had been made possible, the fire at the foremast had been placed under control, and the pumping out of the steering room was succeeding."[155] Even the downcast Abe was looking up.

Just in time to see the next air attack developing, with eight Marine Dauntlesses under 2nd Lieutenant John H. McEniry, Jr., six *Enterprise* TBFs under Lieutenant Coffin, and 14 Wildcats under Captain Foss and Captain Bob Fraser. Naturally Lieutenant Yamamoto's protective Zeros were nowhere to be seen. In fact, they had just left for Rabaul, but were blocked by raging storms over The Slot and had to ditch near Rekata Bay. Yamamoto himself suffered severe injuries and had to be sent back to Japan.[156]

Captain Nishida must have wished that he could make it back to Japan. The *Hiei* got under way but this time her antiaircraft fire was pitiful. She was struggling to find enough men to man her guns, which, since she had so few guns left, is saying something. Seeing that there were no covering Zeros the Wildcats zoomed low over the battleship's deck and machine-gunned her few remaining gunners.

Low clouds ruined Lieutenant McEniry's dive-bombing attack, but Lieutenant Coffin seems to have executed another anvil attack. The 14-inchers roared at the torpedo bombers. Once again the *Sanshikidan* bursts looked spectacular but failed to shoot down a single plane. As Captain Foss led his fighters in more strafing runs, he saw a "wonderful" explosion amidships, "which shot water, steam, fire, and debris high into the air." This was a torpedo, launched by Lieutenant Coffin, which had struck the battleship and exploded on the starboard side under Turret 2 in front of the pagoda in the windlass room.[157] A second torpedo, one apparently dropped by Lieutenant Welles, struck the forward section of the starboard engine room. A third torpedo may have struck the port side forward. A fourth ran erratically. Two more were seen to strike the port side and just sink.[158] All in all, by American torpedo standards, it was an outstanding performance.

For the beleaguered *Hiei* and her crew, the hit to the starboard engine room was devastating. Not only did it damage her engines – about the only thing on the battered battleship that had remained undamaged all day – it blew a giant hole in the starboard side very near the hole that had been flooding the steering compartment, whose hull patch had been ripped off once again. Now the flooding got much worse and all the collision mats, blankets, towels, mattresses, pillows, and cushions Captain Nishida could muster would not plug that giant hole.

Discouraged but determined, Captain Nishida refused to give up hope. Admiral Abe had, however, and sent a written order over in a cutter for Nishida to abandon ship. Nishida crushed the paper in his hands. He stalled, however. Darkness was coming; low clouds were already crippling bombing attacks. He would wait just a little while longer.

Then he got a report that the starboard engine room was completely destroyed by Lieutenant Welles' torpedo.

The color drained from the skipper's face. "Is that so? Totally destroyed?" With the reply, "Yes," his last hope had gone. Quietly, calmly, Captain Nishida ordered the *Hiei* abandoned. Signal officer Lieutenant Sakamoto Matsuzaburo spread the word, then looked for the executive officer Commander Tamura. Sakamoto wanted help in case Nishida refused to leave the ship. Nishida was old school, believing the captain should go down with the ship. So was Tamura. His only response to Sakamoto's request was an icy glare.[159]

The *Hiei* was slowly settling by the stern and listing more to starboard when nine Zeros from the *Junyo* arrived as fighter cover – for all the good it had done today – guided by three D3A dive bombers. A heartbroken Captain Nishida called for the remaining crew to assemble on the fantail. The men coming up on deck from the machinery rooms and the turrets were shocked at the condition of the upper deck, with the holed superstructure, the blackened pagoda, the smashed guns; the blood, bodies, and parts of bodies everywhere – and the smell.

Speaking from atop Turret 4, Captain Nishida praised the crew for their service and devotion, extolled them to continue serving the emperor, and took full responsibility for the fate of the *Hiei*. And blamed bad luck. Then he dismissed them to their abandon ship stations. With his lacerated leg bothering him, someone brought a folding chair for Nishida to direct the abandonment from the top of the turret. Lieutenant Shiga had led his fighters back to the *Junyo*, who shut down air operations in the face of the foul weather. Shortly after Shiga left, true to form, came eight SBDs led by Major Sailer. The worsening weather crippled this strike. Only Sailer and one other were able to even find the *Hiei* and her escorts and Sailer could not get the battleship lined up for an attack, so he dropped his bomb off the *Yukikaze*, which missed, though the concussion cracked a boiler foundation. Two of Sailer's Dauntlesses disappeared in the murk and growing darkness, the only losses of the day. Sailer himself was lucky to make it back to Henderson.

The evacuation went smoothly. As his last orders, Captain Nishida ordered the flooding of the magazines and the opening of the Kingston valves.* He still refused to leave the ship and the *Yukikaze* refused to fire scuttling torpedoes while he was aboard. Admiral Abe sent a written order over to the *Hiei* in a cutter. It read, "This is an order. You are requested to come on board *Yukikaze* to report. If you wish, you will be sent back to *Hiei* again."[160] It was not enough, and four officers climbed to the top of the turret and physically dragged a protesting Nishida off the ship.[161]

With everyone else now off the *Hiei*, Captain Nishida arrived at the *Yukikaze* at 6:00 pm. He was greeted by the destroyer's skipper Commander Kanma Ryokichi and

---

* Kingston valves are seacocks on the bottom of the ship that can be opened to allow in seawater to various parts of the ship that might need flooding, such as ballast tanks and fuel tanks, or vice versa, such as a tank that might need to be cleaned.

shown to a small cabin behind the bridge. There, Nishida was shocked to see Commander Chihaya, exclaiming, "I thought you were dead!" As Chihaya tried to explain, Nishida overheard Admiral Abe questioning one of the *Hiei*'s engineering officers about the destroyed engine room. The officer thought there must have been some mistake because the engine room was still operational. He didn't understand why the ship was abandoned.[162] Nishida sank down into his chair in shock.

The *Hiei*'s skipper was even more horrified when he heard Commander Kanma order, "Both engines ahead full; prepare to fire torpedoes to starboard." Nishida bolted from the cabin to Admiral Abe, protesting, wanting to at least be returned to his ship. Abe told him to be silent.[163]

Captain Nishida returned to the cabin, the color drained from his face, slumped into the chair, and wept. "This is against my will! I made up my mind to go down with my own ship – only the commanding officer instructed me to come on board *Yukikaze* to report – I came over here … he betrayed me!"[164]

Admiral Abe just wanted this to be over, consequences be damned. He had been trying to be done with the battleship since the morning, had repeatedly ordered her scuttled, and had denied her the means to be towed to safety by sending the *Nagara* and *Kirishima* away. Nevertheless, Admiral Abe asked Combined Fleet for permission to scuttle the battleship, which seems rather odd since her Kingston valves had already been opened, only to be ordered "not to do so" by Combined Fleet.

Seemingly much more interested in saving the *Hiei* than Admiral Abe was, Admiral Yamamoto and his staff had spent much of the day discussing what to do with the crippled battleship, yet not exactly doing much to help her. Though aircraft carriers had supplanted battleships as the decisive strike instruments of navies, battleships had been the backbone of major navies for decades and remained objects of emotion and prestige. That was one reason Pearl Harbor was so traumatic for Americans – with all the Pacific Fleet's battleships sunk or immobilized, it felt like the entire navy was gone. The Japanese had a similar emotional attachment to their battleships. Additionally, while she was not the *Yamato*, the *Hiei* in particular was the object of more than the usual emotion because she had hosted the emperor in his last review of the Imperial Japanese Navy in 1940. Finally, Combined Fleet had shown a definite reticence to commit its battleships to anything but the "Decisive Battle." Guadalcanal wasn't it, as far as they were concerned. Losing a battleship in this seemingly indecisive action would cripple them when the "Decisive Battle" finally arrived.

With all this in mind, Admiral Yamamoto and his staff decided "to make every effort to rescue her after nightfall."[165] But what those efforts would entail bogged down in "long, involved meetings."[166] The *Hiei*'s position was hardly hopeless – she had escorts with her and was within range of land-based air cover, for all the good it had done. It was initially decided to leave the *Hiei* where she was, with the submarine *I-16* watching her. Then Yamamoto expressed concern the US would take photographs of the disabled battleship and use them for propaganda purposes. Sidestepping the logic of sinking one of your own irreplaceable fast battleships because you're afraid the enemy might take a picture of it, the staff abated his concerns by pointing out to him that the Americans had probably already taken pictures. Then they wondered if she could draw away American air attacks from Admiral Tanaka's convoy. At the end of the day, Yamamoto and his staff decided, unsurprisingly, to do nothing.[167] This amounted to a death sentence for the *Hiei* since the flooding was no longer being mitigated by damage control and her seacocks had already been opened. Evidently, those rather important details had never reached Yamamoto or his staff.

Admiral Abe decided that he couldn't wait around for the *Hiei* to sink and ordered the *Yukikaze* to head west. As the destroyer trudged along, Captain Nishida no doubt looked out over the stern to see his proud ship *Hiei*, now abandoned in more ways than one, down by the stern and listing to starboard, receding in the distance and finally disappearing in the dark.

The *Hiei* was never seen again. The *I-16* was unable to find her in the darkness. The *Yukikaze* returned at about 1:00 am and found only a large oil slick. Abandoned by people who could and probably should have done more to save her – "a matter of nerves" was how naval historian Vincent P. O'Hara described it – the *Hiei*, all alone in the dark, ended her agony in her own time.[168]

The old adage holds that no battle plan survives contact with the enemy. A corollary holds that sometimes the plan doesn't last even that long.

Night came on November 13 with the corollary holding true both ways. Commanders depend on information and communications, and at this point South Pacific commander Admiral Halsey had neither. For the past 24 hours, he had been aware that the outcome of the campaign, if not the war, hung in the balance; and he could do nothing more to affect it for the time being but wait. Halsey recalled:

> Back on the *Argonne*, in Nouméa, all we knew was that the battle was raging. I had sent Callaghan and Scott into it, and now I could do nothing but wait for the results. The waiting was hard, as always. I walked the decks, re-examined reports and charts, and conferred with my staff. I must have drunk a gallon of coffee and smoked two packs of cigarettes. When the tension became unbearable, I skimmed through the trashiest magazine I could find.[169]

It was daylight before the first messages came trickling in, piecemeal and frightening: "Steering room flooded and rudder jammed hard right by torpedo hit starboard quarter X Cannot steer by engines X Request tow"[170] – this from the *Portland*.

A half-hour later: "Need help" – from the *Atlanta*. The bad news continued to come in. At 9:00 am the *Helena* signaled: "Helena San Francisco Juneau OBannon Fletcher

Sterett in company proceeding course 175 X Helena senior ship X All ships are damaged so request maximum air coverage."

Why was the *Helena* signaling and not Admiral Callaghan's flagship? Something must have happened to him. That wasn't encouraging. But, infuriatingly, nothing else came in until the afternoon, when Guadalcanal, after debriefing the survivors, sent as full a report as they could:

Ten miles north Savo Island five enemy DDs [destroyers] attempting assist Kongo-class BB [battleship] which has been hit by seven torpedoes and 1000 lb bomb X After part of ship burning fiercely X Ship believed hostile DD beached and smoking north coast Olevuga Island X Large vessel burning Indispensable Strait x USS Cushing burning five miles SE Savo Island and USS Monssen dead in water both abandoned X Atlanta and Portland badly damaged X USS Laffey sunk X 700 survivors picked up 25% of these wounded.

Ten minutes later came another discouraging signal: "Atlanta unable to control water X Abandoning and sinking her with demolition charges X I am proceeding under tow to Tulagi." This was from the *Portland*. Why wasn't Admiral Scott's flagship *Atlanta* signaling? Where was Scott? Something must have happened to him, too. This sounded bad. And it was.

Yet sending them to battle had been an absolute necessity – and successful, as General Vandegrift made clear in a signal for Admiral Halsey:

To Scott, Callaghan, and their men goes our greatest homage X With magnificent courage against seemingly hopeless odds, they drove back the first hostile stroke and made success possible X To them the men of Guadalcanal lift their battered helmets in deepest admiration.

But it was not over yet. Admiral Halsey had sent Admiral Kinkaid and the *Enterprise* task force to sea from Nouméa with the idea that the carrier would be in range of The Slot and Ironbottom Sound on November 13 to break up the projected invasion. In order to protect the last operational US carrier in the Pacific, he had given Kinkaid instructions concerning a specific line of latitude 11 degrees 40 minutes south.[171] But because the *Enterprise* task force was maintaining radio silence, Halsey had heard nothing from them since.

A little after 4:00 pm, Admiral Halsey signaled Admiral Kinkaid to separate Admiral Lee and his two battleships and an escort of four destroyers into a separate task force. They were to dash into Ironbottom Sound to help defend Henderson Field on Halsey's order only. Halsey formally ordered this new force, Task Force 64, into the Sound shortly before 5:00 pm, intending for it to arrive early on December 14. This plan sounded simple enough, but it had a few issues.

First, as Admiral Halsey knew, he was breaking multiple rules of naval warfare by sending battleships into restricted waters such as Ironbottom Sound. He just didn't have anything else left. This was his last card and he knew it, later writing, "Lee's ships were my only recourse, so I ordered them in."[172]

The bigger problem was a misinterpretation of his orders. Admiral Halsey thought he had told Admiral Kinkaid to stay near 11 degrees 40 minutes South, but not to cross it. Kinkaid had just heard "do not cross it." Being very conservative with the last American carrier in the Pacific, Kinkaid stayed well south of that line.[173] The issue was compounded by the usual unfriendly winds in that region that had required the *Enterprise* to turn to the south to conduct flight operations.[174] Halsey sending the *Enterprise* out late from Nouméa had certainly not helped things.

As a consequence, Task Force 16 was some 150 miles south of where Halsey thought it would be. Admiral Kinkaid sent Admiral Lee and Task Force 64 forward, but there was no way they could arrive in time. Kinkaid sent the destroyer *Mustin* 50 miles east to message Admiral Halsey: "From Lee's present position impossible for him to reach Savo before 0800 tomorrow."[175] Meanwhile, after breaking away from the *Enterprise*, Admiral Lee ignored radio silence to radio Admiral Halsey, "What do you think we have? Wings?"[176]

The news was "a shock" to Admiral Halsey, learning his plan for the battleships had fallen apart already. One of his staffers, Charles Weaver, said that when he gave the admiral the news, "You can well imagine the blast I got from my seniors who were sure that Lee was in good position to intercept."[177] Halsey himself would later say he received the news with "great disappointment."[178] Late that night the South Pacific commander was forced to message General Vandegrift, "Sorry Lee cannot comply too far."[179] It was an embarrassing admission for the man who had promised Vandegrift, "I'll promise you everything I've got."

This would not be the last time one of Admiral Halsey's orders was misunderstood. The latest scouting reports still placed the main Japanese forces near Ontong Java atoll, well north of Guadalcanal. As best as anyone could tell, some Japanese might visit Ironbottom Sound that night, but not the main invasion force or Admiral Kondo's Advance Force.

So, if the scouting reports were true, this would be a quiet night for once for the Marines on Guadalcanal. And the misunderstanding would be a case of no harm, no foul.

Hopefully.

CHAPTER 4

THE RECKONING BEGINS

Night came to Guadalcanal as it normally did – hot, sticky, oppressive, and dark – with the added feature of the aftermath of torrential rain this Friday, September 13. After the hectic hours harassing the *Hiei*, among other more mundane missions like scouting, the Marine, Army, and Navy pilots were happy to get that most precious wartime commodity among servicemen – sleep.

Among those catching some badly needed shuteye was 2nd Lieutenant Emil Novak of the Army Air Force's 67th Fighter Squadron.[1] Though his squadron of P-39 Airacobras had been deployed to Henderson Field since August, he was new, having arrived only a few days earlier. The uncomfortable environment of Guadalcanal was also new to him and may have made him a light sleeper, at least temporarily. This is probably why it was Lieutenant Novak who was stirred from his slumbers by the low growl of an airplane at around 1:30 in the morning. No doubt it was a seaplane aloft to look for and pick up downed pilots; he knew Guadalcanal had two planes for such purposes. A little while later, however, he detected a greenish light bathing the area, illuminating it with flares. Why would the rescue pilots drop flares?

Lieutenant Novak grabbed his shoes and flight coveralls and bounded from his tent. He was halfway to the nearest shelter when the world exploded – again. This time, the explosion resulted from the impact of 8-inch incendiary shells fired from the cruisers *Suzuya* and *Maya*. Admiral Mikawa and his cruisers had sailed into Ironbottom Sound completely undetected and were now bombarding Henderson Field.

With Admiral Abe's battleships turned back the night before, successfully if not skillfully, the task of reducing Henderson Field to rubble had fallen to Admiral Mikawa, at least to the extent a dirt airfield with tents and bamboo huts could be reduced to rubble. Mikawa had never lost a battle with the Americans, but the failure from the night before put more pressure on him to pick up the slack.

The original plan had always assigned this night's scheduled bombardment to Admiral Mikawa's tiny 8th Fleet. In a rare display of restraint, for this operation the fleet was divided into only two parts: the "Main Body" and the "Support Force." The Main Body under Mikawa's direct command contained the luxurious heavy cruiser *Chokai*, which was again performing her traditional role as fleet flagship, leading the heavy cruiser *Kinugasa*, light cruiser *Isuzu*, and the destroyers *Arashio* and *Asashio*. The Support Force under Rear Admiral Nishimura Shoji had the heavy cruisers *Suzuya* and *Chokai*'s sister ship *Maya*, the light cruiser *Tenryu*, and the destroyers *Yugumo*, *Makigumo*, *Kazegumo*, and *Michishio*. In an arrangement only the Combined Fleet could have concocted, the Main Body was to support the Support Force by protecting it from interference, while the Support Force was to perform the main mission by bombarding Henderson Field.

Admiral Mikawa's cobbled-together fleet left its anchorage in the Shortlands at 6:30 am on November 13. The vice admiral hoped to evade detection by not sailing directly down The Slot from the Shortlands to Lunga, but to steer well north of it and come down through Indispensable Strait. But he could not evade General MacArthur's 5th Air Force B-17s, who attacked the Shortlands and caught the force soon after it left the anchorage. Near misses off the stern of the *Michishio* damaged her machinery and left her dead in the water. Mikawa's ships continued on as the *Michishio* was towed back into the anchorage.[2] But the encounter was too close to the Shortlands to give clues as to where he was going.

As always, Admiral Mikawa had planned and prepared well. US scouts did not reach as far north of The Slot as Mikawa had detoured. To that must be added Mikawa's usual store of good luck: American air power was mostly focused on the *Hiei*, and Mikawa was coming in under cover of a storm. His ships got into the air range of Henderson Field just as the sun set. His timing was perfect. No one had seen him coming.

Admiral Mikawa's Main Body positioned itself northwest of Savo Island to look for any ships trying to interfere. The Support Force launched two floatplanes, one each from the *Suzuya* and *Maya*, to guide them in their lobbing of 8-inch Type 3 shells into Henderson Field, waking its inhabitants such as Lieutenant Novak. If the flares didn't wake them, the incoming shells, which Lieutenant McEniry thought sounded like "a freight train going overhead," certainly would.[3]

Henderson Field was chaotic under the Japanese guns, with men running, falling, shouting, screaming, trying to find the nearest shelter. Lieutenant Novak yelled for his three tentmates as he dove into the foxhole. One quickly joined him. A second, crawling on his hands and knees, could not see the shelter and ended up in a tiny depression in the ground lying prone to avoid the flying shrapnel. The third, 1st Lieutenant Danny Miller, understood how embarrassing it would be if he ran out of his tent into the shelter – or even if he was killed – without being properly dressed. As the explosions boomed and the shrapnel flew outside his tent, Miller was calmly digging into his flight bag for a clean pair of socks. Then he put on a clean flight suit, sat down to deliberately tie his shoes, and topped it off, literally, by putting on his flight helmet. Now ready to face the world, Miller strolled out of his tent, across the yard, taking no visible notice of the blasts, fire, and white-hot steel flying around him, and into the shelter.[4] As the old saying goes, it's better to look good than to feel good.

Captain Dooley was not one to be embarrassed if he was not properly dressed for an air raid shelter, but he did at least want to have his pants on. He had grabbed his trousers when he raced from his tent, intending to put them on when he got to the shelter. But once Dooley got there, he found the day's heavy rains had left about 8 inches of water in it. Not wanting to soak his pants in the dirty water in order to put them on, he climbed back out of the hole, only to have a shell explode nearby that sent him diving back in. Every time Dooley climbed out, another shell would land close by. Dooley ended up enduring the shelling pantless and soaking in the muddy water.[5]

Water was not a problem on Edson's Ridge, where the executive officer of Marine Scout Bombing 132, Major Ben Robertshaw, was rousing his three tentmates as the first shells landed. Two followed Robertshaw to the shelter. The third, 2nd Lieutenant Archie "Hap" Simpson, was too exhausted after multiple long search missions to get out of bed, hoping to just sleep through the bombardment – not exactly unheard of – until one blast sent him sprawling to the ground. His decision made, Simpson scampered to the shelter, where he found Robertshaw nonchalantly giving scholarly lessons on the differences in the sounds between land-based and naval artillery shells, and how to tell by the differences in sound if a shell would be short, over, or on target, assuming you were the target. The lessons did not comfort Simpson.[6]

Some did find comfort, of a sort, in the idea that this shelling was nothing compared to the original bombardment from the battleships *Kongo* and *Haruna* a month earlier. Nonetheless, such logic did not keep others from going into an understandable panic, such as one sailor who, having survived the sinkings of both the *Wasp* and the *Barton*, burst into one shelter almost catatonic, unable to say a word.[7] Others, like Major Robertshaw and Lieutenant Miller, were in anything but a panic.

Some survivors of Admiral Abe's attack the night before thought the Japanese were coming after them personally. The *Atlanta*'s Bill McKinney "had the feeling that they knew where we were and planned to finish us off." Nevertheless, he watched his tormentors and their "little winking pinpoints of blue light as their salvos thundered toward us. It was a fearful experience."[8]

General Vandegrift signaled Nouméa, "Being heavily shelled."[9] Admiral Halsey was already incensed; now he was embarrassed. He simply had nothing with which to respond. The closest major US Navy ship was the cruiser *Portland* at Tulagi. Even under normal circumstances she could not take on the *Suzuya*, *Maya*, and their escorts by herself, not even counting the *Chokai*, *Kinugasa*, and their escorts further out.

Moreover, these were hardly normal circumstances for the *Portland*. Her crew was still trying to restore some semblance of navigability after she had suffered the Japanese torpedo hit. She was simply in no condition to fight. But while the *Suzuya* and *Maya* were bombarding Henderson Field, they had their searchlights sweeping Ironbottom Sound for targets. Captain DuBose had his gunnery officer Commander Shanklin get a target lock on Admiral Nishimura's cruisers and told him to fire only if the searchlights stopped in their direction.[10] As it was, two PT boats, one commanded by Lieutenant John Searles, the other by Lieutenant Henry S. Taylor, launched themselves like a pair of angry midges at the cruisers, firing six torpedoes. Searles and Taylor thought they had gotten a few hits; they didn't. They returned safely.[11]

After about 35 minutes of hell in which the *Suzuya* launched 504 and the *Maya* 485 8-inch shells, starting out with Type 3 incendiary but switching to Type 91 armor-piercing when the incendiaries ran out, Admiral Nishimura's Support Force sailed out of Ironbottom Sound and headed back toward the Shortlands with their escorts. Admiral Mikawa's *Chokai* had thrown her weight into the bombardment by tossing 385 Type 3s and Type 91s of her own at Henderson Field before heading back with the Main Body.[12]

Nishimura Shoji was not the most astute of admirals.[13] But though he had seen some fires and chain explosions, he determined Henderson Field was still usable.[14] This was correct, mostly because his bombardment had completely missed Henderson Field proper and the aircraft parked there, which were the biggest threats to Admiral Tanaka's transports. Most of the Japanese shells landed instead around the satellite Fighter 1 strip, where most of the fighters were located. The 67th Fighter Squadron watched 15 of its 16 P-39 and P-400s suffer damage from the shelling. The only one left undamaged was "the oldest, most bent up klunker" of a P-400.[15] But most of the Airacobras were not irreparably damaged. Two Wildcats were burned out, three more Wildcats and one Dauntless were badly damaged, and 17 Wildcats suffered light damage. The runway Fighter 1 now featured two large craters. Fortunately, however, repairing a dirt airfield is not particularly difficult.

This was not going according to the Japanese plan. With a few notable exceptions, such as Admiral Mikawa, Japanese commanders had shown throughout this Pacific War that when things did not go according to plan, they were not good at making adjustments.

When the sun rose over the Solomons on November 14, the rain was gone and it was set to be a bright, clear day with perfect flying conditions. An incensed Cactus Air Force, supported by the carrier *Enterprise*, planned to do a lot of it, early and often.

The night before, Brigadier General Woods had briefed the pilots at Henderson on what the plan would be, what they would be facing, and what was at stake. He concluded with, "We lay the fate of Guadalcanal in your hands and know that each of you will do his best."[16]

Before dawn, a combat air patrol of four Wildcats took off from Fighter 1, maneuvering around the craters with the help of a light shone by the ground crew. Then six Marine Dauntless dive bombers launched from Henderson, fanning out over three search sectors of New Georgia, Santa Ysabel, and Malaita. While passing Savo Island, they saw that the battleship they had spent yesterday mauling was gone, replaced by an oil slick some 3,000 yards wide.

At 6:30 am, two Marine Dauntlesses flown by 2nd Lieutenants William Hronek and Horace C. Baum of Marine Scout Bombing Squadron 132 reported two light cruisers and five destroyers just south of New Georgia, bearing 280 degrees True, course also 280 degrees True, speed 16 knots, distance 140 miles from Lunga.[17] It was not a completely accurate report, but it was good enough to identify Admiral Nishimura's Support Force, desperately trying to catch up to the Main Body, which was also speeding away, trying to get out of range of the vengeful pilots at Henderson. At this point they were no more than halfway to the limits of that range.

It would prove to be a productive day for Hronek and Baum, but first it was time for the 1st Marine Air Wing to get to work. For the American aviators it was time for payback. Around 7:00 am, the first payment of that payback took off: Major Joe Sailer with six Marine Dauntlesses, Captain Dooley and six Marine and *Enterprise* Avengers, with Captain Joe Foss and eight Wildcats for escort.

In the meantime, the *Enterprise* had been trying to make up for lost time by speeding northwest through the night at 25 knots to reach a point southwest of Guadalcanal. Admiral Kinkaid had heard nothing of the presence of Admiral Mikawa's cruisers, nor had Admiral Halsey or Admiral Fitch. But Halsey had ordered Kinkaid to position the *Enterprise* task force 100 miles south of the Solomons in order to "Locate and destroy transports." Admiral Lee, in turn, was ordered to keep his battleships positioned 50 miles south of the Solomons, between the *Enterprise* and any possible Japanese surface forces – a very fortunate precaution.[18]

As she was speeding northwest, the *Enterprise* ran into more squalls, which cut her visibility and delayed flight operations until 6:08 am, when she could then launch eight Wildcats for a combat air patrol. Then came ten Dauntlesses for scouting, giving them the option to land at Henderson Field if necessary, and three for an antisubmarine patrol. Having put his air group in motion, Admiral Kinkaid cut speed to 22 knots and waited for the results, which were initially heartstopping. At 7:07, one of the scouts reported ten unidentified planes at low altitude 140 miles due north of the *Enterprise* herself. The *Enterprise* task force assumed an antiaircraft formation, and at 7:37 Admiral Kinkaid ordered aloft a ready strike he had already prepared – 17 SBDs under Scouting 10 skipper Lieutenant Commander James R. "Bucky" Lee escorted by ten Wildcats under Lieutenant Commander Jimmy Flatley. They were ordered to head north, listen to the radio for scouting reports, then attack the best target, landing at Henderson Field if necessary. Once the strike was launched, Kinkaid turned the *Enterprise* around and headed south, in a desperate attempt to avoid a Japanese airstrike.

The reported ten unidentified planes never materialized, but starting at 8:25 a bogey kept appearing intermittently on radar. Lieutenant MacGregor Kilpatrick was vectored toward it, leading four Wildcats. The unknown aircraft turned out to be a giant four-engine Kawanishi H6K Type 97 Large Flying Boat – "Mavis" – flown by flight leader Lieutenant Commander Wada Ryu, who cleverly tried to minimize his radar signature by periodically ducking below radar. But the Mavis was largely a flying gas tank. Only one pass from

Kilpatrick's Grummans and the flying boat exploded and went down in a smoke pall that could be seen from the *Enterprise* more than 40 miles away. At 8:53 Kilpatrick sent the laconic but informative message, "Bogey found and downed."[19]

Kilpatrick's interception was far easier than the airstrike's assignment, which, being a little light on the details, was not for the faint of heart. "We don't know where we are going," thought SBD pilot Ensign Leonard Robinson to himself. "We don't even have target assignments."[20] It was with such comforting thoughts that the *Enterprise* fliers headed into the great unknown.

Admirals Mikawa and Nishimura had hoped to keep their position undetected by following a mirror course to their approach to Guadalcanal, heading well south of the Solomons instead. Those hopes were dashed when the submarine USS *Flying Fish* let loose with six Mark 14s at one of the heavy cruisers. Being American Mark 14s, naturally none of them hit. Then the ships were spotted by the scouts from Henderson Field. Nishimura's Support Force caught up to Mikawa's Main Body around 7:50 am, hoping for mutual support.[21] They were going to need it. Major Joe Sailer's strike from Henderson Field caught up to Mikawa's marauders around 8:00.[22] Sailer carefully reported them in to Henderson as four heavy cruisers and three destroyers, bearing 280 degrees True, distance 170 miles, with no enemy fighter protection.[23]

At around 8:30, Major Sailer led his SBDs through their pushover points diving on an "*Atago*-class cruiser." Screaming down from the skies, the Dauntlesses claimed two hits with 1,000lb bombs and three near misses. Sailer himself claimed one hit near the bow, while a bomb dropped by 2nd Lieutenant Robert E. Kelly plunged through the forward part of the bridge, through the superstructure, all the way down to the lower deck below the waterline, where it exploded.[24]

Lieutenant Kelly's hit on their unfortunate target, the cruiser *Kinugasa*, was devastating. The blast literally decapitated the ship, killing both the fiery skipper Captain Sawa Masao and his executive officer, leaving the torpedo officer in command. It also blew out large sections of the hull below the waterline, causing major flooding that quickly gave the old cruiser a 10-degree list to port. Shrapnel ignited the forward gasoline storage, starting a nasty fire.[25]

Meanwhile, Captain Dooley had split up his Avenger torpedo bombers; three Marine TBFs attacked the port side, and three Navy TBFs attacked the starboard side in an anvil attack on a "*Mogami*-class cruiser," sometimes incorrectly identified as the *Kinugasa*, but actually Admiral Mikawa's flagship *Chokai*. The Marines claimed two hits and the Navy aviators claimed three hits, the total of which would normally sink any cruiser, but *Chokai* seems to have made no turns and actually outran the anvil attempt, suffering no damage. All aircraft returned safely to Henderson.

Meanwhile, the *Enterprise* fliers were having issues. At 7:50 am, the dawn search of Lieutenant (jg) Robert D. Gibson and Ensign Richard M. Buchanan of the *Enterprise* chased down the fleeing Japanese cruisers south of Rendova Island. Unable to see the Marine attack, Gibson and Buchanan began shadowing the Japanese ships from the cover of a cloud, and at 8:21 Gibson began transmitting contact reports, the first of which stated that there were nine enemy ships, including one possible converted carrier.[26] He added, the "weather conditions [are] favorable for dive bombing."[27] The final report identified the force as two battleships, two heavy cruisers, one carrier, and four destroyers. But some of the reports were garbled and the locations received were 30 miles off the mark.[28]

The idea of a Japanese carrier out there piqued the *Enterprise*'s interest. Bucky Lee was asked if he knew about the reported ships. He replied that he knew everything except their position, which the *Enterprise* provided. Skipper Captain Osborne B. Hardison then ordered Lee to attack that force, then return to Henderson Field because he would not have the fuel to return to his carrier. Unfortunately, no one had tuned the radios of Jimmy Flatley's escorting Wildcats to the search-attack frequency. Lee's Dauntlesses headed northwest alone.

Lieutenant Commander Flatley was in the dark and down two Wildcats. Ensigns Chip Reding and Hank Leder had spotted two "float Zeros" that were threatening the Dauntlesses and peeled off to intercept.* It was actually one Type 0 Reconnaissance Seaplane – a "Jake" – flown by veteran pilot Lieutenant (jg) Ikeya Nobuo of the *Chitose* operating out of Shortland. Ikeya flew into a cloud and escaped, while Reding and Leder could not find their way back to Flatley's group.†

In the meantime, Lieutenant Gibson decided he had done enough reporting and now it was time to do some attacking. He chose a "*Nachi*-class cruiser" that had dropped behind the others and was trailing an oil slick.[29] The cruiser, the already heavily damaged *Kinugasa*, was completing a large, slow loop to port, but had put out her fires, had corrected her list by counterflooding, and was now trying to get back on course and catch up with the rest of Admiral Mikawa's force. The destroyers *Makigumo* and *Kazigumo* were on hand to assist the stricken ship.[30]

At 9:15, Ensign Buchanan followed Lieutenant Gibson as he approached at 18,000 feet from astern and dove on the limping cruiser. In the face of heavy antiaircraft fire, they released their 500lb bombs at 2,000 feet and pulled up at around 1,000 feet. Gibson then maneuvered his SBD to present the most difficult target possible for the *Kinugasa*'s gunners, who, in desperation, anger, or both, fired the cruiser's 8-inch main battery at the fleeing Dauntlesses.[31] Gibson later explained, "When you're jinking out of an enemy fleet, it's the most exciting part of your day."[32]

Lieutenant Gibson's radio operator/gunner Aviation Radioman 2nd Class Cliff Schindele radioed another laconic message – three times, to make sure it was heard – "Dove on *Nachi*-class cruiser. Left ship burning. Continuing to CACTUS."[33] On their return Ensign Buchanan found out just how exciting his day had been; his fuselage had an

---

* Allied pilots generally referred to any single-engine monoplane with floats as a "float Zero." Technically, the only real "float Zero" was the Nakajima A6M2-N Navy Type 2 Interceptor-Fighter-Bomber – "Rufe" – that was literally a Zero with floats.

† The Type 0 Reconnaissance Seaplane should not be confused with the Type 0 Observation Seaplane.

8-inch hole, compliments of a dud from the *Kinugasa*'s main battery. Gibson reported that his bomb hit on the starboard side forward of the superstructure, while Buchanan said his struck on the port side amidships. In actuality, neither bomb hit, but both were unusually damaging near misses. Buchanan's bomb ruptured hull plating on the port-side that caused the flooding to restart and rapidly increased the list back to 7 degrees. Gibson's seems to have reignited the fire in the gasoline tanks. As if that were not enough, the concussions jammed the rudder.[34]

As Lieutenant Gibson and Ensign Buchanan had conducted their attack, another pair of *Enterprise* scouts, Ensigns Robert A. Hoogerwerf and Paul M. Halloran, had done exactly the same thing. Approaching from the southwest, at 10:23 they spotted the wakes of Admiral Mikawa's ships, who by this time were scattered. They found one cruiser, the *Kinugasa*, low in the water and blazing, with two destroyers in attendance. Ten miles west they found what they identified as a light cruiser and one destroyer, while 5 miles south they identified a heavy cruiser and one destroyer heading west.

Ensigns Hoogerwerf and Halloran circled the force twice at 17,500 feet to pick the best targets, then split up. Hoogerwerf dove on the undamaged heavy cruiser from astern, releasing his bomb at 3,000 feet. His bomb never caught up to his target, Admiral Nishimura's flagship *Suzuya*, exploding in the ship's wake about 15 feet astern and causing no damage. As Hoogerwerf was escaping to the south, he thought he saw an explosion on the light cruiser, which was covered in black smoke. He cheered the success of Halloran, but his efforts to raise Halloran on the radio met only with silence. Hoogerwerf headed back to the *Enterprise* alone, where he was scolded for not radioing in his sighting and attack.[35]

Neither Ensign Halloran nor his gunner Earl Gallagher was ever seen again. Dropped from astern, his bomb had missed his target, actually the heavy cruiser *Maya*. But as Halloran pulled up, his starboard wing clipped the *Maya*'s mainmast, pitching his Dauntless into the port side of the superstructure near the high-angle 4.7-inch mount. As the SBD crashed, it spewed flaming gasoline, setting off the ready ammunition, wrecking the 25mm mounts, two high-angle 4.7-inch mounts, and the port-side searchlight towers. The resulting fire was so serious that as it approached the torpedo mounts the cruiser was compelled to jettison 16 torpedoes. The fire was eventually brought under control and *Maya* made it back to Shortland, but 37 of her crew had been killed.[36]

Now came the turn of Lieutenant Commander Lee's strike from the *Enterprise*. Lee had been busy shedding aircraft from his formation. He had his dive bombers turn left – 300 degrees True – to try to get between Mikawa's fleeing ships and their base at Shortland, but most of Lieutenant Commander Flatley's escorting fighters, including that of Flatley himself, had missed the course change and kept going northwest. Then one of Lee's Dauntlesses and both of his remaining fighters had to turn around for lack of fuel. Naturally, just after the two Wildcats left, the Dauntlesses were attacked by two so-called "Float Zeros," probably Jake floatplanes launched from the cruisers. They were driven off, with one possibly shot down.

Some 10 miles southwest of Rendova, Lieutenant Commander Lee sighted the burning, badly listing *Kinugasa*, still trailing that oil slick. Uncomfortably accurate antiaircraft fire from her attending destroyers *Makigumo* and *Kazigumo* convinced Lee that the cruiser was not worth the effort to attack her. He wanted something bigger.

At around 11:15, he found it: an enemy force "of about six cruisers and four destroyers" 25 miles northwest of the *Kinugasa*, a cool 330 miles from the *Enterprise*, and clearly taxing their engines in their flight. Lieutenant Commander Lee divvied up the targets. Lieutenant Commander James A. Thomas was directed to take five Dauntlesses from Bombing 10 and attack the heavy cruisers; Lieutenant Stockton Birney Strong was to take five from Scouting 10 and attack the light cruisers; while Lee himself would take six more from Scouting 10 to look a little longer for that reported carrier before returning to these targets in hand.[37]

At 11:30 Lieutenant Commander Thomas led his group down on Admiral Mikawa's flagship and US Navy nemesis *Chokai*. In the face of heavy antiaircraft fire, everyone missed, but Ensigns Jefferson H. Carroum and Edwin J. Stevens achieved damaging near misses: Carroum 10 feet off the starboard bow, Stevens 30 feet off the starboard side. Mikawa's flagship suffered a few flooded compartments in the bow area and had to temporarily shut down Boilers 4 and 6, but she had no casualties and still made 29 knots toward Shortland and relative safety.[38]

Lieutenant Strong chose the light cruiser *Isuzu* as the target for his bombers, but they didn't have much more success than Lieutenant Commander Thomas had had. Two near misses ruptured hull plates and started flooding that flooded her No. 3 boiler room, reducing her speed to 15 knots. Destroyer *Asashio* was left behind to help her get to Shortland, but the damage was not overly serious and she made it without too much trouble.[39]

Lieutenant Commander Lee came back from his fruitless search for the carrier to attack the light cruiser *Tenryu* with no success whatsoever. All of the remaining Dauntlesses headed for Henderson Field. En route, Lee and Thomas saw the last of the *Kinugasa*, keel to the sky, bubbling under the waves.[40] The gravely damaged cruiser had capsized to port at 11:22, taking 51 of her crew with her. Destroyers *Makigumo* and *Kazigumo* rescued the survivors and headed toward Shortland.

Bucky Lee's escorts were having a very unpleasant morning. A frustrated Lieutenant Commander Flatley led his Wildcats back to the *Enterprise*. Ensigns Chip Reding and Hank Leder, who had split off to go after Lieutenant Ikeya's Jake, were so thoroughly lost they actually resorted to asking for directions. Coming across Admiral Lee's battleships *Washington* and *South Dakota* southwest of Guadalcanal, Leder flew low over the *Washington* and dropped a note: "Please point your ships in the direction of our carrier." Admiral Lee turned his massive strategic asset capital ships to the south, something that probably wouldn't have happened in most navies.[41] "Thank you" assumed, Reding and Leder headed south and reached the *Enterprise* around 12:30 pm.[42]

The day may have been half over, but the mission was not, thanks again to the work of 2nd Lieutenants Hronek and Baum. At 7:00 am, a half-hour after spotting Admiral

Mikawa's force, Hronek reported sighting one carrier, two cruisers, and one battleship, bearing 300 degrees True – northwest – in The Slot off New Georgia, course 120 degrees True – southeast – speed 15 knots.[43]

Hronek and Baum were not alone, however. At 7:15, a second pair of Marine scouts, 2nd Lieutenants Walter A. Eck and Andrew Jackson, reported two battleships, one light cruiser, and 11 destroyers very close to Hronek's contact. Then, at 7:30 a Royal Australian Air Force Lockheed Hudson flying out of New Guinea reported sighting a dozen transports off New Georgia.[44] A pair of Dauntlesses from the *Enterprise* piloted by Lieutenants (jg) Martin D. "Red" Carmody and William E. Johnson spotted the convoy at 8:49. Carmody radioed, "many enemy transports, two heavy cruisers, three light cruisers, and six destroyers" in roughly the same position as the other sighting. Sifting through this relatively shallow stream, General Woods and his intelligence analysts quickly concluded this was the invasion convoy. Finally, this was it.

Admiral Tanaka, the veteran commander of the 2nd Destroyer Flotilla, was ready, or at least as ready as he could be. He had never liked this operation – an opinion he was not shy about sharing – and still didn't, but he executed it to the best of his considerable ability. He was without his normal flagship *Jintsu* and so was aboard the destroyer *Hayashio*. With his flagship were the destroyers *Oyashio*, *Kagero*, *Umikaze*, *Kawakaze*, *Suzukaze*, *Takanami*, *Naganami*, *Makinami*, *Amigiri*, and *Mochizuki*.

With them were the 11 best, most modern transports the Imperial Japanese Army could requisition, carrying half of the 38th Nagoya Division under Major General Watanabe Suketomo.[45] The 11 transports were divided into two groups. The First Section consisted of the *Nagara Maru*, *Hirokawa Maru*, *Sado Maru*, *Canberra Maru*, and *Nako Maru*. The Second Section had the *Yamazuki Maru*, *Yamaura Maru*, *Kinugawa Maru*, *Shinanogawa Maru*, *Brisbane Maru*, and *Arizona Maru*. The First Section was to unload at Tassafaronga, the Second, with transports that were slower by a few knots, at Aruligo Point near Cape Esperance.[46]

The convoy had left Shortland at 6:30 pm on November 13 and deployed into one long column sailing directly down The Slot. Morale was high because, as *Hayashio* skipper Commander Yamamoto Tadashi explained it, the crews and troops "thought that the bombardment groups had succeeded in destroying [the American] planes the night before."[47] They never tell the lower ranks or the enlisted men anything.

Unfortunately, the Allied scouts never told anyone that the convoy had air cover. Lieutenant Miyano Zenjiro was leading six Zeros of the 204 Air Group flying out of Buin. At 9:08 am, Carmody and Johnson dove on one of the transports, but scored no hits.[48] Carmody strafed one of the destroyers before seeking cloud cover. On the way out, he noticed Zeros strafing nearby while his gunner John Liska saw a plane careen into the water. Neither Johnson nor his gunner Hugh P. Hughes, Jr., was ever seen again. The crashing plane was either Johnson's or the Zero flown by Petty Officer 2nd Class Hoshino Koichi that Johnson's Dauntless had shot down. Hoshino's body was never recovered.[49] All the surviving aircraft returned to their respective bases.

Admiral Tanaka's second combat air patrol of the day consisted of six Zeros from the *Hiyo* operating out of Buin under Lieutenant (jg) Iwaki Manzo. Iwaki's pilots entertained themselves by hounding a B-17 on a scouting mission from Espiritu Santo that had just appeared over the convoy. This Flying Fortress was the *Typhoon McGoon* piloted by Captain James E. Joham of the 98th Bombardment Squadron. It was six Zeros versus one Fortress, hardly a fair fight but for whom is unclear. Starting at around 9:30, the six Zeros kept making passes at the bomber and kept failing to shoot it down. For their part, Joham's gunners claimed five of the six fighters were shot down; given that Joham described the aircraft as "three with fixed landing gear" and three "ME109s" from "carriers," it is not surprising that his crew actually shot down none.[50]

But Captain Joham did get off contact reports. The first at 9:50 simply said, "two carriers, 23 other ships." There was that word again: "carriers." He later elaborated that there were two forces: one of one carrier, two heavy cruisers, two light cruisers, and seven destroyers bearing 300 degrees True, distance 150 miles from Lunga; the other of one carrier, one battleship, two heavy cruisers, two light cruisers, and five destroyers on the same bearing but 10 miles closer.[51] Then he broke off to make some repairs at Henderson Field before returning to Espiritu Santo.[52] His reports jolted the New Hebrides base, who at 10:18 sent up 16 B-17s in two flights to attack Admiral Tanaka's carriers.[53]

Admiral Tanaka didn't have any carriers but most likely wished he did. As Lieutenant Iwaki was sparring with Captain Joham, the sun could be seen glinting off a flight of aircraft in the distance to the south. Tanaka had his transports take evasive action. The destroyers were ordered to deploy into a screen and make smoke. But the American planes were not even targeting the convoy; they were Lieutenant Commander Lee's group heading for Admiral Mikawa's ships.[54] Tanaka's blood ran cold. The transports were reorganized into a formation of three columns. The five ships of the faster First Section were placed in the starboard column to the south. The *Yamazuki Maru*, *Yamaura Maru*, and *Kinugawa Maru* of the Second Section were placed in the center, while the *Shinanogawa Maru*, *Brisbane Maru*, and *Arizona Maru* were placed in the port column to the north. Tanaka's destroyers were positioned in front and on either side.[55] This was a formation for maximum defense. That defense was augmented by six Zeros under Lieutenant Iizuka Masao of Base Air Force's 253 Air Group from Rabaul, after a stop in Buka to refuel. Tanaka knew he would need all of it and more.

But that was all he had when at 11:00 he saw the sun glinting off yet more metallic birds in the sky. This time they weren't going after Admiral Mikawa; they were going after him. Admiral Tanaka ordered his destroyers to make a smoke screen to protect the transports.[56] It was a typical tactic of the Imperial Japanese Navy. And when it came to hiding a ship, a smoke screen was effective, unless, of course, the enemy could fly over it.

The 38 pilots in question were probably wondering what was the point of the smoke screen when they approached the convoy. Major Sailer led ten Dauntlesses, while Major Richard led nine, including two from the *Enterprise*, up to 12,000 feet. The carrier's Lieutenant Coffin led seven Torpedo 10 Avengers. Protecting this small aerial armada were eight Marine Wildcats under Captain Fraser and four Army Airacobras under 1st Lieutenant Martin E. Ryan, positioned 1,000 feet above the dive bombers.[57]

But having positioned themselves at high altitude, Lieutenant Iizuka and his Zeros were also ready. They dove on the American attackers. The Marines saw their opponents, and Captain Fraser had his Wildcats turn their noses up to face the Zeros head on. There were quick bursts of machine-gun and cannon fire as the two fighter formations passed through each other. Iizuka chose to have his Zeros continue down toward the bombers. He chose poorly. The Marines turned around and followed the Japanese down and sent bullets into them.[58]

Major Sailer selected the southern column, the First Section, as the target of his SBDs. Chased by Lieutenant Iizuka's Zeros most of the way down, Major Sailer and his men thought they had targeted two different transports, but actually they all targeted the *Sado Maru*.[59] After dropping their bombs, they all raced back for Henderson.

Leading six Dauntlesses, Major Richard targeted a transport "larger than the *Lurline*," the transport on which Richard and his men rode to the South Pacific; his group reported five hits complete with explosions. Fresh from battering the *Kinugasa*, the *Enterprise*'s Lieutenant Gibson led the other three in a dive on a transport in the center column, claiming two hits and one near miss. Actually, none of Richard's charges had gotten any hits. On the bombers' way out, Airacobras held back the vengeful Zeros, though the Japanese did hole 2nd Lieutenant Novak's fuselage.[60]

This attack was not well coordinated, but in the process of twisting and turning to avoid bombs, the transports had become scattered, just as Lieutenant Coffin's torpedo-carrying Avengers arrived. Selecting two transports in the southern column – again – Coffin's Grummans bore in, braving "moderate" antiaircraft fire, mostly from the destroyer *Takanami*, leading the First Section.[61] The destroyer would inaccurately claim one carrier attack plane shot down, though Coffin's tail caught some bullets and George Welles ended up with some shrapnel in his lap. A Zero tried to rattle Avenger pilot Lieutenant (jg) Dick Batten with a head-run, only to be "virtually disintegrated" by Captain Fraser.[62]

Lieutenant Coffin himself led four TBFs into plunking two torpedoes into the port side of what was apparently the *Nagara Maru*, while MacDonald Thompson led three more Avengers in plunking one into the starboard side of what was apparently the *Canberra Maru*.[63] After seeing the dive and torpedo bombers safely away – and against the orders of General Woods and Lieutenant Colonel Bauer – several Wildcats returned to strafe the transports, with the packed troops right out there in the open.[64] All of the strike aircraft returned to Guadalcanal.

After having been optimistic all morning, the Japanese received this attack as something of a gut punch. Admiral Tanaka's lookouts counted 41 planes – eight B-17s, eight torpedo bombers, eight fighters, and 17 carrier bombers.[65] Three of Lieutenant Iizuka's Zeros were shot down; a fourth had to land at Buka. That they managed to mistake single-engine aircraft for giant four-engine B-17s, of which there were none in this attack, suggests just how rattled the Japanese were. Tanaka had designated his oldest destroyers, the *Amagiri* and the *Mochizuki*, as the "Recovery Unit." The Recovery Unit had to recover 1,562 men from the *Nagara Maru* and *Canberra Maru*, both of which were doomed by the torpedoes and sank in short order. What exactly happened to the *Sado Maru*, the target of Major Sailer's Dauntlesses, is unclear, but she lost steering control, possibly from near misses near her stern. Naturally, she was the one carrying the man commanding the army reinforcements, General Watanabe, who could not have been entirely pleased with this turn of events. The *Suzukaze* took him off; then the *Amagiri* and the *Mochizuki* proceeded to escort the limping transport back to the safety of Shortland, where she was promptly sunk in an Allied air attack.[66]

The *Enterprise*'s pilots had been making major contributions this day, and the carrier herself was about to toss in more. After launching her airstrikes, Admiral Kinkaid had signaled Admiral Halsey, "Retiring south to fuel [destroyers] tomorrow. If there is an air group available Guadalcanal can return to pick it up but not advisable."[67] Kinkaid really wanted to keep America's last operational carrier in the Pacific out of harm's way.

But she was about to be dragged back in. Lieutenant (jg) Ikeya of the *Chitose*, who had evaded Ensigns Reding and Leder, had come upon the *Enterprise* with his Jake and made a contact report at 10:40 of one carrier, two battleships, and five cruisers and destroyers. *Magic* deciphered the message and Pearl Harbor sent out a message to this effect at 12:21.[68] Now Kinkaid's concern was even more pressing. Ikeya himself returned to Shortland at 5:30.[69]

Lieutenant Commander Flatley had returned with his six fighters around 11:30 am, quickly followed by Lieutenant Carmody's SBD, which had only 5 gallons of fuel left.[70] An hour later came Ensigns Reding and Leder in their Wildcats. After getting up at 4:00 am, enduring an attack and a 5½-hour flight, Gunner John Liska grabbed a sandwich and coffee while an exhausted Carmody went straight to bed.[71]

From where the *Enterprise* pilot was dragged almost immediately by Commander Crommelin, the air officer. Crommelin and Captain Hardison organized a new airstrike to hit the transports and land at Henderson.[72] Briefing the pilots, Crommelin was grim and perhaps a little melodramatic. If the transports landed their troops, "It will be the worst massacre for the United States," he said. "You get those transports!"[73] Flatley would take 12 Wildcats, Lieutenant (jg) Ralph H. Goddard would lead five Dauntlesses of Bombing 10, and Lieutenant (jg) William C. Edwards had three more Dauntlesses of Scouting 10. Turning aside Lieutenant Carmody's pleas for rest after attacking the convoy, Crommelin told him, "Oh, no, you're going to take them back."[74] *We're throwing everything at them, even the kitchen sink*, Carmody thought.[75] The aircraft began taking off at 1:05. Then the *Enterprise* sped south at 27 knots, finding at around 2:00 pm a convenient storm front in which to hide from prying Japanese eyes.[76]

Prying Japanese eyes were on Henderson Field as well. The returning pilots had had to deal with Japanese snipers taking shots at their cockpits as they landed. Lieutenant Commander Emura, the Japanese lookout on Mount Austen, was stunned at how the number of aircraft at the base complex had swelled. That afternoon he reported more than 40 fighters, 40 carrier bombers, and three large planes had landed at Henderson.[77]

The airbase was in fact in a state of barely organized chaos. "[The] big shots were running around, pulling their hair and yelling orders," said 2nd Lieutenant Hap Simpson. "We would go up and drop a bomb on them, then come back and get another one, and go back again."[78] Birney Strong called it "a sort of merry-go-round." "[T]ake off, fly out a hundred miles, drop bombs, return to Henderson Field, gas, rearm, fly out again, and attack again."[79]

Understandably, given the urgency and the speed with which the ground crew were forced to work, virtually every airstrike was a mixture of Navy, Marine, and Army aircraft. Lieutenant Commander Lee led three Dauntlesses from Scouting 10 and two from Marine Scout Bombing 132 against the convoy. Finding the transports northwest of the Russells, they claimed two hits on two different transports and, encountering no air opposition, headed back to Henderson.[80]

There was more. Scouting 10 executive officer Lieutenant Bill Martin led nine Scouting 10 Dauntlesses escorted by Lieutenant Sutherland with six Wildcats from Fighting 10 and one each from Marine Fighter Squadrons 112 and 122. After making yet another fruitless search for the mythical aircraft carrier, Martin returned to dive on the convoy from 16,000 feet, claiming four hits on two targets, then returned. Again there was no aerial opposition.[81]

"Mythical aircraft carrier" might be too strong a term. There was indeed an aircraft carrier, just not where anyone had reported it to be. Providing long-range fighter cover is never easy; it tends to lose effectiveness the further one gets from the airbase. Admiral Tanaka had to rely on Base Air Force fighters coming all the way from Rabaul. Theoretically, there was a closer airbase: Admiral Kakuta's carrier *Junyo*, who had tried to provide a fighter defense to the *Hiei* the day before. As such, she could have provided fighters to help defend the helpless convoy, and much more easily than Lakunai, Vunakanau or Buin. But she had things to do.

At 9:00 am this November 14, the *Junyo* launched three Vals under Lieutenant (jg) Kato Shunko, escorted by nine Zeros under Warrant Officer Kitihara Saburo. Their job was to scout Tulagi for Admiral Kondo and see if the two ships disabled in the night battle of November 13 were still there. At 10:40, the formation reached Tulagi and found that, indeed, those two immobilized ships were still there, one of which they correctly identified as a *Portland*-class heavy cruiser. With that pressing question answered, Kato and Kitihara led their charges back to the *Junyo*.[82] After that single mission, exhausting though it may have been, the carrier did not perform another for the rest of the day. Naturally, the airmen of Henderson Field and the *Enterprise*, as well as the crews of the *Portland* and *Aaron Ward*, were most grateful.

Meanwhile, Admiral Tanaka was paying the price. The *Nagara Maru* and the *Canberra Maru* were sunk; the *Sado Maru* headed back to Shortland. Now, with no air cover, the *Brisbane Maru* took a 1,000lb bomb hit that started an inferno. Tanaka assigned the destroyer *Kawakaze* as another "Recovery Unit" to stay with her. The destroyer ended up recovering 550 survivors when the blazing transport was abandoned.[83] Tanaka reorganized his rapidly diminishing convoy around seven transports and eight destroyers and grimly continued on.

Now Lieutenant Suganami Masaji of Base Air Force's 252 Air Group and a veteran of both Pearl Harbor and Midway as a pilot on the *Soryu* led six Zeros from Vunakanau that now arrived as air cover. But they could not stop a Scouting 10 Dauntless piloted by Ensign Charles B. "Skinhead" Irvine. Delayed from accompanying the earlier strikes by engine trouble, he took off at 2:55 and managed to get a direct hit, returning safely to Henderson.[84]

Having missed Ensign Irvine, Lieutenant Suganami and his fliers went after a flight of seven B-17s under Major Allan Sewart, commander of the 26th Bombardment Squadron. They were the first part of the two-part strike sent out to look for the mythical aircraft carriers, but Admiral Fitch had changed their target midflight to the convoy. Suganami's Zeros could not intercept the Flying Fortresses before they dropped their 500lb bombs, getting one hit. Nor could they shoot any down, though they claimed four.[85]

Meanwhile, Warrant Officer Tsunoda Kazuo had arrived with eight Zeros of the 582 Air Group. Four immediately went off on a fruitless chase of Major Sewart's B-17s. Tsunoda and the other three watched a confusing dogfight below between Lieutenant Suganami's Zeros and Lieutenant Sutherland's eight Wildcats in which neither side suffered any loss. Low on fuel, Suganami and his pilots headed back to Vunakanau. But as soon as they were organized for the long flight back, Suganami ordered his pilots, much to their dismay, to continue on while he turned around to continue patrolling over the convoy.[86]

As Lieutenant Suganami headed back to the transports, the second strike from the *Enterprise* arrived, having circled round to approach the convoy from astern. Lieutenant Commander Flatley assigned targets. Lieutenant Goddard's five Dauntlesses dove on the remnants of the First Section and thought they had gotten two hits; in reality, they'd gotten none. Lieutenant Edwards' three Dauntlesses fought their way through four of Tsunoda's Zeros to get to the convoy's left flank, where the Second Section was located. Lieutenant Carmody and Lieutenant (jg) Robert F. Edmondson each selected a different transport for his 1,000lb bomb and each got a hit.[87] Pulling out of his dive, Edwards roared over the open transports on a strafing run. "We were real close," Edwards' gunner Wayne "Slim" Colley later said. "I could see the troops on deck, just loaded." They lashed the decks with their machine guns until it was "a bloody damn mess."[88]

Warrant Officer Tsunoda's Zeros were a problem, but not a major one. Carmody and Edmondson had managed to hold them off with their tail gunners. Lieutenant Commander Flatley's fighters did not have much of a problem, either. Gaining altitude to intercept, Tsunoda himself, thinking the Grumman Wildcat fighters carried bombs that he wanted to stop from falling on his ships, chose as his target the fighter at the tail end of the group, flown by Ensign Lynn Slagle. He chose poorly. Slagle was not carrying any bombs, nor were any of the other Wildcats. Worse, Slagle had already lined up Tsunoda in a head-on shot and tore through the Zero's wings. Tsunoda turned away, his fighter smoking, his controls unresponsive. But Tsunoda was filled with "indescribable joy" as he had successfully kept Slagle from dropping the bomb he didn't have.[89] For that victory of priceless value, Tsunoda ended up ditching near the retreating *Sado Maru* and was fished out of the water by the destroyer *Amagiri* which was already packed with survivors.

The targets of Lieutenant Edwards' Dauntlesses were the *Shinanogawa Maru* leading the column and the *Arizona Maru* bringing up the rear. The hits were devastating, leaving both dead in the water and afire. Both transports were abandoned. Admiral Tanaka again augmented his "Recovery Unit," with the destroyer *Naganami* recovering 570 from the *Shinanogawa Maru* and the *Makinami* rescuing 1,020 from the *Arizona Maru*.[90]

Admiral Tanaka was soon going to need a Recovery Unit for himself as this mission was rapidly becoming a nightmare firmly imprinted in his memory:

[T]he general impression is indelible in my mind of bombs wobbling down from high-flying B-17s, of carrier bombers roaring toward targets as though to plunge full into the water, releasing bombs and pulling out barely in time; each miss sending up towering columns of mist and spray; every hit raising clouds of smoke and fire as transports burst into flame and took the sickening list that spells their doom. Attackers departed, smoke screens lifted and revealed the tragic scene of men jumping overboard from burning, sinking ships.[91]

He was not the only one. Lieutenant Commander Flatley's fighters watched what one of the fighter pilots called the "terrible picture of destruction" wrought by Carmody and Edmondson.[92] Then the Wildcats, in pairs, began strafing runs on the open ships. The conditions for the Imperial Japanese Army troops on the transports – "crowded with soldiers," was how one report described them – seems to have been highly unpleasant. Packed in tightly, the soldiers were helpless to duck or dive away from the bombs and strafing. It was so bad that the American attackers even expressed sympathy. Some vomited at the sight and the thought of what war had forced them to do to these men. Hap Simpson wrote, "We sank many of their ships that day, and it certainly looked good to see them sinking and burning. However, not too good, because we would get down real low on our dive, and we could actually see them, the men on the troop ships. They must have packed them on these ships ..."[93] Even accounting for the many atrocities already committed by the Imperial Japanese Army, of which the American pilots were well aware, for an instant the Americans could see their adversaries as human beings, helpless in inhuman conditions.

But the inhuman conditions were not going to end for either side any time soon. Now came eight B-17s under Major Donald Ridings, commander of the 72nd Bombardment Squadron, as the second part of that strike sent out from Espiritu Santo. Bombing the convoy from the unusually high altitude of 20,000 feet, they could only get a few near misses with their 500lb bombs. An interception attempt by the remaining Zeros came to nothing. All the Flying Fortresses returned to Espiritu Santo to face the rage of Admiral Halsey for bombing from such a high altitude, but it was Army Air Force doctrine, even if it clearly didn't work.[94] All of the aircraft from the *Enterprise* strike landed at Henderson Field. Tsunoda's fighters lost two of their number, with both pilots rescued.[95]

It was now 3:00 pm, and Admiral Nimitz broadcast a message from Pearl Harbor: "Looks like all out attempt now underway to recapture Guadalcanal regardless losses." The men of Henderson Field were shocked. Thirty minutes later, another strike of seven Bombing 10 SBDs under Bombing 10 skipper Lieutenant Commander Thomas took off. The mission went awry even before the start. Thomas got into an argument with Ensign Leonard Robinson. Thomas wanted to leave immediately so they could dive out of the sun, while Robinson wanted to wait for fighter cover. They took off, but Thomas seems to have been promised fighter cover, and he slowed their ascent to altitude. It may have been to let the fighter catch up with the strike, but Lieutenant Gibson later explained, "This was a trait that [Thomas] had shown since I joined the squadron." It hampered performance, Gibson said, because "Barely flying above stalling speed reduces the controls to a mushy feeling[.]"[96]

The Bombing 10 Dauntlesses sighted Admiral Tanaka's transports around 4:00 pm some 10 miles northeast of the Russell Islands. By this time, Tanaka had been informed of American ships to the southwest, so he had tried to turn the ambulatory ships to the northeast, heading toward Santa Ysabel. Lieutenant Commander Thomas reported an estimated ten transports and three destroyers were sighted. Of those transports, two were burning to the northwest, one or two were headed west, three or four were dead in the water, and the remainder were still headed toward Guadalcanal.

But Lieutenant Commander Thomas does not seem to have had the complete confidence of his air group. Ensign Robinson, knowing they didn't have fighter cover, wanted to attack right away. Lieutenant Gibson believed they were "way below an optimum altitude" for commencing a dive-bombing attack. So did Lieutenant Vivian Welch, who was commanding a section of four Dauntlesses, and he led his charges to 12,000 feet. Thomas still wanted to dive out of the sun and led Gibson and Ensign Stevens around to try to dive from the southwest. It was a mess.

Their failed efforts were exploited by an effective air defense by six Zeros from the *Hiyo* operating out of Buin under the command of respected veteran Lieutenant Commander Kaneko Tadashi. Tadashi himself led wingman Chief Petty Officer Tanaka Jiro in attacking Lieutenant Commander Thomas' section. After accurate gunfire by Thomas' gunner Aviation Chief Radioman Gordon C. "Skip" Gardner, Kaneko's Zero "burst into flames, went over on its back, and fell into the sea."[97]

Tanaka Jiro then went after Lieutenant Gibson and got 27 shells into the Dauntless before Cliff Schindele hit the Zero. Tanaka flew alongside Gibson for a few minutes, barely a yard off his wing. "The two of us flew straight ahead while we looked eyeball to eyeball for more than a minute." He waved his wings in a sign of respect for Gibson's flying ability, which Gibson returned with a wave. Then Tanaka flew off, eventually ditching.

Gibson nursed his Dauntless back to Henderson, where the mechanics "just looked at it and shoved it over into the graveyard ditch. It wasn't worth repairing."[98]

Tanaka's would not be the only salute of the day. Warrant Officer Mori Mitsugu led the other four Zeros of this combat air patrol against Lieutenant Welch's bombers, with, apparently, some help from the 252's Lieutenant Suganami Masaji, who had turned around to protect the transports in what appears to have been a personal suicide mission. Mori didn't last long. He came head on at Ensign Robinson, catching the Dauntless in a crossfire with Petty Officer 2nd Class Motegi Shigeo behind him. Robinson sent Mori into the sea with a blast from his cowl guns, but Motegi sent a 20mm shell into Robinson's engine, setting it afire. Robinson put the fire out and restarted his engine, but Motegi hung onto him like a leech, blasting away no matter what evasive moves Robinson tried. Eventually, Motegi used up all his 20mm ammunition and 600 rounds of 7.7mm bullets, but the Dauntless still held on. Motegi flew his Zero – "It was a beautiful plane, sort of a chartreuse color with a big red sun on the side" – on Robinson's starboard side. Then he showed off to the American aircrew with some barrel rolls and flying upside down before rocking his wings in a salute and heading back to the convoy. "He gave us quite a show," said Robinson, who returned to Henderson with 68 holes in his Dauntless.[99]

That was about the only good news from this mission. The Dauntlesses of Lieutenant Welch, Lieutenant (jg) Donald Wakeham, and Ensign Carroum had gotten caught in a crossfire of three Zeros, one of which was apparently the 252's Lieutenant Suganami. No one saw what happened to Wakeham's Dauntless. The last time Welch was seen he had just dropped his bomb on his target. Carroum was forced to ditch by a burst of antiaircraft fire that killed his engine. Carroum managed to get to one of the Russell Islands but his gunner Aviation Radioman 3rd Class Robert C. Hynson, Jr., did not survive.[100]

It was a costly mission – three SBDs shot down, two, it is believed, by Lieutenant Suganami, and five men dead – for no bomb hits.[101] Ensign Robinson had been right about waiting for that fighter escort. The Japanese lost three Zeros and one very respected pilot.

In the interim, Henderson Field was assembling the largest airstrike it could muster. One Navy Dauntless joined 16 Marine SBDs, all under the command of Major Joe Sailer, three *Enterprise* Avengers armed with bombs led by Lieutenant Coffin, and 14 Marine Wildcat fighters under Major Fontana and Captain Foss. At the last minute, Lieutenant Colonel Bauer, the very popular head of fighters at Henderson Field, decided to join the strike, telling Foss, "I'm not going to let you fellows have all the fun."[102]

The strike took off from Henderson Field under shelling from Japanese artillery; the Imperial Japanese Navy had begged the army to bombard the airfield to try to suppress it, but the artillery was critically short of shells and was little more than an irritant. Flying in separate groups, the airstrike found the convoy "in disarray," reflecting the rays of the setting sun. Also reflecting the rays of the setting sun: six Zeros of the 204 Air Group under the respected veteran pilot Lieutenant Commander Kofukuda Mitsugi that had just arrived from Buin at 5:15. The Zeros were joined in short order by eight Mitsubishi F1M "Pete" floatplanes – two from the *Kunikawa Maru*, two orphans from the *Hiei*, three from the *Sanyo Maru*, and one from the *Sanuki Maru* – operating out of Rekata.[103]

The result was, as Major Fontana said it, "one mass dogfight," part of an engagement that again reached heights of savagery. Staff Sergeant Thomas C. Hurst aimed head-on for a Pete from the *Sanyo Maru*, and got the floatplane's engine smoking, only to see the floatplane turn up in what Hurst called a "suicide maneuver" and ram the Wildcat, knocking a wing off. Hurst was forced to bail out some 10 miles north of the Russell Islands, where he eventually hooked up with Jeff Carroum and made it back after several weeks.

The Zeros' real targets were the Dauntless dive bombers, but the SBDs' tail gunners kept them at bay, possibly even shooting down one. They managed to strike the *Nako Maru* with multiple bombs, at least one of which was dropped by Master Technical Sergeant Don Thornbury. The transport became an unnavigable inferno wracked by explosions of ammunition. Admiral Tanaka designated the destroyer *Suzukaze* as yet another part of the oft-used Recovery Unit, taking off 1,100 survivors before abandoning the transport.[104]

Lieutenant Coffin's Avengers made a level bombing run from 6,000 feet but apparently achieved no hits, though Aviation Mechanic 3rd Class Clarence T. Wall, turret gunner for Lieutenant (jg) Jerry Rapp, did manage to take down one Zero.[105]

Having kept the Zeros at bay, Lieutenant Colonel Bauer, Captain Foss, and 2nd Lieutenant Thomas W. Furlow circled at the edge of the convoy looking for Dauntlesses in trouble. Once the bombers were away, they decided to use their machine guns to lash the *Shinanogawa Maru* and *Arizona Maru*, whose army passengers were still streaming over the sides to be picked up by the *Nakinami* and *Makinami*. Then they assembled for the trip back, only to realize they had picked up two Zeros on their tail.

Bauer turned around and quickly shot down the leader while Foss and Furlow unsuccessfully chased the wingman. When they came back, Foss found Bauer in the water. He was shot down apparently as a last act of vengeance by Lieutenant Suganami, who was never seen again. Foss circled low to drop a life raft, but it would not release. Bauer jumped out of the water and pointed toward the southeast. "Go home!" was his message. Foss tried to alert Henderson Field but could not get through.[106] They raced back, hoping to go out again in a floatplane while it was still light, but they were delayed and did not reach the site until well after dark.

Joe Bauer was never seen again. To quote Guadalcanal historian Eric Hammel, "It is a testimony to Joe Bauer's towering achievements as a man and a leader that no fighter pilot based at Cactus that week thought the destruction of six Japanese transports was worth the loss of the Coach."[107]

Six transports were sunk or abandoned. On the last strike, two Wildcats were shot down. Three Petes went down – one from the *Hiei* missing, one from the *Sanyo Maru* lost in the collision with Hurst, and a second from the *Sanyo Maru* set afire and forced to ditch, its crew rescued by the destroyer *Kagero*. Four Zeros were shot down; the remainder returned to Buin.[108]

One transport headed back barely navigable. Of the 11 transports that originally set out only four remained on course to Guadalcanal and these were likely damaged by bombs and strafing. Some 5,000 troops had been aboard the ships sunk or abandoned. Most were rescued, but nothing could be done about the supplies.

Admiral Tanaka gave his assessment of his mission: "[P]rospects looked poor for the operation."[109]

The old adage holds that no battle plan survives contact with the enemy. A corollary holds that sometimes the plan doesn't even last that long. Admiral Halsey had experienced the corollary the hard way with Admiral Lee's battleships.

But the adage had a different application when it came to the Imperial Japanese Navy. The battle plan did not survive contact with the enemy, true. But the plan wasn't dead, either. Unwilling, perhaps unable, to make major adjustments, throughout the course of the war the Japanese would push a battle plan forward even after it had fallen apart completely. Decaying, rotting, bits and pieces falling off here and there as it continued mindlessly shuffling forward toward a singular goal that became increasingly vague as it slipped further and further out of reach.

In the aftermath of this catastrophic day for Admiral Tanaka, during which six of his 11 transports had been sunk and a seventh sent limping back to Shortland, it's hard to understand why the Japanese did not abort the operation to reinforce Guadalcanal. But Admiral Yamamoto specifically ordered Tanaka to continue.[110] If the Imperial Japanese Navy was not exactly nimble when it came to adjusting to changing conditions, no one was less nimble than Kondo Nobutake.

Admiral Kondo's objective had always been to get the transports to Guadalcanal and he still planned to get them there, whatever transports were left. Once again, Kondo planned to suppress Henderson Field with a naval bombardment, which had not exactly been the Combined Fleet's finest moment in the last 48 hours. Admiral Abe had not bombarded it at all and had lost a battleship in not doing so, and while Admiral Mikawa had actually tried to bombard it, he had missed it completely.

To that end, Admiral Kondo formed what would be creatively called "The Emergency Bombardment Unit."* It is worth pointing out that even at this critical junction there was a reluctance on the part of senior commanders to commit their main battle line units, such as the *Yamato*s and *Nagato*s, as these were still being preserved for that "decisive battle" for the Pacific and they remained convinced that Guadalcanal was not it.

---

* Whether it was a unit for emergency bombardments or an emergency unit for bombardments was never made clear.

This was traditional Japanese naval thinking and Admiral Kondo was a very traditional Japanese naval officer. He had at his disposal three battleships – the *Kirishima* remaining from the aborted November 13 bombardment, and her remaining sister ships *Kongo* and *Haruna* from the not-aborted October 15 bombardment. Kondo could have taken all three battleships to perform a bombardment to end all bombardments on Henderson Field. Kondo could even have taken all three battleships to have the *Kirishima* bombard Henderson Field while the other two protected her from any and all opposition. But that was just not the Japanese way. The Japanese way was division, deception, and unexpected forces popping up in odd places to hopefully surprise the enemy. As such, Kondo planned instead to have the *Kirishima* bombard Henderson Field while the *Kongo* and *Haruna* would sit around doing nothing. Indeed, sit around doing nothing just far enough away from the *Kirishima* so that if things got hairy for the *Kirishima*, the *Kongo* and *Haruna* could speed down and arrive just after the nick of time, too late to do any good. The Imperial Japanese Navy called it "providing distant cover," usually emphasizing the "distant" part of that equation. Certainly the US Navy would be surprised to unexpectedly come across two Japanese battleships sitting around doing nothing. The logic was impeccable, and was largely responsible for the straits in which the Japanese found themselves this day.

So while the *Kongo* and *Haruna* would stay behind, refueling a few destroyers and basically acting as tankers with turrets, the "Emergency Bombardment Unit" would also have Admiral Kondo's flagship heavy cruiser *Atago* and her sister ship *Takao* alongside the *Kirishima*. Escorting them would be Admiral Kimura's 10th Destroyer Flotilla with flagship light cruiser *Nagara*, and destroyers *Ikazuchi* and *Samidare* – all survivors of the aborted bombardment two nights earlier. Joining them in this screen would be Rear Admiral Hashimoto Shintaro's 3rd Destroyer Flotilla with the flagship light cruiser *Sendai* and destroyers *Ayanami*, *Uranami*, and *Shikinami*; and Admiral Takama's 4th Destroyer Flotilla, still a light cruiser short after the sinking of the *Yura*, with flagship destroyer *Asagumo* and large antiaircraft destroyer *Teruzuki* – both survivors of the night battle 48 hours earlier – and destroyers *Shirayuki* and *Hatsuyuki*.

Admiral Kondo had them start heading down toward Ironbottom Sound at 5:30 am but progress slowed to a crawl early on while refueling took place.[111] When that was completed around 10:00 am, Kondo signaled, "Follow me," and the Emergency Bombardment Force set off again, centered on a column of *Atago* followed by *Takao* and then *Kirishima*.[112]

It wasn't until late afternoon that things started going awry. At 2:55 pm, a scout plane reported two cruisers and four destroyers 100 miles south of Guadalcanal. At 4:29 pm, when the force was east of Santa Ysabel, Admiral Kondo's flagship *Atago* had to dodge three torpedoes, one of which had passed under the destroyer *Asagumo*, another of which struck the *Kirishima* but failed to explode. They came compliments of Lieutenant Commander Lawson P. "Red" Ramage and his submarine *Trout*, who had been stalking Kondo's group most of the day. Over the past 36 hours the *Trout* had made a real nuisance of herself to the admiral's forces. She reported the contact over the radio in plain language.[113] So now Kondo knew he had been sighted and had better prepare for a fight.

Sightings came in for the rest of the day and into the evening. At 5:35 pm, Admiral Kondo signaled his ships, "Tonight we face a high probability to encounter a number of enemy cruisers and destroyers in the vicinity of Savo Island; in that case the bombardment will be temporarily suspended until the enemy surface force has been destroyed. The primary objective will be realized thereafter."[114] Kondo then stressed that each skipper should be flexible and ready to deal with any contingency without any preconceived notions.[115] These orders prompted an argument on board the *Kirishima*, slated to be the star of this particular show as the *Hiei* had been two nights before. In the event that the incendiary ammunition currently in the main guns had to be changed to armor-piercing ammunition, Captain Iwabuchi did not want another chaotic changeover which had been the previous experience. He and his gunnery officer decided to simply fire off the Type 3s already in the hoists, as the *Hiei* had done. It had worked so well for her, after all, and could be done in around three to five minutes.[116]

At 6:25 pm a shadowing seaplane reported a force headed for the convoy. Combined Fleet ordered Admiral Tanaka to exercise caution, but he was already positioning the remnants of the convoy to keep Admiral Kondo between it and the advancing force. For his part, Kondo reassured Tanaka that his plan was to clear Ironbottom Sound of enemy ships and bombard the airfield.

But what enemy ships? There was a bewildering number of search reports. Admiral Tanaka had been told of a force of four enemy cruisers and four destroyers east of Guadalcanal.[117] At 7:30 pm the *Kirishima*'s floatplane reported "two unidentified cruisers and four destroyers sighted 50 miles ahead of your force."[118] At 8:45 pm another search plane reported two enemy cruisers and four destroyers headed north at 25 knots 16 miles west-southwest of Cape Esperance.[119] At 9:30 pm came yet another report, this time from the R-Area Air Force, reporting two cruisers and four destroyers 50 miles west of Kondo. This was apparently Tanaka's convoy.[120] As it was, Admiral Kondo was aware of three enemy forces in the area. One consisted of a carrier, two battleships, a cruiser, and four destroyers; this was Admiral Kinkaid's Task Force 16. A second consisted of four cruisers and four destroyers; this was the (inaccurately reported) remnant of the late Admiral Callaghan's retreating cruiser force, heading away from Guadalcanal. A third, headed toward Guadalcanal, consisted of two cruisers and four to eight destroyers.[121] It was this third force that concerned Kondo. It was just a few cruisers and destroyers, however – nothing his escorts could not handle.

Admiral Tanaka breathed a sigh of relief when he spotted the "Emergency Bombardment Unit" finishing its transit of Indispensable Strait and now positioning itself between the rump of his convoy and any possible surface opposition. But six ships of that Emergency Bombardment Unit – destroyers *Asagumo*, *Teruzuki*, *Ikazuchi*, and *Samidare*; Admiral Kimura's light cruiser *Nagara*; and, especially, the battleship *Kirishima* – now entering the area of their savage combat two nights earlier, may have been not so much relieved as haunted:

> [O]n six of his (Admiral Kondo's) ships, the topside crews remember vividly speeding north from Savo 36 hours before, leaving *Hiei* blazing like a small volcano. The loss of a battleship had to shake even the nonneurotic crews as they go[t] back to the scene.[122]

Even the ships themselves noticed. Magnetic compasses began spinning uncontrollably as they began passing over the graves of so many ships, especially the *Furutaka*, the *Fubuki*, the *Akatsuki*, the *Yudachi*, the *Hiei*. Were they trying to send a warning from the depths?

> Remember me as you pass by
> As you are so once was I
> As I am now so you shall be
> Prepare yourself to follow me.*

The compasses were also spinning on the American ships, as if the prior victims like *Astoria*, *Quincy*, *Vincennes*, *Blue*, *Duncan*, *Atlanta*, *Cushing*, *Laffey*, *Barton*, and *Monssen* were speaking to them from the depths as well. Was it a warning, too? Or were they cheering?

So far on this day the Americans had reason to cheer. As Admiral Lee's force approached The Slot from the southwest, the men were tense, nervous, and scared – like anyone about to enter combat is – but there was reason to be optimistic. The flagship received reports of "gunfire over the horizon north and northwest of the Russell Islands. Glows such as of a ship afire, glows flaring up such as by explosion."[123] It was two of Admiral Tanaka's transports damaged in the afternoon attacks, still burning – a good start, but the day wasn't over yet. The American task force still had to make its planned counterclockwise loop around Savo to look for the Japanese. Captain Glenn B. Davis of the *Washington*, like many a good commander, tried to both prepare and reassure his crew.

> This is the captain speaking. We are going into an action area. We have no great certainty what forces we will encounter. We might be ambushed. A disaster of some sort may come upon us. But whatever it is we are going into, I hope to bring you all back alive. Good luck to all of us.[124]

In a campaign that had been an exercise in improvisation from the start, this mission was just one more. Lee's force was simply the best the Americans could slap together on short notice. The four destroyers selected – *Walke*, *Benham*, *Preston*, and *Gwin* – had

---

* Epitaph of Edward, the Black Prince (1330–76), eldest son of King Edward III of England. The *Kongo* class had originally been designed in England and *Kongo* had in fact been built there.

been chosen simply because, out of all the destroyers with the *Enterprise*, they had the most fuel. They were from four separate squadrons, four separate classes, and none of them had ever worked together. The skipper of the *Walke*, Commander Thomas Fraser, was placed in command of all four destroyers simply because he outranked the other skippers; but with his own ship to command, it was anticipated that he would not be able to exercise it much. For the part of the battleships, who had also never worked together, the *Washington* had only fired her main guns at night once, in January 1942; the *South Dakota* had never fired her main guns at night, though she had fired them three times overall.*

The six ships shifted into a column formation, the four destroyers *Walke*, *Benham*, *Preston*, and *Gwin*, in that order, 500 yards separating each of them, some 3 miles ahead of the *Washington* and *South Dakota*, separated by a little more than a mile, as they approached Savo Island from the southwest.[125] Aside from their fuel reserves and having four 5-inch guns each, these four destroyers had little to recommend them operating as a group. The *Gwin* was the most modern, with good fire-direction radar and the most modern rapid-firing guns. Naturally, she was placed in the rear of the destroyers and was assigned to fire starshells for the other ships.[126] Then again, the starshells were needed because the *Benham* had no radar at all, the *Preston* had been asked to deactivate her SC radar to prevent alleged interference with the battleships' radars, and both had to rely on optics for a night battle. Additionally, the *Benham* had a brand new skipper who had only assumed command when the ship left Nouméa.[127]

But the battleships were state-of-the-art by any standard in any navy, though not without their own issues. Both the *Washington* and *South Dakota* carried nine 16-inch guns in three triple turrets, though two guns in the *South Dakota*'s Turret 2 had been damaged by shrapnel from that bomb hit on top of Turret 1 in the Santa Cruz action and, after a fashion, their use was determined to be unsafe.[128] *Washington* had 20 5-inch dual-purpose guns in ten dual mounts, five to a side; the *South Dakota* had 16 such guns in eight dual mounts, four to a side. Both ships had the most modern radars – FC fire-control, FD fire-direction, and SG surface search, though the *Washington*'s SG radar was mounted on the front of her tower mast, which created a problem in that the mast blocked the radar's sweep to the rear, leaving a 60-degree blind spot behind the battleship. Both had well-respected skippers – Captain Davis of the *Washington* and Captain Gatch of the *South Dakota*, although the same bomb that had disabled the two guns in the *South Dakota*'s Turret 2 had also badly wounded Gatch, and he was going into this battle heavily bandaged, with his neck immobilized and his arm in a sling – over his head.[129] Most importantly, in Admiral Lee, they had perhaps the most respected and experienced radar theoretician in the US Navy. While this was his first flag command, Lee knew how the various radars worked better than their operators did.

---

* The first time all nine of the *South Dakota*'s 16-inch guns were fired at the same time as part of a test, the wave of pressure from the blast tore the pants off her skipper Captain Gatch. Hornfischer, *Neptune's Inferno*, 6458.

So hastily assembled had this force been that Admiral Lee had not been given a radio call sign. After the battleships and their escorts had completed their sweep of the west side of Savo Island and began looping toward the southeast, cutting speed to 17 knots because of unfamiliarity with these restricted waters, Lee asked Guadalcanal for the latest information, but without that call sign, he had to refer to himself by his surname.[130] That did not impress the radio operators on Guadalcanal, who tersely replied, "We do not recognize you." Their response compelled Lee to draw on his days at the Naval Academy, where, as a student Marine, General Vandegrift had known him by his nickname "Ching," given as a result of his well-known interest in China and the Far East. "CACTUS, this is Lee. Tell your boss 'Ching' Lee is here and wants the latest information."

As he was waiting for a response, Admiral Lee heard talk over the voice radio from three PT boats patrolling northeast of Savo Island. "There go two big ones, but I don't know whose they are!" said one of the PT boat skippers, following it with a report on the battleship's position, course, speed, and distance in a code Lee did not have. Understanding that the PT philosophy of "Shoot first and maybe ask questions later at the court martial" made this a dangerous situation, he had his flag secretary Lieutenant Commander Richard Zern radio the boats, "This is Lee." That did not impress the PTs. "Who's Lee?" At least they did ask a question, which the admiral himself answered on the radio. "Tell your boss this is 'Ching' Lee." At 10:30 he shot another message off to Guadalcanal, "Refer your big boss about 'Ching' Lee. Chinese, catchee? Call off your boys!" The skipper of one of the PT boats stated, "Your identity established. We are not after you."[131] About ten minutes later, Guadalcanal reported, "The boss has no additional information."[132] This was disappointing but hardly surprising. A little later, Lee received a warning based on radio intelligence to expect an escorted convoy to arrive off Savo between 12:30 and 2:30 am.[133]

While Admiral Lee was trying to keep his American ships from being torpedoed by American boats, Admiral Kondo implemented the battle plan he had signaled to his ships that afternoon. With his 14 ships, he could have entered Ironbottom Sound and kept any opposition at bay while *Kirishima* blasted Henderson Field. But Kondo was a traditional Japanese admiral who would do it the traditional Japanese way. He divided his 14 ships three ways, which soon became four ways. Kondo retained direct control of the "Bombardment Unit," which consisted of his flagship heavy cruiser *Atago*, her sister *Takao*, and the battleship *Kirishima*, attended by Admiral Takama's destroyers *Asagumo* and *Teruzuki*, which at the present time were in line behind the *Kirishima*. Admiral Hashimoto would take his 3rd Destroyer Flotilla with the flagship light cruiser *Sendai* and destroyers *Ayanami*, *Uranami*, and *Shikinami* and form a so-called "Sweeping Unit" to go clockwise to the east around Savo Island. Admiral Kimura would take his 10th Destroyer Flotilla with the flagship light cruiser *Nagara*; destroyers *Ikazuchi* and *Samidare*; and destroyers *Shirayuki* and *Hatsuyuki* whom Takama had ordered to join up, to form the "Screening Unit," and would follow the Sweeping Unit to deal with any enemy ships it had revealed.[134] Hopefully this would all be complete before the Bombardment Unit had to enter to commence the bombing of Henderson Field.

It was about ten minutes later at 11:10 pm when Admiral Hashimoto on the *Sendai* reported the *Shikinami* had spotted two enemy cruisers and four destroyers north of Savo Island at bearing 200 degrees. The *Uranami* reported them as "new-type cruisers." In response, Hashimoto now divided his force of five ships two ways, sending the *Ayanami* around the west side of Savo to sweep for more enemy ships. Even by Japanese standards, this division of force in such a small area shared with the enemy was extreme, bordering on ridiculous.[135]

Admiral Lee suspected that the Japanese were trying to sneak up behind him. The *South Dakota's* radio team had been picking up voices on the Japanese radio channels. The feeling grew stronger with a report from the PTs that "Three ships just rounded north of Savo headed west."[136] When he completed the east leg of his circuit around Savo at 11:52 and headed west, he could be comforted that they would no longer be in the blind spot of his search radar.

Sure enough, at 11:55 pm the *Washington's* search and main battery radars detected an unknown ship 18,000 yards to the northwest, off the starboard bow. Admiral Lee saw the return and muttered to his flag captain, "Well, stand by, Glenn, here they come."[137] The contact was lost two minutes later amidst interference from Savo Island, but was picked up by the secondary battery radar.[138] The main battery director was behaving erratically, but it was back online in short order.[139] With one good target in hand, Lee waited for other targets to show up to give him a better picture of the situation before opening fire. In the meantime, Captain Davis ordered full watertight integrity for the *Washington* and had gasoline and paint stowage flooded with carbon dioxide.[140] By this time, destroyer *Gwin* had also prepared for battle by jettisoning all flammable materials, pre-positioning emergency equipment and food, and telling the crew to put on fresh clothes to minimize the chance of any wounds becoming infected.

The radar contact was of Admiral Hashimoto's flagship *Sendai* and the destroyers *Shikinami* and *Uranami*, sailing as close to Savo as they could to help camouflage themselves. At 11:12 *Uranami* spotted Admiral Lee's force heading west at 18 knots about 10 miles southeast of Savo.[141] Hashimoto promptly reported it to Admiral Kondo, who was being inundated with contact reports. At 11:00 pm, he had received a very-delayed report from the R-Area Air Force describing the enemy as four destroyers and two heavy cruisers or battleships. Kondo refused to believe it was battleships as ever since American battleships returned to Pacific waters, they had stayed with the American carriers, who always pulled back at night. It must be heavy cruisers.

Nevertheless, Admiral Kondo saw the situation as the Sweeping Unit and the Screening Unit were both about to chase an enemy force heading west toward his exposed Bombardment Unit. This was not going as Kondo had planned, so he changed Admiral Kimura's orders from sweeping down the east side of Savo to sweeping down the west side, hoping to trap in a surprise pincer movement the two cruisers and four destroyers the scouting reports had mentioned.* Destroyer *Ayanami* would continue acting as a sweeping

---

* In most major armed forces, a guiding principle is "March divided, fight concentrated." The Imperial Japanese Navy had it reversed.

unit for the Sweeping Unit and sweep the west side of Savo for enemy ships before Admiral Kimura and his Screening Unit would also sweep the west side of Savo for enemy ships.[142] Kondo was very concerned about his different units running into each other, so the Bombardment Unit turned northeast and would mark time northwest of Savo. The Screening Unit slowed down to maintain 10-mile distance from the *Ayanami*.[143]

While this was going on, high up in the *Washington*'s tower mast, the main battery director officer announced at 12:12 that, through his spotting telescope, he had a visual on two ships, one of which was a *Tenryu*-class light cruiser.[144] The *South Dakota* had already gotten a visual.[145] Admiral Lee had delayed a bit, but he was no Admiral Callaghan. He signaled, "When you are ready open fire." They were. And they did.

At 12:17, the nine 16-inch guns of the *Washington* thundered across Ironbottom Sound. Nine red tracers were "grouped together for all the world like a flight of airplanes" flying over the water, into the low-hanging clouds overhead, then coming back out some 11,000 yards away toward the *Sendai* in the first combat use of the US Navy's 16-inch gun.[146] Doing a little bit of multitasking, three of the five dual 5-inch mounts on the starboard side opened up on the *Shikinami* at a range of 15,000 yards. One 16-inch salvo landed on one side of the *Sendai*; the next landed on the other. The *South Dakota* joined the flagship with her seven operable 16-inch guns firing at *Shikinami* at a range of 15,700 yards. The *Preston* and *Gwin* saw the exchange between the battleships and Admiral Hashimoto's ships and tried to engage with torpedoes, only to find they were out of range. That didn't stop *Gwin* from launching one torpedo from her after quintuple mount – accidentally, due to a short circuit in the torpedo director.[147] The *Gwin* also tried to support the battleships with starshells, but she was out of range for her guns as well.[148]

Admiral Hashimoto had seen enough. He turned his three ships around and proceeded back to the northwest behind a smoke screen.[149] The radar techs on the *Washington* thought they saw the *Sendai*'s radar return flicker, interpreting that as sinking. The lookouts disagreed, guessing the target had laid a smoke screen.[150] The *South Dakota* thought the flagship had set an enemy battleship "ablaze from stem to stern."[151] In fact, the flickering was due to the giant shell splashes interfering with the radar returns; the *Sendai* was not damaged. Captain Gatch on the *South Dakota* thought he had sunk the *Shikinami*, but after eight 16-inch salvos she, too, was untouched.[152] The radio operators on the *South Dakota* had been listening to the Japanese radio channels for hours. Now the Japanese voices suddenly "became excited and very numerous," which they found most amusing. The radio-direction finding team was able to analyze the messages and deduce at least 13 Japanese ships present.[153] Now they knew they were outnumbered. But not outgunned. Definitely not outgunned.

As Admiral Hashimoto's targets disappeared from radar, the *Washington* stopped firing. She had fired 42 rounds of 16-inch ammunition.[154] Hashimoto, trying to reconcile the belief he was facing 8-inch-armed cruisers with the immense shell splashes he had seen, later told his superiors he had completed his mission of springing the enemy trap and that, when he bravely turned his tail and fled, he had actually "diverted enemy in order to decoy

MAP 4: THE SECOND NAVAL BATTLE OF GUADALCANAL, NOVEMBER 14–15, 1942

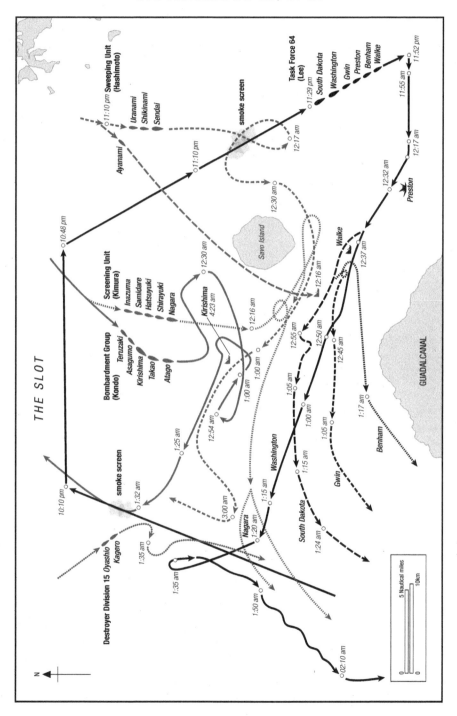

enemy to our main strength."[155] Admiral Lee ordered his force to change course slightly to the northwest, 300 degrees True, and increase speed to 23 knots,[156] heading for the very familiar channel between Savo and Guadalcanal.

But the Americans were not the only ones going between Savo and Guadalcanal, nor the first, as the American destroyers, a little less than 3 miles ahead, were not quick to realize. Destroyer *Walke* changed course to 270 degrees True – due west – and cut speed to 17 knots, without telling anyone – perhaps not the smartest decision in a night battle.[157] She was watching a moving shadow ahead 20 degrees on the starboard bow, what she thought was a cruiser with a single raked stack.[158] This was the destroyer *Ayanami*, who in this battle was playing the role the *Yudachi* had played two nights earlier by attacking the American column on her own. She signaled Admiral Kondo she was beginning her attack.[159] The *Walke* did have a fire-direction radar, but the *Ayanami*'s savvy skipper Commander Sakuma Eiji was staying as close to Savo Island as he could to hide from human and electronic eyes.

And he was succeeding. At 12:22 the *Walke* opened fire at a range of 15,000 yards, but the interference from Savo gave her radar problems in getting a good target lock. The *Benham*, with no radar whatsoever, could not see a ship and focused on firing where the *Walke* had fired; and the *Gwin* chimed in with starshells, as she had been assigned to do.[160] But they could not overcome the shadow of Savo and mistook the *Ayanami*'s return fire as coming from shore batteries. After two salvos of starshells, the *Gwin*'s thoroughly annoyed captain Lieutenant Commander John Fellows ordered his gunners to switch to high-explosive rounds. Still unable to get a lock on the Japanese ships against the backdrop of Savo either visually or with radar, Fellows told his gunnery officer to estimate the firing solution based on the gun flashes of the Japanese, who were using flashless gun powder, though that powder did produce a small red flame.[161] The results were less than impressive and the *Gwin* stopped shooting. Then the *Washington* started at the *Ayanami* with her secondary battery and began getting hits. The *Walke* thought she saw *Ayanami* burst into flames and stopped shooting.

Meanwhile, at 12:27 the *Preston* sighted a large ship, bigger than a destroyer, faintly illuminated by moonlight, emerging from around the southwest corner of Savo Island at a range of about 9,000 yards. Skipper Commander Max C. Stormes locked on using the optical fire-control equipment and opened fire. The *Walke* also shifted fire to this new target, which was off the starboard bow at a range of about 7,500 yards. Admiral Lee now rather belatedly signaled Admiral Halsey, "We are engaging enemy."[162]

This ship was veteran Admiral Kimura's flagship light cruiser *Nagara* – old, ugly, outclassed, but, under skipper Captain Tawara Yoshioki, arguably the best-handled ship in the previous 48 hours of combat. After reporting to Admiral Kondo that she was engaging one cruiser and three destroyers, she was about to punch well above her weight yet again, this time with some unwitting help.[163]

The *Walke* pumped out 5-inch shells for about three minutes, seeing fires on the Japanese light cruiser before the *Nagara* disappeared around Savo Island. Then the destroyer turned her guns to port at gun flashes she saw some 7,500 yards behind her, believing it a continuation of the gun battle she had witnessed earlier. Meanwhile, the *Preston*'s first salvo was short; she adjusted and thought she was registering punishing hits on her target. A burst of 25mm fire from the *Nagara* decimated the after repair party and killed a cook.[164] But that seemed like a pitiful response from the *Nagara*. The gunnery officer shifted away from the *Nagara* to another target after the *Preston*'s rangefinder operator yelled, "It's burning!"[165] Only one problem: it wasn't.

The *Preston* had indeed been witnessing punishing hits – on the *Ayanami*, whose dark silhouette seems to have merged with that of the *Nagara* and other ships in the dark shadow of Savo. The *Ayanami* was burning; the *Nagara* was not. And the *Nagara* now unloaded on the hapless *Preston*. One 5.5-inch shell created a devastating domino effect, exploding between the two firerooms, killing everyone in both and spewing hot, dirty firebrick and debris all over the main deck, starting several fires. The blast also toppled the second stack onto the searchlight platform, which in turn collapsed onto the starboard torpedo tubes, igniting the TNT from torpedo warheads cracked open by the shock of the explosion and starting even more fires. A second hit was, by comparison, anticlimactic – it hit just behind 5-inch Mount 2 but did not explode, severing the power and communication cables to Mount 2, killing one and injuring another.[166] As one Solomons Island historian quipped, "*Nagara*'s gunners, veterans of the cruiser action 48 hours before, seemed to have learned how to avoid night blindness."[167]

The situation rapidly deteriorated. Radar Fire Controlman 3rd Class Jim Cook was in the gun director facing backwards and to starboard, away from the action forward to starboard, when he suddenly saw three large shell splashes to port – the opposite side of the fighting. Where did *that* come from?

Then there were several greenish explosions aft. One shell penetrated to the engine room and exploded on one of the generators. Another landed between the secondary control station and 5-inch Mount 3. Still another detonated right on Mount 4. The concussion jammed Mounts 1 and 2 in train. Almost everyone aft of the after machine gun was killed, including the executive officer. The entire after part of the destroyer was a blazing wreck.[168] In the director, Jim Cook felt something bonk him on the top of his helmet. Then another. As he ducked, he saw it was raining potatoes and onions. The ship's vegetable locker had been caught in the explosions.[169]

During this shower of spud missiles, Radioman 3rd Class Myron Lindley was in the radio room when he felt a great jolt. The emergency lights came on. Then Lindley felt a second jolt, one that left the deck shaking for several seconds. Lindley had barely stepped out of the room to see what was happening when the *Preston* started listing to starboard.[170] Not a good sign; when a ship starts listing that quickly, it's about to sink.

And Commander Stormes knew it, ordering "All hands abandon ship." With the communications out, the order was passed on by shouting. The *Preston* groaned and twisted as she quickly heeled over to starboard and started rapidly settling by the stern. There was very little time. Jim Cook threw himself out of the director and half-fell, half-climbed down to the main deck. He tried to follow Stormes, but the *Preston* was rolling over to starboard and, as his deck tipped him over, Cook had to climb to the port side of the ship and run down the exposed hull straight into the water.

Cook had no choice. Less than 30 seconds after the order to abandon ship had been given, the *Preston* rolled over onto her starboard beam and her bow stood up straight in the air. Cook had joined up with the destroyer's chief radioman in the water, only to look up and see the monstrous hull of the *South Dakota* headed straight for them. There was nothing they could do but wait for the inevitable. The battleship veered slightly to starboard to avoid the bow of the *Preston*, now standing like a steeple in the water. This maneuver saved Cook, but many of the destroyer's survivors were unavoidably run down or drowned in the behemoth's bow wave or wake.

Crewmen on the *South Dakota* tried to help their comrades in the water by tossing down life rafts and flotation rings as the battleship passed by. The *Preston*'s torpedo officer Ensign Ted Marx was almost conked on the head by a cork life ring thrown from the deck. Marx had left the bridge with Commander Stormes and they jumped over the port side together, but then they became separated. Stormes was never seen again. The *Preston*'s bow continued to float upright for about ten minutes before slipping beneath the waves for the final time.

The second jolt and shiver felt by Radioman Lindley had been at least one torpedo. The *Ayanami* had, in fact, launched six Type 90 torpedoes at 12:30, aimed at the third ship in line, believed to be a cruiser but actually the *Preston*.[171] Five minutes later, Admiral Kimura ordered his ships to launch theirs at the *Walke* and *Benham* at an angle of 20–30 degrees off the starboard bow.[172] The result was a spread of 35–40 mostly Type 90s – not quite the Type 93 Long Lance, but effective nonetheless – headed for the American destroyers. The *Gwin* had seen a large explosion on the *Preston* at around 12:32, which was the torpedo hit.

The *Ayanami*'s torpedoes had sunk the *Preston*, with an assist from *Nagara*'s guns. But both ships had been to starboard. Who had fired the shells that hit the *Preston* from the unengaged port side? According to the Office of Naval Intelligence, "[A]n enemy heavy cruiser came in on the port side of the column 'virtually undetected,' and the *Preston* was hit on the port side by part of an 8-inch salvo (probably three shells)."[173] The only evidence of this cruiser was of gunfire witnessed aft to port by the *Walke* (to which she responded with gunfire); the shell hits to the *Preston*; and the indication in the statement of *Benham*'s skipper, Lieutenant Commander John Taylor, that he thought he saw a cruiser to port firing on the aft destroyers. There were two Japanese 8-inch-armed heavy cruisers in this action, *Atago* and *Takao*. Neither of them was to port of the *Preston*. For that matter, no Japanese ships at all were to port of the *Preston*.

Nevertheless, the *South Dakota* witnessed a rather curious exchange. She saw what appeared to be a barrage of 5-inch shells straddle the *Washington* ahead of her. In response, she asked Admiral Lee, "Are you damaged?" The flagship responded, "We are OK."[174] The shells were coming from the shadow of Savo. The *Washington* fired to starboard almost blindly into those shadows.

Radioman 2nd Class Henry Stewart was in the *South Dakota*'s tower mast watching the action with Executive Officer Commander Archibald E. Uehlinger. "I saw the *Washington* open fire to her starboard, the USS *Preston* a destroyer was hit and burning," Stewart would later write. "[A]nd to us it looked as if the *Washington*'s fire had caused the accident."[175]

Commander Uehlinger turned to Stewart and asked, "You didn't see that did you son?"

"No, Sir."[176] From this point forward in the engagement, Admiral Lee and Captain Gatch were *very* concerned about friendly fire. In fairness, however, the gunfire the *Walke* had seen astern to port was actually the *Washington*, and the barrage of 5-inch gunfire the *South Dakota* had seen bracketing the *Washington* had come from the *Walke*. There was plenty of blame to go around here. World War II night battles were inherently chaotic.

This night so far had belonged to the older Type 90 torpedoes on the *Fubuki*-class destroyers and the *Nagara*. When the *Ayanami*'s Type 90 hit the *Preston*, leading US destroyer *Walke* was turning to port to unleash torpedoes of her own to starboard at Admiral Kimura's column. The destroyer was bracketed twice by Japanese gunfire, but no hits. Seaman 2nd Class J.O. Pinion, one of the starboard lookouts, was watching the light show created by the tracers and gunfire when executive officer Lieutenant Commander Reader Scott pulled him back, yelling "Get down!"

No sooner had they flattened themselves on the deck than the *Walke* was rocked by a massive blast forward, followed by explosions in the radio room, near the foremast, and around 5-inch Mount 3. Once the ship's initial convulsions had stopped, Pinion tried to get up, only to be crushed by a deluge of hot water and fuel oil.[177] The gun captain of Mount 3, Cox Peter Trella, knocked unconscious by the initial blast, quickly came to, tried to get up, and was also pummeled back to the deck by an avalanche of water and oil. He shouted, "Let's get out of here!" and he and his crew left the mount.[178]

Lieutenant John Walsh, the communications officer, was on the bridge when the explosion threw everyone into the air, slamming him into a beam in the ceiling that broke his fifth cervical vertebra. Walsh then slammed back down to the deck, tearing ligaments in his left leg and shattering his left kneecap. His steel helmet, which he usually didn't wear but had tonight, had saved his life – crashing into the beam had left the helmet "creased like a fedora hat[.]"[179] A shell striking just beneath the bridge left the deck quaking and Walsh fumbling for a handhold with which to pull himself up. He found himself drenched in a wet, sticky liquid. Walsh tasted it and was thankful to learn he was not covered in blood, just oil – on a blazing ship.[180]

The *Walke* had been hit by a torpedo – from Admiral Kimura's ships, but exactly which one is unknown – on the starboard side under 5-inch Mount 2. The explosion started a fire that quickly detonated the 20mm magazine, blowing off the forecastle and superstructure as far as the bridge. That's about 100 feet of bow – gone just like that. It exposed the bulkhead of the forward fireroom, which was not designed for the hydrodynamic pressures of battle speed and so it buckled, as did the deck amidships.

Watertight integrity was completely destroyed. An instant after the torpedo hit, a salvo of 5.5-inch rounds from the *Nagara* blasted what was left of the superstructure.

The damage was catastrophic. The *Walke's* speed drove her shattered bow deeper and deeper into the water. She was basically steaming into the depths. Commander Fraser stayed on the bridge to take a formal damage report, after which he immediately ordered, "Abandon ship!" Then he disappeared, never to be seen again.[181]

The situation was chaotic because of the speed of the disaster, the lack of communication, and the continuing rain of Japanese shells. Lieutenant Walsh was working his way toward a rail to jump over the side but was stopped cold when he saw a big hole in the hull where he was about to jump. He tried to call attention to it, but between the chaos and the 5-inch Mount 4 still shooting at their tormentors, a few lookouts did not hear him and jumped straight into the hole and their deaths. Walsh noticed the oil that was covering him had ignited and he had to beat out the flames, after which he noticed he had been blown out of his shoes. This made his jumping into the water a few seconds later much easier.[182]

Closer to the stern, the depth charges were checked and reported to be set on "safe" so they would not explode in the water when the ship sank.[183] Cox Peter Trella had quickly located his brother, Fireman 1st Class Paul Trella, and they headed aft to join a large group about to abandon the blazing, sinking destroyer. But Chief Boatswain's Mate John Bussard scoffed at the notion that they should abandon ship just because the *Walke* was completely ablaze, was being buried by Japanese shells, had its bow blown off, and was steaming into the depths. With undisguised contempt, Bussard sneered that he would be going forward to the galley to get a cup of coffee. After he left, the Trellas and the group dove off the fantail into the water. Many, many people have said they would give their lives for a cup of coffee. John Bussard actually did; he was never seen again.[184]

While the Trellas and their mates were jumping off the stern, the wounded were placed in a life raft that was released from the stern. Seconds later, the shattered *Walke* drove her bowless hulk under for the last time, sticking her stern straight out of the water for a few seconds before disappearing.

But not forever. The severed bow section somehow bobbled back to the surface, and the gunners of 5-inch Mount 1 managed to escape. The bow stayed afloat and provided shelter for some of the survivors. They needed it, for one of the unwritten rules of the US Navy was about to assert itself: even though the depth charges are not supposed to explode because they are set on "safe," they explode anyway. And the *Walke's* did, the shock waves radiating through the water, slamming into the sailors swimming for their lives. Battleship *Washington* dropped a few life rafts, but she had been unable to avoid sailing through the survivors and ended up running some of them down.

Though immediately behind the *Walke*, destroyer *Benham*, at least, did not run over her survivors. Lieutenant Commander Taylor ordered hard to port to clear the *Walke's* wreckage. She was passing the hulk only to take another of Admiral Kimura's torpedoes on the starboard side just a few yards from the bow. The explosion blew off the bow as far as the bulkhead for the magazine for 5-inch Mount 1. The destroyer rose forward, heeled about 5 degrees to port, then rolled to starboard about 30 degrees, settling by her severed bow and righting herself slowly. The concussion of the explosion resonated down the keel, shaking the ship so violently that almost no one was left standing. The *Benham* slowed down rapidly from 27 down to 5 knots, placing additional hydrodynamic stress on her shaken hull. Midships plates and longitudinals buckled somewhat. There was a crack in the main deck right above the forward fireroom, evincing that, like the *Juneau*, the *Benham*'s keel had snapped as a result of the torpedo hit.[185]

The torpedo's explosion also threw up a geyser of water that rose about 20 feet higher than the director and – again, as what goes up must come down – did indeed come back down with crushing force, driving the stern under temporarily so that the crew of 5-inch Mount 4 was waist deep in water. Chief Torpedo Mate Jon Chapman was washed overboard. Several other torpedomen, the chief machinist's mate, chief boatswain's mate, and several members of the after damage control party were badly injured.[186] And just when that deluge ended, the *Preston* exploded as she took the *Ayanami*'s torpedo, sending up another geyser of water and oil that now crashed down on the *Benham*'s stern.[187] There were more injuries, but through all this, fortunately, no one was killed.[188]

With the destroyer almost dead in the water and with what looked like a very large Japanese ship about to overtake her from the starboard quarter, Lieutenant Commander Taylor ordered the dazed helmsman to turn to starboard and head back toward the east. The *Washington* sped by – she was the very large "Japanese" ship Taylor had seen – on an opposite course. The *Benham* had the *Gwin* relay a signal to Admiral Lee: "We have torp hit forward and a bad buckle in the fire room. There is possibility ship may break up. We are making 8 knots to rendezvous."[189] Taylor thought it better to stay and get some protection from the behemoth, so he turned around again and headed west. As he did so, the *Benham* felt several underwater explosions – probably the *Walke*'s depth charges, but it could also have been the *Preston*'s.

Last in the line of destroyers, *Gwin* had been having a decent night. She had gotten another lock on the *Ayanami* and resumed fire, collapsing the Japanese destroyer's forward stack and disabling 5-inch Mounts 1 and 3, reducing the Japanese destroyer to one functioning 5-inch mount.[190] The *Ayanami* countered by sending a 5-inch shell into the *Gwin*'s after engine room on the starboard side about 4 feet above the waterline.

The shell detonated in the vicinity of the control station, killing all the personnel on the upper level. The lights to 5-inch Mounts 3 and 4 went out, but emergency lights came on so that neither gun's ability to fire was impaired. Though the explosion was in the after engine room, it broke all the shear pins holding the torpedoes in the forward quintuple torpedo mount. One fell out, bouncing off the weather deck rail before dropping into the sea; two others just slipped out and fell into the sea; the remaining two came halfway out. The fires in the after engine room were quickly extinguished.[191]

Now under enemy fire, skipper Commander John Fellows shouted, "Left full rudder!" This was a by-the-book evasive maneuver for such emergencies in which the odd ships in a column turn to starboard and even ships to port. It had been drilled for so long that by now it was instinctive. The only problem was that a port turn would be right into the flaming hulk of the *Preston*. With no time to ask for permission, executive officer Lieutenant Commander William Cox saw the danger and sprung to the helmsman's side, barking, "Hard right! Hard right!" The *Gwin* cleared the wreck and Cox asked for his skipper's forgiveness for countermanding his order. Fellows said nothing of it.[192]

But though she had cleared the wreck, the *Gwin* was not safe from it. The fires detonated some of the *Preston*'s torpedoes, resulting in a large explosion that sent debris down on the *Gwin*. One torpedoman on the *Gwin* even caught a pair of jeans, blown off the *Preston*, around his neck.[193] Once she had passed the *Preston*, the *Gwin* returned to course 300 degrees True. As she did so, she felt a number of underwater explosions. The *Preston*'s depth charges were detonating, giving the *Gwin* "quite a shaking up."[194] She resumed fire on the *Ayanami* and sent several shells into the impudent destroyer's engine rooms and steering gear, leaving her heavily damaged, burning brightly, and slowing down.

Next the *Gwin* took a weird hit. An unknown caliber shell apparently ricocheted off the water and struck the starboard side near the depth charge rack. It left a jagged hole about 2 feet square and distorted the starboard depth charge rack so two 600lb depth charges burst open, spilling their explosive contents on the deck. It was quickly cleaned up, and the destroyer stopped firing because she could not find any more targets. Nor could she find the *Benham*. A torpedo then crossed her stern, missing by about 30 yards.

This torpedo had come from the screening group led by Admiral Kimura in the *Nagara*, the old light cruiser once again making a major pest of herself. He ordered a 180-degree turn to port, toward Savo Island, to keep up with the American column. At 12:38 am, during the four minutes it took his group to fully reverse course, Admiral Hashimoto's *Sendai*, *Shikinami*, and *Uranami* sped past him toward the west. When Kimura was finished pointing his column toward the west, he ordered the torpedo tubes reloaded for a second massed torpedo attack.[195]

While passing Admiral Kimura's group, Admiral Hashimoto had also passed the plucky *Ayanami*. By now the destroyer was ablaze and dead in the water just east of Savo Island. Even so, Commander Sakuma was pretty proud of himself. He radioed Admiral Kondo saying his destroyer, all by itself, had sunk one heavy cruiser and one destroyer with torpedoes and set on fire a third destroyer with gunfire. It took some time for the message to reach the Japanese admiral, but when it did at 12:45, the bridge crew of the *Atago* started cheering. The Americans were obviously being crushed. Then they received a message from the *Sendai* that the *Ayanami* was afire. They stopped cheering.[196]

Still Admiral Kondo was very satisfied with the results so far. He would continue to keep the *Atago*, *Takao*, and *Kirishima* in a holding pattern northwest of Savo until the Sweeping and Screening Groups had finished with the Americans. Then he could proceed with the bombardment without interference.

But not yet; some elements of that interference were still there. Flagship *Washington* was tracking practically everyone on her search radar – except anyone in that blind spot aft. Admiral Lee hoped that the *South Dakota* was in that blind spot. But he wasn't sure, and until he was sure, he would not fire. He would not have a repeat of the *Preston* incident.

This concern over the location of the *South Dakota* came about because the battleships had been separated by the disaster that came over their leading destroyers. Seeing burning wrecks and bobbing heads in his way, Admiral Lee had the *Washington* swerve to port to keep the fires between his ship and the Japanese; that way, he could still use the camouflage provided by the dark bulk of Guadalcanal. As the flagship came upon the swimming survivors, the sailors of the *Washington* tossed some life rafts over the side. From the dark water below, the sailors heard shouts of "Get after 'em, *Washington!*"[197]

The *South Dakota*, on the other hand, was having a frustrating night. At 12:33, just after she finished shooting ineffectually at the *Sendai* and her friends, the battleship suffered a major electrical failure. The concussion of the main guns firing caused a short circuit in the feeder cable to one of the secondary battery directors. It would have tripped the breakers serving the secondary battery – except the circuit breakers, "counter to damage control procedures," had been tied down, which had the effect of putting the electrical system on one circuit, instead of several working in parallel.[198] So the surge spread to other areas of the ship, especially the stern area, like a virus. The result was that all the power gyros and all the fire control equipment – the directors, the radars – lost power. For three long minutes.[199]

Radar may have been a new-fangled device, but the men of the *South Dakota* had come to rely on it and they quickly found they could not manage without it. As Captain Gatch later reported, "After this ship lost both SG and SC equipment, the psychological effect on the officers and crew was most depressing. The absence of this gear gave all hands a feeling of being blindfolded" – blindfolded while driving a battleship at high speed.[200]

It was now that the *South Dakota* came upon the wrecks of the US destroyers. She tried to follow the *Washington* to port, but quickly found she could not clear the fiery hulk of the *Preston*. With little choice, Captain Gatch had her swerve to starboard instead. She avoided the *Preston's* burning wreck, but in so doing had placed herself between the fire and the Japanese. In other words, she was backlit by the fire. The Japanese had gotten a quick glimpse of her and her position and could maneuver themselves for an attack, all while she was handicapped with her radar out and her main guns frozen.

The electricity returned to the *South Dakota* at 12:36, though electrical problems and even electrical fires continued to plague the ship for the next few hours. Nevertheless, the radar blackout had thoroughly disoriented the men of the battleship. In the interim, the pictures on the radar screens had changed. Which blip was the *Washington*?

The question was temporarily mooted at 12:41 when the search radar went out yet again. While they were trying to fix the search radar, the main battery director had a gunnery radar lock on a ship an estimated 15,500 yards directly behind the *South Dakota*.

The aft turret, the only one that could bear on the target, boomed out three 16-inch shells. The battleship seems to have been aiming at the *Ayanami*, but the shells landed awfully close to the *Gwin* – so close that Lieutenant Commander Fellows felt compelled to turn on his recognition lights. The *South Dakota* stopped shooting, but only after firing one more three-gun salvo that caused the crippled destroyer's crew to hold their breaths until the shells finally landed wide.[201]

At 12:44, the *Gwin* radioed Admiral Lee, "I am all right, with one hit in engine room." The admiral responded one minute later by radioing all his destroyers, "Retire – retire."[202] Only the *Gwin* acknowledged, saying she could not find the *Preston*.[203] She headed west around Cape Esperance then turned to the south.[204] At grave cost to themselves, the destroyers had done their job – except for their inability to launch any torpedoes which none of them had managed to do: they had sprung the trap the Japanese had set, taking the sting meant for the battleships. The *Washington* and *South Dakota* would finish this off. Alone.

Indeed, the *South Dakota* felt like she was alone, mostly because her change of course and the failure of her search radar caused her to lose track of the *Washington*. Her frustrating night continued, as now she was being hurt by her own gunfire. The first salvo that landed near the *Gwin* set fire to two floatplanes and parts of her fantail. The second salvo conveniently extinguished most of the fires set by the first salvo and blew the two burning planes over the side.

But as small as this matter may seem, it loomed rather large. Their fires pinpointed the *South Dakota* in the darkness for the Japanese. Far worse, this failed attempt to hit the *Ayanami* distracted the bridge crew from the approaching Japanese. Admiral Lee had issued instructions prohibiting the battleships from coming within 7,000 yards of Japanese ships with the idea of staying out of the range of their searchlights.[205] But with her search radar out, the *South Dakota* was blinded as to the locations of the Japanese ships. The search radar came back on, and at 12:47 it reported four ships on a relative bearing of 70 degrees, range 5,800 yards.[206] The report was not immediately acknowledged because the bridge was dealing with the gunfire astern.[207]

It was for this very reason that battleships were not usually employed in restricted waters. But the Americans were out of ships. What choice did they have?

At 12:48, the shutters on two pairs of searchlights, each pair arranged vertically, snapped open and bathed the battleship in their blinding, icy light.[208] They were from the *Sendai*. The *Washington*, who already had a radar lock, immediately opened fire on her. Within a minute, the light cruiser let loose on the brightly lit *South Dakota* at a range of only 5,000 yards.

The *South Dakota* was still having problems. Her gunners believed that the main battery radar was giving them incorrect range information. They requested the fire directors controlling the secondary battery take over the main battery as well. There was a slight problem: of the four secondary battery directors, the radars in 5-inch Directors 1 and 4 were out, while those in 2 and 3 were "doubtful." It took some 30 seconds after the

Sendai opened fire for the *South Dakota*'s starboard 5-inch guns, operating under Secondary Director 3, located starboard aft, to respond.[209] By that time, the light cruiser had drawn first blood from the battleship, sending a 5.5-inch shell through the 1.1-inch clipping room in the foremast, exploding as it exited to port.[210] Apparently having seen the hit to the mast, Admiral Lee radioed Captain Gatch, asking, "Are you alright?" He replied, "Everything seems okay."[211]

The *Sendai* decided to turn her lights out, only for the *Nagara* to snap on her own searchlights and briefly illuminate the *South Dakota* while pumping out 5.5-inch munitions. Captain Gatch felt more hits to his battleship, but no one could locate them.[212] In fact, one 5.5-inch shell had plowed through the 1.1-inch director without exploding.[213] A second had passed through forward air defense control and damaged Main Battery Director 1, again without exploding.[214] Whether from the *Sendai* or the *Nagara* no one can say. During this time, the *South Dakota*'s technicians had managed to get Secondary Director 3 to control the main battery and fired a few salvos off in her direction. The *Nagara* made smoke and headed away.[215]

The flagship *Atago*, sister ship *Takao*, and battleship *Kirishima* were now heading west, still marking time until the enemy forces were cleared out. On the bridge, Admiral Kondo was monitoring the action with his chief of staff Rear Admiral Shiraishi Kazutaka and the cruiser's skipper Captain Baron Ijuin Matsuji, one of the few noblemen in the Imperial Japanese Navy. Kondo was satisfied with the way the battle was going. To the south, the dark backdrop of Guadalcanal was marred by even blacker shadows, one of them intermittently lit. The *Takao* reported that the shadows were one battleship and three destroyers.[216] Kondo did not believe it could possibly be a battleship and felt it had to be a cruiser.

The *Takao* was not alone in her belief. A report came in from an apparently shocked Admiral Kimura: "We have illuminated a battleship!"[217] This was followed moments later by "Two enemy battleships off Cape Esperance, heading west along north coast of Guadalcanal!"[218] Kondo still refused to take the report of enemy battleships seriously. He ordered his Bombardment Force to prepare to reverse course to 130 degrees – east southeast – to make the run to Lunga and shell Henderson Field.

The Japanese admiral informed Admiral Hashimoto of his plan, and ordered Hashimoto to help the disabled *Ayanami*. Hashimoto sent the *Uranami* to assist the *Ayanami* while he had his Sweeping Force, led by the *Sendai*, turn to the north to head back toward Lunga. In so doing, he cut directly in front of Admiral Kimura's Screening Force, led by the *Nagara*. Admiral Kondo's worst nightmare about mixing his disparate forces became a reality. Kimura was compelled to turn his force to the north and do a complete circle to starboard in order to avoid a collision. These maneuvers effectively took both the Sweeping Force and the Screening Force out of the fight. Kondo's Bombardment Force was now exposed.

They were in the middle of their reversal of course, with the *Atago* now pointed toward the north, when the flagship spotted a large dark object some 11,000 yards away, relative bearing 125 degrees. At 12:52 am, a lookout shouted, "*Kirishima* is firing!" Admiral Kondo looked back and saw his battleship, who had not even started her turn, unloading with first her secondary battery and then her main battery – and hitting the enemy ship's superstructure. The excited lookouts shouted, "*Kirishima* has scored a hit to enemy bridge with her first salvo!" It looked to them like the *Kirishima* had blown off the top of the target's mainmast.

Not quite, but the reality was bad enough. The target, the *South Dakota*, had taken two 6-inch shells, one of which did not explode but disintegrated, and one 14-inch incendiary shell in and around the radar plot. One officer was killed and the plot was gutted by fire caused by the incendiaries, most of which passed through the compartment and over the side. A steam pipe outside the compartment was smashed as well.[219] It was a good start for the *Kirishima* against her much more modern opponent. She had spotted the *South Dakota* even before her flagship had, and after Captain Iwabuchi announced a gun battle to starboard and ordered the battleship to go to full speed, she was ready.[220] But the next few salvos were straddles and she had to stop firing to begin her turn – the same turn the *Atago* had just completed, settling on a course of 130 degrees True heading back for Lunga.[221]

In preparation for their screening duties during the bombardment, the two destroyers *Asagumo* and *Teruzuki* moved to the front of the column.[222] One of the flagship's lookouts shouted, "A battleship off starboard." Admiral Shiraishi asked if it could be the *Hiei*; no one knew what had happened to her. It was time to shine some light on the situation. Captain Ijuin ordered, "Stand by for a gun and torpedo action to starboard!" "Ready to illuminate," one of the crew shouted. "Commence illumination," the captain responded. The shutters on one of the *Atago*'s searchlights snapped open, followed by one on the *Takao*. The two beams met at the unknown ship.

Admiral Kondo peered through his binoculars and examined the unknown ship in the icy glare of the searchlights: big turrets, high freeboard, layered bridge, a tall tower mast reminiscent of the *Yamato* …

That's no cruiser. It's a battleship. Kondo was stunned.[223]

She was officially identified – wrongly – as a *North Carolina*-class battleship, a new breed of battleship that had entered service since the war started. This was the reckoning the Japanese had dreaded. American industry was starting to overtake the Combined Fleet's advantage in numbers. It would only get worse. Admiral Yamamoto's six months of running wild was long gone. This new battleship was proof. But the strategic implications could wait. The *Atago* began to turn to port to aim her torpedoes.

Torpedo officer Lieutenant Watanabe Yoshiro directed his men to "stand by for torpedo action starboard and engage enemy battleship steaming on parallel course" going away from us. On second thought, no, she's not moving at all. On third thought, no, wait, the target is coming toward us. After Watanabe had thus narrowed the possibilities, at 1:03 – 11 minutes after the *Kirishima* had started firing, and moments after the *Takao* had started firing – Captain Ijuin ordered the torpedoes launched and the main battery to open fire. Eight Long Lances leapt out of the tubes in roughly the general direction of the *South*

Dakota, consistent with Watanabe's directions. Surprisingly, they all missed. A few of them even exploded prematurely.[224]

But the *Atago's* main battery, joined by the guns of the *Asagumo* and *Teruzuki*, was much more successful. The *Takao* was already shooting, and the *Kirishima* resumed fire after the *Atago's* searchlight pinned the American battleship. The *South Dakota* took a pounding.

Captain Gatch's technicians had managed to get Secondary Battery Director 1 working and controlling Mount 1 that was firing starshells, just in time for the director to be knocked out, apparently by the *Takao*.[225] Two hits were felt below decks; these were two 14-inch high-explosive shells from the *Kirishima's* first salvo after resuming fire, striking the hull near Turret 1 and amidships, rupturing some hull plating. Only able to respond with his 5-inch guns, Gatch ordered the *South Dakota* to go to full speed.

The *Atago* and *Takao* shut down their searchlights, only to be replaced by those of the *Kirishima* pinning the *South Dakota*, allowing the pummeling to continue. The American battleship felt more hits below decks. One 8-inch shell bounced off 5-inch Mount 5 on the starboard side, then plowed through the superstructure into the back of 5-inch Mount 4 without exploding. The shell was found on deck and heaved over the side. A 14-inch incendiary slashed through Secondary Director 3, the stack, and Secondary Director 2 without exploding but spreading incendiary tubes everywhere that started small, short-lived fires. This hit damaged the *South Dakota's* radio antennae, so her calls to the *Washington* for help were met with silence.

The *Atago* ceased firing. After a false alarm of approaching torpedoes, Admiral Kondo got a good look at their target, pinned as she was in the *Kirishima's* searchlights. He could see that their target was burning and heavily damaged, possibly even sinking.

"There is another ship forward of the first, a big battleship!" The call came from one of the *Atago's* lookouts. Once again Admiral Kondo was stunned: now there were two of them!

They identified the second battleship – wrongly, again – as an *Idaho*-class and determined that she was sinking by the bow, already awash up to her main deck. That last part was almost immediately proved to be false when one of the lookouts shouted, "*Kirishima* is totally obscured by shell splashes!" When Admiral Kondo and the other officers swiveled their heads aft toward their battleship, they saw a virtual wall of water surrounding her in the form of nine 100-foot geysers.[226] The battleship was not hit, but she was straddled. Keeping a log on the battleship's bridge, Lieutenant (jg) Kobayashi Michio later remembered when the geysers came crashing down, drenching the battleship's senior officers and trashing the log he had been keeping.[227] It was an ominous turn of events.

Then one 16-inch shell detonated in the pagoda, turning the navigation bridge and the forward telegraph room into "a scene of total destruction."[228] A 5-inch salvo hit between the forward stack and the pagoda, starting another series of fires and smashing the starboard side searchlights that had pinned the *South Dakota*. That was just a taste.

The "*Idaho*-class battleship" "sinking by the bow" was Admiral Lee's flagship *Washington* in picture-perfect shape. While the *South Dakota* had grabbed Japanese attention by backlighting herself with the burning US destroyers and setting her own floatplanes on fire, the *Washington* had kept herself hidden in the darkness by keeping the burning ships between herself and the Japanese. Her main battery director had gotten a lock on the largest blip on her radar, the third ship in the Japanese column, but because Admiral Lee did not know where the *South Dakota* was, he would not open fire on the target for fear of another friendly fire incident like the *Preston*. When the Japanese pinned the *South Dakota* in their searchlights, they revealed her location to Lee. Now absolutely certain his target was Japanese, he gave the order to open fire. The range was 8,400 yards – "body punching range for guns that could reach five times that distance."[229] One of the *South Dakota*'s turret officers, Paul Backus, was horrified. "Throwing 14-inch and 16-inch shells at that kind of range – Jesus."[230]

As if in shock just as much as their admiral, the *Atago* and *Takao* were sluggish to respond. The *Kirishima* never did respond. She was blinded by the searchlights and could not get a clear fix on the *Washington*, so she just kept firing at the *South Dakota*.[231]

Her gunnery officer firing in 3-gun salvos as soon as each turret was ready, the *Washington*'s blasts were more than close; they were brutal.[232] Two 16-inch rounds struck amidships, just above the secondary batteries, resulting in large explosions leaving two holes each 30 feet wide. The upper deck was now ablaze, with fires threatening the *Kirishima*'s aft secondary magazines. Executive Officer Commander Ono Koro ordered them flooded.

Captain Iwabuchi and Damage Control Officer Lieutenant Commander Hayashi Shiro thought the *Kirishima* had dodged a blow when two shells splashed off the starboard beam, though they produced a strange vibration. This was because these 16-inch shells had plunged into the water all right – and burrowed themselves into the battleship's hull beneath the waterline before detonating. These devastating hits opened the *Kirishima*'s middle and lower decks to the sea, and the starboard engine room began flooding. Not quickly, but steadily, relentlessly – even more relentless than the *Washington*'s continued pounding. More 5-inch rounds hit the upper levels of the pagoda, starting several fires. Two more 16-inch shells hit 14-inch Turret 1 almost simultaneously, combining for an impressive explosion. Captain Iwabuchi shouted, "Flood No. 1 turret magazines immediately!"[233] He had saved his ship – for now. Turret 1 was now wrecked and useless, while Turret 2 was probably damaged but definitely still operable.

On the next salvo the *Kirishima*'s stern area was pummeled. Three 16-inch shells smashed the officers' cabins. One more hit just below the waterline – again – caused flooding in the rudder control room, shorting out one of the generators and jamming the rudders 10 degrees to starboard. Yet another passed through the torpedo bulge and the main belt to explode in the starboard aft hydraulic pump room.

As the *Kirishima* shuddered with every blow, her men were aghast at the vicious punishment they were receiving. The Imperial Japanese Navy had never faced, had never even heard of, a ship like the one shooting at and hitting them now. Sure, the Japanese had built the colossal *Yamato* and the even bigger *Musashi*, but could the twin monsters do *this*? The main guns on this American beast were penetrating the Japanese battleship's armor, as Captain Iwabuchi and his men were finding out with every hit, after hit, after hit. Of course there were misses, but the shots that didn't hit were usually close enough that their concussions ruptured hull plating or, worse, as had already happened, actually hit the *Kirishima* below the waterline like torpedoes and caused dangerous flooding. The Japanese lookouts and gunners could not see their avaricious adversary well enough to dish out even a fraction of what they were taking. If the *Hiei* had been pecked to death, the *Kirishima* by comparison was being punched hard in the mouth – over and over and over again.[234]

Things did change, for a moment. Admiral Lee received a report that the target of his main guns had sunk. Two salvos from the *Kirishima* later, Lee got the idea that the report was wrong, although the Japanese battleship only fired from three turrets. So after a 90-second interlude, the admiral said, "If you can see anything to shoot at, go ahead."[235]

It took a few salvos for the *Washington*'s main battery director to reacquire the *Kirishima*, but on the third salvo after resuming fire, the US flagship scored with a double 16-inch hit on the *Kirishima*'s 14-inch Turret 2 that left it disabled. A third detonated under the waterline – again – and knocked out the starboard forward hydraulic pump room.

Watching this exchange from his flagship *Atago*, Admiral Kondo was deeply concerned for his battleship, not that the *Atago* didn't have her own issues. Though she had turned her searchlights off, they had attracted a few of the 5-inch guns of the multitasking *Washington* to go alongside the secondary battery of the *South Dakota*. Captain Ijuin was wondering why the *South Dakota* was not firing with her main guns, but was not questioning his divine providence, especially after the *Atago* began taking some hits. A 5-inch shell from the *South Dakota* detonated in the starboard soy sauce store, starting a fire on the cruiser's bow.[236] A second 5-inch shell hit the port side but bounced off the cruiser's armor belt.[237]

At 1:08, a lookout on the *Atago* reported, "*Kirishima* is burning and she is gradually lagging behind."[238] This was not going according to plan. The *South Dakota* seemed to be sinking, or so Admiral Kondo thought. Now he needed to save his battleship. He ordered a port turn to the north hoping to get the *Kirishima* away from her tormentor. The *Takao* followed her into the turn, but the blazing *Kirishima* struggled to keep up. She was rapidly losing the ability to fight, as her only main battery guns still firing were the aft Turret 4, and even that was about to seize up, as Turret 3 already had, due to the loss of hydraulic pressure caused by the destruction of the pumps. A parting salvo from the *Washington* landed just off the *Kirishima*'s stern as she staggered northward.

Informed that the *Washington*'s forward turrets had reached the stops that prevented them from shooting up the battleship's bridge structure, Admiral Lee had ordered, "Cease firing" at 1:07. He warned his lookouts to be wary of Japanese destroyers approaching from off the bow. The *Washington*'s search radar continued tracking the *Kirishima* for another ten minutes, during which the Japanese dreadnought was observed making a 500-degree turn to port.[239]

Admiral Kondo now had multiple serious problems: he had two American battleships running free in the area of the convoy, which he had to protect while also bombarding Henderson Field. He ordered his column to reverse course via two port turns, but the *Kirishima* could not follow. The *Atago* sighted a battleship 15 degrees off the port bow about 6 miles away. Captain Ijuin launched four torpedoes at this target, the *South Dakota*. Around this time, Captain Gatch decided his battleship was too damaged to be effective so he sheared to port of the *Washington* and headed southwest to clear the area, "to the great relief of the Task Force commander," Admiral Lee later wrote.[240]

The relief was shared by Captain Gatch. The *Kirishima* may have been a blazing wreck, but she still had fight in her. And while she could never get a fix on the *Washington*, she could on the burning *South Dakota*. The battleship fired one last 14-inch salvo of armor-piercing shells from her aft turret at the *South Dakota*. One burrowed through the main deck to detonate against the barbette of Turret 3, denting it, damaging the right-hand gun on Turret 3, gouging a hole in the main deck, perforating one of the after bulkheads, and destroying some kitchen supplies – but never penetrating the barbette or the magazine.[241] It just angered the officers and men on the battleship. Turret 3's commander was irate. "Never mind how bad we're hit," he said. "I don't give a damn if the guns blow up. I'm going to fire." He didn't; the main guns were frozen by yet another electrical failure.[242] A frustrating night, but it could have been worse. Several explosions were seen 1,000 yards astern, apparently either Ijuin's torpedoes detonating in the battleship's wake or a few parting gifts from the *Atago*.[243] For his part, Lee kept his flagship on course to draw the Japanese away from his damaged ships and to possibly find that Japanese invasion convoy.

This further complicated Admiral Kondo's already complicated position. The *Atago* had sighted the second battleship. Both *Atago* and *Takao* let loose with eight Long Lances each at the American flagship. Kondo ordered his column to course 300 degrees True – roughly northwest – parallel the *Washington*'s course to keep a blocking position with the convoy. Lookouts thought they had seen explosions when the torpedoes were supposed to have hit, but they appear to have been premature explosions; the wakes of the battleships were apparently strong enough to detonate torpedo warheads. The convoy was soon sighted off the starboard bow, far too close for comfort. Kondo ordered it to turn away and had his cruisers turn to port to head due west on a slightly converging course with the *Washington*.[244] Admiral Tanaka had his own concerns about American battleships running loose anywhere near his convoy, so he sent destroyers *Oyashio* and *Kagero* forward to attack any American ships that approached.[245]

Admiral Lee, who had ideas of wreaking havoc with the invasion convoy, decided to approach. He turned to course 340 degrees True – north-northwest. Thinking the engagement was about to recommence, Admiral Kondo had his cruisers parallel the *Washington* again. The *Atago* fired three more Type 93s at the flagship. They missed. She also opened fire with her main guns. "Looks like someone opening fire on us on the starboard quarter," reported the main battery director on the *Washington*.[246] The main guns were trained on the *Atago*, relative bearing 150 degrees with a perfect firing solution, but, much to the gunners' frustration, Lee would not let them open fire. He did not want to give away his position with gun flashes, and he had lost track of the *South Dakota* once again.

So had the destroyer *Gwin*, even though she was almost right behind her. She radioed the flagship, "We bear 200 degrees from you. Proceeding on one engine," but she had mistaken the *South Dakota*, whom she was following, for the *Washington*.[247] The *Gwin* was having trouble getting to 15 knots and was dumping ammunition in an attempt to lighten the ship.[248] About a half-hour later, the bowless *Benham* radioed the flagship, "I am on your port quarter." She, too, had mistaken the *South Dakota* for the *Washington*.[249]

Meanwhile, in the midst of all this drama west of Savo, Admiral Hashimoto in the *Sendai* radioed Admiral Kondo that Lunga Point was clear so the *Kirishima* could proceed with the bombardment. It was a timely reminder to Kondo that he was still supposed to bombard Henderson Field and that he still had the *Sendai* and *Nagara* groups under his command. Kondo immediately signaled, "all units [to] attack" two enemy battleships 6 miles north of Cape Esperance.[250] This seems to have been the first indication that Admirals Hashimoto and Kimura had of the urgency of the situation west of Savo. Hashimoto's group was still east of Savo, so there was no hope of them taking part. But Kimura, just west of Savo with a few of his ships still reloading torpedoes, had his *Nagara* and his remaining destroyers immediately head west. Between Kondo's cruisers to the northeast, Tanaka's destroyers to the northwest, and now Kimura's ships to the east, there were three groups of Japanese ships converging on the *Washington*. It was a fairly dangerous situation, but not one of which Lee was unaware or for which he was unprepared.

In contrast, Admiral Kondo seems to have been a little slow on the uptake. He officially canceled the bombardment, since his battleship and his heavy cruisers were somewhat preoccupied. In preparation for action to protect the convoy, Kondo had the *Atago* and the *Takao* make smoke. Admiral Lee saw the cruisers from the *Washington*. More disconcertingly, he also saw two Japanese destroyers, *Oyashio* and *Kagero*, off the starboard bow making smoke and turning away …

Captain Davis immediately ordered a hard starboard turn, and the battleship heeled over as she made her sharp turn, disrupting the water so much that her wake occasionally registered on radar and frequently detonated Japanese torpedoes. At the direction of Admiral Lee, the turn was about 270 degrees, taking the battleship to course 180 degrees True – due south. Were those ships closing in from the east, northeast, and northwest? Lee was going to give them the slip by heading south. He had decided to withdraw. He had delayed the convoy long enough to prevent it from completing its unloading before dawn, when Henderson Field could handle it. Lee radioed the task force, "We are retiring," but only the *Benham* received it.[251] Davis ordered emergency power, bringing the *Washington* up to 27 knots.[252] As the leviathan pulled away, there were several large explosions in her wake, the waves causing the torpedoes launched by the *Oyashio* and *Kagero* to detonate. Davis had guessed correctly.

Admiral Lee kept his flagship well to the west of his damaged ships to continue to draw the Japanese away, which worked – almost too well. While Admiral Kondo kept his heavy cruisers to the north in a blocking position protecting the convoy, the chase was on with Admiral Tanaka's *Oyashio* and *Kagero* off the *Washington*'s starboard quarter and Admiral Kimura's *Nagara* and his destroyers off the port quarter. The *Nagara* herself launched torpedoes at "a new type battleship which appeared to have rudder trouble" and heard three explosions.[253] Not hits, the torpedoes had detonated in the battleship's wake. The *Oyashio* launched six more torpedoes at 1:39, and the *Samidare* of Kimura's group launched more six minutes later.[254] The torpedoes were launched at a receding stern profile, but despite the *Washington*'s evasive maneuvers that took her very close to Lamon (Laumuan) Island of the Russell Island group, four or five torpedoes came "uncomfortably close."[255]

By this time, Admiral Kondo had lost sight of the *Washington* and, for that matter, any of the American ships. Now he remembered he still had two destroyers with him in the *Asagumo* and *Teruzuki*. At 1:45, he unleashed them on the retreating Americans, but they had no chance to catch up.[256] At the same time, Kondo sent the battleship *Kirishima* a message explicitly directing her to withdraw. There was no response.

Admiral Hashimoto's report was taken to mean the coast was clear – literally – for Admiral Tanaka's transports. That part of Admiral Kondo's mission was successful; the other part, the bombardment of Henderson Field, not so much. Kondo was well aware of the wrath of the Cactus Air Force and wanted to put as much sea between his forces and Henderson as he could. His ships were almost out of torpedoes as well. So, at 2:04 he ordered everyone to withdraw once they had completed their attacks. He himself had the *Atago* and *Takao* take off around 2:30. The *Nagara* and *Kagero* had managed to keep the *Washington* in sight until 2:40 or so, and then they also pulled back, the *Kagero* under a smoke screen.[257] The only exceptions to the withdraw order were the *Asagumo* and *Teruzuki*. They were told to look for the missing *Kirishima*.

Even though the *Washington* could track on radar the Japanese retiring to the north, she was still very skittish. The bridge received multiple reports of torpedo boats stalking the battleship. On the PT boat circuit, Admiral Lee radioed a simple message: "Stop firing at us." Guadalcanal responded with the obvious, "Friendly PT boats are not firing at you."[258] That seemed to clear things up.

Things cleared up even more when Admiral Lee, after sending five messages over roughly a half-hour, was able to raise the *South Dakota* on the voice radio. Captain Gatch informed Lee that she was making 26 knots. The *Washington* was making a little more than that. They would reunite sometime after daybreak.

Further north, there was also a reunion, one not nearly as happy. After some 40 minutes of steaming eastwards in the night, at 2:43 am the *Asagumo* and the *Teruzuki* found the *Kirishima* about 5 miles west of Savo Island.[259] All alone in the dark, grievously hurt, the dreadnought was a horrific sight. Bludgeoned almost beyond recognition by the *Washington*, the battleship was listing to starboard with fires in her midships, pagoda, and forward main turrets. She could not fight. She could not move. The *Kirishima*'s condition was grave, her grip on life slipping slowly but surely.

The *Kirishima* could not move because of the *Washington*'s last salvo. It had missed, but at least one of the American flagship's shells had detonated under the *Kirishima*'s stern. Fragments had nibbled away at the starboard rudder, already jammed 10 degrees to starboard, but the real damage was to the port rudder, blown 80 degrees to starboard by the explosion. Though the port rudder was now turned to the right, it acted as a drag on the port side, forcing the *Kirishima* into an unwanted left turn. The search radar on the *Washington* had detected the *Kirishima* making a 500-degree turn – almost one-and-a-half circles. Moreover, the concussion destroyed most of what watertight integrity remained in the rudder machinery room, which flooded completely. "[A]ll engines were still operable with their full power," Captain Iwabuchi would later report, "but the steering gear room was completely flooded, so we couldn't make way at all."[260]

Both forward main turrets were ablaze, as were some of the aft secondary guns. On instinct borne of years of experience, Commander Ono ordered the remaining forward and aft magazines flooded to prevent explosion. As a result of this, however, the *Kirishima* was now listing to starboard. Ono ordered voids in the port side of the hull flooded to correct it, exactly what these open spaces were intended for, and the *Kirishima* quickly righted herself. Problem solved.

Elsewhere, things were not as easily rectified. With the rudders inoperable, they tried to steer the *Kirishima* with her engines, but the engines could not compensate for the port-side drag, so their efforts literally went nowhere. They tried to send divers into the steering compartment to see what could be done with the rudders, but the same explosion that had jammed the port-side rudder had also jammed the watertight hatches to the flooded steering room. "An attempt to prevent the flooding of the steering gear room also failing," Captain Iwabuchi would later report, "the ship became hopeless."[261] The battleship heeled to port. Commander Ono ordered starboard voids flooded, and the list was corrected again.

While Commander Ono was working diligently if not effectively to save his ship, Captain Iwabuchi was devising a plan to save his ship or at least to keep her in the fight. Able to steam only in circles, the *Kirishima* needed a tow to safety, either by the attending *Asagumo* and *Teruzuki* or, better yet, the *Nagara*, but instead Iwabuchi wanted to identify a place where she could be beached and then fire off her remaining 14-inch shells as a land battery.[262] How Iwabuchi planned to fire off those 14-inch shells when all his 14-inch guns were disabled was somewhat uncertain. Where was that Admiral Jojima when you needed him?

With all of her signaling devices destroyed, a simple flashlight was used to signal the *Asagumo* and the *Teruzuki* to approach. Heavy wire ropes were passed to them for towing the crippled battleship together. Captain Iwabuchi had a message forwarded to the *Nagara* as well asking for a tow. While this was going on, Iwabuchi was made aware that the engine rooms were becoming suffocating, with smoke and heat drawn in through the vents. With internal communications mostly down, the skipper sent runners to order the machinery spaces abandoned, but it was too late for some 90 percent of the men.[263] Eventually, only the center engine could function, and then only at the slowest speed. It was something of a tragic irony, since by this time most of the fires had been brought under control.[264]

The *Kirishima* heeled over to port and Commander Ono ordered additional starboard voids flooded again to rectify the list. It was standard damage control procedure for dealing with a list, with a few exceptions. Unfortunately for the *Kirishima*, no one seems to have grasped that the alternating lists meant this was one of those exceptions.

The *Kirishima* was in a similar predicament to that of the *San Francisco* two nights earlier. The *San Francisco* had a high volume of water trapped on, but not completely filling, the middle decks, making her somewhat top heavy. Every time the cruiser moved, the water would slosh from one side to the other, threatening to capsize the ship; the free surface effect in action once again. On one turn, the *San Francisco* heeled over a dangerous 40 degrees. She was eventually able to drain the middle decks. The *Kirishima* had taken two 16-inch hits below the waterline, which opened up her poorly compartmentalized middle deck to flooding. It was this water sloshing back and forth on the middle deck that was causing the battleship to list back and forth. Flooding the voids to correct the list caused the *Kirishima* to sink lower in the water – allowing yet more water into her middle deck to slosh back and forth. In short, every void Commander Ono flooded was actually another nail in the *Kirishima*'s coffin.

The battleship tipped to starboard. Soon it became difficult to stand on the bridge. Commander Ono shouted, "Commence counterflooding port voids!" Unsurprisingly, the list worsened. This was just in time for the destroyers to start towing the *Kirishima*. But though the lines held taught, with her magazines flooded, her voids flooded, her middle deck sloshing, and her port rudder dragging her back, the battleship would not budge. The destroyers flashed, "Towing is impossible."

Captain Iwabuchi and Commander Ono may not have understood the nature of the severe damage to the *Kirishima*, but it seems the *Nagara*'s Captain Tawara did. He flatly refused Iwabuchi's request to tow the battleship. Iwabuchi appealed to Admiral Yamamoto, asking him to make Tawara tow the battleship. It is not known whether Yamamoto saw the message.[265] The issue was moot anyway. It was too late.

The *Kirishima* wasn't moving, but her starboard list kept worsening. In desperation, Commander Ono ordered all the remaining port voids flooded. It did no good. The battleship continued to heel over to starboard. Silence fell over the already-dazed bridge with the shocking realization that their *Kirishima* was sinking and there was nothing they could do to stop it. Even so, Captain Iwabuchi, whose grip on rationality seems to have been slipping along with the life of his ship, only gave the order to abandon ship at the suggestion of Ono. Runners were sent to convey orders for all sailors to report to the main deck while the *Asagumo* and the *Teruzuki*, now joined by the *Samidare*, were signaled to come alongside to remove the crew.

As the officers and sailors arrived on the darkened main deck from below and above, they were appalled at the gruesome condition of their ship: bodies everywhere, the searchlight platform collapsed, the pagoda shredded so badly the original tripod mast on which the platforms had been bolted was visible in places, some fires still raging. To take up the survivors, the *Asagumo* moved to the *Kirishima*'s starboard quarter while the *Teruzuki* tied up to port.

But they didn't take the survivors just yet. Abandoning ship was a rather ritualistic affair in the Imperial Japanese Navy. First, the naval ensign was lowered while Captain Iwabuchi led the crew in singing the Japanese national anthem *Kimigayo* and giving three banzais. The emperor's portrait was removed to the *Asagumo*. Then the wounded were taken off, which was both difficult and time-consuming on a darkened and badly listing ship. To try to buy some time, Iwabuchi ordered the port engine room flooded. It had no effect, not immediately at any rate. Nevertheless, the evacuation proceeded in an orderly fashion. After the wounded had been taken off, everyone else began to follow.

All of a sudden, the *Kirishima* pitched over from starboard all the way to port. Flooding the port voids had at last succeeded – too well. The internal floodwaters had quickly sloshed over to the port side, loose equipment slid from the starboard side to port with a grinding roar, and the battleship's bow lurched upward. The *Asagumo* had to cut herself free, while the *Teruzuki* had to go into a full reverse and just barely avoided being crushed by the capsizing battleship.

The *Kirishima* joined her sister *Hiei* and rolled over to port to sink by the stern at 3:23 am.[266] The 300 survivors who were still aboard, including Captain Iwabuchi and Commander Ono, were unceremoniously dumped into the water, almost as if the battleship was rejecting the skipper who had wanted to shamefully end the *Kirishima*'s life by running her aground. Most of those in the drink, including Iwabuchi and Ono, were picked up by the *Samidare*, who was becoming very experienced at fishing survivors out of the water. The rescue work was completed by 4:30 and all three destroyers headed north to join Admiral Kondo.[267]

However you slice it, having your ship shot out from under you is not a pleasant experience. It's not like jumping into a pool with your clothes on – unless that pool is of indeterminate depth, and full of oil, blood, human waste, and debris. Worst of all was the oil. Several inches thick on the water's surface, it stung eyes, nose, and skin.

The lucky few had a spot in a raft or lifeboat, but those were normally reserved for the wounded. Maybe some had a floatation ring to keep them afloat or perhaps a life vest. Regardless, there was little to do but cling on to hope and wait as the hours passed.

Even in the dark, the survivors of the *Walke* and *Preston* had noticed two very important and disconcerting details: they were in waters off a Japanese-held coast near Cape

Esperance, and the tide was carrying them ever closer to that coast. At various times they tried paddling away from the coast but it did little good. There was nothing they could do about it except hope they were found before they made landfall.

Some lucky survivors of the *Walke* were on the still-floating bow of the destroyer or in rafts. However, about 15 in one raft were not feeling particularly lucky when, roughly an hour after the *Walke* was sunk, they were found by a surfaced Japanese submarine. Mustering as much authority as a whisper could manage, the mortally wounded Lieutenant Commander Scott told everyone, "Bow your heads," following it up with "No talking!" Expecting to be victims of another Japanese war crime, the men obeyed. Two Japanese crewmen swept a blue light over the raft twice. Evidently concluding the occupants were dead, the men went back into the submarine, which backed off and submerged.[268]

Later, around 4:00 am, survivors of the *Preston* detected four successive explosions from the empty waters somewhere west of Savo Island. These were evidently the forward magazines of the sunken *Kirishima*, now lying on the bottom upside down, detonating as a result of an explosive decompression, utterly shattering her bow.[269]

But nothing could top what they saw about an hour before dawn. Two very noisy ships passed by the survivors and anchored a few hundred yards off the Japanese-held beach.[270] Transports: what were they doing here?

Those ships also caught the attention of Henderson Field. As the sky was just lightening, Major Joe Renner took off in a JF2 Duck and Captain Joe Foss took off with eight F4Fs in order to be over the Russell Islands at daybreak so they could look for Lieutenant Colonel Bauer and Staff Sergeant Hurst. Outbound, they found three ships off Guadalcanal. Captain Foss saw a fourth, "full of men," 7 miles west of the island and headed for Aruligo Point. Foss called it in, then they continued their rescue mission.[271] As they did so, they encountered two Petes from the *Sanuki Maru* operating out of Rekata Bay. Both biplanes, one of which was flown by veteran pilot Lieutenant (jg) Watanabe Kaneshige, who was the acting commander of the *Sanuki Maru*'s air group, were shot down with no survivors. But they did not find Bauer or Hurst.*

Back at Henderson, SBDs were launched on scouting missions. The new fighter strip, Fighter 2, officially became operational with the takeoff of four Airacobras under Army Air Force 1st Lieutenant James T. Jarman of the 67th Fighter Squadron. The crew of Pistol Pete was kind enough to help inaugurate Fighter 2's new online status by lobbing several shells into it.[272]

Lieutenant Jarman examined the ships from 1,200 feet but saw no signs of life among them and could not even tell whose ships they were. He flew over them again, this time at 400 feet. He spotted some rafts and swimmers, but it was still unclear if they were American or Japanese. Jarman tried a third time. Now the ships got under way, heading for the beach, and opened fire with their antiaircraft guns at his Airacobra. Jarman flew back to

---

* The Type 0 Observation Seaplane should not be confused with the Type 0 Reconnaissance Seaplane.

Fighter 1 to report in person that there were Japanese transports near Tassafaronga some 7 miles west of the Marine perimeter.[273]

The response was immediate. At 5:55 am on November 15, Major Joe Sailer took off with eight Dauntlesses to attack the ships. By the time he arrived over the transports, all four had run themselves aground on the beaches. Men could be seen streaming from the ships into the jungle.[274] He noted "much Japanese activity," including what evidently were four antiaircraft guns on shore.[275]

These ships were the remnants of Admiral Tanaka's convoy that had proudly left Shortland with 11 transports. Off Aruligo Point was the *Yamazuki Maru*. In Doma Cove was the *Yamaura Maru*. And together near Tassafaronga at the mouth of the Bonegi River were the *Kinugawa Maru* and *Hirokawa Maru*.[276] The Japanese seem to have chosen these locations because they were closest to deep water.[277]

This was not the preferred method for unloading cargo; in fact, it was an act of desperation. Admiral Tanaka had originally planned for their unloading to begin around midnight and be completed in two hours, enough time for the transports to get away. But Admiral Kondo's aborted bombardment and the airstrikes of the previous day had delayed the transports so much the unloading could not start until dawn.[278] Tanaka had just spent a day watching what Henderson Field could do to his transports in the water. He could not let these last four sit offshore; they would be helpless in the face of air attacks and might never be unloaded. At least if the transports were run aground, the troops and supplies would have reached dry land and could still be unloaded via the cargo booms on the ships. The ships themselves would probably never sail again, like the *Kyushu Maru*, beached a month earlier and abandoned in what was now the midst of these transports.

"The concept of running aground four of our best transports was, to say the least, unprecedented, and I realized full well that their loss would be regrettable," Admiral Tanaka would later write. "But I could see no other solution."[279] At 3:00 am he radioed his plan to run the ships aground to Admiral Mikawa and Admiral Kondo. Mikawa rejected it outright, saying it would make landing of troops and supplies more difficult. Mikawa's reaction did not sit well with Tanaka, who seems to have considered Mikawa something of a know-it-all.[280] But Kondo, with the backing of Admiral Yamamoto, said, "Run aground and unload troops!"[281]

Though he had been given no specific instructions as to grounding the ships, Admiral Tanaka seems to have accepted a suggestion from Admiral Mikawa that he keep the ships offshore all night and beach them in the morning, "if the enemy situation so warranted."[282] The visit by Lieutenant Jarman seems to have propelled them into action and the ships had driven themselves high onto the beaches, in some cases the bows jutting upward at a 30-degree angle.[283] From these awkward positions the troops were climbing down netting and crates of equipment were being unloaded onto the beach.

Admiral Tanaka was long gone, hurrying back toward Shortland. Clearly he wanted to wash his hands of this catastrophe. Once the ships were in position, Tanaka had rounded up his remaining destroyers. They were full of the survivors of the sunken and abandoned transports, but only *Suzukaze* landed any troops. Then the destroyers left.

The only air cover available were eight Mitsubishi F1Ms – biplanes with floats – of which six came from the *Chitose*, one the *Sanuki Maru*, and one the *Kunikawa Maru*.[284] As far as air defense goes it was a pitiful commitment of resources. What the carrier *Junyo* was doing in all this is anybody's guess. She provided no air cover and it showed. Major Sailer's bombers claimed three hits on the beached *Kinugawa Maru* and *Hirokawa Maru* off Tassafaronga.

Meanwhile, American ground troops were mobilizing. American spotters pinpointed three of the transports for artillery. The men of Battery F of the Army's newly arrived 244th Coast Artillery Battalion dragged two 155mm (6.1in) guns to the beach at Lunga, within range of the beached *Kinugawa Maru* and *Hirokawa Maru*. A half-hour later came Marines of the veteran 3rd Defense Battalion with two 5-inch guns. They started pounding the two vessels.[285]

Lieutenant (jg) Tom Ramsay led three SBDs from the *Enterprise* aloft at 6:30. While they headed for 12,000 feet, Lieutenant Coffin, who had taken off after Ramsay, arrived over the ships all alone in a Grumman Avenger with four 500lb bombs. Three failed to drop, but one landed on the stern of one transport.[286] Ramsay's Dauntlesses plowed through the eight Petes and got two hits and a near miss. The Petes left after that, leaving the beached ships completely without air cover.[287] Ramsay's group returned to Henderson Field to rearm less than an hour after taking off.[288]

Lieutenant Jarman led four Airacobras armed with bombs, not only bombing the vessels, but strafing the thin-skinned ships with 20mm cannons and .30- and .50-caliber machine guns.[289] On his way back over Ironbottom Sound, Jarman saw debris, an oil slick, and a detached bow floating in the water.[290]

At 7:00 am, the *Enterprise*'s Lieutenant Stockton Birney Strong and Lieutenant (jg) Glenn Estes were sent up in their Dauntlesses to scout the area and attack the best targets they could find. They found four burning transports in The Slot some 100 miles northwest of Lunga, and, of course, the beached transports. Strong hit one of the beached ships with a 1,000lb bomb. Estes used his to trash a pile of landed supplies, resulting in a large explosion seen by the survivors of the *Walke* that sent smoke 300 feet into the air. Both SBDs landed around 9:30.[291]

Two more *Enterprise* Dauntlesses took off at 7:30, got near misses on the transports, and returned. Four more SBDs – two Marine, two from the *Enterprise* – took off at 8:15. "Just as soon as you got your landing gear up and could see over the trees, you could see the transports," remembered *Enterprise* pilot Lieutenant (jg) Bruce McGraw. On this run, he planted his bomb amidships, resulting in a spectacular explosion and several secondary explosions and fires.

It was the pattern for Henderson Field on this day: take off, hop over to the beached ships, attack them, then return to rearm, often within an hour. But as bad as this was for the Japanese ashore, it was about to get worse.

At 8:30 am, General Vandegrift had contacted the destroyer *Meade*, who was at that moment in Tulagi, to where she had escorted the cargo ship *Kopara* that morning. Vandegrift ordered the *Meade* to shell the transport beached at Doma Cove, the *Yamaura Maru*.[292] The *Meade's* skipper Lieutenant Commander Raymond S. Lamb was all too happy to help. He contacted Lieutenant John A. Thomas, who was flying the *San Francisco's* SOC floatplane, to act as a spotter for him, and left Tulagi at 9:15 to speed across Ironbottom Sound at 25 knots.[293] With Thomas' help, the *Meade* quickly located all the transports. She ignored the derelict *Kyushu Maru* and decided the *Yamazuki Maru* on Aruligo Point was such an inferno as to already be a total loss.[294]

At 10:12 am, the *Meade* opened fire on the *Yamaura Maru* at a range of 12,500 yards. In ten minutes she was burning so fiercely that Lieutenant Commander Lamb thought she was finished, so he targeted the ships off Tassafaronga, either the *Kinugawa Maru* or the *Hirokawa Maru*. Shortly thereafter, Lieutenant Thomas reported that the *Yamaura Maru* was only slightly damaged despite the fires on board. The *Meade* blasted her again. Seeing her sufficiently burning, Lamb switched back to the hulks at Tassafaronga for ten minutes. Then he decided to try out the *Meade's* new 40mm Bofors guns by strafing the beach.

Lieutenant Thomas reported that both the *Kinugawa Maru* and the *Hirokawa Maru* were "burning with many internal explosions" but that the *Yamaura Maru* was still holding on. The *Meade* headed back over to Doma Cove, raking the shore with her 40mm Bofors the entire way. At 10:54 the *Yamaura Maru* broke in two. Thomas reported no more targets and no Japanese troops visible. With his gunners exhausted – they had fired some 600 5-inch rounds – Lieutenant Commander Lamb considered his mission finished for the time being and turned the destroyer away.[295]

While the *Meade* was busy destroying three of the beached transports, Henderson Field decided to prevent the salvage of the four derelict transports the *Enterprise's* Lieutenants Strong and Estes had found in The Slot some 100 miles northwest of Lunga: *Brisbane Maru*, *Nako Maru*, *Arizona Maru*, and *Shinanogawa Maru*.

At 10:20 am, four *Enterprise* TBF Avengers under Lieutenant Larsen escorted by six Marine F4F Wildcats under Major Campbell took off with orders to torpedo the hulks. It was a grisly trip. They flew over "seventy miles of wreckage ... along the groove – debris of ships, corpses, oil streaks, life rafts, and an occasional burning hulk."[296]

The burning hulks were their targets. They found the *Arizona Maru* and the *Shinanogawa Maru* close together, with the *Brisbane Maru* and the *Nako Maru* visible off in the distance. Lieutenant (jg) George Welles and Ensign Bob Oscar of Torpedo 10 targeted the nearer two. Welles watched Oscar's perfectly dropped Mark 13 plow into the stern of one ship and sink without exploding, though it likely left an unsightly dent. Welles' own torpedo hit without exploding as well – another legendary performance by the Mark 13.

Lieutenant Larsen and Lieutenant (jg) Larry Engel aimed their Mark 13s at the *Nako Maru*. Engel's gunner John King later said, "Larsen missed by a mile" with his torpedo, but Engel's Mark 13 detonated amidships on the derelict. Larsen and Engel circled the *Nako Maru* until it sank, then rejoined Welles and Oscar for the trip back.[297] As they did so, they saw another transport sink in the distance.[298]

Espiritu Santo was getting into the act, sending up two groups, each of seven B-17s, into the area. One plunked another bomb into the two remaining derelicts in The Slot. The other didn't think the beached ships were worth the bombs and went back. Later that afternoon, a Marine SBD on a scouting mission put one more in the hulks. One sank that night, but the remaining gutted transport drifted until November 19, when she finally took the plunge off Malaita.[299]

The bloodbath on the beaches continued. Army Air Force Airacobras from the 67th Fighter Squadron continued to strafe the beached hulks, the troops that made it ashore, and concentrations of supplies the Japanese had managed to land. At 11:45, Lieutenant Coffin led his four Avengers back to join in by dropping concoctions of bombs and incendiaries they called "Molotov bread baskets." Lieutenant (jg) Bob Gibson led his three *Enterprise* Dauntlesses hunting for targets. Gibson got a close miss on the *Yamaura Maru* at Doma Cove.[300] Wingman Ed Stevens tried to drop his bomb, but it would not release. The other wingman, Lieutenant (jg) Ralph Goddard, did not have that problem, but he had been assigned to bomb an antiaircraft battery. He could not find it, but he did see a road leading from the beach to a circular area. He dropped his 1,000lb bomb there. The result was "an explosion of gratifying proportions," sending smoke rising up to 2,000 feet.[301] Guadalcanal Radio later called it, "Greatest sight ever seen on Guadalcanal. Still burning 16 hours later. Heavy black smoke. Estimated to be oil, ammunition, and stores."[302] Both Goddard and Gibson strafed the areas around their targets, and returned to Henderson around 3:40 pm.

The work of Henderson Field was by no means complete. Lieutenant Jarman took to the air in his Airacobra. Something about that debris and oil he had seen in Ironbottom Sound that morning was bothering him, but what was it? When he arrived over Savo Island, he finally figured it out – there were people in the water. Hundreds of people, survivors of the *Walke* and *Preston*, who had been in the water since the previous night, some 15 hours of soaking, trying to avoid Japanese or Japanese-held beaches, dealing with their wounds, fighting off sharks. And they were within sight of the destroyer *Meade* and the aircraft who had been attacking the beached ships all day. Jarman tried to get the destroyer's attention, but after two passes failed, he resorted to firing his 20mm cannons and machine guns in front of the *Meade*'s bow.[303] Lieutenant Commander Lamb likely did not appreciate that until he understood the reason. Jarman headed back.

He was replaced by Ensign Robbie Robinson and gunner Skip Gardner of the *Enterprise*, flying "inner air patrol" for the destroyer *Meade*. Robinson would fly low over groups of survivors, with Gardner marking some locations with smoke bombs for the destroyer, the YP boat, the PT boat, and the Higgins boats who came to fish everyone they could out of the water. Robinson and Gardner located more than 100 survivors; Gardner himself was later cited for finding at least a dozen individual swimmers, not with any group, who would otherwise have been lost.[304] Also joining in the rescue effort was Lieutenant Thomas in the *San Francisco*'s Seagull, several seaplanes from Guadalcanal, and eight *Enterprise* Wildcats under Lieutenant Commander Jimmy Flatley who provided air cover. By 2:30 pm, they rescued six officers and 129 men from the *Walke*, ten officers and 121 men from the *Preston*, and one man who fell overboard from the *Benham*.[305] But nothing on Guadalcanal was ever easy or cheap. In the late afternoon, Thomas' floatplane crashed in the water. The *Meade* quickly came over to the wreckage, but there were no survivors.[306]

Sailor Jim Cook of the *Preston* had just climbed aboard the *Meade* and was standing in an internal passageway when a Zero came in and strafed the ship. Cook was wounded in the left arm and left calf. Two *Meade* crewmen and three *Walke* survivors were killed. Several more survivors were wounded. The Zero, apparently Leading Seaman Ueno Masahiro's of the *Hiyo*, was shot down.[307]

Ueno was part of a two-pronged airstrike launched from Buin, possibly in response to the activities of the *Meade*. The first, seven Zeros of the 253 Air Group under Lieutenant Ito Toshitaka, launched at 12:30, meant as a decoy to draw the combat air patrol away from the second group, seven Zeros of the 252 and *Hiyo* air groups escorting seven D3A dive bombers, led by Lieutenant (jg) Kurihara Ichaya launched at 1:30. Ito's diversion worked but the strike fizzled as none of the Aichis could find the *Meade* – though Ueno found her – and turned back. Seven *Enterprise* Wildcats were scrambled to join Lieutenant Commander Flatley's eight Wildcats already in the air. The result was a scuffle in which one Grumman was shot down, the pilot recovered, and Ueno's Zero destroyed.[308] With that, the Japanese reinforcement effort came to a close.

This operation, intended to land some 12,000 men and some 10,000 tons of supplies on Guadalcanal, was an abject catastrophe for Japan. The Imperial Japanese Navy had lost two battleships, a heavy cruiser, three destroyers, and ten very valuable transports. At such a disastrous cost, the outcome was 2,000 men landed and some 5 tons of supplies – 360 cases of ammunition for field guns and 1,500 bales of rice – enough for about four days.[309]

Admiral Tanaka would later write, "My concern and trepidation about the entire venture had been proven well founded."[310]

As the ships of the Japanese 2nd Fleet entered Truk Harbor, Admiral Ugaki thought, "It was lonely indeed that we couldn't see the *Hiei* and *Kirishima* among them." When Admiral Abe stepped ashore, he looked even worse. According to Ugaki, "He looked sad with a bandage on his lower jaw. With a sorrowful face he reported losing two ships under his command." Apparently the *Akatsuki* and *Yudachi* did not count – not uncommon for battleship admirals, it would seem. "He seemed to suffer especially for his sunken *Hiei*,"

Ugaki wrote. "He even confided that he thought he would have been better to have gone down with *Hiei*."[311]

Admiral Yamamoto was furious over the loss of the *Hiei*, understandably believing that Abe had jumped the gun in ordering her scuttled before checking in with Combined Fleet. Both Abe and Captain Nishida were hauled before two admirals who comprised a quickly convened secret court of inquiry. Abe and Nishida were called to testify but did not offer a defense. Abe was cited for his "disgraceful leadership."[312] Both were given face-saving jobs, then shunted off into "retirement," or what Hara called the equivalent of a dishonorable discharge. They kept their pensions but were barred from public office.[313]

Admiral Kondo was next to face Admiral Yamamoto's wrath. The choice of Kondo as deputy commander of the Combined Fleet had not been a popular one, nor had been his choice to head the second attempted bombardment of Guadalcanal. He was seen as overcautious and "lacking in spirit."[314] He was never again given a seagoing command.

During the entirety of the battleship engagement, the cruiser *Portland* stayed tied up to a palm tree off Tulagi, hoping no one would notice her. And no one did, the *Junyo* scout's report apparently not attracting much interest. The crew was busy cleaning out damaged compartments and scrounging I-beams from abandoned Japanese equipment to shore up the hull in those compartments. The attack by the PT boats did not discourage the cruiser from fueling the boats when needed during this time. On November 16, underwater shipfitters arrived from Espiritu Santo. They worked with the cruiser's own divers to cut away the warped steel on the stern and return it to some semblance of operation. It was difficult work even for this team of highly skilled technicians, but two days later it was completed successfully. The grateful crew of the *Portland* watched as these trouble-shooting shipfitters headed off for their next assignment aboard a PBY Catalina – which promptly crashed on takeoff, with no survivors.[315]

It was another six days of around-the-clock repairs before the *Portland* was ready to leave Tulagi, towed by the tug *Navajo* and escorted by the ubiquitous *Meade* and destroyer-minesweeper *Zane*. Unfortunately the jury-rigged steering broke down outside Tulagi and she had to return for some more jury-rigging. She finally left Tulagi at 8:00 pm on November 22 and was not so much towed, as she steamed on her own with the *Navajo* alongside, just in case, all the way to Sydney for more temporary measures before she returned to the US for a permanent repair job.[316]

The *Portland*'s trip might have been slow and boring, but at least it lacked the unwanted drama experienced by other ships such as destroyers *Gwin* and *Benham*. At 2:45 am, the *Benham* had radioed Admiral Lee, "Making 10 knots. Forward fire room has buckled and may carry away."[317] Some 15 minutes later, the *Gwin* estimated she was 5 miles from the *Benham* and adjusted speed to join her at dawn.[318] Lee ordered both to make for Espiritu Santo. The *Benham* doesn't seem to have received the order, but a little more than a half-hour later she radioed the *Gwin*, "My speed is two knots.

Bow may drop off. Close me." The *Washington* picked up the message. Lee responded by contacting the *Gwin* with the instructions, "Proceed as previously directed. Use your discretion." At 3:30, Lieutenant Commander Fellows responded that he was trying to find the *Benham*.[319]

The two destroyers were able to link up as the sun was coming up at 4:15, when the *Gwin* took station 1,000 yards on the *Benham*'s port quarter as they left together.[320] The *Gwin* was hobbled but the *Benham* with her broken back, down 2 feet at the bow and up 1 foot at the stern, was truly struggling. They varied their speed between 5 and 15 knots depending on how the *Benham* was handling in what were thankfully smooth seas, but the fractured destroyer creaked and groaned anyway. They even tried having the *Benham* go in reverse, but that just made things worse.[321]

Throughout the day, Lieutenant Commander Taylor and his crew did everything they could to try to save their ship. Ammunition and anything else heavy were dumped over the side. The cracks in the decks and bulkheads were marked. Plates were welded over the crack in the main deck.[322] Taylor evacuated the forward part of the *Benham*.[323]

But men in peril on the sea are always at the mercy of the sea, and on this day the sea was merciless. Around noon, the swells increased to about 3 feet.[324] With the *Benham* only held together by her exterior hull and interior bulkheads, the increased stress was just enough to twist her cracks open more and more. By around 4:00 pm, it became too dangerous to proceed, and Lieutenant Commander Taylor stopped the destroyer, requesting the *Gwin* approach to take off the crew. The sea was too rough for directly transferring the crew, so rafts, lines, and, for the injured, the whaleboat were used. Some even swam.

By 6:24 the entire crew had been taken off. At 6:33, the *Gwin* set about hastening the *Benham*'s end with one Mark 15 torpedo; it exploded prematurely. So, two minutes later she fired another one; it missed ahead. At 6:49 she fired a third; it ran wild and disappeared. At 7:13 she fired a fourth; it missed astern.[325] It was another legendary performance by the Mark 15, arguably exceeding the standard set with the attempted scuttling of the *Hornet*. Resigned to gunfire, the *Gwin* hit one of the *Benham*'s magazines with a 5-inch shell at 7:35 pm and the destroyer sank.[326]

But the sacrifice of the destroyers had not been wasted and in fact was considered necessary. The *South Dakota*'s Captain Gatch believed the destroyers "indirectly deceived" the Japanese into firing their torpedoes too soon. The *Washington*'s Captain Davis agreed, believing – correctly – that the Japanese had mistaken the destroyers for larger targets. "This probably saved the battleships being hit by torpedoes," he said. Apparently caring for his destroyers more than Admiral Abe did, Admiral Lee took to asking Gatch if his use of the destroyers had been proper. "As things turned out, I thought it was," Gatch replied. Lee was very appreciative of their sacrifice, writing, "In breaking up the enemy destroyer attack, our destroyers certainly relieved the battleships of a serious hazard and probably saved their bacon."[327]

Their bacon was indeed saved, but things were frying beneath the surface on the two battleships. At 6:49 am, the *Washington* secured from battle stations. Admiral Halsey initially ordered the *Washington* to head toward Espiritu Santo and rendezvous with fully fueled destroyers. Then this new force was to keep themselves in a position to reach the Savo Island area by 10:00 that night. However, the attacks on the transports were so successful and the Japanese retreat so complete that this order was countermanded.[328]

So the American flagship did not catch up to the riddled *South Dakota* until 9:51 am on November 15.[329] The *South Dakota* blinkered a message to her undamaged cousin: "We are not effective. Turret 3 out. Fire control badly damaged. Only one radar operative. Fuel tank holed."[330] With the *South Dakota* trailing a slick of bunker oil, the two made for Nouméa. Initially they braved Torpedo Junction with no destroyer escort until 10:40 that night, when the destroyers *Dale*, *Lardner*, and *Stack* joined and formed an antisubmarine screen.[331]

Two days later this small force reached Nouméa, at which point the crews of the *Washington* and *South Dakota* started fighting with each other in the bars and streets. The *South Dakota* sailors thought the *Washington* had abandoned them; in turn, the *Washington* sailors believed they had saved the ineffective *South Dakota*. A *Washington* sailor would later say, "War was declared between the two ships. It was that simple." The US Navy was and is not necessarily one big happy fleet. A furious Admiral Lee forced a truce, issuing a special Order of the Day decreeing, "One war at a time is enough!" Shore leave for the crews was staggered until the *South Dakota* left for full repairs in the US, at which point the battleship got most of the press for the victory, while the *Washington* was largely unnoticed by the news media.[332]

The final drama was reserved for the survivors of Friday the 13th, who arrived off Espiritu Santo the afternoon of November 14. Upon their arrival, Admiral Turner sent an aide to summon the acting skipper of the *San Francisco*. Lieutenant Commander Schonland promptly got into the *Helena*'s whaleboat for the trip to the *McCawley*. As he stepped onto the gangway, Turner's flag lieutenant told him Turner wanted to see the officer who was on the *San Francisco*'s bridge during the battle, not him. No good deed goes unpunished, at least with the acerbic Turner. A humiliated Schonland returned to the cruiser and McCandless went over to report on the battle.[333]

After some badly needed rest, emergency repairs, a concert by the *Helena*'s band, and the assignment of a new commanding officer – Captain Albert Finley France, Jr. – the cruiser went to Nouméa. Admiral Halsey came on board to inspect the cruiser's damage. He gripped the selfless Lieutenant Commander Schonland by the shoulders and declared, "Men like you, Schonland, are going to win this war."[334] Halsey's staff material experts put the *San Francisco* and her damage through a fine-toothed comb and determined that nothing short of a full-fledged navy yard could repair the damage. She was sent off to Mare Island.[335]

Much less happy was the arrival of the *Helena* in Nouméa on November 16. The previous day, Admiral Halsey had ordered Captain Hoover to sail there immediately. That was not a good sign, Hoover knew.

Admiral Halsey grilled the skipper over what he had done to rescue the men of the sunken *Juneau*. No, Captain Hoover had not stopped for survivors; it was simply too dangerous. He had reported her sinking to the B-17, but the report by pilot Lieutenant Gill had been buried on an intelligence officer's desk. He had reported it to Admiral Turner but had not mentioned survivors. He had reported it to Admiral Fitch, who did nothing.[336]

There was more than one party who dropped the ball here, including Captain Hoover, to be sure. Admiral Halsey did not learn of the loss of the *Juneau* until he read Hoover's list of ships arriving in Espiritu Santo. Wondering where the *Juneau* was, he asked his chief of staff Captain Miles Browning to find out. He checked with Admiral Turner, who had just been given a report that a search plane had found some 60 men in the water. Turner cross-referenced the report with Hoover and determined these were the survivors of the *Juneau*. Turner reported to Halsey that the *Juneau* was sunk and Hoover had not stopped for survivors.[337]

No one who witnessed the explosion of the *Juneau* believed there even could be survivors – but there were, over 100 of them, and even though B-17s and PBYs flew over them time and again, none thought to send them any help. The survivors were suffering in a special kind of hell, trapped at sea, with no food, especially no drinkable water, blasted by the searing sun, and circled by hungry sharks. Some died of their wounds, others were driven mad, and still others just gave up. As historian Eric Hammel put it so eloquently, "Every death was the culmination of intense agony and the most brutal mental and physical suffering imaginable."[338]

The tragedy was seemingly an opportunity for Captain Browning. Admiral Halsey's chief of staff was a brilliant man who has also been described as "brawling and ill-tempered" and "a psychotic misanthrope" – and who harbored a grudge against Captain Hoover from their time at the Naval Academy.[339] Browning made sure the investigation and subsequent report put Hoover in the worst possible light.

But the use of bureaucracy to settle old personal vendettas did nothing to help the survivors of the *Juneau*, who were still in the water and suffering. An appalling eight days after the *Juneau* was sunk, a PBY Catalina picked up ten survivors. Lieutenant O'Neil and the medical staff that had gone to the *San Francisco* had survived as well. Everyone else, out of a total crew of 697, had perished, including all five brothers from the Sullivan family, two brothers from the Rogers family, and two from the Coombs family.

Captain Hoover was an aggressive, highly respected skipper now experienced in night fighting and destined for flag rank. But he was not well versed in bureaucracy the way Captain Browning was. So, for not stopping to rescue the survivors of the *Juneau*, Admiral

Halsey removed Hoover from command of the *Helena*. The decision devastated the crew of the cruiser. Much later, Halsey would write of his decision, "I was guilty of an injustice," admitting "Hoover's decision was in the best interests of victory."[340] The media with the full connivance of the Navy wanted a head. It would be Hoover's. Even a later court of inquiry that exonerated him could not save his career.

Ancient Carthage, those people known for burning babies to death as offerings to the god Baal Hammon, had a habit of crucifying – literally – a commander who lost a battle. It was a stupid habit, as it did not allow them to learn from their mistakes. Carthage paid dearly for this policy in its wars with Rome.

Like Carthage, the US Navy had just crucified – figuratively – a commander, albeit one who had won a battle. They did this for no other reason than the irrational vengefulness of a talented bureaucrat.

And like Carthage, the US Navy would pay dearly.

CHAPTER 5

JUST WHEN YOU THINK

As long as humanity has had armies, there has been the adage, "An army marches on its stomach." Before an army can fight, it must be fed. Quite simply, if it is hungry, it will lose effectiveness on the battlefield, which was exactly the situation facing the Japanese in the Solomons. While they had done their homework for the Java Sea Campaign and were prepared for almost any contingency, their advance in the Solomons was much more opportunistic, much less prepared. They established their main bastion at Rabaul, home to a fine harbor and an equally fine set of active volcanoes which occasionally hampered air operations. They had then moved to extend their line down the Solomons to Tulagi and Guadalcanal, but do not seem to have considered how they would support it.

Once the US had captured the Lunga airfield in August 1942, Japanese efforts on Guadalcanal were in trouble. Any troops they sent to recapture the airfield, any supplies sent to those troops, had to run the gauntlet of American air power. The airfield had to be suppressed; the supplies had to have air cover. But to provide air support, Japanese aircraft had to travel some 650 miles from Rabaul to Guadalcanal and hope they wouldn't be shot down or have engine trouble. They did have a few bases around Bougainville – Buka, Buin (called "Kahili" by the Allies after a nearby village) – but the Japanese had not set up the necessary intermediate bases to strengthen the line from Rabaul to Guadalcanal. They would repeatedly set up seaplane bases in Rekata Bay near the northern tip of Santa Ysabel. But seaplanes are always less effective, as they would prove time and time again during the course of the campaign, than regular land-based aircraft.

With their supply line effectively cut the Japanese 17th Army on Guadalcanal was now in desperate shape. The experience of Admiral Tanaka's convoy had, once again, showed the dilemma: they needed troops and supplies to take the Lunga airfield, but that same airfield prevented them from getting those troops and supplies. By this time, the 17th Army had no more than five artillery pieces, and could not afford to fire more than ten rounds a day unless they wanted to risk being left without ammunition with which to defend themselves. There had been plenty of ammunition for the artillery on Tanaka's transports, but most of it ended up on the bottom of The Slot or exploding on the beaches of Doma Cove. The small arms ammunition situation was only marginally better.

But it was food that was truly lacking. Of the some 28,000 Japanese troops of the 17th Army on Guadalcanal, only about 4,200 were estimated to be in any shape to fight. Starvation rations did not help the body's immune system, and the vast majority of the Japanese troops were stricken with malaria. Those soldiers who could walk were assigned to scouting, patrols, and attacks. The vast majority, too weak to walk, were put in defensive emplacements.[1]

Imperial General Headquarters recognized the problem, but did not know how to solve it. Back in August, it was the Imperial Japanese Navy that had wanted to recapture Guadalcanal and the Imperial Japanese Army that had focused on New Guinea. Now, it was the Navy that thought the important theater was New Guinea while Guadalcanal wasn't worth the already staggering cost and the Army that insisted on recapturing the island. Imperial General Headquarters, forced to negotiate between the two rival services, concluded that things had to change.

Imperial General Headquarters had already realized that General Hyakutake could not manage campaigns in both New Guinea and Guadalcanal at the same time, so the campaigns were split. General Hyakutake kept the 17th Army on Guadalcanal. A new army, the 18th, was formed to handle operations on New Guinea and handed over to Lieutenant General Adachi Hatazo. Lieutenant General Inamura Hitoshi was appointed to coordinate and oversee these two armies as commander of the new 8th Area Army, the Imperial Army's equivalent of an army group. Inamura was recognized as a good administrator and it was hoped that he would be able to improve the rapidly worsening situation. Summoned to the Imperial Palace to officially receive his new appointment, as the general was bowing himself out, the emperor said, "Inamura! I understand that my soldiers are suffering terribly on Guadalcanal. Go as soon as you can. Even one day is important." There were tears in his eyes.[2]

General Inamura arrived at Truk on November 21, 1942, on his way to Rabaul. On the *Yamato* he was to be briefed by the ubiquitous Colonel Tsuji and meet with the Combined Fleet staff.[3] The new area army commander's initial orders were to recapture the Solomons and drive the Allies from New Guinea. But the defeat of the early November offensive on Guadalcanal prompted a reorientation. On November 18, the objectives in New Guinea were limited to protecting "important areas," which were essentially Lae, Salamaua, Madang, and Wewak, while retaking Guadalcanal was kept on the agenda.[4]

Also on the agenda was the assessment of a possible site for a new airfield at Cape Munda, near the southwestern end of New Georgia, only about 170 miles from Guadalcanal, roughly halfway between Guadalcanal and Bougainville. On November 13, the old destroyer *Hakaze* had dropped off airfield surveyors and three companies of the

6th Sasebo Special Naval Landing Force to secure and assess the Munda site.[5] They found it suitable for an airfield. Construction on the Munda site was now formally approved at this meeting and began in short order.[6] This would be another, crucial base for Base Air Force. Needless to say if the Munda airfield had been developed six months earlier recent events may have taken a very different course.

Inamura was able to secure some reinforcements for his new command; the 6th Kumamoto Division from China, the 65th Brigade, and, most importantly, the 6th Air Division of the Japanese Army Air Force, consisting of 110 aircraft. The plan, given the catchy title of "South Pacific Number 8 Operation," started, prudently, with the strengthening of that supply line with intermediate airbases – Rapopo, near Rabaul, for the Army; Vila, on Kolombangara Island in the middle Solomons, for use by both the Army and the Navy; Ballale, an island just off Shortland where airfield construction had begun on November 3; and the aforementioned Munda for the Navy.[7] With the new Army aircraft and 135 aircraft from the Navy, these bases would help regain air superiority. The Navy would transport reinforcements to the 17th Army while barring Allied reinforcement of Guadalcanal. The plan would culminate in an offensive to retake the island around January 20, 1943.[8]

It was a plan that taxed Japanese shipping capacity perhaps to the breaking point, but the Imperial Navy had more immediate concerns. In New Guinea, General MacArthur had launched his offensive to take Buna, the main Japanese base on the north coast of Papua.

This offensive was the result of another of those times when General MacArthur's performance was "horrid." Buna had been unoccupied by anyone until July. Allied intelligence had long believed the Japanese were interested in Buna, but MacArthur made no effort to get there first. When intelligence revealed a Japanese invasion convoy leaving Rabaul on July 13, Colonel Kenneth Wills, senior intelligence staff officer for the Australian 1st Army, determined it was headed for Buna.[9] However, MacArthur's chief of staff, the "highly irritable" General Sutherland refused to believe it, saying he had no hard evidence that Buna was their destination.[10] The convoy was spotted on July 19 heading directly for Buna by a B-17 from the 19th Heavy Bombardment Group, resulting in an attack by one B-17 and five B-26s on July 21.[11] Sure enough, that night, the Japanese landed at Buna. Multiple heavy air attacks the next day by 5th Air Force B-17s; 22nd Medium Bombardment Group B-25s and B-26s; and 35th Fighter Group Airacobras against the Japanese transports off Buna were too little, too late, and futile.[12] The Japanese were at Buna in force. At least Sutherland now had his hard evidence.

Having given Buna away, General MacArthur would have to pay dearly to get it back. Worse than having given away a major strategic position, as it had been with the disasters at Clark Field and Bataan, MacArthur had made a very public miscalculation. That was not just intolerable; it was impossible. Someone else must be at fault. As MacArthur had shown after Clark Field, he and his senior staff would be utterly ruthless and unreasonable in their search for scapegoats. Back then, he had blamed Admiral Hart, his Asiatic Fleet, and the US Navy. Now he blamed the Army Air Force, sacking three generals, including his air commander Lieutenant General George Brett.[13] MacArthur and his senior staff would also whip everyone to correct his mistake or at least cover it up.

In mid-November, General MacArthur began his latest offensive in the now four-month-old campaign to correct his mistake. Leading the attack up the Kokoda Trail had been the 16th and 25th Brigades of the Australian 7th Division. As the Australian troops neared the northern coast of Papua, MacArthur brought in the 126th and 128th Infantry Regiments of the US 32nd Infantry Division. His plan called for the 7th to take Gona and Sanananda while the 32nd would take Buna. It sounded simple enough.

But, as in the Philippines, General MacArthur and his senior staff had badly misjudged the strength of the Japanese. MacArthur relied on his staff intelligence officer, Brigadier General Charles Willoughby, whom Papuan campaign historian Peter J. Dean says "demonstrated high levels of mediocrity" and was "one of the poorest, if not the worst, senior Allied intelligence officers of the war."[14] But he also had a sycophantic quality that was clearly important to MacArthur.[15] Willoughby had determined the Japanese had about 1,500–2,000 troops in the area of Buna and Gona, and that even these troops gave "little indication of an attempt to make a strong stand against the Allied advance."[16] From his own intelligence estimates, 32nd Division commander Major General Edwin F. Harding expected "easy pickings with only a shell of sacrifice troops left to defend [Buna]."[17] Colonel Wills and the Australian intelligence staff, who "consistently proved more apt at analyzing Japanese strengths and intentions," knew better.[18] Naturally, General MacArthur didn't listen to them.

In fact, the Japanese had some 6,500 fresh troops in the 11-mile-long coastal strip from Buna northwest to Gona. They were well dug in, with a line of concealed bunkers made from coconut logs, some reinforced with steel, almost all with connecting trenches. Their fields of fire dominated the few trails leading from the swamps through which the Allied attackers would have to move.[19] General Sutherland "glibly" called these fortifications "hasty field entrenchments."[20]

To top it off, the Australian 7th Division was badly understrength, while General Harding's 32nd Infantry Division was half-trained, inexperienced, and underequipped, consisting of Michigan and Wisconsin National Guardsmen who had never received jungle combat training.[21] General MacArthur ordered Harding to attack "regardless of cost."[22]

As hard as it may be to believe that with this preparation, more worthy of General Kawaguchi or General Hyakutake than one of the best generals of the war, the offensive, launched November 16, would stall, but stall it did: in the proverbial and literal quagmire. The swampland, as it was on Guadalcanal, was distinctly unhealthy, striking down the Allied troops with malaria and dengue fever in generous quantities. Then the Japanese took their proverbial and literal pound of flesh. The attack bogged down after about a week. MacArthur accused the 32nd Division of a lack of "fight."[23]

On November 21, General MacArthur busted some heads. He summoned Lieutenant General Robert L. Eichelberger, commanding the 32nd's parent unit, I Corps, to his headquarters.

"Bob," said General MacArthur in a grim voice, "I'm putting you in command at Buna. Relieve Harding. I am sending you in, Bob, and I want you to remove all officers who won't fight. Relieve regimental and battalion commanders; if necessary, put sergeants in charge of battalions and corporals in charge of companies – anyone who will fight. Time is of the essence; the Japs may land reinforcements any night."

"Bob," he said, "I want you to take Buna, or not come back alive." He paused a moment and then, without looking at [Brigadier General Clovis] Byers, pointed a finger. "And that goes for your chief of staff too. Do you understand?"

"Yes, sir," the corps commander answered.[24]

And General MacArthur meant it. Later in the campaign, when informed that General Eichelberger was risking his life at the front, MacArthur "cold-bloodedly" remarked, "I want him to die if he doesn't take Buna."[25]

It was a sorry performance, with Douglas MacArthur at his absolute worst. His arrogance and overconfidence had gotten him into trouble yet again. So now he drove his subordinates and his troops with a ruthlessness not usually seen outside the Imperial Japanese Army. All to correct his mistake. But Douglas MacArthur was right about one thing: the Japanese could land troops at any time.

Because as poorly as the offensive was going for the Allies at the moment, it sent shockwaves through Combined Fleet. A furious Admiral Ugaki called the Army "careless" and commented that, if the Buna airfields were lost, "air raids upon Rabaul would be intensified, ultimately making it impossible for us to hold there."[26] Inamura agreed to divert the Army's 21st Brigade to Buna.[27]

General Inamura then headed off to Rabaul, where he arrived on November 22. Inamura immediately radioed General Hyakutake on Guadalcanal, telling him that two fresh divisions would arrive within a month and requesting a complete report "without hiding anything."[28] Hyakutake didn't hide anything, reporting that his troops had been living on grass roots and water for a month. Moreover, "an average of 100 men starve to death daily. This average will only increase. By the time we get two division reinforcements, doubtful how many troops here will be alive."[29] Inamura could only offer promises of help, adding that their bravery was "enough to make even the gods weep."[30]

Three days after his commanding officer had visited Truk, General Adachi came in for a briefing by Combined Fleet. Coming over from China, Adachi had very little understanding of the South Pacific situation. By this time, the Japanese on Guadalcanal were being pushed westward out of their lines on the Matanikau River. Included in this retreat was the 16th Infantry Regiment, which came from Admiral Yamamoto's home town of Nagaoka. Trying to lighten the dark mood, Yamamoto joked about "the poor conduct" of the 16th Infantry. Admiral Ugaki told him to shut up.[31]

Not getting the hint, Admiral Yamamoto added that he was "encouraging them to clear the past dishonor. But most probably, they will never come back alive." With a smile he concluded, "I, too, will not be able to go back home unless Guadalcanal is recaptured, so I am depending on your army."[32]

General Inamura formally assumed command of the 8th Area Army on November 26. That same day, Major Hayashi Takahiko arrived from Guadalcanal with a formal report from General Hyakutake. The 17th Army was almost out of meat and vegetables, and its supply of rice and barley would be exhausted that very day. Some units had not been resupplied for six days. Medical supplies were also exhausted, since the army suffered through being deployed mostly in jungle areas devoid of sun or on reverse slopes. Naturally, in his view, the blame for this situation fell entirely on the Imperial Japanese Navy for a lack of support, especially air support, and an inability to cut the Americans' supply lines.[33] That the Japanese Army Air Force had until now contributed none of its own aircraft in support of its own 17th Army was apparently left out of this report.

The food situation had reached crisis proportions: "Starvation Island" indeed. The redoubtable Captain Monzen Kanae, who had been commanding Japanese naval troops on Guadalcanal since before the American landing, sent a hand-written note to Admiral Ugaki stating, "Hardships and shortages have reached beyond the limit this time."[34] The Japanese needed to get food to the 17th Army. Since the Americans kept attacking supply convoys, the Japanese would be forced to try other methods.

Back on November 16, Combined Fleet ordered most of its submarines in the area to prepare to transport food to Guadalcanal in what would be called "mole (*mogura*) runs."[35] A submarine could transport 20–30 tons of food on one trip, enough to feed the army on Guadalcanal for a whole day, assuming the troops could manhandle the crates from the beach through miles of jungle to the front lines.

It was not a plan that found favor with the submariners. On his flagship, the light cruiser *Katori* at Truk, Vice Admiral Marquis Komatsu Teruhisa, head of the Japanese 6th Fleet, its submarine force, had to justify the idea to his angry staff. "Our Army troops … are starving on Guadalcanal. They used the last of their rations several days ago. More than a hundred men are dying from hunger daily. Many of the rest are eating grass. Very few men are fit for fighting." Komatsu looked around the wardroom. "What are we to do," he asked, "let our countrymen starve to death in the jungle?" The answer was obvious: "We must help them, no matter what sacrifices must be made in doing so!"[36] Nevertheless, the submarine crews absolutely hated it, calling themselves "*Marutsu*," the Imperial Japanese version of FedEx.[37]

In running supplies, submarines presented a new set of difficulties. The first supply effort on the night of November 24 was foiled by the presence of PT boats and aircraft. The next night, *I-17* landed about 11 tons, but had to cut the mission short when the US destroyer *McCalla* showed up.[38] Every night thereafter to the end of the month, they would land 20–30 tons. But it was a very expensive effort in terms of fuel and submarine commitment for a relatively paltry return. Worse, as more and more Allied naval units showed up, it was also becoming increasingly dangerous.

Then the Japanese began implementing a plan for something they called "Chain Transportation," moving supplies in little night trips along a "secret course" – a chain of bases in the Solomons from Rabaul to Guadalcanal – using tiny cargo ships of 500 tons or less that they called "sea trucks."[39] The concept was sound. But the groundwork for it should have been laid long ago, before the campaign – for reasons that now became apparent.

As their first new base in the chain, the Japanese chose Wickham Anchorage, on the island of Vangunu off the southeast coast of New Georgia. On December 26, two sea trucks, *Takashima* and *Iwami Maru*s, arrived in Wickham carrying dehydrated rations, sealed drums of rice, a machine gun section and a signal unit. Both ships were camouflaged – poorly – by a few palm fronds, which fooled neither New Georgia coastwatcher Donald Kennedy nor an Airacobra scout that found them at 10:15 am. About four hours later came an airstrike centered around seven SBD Dauntlesses, who pummeled both ships with bombs. The *Iwami Maru* quickly sank, while the *Takashima Maru* lingered until late that night before foundering.[40] The next night, December 27, destroyers *Urakaze*, *Tanikaze*, *Isonami*, *Inazuma*, *Arashio*, and *Yugure* successfully dropped off 600 army troops at Wickham without incident.[41] The following day the sea trucks *Kiku Maru* and *Azusa Maru* brought 300 naval infantry, food, and heavy antiaircraft guns to Wickham. They, too, were camouflaged – poorly – by palm fronds. This did not fool a pair of P-38s flying reconnaissance on the morning of December 29. Just before 10:00 am, a dozen Dauntlesses arrived from Henderson Field and promptly destroyed both ships before they could offload more than a tiny fraction of their cargo.[42] Now, instead of starving troops on Guadalcanal, the Japanese had starving troops on both Guadalcanal and Wickham. So much for Chain Transportation.

The Japanese were thus forced to switch to Plan C: continuing the tried-and-tested method of "Rat Transportation" – running food into Guadalcanal at night on destroyers. (It's hard to escape the conclusion that none of the Imperial Navy crews actually enjoyed running supplies, given their unflattering nicknames for it.) But with a rather bizarre twist. They would put 330 pounds of rice and barley into an oil drum that had been scrubbed clean – hopefully. They would load 200–240 of these half-filled drums, joined by ropes, onto the fantail of a destroyer. When the destroyer was close to the Guadalcanal shore, the drums would be pushed overboard, to be pulled ashore by the troops on Guadalcanal. The destroyers could then be away before daylight. It would take twenty such destroyer runs per month to feed 20,000 men. It was not a perfect plan. The same fuel and efficiency issues of the original Tokyo Express were present with this new version. Munitions remained an issue, since they were too heavy to be transported by this method, and while the tides were predictable, the currents were not. To be blunt, this was a method borne of desperation. There was simply no other option.

The first of five planned runs would be handled by none other than Admiral Tanaka and his veteran 2nd Destroyer Flotilla, minus his normal flagship *Jintsu*. As befitting a Japanese admiral, Tanaka proceeded to slice and dice his command into smaller, bite-sized pieces. His temporary flagship, the brand new destroyer *Naganami* would, with her sister

Takanami, form his own Screening Unit. They would carry no drums of food because, as previously noted, a Screening Unit's job was, theoretically, to screen the Transportation Units, who were carrying the actual drums of food. The 1st Transportation Unit would consist of the destroyers *Makinami*, *Oyashio*, *Kuroshio*, and *Kagero*, each carrying 240 drums, to be dropped off at Tassafaronga. The 2nd Transportation Unit, with the *Suzukaze* and *Kawakaze*, would each carry 200 drums to be dropped northwest of Tassafaronga at the mouth of the Umasani River. Carrying the drums made the destroyers too heavy to carry their torpedo reloads and made using their torpedo tubes problematic, basically halving their combat effectiveness, hence the need for the screen.[43] The *Takanami* was slated to escort the leading 1st Reinforcement Unit, while Tanaka's flagship *Naganami* would escort the 2nd. Most of the admiral's destroyer skippers were unhappy with this choice of dispositions, since Tanaka would not be leading the formation, which is where the admiral would traditionally be stationed.[44]

Of course, upholding tradition in the face of changing conditions was a major reason why the Imperial Japanese Navy had been reduced to dropping drums half-full of food into the water and the Imperial Japanese Army had been reduced to hoping they could pull the drums in. Not to be able to fight, but just to be able to stay alive.

Admiral Tanaka's supply convoy of destroyers left Shortland at 12:30 am on November 30. They passed through Bougainville Strait and turned east, heading toward Roncador (Keulopua) Reef, looping to the north of the Solomons. Moving at 24 knots, the force was shadowed by a B-17, frustrating Tanaka from turning south until around noon. He needn't have worried; the reconnaissance plane did not report him. Under cover of a friendly squall, the force headed south to Ramos Island, passing west of Rua Dika and Buena Vista Islands before heading down Indispensable Strait, upping the speed to 30 knots for the final run to Guadalcanal.[45]

That afternoon, Japanese scout planes reported 12 destroyers and nine transports. Admiral Tanaka passed the words to his crews, adding, "There is a great possibility of an encounter with the enemy tonight. In such an event, utmost efforts will be made to destroy the enemy without regard for the unloading of supplies."[46] In other words, feeding the starving troops was not the top priority. It never was.

Admiral Tanaka received no other reconnaissance reports throughout the day. His 2nd Destroyer Flotilla was, he still believed, the best in the Imperial Japanese Navy, even without his normal flagship *Jintsu*. They had trained together, fought together. They were tough veterans who did not need much in the way of orders but would properly carry out any orders he issued. At 6:45 pm, Tanaka organized his ships into a column. The *Takanami*, as planned, was in the lead. After her were the destroyers of the 1st Unit, the 15th Destroyer Division with the *Oyashio*, *Kuroshio*, *Kagero*, and *Makinami*, carrying division commander Captain Sato Torajiro. Behind that was Tanaka's *Naganami*, and the 2nd Unit, the 24th Destroyer Division, with the *Kawakaze* and *Suzukaze*, under the command of Captain Nakahara Giichiro.[47]

Coming from the north, the Japanese force entered Indispensable Strait and sighted Savo Island at 9:40 pm. An hour later, Admiral Tanaka's delivery destroyers looped to the south of Savo Island and headed eastward into Ironbottom Sound some 3 miles off the shore of Guadalcanal. The *Takanami* as planned split off and moved ahead about 4½ miles from shore, scouting the area ahead of the main force. Carrying Captain Shimizu Toshio, commander of the 31st Destroyer Division, and skippered by respected veteran Commander Ogura Masami, Tanaka considered the three-month-old *Takanami* the ideal ship to keep watch. She reported that everything was clear.[48]

Having found the lighted markers off Doma Cove, at 11:00 pm the flagship veered to starboard to lead the *Kawakaze* and *Suzukaze*. The three destroyers bringing up the rear slowed to dump their drums, dropping back from the rest of the force. Tanaka thought he saw the running lights of US scout planes over Ironbottom Sound, so he ordered the *Naganami* to speed on ahead to help the *Takanami* with scouting.[49] What were the Americans doing?

Few Japanese skippers accepted how things had changed since Midway.[50] Fewer still knew how to adapt when things changed. The exception was Tanaka Raizo.

At 11:12, the voice radio squawked, "Sighted what appear to be enemy ships, bearing 100 degrees." This was quickly followed by, "Seven enemy destroyers sighted." The voice was from the destroyer *Takanami*.[51]

The reaction from Admiral Tanaka was cool, calm, and immediate.

"Stop unloading. Take battle stations."[52]

To the Americans the battles of mid-November had represented a turning point in the Guadalcanal campaign. But the losses to the US Navy had been staggering – 18 ships sunk or so badly damaged that they would be down for an extended period. With the exception of destroyers, Vice Admiral Halsey's only available warships were the carrier *Enterprise*, still under repair; battleship *Washington*, and light antiaircraft cruiser *San Diego* at Nouméa; and the heavy cruisers *Northampton* and *Pensacola* at Espiritu Santo.[53] To keep the pressure on, Halsey needed more ships. Indeed, help was on the way. After the naval battles of Guadalcanal, Admiral King had stormed in to the Joint Chiefs of Staff to demand the transfer of ships from the Atlantic and Mediterranean to replace the losses in the Pacific.[54]

Admiral King won the immediate transfer of two cruisers, three escort carriers, and five destroyers to the Guadalcanal area, with more to follow. But it would take a while for them to arrive. Meanwhile, naval protection remained fragile, which necessitated major reorganizations in the South Pacific.

On Guadalcanal itself, Henderson Field was adding a mile-long strip so it could house B-17s and other heavy bombers. Since the naval battles of mid-November, the Cactus Air Force had increased in size from 85 to 188, including heavy bombers for that new airstrip as well as reconnaissance and antisubmarine aircraft.[55] It represented a critical mass of aircraft that could menace the Japanese up and down the Solomons.

In the interim, Admiral Halsey was promoted to full admiral, a recognition of his success and the growing importance of his command. They still had only one operational carrier, *Enterprise*, whose task force was now under Rear Admiral Frederick C. Sherman, former skipper of the *Lexington*, for the time being. But by November 25, the freshly repaired *Saratoga* under Rear Admiral DeWitt C. Ramsey was at Nandi in the Fijis and due to return. Also at Nandi were the older battleships *Colorado* and Pearl Harbor survivor *Maryland*, under Rear Admiral Harry W. Hill, waiting for assignment; the newly repaired *North Carolina*, set to join Admiral Lee's *Washington* and the just arrived *Indiana* to form a task force of battleships; as well as the light antiaircraft cruiser *San Juan*. Two little escort carriers, *Altamaha* and *Nassau*, were also in the area ferrying aircraft to Espiritu Santo and Nouméa.[56] Eight destroyers were assigned to patrol the route between the Solomons and the bases at Espiritu Santo and Nouméa, the infamous Torpedo Junction.[57]

But battleships and aircraft carriers would not be fighting in the waters of Ironbottom Sound. PT boats would, if they could stop their unfortunate habit of shooting torpedoes at anything that appeared, enemy or otherwise. By November 30, 15 of them were housed at Tulagi, along with the PT boat tender *Jamestown*.[58] Cruisers would be fighting there, too. The heavy cruiser *New Orleans* and the light cruiser *Honolulu* had come from Pearl Harbor to join the *Northampton* and *Pensacola* at Espiritu Santo on November 25. The heavy cruiser *Minneapolis* arrived two days later.[59]

While this collection of ships at Espiritu Santo sounds impressive, it was in reality the only force that Admiral Halsey could hastily slap together. It was urgently needed because the Japanese appeared to be up to something. The amount of shipping in and around the Shortlands was something of a tipoff as to Japanese intentions. After the battles of mid-November, the number of Japanese cargo ships was very low, bottoming out at a dozen. But those numbers began to grow again on November 24. On November 27, the number of cargo ships in the Shortlands was estimated to be 25–30.[60] Clearly a supply or reinforcement attempt had to be in the offing.

To stop this effort, Admiral Halsey had this mass of cruisers: *Minneapolis, New Orleans, Pensacola, Honolulu, Northampton*. But who should command them? With the deaths of Admirals Scott and Callaghan and the sacrifice of Captain Hoover to office and national politics, there were no flag officers experienced in handling surface forces at night. Admiral Kinkaid, having been recently replaced by Admiral Sherman as commander of the *Enterprise* task force, was available, so Halsey tabbed him to command this new force, designated Task Force 67.

Admiral Kinkaid had done a creditable job commanding the *Enterprise* task force, but he was a "black shoe admiral," to use historian John Lundstrom's term – a non-pilot, who usually wore black shoes; commanders who were pilots usually wore brown boots. This cost Kinkaid credibility with some people, as it had Admiral Fletcher, and some wondered if this lack of aviation training had played a role in some of his less successful decisions.

Be that as it may, Admiral Kinkaid got the job to head Task Force 67. Kinkaid arrived in Espiritu Santo on November 24, while his cruisers assembled. Oddly, in a campaign that featured four major night combat engagements, three of which involved cruisers, neither Kinkaid nor any of these particular cruisers had taken part. They had been serving as escorts to the aircraft carriers. When the various carriers were sunk, it had the perverse effect of freeing these ships for surface action, just as it had aircraft for Guadalcanal. The destroyers *Fletcher*, *Drayton* (who had arrived with the *Minneapolis*), *Maury*, and *Perkins* were then thrown together to form a totally inadequate screen.

Admiral Kinkaid spent three days working up his general plan of battle, completing it on November 27. Under this operational plan, given the catchy title of "Oplan 1-42," Kinkaid divided this new Task Force 67 into one group of destroyers and two groups of cruisers, each led by a ship equipped with the SG search radar. One group of cruisers would be led by Rear Admiral Mahlon S. Tisdale in the light cruiser *Honolulu*, the other by Rear Admiral Carleton H. Wright in the heavy cruiser *Minneapolis*. The destroyers would be led by Commander William M. Cole in the Guadalcanal veteran *Fletcher*. This SG radar-equipped ship would lead the other destroyers to scout some 10,000 yards ahead of the main force.

The plan was to exploit the advantage conferred by radar with a surprise torpedo attack by destroyers executed on their own initiative, without the need for permission from command. Once their attacks were complete, the destroyers would clear out, possibly rotating back behind the cruisers to use their guns once the cruisers were finished. The cruisers would remain at a distance of 10,000–12,000 yards from the enemy, outside the range of enemy torpedoes – they thought – and would not open gunfire until the torpedoes were due to strike. The cruisers would then bombard the enemy from this standoff distance. Use of searchlights was specifically forbidden. A skipper could flash recognition lights only if fired upon by a friendly ship. Floatplanes would be flown off to Tulagi before the engagement, from where they could be called upon to perform scouting and illumination. Any illumination they provided over a shore was to be at least a mile beyond the shoreline in order to avoid illuminating friendly ships.[61]

Oplan 1-42 was striking on multiple levels. Admiral Kinkaid tried to avoid repeating mistakes made in earlier battles of the campaign, incorporating some painfully learned lessons. These included getting the floatplanes off the ships so they would not be the fire hazards as they had been at Savo Island; ensuring destroyers cleared out so they would not be caught in the crossfire like at Cape Esperance; not using searchlights or recognition lights that attract enemy fire as they had in the Friday the 13th engagement; and placing the radar-equipped ships in front, as they should have been in that same action. But much was borrowed from the Japanese as well, reflecting a healthy willingness to copy from the enemy that which had been effective: the use of torpedoes before gunfire to preserve surprise and concealment as long as possible; the opening of gunfire to be concurrent with the torpedoes hitting their targets; the independence of destroyers in torpedo attacks; and the use of floatplanes for scouting and illumination.

Admiral Kinkaid's Oplan 1-42 was an excellent piece of careful consideration, self-reflection, and research. Naturally, after putting so much time and effort into preparing this tactical plan, Kinkaid was immediately reassigned to the North Pacific to help retake from the Japanese those two Aleutian bastions of infinitesimal strategic value – Attu and Kiska. In fairness, Kinkaid wanted to be reassigned. He was upset at losing command of the *Enterprise* task force and viewed his new assignment as something of a demotion. His replacement would be Rear Admiral Wright. This seemed logical. "Bosco" Wright had been Kinkaid's subordinate and was intimately involved in the development of the plan. Naturally, after taking command himself, Wright scrapped much of it.

Admiral Wright had no time to settle in to his new command. On November 29, a coded Japanese transmission was sent alerting the 17th Army on Guadalcanal to the supply operation. The transmission was promptly decoded by *Magic*.[62] That was as much confirmation as one could hope for. That afternoon, at 4:52 pm, Admiral Halsey signaled Wright, "Be prepared to get underway as soon as possible with all your force present and intercept enemy destroyers at CACTUS night of [November] 30–[December] 1. Report your force and readiness."[63] Wright responded, "*Minneapolis, New Orleans, Pensacola, Honolulu, Northampton, Fletcher, Maury, Perkins, Drayton* ready midnight 29th."[64]

At 7:35 pm, Admiral Wright signaled his ships to prepare to leave at midnight and that Oplan 1-42 was "effective," but less than a half-hour later he was backing off the latter:

Present intention destroyers concentrate two miles ahead of guide before entering Lengo Channel. Upon clearing channel and until contact is made destroyers on bearing 300 true from guide distance 2 miles. Cruisers in line of bearing 320. Maneuver by turn movements to pass about 6 miles from coast. Expect to direct commence gunfire at range about 12,000 yards. Situation will probably not permit withholding gunfire to complete torpedo attacks. Any vessel having known enemy within six thousand yards is authorized open fire.[65]

Admiral Halsey ordered Admiral Wright to take his force east and north of San Cristobal to enter Lengo Channel and be off Tassafaronga by 11:00 pm on November 30. Wright responded that he planned to leave at midnight and be off Tassafaronga by 1:00 am on December 1. That itinerary was not good enough for Halsey, who was concerned the convoy might consist only of destroyers and thus responded, "Enemy may arrive sooner than expected." He added, "Hurry arrival."[66] This meant completing the 600-odd-mile run to Tassafaronga in 23 hours. Wright was concerned that his ships would have to average more than 26 knots, requiring the use of all their boilers for the full 23 hours.[67]

So, come midnight, Task Force 67 was north-bound with a long way to go and a short time to get there. Even so, they passed east of San Cristobal, hoping to avoid Japanese scouts. They didn't; as noted above, a reconnaissance plane radioed Admiral Tanaka, "12 american warships and 9 transports approaching Guadalcanal."[68]

The Japanese were not the only ones watching. The indefatigable coastwatcher Paul Mason, scanning the Shortlands anchorage, found that a dozen destroyers had vanished during the night. He notified Guadalcanal, who passed it on to Admiral Halsey and Admiral Wright. But no one seemed interested in where those destroyers could have gone.[69] Also uninterested had been the crew of a B-17 on a scouting mission north of the Solomons that seems to have passed over several destroyers at around 10:00 am.[70] And didn't report them.

During the afternoon of November 30, Admiral Wright directed that his ships were to go to battle stations at 8:00 pm that night.[71] A little while later, at 4:25 pm, all ten scout planes were flown off from the cruisers to Tulagi carrying 160 gallons of fuel and four parachute flares.[72] When ordered to do so, they were to launch from Tulagi and search between Lunga Point and Cape Esperance starting at 10:00 pm, to report all enemy ships sighted to the admiral, but not to release the aforementioned flares unless he so ordered.[73] Wright had pushed his ships so hard that 90 minutes had been knocked off the travel time; expected arrival off Tassafaronga was now 11:30 pm.[74]

The admiral kept fine-tuning his plan, though how fine it was tuned was up for debate. "About the last visual dispatch we got before dusk settled in were instructions stating not to commence firing without permission," said Lieutenant Joseph C. Wylie, executive officer of the *Fletcher*.[75] Yet another part of Oplan 1-42 scrapped. Meanwhile, Tulagi, in order to avoid another friendly fire incident, ordered its PT boats to return to port because of the approach of Wright's task force.[76]

But a friendly collision incident was almost in the making. As Admiral Wright's force approached Lengo Channel, they were in a column led by the destroyers *Fletcher*, *Perkins*, *Maury*, and *Drayton*, followed by the flagship *Minneapolis*, then the cruisers *New Orleans*, *Pensacola*, *Honolulu*, and *Northampton*. Wright had been informed that a friendly supply convoy was around here somewhere, but he did not know precisely where until the convoy of three freighters and five destroyers suddenly materialized out of the dark headed straight for him. "Collisions were narrowly avoided."[77]

Two of the destroyers escorting the convoy, the destroyers *Lamson* and *Lardner*, forming 9th Destroyer Division, had received orders from Admiral Halsey at 6:50 pm to put themselves at Admiral Wright's disposal.[78] At 7:37 pm, Wright messaged them, "form astern of last unit of this formation. My speed 20."[79] The *Lamson* and *Lardner* fell in as directed at around 9:00 pm. Commander Laurence A. Abercrombie of 9th Destroyer Division now became the senior destroyer commander present. Except he had no idea of Wright's plan; Wright did not want to radio the plan to him, and flashing it by Aldis lamp could take an hour. So there was no way for Abercrombie to effectively command the destroyers. Abercrombie would later write, "No information was obtained concerning the disposition of enemy forces, what might be encountered, no operation orders, no special instructions, no recognition signals, no reference or rendezvous points or anything pertaining to the night's operations."[80] Wright just told him to rely on "good sense and tactical signals."[81]

But adding two more ships to a task force at night when those ships were unfamiliar with the plan or the other ships or the officer in tactical command was asking for trouble in the form of a friendly fire incident. This had almost happened with the ships already in the force and already familiar with the plan. At 9:35 pm, the *New Orleans*, struggling with its radar, radioed Admiral Wright, "We think we have about 4 contacts on the port bow in column."

This description of the contacts must have sounded disturbingly familiar to Commander Cole of the *Fletcher*, leading the four destroyers. He asked, "Is that us?"[82] It was. Fortunately for him, the *New Orleans* had more sense than, say, the PT boats currently cooped up in Tulagi. But it was indicative of how Admiral Wright had deviated from Oplan 1-42 – the *Fletcher* or some other SG-equipped destroyer was originally supposed to be 10,000 yards out in front. She was not even half that, and consequently could not effectively scout even with her SG radar.

Admiral Wright's force cleared Lengo Channel at 10:25 pm.[83] The cruisers changed course by head of column to 320 degrees True, with the destroyers on parallel courses, to parallel the coast of Guadalcanal some 25 miles away. About 15 minutes later, pursuant to orders given earlier by Admiral Wright, all ships turned to course 280 degrees True, in the process forming a line abreast, with the line at an angle of 140 degrees – this was called a line of bearing.[84] This was done so the ships could approach the Guadalcanal coast together and perform a maximum sweep of the coast with their search radars, but 11 ships charging in a line – an angled line, actually, known as an echelon – was an impressive sight reminiscent of the ancient Athenians charging at Salamis.

And the charge found something. At 11:06 pm, the radar operators on the *Minneapolis* saw something that looked like "a small wart on Cape Esperance." The wart grew larger until it finally detached itself from the land. It was almost due west, 284 degrees True, at a distance of 26,000 yards.[85] The wart then started splitting up until, by 11:15, seven blips were clearly visible, heading to the southeast at a speed of 15 knots.[86] At 11:08, Admiral Wright ordered "Ships right to 320 degrees True" to reform the column.[87] He immediately informed the rest of his force of the radar contact, almost due west, distance 32,000 yards.[88]

At 11:10, the destroyer *Fletcher*, leading the Allied force, picked up blips at 14,000 yards. Commander Cole had the destroyers increase speed to 25 knots. As the range closed, the Japanese formation became clear – a column with a lone ship on the port beam of the leader. It was running parallel to the coast of Guadalcanal – course about 150 degrees True – about 1.5 miles into the water. He ordered the *Fletcher* to course 290 degrees – northwest. He watched the port torpedo director as the range closed and the angle became a perfect port beam shot – 270 degrees – for Mark 15 torpedoes running at 36 knots for 9,000 yards, which was the intermediate setting.

Ready to launch his torpedoes, at 11:16 pm, Commander Cole radioed Admiral Wright, "Interrogatory William," which was code for a request to fire torpedoes.[89] Wright responded, "No," elaborating, "Range to our bogey is excessive. 14,600 yards."[90] Lieutenant Wylie called Wright's response "the most stupid thing I have ever heard of."[91] It seems two different pictures were emerging on the *Fletcher* and on Wright's flagship *Minneapolis*. And neither ship could grasp what the other was seeing.

Admiral Wright had checked with his radar plot and found the closest target was still 14,600 yards away. Commander Cole had checked with his radar and found he had a perfect beam torpedo shot on a target 7,000 yards away.[92] Who was correct? There is the possibility that both were, as it has been suggested that Wright simply spaced it and forgot the *Fletcher* was almost 3 miles ahead of the *Minneapolis*.[93] "Do you have them located?" Wright asked his destroyer skipper. "Affirmative. Range is all right for us," Cole replied.[94] Was it? At its fastest speed the Mark 15 could only travel 4,800 yards. In the November 13 action, the *Fletcher* herself had fired ten torpedoes at a range of 7,000 yards and missed – rather embarrassing, but whether it was more embarrassing that she missed with ten torpedoes or that her target had been the USS *Helena* no one could say.

Admiral Wright had, in divergence with Oplan 1-42, tied his destroyers' hands; his command was paralyzed with indecision. To his credit, Wright understood this and checked with the radar plot again. The operators could distinguish four and guessed they were destroyers. Wright's instinct told him the same thing; the Japanese would not lead with transports, except at Cape Esperance, where almost everything the Japanese did was wrong. The admiral shared his information with Cole. "Suspect bogies are DDs. We now have four." Both Wright and Cole were aware the clock was ticking; the seconds had turned into minutes, four of them to be exact. The admiral finally approved: "Go ahead and fire torpedoes."[95]

Commander Cole relayed the admiral's approval to his lead destroyers. But during those four minutes Cole had watched in frustration as his perfect firing solution slipped away. The targets were now passing him in the opposite direction. He had to have the torpedoes reset for a stern chase, the long-range setting but with a slower speed – 27 knots, at which speed Japanese ships could actually outrun the torpedoes. He fired his first half-salvo of five torpedoes at three-second intervals off the port quarter.

Then the voice radio on the bridge crackled to life with the voice of Admiral Wright. "Stand by to roger." Time seemed to freeze during the slight pause that followed. "Execute roger. And I do mean roger!"

Admiral Wright was taking no chances; there was no mistaking the meaning of "roger" here, as there had been at Cape Esperance. He immediately sent a plain-language message to Admiral Halsey: "Am engaging enemy surface forces."[96] The nine 8-inch guns of the *Minneapolis* roared at once, the concussion staggering the cruiser's skipper Captain Charles E. Rosendahl. Lieutenant Russell Sydnor Crenshaw, Jr., the gunnery officer of the *Maury*, was struck by the flash of the guns. "The flash was dazzling, lighting up the ocean for hundreds of yards. Anyone caught with his eyes open could see nothing except the brilliant orange blob the flash had etched into the retina."[97] The 5-inch secondary battery started launching starshells for illuminating their targets.

There was thunder and light from the main batteries of the *New Orleans* and the *Northampton* within a minute. The *Pensacola*, with no SG radar, struggled to find a target, opening fire four minutes after the flagship. The *Honolulu* opened up a minute after that. Here was another departure from Admiral Kinkaid's painstakingly crafted

Oplan 1-42: they had opened gunfire not only before the torpedoes could hit the targets, but barely after the torpedoes had been launched.

Commander Cole on the *Fletcher* finished launching the last five of his ten torpedoes, then opened gunfire on the rightmost target in the enemy column. After some 60-rounds of 5-inch shells, her fire control radar lost the target lock and she stopped shooting.

The *Perkins*, 500 yards behind the *Fletcher*, launched a full salvo of eight torpedoes at the closest target, which was the lone destroyer flanking the lead Japanese ship. Then she poured 50 rounds of 5-inch ammunition at the same target. Skipper Lieutenant Commander Walter C. Reed saw a large explosion. Was it one of his torpedoes hitting the target? He couldn't tell.[98]

Next astern, the *Maury* had no SG radar and so held her torpedoes until a target presented itself visually. She was able to get a target lock with her gunnery radar – which promptly shorted out. Using the firing solution from the range-keeper, she fired 20 salvos, sweeping back and forth hoping to hit something. But her target was obscured by smoke and the Americans' own starshells bursting between the destroyer and her target, blinding the *Maury*'s gunners. She thought she might have glimpsed her target – a "small merchantman," maybe?[99]

The SG radar of the *Drayton* detected five ships, but plotting the contacts showed their speed to be zero. Either the Japanese ships were stopped, the radar was malfunctioning, or it was picking up land, probably Cape Esperance.[100] Skipper Lieutenant Commander James E. Cooper couldn't imagine the enemy ships would be stopped, but he took no chances and launched two torpedoes at 8,000 yards at a target she found to the right of the main group, holding the rest of her torpedoes until the situation better materialized. She opened fire on the same target with about 100 5-inch shells; she never saw her shells hit anything and never saw any enemy ships.[101]

The flagship *Minneapolis* was pouring on the gunfire. The first salvo was somewhat over, but the second was on target, and the next two were straddles. Captain Rosendahl watched as the target, identified as a transport, "violently disintegrated."[102]

The *New Orleans* was firing her guns by radar control, at an enemy destroyer 8,700 yards away on her port bow. The lookouts noticed this target was drawing fire from other cruisers as well. Should they maybe fire at something else? The question became moot when the lookouts reported the destroyer blew up after the *New Orleans*' fourth salvo.[103]

Next in the column, the *Pensacola* took four minutes to find a target. She had no SG search radar, but she used her fire control radar to search on the bearing and range reported by the leading destroyers. Using this improvised method, she detected an object her officers believed to be a light cruiser, potentially the *Yubari*, some 10,000 yards off the port bow moving at 17 knots, left of the ships under fire from the *Minneapolis* and *New Orleans*. The *Honolulu* and *Northampton* behind *Pensacola* had opened up on this target as well. The *Pensacola* joined them, only to fire her first three off target. She shot up starshells of her own to better illuminate the target, and after her fourth or fifth salvo, the lookouts reported the cruiser had sunk.[104]

The rapid-firing light cruiser *Honolulu* took two minutes after Admiral Wright's order to find a target. The starshells revealed what she identified as a Japanese destroyer off the port bow at a range of 9,600 yards. The cruiser put those 15 rapid-firing 6-inch guns to work for 30 seconds. The rangekeeper reported the target was staggering to a stop. Another 60 seconds of rapid fire and lookouts reported the destroyer had sunk.[105]

The last cruiser in the column, heavy cruiser *Northampton*, had no SG search radar and thus struggled to find a target. She had to train her fire control radar on the shell splashes from the other ships and was finally able to locate a destroyer. She unloaded her main battery on the target and was rewarded with reports from her lookouts of several hits.[106]

But the rear destroyers *Lamson* and *Lardner* were hamstrung by being the last in the column and, having no real idea of Admiral Wright's battle plan, could not find targets. The *Lamson* fired starshells to try to shed some light on the situation. And shed some light she did, temporarily blinding the Americans and achieving little.[107] In the uncertain illumination and against the dark background of Guadalcanal, she sighted three shadows, again off the port bow heading in the opposite direction. The *Lardner* took these ships under fire at a range of 9,000 yards, but after three salvos the wraiths disappeared in the darkness.[108]

So far, it seemed to be going well, with one notable exception: the cruisers' floatplanes at Tulagi. They were trying to take off, but the seas were calm, smooth, and glassy. While that might be good for ships, it's bad for seaplanes. The water has a suction effect on the pontoons and other floats of seaplanes. Choppy seas reduce the contact between the water and the floats and thus reduce the suction. But the seas were so smooth that even at full power, the scout planes could not generate enough lift to overcome the suction effect of the water. This phenomenon had been known for over a decade, with a relatively simple solution: send a small speedboat to zigzag in front of the seaplane, forming ripples and chops that create separation between the water and the floats, reducing the suction and allowing the seaplanes to take off. There were 15 PT boats close by at Tulagi that could fill the zigzag function, but the idea of asking any of the PT boats to help was apparently beyond comprehension for the ten floatplane crews. The pilots spent an hour cursing and swearing as their pontoons remained stuck to the sea.[109]

Nevertheless, things seemed to have gone well for the Americans. Admiral Wright's column continued sailing in a straight line while raking the area to port with explosives and starshells. Although blinding gunflashes, smoke, shell splashes in and around the enemy, and the uncertain light from the starshells that played through the low clouds and smoke made it very difficult to see the results, the cruisers especially were putting out a tremendous volume of gunfire and knocking down Japanese ships like mechanical ducks in a shooting gallery. Lieutenant Crenshaw on the *Maury* was impressed, but he had a creeping uneasiness:

Starshells streaked in from the left and filled the sky with dazzling flares from the quarter forward to the beam. As their number increased, the eerie white light brought a type of daylight to the scene. A wall of smoke and shell splashes blanketed the target area, but no ships could be seen. A few flashes, which might be gunfire, appeared to the right of the main enemy group.[110]

There were a lot of shells, a lot of torpedoes, a lot of explosions, a lot of smoke, a lot of starshells, a lot of splashes. The air was full of sound and fury – but signifying nothing; hitting nothing.

Nothing but empty sea.

This would be the third time the Japanese had been surprised during the Guadalcanal campaign. There was Admiral Goto at Cape Esperance, Admiral Abe at Guadalcanal, and now, Admiral Tanaka. But Tanaka Raizo was not Goto Aritomo, who never understood what he was facing, or Abe Hiroaki, who panicked and froze. No, Admiral Tanaka, already a controversial figure within the Imperial Japanese Navy, did not panic, did not freeze. He was firmly in command.

Nevertheless, the admiral did have his hands full. The *Kawakaze* and *Suzukaze* had been stopped and were lowering their boats to release the drums; the *Makinami*, *Kagero*, *Oyashio*, and *Kuroshio* had actually passed the *Takanami* and were putting crewmen in boats to prepare the drums when Admiral Tanaka's order to stop unloading came in.[111]

But this was the 2nd Destroyer Flotilla. Admiral Tanaka and his men had been through difficult situations before, including virtually having to take on an entire Allied cruiser column by themselves in the Battle of the Java Sea due to the ineptitude of Tanaka's superior. They would manage – and they did.

Flares and starshells started falling. "The minute these parachute flares burst into light, enemy ships opened fire on the nearest ship, which was the *Takanami*," Admiral Tanaka would later write.[112] There were no parachute flares, not yet, anyway. The scouting destroyer was surrounded by shell splashes. Tanaka did not hesitate: "Close and attack."[113]

The order was not quite that simple. Captain Toyama Yasumi, Admiral Tanaka's chief of staff, ordered the destroyers to reverse course and increase speed to 24 knots to throw off the enemy aim. He had also ordered them to not use gunfire unless absolutely necessary, an order which was about to pay immediate dividends.[114] Oddly, for whatever reason, the *Takanami* did not follow this order and started returning fire with her 5-inch battery as she turned to port back the way she had come.

The Japanese were outgunned and outnumbered, and not even sure of what they were facing. But they did have one critical advantage. Like Savo Island and like the November 15 action, the Japanese ships were between the Americans and the land, which made spotting them against the dark backdrop of Guadalcanal much more difficult. One would think that the Americans' SG search radar would neutralize that advantage. But shell splashes show up on radar, and the American gunfire was so heavy that the shell splashes were cluttering the radar images and confusing the operators.

Between the poor visibility and the cluttered radar screens, the Americans did not notice the Japanese turning around. Near Doma Cove, Captain Nakahara's destroyers *Kawakaze* and *Suzukaze* dumped their drums, rang up emergency full speed, and reversed course to port. Closest to the Americans, the *Takanami* turned around to port as well. Admiral Tanaka's flagship *Naganami* turned to starboard, away from the enemy, which seemed to violate his own order to "Close and attack," leaving many of the men on his ships grumbling, but there was a method to his madness. Near Tassafaronga, Captain Sato's *Makinami*, *Kagero*, *Oyashio*, and *Kuroshio*, struggling to dump their drums, did not reverse course yet but made a turn to port to unmask their weapons. The course changes threw off the American aim. The shells landed where they were supposed to land, where the Japanese were supposed to be, except the Japanese were not there, and the avalanche of shells splashed almost entirely in empty water.

But the Japanese were struggling with visibility as well. "[N]umerous illuminating shells and parachute flares suddenly set off by the enemy brightened our vicinity so that it was extremely difficult to make out the formation of the enemy fleet," Tanaka would later write.[115] The continuous flashes of gunfire from the US Navy ships, however, were as good as bullseyes for the Japanese.

It felt like an ambush. The Japanese squadron was too scattered to mount a coordinated response. But this was the 2nd Destroyer Flotilla. These Japanese destroyers were veterans and trained to think independently and take the initiative. They knew better than anyone the ancient Japanese credo: *when in doubt, launch torpedoes.*

***

In the Imperial Japanese Navy, launching torpedoes carried not so much an air of tension as an air of expectation. They were trained well in the use of torpedoes, they knew they had excellent torpedoes, and they were very happy to use them. In the US Navy, the air was of tension, perhaps leavened with dark humor. Would their torpedoes actually launch? Would the torpedoes actually reach the target? Or would they speed off in some random direction? Or even circle back? If they reached the target, would they even explode?

Commander Cole and his crews watched the clock, timing the runs of the torpedoes they had launched while the *Fletcher* led the four destroyers westward at 25 knots. He saw three Japanese rounds splash just 100 yards in front of his destroyer; another three splashed 200 yards to port. Clearly it was time for evasive maneuvers. Cole increased speed to 30 knots and set course 350 degrees True, north-northwest, hoping to pass west of Savo Island and loop around. The *Perkins* was straddled and saw a torpedo cut in front of her. Her captain Lieutenant Commander Reed wisely made smoke and followed the *Fletcher* to the north. In their wake followed the *Maury*, who saw shell splashes from the *Takanami*, and torpedoes, but no one was hit.[116]

The lookouts could see a row of explosions at the time the torpedoes were expected to hit their targets, which brought some satisfaction among the destroyer crews that their Mark 15 torpedoes had finally hit something. To be sure, they had hit the beach and not any Japanese ships, but at least they had hit something, which was more than could usually be expected from the Mark 15.

Watching the action from the bridge of the *Minneapolis*, Admiral Wright must have felt some satisfaction. The plan had been executed – not exactly as written, but executed – and the battle was going well, or seemed to be, anyway. The cruiser column continued onward in a straight line …

The *Minneapolis* was suddenly rocked by a massive underwater explosion on the port side forward of Turret 1 in, of all places, the aviation gasoline compartment. An instant later the ship convulsed from a second underwater explosion in the No. 2 fireroom. The forecastle became an instant inferno, although this was quickly doused as the massive geysers of water sent up by these torpedo hits came crashing down, drenching the bridge.

Almost immediately, Admiral Wright could feel that the *Minneapolis* now seemed to be dragging, plowing through the water rather than cutting through it, as well as being pulled to the right. Through the smoke now engulfing the bridge, the admiral glimpsed the bow. More accurately, he glimpsed where the bow was supposed to be, but wasn't.

For the heavy cruiser *Minneapolis*, the bow had been blown off. And for Admiral Wright and the Americans, the bottom had fallen out.

In the Battle of Friday the 13th, later christened by Western historians as The First Naval Battle of Guadalcanal, the battleship *Hiei* and the destroyer *Akatsuki* had "taken one for the team," so to speak, by turning on their searchlights, thereby both illuminating enemy ships and drawing enemy fire on themselves. On this night, it was the destroyer *Takanami* drawing enemy fire – fire from, at one time or another, every American ship in Admiral Wright's force. This was not unexpected. As the ship closest to the Americans, the *Takanami* had the biggest radar signature, and, after she started using her guns, she was the most visible ship. All the other Japanese ships were visible only intermittently, if at all. Although certainly unpleasant for Captain Shimizu, Commander Ogura, and their men, it made Admiral Tanaka's decision to have the *Takanami* take point in the Japanese force instead of his own flagship *Naganami* – an unpopular decision with his own crew – seem very prescient. More importantly, it protected the other Japanese ships. The American fire ended up being overconcentrated. While the skippers all thought they were taking on different ships, they were actually shooting mostly at the *Takanami*.

The Japanese destroyer was smothered within minutes by a hurricane of hot steel, mostly from the *Minneapolis* but also the *New Orleans*, *Northampton*, *Perkins*, and *Maury*. Shortly after she reversed course, smashed and burning; her smoke generator billowing in a futile attempt to hide herself, the *Takanami* staggered to a halt, causing the five torpedoes of the first half-salvo fired by the *Fletcher* and all eight torpedoes launched by the *Perkins* to miss. *Perkins* reported a large explosion on the Japanese destroyer at this time, thinking it was a torpedo hit, but it was apparently the *Takanami*'s torpedo reloads detonating.[117]

Nevertheless, the Japanese destroyer did not sink and, indeed, gave far more than she got. Without waiting for permission to open fire, Commander Ogura, having an idea of the long odds he faced, fired off 70 rounds of 5-inch shells.[118] And, more importantly, he launched eight Type 93 torpedoes aimed at the head of Admiral Wright's cruiser column.

It was two of the *Takanami*'s devastating Long Lances that had blown off the bow of Admiral Wright's flagship *Minneapolis*. Incredibly, and a testimony to the toughness and professionalism of the US Navy crew, the cruiser actually got off two more salvos from her main battery before her power went out. Three of the four firerooms were flooded, and she was having difficulty getting feed water to the fourth.[119] At 11:33, six minutes after the torpedo hit, Wright tried to radio Admiral Tisdale in the *Honolulu* to take over, but communications were out as well.[120] The *Minneapolis* struggled to head toward Lunga Point, in case she had to beach herself to prevent sinking.

Just astern of the burning, disabled American flagship was the *New Orleans*. Seeing the *Minneapolis* stopping dead in the water just ahead of him, Captain Clifford H. Roper immediately ordered "right full rudder." The *New Orleans* started lumbering to the right when, about 30 seconds after the *Minneapolis* was hit, she suffered a cataclysmic explosion of her own between the two forward 8-inch turrets. The aviation gasoline stowage – like the *Minneapolis* – and forward magazines had detonated as a result of a hit by another of the *Takanami*'s Long Lances. The blast blew the bow of the *New Orleans* clean off as far aft as the barbette of Turret 2. With the guns of Turret 1 pointing skyward as a last defiant gesture of its now-dead crew, the severed bow floated down the *New Orleans*' port side with loud bangs as it scraped and gouged and tore holes in the hull, knocking a blade off the port propeller before disappearing in the dark off the port quarter.

High up in Battle II, executive officer Commander W.F. Riggs, Jr., saw the devastation up front. Unable to reach the captain or the bridge, he guessed that everyone there had been killed, so he took control and ordered rudder control shifted to steering aft. Riggs then ordered "right rudder" to try to comb any more torpedoes in the water, and to put some distance between the ship and the Japanese – at least as much as she could at her now-reduced speed of 5 knots – and make for Tulagi.[121]

Despite the traumatic disfigurement of their ship and the deaths of everyone in the severed bow and Turret 2, the crewmen never wavered in performing their duties. When the inrush of waist-deep water threatened to sweep the 5-inch gunners away, Chief Gunner's Mate Sam Matulavich thundered, "Get back to your guns!" And they did.[122] In part because they saw the dark humor and even took some pride in what was truly an impressive accomplishment and, indeed, the beginning of a legend. Thanks to the cruiser's detached bow banging against the port side, the *New Orleans* was now the only ship in US Navy history to have rammed herself.

Around this time, some US cruiser floatplanes arrived – finally – over the battle zone. One of the pilots saw what he believed to be three burning Japanese transports; they were actually the *Minneapolis*, *New Orleans*, and *Takanami*. Some of the pilots paid special attention to a dark strip of water between the Guadalcanal shore and the area lit by the American starshells. South of the US cruiser line, they spotted six ships that looked like destroyers heading northwest back toward the combat action. They could not warn their admiral of this incoming enemy, and they could not drop flares to illuminate the enemy; Admiral Wright had said they could drop flares only on his instructions, and his communications were out.[123]

Behind the *New Orleans* was that strange-looking heavy cruiser, the *Pensacola*. Most US heavy cruisers had nine 8-inch guns in three triple turrets, two forward and one aft. But, like most Japanese heavy cruisers, the *Pensacola* carried ten 8-inch guns, albeit in four turrets – two triple turrets, one forward and one aft; and two twin turrets, one forward and one aft. For a US cruiser, it was an unusual look, made even stranger by the *Pensacola*'s tripod mast being much taller and bigger than those of other US cruisers, which would carry some consequences.

With the damaged *New Orleans* in front of her, the *Pensacola* veered 20 degrees to port to avoid the suddenly slowing cruiser. It was a curious decision. Skipper Captain Frank L. Lowe had moved to Sky Forward, one level above the bridge, where he would have better visibility in an air attack. Of course, it was night and there was no air attack, but that was Lowe's plan and he was sticking to it. He commanded the *Pensacola*'s guns from there while the executive officer Commander Harry Keeler, Jr., conned the ship from the bridge.[124] So it was Keeler who chose to turn to port, possibly because the *New Orleans* in her truncated state had started slowly turning to starboard. But Keeler's port turn placed the *Pensacola* between the burning *Minneapolis* and *New Orleans* and the Japanese – and thus backlit his ship.

At this point, the Japanese were not the only danger. As the *Pensacola* passed the disabled *Minneapolis*, the flagship fired one of her main battery's last salvos – right over the *Pensacola*'s smokestacks.

The *Pensacola* now returned to her original heading of 300 degrees True, on the prowl for the enemy. So focused was she on finding a new target that it apparently never occurred to anyone that, with Japanese torpedoes in the water, maybe the *Pensacola* should instead try some evasive maneuvers. Instead the cruiser kept a straight course. It was easier for the guns to target that way and her aft fire control radar now showed a target some 6,000 yards away. She could never get a clear visual, however, and after seven main battery salvos the target disappeared from radar. Captain Lowe believed the target had been sunk. The target, Admiral Tanaka's flagship *Naganami*, would have disagreed. Time for the *Pensacola* to look for more targets.[125]

And she quickly found one. To the right of the previous target but still on the port bow was another unidentified ship, moving at 32 knots on a course of 295 degrees True at a distance of 12,000 yards. This was actually the *Suzukaze*.[126] Now at the head of the reduced cruiser column, the *Pensacola* opened up with 8-inch gunfire. Her first salvo knocked the after fire control radar offline, and the forward fire control radar could not pick up the target. She fired three salvos anyway, after which the target disappeared.

Small splashes then started appearing close by on the port bow of the *Pensacola*. Who was doing the shooting? They spotted an unidentified ship to starboard. The *Pensacola* fired two starshells over her to see who it was. It was the *Honolulu*, who promptly flashed her recognition lights.[127] So who was shooting at them?

The question was quickly forgotten, as the cruiser now paid a price for her straight-as-an-arrow course. At 11:39 pm, the *Pensacola* was rocked by a very large underwater explosion, port side aft, under the mainmast. Yet another Japanese torpedo had struck the fuel tank just forward of Turret 3. Blazing oil was spewed high over the superstructure and all over the main deck. The main battery lost its power and the ship lost its lights. Oil covered the mainmast, which quickly turned into a torch, incinerating the crew in Battle II. The cruiser heeled over 13 degrees.[128] The fires spread quickly across the main deck and the stern. The US Navy takes pride in its damage control, and this night showed the reason why. The engineering spaces were heavily damaged, but the *Pensacola* still had one fireroom and one engine room. Her engineers acted quickly and restored power to one propeller shaft so the *Pensacola* could join the parade of damaged cruisers heading for Tulagi.[129]

Just who was responsible for the torpedo hit on the *Pensacola* is uncertain. What is known is that Commander Keeler's decision to have the cruiser pass the burning *Minneapolis* and *New Orleans* to port, while perhaps unavoidable, had disastrous consequences. In the flames of the flagship and her sister, the Japanese saw the tall, heavy tripod mast of the *Pensacola* – and concluded that the silhouette was, unmistakably, a *Texas*-class battleship.

On the *Naganami*, Commander Kumabe Tsutae shouted to his torpedo officer, "Get the big one!" The destroyer completed her reversal of course to starboard that would leave the other sailors grumbling but paralleled the course of the target. When the range was down to 4 kilometers, Kumabe had the destroyer sheer to port to unmask her torpedo batteries. Then the *Naganami* launched eight torpedoes. They couldn't miss at that range. Kumabe then called the engine room to give everything they had, and the flagship sped off toward Cape Esperance and The Slot at, Admiral Tanaka estimated, 45 knots. Large-caliber shells deluged the destroyer, but, incredibly, the *Naganami* was not hit.[130]

She was not the only one to see the *Pensacola* and determine that she was, unmistakably, a *Texas*-class battleship. Off Doma, the *Kawakaze* had led the *Suzukaze* in a quick turn to port, barely avoiding a deluge of enemy gunfire, and was heading back toward Cape Esperance when the *Minneapolis* and *New Orleans* were hit, their fires silhouetting the supposed battleship. Their fires also revealed two bubbling wakes headed for the *Suzukaze*, who almost hit a reef while swerving to port to avoid them. The torpedoes exploded against the reef, and the *Suzukaze* returned to her previous course.[131]

It was another of those ironies of war that the torpedoes that had inconvenienced the *Suzukaze* came from the US destroyer *Drayton*. Lieutenant Commander Cooper had not

MAP 5: THE BATTLE OF TASSAFARONGA, NOVEMBER 30, 1942

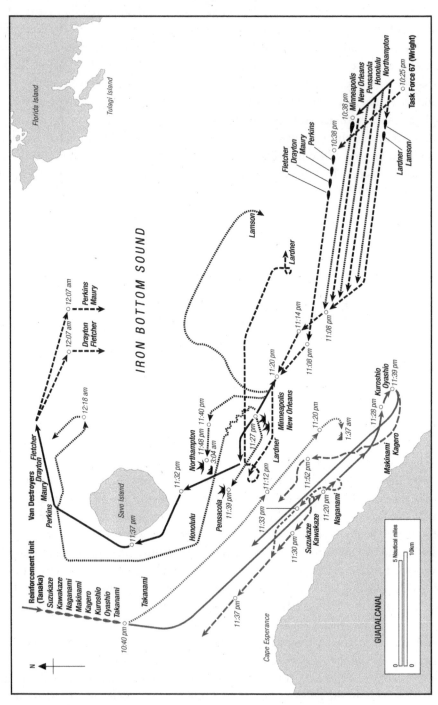

trusted his search radar when it showed targets with a speed of zero. It was an understandable judgment call, playing the odds, but that was indeed the actual speed of his targets, the *Kawakaze* and the *Suzukaze*, who had been stopped as they tried to release their drums. Maybe if Cooper had launched more than two torpedoes, he could have bagged one or both of these destroyers; then again, given that he was using Mark 15 torpedoes, maybe not.

The *Suzukaze's* evasive maneuvers prevented her from positioning herself to launch her torpedoes, but the *Kawakaze,* with exquisite care, plotted a firing solution and launched a full salvo of eight Type 93s at the *Texas*-class battleship.[132] The *Kawakaze's* crew ended up cheering a massive explosion at the precise time when their torpedoes were supposed to hit, which was also the time when torpedoes from Captain Sato's group, specifically those of the destroyer *Kuroshio*, were supposed to hit the alleged battleship. *Kuroshio* herself had been a target of the first half-salvo of torpedoes from the *Fletcher*, but the Japanese destroyer sped clear before they arrived. The *Fletcher's* second half-salvo had targeted the *Kagero* and she, too, had sped clear. As Sato's destroyers had angled to the left, skipper Commander Takeuchi Hajime had taken a chance with two torpedoes aimed at the battleship at a range of 18,000 yards. Lieutenant Commander Higashi Hideo of the *Oyashio* led the *Kuroshio* in completing the course reversal. After Higashi had sped past the disabled *Takanami* and was clear of her smoke, he carefully aimed eight torpedoes at the "battleship" *Pensacola* as both destroyers sped off into the night. Sato's *Makinami* could not launch torpedoes because she was struggling to clear the drums from around her torpedo tubes, so she led the *Kagero* in a course reversal to approach the battleship. Guadalcanal historian Richard Frank would say that in this attack, Sato "executed one of the most professionally skilled performances of any Japanese destroyer commander during the war"[133] – except for the part in which the course reversals set Sato's destroyers on an imminent collision course with the *Fletcher's* torpedoes that they had escaped earlier.[134] But nobody's perfect. And at this point in the war, the US Navy could not buy a Mark 15 torpedo hit.

For those keeping score, at this time, the heavy cruiser *Pensacola*, identified by the Japanese as – unmistakably – a *Texas*-class battleship, was, all by herself, stalked by five destroyers – the *Naganami, Kawakaze, Kuroshio, Oyashio,* and *Kagero* – and the target of 26 Japanese Type 93 torpedoes, 25 of which missed. That one successful torpedo, however, left the *Pensacola* grievously hurt, being eaten alive by fire. But she was not dead yet.

The jumbled mess now in the front of Admiral Wright's cruiser column added more confusion to an already confusing night for the light cruiser *Honolulu*. She had started the night targeting a destroyer, which turned out to be the *Naganami*. Directed by fire control radar, she unleashed the murderous rapid fire of her 6-inch guns on Admiral Tanaka's hapless flagship. Much to Tanaka's surprise, however, this avalanche of white-hot steel missed entirely – accurate on range but not deflection, which is the opposite of what artillery fire normally is. The smoke and starshells prevented the *Honolulu* from actually seeing her target, so she depended entirely on the fire control radar, which is being confused by the forest of shell splashes, causing the light cruiser's gunners to target not the *Naganami* but their own shell splashes.

The *Honolulu's* gunners were so confused that they believed the range to the *Naganami* was decreasing when it was actually increasing. Compounding the confusion was the *Naganami's* reversal of course behind the disabled *Takanami*. The change in the *Naganami's* bearing caused the *Honolulu* to believe she was slowing down and finally stopping, when it was the *Takanami* that was actually stopped. And the cruiser, thinking the *Naganami* and the *Takanami* were one and the same, inadvertently switched targets to an enemy ship that had been over-targeted and already disabled.[135]

Seeing the flagship *Minneapolis* and sister ship *New Orleans* hit added to the confusion. Admiral Tisdale was waiting for a message from Admiral Wright ordering him to assume command because of the damage to the flagship, but no order was forthcoming. Wright had no communications at that moment, so Tisdale radioed Wright asking for instructions, only to be met with silence. The *Honolulu's* skipper Captain Robert H. Hayler ordered "right full rudder" to avoid both the chaos in front of him and the *Pensacola's* mistake, thus keeping his ship hidden from the Japanese in the dark on the other side of the burning cruisers. Guessing the *Minneapolis* and *New Orleans* had been torpedoed, Hayler also wanted to comb any incoming torpedoes. He increased speed to 30 knots to keep his tactical flexibility.[136] But as he passed the *Minneapolis* and *New Orleans*, he was obliged to stop firing for fear of hitting the burning American cruisers. When the *Honolulu* finally cleared them, she could not locate any targets.

The veteran cruiser *Northampton* was still firing on the *Takanami* when the cruiser column disintegrated in front of her. She followed the *Honolulu* in a turn to starboard to avoid the damaged cruisers and, like the *Honolulu*, also had to check her fire, in the *Northampton's* case on the *Takanami*, because the cruisers obstructed the line of fire. She headed north-northwest – course 350 degrees True – and picked up the *Naganami* but lost track of the *Honolulu*. The *Northampton* fired nine main battery salvos at the destroyer and concluded that she had sunk the *Naganami*, which would have surprised Admiral Tanaka.

Attempting to follow the *Northampton* were the *Lamson* and *Lardner*. These two late-assigned destroyers had done their best to help in the battle, but were handicapped by a lack of information and preparation that was entirely out of their control.

The dangers created by this deficiency were starkly revealed at 11:29 pm, when the *Lardner* was raked by 40mm and even some 5-inch fire from the *New Orleans*.[137] Even though no one had given them the nighttime identification signals, the destroyer flashed her recognition lights, identified herself by voice radio, and even described the position of the attacking ship. The shrapnel continued flying for another eight minutes. The *Lardner's* skipper Lieutenant Commander William M. Sweetser hauled out to the east.

As, ultimately, did the *Lamson*. When the *Northampton* sheared out of line, the *Lamson* did as well, only to take a lashing by 40mm and machine-gun fire, from either the *Northampton* or the *New Orleans*. After that unfriendly welcome, skipper Lieutenant Commander Philip H. Fitz-Gerald also hauled out to the east. A frustrated Commander

Rear Admiral Daniel J. Callaghan as skipper of the flagship cruiser *San Francisco*, c.1941–2. Killed aboard this vessel during the November 13 action, the inexperienced Callaghan nevertheless accomplished his mission of keeping the Japanese battleships away from Henderson Field. (Naval History and Heritage Command)

Rear Admiral Willis Augustus Lee aboard the battleship *Washington*, c.1942–3. Lee was an expert on the use of radar, an advantage he exploited to the fullest against the Japanese Admiral Kondo and his battleship *Kirishima* on November 15, 1942. (Naval History and Heritage Command)

Rear Admiral Norman Scott, c.1942. Scott fought a victorious if imperfect battle off Cape Esperance in October 1942 but was passed over for command of the US Navy surface forces facing the Japanese for the November 13 engagement because of seniority issues. He was killed aboard his flagship *Atlanta*, possibly by friendly fire. (Naval History and Heritage Command)

Vice Admiral William F. Halsey being sworn in as Commander, South Pacific Force, by his controversial Chief of Staff, Captain Miles H. Browning, November 27, 1942. (Naval History and Heritage Command)

From left to right, Commander Herbert E. Schonland, Admiral Chester Nimitz, and Lieutenant Commander Bruce McCandless on board cruiser *San Francisco* in Pearl Harbor, December 1942. After the death of the cruiser's skipper, Captain Cassin Young, command fell to Schonland, but because he was managing damage control with no time to get to the bridge or bring someone else up to speed on the damage situation, he had McCandless, the communications officer, conn the ship for the remainder of the action on November 13. Both received the Medal of Honor. (Naval History and Heritage Command)

Admiral Kondo Nobutake, commander of the Japanese 2nd Fleet. A popular and respected officer, he was a "British-gentleman sort of man [who] was amiable and affable to everyone and was known as a scholar." He was inept and slow to adjust during the November 15 battleship action off Guadalcanal. (Naval History and Heritage Command)

Rear Admiral Tanaka Raizo was involved in transporting troops and supplies to Guadalcanal for almost the entirety of the campaign. His complaints to superiors about the conduct of that campaign went unheeded but nevertheless proved prescient when his November convoy was almost completely destroyed by Allied air power. Not even his spectacular victory at Tassafaronga on November 30–December 1, 1942, was enough to overcome the resulting ire of his superiors and he was shipped off to Burma. (Naval History and Heritage Command)

Japanese transports *Hirokawa Maru* and *Kinugawa Maru* beached and burning off Tassafaronga after Allied attacks, November 15, 1942. (Australian War Memorial/Public Domain)

The Japanese light cruiser *Nagara* operating off Shanghai, China, in 1936. Off Guadalcanal during the critical period of November 13–15, 1942, she was a US Navy nemesis. (Naval History and Heritage Command)

The Japanese Battleship *Hiei* in Tokyo Bay, July 11, 1942. Her foremast is actually a prototype of the tower mast seen on *Yamato*-class superbattleships, but it still manages to look like a pagoda, as the foremasts on Japanese battleships typically do. She was sunk after the November 13 action. (Naval History and Heritage Command)

USS *Laffey* was the second ship in the American column on November 13, and engaged the destroyer *Akatsuki* and then the battleship *Hiei*, coming within mere feet of being run down by the latter, but nevertheless causing heavy damage to the battleship's bridge. *Laffey* was then engaged by four Japanese vessels and finished off by a Type 93 torpedo. The ship in left background is the light cruiser *Helena*, who was also heavily involved in the November 13 action. (Naval History and Heritage Command)

US Navy light antiaircraft cruiser *Atlanta* in the South Pacific, October 25, 1942. She was mortally injured during the November 13 action and had to be scuttled the next night, some 12 hours after her sister ship *Juneau* was sunk by the Japanese submarine *I-26*. (Naval History and Heritage Command)

Left *Hiei* under bombing attack from American B-17 Flying Fortresses of the 72nd Bombardment Squadron, 11th Bombardment Group, north of Savo Island late in the morning of November 13, 1942. Damaged in surface action the night before, the battleship is circling because her rudder is jammed hard to starboard. She is also trailing a large oil slick. (US Air Force)

Main image US Navy heavy cruiser *San Francisco* off Mare Island Navy Yard, December 14, 1942. Circles mark some of the shell hits she took in action off Guadalcanal on November 12–13. (Naval History and Heritage Command)

Below The battleship *Washington* fires a salvo at Japanese battleship *Kirishima* on November 15, 1942. (US Navy)

Below opposite Admiral Kondo's flagship heavy cruiser *Atago* (foreground) leads sister ship *Takao* and the battleship *Kirishima* (rear), into to action off Guadalcanal, November 14, 1942. (Public Domain)

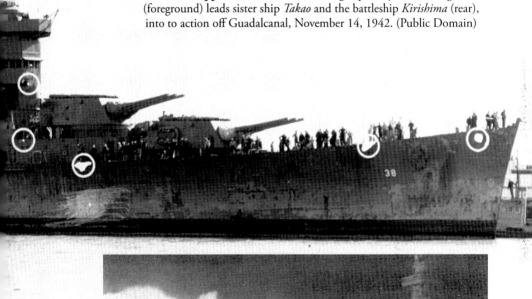

During the November 15 action, *Benham* was hit by a Japanese torpedo that blew off her bow forward of the Number 1 5-inch mount. She survived the combat, but the torpedo had broken her keel and she started falling apart in heavy seas later that day and had to be abandoned and scuttled. Amazingly, her entire crew survived her sinking.
(Naval History and Heritage Command)

South Dakota was paired with *Washington* to repel the Japanese on November 15, but suffered electrical issues that disabled her radar and main guns for much of the engagement.
(Naval History and Heritage Command)

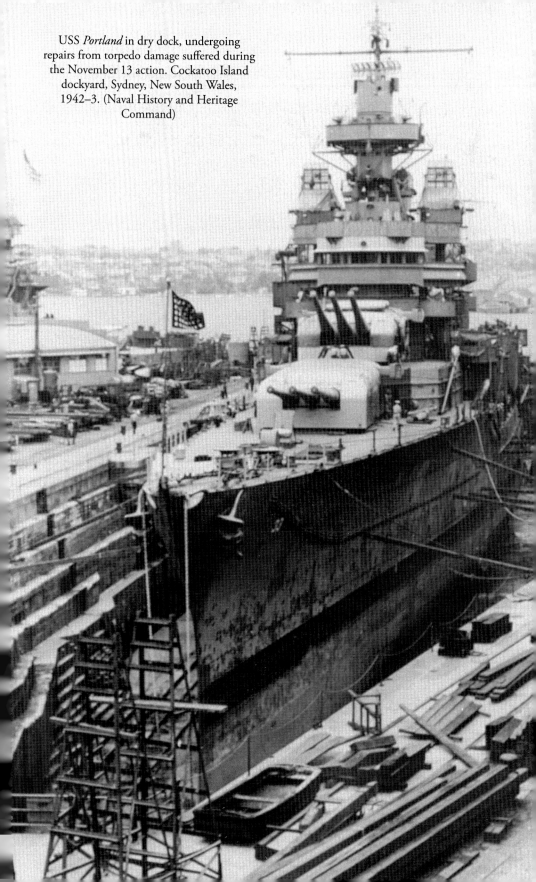

USS *Portland* in dry dock, undergoing repairs from torpedo damage suffered during the November 13 action. Cockatoo Island dockyard, Sydney, New South Wales, 1942–3. (Naval History and Heritage Command)

Above The burnt-out wreck of the transport *Yamazuki Maru* off Aruligo Point, Guadalcanal. It was rendered a total loss by Allied air attacks on November 15, 1942. (National Museum of the US Navy)

Left Vice Admiral Carleton H. Wright. As a rear admiral, he was handed command of a cruiser task force at the last minute. Though Wright handled it competently, his moment's hesitation was a factor in the disastrous Battle of Tassafaronga on November 30, 1942. Wright never held a surface combat command again. (Naval History and Heritage Command)

USS *Minneapolis* at Tulagi on December 1, having had her bow shattered by a torpedo at Tassafaronga. (Naval History and Heritage Command)

US Navy cruiser *New Orleans* enters Tulagi harbor on December 1, 1942, some eight hours after a Japanese torpedo at Tassafaronga had blown off her bow forward of Number 2 8-inch turret. (US Navy)

Stern view of *New Orleans*, camouflaged in Tulagi pending repairs. Her stern is riding high while what remains of her bow is low in the water. (Naval History and Heritage Command)

A burning Japanese bomber, likely the Mitsubishi G3M "Nell" of Lieutenant Commander Higai Joji, plunges to its doom off Rennell Island on the night of January 29, 1943. The bomber's wreckage burned on the water for several minutes, backlighting the heavy cruiser *Chicago* for other attacking Japanese bombers. (Naval History and Heritage Command)

Heavy cruiser *Louisville* (right) tows heavy cruiser *Chicago* (left), which was torpedoed and disabled by a Japanese air attack off Rennell Island the night of January 29, 1943. Not easily visible against the bulk of the Louisville is a tug, probably the *Navajo*, trying to take over the tow. (Naval History and Heritage Command)

USS *Chicago* on the morning of January 30, 1943, damaged and down by the stern after taking several Japanese aerial torpedo hits the previous night off Rennell Island. (Naval History and Heritage Command)

Army Intelligence officers examine the wreck of Japanese submarine *I-1* off Kamimbo, Guadalcanal Island, February 11, 1943. After suffering damage from Royal New Zealand Navy corvettes *Kiwi* and *Moa*, the submarine was beached in sinking condition. Japanese naval code books on board the wreck were captured.
(Naval History and Heritage Command)

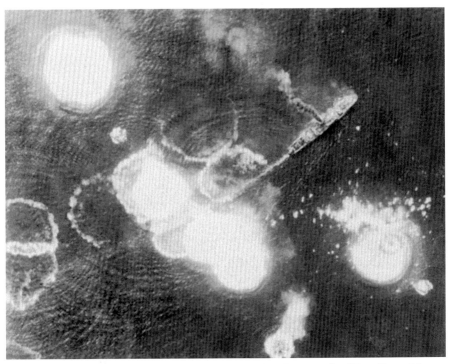

Unidentified Japanese transport under heavy Allied bombing attack off Lae, Papua New Guinea, March 3, 1943. (Australian War Memorial/Public Domain)

The Grumman TBF Avenger became a tough, reliable mainstay in US Navy aerial torpedo attacks. This is the TBF-1 Avenger "Daisy Mae" of Marine Scout Bombing Squadron 131 based at Henderson Field, Guadalcanal, 1943. (NARA)

Imperial Japanese Navy transport *Taimei Maru* under attack by Allied aircraft of the 5th Air Force off Lae, Papua New Guinea, March 3, 1943.
(Australian War Memorial/Public Domain)

The so-called Battle of the Bismarck Sea saw the advent of low-level bombing and strafing tactics that would prove effective for the rest of the Pacific War. Here, two modified US Army Air Force B-25 Mitchell gunships stalk an unidentified Japanese transport off Lae, Papua New Guinea, March 3, 1943. (Alamy)

SG radar image from the light cruiser *Denver* during the Battle of Vila-Stanmore, at 1:05 am, March 6, 1943. The *Denver* is the image at the center, with spots to her lower left being other US ships. The big blob to the right is New Georgia, the big blob to the left is Kolombangara. The two small spots to the right of Kolombangara are Japanese destroyers. The smaller is the *Murasame*, which has just been disabled and is dead in the water. The bigger is the *Minegumo*, which is still moving and is thus giving a bigger radar return. Shortly after this image was taken, the *Minegumo* was disabled. (Naval History and Heritage Command)

Abercrombie later opined, "I was completely perplexed throughout the operation and due to the incorrect recognition signals the two ships of this unit were fortunate in extricating themselves without damage from precarious positions."[138] To put it mildly. Abercrombie thought the safest bet was to have his destroyers head toward Lengo Channel and hold a blocking position. Russell Crenshaw of the *Maury*, in his respected analysis of the Battle of Tassafaronga, would later say this act "can only be described as prudent. No one had given him any orders at all."[139]

On the *Northampton*, skipper Captain Willard A. Kitts believed he had sunk two destroyers – not the *Lamson* or *Lardner* – so his ship had a good night. Others had not; the *Minneapolis* and *New Orleans* were badly hit, and now Kitts saw the *Pensacola* hit – by torpedoes, he thought. His ship was not, although she was about to be hit, or rather, to hit Savo Island if he did not change course, so he headed more toward the west – course 280 degrees True – hoping to round Savo keeping the island to starboard. The *Northampton* sailed along for nine minutes, seeing the burning ships behind her, hoping to see more targets ahead of her.

She saw something ahead of her, all right, but not targets. And not likely ahead of her, either, though that's what her after action report stated. No, at 11:48, Captain Kitts saw two torpedoes coming from – allegedly – due west, just off the port bow. They were very close together, one running about 10 feet below the waterline, the other almost on the surface. "Left full rudder," Kitts barked. Too late.

There was a massive underwater explosion on the port side near the stern, whether from one or two torpedoes is unclear. As the executive officer on the *Honolulu* described it, "A huge smoke and fire cone rose about 250 feet and [*Northampton*] seemed to be aflame instantly."[140] The *Northampton* shook for several seconds afterwards. That was a bad sign.

And more were to come. The explosion was in the after engine room, flooding it, and rupturing the fuel and water tanks around it. Burning fuel spewed all over the mainmast – again – the boat deck, and, through cracks in the aft magazines, the second and main decks. It was a weird coincidence how fuel had been set alight by Japanese torpedoes on three US Navy ships in one night. The 5-inch ready ammunition on the boat deck began to burn; explosions would not be far behind. The burning fuel quickly turned the aft area into a raging inferno. As if that were not enough, three of the *Northampton*'s four propellers were disabled, leaving only the outer starboard propeller operating, which drove the cruiser into a port turn. Power and lighting in the after part of the cruiser were knocked out. To top it off, the cruiser heeled over 10 degrees to port. Another bad sign, a very bad sign.

Pumps started working on the flooding. The engineers managed to get that one propeller turning, and the *Northampton* began turning to port – toward a Japanese-held shore of Guadalcanal, Captain Kitts quickly noticed. Since communications with the after part of the ship were also out, Kitts used the ship's loudspeakers to direct the engine room in a course change, and the *Northampton* – in blazing, flooding agony; barely conscious of the world around her; desperate to find some place of relative refuge to make her misery stop – joined the parade of maimed cruisers milling around in Ironbottom Sound.[141]

Precisely who hit the *Northampton* is, once again, uncertain. Precisely what Captain Kitts saw off the port bow is unknown because there were no Japanese ships to the west of the *Northampton* that could have fired the torpedoes he reported seeing. But eight torpedoes were headed in her general direction, courtesy of Commander Higashi's destroyer *Oyashio*. In a bit of irony, Higashi had aimed his torpedoes at a *Texas*-class battleship, that is, the *Pensacola*. The torpedoes missed and kept on running; then the unfortunate cruiser *Northampton* blundered into them.[142] Naval historian Vincent P. O'Hara called it "the final crowning of a cursed night for the U.S. Navy."[143] Adding to the irony, the destroyer *Kuroshio* had actually targeted the *Northampton* with four Long Lances launched at 11:45, but they had not reached the cruiser before the *Oyashio*'s torpedoes hit. Seven minutes later, *Kagero* launched four torpedoes at an enemy "battleship" – *Pensacola* or *Northampton* – but got no hits.[144]

At Admiral Tisdale's direction, the *Honolulu* had just changed course to 345 degrees True to search northwest of Savo Island when he saw the explosion on the *Northampton*. The flagship *Minneapolis* had been hit; and there was no word from Admiral Wright. The *New Orleans* had been hit. The *Pensacola* had been hit. Now the *Northampton* was hit. What the hell was going on?

Admiral Tisdale tried to raise the *Northampton* on the voice radio. "Can you move?" he asked. No response. The *Northampton* was not showing up on the SG search radar, either. This was not encouraging. With only silence coming from the flagship, Tisdale concluded he had better take charge. He ordered the *Honolulu* to go to flank speed and rounded Savo Island back toward the east, searching for foe or friend. One of the Seagull floatplanes overhead made an alarming report that they could see the wake of a large, unidentified ship at high speed rounding Savo Island. It took some time but eventually Admiral Tisdale and his staff on the *Honolulu* determined correctly that this large unidentified ship at high speed as reported to the *Honolulu* was, in fact, the *Honolulu*.[145]

At one minute before midnight, the *Minneapolis* made her reappearance on the voice radio, with a serious understatement: "To any ship, we need assistance." She was painfully inching her way toward Lunga, difficult enough in her situation without random flotsam tossed in her way. But nothing was easy around Guadalcanal. At 11:49 the *Minneapolis* nearly plowed into something that in the darkness looked like a capsized, partially submerged ship. As Captain Rosendahl described it, "This derelict was unmistakably a destroyer bow with a lengthy section of other structure attached to it," with, according to Admiral Wright, the "[v]isible part of keel variously estimated at 300 to 500 feet."[146] Even in her crawling state, the *Minneapolis* managed to avoid this "unmistakabl[e...] destroyer bow," which was indeed a mistake; it was the severed bow of the *New Orleans*, almost crashing into its second ship that night.[147]

One minute into December 1, Admiral Wright finally got his message through, instructing Admiral Tisdale to assume command. In so doing, Wright now plopped this mess of gargantuan proportions onto Tisdale's plate. Tisdale did not shrink from it, having a good idea of the magnitude of this disaster, if not the specifics. At 12:20 am, the *Pensacola* radioed, "My position one half way between Tulagi and Cape Esperance; my speed 8 knots."[148] This answered one question – to a degree. At 12:29, Commander Cole on the *Fletcher* radioed, "Where are our other ships?" *Honolulu* answered, "We do not know position of other ships." Evidently the *Pensacola*'s message didn't register. Five minutes later she added that she saw two burning ships "believed to be ours."[149] They were the *Pensacola* and *Northampton*.

The SOC floatplanes flying overhead could see the burning ships, but they had more interesting things in sight. At 12:37 am, one radioed Admiral Tisdale, "Request permission to illuminate enemy destroyer landing troops on Guadalcanal."[150]

Admiral Tisdale radioed, "We are swinging left to fire on destroyer landing troops on Guadalcanal," and ordered Commander Cole and his destroyers to assist. The *Honolulu* raced down the west side of Savo toward the target, but Tisdale had his doubts. There were some 20 minutes of radio exchanges between the *Honolulu* and the Seagull. The light cruiser asked the floatplane if it was sure the target was a Japanese destroyer. The SOC replied, "It appears to have its bow on the beach,"[151] which did not answer the question.

Once the *Honolulu* and Commander Cole's destroyers were in position, permission was granted, and the Seagull dropped a flare, which illuminated the target – and every American ship in the area. That might have been a necessary evil, except the alleged destroyer turned out to be an abandoned wreck from Admiral Tanaka's ill-fated convoy a few weeks earlier. At 1:05, just after detaching the *Maury* and *Perkins* to stand by the *New Orleans*, a disgusted Tisdale ordered, "All SOC planes return to Tulagi."[152]

In the meantime, the new commanding officer had to deal with all his disabled ships. At 12:50 am, he had asked Guadalcanal, "Can you send boats toward Savo?"[153] Guadalcanal responded by dispatching the tug *Bobolink* and four PT boats – out of 15 available – from Tulagi.[154] The *New Orleans* and *Pensacola* were already crawling for Tulagi but the small boats would be needed for salvage and to pick up any US sailors who had ended up in the water. Tisdale ordered the *Northampton* to retire.[155]

Captain Kitts wished he could comply, but his *Northampton* was in extreme distress. Damage control teams worked through the darkness in the after part of the cruiser and were confronted with a seemingly endless series of flooding compartments. The pumps had all been put to work at maximum capacity, but the torrent continued. When the list reached 16 degrees, Captain Kitts stopped the *Northampton*, hoping to reduce the inrush of water.

If it did, it was not enough. A little after 1:00 am, the list reached 20 degrees and the engine had to be shut down because the supply of lubricant had failed. With the engine went the power supply to the pumps. Now they could no longer even slow down the flooding, let alone stop it. They managed to get power to the voice radio and Captain Kitts reported to the rest of the force, such as it was, that he was preparing to abandon ship. When the relentless flooding caused the list to reach 23 degrees, all personnel were ordered topside and life rafts and nets were thrown in the water. At 1:30, Kitts ordered everyone off the *Northampton* except a salvage crew.[156] He wasn't giving up quite yet.

Nor was Admiral Tisdale. Still unsure of how many Japanese ships, if any, were in the area, he had the *Honolulu* sweep to the east. The *New Orleans* reported a surfaced submarine. Those torpedoes had to come from somewhere. So now the *Honolulu* swept to the west and the south. She was joined by the destroyers *Fletcher* and *Drayton*, who fell in astern.

But they found no Japanese ships. Admiral Tanaka's ships were long gone, having sped off around midnight, with the flagship *Naganami* outrunning a Parthian shot of four torpedoes launched by the *Drayton* as the American destroyer headed up the west side of Savo. Tanaka had his ships rendezvous at a prearranged point some 50 miles away, but repeated hails brought no response from the *Takanami*. That wasn't good. He sent the *Oyashio* and the *Kuroshio* to the destroyer's aid. En route, they found that enemy battleship, at whom the *Kuroshio* launched her last two torpedoes. They did not hit the battleship, or the cruiser, probably the *Northampton*, that was mistaken for the battleship.[157]

Continuing on, at 1:15 the two Japanese destroyers found the *Takanami* in severe distress and all alone in the dark. The *Oyashio* lowered lifeboats and the *Kuroshio* positioned herself alongside the dying destroyer, but then, according to Admiral Tanaka, "an enemy group of two cruisers and three destroyers appeared at such close range that neither side dared fire."[158] They had spotted the *Honolulu* with the *Fletcher* and *Drayton* following, though where the admiral got the idea they were so close that "neither side dared fire" is anyone's guess. The encounter did scare off the *Oyashio* and *Kuroshio*, leaving the *Takanami* and her survivors to their fate.

The *Takanami* had been the target of more than 180 5-inch shells from the *Perkins*, *Maury*, *Minneapolis*, and *New Orleans*; 155 8-inch shells from the heavy cruisers; and 90 6-inch rounds from the *Honolulu*.[159] Her crew had suffered 197 killed, including Captain Shimizu and Commander Ogura; 48 survivors reached Guadalcanal, 19 of whom were captured by Americans. Tanaka said the loss of the *Takanami* and her officers and crew "was a matter of deep regret."[160] He later expressed the true depth of that regret:

> We were able to defeat Admiral Wright's ships in this action only because of the *Takanami*. She absorbed all the punishment of the enemy in the opening moments of battle, and she shielded the rest of us. Yet we left the scene without doing anything for her or her valiant crew.[161]

Tanaka was "glumly silent" as his destroyers sped back up The Slot while he considered going back in to help the *Takanami*.[162]

While the *Honolulu*, *Fletcher*, and *Drayton* may have missed the *Oyashio* and *Kuroshio*, they did not miss the *Northampton* as they passed close by. While his light cruiser sped on at 30 knots, Admiral Tisdale detached the two destroyers to stand by the dying heavy cruiser. Her fires aft could not be contained, and the clutching fingers of Ironbottom

Sound entering her hull were relentlessly pulling her further and further toward the depths, the cruiser's list reaching 35 degrees by 2:40 am. Captain Kitts ordered the salvage crew off. The end was not long in coming. At 3:04 am, the *Northampton*, veteran cruiser with a magnificent fighting record, rolled over to port and sank stern first, her bow pointing 60 degrees into the sky as she gracefully slid beneath the waves.[163]

The *Fletcher* and *Drayton* spent three-and-a-half hours picking up *Northampton* survivors. The *Fletcher* rescued 646, the *Drayton* 127, and after making a fruitless search for the *Honolulu,* both headed for Espiritu Santo.[164]

By now, all the destroyers were involved in rescue work. The *Maury* was leading the *Perkins* heading east at 25 knots when lookouts spotted a ship off the starboard bow in the darkness some 5,000 yards away – a very weird-looking ship. To the right it looked like a warship, but to the left it looked possibly like a freighter or a transport. Whatever it was, it had a straight bow.

Could be a Japanese transport, skipper Lieutenant Commander Gelzer L. Sims thought. He ordered all guns and torpedo tubes trained on the target. But, just to be safe, he ordered his signalman to flash a challenge from his blinker gun. The proper answer to the challenge would be flashing the recognition lights or shooting up a green-colored flare, known as a Very light, followed by a white flare and another white flare. Sims waited and watched through his binoculars.

From the right side of the unknown ship came three flares – white, green, green – precisely the opposite of what it was supposed to be. "Stand by to fire torpedoes," Lieutenant Commander Sims growled. The range had dropped to 2,500 yards.

Then green and white flares shot up from all over the unknown ship, most in the proper order of green-white-white. "Hold fire," Sims said, and had the *Maury* and *Perkins* veer to the left.[165] While the *Perkins* patrolled for Japanese submarines Sims had a conversation with the ship, now identified as the *New Orleans*, by bullhorn.

The *New Orleans* was in much better shape than *Northampton* – better shape, in fact, than all the other damaged ships, which may seem counterintuitive because the *New Orleans'* bow all the way up to Turret 2 was simply gone. But, unlike the *Minneapolis*, her bow was completely cut off, not dragging her exposed forward sections down into the water. So the flooding from her open bow area was limited and there was no immediate danger to her buoyancy. Moreover, her fires were out. She was heading for Tulagi at 5 knots.[166]

Spotting a flaming ship ahead that looked like it needed help more than the *New Orleans* did, Lieutenant Commander Sims had the two destroyers proceed. It turned out to be the *Pensacola*, still burning, still listing to port 13 degrees.[167] The magazine for Turret 3 had been flooded as a precaution, but the intense heat of the fires boiled the water away. Powder detonations blew off parts of the barbette and sent them flying at the damage control teams. Then the 8-inch shells inside the magazine started cooking off. If all the 8-inch shells exploded at once, the ship would probably be destroyed. And all 150 8-inch shells did indeed explode – one at a time.[168] Nerve-wracking though they may have been,

150 little explosions were much preferable to one giant explosion. The *Perkins* went alongside the cruiser to help with fighting her fires, while the *Maury* screened ahead as the *Pensacola* made painfully slow progress for Tulagi at 9 knots on one operable engine. As soon as they entered Tulagi at 3:44 am, the *Maury* headed back to help the *New Orleans*.[169]

Meanwhile, the *Minneapolis* was still having major problems. Her exposed bow sections being dragged down by her dangling bow, she was taking in serious water. Determining that if she was close to Guadalcanal she could end up grounding on a Japanese-held beach, Captain Rosendahl turned toward Tulagi instead. But this confused the orders given to the destroyers *Lamson* and *Lardner*.

At around 1:30 am, Guadalcanal relayed orders to them to help the *Minneapolis*, who was supposed to be headed for Lunga. She wasn't, and *Lamson* and *Lardner* found nothing. Guessing the damaged cruiser had made for Tulagi instead, Commander Abercrombie had the destroyers make for Tulagi as well. They finally found the *Minneapolis* a few minutes before 3:00 am and, after the *Lamson* did one last sweep for enemy ships, proceeded to escort her into the tiny base.[170]

This tiny base was now the salvation of so many damaged ships. As dawn broke, the *Maury* pulled up alongside the *New Orleans* and hooked herself up to serve as an anchor for the cruiser; with her bow gone, the *New Orleans* no longer had anchors of her own. Shortly thereafter the *Minneapolis* staggered in, assisted by the tug *Bobolink* and attended by the *Lamson* and *Lardner*. She went deep into the inner harbor at Sasapi, tied up to some coconut trees, and covered with camouflage, just as the *Portland* had done a few weeks earlier.[171] The *New Orleans* was moved even deeper into Tulagi, up McFarland Creek, where she was moored next to the PT boat tender *Jamestown* and was also camouflaged – so effectively that one observer said she looked like a "botanical garden."[172] The *Pensacola* just anchored in the bay.[173] Her fires were not extinguished until around 7:00 am.

It was an hour later when the *Honolulu*, having completed yet another unsuccessful sweep for enemy ships or more survivors, sailed into Tulagi. It was there that Admiral Tisdale finally received the grim tally from Admiral Wright – *Northampton* sunk; *Minneapolis*, *Pensacola*, and *New Orleans* in no condition to move. Admiral Wright then ordered the *Honolulu* to return to Espiritu Santo, screened by the *Lamson* and *Lardner*.[174] Picking up the *Fletcher* and *Drayton* along the way, they arrived at Espiritu Santo on December 2.

Tulagi was where some semblance of recovery began. It did not have much in the way of resources yet for surface ships, but it did have a lot of coconut logs. The *New Orleans* used them to build a cofferdam, the *Minneapolis* to build a false bow. It was a victory for both cruisers, but especially the *Minneapolis*, who in the interim had suffered a gas explosion forward that flooded several compartments. They left Tulagi on December 12, six days after the *Pensacola*. It would take almost a year for all three cruisers to be fully repaired.

There was no repairing the reputation and career of Admiral Wright. Thirty years of preparing for an independent combat flag command were ruined in the first thirty minutes of that command. The scorecard of ships sunk might not look bad – the Americans had sunk one ship (Wright believed he had sunk four); the Japanese had sunk one ship (well, one-and-a-half if one counts the bow of the *New Orleans*). Wright had made mistakes, to be sure – not releasing his destroyers to attack with torpedoes, not taking evasive action – but nothing commensurate with the disaster that befell his force. It certainly had not helped that he had a hastily assembled team of ships that had never trained or worked together.

Nevertheless, regardless of the circumstances, losing one cruiser sunk with severe damage to three others in battle with a clearly inferior enemy force was an abject humiliation that could not be tolerated. And Admiral Wright knew it. Moreover, even if his superiors still had confidence in him, his men did not.

A conscientious officer, Admiral Wright got together with Admiral Tisdale to try to make sense of it all and prepare his after action report. The report would be far more noteworthy and influential than most such reports. For starters, Wright took complete responsibility for the defeat; he absolved the skippers of the damaged cruisers "from any blame for the torpedoing of their ships."[175] Admiral Spruance, victor at Midway and Admiral Nimitz's chief of staff, later remarked that Wright's acceptance of responsibility despite his being new to the job, having no choice as to his route, and dependent on someone else's plan indicated a "high military character."[176]

Even so, the report and its later endorsements by Admiral Halsey and Admiral Nimitz indicated that the Pacific Fleet still did not quite get it. Admiral Wright described the gunnery performance as "very impressive" in volume. With the benefit of hindsight, Samuel Eliot Morison later called it "abominable."[177] The problem, as was determined later, was not with the crews, but with the relatively slow rate of fire and train for the 8-inch-armed pre-war cruisers, whose turrets could not turn fast enough to keep up with speeding Japanese destroyers.[178] Wright would compare the 6-inch-armed *Honolulu* with its rapid-fire guns and state-of-the-art fire control, with the two 8-inch-armed cruisers – except the *Honolulu*'s gunnery that night was, if anything, even worse than that of the heavy cruisers because her gunners kept chasing her own shell splashes on radar.

The primary culprit on this night was the torpedo, specifically, the Japanese Type 93 "Long Lance" torpedo. Of Japanese torpedoes, Admiral Wright got so close to understanding:

[T]he observed positions of the enemy surface vessels before and during the gun action make it improbable that torpedoes with speed-distance characteristics similar to our own could have reached the cruisers at the time they did if launched from any of the enemy destroyers or cruisers which were observed to be present.[179]

Wright surmised some of the torpedoes must have been launched by submarines; he could not conceive of the superiority of the Long Lance. Nor could Admiral Nimitz.

What Admiral Nimitz could admit was the superiority of Japanese torpedo technique, though he did not seem to grasp the substance of that superiority. As Morison commented, "American commanders of cruiser-destroyer task forces had the bad practice of tying their destroyers to a cruiser column instead of sending them off on an independent torpedo shoot before gunfire was opened."[180] In short, it was not just the torpedoes themselves, but how they were used. The irony here is that Admiral Kinkaid's plan, developed with Admiral Wright, had actually adopted the idea of independent torpedo attack before gunfire. But Wright, for reasons known only to him, made a conscious decision to throw that away.

Admiral Nimitz's solution to these problems was summed up by this phrase: "[T]raining, TRAINING and M-O-R-E T-R-A-I-N-I-N-G. Each commanding officer is called upon to do his share."[181] The second clause of this quote is often omitted, but it is important in understanding the philosophical foundation here.[182] In response to Nimitz's statement without the omitted clause, it has been suggested that it was the commanders who needed the training, much more than the men under their command. In fact, once the omitted clause is included, it becomes clear that training for commanders is part of what Nimitz was advocating. The commanders needed to break their habit of micromanaging their destroyers.

But Admiral Nimitz was careful to discuss the nature of the enemy Admiral Wright faced, stating that Wright, "led his force into action resolutely and intelligently and opened fire at a range that should have permitted avoiding surprise torpedo attack." He went on to note: "As in previous engagements, we are made painfully aware of the Japanese skill, both in night and day action, in the use of guns and torpedoes. To date there has been no reason to doubt his energy, persistence, and courage."[183]

And perhaps no Japanese flag officer embodied that "energy, persistence, and courage" more than Tanaka Raizo. Unlike most Japanese flag officers confronted with an unexpected enemy, Admiral Tanaka had been calm, cool, flexible, and resourceful. Tanaka had changed the simple if desperate resupply operation into a simple if opportunistic attack – with Type 93 torpedoes. Once the presence of the enemy was confirmed, under the direction of Tanaka but more or less operating as independent groups, the Japanese destroyers simply turned around, launched their torpedoes, and, except for the *Takanami*, departed. Tanaka and his men made the best of a bad situation. No force of ships was even remotely as devastated by a Japanese torpedo attack as Admiral Wright's was by Admiral Tanaka.[184]

Of course, the supplies had not been delivered, so the Japanese army on Guadalcanal was going to starve for at least one more day. Admiral Tanaka's superiors were furious with him for not dropping off the supply drums. Tanaka accepted the criticism:

It was an error on my part not to deliver the supplies according to schedule. I should have returned to do so. The delivery mission was abandoned simply because we did not have accurate information about the strength of the enemy force. [...] I saw no percentage in having our seven destroyers, low on ammunition and decks loaded with cargo drums, fight another running battle against [what he believed were] eight US destroyers.[185]

Tanaka Raizo was far more respected by the US Navy than by the Imperial Japanese Navy, in which he was known as a "B admiral." His outspoken nature, more than any performance issue, seems to have been the reason for this low opinion. For no one knew how close Tanaka had come to a complete wipeout at Tassafaronga – not even Tanaka himself, until years later.

"Had I but known that only one cruiser and four destroyers remained in fighting trim!"[186]

Admiral Wright had suffered a humiliating defeat, his career effectively over, but he might have drawn some comfort in that his lone victory out of Tassafaronga – keeping the Japanese from delivering their supplies – had a far, far greater effect than he or anyone could have anticipated.

Those Japanese troops on Guadalcanal still needed to be fed. Admiral Tanaka took his failure to deliver the supplies hard and began preparing for another run as soon as he returned to the Shortlands. He gained reinforcements in the form of the destroyers *Arashi*, *Nowaki*, and *Yugure*, which more than made up for the loss of the *Takanami* and brought his force up to ten destroyers.[187]

Admiral Tanaka's upgraded Tokyo Express left the Shortlands at 1:00 pm on December 3 for Drum Run 2.0. It featured seven transport destroyers covered by three designated escorts – flagship *Naganami*, *Makinami*, and *Yugure*.[188] Coastwatchers reported the force's passing, and an Allied scout plane kept it under surveillance. The Americans prepared a warm welcome – eight Dauntlesses and seven Avengers caught the ten destroyers around dusk some 160 miles from Kamimbo. Their attack was complicated by the decreasing light and by the Japanese air cover. But that air cover consisted of a dozen Mitsubishi F1M floatplanes – biplanes with float pontoons. They were no match for the Americans' escorting Wildcats, shooting down one F4F at a cost of five of their own. Yet the attack runs by the Dauntlesses and Avengers at "very close range" were mostly ineffective, with one SBD and one TBF shot down to gain just a near miss that slightly damaged the destroyer *Makinami*. After the debacle at Tassafaronga, there was almost nothing in the way of surface opposition available, so Admiral Tanaka succeeded in dumping 1,500 drums of supplies. For the Japanese, that was much-needed good news indeed. The bad news was that only 310 of the drums reached the beleaguered army troops. Aircraft from Henderson Field found the floating drums great for target practice.[189]

Upon returning to Shortland the next day, a frustrated Admiral Tanaka met with Admiral Mikawa, whose flagship *Chokai* was in for a visit. Tanaka was blunt, telling his superior that these drum runs were hopeless and recommending the evacuation of Guadalcanal.[190]

Seeing as how the first two supply runs were less than complete successes, but were still, in the Japanese view, the best option available, the drum runs were further modified.

The Tassafaronga action convinced Combined Fleet that more escorts were necessary, so three more destroyers – the *Tanikaze*, *Urakaze*, and *Teruzuki* – were now assigned to the drum runs, although the state-of-the-art *Teruzuki*, who was becoming a sort of troubleshooter for Combined Fleet, was delayed in arriving when she hit a reef at Truk.[191] The technique of dropping the drums off was changed as well, the most notable change being dropping them closer to shore.

So December 7 – the first anniversary of the Japanese attack on Pearl Harbor – saw the third drum run leave the Shortlands with now 11 destroyers, of which three were designated escorts. This run was not under Admiral Tanaka but instead under Captain Sato aboard the *Oyashio*.[192]

Once again, coastwatchers reported the force's passing, and Henderson Field prepared an even warmer welcome. The redoubtable Marine Major Joe Sailer talked his way into leading this one last bombing mission before he would take over a new assignment as executive officer for the commander of Henderson Field, Colonel William J. Fox – an assignment Sailer dreaded.[193] His specific goal in this mission was to hit a destroyer, something he had never done in his very distinguished career.

Major Sailer, leading 13 Dauntlesses escorted by four Wildcats, went up from Henderson at about 5:20 pm. Maybe 80 minutes later, they found the destroyers "of the new, large type" in columns of six and five.[194] Sailer had his section dive on the port column of ships. His own dive was normal, but his bomb was only a near miss that "caused the ship to rise in the water perceptibly."[195] His target was the destroyer *Nowaki*, which during this attack suffered ruptured hull plating, killing 17 men, flooding an engine room and a boiler room, leaving the destroyer without power. The *Nowaki* had to be towed back to Shortland by the *Naganami*, escorted by the *Ariake* and the *Arashi*, herself damaged slightly in the attack.[196]

But Major Sailer struggled to pull out of his dive. He explained over the voice radio that his dive flaps would not retract, so his airspeed was severely limited, and he could not make it back to Guadalcanal; he may have been nicked by antiaircraft fire. Sailer announced he would try to ditch near the southern end of New Georgia.[197]

But the convoy was defended by eight Pete floatplanes, whom the escorting Grumman Wildcats had completely missed. One of the F1Ms dove on Major Sailer's limping Dauntless and raked it with machine guns "from tail to nose."[198] A horrified Lieutenant Hap Simpson, flying in Sailer's section, watched as the fatally injured SBD rolled over and "plunged head on into the sea and sank immediately."[199] Neither Sailer nor his gunner was ever seen again. His loss was a heavy blow to the Cactus Air Force.[200] John McEniry later said the pilots "all felt a real sense of loss," while Simpson wrote that the death of Joe Sailer, a veteran ace of 19 attack missions, "was a real tragedy for us."[201]

Heavy hearts would not stop the war from continuing, however, nor would they stop Captain Sato's convoy. There were still no US Navy surface ships available after Tassafaronga, but plenty of PT boats were available. Given their propensity for attacking anything that moved, enemy or not, Admiral Halsey's crew decided it was time to have the PT boats shoot at Japanese ships instead of American ships.

Now eight of the precocious little craft were waiting for Captain Sato's ships. Four boats were designated as scouts – *PT-40* and *PT-48* were positioned between Savo Island and Cape Esperance. Behind them, *PT-43* and *PT-109* sat between Cape Esperance and Kokumbona. The remainder – *PT-36*, *PT-37*, *PT-44*, and *PT-59* – were designated as the striking force and hid behind Savo.[202] Flying overhead in the dark was one SOC floatplane, left over from the cruisers sunk and damaged at Tassafaronga, that would scout and illuminate the enemy.[203]

At 11:20 pm, *PT-40* and *PT-48* detected Captain Sato's ships coming in between Savo and Cape Esperance, exactly as they were supposed to do. What they were not supposed to do was suffer a critical engine breakdown as they began combat maneuvers, but that is precisely what happened to *PT-48* when she lost one of her three engines. She tried to withdraw southward toward Guadalcanal when another engine went out. *PT-40* spent her time trying to protect *PT-48* by laying a smoke screen and diverting the attention of two incoming Japanese destroyers by speeding off toward the southeast with her three good engines. Not an auspicious beginning.[204]

But the Japanese seemingly had far more respect for the American PT boats than did the Americans themselves. Captain Sato, who barely a week earlier had faced down five cruisers, one of which he mistook for a battleship, turned his ships around at 11:30 pm, spooked by a pair of PT boats, one of which was disabled.[205]

Fifteen minutes later, Captain Sato thought better of it, decisively turned around again, and bravely charged in to deliver the supplies to the starving 17th Army.[206]

He promptly ran into the four-PT-boat striking force. The Japanese ships opened fire, but the PTs were determined. *PT-37* fired two torpedoes at the leading ship. *PT-59*, skippered by Lieutenant (jg) John M. Searles, then launched two of her own at the nearest destroyer, Captain Sato's command ship *Oyashio*. The destroyer turned and the torpedoes missed, but a shocked Sato watched as *PT-59*, in the process of turning away from her much larger foe, came within 100 yards and raked the *Oyashio*'s bridge and deck with .50-cal and 20mm gun fire.[207] The *Oyashio* responded in kind, and succeeded in hitting the *PT-59* ten times before the boat made it back to Tulagi.

As *PT-59* was making its getaway, *PT-36* and *PT-44* charged in and fired four torpedoes each before turning tail for Tulagi. None of the PTs' torpedoes hit, but the commotion caught the attention of *PT-43* and *PT-109* near Kokumbona, and they now bravely charged in.

Still leading eight heavily armed destroyers, Captain Sato was unnerved. Two of these roughly 80-foot plywood boats were bad enough. Now another six had just appeared. Sato obviously had only one choice in the face of such overwhelming firepower: retreat – without delivering the supplies. Rushing to the scene in the recently arrived *Teruzuki*, Admiral Tanaka was informed that Sato "was prevented from completing his mission by the presence of enemy planes and more torpedo boats."[208] On the basis of this information, the tenacious Tanaka agreed with Sato's decision.[209]

But the Japanese were not finished. Around midnight on December 9, 1942, Lieutenant Commander Togami Ichiro raised the periscope of his submarine *I-3* some 3 miles north of Kamimbo and looked around. Seeing nothing, Togami lowered the periscope and the *I-3* surfaced. They contacted the Japanese army ashore while crewmembers came on deck to prepare the *Daihatsu* landing barge to transport the supplies.

Lieutenant Commander Togami's periscope sweep was less than thorough. He missed Lieutenant Searles' *PT-59* who, with *PT-44*, was waiting for him. American radio intelligence had – again – figured out exactly when the next supply run would occur. Searles and his compatriot from the *PT-44*, Lieutenant Frank Freeland, were told they had a date with a submarine.

Likely not pleased by his punctuality for this particular date, Lieutenant Commander Togami ordered the *I-3* to crash dive, leaving the *Daihatsu* bobbing on the surface. The *PT-44* went over to strafe the barge while Lieutenant Searles had the *PT-59* head close to shore and sit still, guessing the submarine would be back to complete its mission as soon as it got quiet.

As the *PT-44* stopped to reload its guns the *I-3* rose from the depths once again, just 400 yards away. *PT-59* quickly launched two torpedoes. One passed under the stern of *PT-44*.

But then the other one struck the *I-3* near the stern. There was an eruption of water that was immediately followed by an explosion, then a large oil slick that spread for 90 minutes. And thus the *I-3* passed from the mortal world along with 90 of her crew.[210] There would be no more submarine runs to Guadalcanal for a while.

But there would be another drum run. Admiral Tanaka made arrangements to set out on December 11. He had assembled three ships of the 15th Destroyer Division (*Kuroshio*, *Oyashio*, and *Kagero*); two ships of the 17th Destroyer Division (*Tanikaze* and *Urakaze*); two ships of the 24th Destroyer Division (*Kawakaze* and *Suzukaze*); plus the *Arashi*, *Ariake*, and *Naganami*.[211] No fewer than five of the destroyers would be escorts. This was an odd collection of ships for the Japanese, ships who had mostly not served or practiced together. But times were desperate – so desperate that Admiral Yamamoto had sent Tanaka a personal message.[212] They had to get through. Tanaka himself would lead them, this time in the *Teruzuki*.

Admiral Tanaka's force was blessed with air cover for most of the day, but after that air cover had departed came 14 Marine SBD dive bombers with 1,000lb bombs, under the direct command of Major Louis Robertshaw and an escort of F4Fs and P-38s. But arriving at 6:55 pm as daylight was disappearing and at the extreme end of their range, the Dauntlesses scored no hits and lost one of their own.[213]

It was after midnight when Admiral Tanaka's convoy rounded Savo Island and headed for Kamimbo. The transport destroyers dropped off some 1,200 drums of supplies and were headed back by 1:15 am on December 12.

While the convoy was moving off, Tanaka was having the *Teruzuki* cover them, running at 12 knots along the coast. Near Savo her lookouts spotted some of the PT boats that had so spooked Captain Sato. They would not spook Tanaka. He was called "tenacious" for a reason. He didn't have his beloved *Jintsu* but he did have the *Teruzuki*, the second commissioned member of what the Japanese called the "Type B" class of destroyers and

Westerners called the *Akizuki* class designed primarily for air defense. They were "the finest class of destroyers Japan fielded during the war," according to respected Imperial Japanese Navy historian Jonathan Parshall.[214] They were also "The largest, most handsome, and, in the Japanese estimation, most successful destroyers in the Imperial fleet," according to respected Imperial Japanese Navy historian Allyn Nevitt.[215] The antiaircraft destroyer's bridge was perhaps a bit too cramped for an admiral, but she was brimming with state-of-the-art – for the Japanese – weapons technology.[216] The admiral had the *Teruzuki* maneuver to go around the PT boats, while engaging them with her guns.[217]

There was "a heavy explosion," port side aft. Admiral Tanaka was flung to the deck of the bridge, unconscious. When he came to, the trusty *Naganami* was alongside, taking off the *Teruzuki*'s crew. At 1:33 am, Tanaka's staff helped him aboard his old flagship and helped make it his new flagship again, while Tanaka was treated for hip and shoulder injuries. The admiral was confined to a bed, from which he continued to command the force and even radioed that the flag had been shifted.[218]

The Tenacious Tanaka had finally met his match: PT boats. Warned by *Magic* – again – of another Japanese supply effort, the PTs had set up a new ambush.[219] Three boats, *PT-40*, *PT-45*, and *PT-59*, the group commanded by Lieutenant (jg) Lester H. Gamble of the *PT-45*, charged in, launched torpedoes, and rapidly departed. It was a torpedo from Gamble's own *PT-45* that had burrowed itself into the stern of the *Teruzuki*.[220] The torpedo's detonation seems to have been unusually large, breaking the rudder and one propeller shaft, thus causing the destroyer to immediately lose navigability. Worse, the blast ignited a nasty oil fire that spread both inside the ship and on the water around it.

A radio report attracted the attention of two more PTs, *PT-44* and *PT-110*, off Kamimbo. Now they both charged in.[221] *PT-44* under Lieutenant Freeland sped behind the burning *Teruzuki* and inadvertently backlit herself for the vengeful *Kawakaze* and *Suzukaze*. One shell, apparently from the destroyers' main batteries, passed through the engine room canopy, disabling the engines and setting the boat afire. Freeland approved a suggestion that they abandon ship or, rather, boat. They had just started jumping overboard when another salvo obliterated the *PT-44*. Only two, one officer and one enlisted man, survived the destruction of the *PT-44*; two officers, including Freeland, and seven enlisted men were lost.[222]

It was cold comfort for the *Teruzuki*. After the destroyer had blazed for some three hours with no progress made in controlling the flames, a scuttling order was apparently issued at 3:15 am, but it was unnecessary. The spreading inferno reached the after depth charge magazine, resulting in a massive explosion at 4:40 am that finished off the antiaircraft destroyer. Nine were killed. The *Naganami* rescued Admiral Tanaka and 56 others. Another 140 were picked up by the *Arashi*, while 156 reached Kamimbo.[223] To add insult to grievous injury, of the 1,200 drums that were dropped, only 220 reached the troops on Guadalcanal.[224]

Admiral Tanaka would later say, "The loss of my flagship, our newest and best destroyer, to such inferior enemy strength was a serious responsibility. I have often thought that it would have been easier for me to have been killed in that first explosion."[225] If Combined Fleet was not already unhappy with Tanaka Raizo for losing the *Teruzuki* or for not delivering the supply drums, then he would soon give them another reason.

The Reinforcement Unit arrived back at Shortland at 11:30 am, when Admiral Tanaka received the following order, "Guadalcanal reinforcements will be discontinued temporarily because of moonlit nights. The reinforcement unit will proceed to Rabaul and engage in transportation operations to Munda for the present." Tanaka ordered the destroyer *Maikaze* to tow the still-disabled *Nowaki* from Shortland to Truk, escorted by the *Arashi*. As ordered, Tanaka himself went with his remaining eight destroyers to Rabaul.[226]

There Admiral Tanaka was hospitalized. Deeply depressed about losing the *Teruzuki* and failing his mission, in pain from his injuries, and probably suffering from the effects of a concussion, Tanaka dictated a memorandum to his superiors recommending the evacuation of Guadalcanal.[227] No one knows what Tanaka expected to come out of his too-frank letter, including Tanaka.

It was a not-so-merry Christmas Day when Admiral Tanaka received a response from Combined Fleet to his missive – he was being reassigned. Reassigned to that hotbed of naval activity: Burma. Tanaka's naval career was effectively over. The Japanese may have been defeated on Guadalcanal, but in the Navy's eyes that was no excuse for actually admitting such defeat.

Even so, Combined Fleet's message in the reassignment of Tanaka Raizo was all too clear: the defeat on Guadalcanal was all *his* fault – at least that's what they wanted everyone to think. And given that Tanaka's reputation is far worse in Japanese circles than in American ones, it seems that their efforts here had some success.

Ultimately, Tanaka's reassignment was good for the Allies, bad for the Japanese, and a tragedy for Tanaka himself because his memorandum had been completely unnecessary.

CHAPTER 6

DELAY, LINGER, AND WAIT

It is the singularly unfair peculiarity of war that the credit of success is claimed by all, while a disaster is attributed to one alone.

Tacitus, *Agricola* 27:1 (AD 98)

In the Southwest Pacific Command, Tacitus' Law had what one might call a variant: *It is the singularly unfair peculiarity of war that a disaster is attributed to all, while the credit of success is claimed by one alone, if that one alone is Douglas MacArthur.*

When the subject of a unified Pacific supreme commander had first been raised, Admiral King had strongly objected to MacArthur ever having operational command over the Pacific Fleet due to the lack of understanding of naval matters that MacArthur had displayed during the disastrous Philippines campaign as well as MacArthur's slander and downright abuse of the US Navy. The compromise had been the creation of separate command areas for the Pacific theater. MacArthur got the Southwest Pacific Command, with Australia, New Guinea, the Solomons, the Bismarcks, the East Indies, and the Philippines. Nimitz got the rest, with the area adjoining MacArthur's command called the South Pacific Command, at this time under Admiral Halsey.

After the victory at Midway, the issue had become a little more urgent because Admiral King had planned operations in the lower Solomon Islands – Tulagi and eventually Guadalcanal – which were in General MacArthur's Southwest Pacific Command area. There was another clash of services, with Douglas MacArthur again the focal point. It was out of this specific disagreement that Admiral King and General Marshall hammered out the "Joint Directive for Offensive Operations in the Southwest Pacific Area Agreed on by the United States Chiefs of Staff" on July 2, 1942. This was a three-phase plan that was codenamed *Pestilence*. Phase One, with the code name *Watchtower*, became the seizure of

Guadalcanal and Tulagi, to be completed by the Pacific Fleet. Phase Two would be the capture of Lae, Salamaua and the rest of the northeast coast of New Guinea, and the central Solomons. Phase Three would involve the reduction and capture of Rabaul. Phases Two and Three were to be under the command of General MacArthur.

That agreement had endured through the parallel Guadalcanal and Buna campaigns. Both of those campaigns were nearing their successful conclusions, though much extremely difficult fighting remained, especially in the Buna-Gona campaign. It was in the context of the bitterly fought Buna campaign that the command dispute rose once again.

With the Australian 7th and US 32nd Infantry Divisions closing in on Buna and Gona from the south and southeast, the Japanese defenders had their backs to the sea. While General MacArthur was no expert on naval operations, he did understand that to fully cut off the Japanese from reinforcement and supply, he had to cut off access from the sea, so he needed naval support. MacArthur's Southwest Pacific Command had its own navy, but it was far too small for the job at hand. He asked Admiral Halsey for naval help in cutting off Buna. Moreover, MacArthur wanted South Pacific units to help him establish a seaborne supply line around the tip of Papua instead of having to negotiate the Kokoda Trail over the Owen Stanley Mountains. Finally, MacArthur would then take Rabaul to protect his flank.[1]

As Halsey explained in a message sent November 28, he was disinclined to acquiesce to MacArthur's request:

> Our common objective is Rabaul. Until Jap air in New Britain and Northern Solomons has been reduced, risk of valuable naval units in middle and western reaches Solomon Sea can only be justified by major enemy seaborne movement against south coast New Guinea or Australia itself. Seaborne supply of bases we take on northern coast of New Guinea not feasible until we control Solomon Sea, in other words Rabaul. Pursuant foregoing and with history past months in view, consider Rabaul assault campaign must be amphibious along the Solomons with New Guinea land position basically a supporting one only. I am currently reinforcing Cactus position and expediting means of operating heavy air from there. It is my belief that the sound procedure at this time is to maintain as strong a land and air pressure against the Japanese Buna position as your lines of communication permit, and to continue to extract a constant toll of Japanese shipping, an attrition which if continued at the present rate he can not long sustain. I believe that my greatest contribution to our common effort would be to strengthen my position and resume the advance up the Solomons as soon as possible.[2]

In short, he meant "no," and his refusal came with the full support of Admiral Nimitz, Admiral King, and even General MacArthur's own naval commander Rear Admiral Arthur S. Carpender.[3]

MacArthur was livid, and with some justification. The lack of adequate naval support made his drive to take Buna and Gona more difficult by giving the Japanese both a supply route and line of retreat. But this was a bed that Douglas MacArthur had mostly made himself. Up until the start of the Pacific War, MacArthur had made bombastic pronouncements about a glorious land war if the Japanese attacked the Philippines, while belittling the US Navy's Asiatic Fleet and its commander Admiral Thomas Hart. Once the Japanese attacked Pearl Harbor, MacArthur disappeared for critical hours, willfully violated orders from Washington to attack Japanese airbases on Formosa, and allowed most of his air force to get destroyed on the ground. Having given away any hope of even contesting the air, MacArthur watched as Japanese air attacks pounded his ground troops and turned the Asiatic Fleet's primary base at Cavite literally into molten slag. MacArthur refused to assemble supply caches on Bataan, to which his troops were supposed to withdraw, on the logic that it was "defeatist." As a result, when he retreated there all the same, his troops had little food, ammunition, or medical supplies.

For all of this MacArthur blamed Admiral Hart and the Asiatic Fleet, upon whom he unleashed a torrent of abuse and slander. It was a sorry, contemptible, performance, one the US Navy had not forgotten. They simply did not trust Douglas MacArthur. But where there's a will, there's a way, and whatever his other attributes, both good and bad, Douglas MacArthur possessed an iron will.

With Guadalcanal almost secured, then Phase One of *Pestilence* was arguably complete and Phases Two and Three could be initiated, which, by the terms of the "Joint Directive," would place command under General MacArthur. Then he was well within his rights to command South Pacific naval assets to block the sea routes into Buna.

To that end, on December 1, 1942, General Marshall sent the draft of a directive for the commencements of Phases Two and Three to Admiral King for comment. It was mostly the same as the "Joint Directive" originally agreed but did contain some significant changes. It specified that the forces required would come from those already assigned to the South and Southwest Pacific Areas, subject to the approval of the Joint Chiefs. It reserved to the Joint Chiefs the right to withdraw naval units in the event of an emergency. Once again, it gave General MacArthur command over Phases Two and Three.[4]

But it did circumscribe General MacArthur's command powers somewhat, specifying that direct control of the naval and amphibious phases of the campaign would be exercised by a naval officer. In essence, MacArthur's authority in these matters would be limited to selecting the objectives, allocating the forces, and fixing the timing and sequence of the operations.[5]

Admiral King had other ideas. He had been considering the necessity and even the utility of proceeding up to Rabaul as he himself had originally suggested. King thought Phases Two and Three might even be unnecessary. If the experience on Guadalcanal was any indication, a direct advance on Rabaul was madness: it would fail or, more likely, bog down in a stalemate. Why not try to outflank Rabaul by simply bypassing the Solomons and occupying the Admiralty Islands northwest of Rabaul instead?[6]

But this was absurd, for reasons that Admiral Nimitz explained. The capture of the Admiralties would not give the Allies control of the Solomons. The enemy's bases there, including the anchorage at Shortland and the new base at Munda, and in New Britain and

New Ireland, he pointed out, were mutually supporting and there was no assurance that the seizure of Rabaul would neutralize them or induce the garrisons to surrender. Furthermore, if the Japanese retained control of the sea lanes south and east of Rabaul, trying to bypass them would only expose Allied forces to a flanking attack. For these reasons, Nimitz concluded, the Allies must accept a step-by-step slog up the Solomons – just as Admiral King had originally suggested, with the next objective Munda or Kahili, depending on the forces available and the state of the Japanese defenses.[7]

Otherwise, Admiral Nimitz concurred with Admiral Halsey: Phase One was by no means complete and would not be finished until air and naval bases had been established on Guadalcanal and the area firmly secured. Furthermore, it was impossible to start on Phase Two because the forces available in theater were not enough to complete the job. They needed reinforcements. Finally, Nimitz declared that when the offensive was resumed it should be directed by Halsey, not MacArthur; because operations in the Solomons would require most of the surface forces of the Pacific Fleet, command should be vested in a flag officer. "Any change of command of those forces which Halsey has welded into a working organization," he told King with an ominous hint, "would be most unwise."[8]

Both Admiral Halsey and General Harmon, commander of Army forces in the South Pacific, supported a step-by-step advance up the Solomons ladder as a prerequisite to the seizure of Rabaul. "To be able to attack the Bismarcks simultaneously from New Guinea and the Solomons," wrote Harmon in a Novermber 25, 1942, letter to General Marshall, "would be ideal." But he admitted that for now the South Pacific naval forces could do little to support MacArthur's advance in New Guinea. "To send surface forces into the western areas of the Solomons Sea with the Jap air as heavily entrenched as it is," he told Marshall, "would be taking a risk beyond the gain to be anticipated even with the best of fortune."[9] In trying to mitigate this danger, Halsey suggested to General MacArthur taking Woodlark Island, between New Guinea and the Solomons, and building a new airbase there. Admiral King was open to the idea and suggested alternatives, including Kiriwina in the Trobriand Islands.[10]

General Marshall came back and turned Admiral Nimitz's argument for a step-by-step advance up the Solomons into an argument for a unified command – under Douglas MacArthur. Because why would you want an offensive across thousands of miles of Pacific Ocean led by the US Navy when it could be led by the US Army and Douglas MacArthur?

The Japanese positions in the Solomons and New Guinea, he pointed out, resembled an inverted "V" with the point aimed at Rabaul. Against each leg of the V the Allies had placed two strong but separate forces, one controlled by MacArthur and the other by Nimitz, thousands of miles away, and each independent of the other. "Skillful strategic direction, coordinating the employment of the two strong Allied forces available," Marshall insisted in late December, "appears mandatory to offset the Japanese advantages of position and direction." Only in this way could the Allies exploit quickly success against either leg of the V and at the same time use their forces, especially the bombers with their strategic mobility, where they were most needed and where they could achieve the most decisive results.[11]

And so it went – back and forth, back and forth, the Army wanting a unified command under General MacArthur; the Navy agreeing to a unified command, but only under Admiral Nimitz.

When General Arnold had returned from his "fact-finding" South Pacific tour in early October, he had reiterated the idea of a unified command. General Marshall passed it along to the Theater Group of the Operations Division of the Office of Chief of Staff. There it was studied by General St. Clair "Bill" Streett and General Albert Wedemeyer. Both agreed with the idea of a unified Pacific command. Wedemeyer suggested an air officer be the supreme commander. Streett, perhaps alone among the Army brass, understood the problems with selection of such a commander in general and with Douglas MacArthur in particular.[12]

General Streett would write, "At the risk of being considered naive and just plain country-boy dumb," he could not help feeling that the major obstacle to a "sane military solution" of the problem was General MacArthur himself. Only with MacArthur out of the picture would it be possible to establish a sound organization in the area. Streett appreciated fully the political implications of removing MacArthur, but thought it could be done safely if the general were given some high post such as the ambassadorship to Russia, "a big enough job for anyone." Then, depending on whether the Navy or the Air Force was considered to have the dominant role in the war, the post of supreme commander in the Pacific could be given either to Admiral Nimitz or Army Air Force General Joseph McNarney.[13]

The idea for a unified command for the Pacific occurred to Generals Marshall and Arnold only once General MacArthur was evacuated from the Philippines. Douglas MacArthur needed something to do that was worthy of Douglas MacArthur. They had fully bought into MacArthur's public persona. The only plausible command would be that of the entire Pacific theater.

Of course, the Army would eventually have a general in Dwight Eisenhower as Supreme Commander Allied Expeditionary Forces in the European Theater, which was primarily a land war. The Pacific theater, while it had its land combat elements and much more of an air element, was primarily a naval war. There was absolutely no legitimate reason to put an Army general in charge of it, especially a land general.

Moreover, it was that same institutional arrogance and myopia that was behind the relentless drive to put Douglas MacArthur in that role of Pacific supreme commander. MacArthur's performance in the 1941–42 Philippines campaign was so horrid, wracked with ineptitude, arrogance, and willful violation of orders that investigation and court martial would have been warranted. That such steps were impossible due to MacArthur's reputation is perhaps understandable, but that does not excuse the refusal by Generals Marshall and Arnold to acknowledge even privately that MacArthur's performance in the Philippines was perhaps below his usual standards, or to understand why the US Navy, slandered, abused, and blamed by MacArthur for the loss of the Philippines, did not want to serve under him.

The perils of the divided command in the Solomons and New Guinea – and, to be sure, there were many, such as the lack of naval support that General MacArthur had just experienced – were entirely the fault of the US Army leadership in Generals Marshall and Arnold for insisting on a US Army command for the entire Pacific theater; and, failing to get MacArthur that command, insisting that in the alternative he get his own independent command.

Be that as it may, they were in a bureaucratic stalemate. The command arrangements for the South Pacific and the Southwest Pacific would stay as they were – for now.

Meanwhile, on Guadalcanal itself the guard was changing. When he first met Admiral Halsey in person on October 23, 1942, General Vandegrift had emphasized that the 1st Marine Division had been on Guadalcanal since August 7, and had reached the point where they simply had to get off the island. At that time the Japanese were in the midst of their combined arms attack that included the Santa Cruz naval battle, so Vandegrift understood it was impossible at that time, but it had to be done at the earliest opportunity.[14]

On November 16, Admiral Turner gave the heads-up that the 1st Marine Division would be relieved by US Army troops very soon. Battalions were to be relieved in the order of their arrival on Guadalcanal proper.[15] That heads-up became official on November 29, when General Vandegrift, along with General MacArthur, Admiral Nimitz, and Admiral Halsey, received a message from Admiral King, revealing that the 1st Marine Division would be relieved and sent to Australia, where it would be handed to MacArthur's Southwest Pacific Command.[16]

It was long overdue and desperately needed. By now, the men of the 1st Marine Division were riddled with tropical diseases, especially malaria. It was a rule of thumb in front-line units that unless one had a temperature of more than 103 degrees there would be no light duty or excuse from a patrol mission.[17] Moreover, the limited food available during the campaign left them malnourished. And that's before the physical and psychological effects of near constant combat were factored in. On December 7 and 8, US Navy doctors examined the men in one regiment to get a quick snapshot of the division's physical shape. It was not good. The doctors determined that 34 percent of the regiment were unfit for any duty which might involve combat. This percentage would have been higher but for the recent infusion of the regiment with 400 replacements.[18]

Corporal Gallant poetically explained:

By the time our relief did come we looked like beggars clad in rags, weak, exhausted, without a care in the world, for we did not care – we did not give a damn.

We had beaten the Japanese. Now we just didn't give a damn. Values we once held – things we once thought so important – no longer meant a thing. Now we knew how little it takes to live; now we knew how much men can do with very little, if they have guts and do not give a damn.

We knew toughness was more of the mind than of the body. We knew if the mind resolved to do it, the body could do it.

So, we looked with tired, cynical eyes at the sea. Nothing could hurt us now. We had nothing but our lives. And we didn't give a damn.[19]

The most extreme, dangerous manifestation of this "I don't give a damn" attitude was signaled by what was known on Guadalcanal as the "Gooney Bird Stare." In other places, it was called "the thousand-yard stare," a symptom of what is often called "shell shock," "battle fatigue," or some variation thereof; or, in medical terms, "combat stress reaction." Put more plainly, it was a symptom of mental breakdown. As Corporal Gallant detailed it:

Constant exposure to danger, bad diet, hunger, months on the line without relief, caused some degree of neurosis in every Marine – irritability, swift and extreme reactions to noise, inability to sleep but for short catnaps, obsession with some subject – such as fried eggs – and numerous other manifestations of mental torment and physical exhaustion.

The Gooney Bird Stare began to appear when the mind was quite near the edge of outer space, ready to topple over into unreality. It was characterized by wide-open, bloodshot eyes, showing the whites all the way around the pupils, raised eyebrows, wrinkled forehead, and complete inattention. A Marine with the Gooney Bird Stare appeared completely, utterly, exhausted, his eyes blank and without expression. His mind was far away, distracted, occupied with some problem outside reality, such as fried eggs. He had cast aside the world and had entered another for long periods. He quit conversing, preferred to be alone, did not like to be bothered and sat in silence for long stretches of time. [...]

It marked the beginning of the end of the controlled mind. It marked a nervous breakdown. The Gooney Bird Stare became a good warning symptom of battle fatigue, showing the man needed rest for a while, then he was as good as new – or almost new, anyway.[20]

The 1st Marine Division needed rest; indeed they had needed rest for a long, long while.

To that end, on December 8, US Navy transports stopped at Lunga and offloaded the last of the Americal Division's three regiments, the 132nd Infantry. It was time for General Vandegrift and his Marines. The next day, December 9, with little in the way of pomp and circumstance, Vandegrift turned Guadalcanal over to General Patch and the US Army. The 5th Marine Regiment filed into the transports. They would leave that day. The 1st Marine Division headquarters would follow a few days later, the 1st Marines on December 22, and the 7th Marines on January 5.[21]

The procession was haunting – and haunted. As Private Robert Leckie described it:

Some of them had been on the lines more than four months without relief, and they came down to the beach at Lunga ragged, bearded, and bony. Some of them had hardly the strength to walk to the boats, and yet, before they left, all of them had visited their cemetery.

It was called "Flanders Field," and it was a neat cleared square cut into the Lunga coconut groves. Each grave was covered with a palm frond and marked with a rough cross onto which mess gear and identification tags were nailed. Departing Marines knelt or stood there in prayerful farewell[…][22]

Corporal Gallant elaborated on the men's appearance:

We wore ragged clothing. Threadbare, faded dungarees with frayed cuffs; dented helmets with dirty liners stained by sweat; filthy shoes, the rough leather, black with saddle soap, worn and scarred. These were our uniforms. These were our work clothes.

The Marines dressed thus for travel were thin, hollow-cheeked, gaunt of frame. Their faces were burned a deep bronze and their eyebrows were bleached by the tropical sun; their hair was ragged with crude barbering. Eyes that not so long ago danced with merriment of youth were now cold, hard, and merciless, quick to freeze in anger.

The faces, deep lines on the foreheads and at the corners of the eyes, were a picture of exhaustion of mind and body. Yet, they still reflected a fierceness, a starved fierceness, taunted and made mean and impatient by circumstance.[23]

From the landing on August 7, 1942, until relief in December, the 1st Marine Division lost 605 officers and men killed in action, 45 who later died of combat wounds, 31 listed as missing and presumed dead, and 1,278 wounded in action, totaling 1,959 casualties of enemy action. As best as can be determined, however, 8,580 Marines were stricken at one time or another by malaria, dengue fever, and other tropical diseases; or conditions such as jungle rot, in medical terms a "tropical ulcer," now understood as an infection contracted from the constant mud.[24] These numbers are somewhat misleading inasmuch as it's impossible to separate Marines suffering combat wounds from Marines suffering from diseases. Many with malaria were hospitalized more than once and were added to the total as cases rather than as individuals. Some of these men were later killed or wounded in action. Others suffered from a milder form of malaria or other illness and did not go to the hospital, so they do not show in the statistics.[25]

These Marines boarding the transport to leave Guadalcanal had suffered fever, chills, and dehydration. They had been plagued with diarrhea, malaria, jungle rot, and at times near starvation. These Marines had survived countless hours of combat, 170 air raids, 64 naval bombardments, and 614 of Pistol Pete's 150mm shells, lobbed into their defense perimeter.[26] All this they had endured in their four months on Guadalcanal.

Among the graves in the Flanders Field (now Lunga Point) Cemetery is one of Private First Class Bill Cameron, killed by a Japanese bomb in late August. His friend Private First Class James A. Donahue placed a plaque on the grave. The plaque showed Donahue's epitaph for Cameron.[27] It was a poem, said to be a variant of one by Frank Bernard Camp written for World War I, that read:

And when he goes to Heaven,
To Saint Peter he will tell:

Another marine reporting, Sir;
I've served my time in hell![28]

The 1st Marine Division's presence on Guadalcanal may have been concluding, but the Guadalcanal campaign was not yet finished.

General Patch was under orders to remove the Japanese from Guadalcanal. He believed he did not yet have enough troops to do so. The Japanese still had some 25,000 men on the island, not in the best shape, however. They were even more wracked with malaria and other tropical diseases than the Americans were. Because of the disaster of Admiral Tanaka's convoy, they had nearly exhausted their ammunition and their food, as well. They formed into something resembling a quarter circle, from the area of Point Cruz and Kokumbona, where the 4th, 16th, and 29th Regiments of the 2nd Sendai Division were deployed. Inland two battalions of the 228th Regiment were positioned on high ground west of the Matanikau River. Curving southeast and crossing the Matanikau, elements of the 124th Regiment commanded by Colonel Oka Akinosuka held a line running from the Matanikau to Mount Austen. Dug in around and on Mount Austen were the remnants of the 38th Nagoya Division, including the 230th, 228th, and 229th Regiments, and the remainder of the 124th.[29]

A November offensive by US Army troops and Marines to drive west across the Matanikau to capture Kokumbona had managed to isolate and destroy a pocket of Japanese troops at Point Cruz before being stopped cold west of the Matanikau. The Imperial Japanese Army may have been largely inept at launching attacks on Guadalcanal – see, for example, Colonel Ichiki, General Kawaguchi, and General Maruyama – and the troops may have been sick and starving, but they could still fight on the defensive with unequaled tenacity. As General MacArthur, General Eichelberger, and their troops were finding out at Buna, they excelled at designing and building improvised fortifications. With the 1st Marine Division leaving, Patch had only the 164th and 182nd Regiments of the Americal Division and the independent 147th Infantry Regiment. It was not anywhere near the three divisions Patch thought he needed.

To break this stalemate, General Patch told General Harmon that he needed more troops. Harmon promptly ordered the 25th Infantry Division, already on its way from Hawaii, to head directly to Guadalcanal to augment the Americal Division. They would arrive during the last two weeks of December and early January 1943. The rest of the 2nd Marine Division was also ordered to Guadalcanal.

For now, however, General Patch decided to try to remove a longtime thorn from the side of the Americans by – finally – taking Mount Austen. This series of ridges had been a first-day objective of *Watchtower*, but the distance – the 1,500-foot-high summit was about 6 miles southwest of Henderson Field – had been badly underestimated, along with the difficulty getting there. Once the Americans were relatively ready to move on Mount Austen, they found the Japanese had gotten there first and planted an observation post with a lovely panoramic view of American operations at Lunga, whether aircraft at Henderson Field or ships in the roadstead. Mount Austen also served as a position for Japanese artillery, especially Pistol Pete, to harass the airfields. Clearing Mount Austen would not only relieve this headache but provide a flanking position on the upper Matanikau for further operations against the Japanese west of Lunga.

The seizure of Mount Austen took on an added urgency in mid-December. On December 12, a group of maybe four Japanese soldiers led by a 2nd Lieutenant Nakazawa infiltrated the American perimeter from the south.[30] Newly arrived Lieutenant John B. George of the 132nd Infantry Regiment told "the story of the 'great Japanese Infiltrating Party'":

> The party then walked through the dispersal area, passing a dump of several hundred thousand gallons of hundred octane gasoline, and continued walking through a bomb body storage area where several hundred tons of bombs were stacked in large clusters.
>
> Still carrying their detonators and blocks of picric acid (the Jap counterpart of TNT) our visitors crept carefully on through the tented area and past the shelters where the high-priced pilots of the 69th Fighter Squadron were sleeping peacefully. Finally they got to the strip, and there, laid out before them, was the entire effective strength of single motor airplanes in the South Pacific area at the time! Without hesitation they tied all their blocks of explosive to the propeller end of a single P-39 and blew this *one airplane* all to hell![31] [emphasis in original]

Not quite; they did also destroy a fuel truck in addition to the plane, an Airacobra, before escaping. Lieutenant George expressed a certain admiration for the Japanese: "Their feat was as bold and brilliant and as rugged in its demands for bravery as it was stupid in execution and mediocre in results."[32] Two days later, a patrol from the 132nd Infantry Regiment ran into a Japanese position on the northeastern slopes of Mount Austen that was supported by machine guns and mortars. On December 15, yet another Japanese infiltration party, this one from the 38th Engineer Regiment led by a 1st Lieutenant Ono, slipped in and damaged more Airacobras.[33]

The next day, General Patch decided these repeated infiltrations were a threat to the operation of Henderson Field, so he ordered the capture of Mount Austen, from where these attacks were believed to have originated and which would secure the left flank of a future push toward Kokumbona. Taking point in said capture was the newly arrived 132nd Infantry, composed of Illinois National Guard troops under the command of Colonel Leroy Nelson. They would be supported by the 105mm guns from the Army's 246th Field Artillery Battalion and 75mm pack howitzers of the 10th Marine Regiment, the artillery regiment of the 2nd Marine Division.

Now the 132nd learned the hard realities of combat on Guadalcanal. First, they had badly underestimated the size of the opposition. Second, hacking a path through primordial jungle usually means dropping off heavy weapons and ammunition which adversely affects effectiveness in combat. The 132nd started its attack but was quickly pinned down on the lower slopes of Mount Austen by snipers and machine-gun fire from concealed positions.[34] Further probing attacks gained only casualties, but apparently convinced the Japanese to pull back. Not that it helped things much for the Americans.

With sporadic jungle fighting, the 132nd had worked its way forward until Christmas Eve, when it finally captured the Japanese Mount Austen lookout post. Then the regiment was stopped cold when it ran into heavy fire from the next Japanese defense line.[35] Set west of Mount Austen, the line contained maybe 50 pillboxes, made of logs and dirt up to 2 feet thick, with only some 3 feet of pillbox projecting above the ground. Little short of a direct hit from a 105mm howitzer could hurt these things. The pillboxes were staggered, interconnected, mutually supporting, and very well camouflaged – like the Japanese defenses at Buna. Each of these positions contained several riflemen and one or two machine guns, usually Nambu Type 96 light machine guns. The entire position was supported by 81mm and 90mm mortars, and was held by some 600 troops of the 2nd Battalion of the 228th Regiment and the 2nd Battalion of the 124th Regiment, all under the command of Major Inagaki Takeyoshi. For reasons known only to the Japanese, the Imperial Army troops nicknamed this well-designed position after a prefecture in the Home Islands: "Gifu."[36]

The 132nd's Lieutenant George saw the fortifications and bunkers – "reception committee shelters" – at the troublesome Gifu firsthand. With tongue firmly in cheek he described how they would welcome "visitors":

These reception committee shelters were sighted [sic] with care so that there would be little or no chance of any visitor approaching unseen or unheard. The visitors would have to make their way through particularly inhospitable stretches of foliage before they approached their "hosts," clawing often at plant stems and turning now and then to remove the sticky, holding whip of a wait-a-minute vine from the cloth of a jacket or the flesh of a cheek or hand. The last few steps toward the waiting hosts would be in clearer, more open, spots in the jungle – not completely clear, but open as though these spots of ground had perhaps offered less appeal to roots of jungle weeds than had the surrounding area. And the first guests these hosts would receive in time-honored style would, at the moment of reception, be breathing thanks for a few feet of clear space in front of them.

But while the hosts were taking every step to prevent the guests from arriving unseen or unannounced, it was none the less their desire that the reception was to be in the nature of a surprise party. Along with the committee housing project there was also heavy effort under way to prevent the excavations from becoming an eyesore and smearing the pretty green landscape with unsightly mounds of yellow clay, framing the entrances to the committee chambers in a highly unartistic way – all out of keeping with the natural tropical garden atmosphere.

So, while some of the hosts dug with shovels and picks, others were busy with baskets woven from vines in which they carried away load after load of yellow dirt to a hidden place to the rear of the line of diggings. There the dirt was scattered around the roots of heavy brush where it would not change the garden picture of the "back yards," or else it was thrown into a little stream where it was washed away, yellowing the clean spring water. So thorough was this operation that scarcely one clod of yellow dirt was left to mar the perfect scene of green and dark shadow which surrounded the picturesque area.

After the rough line of shelters was finished, the sturdy, well muscled little builders got to work industriously upon a series of connecting tunnels, just large enough for the small and wiry bodies of the hosts to move through with comfort. [...] The areas in front of the windows were sodded over carefully so that no dry leaves or other substance could be blown up into the chamber by a sudden gust of wind, and then the square outline of the window was artistically broken up by the bending and sometimes actual transplanting of pretty leaved plants, making the whole dome of the chamber-structure blend perfectly into the shadowy undergrowth.[37]

The fortifications at Gifu were impressive. Lieutenant George would be compelled to admit:

[T]he Japanese were the most skilled fighters in the world as far as the Infantry aspects of sacrificial defense in jungle country are concerned. There are no other soldiers who would give them a run for their money in that type of fighting. Their excellence in that field was only part guts. A lot of it was due to their remarkable entrenching ability. The way they could build pillboxes and covered foxholes and organize them into clever, mutually-supporting positions is perhaps their greatest defense asset. And their skill at camouflage was part of this remarkable entrenching skill.[38]

There was no easy way to attack Gifu. American artillery had little effect unless it got a lucky direct hit. The 132nd had no flamethrowers and could not get close enough to use demolition charges on the bunkers. It became a duel of artillery and infiltration patrols while the 132nd tried to feel for the flanks and rear of the Gifu position. They managed to determine that it was a line of about 1,500 yards, formed into a horseshoe that was relatively weak to the west.

Machine-gun fire from the well-concealed fortifications repeatedly stymied the Americans. To complicate matters, Colonel Nelson, who had commanded 132nd Infantry Regiment since 1937, was reported to be ill with malaria. He was relieved on December 28 and replaced by Lieutenant Colonel Alexander M. George.[39] While Nelson and the 132nd were Illinois National Guard, George was a Regular Army officer, considered to be "somewhat eccentric" by the men of the 132nd.[40]

He proceeded to quickly display such eccentricity. On December 30, Field Order No. 1 from the 132nd Infantry headquarters detailed that Lieutenant Colonel George expected his troops to capture Hill 27, a position to the south of Gifu. Paragraph 3X of the order read: "Upon capture of Hill 27 a perimeter defense will be established and will be defended at all costs."[41] If the troops were resentful at issuance of such an order from a safe headquarters, they may have been mollified on January 1. That was when George decided to inspect his troops while making the point that Japanese small-arms fire was usually ineffective against moving targets. Wearing only a pair of shorts and a fatigue cap, armed with two .45-caliber automatic pistols and a rifle, George inspected the front lines by walking erect in full view of the soldiers of his troops – as well as of the Japanese, who shot at him, and missed. Repeatedly. George finished his tour, his point proven.[42]

Further showing the inefficiency of Japanese target shooting, on January 2 the 132nd captured Hill 27 and defended it at all costs against no fewer than six Japanese counterattacks.[43] Even so, after 22 days of combat on Mount Austen, the 132nd had suffered 112 killed, 272 wounded, and three missing.[44]

Compelled by these losses and the effects of battle exhaustion and tropical diseases to go over to the defensive, the 132nd began preparing a semicircle position to isolate Gifu from the north, south, and east. They would have to wait for reinforcements to clear out the Japanese fortifications.

While General Patch was trying to secure Mount Austen and having only limited success, Admiral Halsey was seeing an ominous buildup of enemy forces in Rabaul.

Heavy troop reinforcements were arriving at the Japanese base. On December 6 scout planes found 30 ships in Simpson Harbor. On December 22 that number was over 100; eight days later it was still 91, of which 21 were warships.[45] The Tokyo Express runs started up again, running to Guadalcanal, New Guinea, and elsewhere. Something was up.

The concentration of shipping created a target-rich environment in and around Rabaul and the various transit routes. For the bombers of General MacArthur's 5th Air Force and for American submarines, the latter's performance in the Guadalcanal campaign since the *S-44* ambushed the *Kako* in August had left something to be desired, due to ineffective torpedoes and even worse employment.

Now, the American submarines started to assert themselves in a true battle of attrition. On the afternoon of December 10, the submarine *Wahoo*, operating submerged off Buka, came across a southbound convoy of three ships in a column, escorted by one destroyer.[46] Skipper Lieutenant Commander Marvin G. Kennedy decided to take out the destroyer, because once the escort was out of the way he could sink the three cargo ships at his leisure. But Kennedy could not get the *Wahoo* into a good attack position, so at 4:00 pm he launched a spread of four Mark 14 torpedoes at the largest of the freighters, the second in the column. The result was three hits to the starboard side of the fully loaded collier *Kamoi Maru*. The destroyer launched a counterattack of some 40 depth charges, some of which came uncomfortably close, but it did nothing to hurt the *Wahoo* or help the *Kamoi Maru*, who lingered awash for a few hours before finally sinking after sunset.[47] At that time, there was some sort of argument on the *Wahoo* about mounting a second attack, this one on the freighter who was picking up the *Kamoi Maru*'s survivors. Kennedy shot the idea down.[48]

Three days later the *Wahoo* got another chance. At 1:21 pm, in the midst of a rain squall off Shortland, she sighted a submarine leaving the anchorage with what she believed was "I2" painted on the side of the conning tower. The I-boat was about 3,000 yards away, moving on the surface at about 12 knots, estimated to have a course of 15 degrees True – just east of north by east – and a speed of 12 knots. The *Wahoo* barely had time to swing around enough to bring her tubes to bear, but seven minutes later launched three torpedoes at a range of 800 yards. She reported seeing an explosion about 20 feet forward of the conning tower 37 seconds later. Lieutenant Commander Kennedy watched the submarine go down "with personnel still on the bridge." Although sound conditions were "terrible" enough that "[e]ven at 800 yards the targets (sic) propellers could not be heard," the *Wahoo*'s sound gear reported, "two and one-half minutes after the torpedo explosion, the submarine collapsed at deep depth with a noise considerably louder than the torpedo explosion."[49] Kennedy reported sinking a submarine.

Lieutenant Commander Inada Hiroshi of the *I-2* disagreed. He was on the bridge when there were two explosions nearby. Thinking his boat was under air attack, Inada ordered an immediate crash dive. "Somewhat later," the *I-2* heard a third explosion.[50] Attributing the explosions to a bombing attack from an aircraft, Inada and the I-boat escaped the area without damage. It is possible the explosions the *I-2* and Lieutenant Commander Kennedy witnessed were the *Wahoo*'s Mark 14 torpedoes exploding prematurely, just as torpedoes with the Mark 6 exploder often did.[51]

On December 16, Admiral Matsuyama Mitsumaru in the old light cruiser *Tenryu*, part of the 18th Cruiser Division that Admiral Mikawa had once derided as "rabble," left Simpson Harbor leading destroyers *Isonami*, *Inazuma*, *Suzukaze*, and *Arashio*; and merchant ships *Aikoku* and *Gokoku Maru*s on a reinforcement run to Madang, New Guinea. En route, the *Gokoku Maru* took a bomb in the forecastle from one of MacArthur's B-17s of the 43rd Bombardment Group. The bomb didn't do much and the reinforcement run was successfully completed on December 18.

Admiral Matsuyama's force was about to head back when they stumbled across the submarine *Albacore* under Lieutenant Commander Richard C. Lake. Lake had been warned by *Magic* of the reinforcement run and set up an ambush. At a range of 2,000 yards, he launched three torpedoes at a transport escorted by what Lake called a "destroyer." The torpedoes missed the freighter, *Gokoku Maru*, but at 9:15 pm two burrowed their way into the stern of the "destroyer" *Tenryu*. The old cruiser's steering gear was wrecked, her engine rooms flooded, and she lost power. Matsuyama had to transfer his flag to the *Isonami*, who with the *Sukukaze* dropped four depth charges on the *Albacore* without effect. The *Suzukaze* took off the cruiser's crew and the *Tenryu*, a pest who had punched well above her weight at Savo Island, sank at 11:20 pm, with 23 killed and 21 injured.[52] With the *Tenryu* gone, Admiral Ugaki determined the 18th Cruiser Division had "lost the meaning of its existence," so it was deactivated.[53]

While that was going on, on December 17, the submarine *Grouper* found a small convoy of transports *Bandoeng* and *Sorachi Maru*s, escorted by the subchaser *Ch-29* about

15 miles northwest of Buka's Cape Henpan, *Grouper* skipper Lieutenant Commander Rob McGregor launched four torpedoes at the *Bandoeng Maru* and two at the *Sorachi Maru*. McGregor missed the latter but got two hits on the former, including one in the engine room. The *Bandoeng Maru*, carrying ammunition, caught fire, staggered to a stop, and sank by the bow at around 4:00 pm.[54]

These Tokyo Express reinforcement and supply runs were getting much more dangerous than those of the previous fall. On December 18, a Tokyo Express run to Finschhafen, New Guinea by the destroyers *Asagumo* and *Mochizuki* found a welcoming gift from MacArthur of B-17s from the 43rd Bombardment Group and B-24s from the 90th Bombardment Group. The *Mochizuki* was damaged by near misses.[55]

That same day, the Japanese submarine *I-4* was trying to make a mole run to Buna. Lieutenant Commander Ueno Toshitake was a veteran of the early days of *Watchtower* as skipper of the Japanese submarine *I-123*. That experience served him well as skipper of *I-4*. Ueno had made two mole runs to Guadalcanal and was adding this run to Buna to his portfolio when he was chased off by a few PT boats and had to abort.

On December 21, the *I-4* was returning to Rabaul, heading north at 14 knots on the surface in the southern entrance to St. George's Channel when, at 6:37 am, lookouts spotted approaching torpedoes. Lieutenant Commander Ueno ordered an emergency turn to try to comb the wakes. He was fortunate in that one of the torpedoes had exploded prematurely and a second missed ahead as the result of a gyro malfunction – another proud moment for American torpedoes.

But Ueno was unfortunate in that a third torpedo hit the submarine's stern, exploding and sending up a large fireball and sending down the *I-4* and her crew to the depths. She was the victim of that survivor of the bombing of Cavite Navy Yard, the Java Sea Campaign, and Operation *Petticoat*, the US submarine *Seadragon*.[56] Under skipper Lieutenant Commander William E. Ferrall, the *Seadragon* had received a warning from *Magic* of the Japanese submarine's approach and had lain in ambush, only to be nearly undone by her own malfunctioning torpedoes. The torpedo that had exploded prematurely had caused the hot run of another torpedo still in the tube, forcing Ferrall to launch it so it would not detonate in the tube.[57]

The *Seadragon* was a busy boat. In the late afternoon of Christmas Day, Lieutenant Commander Ferrall found the Japanese transport *Nankai Maru* west-southwest of Cape St. George plodding toward Vila. Ferrall managed to plunk a torpedo into the transport forward of her bridge, which did not sink the *Nankai Maru* but did flood one, perhaps two, of her holds. Escorting destroyer *Uzuki* under vengeful skipper Lieutenant Commander Takeuchi Hitoshi went after the *Seadragon* with a flurry of depth charges. Thinking he had sunk the undersea assailant, Takeuchi headed back to the disabled *Nankai Maru*. But the fun was just beginning.

The *Uzuki* moved to attempt to tow the damaged freighter. By some bizarre happenstance, the *Uzuki* "collided with *Nankai Maru*'s bow with her midship and was flooded," to use Admiral Ugaki's description.[58] The freighter's bow sliced into the destroyer's hull and flooded two firerooms, reducing the *Uzaki*'s speed to 6 knots.[59] Now both the *Nankai Maru* and the *Uzuki* were crippled. In and around the Solomons, no good deed goes unpunished.

Admiral Mikawa was on the ball and quickly sent out destroyers *Naganami*, *Tanikaze*, *Ariake*, and *Urakaze* to assist the two ships back to Rabaul, preferably without colliding with either of them. The rescuers found the tough *Nankai Maru* able to move under her own power, so she headed back to Simpson Harbor. The *Ariake* took the *Uzuki* under tow and was promptly found by three of MacArthur's Consolidated B-24 Liberators from the 90th Bombardment Group, who pelted the pair with bombs.[60] None hit, but the *Ariake* was bracketed by six near misses that knocked out the Numbers 2 and 3 5-inch mounts, caused a fire, damaged her steering, and left 28 dead and 40 wounded. Needing to make emergency repairs, skipper Commander Yoshida Shooichi had the *Ariake* give up the tow and make for Eber Bay, New Britain, where she arrived just before midnight. The *Urakaze* took over and towed the *Uzuki* into Simpson Harbor, arriving the next morning. With her best speed reduced to 16 knots, the *Ariake* managed to stagger back into Rabaul the same day.[61] Ugaki called this series of incidents "a case of going into the forest to cut wood and coming home shorn."[62] Presumably this made sense to him.

On December 26, B-17s from the 43rd Bombardment Group attacked Simpson Harbor, planted a bomb on the port bow of the old Japanese destroyer *Tachikaze*, and rocked her with near misses, causing heavy damage and killing her commanding officer Lieutenant Commander Hirasata Yasumi.[63] The next day the 43rd's B-17s returned and sank the cargo ships *Italy Maru* and *Tsurugisan Maru* off Rabaul.[64]

There was a lot of Japanese activity and a lot of Allied activity to counter it. But a lot of Japanese activity meant there was something bigger in the offing. Pacific Fleet intelligence was struggling to figure out exactly what, because the Japanese threw a wrench into the Allied works on January 1, 1943, by changing their secret radio communications codes. On January 4, the Pacific Fleet's daily summary reported "as the [Japanese] have changed nearly all ciphers our educated guesses are not as reliable as they had been."[65] But the radio analysts were nevertheless able to pan considerable gold from this temporarily shallow stream. On January 2, radio intelligence determined replacement aircraft were being ferried to the 21st and 26th Air Flotillas (1st and 6th Air Attack Forces, respectively) in Rabaul. The next day, they had identified the relatively new 8th Area Army headquarters, also at Rabaul. Not even a week later, radio analysis determined that Truk now had the commanders of the Combined Fleet, the 2nd, 4th, and 6th Fleets, and the battleships *Kongo* and *Haruna*. But the 3rd Fleet, *Kido Butai*, the carriers themselves, they simply could not find. Ominous in itself.[66]

Also ominous was the restart of Tokyo Express runs to Guadalcanal. On January 2, the newly promoted Rear Admiral Koyanagi Tomiji, former skipper of the battleship *Kongo* on the night of The Bombardment and now Admiral Tanaka's replacement as head of the 2nd Destroyer Flotilla and the Reinforcement Unit, had his flagship *Naganami* lead fellow destroyers *Kawakaze*, *Suzukaze*, *Makinami*, and *Arashio* – all retrofitted with an additional pair of 13mm machine guns to deal with PT boats – escorting destroyers *Isonami*, *Inazumi*, *Kuroshio*, *Kagero*, and *Oyashio*, on a supply run to Guadalcanal.[67]

But Henderson Field had grown and was now a much larger, much more dangerous airbase. A new airfield, called "Fighter 2" for now, christened "Kukum Field" at a later date, had been completed on January 1. It was meant to replace Fighter 1 and its intractable drainage issues, though in practice both airfields were used. The airbase also now had Martin B-26 Marauders, the closest American equivalent to the torpedo-carrying Mitsubishi G3Ms and G4Ms, of the Army Air Force's 69th Bombardment Squadron, though "Army Air Force" and "torpedoes" did not quite go together due to the Army's perceived lack of interest in developing any effective tactics for this "naval" weapon. Also based at the Henderson Field complex were the 12th Fighter Squadron of Bell P-39 Airacobras, the 44th Fighter Squadron with Curtiss P-40 Warhawks, and the 339th Fighter Squadron with actual Lockheed P-38 Lightnings.

It was all part of Allied air assets in the South Pacific developing. Rear Admiral Fitch commanded Aircraft South Pacific, but below him things were reorganized. The 13th Air Force was activated on January 13 and placed under the command of Brigadier General Nathan F. Twining, the brother of General Vandegrift's operations officer Colonel Merrill Twining. The 13th was parent of the veteran 11th and newer 5th Bombardment Groups with eight squadrons of B-17s. It also had two squadrons of B-26s; four fighter squadrons with P-39 Airacobras, one with P-38s, and one with P-40s; one reconnaissance squadron with modified P-38s; and one transport squadron.

And Admiral Fitch was very happy to use them. He sent five B-17s and five P-38s to hit the Japanese base at Kahili on January 2, but en route they came across Admiral Koyanagi's destroyers first at 2:15 pm. They bombed the convoy without success, but their contact report attracted friends. At 6:05 pm, those friends arrived from Henderson Field with nine Dauntlesses, four Wildcats, and five Lightnings. According to Koyanagi, his ships were compelled to move like a "Bon dance," an ancient ceremonial dance that included left and right swinging movements of the Bon Festival of the Lanterns. The Bon dance was effective, mostly. The *Suzukaze* was nicked by a near miss and had to be sent back to Shortland escorted by the *Inazumi*. Two Wildcats and a Dauntless were lost.[68]

Now down to eight destroyers, Admiral Koyanagi's convoy plowed on and straight into a night ambush by no fewer than 11 PT boats, who spent two hours attacking the destroyers. But the Japanese had support from three floatplanes that harassed the boats so much that all 18 torpedoes the PTs launched missed.[69] Koyanagi was able to complete his mission. The next day the 17th Army on Guadalcanal reported recovering 540 drums and 250 rubber bags of supplies – enough for about five days.[70]

Conditions were still bad for the Japanese on Guadalcanal, but at least the Imperial Army was holding its own. The same could not be said for New Guinea. On January 2, Buna finally fell to General MacArthur's forces, after a campaign that was nothing short of brutal – far longer and costlier than it should have been. General Eichelberger explained just how brutal:

> At Buna it was siege warfare, and that, as history records, is the bitterest and most punishing kind of warfare. Considering the number of troops in the front lines, the fatalities closely

approach, percentage-wise, the heaviest losses in our own Civil War battles. Few prisoners were taken on either side, and the record indicates the quality of opposition which our troops met. The battle had to be fought through until, as one Australian writer phrased it, there was "not one Japanese left who was capable of lifting a rifle."[71]

Nevertheless, upon the capture of Buna, General MacArthur proclaimed, "The utmost care was taken for the conservation of our forces, with the result that probably no campaign in history against a thoroughly prepared and trained army produced such complete and decisive results with so low an expenditure of life and resources."[72]

His troops were shocked. Several eminent historians have considered the claim "absurd" and "preposterous."[73] But there was no time to be offended because the campaign continued for another three weeks on Papua, as Gona and Sanananda were cleared. However, as far as General MacArthur was concerned, it was over. He flew back to Brisbane, telling the news media, "The Papuan campaign is in its final closing stage. The Sanananda position has now been completely enveloped. A remnant of the enemy's forces is entrenched there and faces certain destruction … This can now be regarded as accomplished."[74]

Nevertheless, General MacArthur may have privately chastened himself for the conduct of the Buna campaign and his mistakes, not that he'd admit those mistakes to anyone. Even so, he promised "No more Bunas." Indeed, MacArthur learned a lot from the campaign in Papua. As historian Alan Rems opined:

> Like a stereotypical World War I general seated far to the rear, he disparaged commanders and repeatedly ordered costly frontal attacks without full firsthand knowledge of battlefield conditions and regard for casualties. He would later avoid heavy enemy concentrations and protracted static fighting and would not initiate operations before establishing sound logistics. Also, from the experience of the 32nd Division, he gained an appreciation of the need for thorough troop training under realistic jungle conditions.[75]

MacArthur had just completely taken a major position from the Japanese, a first in this Pacific War. Admiral Ugaki's nightmare about the Rabaul fortress coming within range of regular air attacks was coming true.

On January 10, Admiral Koyanagi led another reinforcement convoy out of Shortland. When his flagship *Naganami* developed an engine issue at the last minute, he switched his flag to the *Kuroshio*. The new flagship led the *Kawakaze*, *Hatsukaze*, and *Tokitsukaze* in escorting the *Arashi*, *Arashio*, *Oshio*, and *Makinami*. The Japanese were exceptionally careful with this convoy. The 204 Air Group provided cover in the form of six-Zero shifts until sunset, at which point they landed in Munda to pick up where they left off the next morning. The timing of the convoy was set so that when it passed coastwatcher Donald Kennedy on New Georgia, it was too late in the day for the Cactus Air Force to mount an airstrike.

But the Cactus Air Force did have a new toy in its inventory that it put to very good use. The Consolidated PBY Catalina flying boat, a mainstay of US Navy reconnaissance since before the war, was too slow, too unarmored, and too lightly armed to be effective at aerial combat or using its bomb and torpedo capability – at least during the day. But if the Japanese could use seaplanes at night, why not the US Navy?

To be sure, Catalinas had operated at night since at least February 1942, but usually such missions were limited to desperate circumstances.[76] It was a night-flying Catalina that had found the Japanese invasion convoy during the Battle of the Java Sea, though its contact report was not passed along in time to do the Allies any good. At Midway, the Japanese invasion force endured a nighttime airstrike by torpedo-armed PBYs that damaged a tanker. Even mighty *Zuikaku* at Santa Cruz was near-missed by bombs from a night-flying Catalina. But the PBY's nighttime use was never systemic.

Until now. In December the first elements of Patrol Squadron 12 under Commander Clarence O. Taff came to Guadalcanal. Patrol Squadron 12 was equipped with PBY-5A Catalinas that had not just pontoons but the optional tricycle landing gear so they could take off from Henderson Field. They also for the first time had both airborne radar as well as a radio altimeter, which enabled precise measurements of altitude, which otherwise is dangerous guesswork at night.[77] They still had the same drawbacks other Catalinas had, but with airborne radar and radio altimeters night operations became much more feasible.

For night camouflage these Catalinas were painted, unsurprisingly, black. "Black Cats" became the obvious nickname for Patrol Squadron 12, with the squadron insignia graded based on experience. For the first mission, a simple black cat could be painted on the Catalina's fuselage. After the second, eyes could be added to the black cat insignia. After the third, whiskers and teeth could be painted on. And after the fourth the pilot could add "anatomical insignia of a more personal nature."[78]

Admiral Koyanagi expected an ambush by the American "devil boats," as the Japanese now referred to the PT boats, and he got one. Although Koyanagi's ships had slipped in under a friendly rain squall and eluded two scout groups of PT boats, at 12:15 am Lieutenant Clyde Worth Curley, flying one of those new Black Cats, alerted a strike group of three PT boats under Lieutenant Rollin E. Westholm of the presence of three destroyers in a column, with a fourth that Curley called a "light cruiser." Curley vectored the PT boats toward the incoming destroyers.

Closing to within 400 yards, *PT-43* under Lieutenant Charles E. Tilden launched two torpedoes at the lead ship, but when powder in the port torpedo tube ignited, the *Hatsukaze* and *Tokitsukaze* were able to pinpoint the boat and cut her to pieces, forcing Tilden to abandon her. Westholm's own *PT-112* launched four torpedoes at the third destroyer before being caught in a crossfire and sunk. Lieutenant Clark W. Faulkner in the *PT-43* made his attack on the second destroyer. Between *PTs -43* and *-112*, someone managed to get a torpedo into the *Hatsukaze* under the wardroom on the port side at 12:47 am, killing eight and wounding 23.[79]

A single torpedo hit is usually fatal to a destroyer. Here the *Hatsukaze* not only did not sink, she did not even lose power. Nonetheless, her skipper Commander Watanabe Yasumasa later said, "she was certainly in bad shape," with her best speed reduced to

18 knots.[80] Her Tokyo Express companions laid smoke screens around her while heavy flak drove Lieutenant Curley's Black Cat off for a bit at 1:15.[81] Nevertheless, the supplies were dropped off. The 17th Army later reported 250 drums with 30 tons of food, medicine, and ammunition had made it to the Japanese-occupied shore, although the PT boats claimed to have shot up and sunk another 250 drums.[82] Also making it to the Japanese-occupied shore was the drifting, abandoned hulk of *PT-43*. Japanese troops tried to pull the shattered PT boat onto the beach, but before they could do so the New Zealand corvette *Kiwi* came along and used gunfire to finish off the wreck.

While the mission was finished, Lieutenant Curley was not. Persistent, patient, and smart, he set about hunting for that "light cruiser," which seems to have been the limping *Hatsukaze*.[83] Curley made several low-level passes, dropping float lights – another idea taken from the Japanese – to mark the ship's course for the three PT boats whom he was vectoring in.[84]

This little-known action was something of a turning point. During the early part of the Pacific War, Japanese control of the skies meant their seaplanes had been ubiquitous. Especially during the Java Sea Campaign, the appearance of a Japanese seaplane was a harbinger of doom, impending an air or naval attack brought by the seaplane's contact report. In the Battle of the Java Sea, Japanese cruiser floatplanes kept the Allied task force under almost continuous surveillance, vectoring ships and spotting gunfire, even at night, which shocked Allied sailors, most of whom had never heard of flying at night. The usually unflappable Allied commander Admiral Karel Doorman was so frustrated by the Japanese floatplanes illuminating his ships and marking his course that he cursed them under his breath. Those seaplanes were, arguably at any rate, the difference in the battle.

Then there was Savo Island, the worst defeat in US Navy history – a defeat set up by seaplanes. Again, cruiser floatplanes illuminated Allied ships while the Japanese remained hidden in the dark, setting up a decisive Japanese first punch. The Japanese owned the night, especially night aviation. That was then.

This was now. How times had changed. Now, it was not an Allied commander cursing the seaplanes. It was the Japanese, frantic to get rid of the pestering Lieutenant Curley and his almost invisible seaplane that hung on to the *Hatsukaze* like a leech. On one of the Black Cat's low passes, the destroyer apparently fired its main battery. The Catalina was not the most nimble of creatures, but Curley just sidestepped the blast. The destroyer turned on her searchlight and pinned the PBY for another blast, but Curley simply dove out of the way. And, by circling the destroyer like a vulture, he kept marking the target.

Three PT boats, *PTs -39, -45,* and *-46,* finally managed to get a visual on the limping *Hatsukaze*, forcing her to take evasive action. But even in her hobbled state, the *Hatsukaze* was able to make tight circles and zig when she should zig and zag when she should zag. Between her maneuvers, the smoke screens, and the dark, she made an impossible target for the dozen or so torpedoes launched by the devil boats, who got no hits. The *Hatsukaze* managed to limp away under the protection of the *Tokitsukaze, Kawakaze,* and *Arashi*.[85]

Yet Lieutenant Curley was still not done. Curley landed his Black Cat at Henderson Field, refueled, and went up again. This was a long mission and bound to get longer until

Curley found his prey, which he did. At 3:00 am, Curley saw a smoke screen in The Slot off the Russell Islands, with ships intermittently visible. It was his "light cruiser," the *Hatsukaze* and her protective flock. But because of the smoke he could not get a clear visual on the target, even as clear a visual as was possible at night. So Curley eventually turned away and went back to Guadalcanal.[86] Tenacious, this Lieutenant Curley had been. How times had changed. As designed by Admiral Tanaka, the Rat Transportation – the Tokyo Express – was to drop off troops and supplies on Guadalcanal and speed away from daylight air attacks from Henderson Field. Now they had to speed away from nighttime air attacks from Henderson Field as well. How Midway had changed everything. Japanese dominance was continuing its slow but steady erosion.

Those daylight air attacks were indeed still a problem. While not a seaplane, the Lockheed Hudson was feared by the Japanese as another harbinger of doom when at 6:30 am one from the Royal New Zealand Air Force's No. 3 Squadron found the *Hatsukaze* and her protective trio *Tokitsukaze*, *Kawakaze*, and *Arashi* in The Slot some 115 miles from Guadalcanal.[87] The destroyers watched helplessly as the Hudson invited itself to tag along – and invited some friends to this particular party.

A dozen aircraft from Marine Scout Bombing 233 and about a dozen more from Marine Fighting 121 were fashionably late to the party because the wet and muddy conditions at the Henderson Field complex delayed their launch. By the time they arrived at 8:30 am, they found their hosts had invited a few friends of their own from the 204 Air Group.[88]

Led by fighter ace Warrant Officer Shimakawa Masaaki, eight "clipped-wing" A6M3 Model 32 Zeros dove out of the sun at the Marine fighters. The Americans struggled with communications and some broke formation to attack the Zeros too soon, leaving the Dauntlesses unprotected. But, curiously, Shimakawa and his fellow Zeros were not interested in the bombers and swarmed over the scattered Wildcats. Three Zeros quickly ganged up on Lieutenant Joe Cannon, setting fire to his belly fuel tank that had failed to release and putting his plane to the torch.[89]

So ferocious was the Japanese interception that the Marine fighters formed a horizontal defensive circle, flying round and round. If a Japanese pilot attempted to attack one Wildcat in the circle, he opened himself up to gunfire from the Wildcat behind the first in the circle – that is, unless the Japanese attacked from above or below the circle. But there were not enough Japanese to do that effectively.[90]

The Marine fighters kept going round in circles with the exception of Marine Gunner Ed Zielinski. Zielinski flew in the opposite direction from the rotation of the other Wildcats. In so doing, he ended up making head-on attacks at two Zeros, unnerving their pilots enough to break off the attack. The Marines freed themselves from the Japanese siege and counterattacked for a short time before both sides broke off.

For his trouble, Zielinski attracted an admirer of sorts. As he was flying back to Guadalcanal all alone, he attracted a lone Zero, who sat on Zielinski's wing until he had gotten the American's attention. Then the Zero dove ahead of Zielinski, and looped behind to come into a killing position on Zielinski's tail. But he didn't fire. He did it again. Again, he didn't fire. Probably his guns were out. For his part, Zielinski's guns had been disabled by a tracer. Having taunted his foe, the Japanese pilot, apparently Shimakawa, turned and headed back to base. The dogfight had cost each side a fighter, the Americans Lieutenant Cannon, the Japanese Chief Petty Officer Itsukaichi Sueji.[91]

The American fighters had done their job, keeping the Japanese away from the Dauntlesses. But the Japanese had done their job as well, keeping the Dauntlesses away from the fleeing *Hatsukaze* and her consorts. The SBDs continued on but could not catch up to the destroyers. Neither could a second strike, escorted by fighters under Captain Foss. "On the way home the bombers unloaded on Munda Airfield," Foss later wrote. "There was no air opposition but a lot of antiaircraft."[92]

The Japanese responded with another convoy on January 14. A new commander, Rear Admiral Kimura Susumu, the expert navigator from the Friday the 13th action off Guadalcanal, took to the sea in the big antiaircraft destroyer *Akizuki*, sister to the sunken *Teruzuki*. This flagship, with the destroyers *Kurishio*, *Maikaze*, and *Tokitsukaze*, would guard transport destroyers *Hamakaze*, *Isokaze*, *Tanikaze*, *Urakaze*, and *Arashi*, who were transporting 750 men of the newly formed Yano Battalion under Major Yano Kenji and a battery of 75mm guns.[93] Again, their transit was protected by a thick wall of clouds and rain – and six-Zero shifts of air cover from the 204 Air Group, who landed at Munda at 7:40 pm to spend the night, before an early combat air patrol the next day over the destroyers.[94]

Admiral Kimura's ships did get some more air cover, though not quite what he would have preferred: two Allied Black Cats. One picked up Kimura's destroyers on radar at 10:50 pm in the continuing rainy weather while a second got a visual on the *Akizuki* and four other destroyers. Guadalcanal and Tulagi were warned. Both PBYs made bombing runs on the Japanese ships and succeeded only in getting a few near misses on the *Urakaze* that left her at "reduced speed," according to Kimura.[95]

The Black Cats had done their job. Lieutenant Westholm led 13 PT boats out to challenge the destroyers. But Admiral Kimura had expected this and had a pair of floatplanes from the *Sanyo* and *Kamikawa Maru*s overhead. They made bombing runs on the devil boats that held them off for a bit, but the bad weather had a much greater effect. The PT boats saw the shadows of destroyers backlit by a flash of lightning and launched 17 torpedoes. None hit, and Kimura completed his mission to land troops successfully.[96] To keep the fliers at Henderson Field awake, Washing Machine Charlie showed up – three times. "It was the first multiple plane attack since November," wrote Joe Foss, who at this time was serving as operations officer – and not particularly happy about it. "We stood on a hilltop and watched the raid, which cost us the lives of six mechanics."[97]

This put the Cactus Air Force in a vindictive mood. One of the Black Cats chased the destroyers back up The Slot, but lost contact. A Royal New Zealand Air Force Hudson from No. 3 Squadron picked up the flotilla at 6:30 am and radioed Henderson Field. Up went 15 Dauntlesses of Marine Scout Bombing 142 under Major Robert Richard, escorted by

12 Marine Wildcats of Marine Fighting 121 and Marine Observation 215 and six Army Airacobras from the 12th Fighter Squadron. An hour later they chased down Admiral Kimura's destroyers north-northwest of New Georgia – and perilously close to Munda.[98]

It was here that they were not so politely introduced to a dozen Nakajima Ki-43 *Hayabusa* ("Peregrine Falcon") Army Type 1 fighters from the Japanese Army Air Force's 6th Air Division. These "Oscars," as they were named for Allied reporting purposes, looked and performed so much like their Imperial Navy equivalent the Zero that they ended up dubbed "Army Zeros." For that matter, there were also nine of the regular Navy Zeros from the 204 Air Group and six from the 252.[99]

The result was an aerial melee between the Japanese, in particular the Oscars, and the Wildcats. The Nakajimas were badly undergunned, having only two machine guns apiece, but their maneuverability was a nasty surprise. Three Wildcats were shot down. No one knows how many Oscars the Japanese lost. The six 252 Zeros never entered the combat. The 204 lost three Zeros, with another four damaged. The 204's survivors stopped at the Munda airfield for 20 minutes to assess the damage, then headed back to Buin at 8:35 am.[100]

It was apparently the job of the Airacobras to keep the Japanese fighters off the Dauntlesses, and, at the cost of two of their own, they did, for the most part. Into the teeth of intense antiaircraft fire, the SBDs dove on Admiral Kimura's twisting destroyers below. The Dauntlesses managed no direct hits, but plenty of near misses, which can still be costly. Destroyers *Hamakaze*, *Isokaze*, *Urakaze*, *Tanikaze*, and *Arashi* all suffered hull damage from near misses, which also killed the *Tanikaze*'s skipper Commander Katsumi Motoi.[101] Near misses also jammed the *Arashi*'s rudder and left her dead in the water. One Dauntless was hit by flak and forced to ditch; a second ditched for unknown reasons. The *Maikaze* had to stop to assist the *Arashi* and prepared to take her under tow.

The Hudson continued watching the Japanese from a distance as Admiral Kimura re-formed his force. He ordered the damaged destroyers *Hamakaze*, *Isokaze*, *Urakaze*, and *Tanikaze* to race ahead to Shortland and get out of range of Guadalcanal. Kimura's flagship antiaircraft destroyer *Akizuki* took over protection of the *Arashi*, now being towed by the *Maikaze*, with the *Tokitsukaze* and *Kuroshio* also screening. If any enemy aircraft appeared, they would see the damaged *Arashi* first and likely go after her. In short, Kimura used the damaged *Arashi* as bait.

While the *Hamakaze*, *Isokaze*, *Urakaze*, and *Tanikaze* safely got to Shortland around midday, the *Maikaze* lugged the *Arashi* at a surprisingly speedy 9 knots, with the *Akizuki*, *Tokitsukaze*, and *Kuroshio* around them in a protective screen and Army Nakajimas overhead. But after their earlier dogfight, the Army pilots were all tired and asked for help from Base Air Force. Admiral Kusaka responded by sending up two Mitsubishi F1M2 floatplanes from the 958 Air Group, who took over for the Oscars at 10:00 am and stayed for some 90 minutes. About a half-dozen Zeros from the 204 Air Group arrived 15 minutes after the Petes, staying until about 12:30 pm. This was about the time the *Arashi* freed her rudder, allowing the flotilla to proceed at 20 knots, with cover from another half-dozen or so Zeros from the 204 Air Group, who stayed until 3:10.

By that time, Admiral Kimura's little group was nearing Shortland, so they got an additional gift of air cover of three Mitsubishi F1M2 floatplanes from the 958 Air Group and seven to ten more from Admiral Jojima's seaplane tenders. Perhaps realizing that biplanes with floats can provide air cover only in the loosest use of the term, Base Air Force supplemented them with a dozen Zeros from the 252 Air Group, who arrived only minutes before the long-awaited Allied airstrike.

Seven Boeing B-17s of the 72nd Bombardment Squadron, escorted by four Airacobras flying low escort, four Warhawks from the 68th Fighter Squadron flying at medium altitude, and three Lightnings from the 339th flying at high altitude, arrived at 3:48 pm, about ten minutes after a warning from the Japanese torpedo boat *Hiyadori* who was in The Slot escorting a freighter. As air cover, the F1M2 biplanes with floats would have been questionable even by World War I standards, but four of them gamely lunged at the B-17s. Lieutenant Lloyd Huff led the Warhawks against the Petes. It was no contest. Then the Airacobras joined the Warhawks in swarming the Petes. All in all, five of the biplanes were shot down; others were damaged. They never got close to the Flying Fortresses.[102]

The B-17s lumbered over Admiral Kimura's tiny, twisting ships, thinking nothing but of using the Army Air Force's tried-and-failed tactic of bombing moving ships at sea from high altitude. Moving ships at sea were difficult to hit in any case; if done at high altitude, it was almost impossible. Unsurprisingly, all their bombs missed. On their way out, the Zeros from the 252 Air Group made a few half-hearted hit-and-run attacks against the B-17s and their fighter escorts, with no hits for either side before the Zeros headed back.

Once the Americans were gone, destroyers *Tokitsukaze* and *Kuroshio* moved to pick up two F1M2 crews who had radioed they were going down off Choiseul. Once that was completed, they rejoined the rest of Admiral Kimura's tiny flotilla under the relative protection of five more R-Area Air Force F1M2 floatplanes – one from the *Kamikawa Maru* and four from the *Kunikawa Maru*. The ships glided into Shortland at around 6:20 pm.[103] On this day, the Japanese crews had earned their pay.

As January went on, the signs, insofar as Allied intelligence analysts could tell, became more ominous. On January 14, radio direction finding located the *Zuikaku* and the *Zuiho* in the Home Islands. About a week later, they figured that at least the *Junyo* had reached Truk. Intelligence then showed the *Junyo* sailed from Truk on January 23 with the carriers *Zuikaku* and *Zuiho* and the new super battleship *Musashi*. Details of the latter were sketchy, but whatever it was, it was big. And as best the analysts could tell, the Japanese were calling it "Operation *Ke*."[104]

To Admiral Nimitz, Admiral Halsey, Pacific Fleet intelligence, and everyone else, it looked like a new offensive. The Pacific Fleet's daily summary for January 7 stated:

> It is beginning to seem possible that the Japanese are shifting from [the] offensive to [the] strategic defensive in the New Guinea, New Britain, Solomon area; [the] accumulation of airfields would release [carriers] for operations elsewhere [and the] threat of raids may thus become more real in the next month or so.[105]

As the Japanese moved their pieces into position, the Allies sought to pick off a piece here and there. Japanese transport *Kimposan Maru* was making the long trip from Yokosuka straight to Rabaul. Late in the day on January 16, 1943, her journey ended prematurely west of Kavieng when a torpedo from the US submarine *Greenling* under Lieutenant Commander Henry C. Bruton burrowed into the transport's engine room and, for once, actually detonated. The *Kimposan Maru* went dead in the water, sinking fast by the bow, 31 of her crew dead. Her distress call reached the Japanese submarine chaser *Ch-17*, heading back to Rabaul from picket duty. The little patrol craft turned around and went to the dying ship's aid, dropping depth charges that forced the *Greenling* deep, then rescuing the *Kimposan Maru*'s survivors.[106] Two days later, it was one of MacArthur's B-24 Liberators, again off Kavieng, that planted a bomb on the freighter *Senzan Maru*, detonating her cargo of gasoline and sending her to the bottom.[107]

A nick here, a scratch there, would start to add up. In late December at Shanghai, the Japanese had put together what was called the "No. 6 Go Transportation Operation: Convoy No. 35." Its mission was to transport to the South Pacific the Imperial Japanese Army's 6th Kumamoto Division, a veteran unit of the war in China and notorious for its role in the Rape of Nanking. The convoy had three parts: A, B, and C.[108] On December 21, 1942, Part A, consisting of the *Teiyo* and *Myoho Marus* and *Shinsei Maru No. 1*, had left Shanghai, followed later that day by Part B, with the *Kenkon*, *Oigawa*, *Kyokusei*, and *Panama Marus*. On Christmas Day, Part C went to sea with the *Meiu*, *Somedono*, *Surabaya*, and *Shinai Marus*. Initially, each part was escorted by an old destroyer from China Area Fleet, but Combined Fleet eventually took over the escorting. Assigned to these convoys were destroyers *Hokaze* and *Nagatsuki*, later joined by destroyers *Shirayuki* and *Shigure*, subchasers *Ch-2* and *-11* and auxiliary gunboat *Choan Maru No. 2*.[109]

Combined Fleet was right to add the extra escorts. On January 19, 1943, US submarine *Swordfish* under Lieutenant Commander Jack H. Lewis came across Part A northeast of Buin. The *Swordfish* welcomed the convoy to the Solomons by torpedoing the transport *Myoho Maru* in the early afternoon.

Having received the convoy's distress signal, Admiral Mikawa sent out Admiral Kimura in the destroyer *Akizuki* with the minelayer *Hatsutaka* to assist the convoy in reaching Shortland. But at 9:30 that night, the *Akizuki* sighted a surfaced submarine. Guns blazing, the big antiaircraft destroyer turned toward the submarine and went to full speed to run it down. But it was not the usual submarine. It was the very large and very veteran USS *Nautilus*. The *Nautilus* had a veteran skipper in Lieutenant Commander William H. Brockman, Jr. Together they had stared down the mighty *Kido Butai* at Midway, harassing the task force and indirectly helping to lead the pivotal US airstrike to its doomed targets.[110] Brockman was not going to be intimidated by a destroyer coming right at him. And he wasn't.

Lieutenant Commander Brockman beat the *Akizuki* to the punch at 9:53 with two torpedoes into the destroyer's starboard side. One hit under the Number 2 3.9-inch mount with a not entirely satisfying plunk before sinking into the depths; it was the *Nautilus*'s second dud in a week.[111] The other hit under the bridge with a far more satisfying explosion, ripping a 26-foot gash in the starboard side, flooding a boiler room and the starboard engine room, and causing severe vibrations to the keel. The *Akizuki* suffered 14 killed, with Admiral Kimura and 62 others injured. Despite the whipsawed keel and being seriously down at the bow, the *Akizuki* could still make 20 knots using emergency steering. She staggered into the Shortlands two days later for emergency repairs, especially the compromised keel, before heading back to Japan.[112] But the *Akizuki* was much better off than the *Myoho Maru*, who sank, taking with her 61 of the 922 Imperial Army troops on board.[113] The remainder of Part A arrived in Shortland on January 20.[114]

This was the same day Part C stumbled across the US submarine *Silversides* under Lieutenant Commander Creed C. Burlingame on the route between Truk and Shortland. Just before 6:00 pm, the submarine launched a half-dozen torpedoes at three ships in the convoy, hitting, at least, *Meiu* and *Surabaya Maru*s. *Meiu Maru* sank about 80 minutes later, taking with her about 400 of the nearly 3,000 troops she was carrying. The *Surabaya Maru*, carrying about 1,100 troops, was hit portside forward, took on a serious list, and started settling slowly. *Ch-11* and *Choan Maru No. 2* rescued all but 462 of the troops, but had to leave the wrecked transport behind in order to deliver them to Shortland. The next day the destroyer *Asagumo* found the derelict transport and scuttled it.[115]

This was also the same day Part B stumbled across Lieutenant Commander Robert J. Foley's submarine USS *Gato*. At about 6:00 pm, the *Gato* torpedoed the *Kenkon Maru*. The Mark 14s caused a fire and detonated ammunition she was carrying, forcing her abandonment and later scuttling. While the *Shirayuki* was able to rescue some survivors including seven crew and 36 troops, an unknown number were killed.[116]

The *Gato* was a busy boat. On January 29, off New Georgia, she encountered the cargo ship *Nichiun Maru*, only recently requisitioned by the Imperial Japanese Army on January 1. Lieutenant Commander Foley fired two torpedoes and got one hit, quickly sinking the *Nichiun Maru* by the bow. The submarine managed to evade the cargo ship's escort subchaser *Ch-22* and escaped.[117]

While the numbers and movements of Japanese supply ships in and around the Solomons had curiously increased, Japanese air activity was about to increase as well. At 1:13 pm on January 25, radar on Guadalcanal detected and started tracking a large flight of unidentified aircraft. Four Marine Observation 251 Wildcats under Lieutenant Herb Peters, already on patrol, were vectored over to check them out, though who they were was not so much the question as what they were. The Wildcats made contact seven minutes later, at which time some of the incoming aircraft – 17 Betty bombers of the 705 Air Group – abruptly turned around and hightailed it away, with all but one making it back to Rabaul,[118] revealing, according to Lieutenant Peters, a "flight of approximately 30 enemy fighters ... in loose formation at altitudes of 18,000 to 25,000 feet in the vicinity of Savo Island."[119] Badly outnumbered, Peters led his four Wildcats into the clouds overhead to make diving passes at straggling Zeros. Eight Marine Fighting 121 Wildcats under Joe Foss were scrambled to assist Peters' hard-pressed pilots.

This was supposed to be the last day on Guadalcanal for Joe Foss and Marine Fighting 121. "Just because we're leaving is no reason we shouldn't pay attention to business and put on a show of shows today," Foss had told his pilots. They took off and moved to 18,000 feet, where they were joined by four Lightnings of the 339th Fighter Squadron.

As the flight approached Savo Island, Foss noticed a dozen Zeros "playing around, doing nip-ups and chasing each other." Foss had his pilots head for them – and then held them up. He had seen a hole in the overcast above. Foss later recalled, "Thinking it was funny for the Zeros to be playing around, I climbed to see what was above. There were about twenty more Zeros. Half a mile further away were about twenty-four dive bombers, and behind them were more planes – I couldn't see what they were."[120]

So the fighter ace raced back down and pulled the reins on his pilots. "We aren't going out there. They want us to attack those Zeros so the gang above can send its dive bombers and fighter escort right to the field while we're busy. Let's stay tight formation and circle."[121]

Joe Foss was not entirely correct. There were no dive bombers. This was Base Air Force's attempt at a fighter sweep. The G4Ms were to lure the American fighters into the air to face an incredible 76 Zeros – 18 each from the 252, 253, and 582 air groups; and 22 from the 204 Air Group. Heading down The Slot, the 18 from the 582 Air Group got lost in the increasing clouds and aborted, leaving a still-incredible 58 Zeros. Lieutenant Peters' fighters had sparred with elements of the 253 Air Group. The 253's job was to tie up the defending fighters while the 252 Air Group under Lieutenant Suho Motonari dove on the Lunga air complex to begin devastating strafing runs without interference. The job of the 204 under Lieutenant Commander Kofukuda Mitsugu was, apparently, to help engage the enemy interceptors or strafe the airfield as needed.[122]

But Joe Foss had stopped the Japanese cold: not hurt them, per se, but stopped them. The four P-38s split into pairs to form the opposite sides of the defensive circle. Foss's Marine Wildcats followed, as did seven more Marine Fighting 121 Wildcats under Captain Greg Loesch that had just scrambled. They went into the defensive circle around the edge of that hole in the clouds, just beneath the overcast, between the Japanese and the Henderson Field complex. They kept going round and round like a merry-go-round in the sky, with the Lightnings slightly outside of the Wildcats.

Six Zeros dove beneath the circle by 1,000 to 2,000 feet, hoping to tempt the Americans to break formation and go after them. Foss himself instinctively started to go after them, then quickly thought better of it. "Just continue wheeling and keep your eyes on them," he radioed his pilots, perhaps more as a reminder to himself.[123] But he kept a tight leash on both. It had been about three months since the late, great Colonel Bauer had told his Cactus Air Force fighter pilots, "When you see Zeros, dogfight 'em!" But Foss was old school – if less than a year earlier could be considered old school. He had seen the Zeros in action too many times to take them lightly, especially when he was outnumbered. Foss would avoid dogfighting if he could. Such was the respect Foss had earned from all the pilots, Marine and Army, that no one dared question him, let alone break the circle.

This was the paradox of "What happens when an irresistible force meets an immovable object?" turned on its head, the heretofore irresistible Zeros meeting Joe Foss's immovable defensive circle. Except Foss and his pilots were not resisting, and the Japanese were not trying to move them, so completely flummoxed were they by the blocking defensive circle.

The 253 Zeros needed to tie up the American fighters to clear the way for the 252, but they could not get the Americans to break their circle. If the 252 dove on the airfield anyway, the Americans could indeed break the circle and catch them from behind. The 253 could dive on the airfield, getting the Americans to break formation that way, and have the 252 engage the Americans – except that was not the plan and, without radios in their Zeros, the Japanese could not change the plan inflight. The Japanese could break the circle by attacking it from above or below, as was the standard tactic – except the overcast prevented the Zero pilots above from seeing the circle. Small groups of fighters would dive through the clouds at random times hoping to catch an American in their sights, but when they did not, the Zeros just melted back into the clouds.

The original dozen Zeros from the 253 Air Group headed back for the clouds as well, hoping to try something else to break the stalemate. In so doing, two shot between the Wildcats and one of the pairs of Lightnings, the pair flown by Army Lieutenants Besby Holmes and Ray Bezner, who promptly turned the aerial merry-go-round into something far deadlier. Bezner surprised one, whose evasive maneuvers only exposed his Zero's underside to Bezner's 20mm cannon and four .50-cal machine guns. One burst later, the Zero was spiraling toward the sea. The Zero's partner turned to wreak vengeance on Bezner, only to fly into the gun sights of Holmes. One long burst later, this Zero was smoking and heading for the water below. The Japanese pilots were apparently Petty Officers 1st Class Iwamoto Shin and Fukutome Tsugio of the 253 Air Group.[124] Theirs would be the only Zeros shot down.

The Japanese now saw that American reinforcements were close at hand, including eight more Wildcats of Marine Fighting 121 under Commanding Officer Major Don Yost, plus one flight of Airacobras and another of Warhawks. Frustrated and with fuel becoming an issue, the Japanese headed back – or at least the 204 and 253 did. With no radios and unable to see the other air groups below the clouds, Lieutenant Suho may not have even realized when they had left; he waited a little too long to escape the worsening weather. Five had to ditch off Guadalcanal, their pilots making it to shore. A sixth ditched and was lost; a seventh had to crash-land at Munda. The remaining 11 made it back to Ballale, an island just off Shortland where the Japanese had recently completed a new airfield. Of the 253, Warrant Officer Nakajima Mitsunori had to ditch and was captured.[125]

It was the ultimate irony that this was perhaps the finest moment in the flying career of Joseph Jacob Foss. A fighter ace with 26 kills to his credit, having just tied Eddie Rickenbacker's record, Foss had managed to have his badly outnumbered pilots turn back a Japanese attack – not with his skilled use of machine guns, but with ingenuity, quick thinking, and coolness under fire. Such qualities would serve Foss well as he continued having spectacular successes in the years ahead.*

For the Allies, the attempted fighter sweep on January 25, the first major raid since November, was just another piece of evidence that the Japanese were gearing up for another offensive. The Japanese were obviously trying to regain air superiority over Guadalcanal.

Another attempted fighter sweep came two days later. For the Americans on Guadalcanal, January 27 started with not so much Washing Machine Charlie as a full laundromat of at least 14 Mitsubishi G4Ms from the 751 Air Group arriving between 3:00 and 4:30 am to wake up the Americans with breakfast treats of 151 133lb bombs and 9,060 rounds of machine-gun fire. The Marine antiaircraft gunners thanked the Bettys for their generosity by shooting down one and damaging seven more.[126]

That was just breakfast. The Japanese planned brunch as well, with the Japanese Army Air Force's 6th Air Division mounting its first air attack on Guadalcanal. Two Mitsubishi Ki-46 command reconnaissance planes of the 76th Independent Air Squadron scouted the way ahead of a strike with an absurd number of fighters – at least 74 Nakajima Ki-43 fighters from the 1st and 11th Air Squadrons and the 12th Air Battalion's headquarters – escorting all of nine Kawasaki Ki-48 Army Type 99 Twin-engined Light Bombers – called "Lily" by the Allies – of the 45th Air Squadron.[127]

This bizarre concoction was the doctrine of the Japanese Army Air Force: send a ridiculously large number of fighters to escort a pitifully small number of bombers capable of dropping a pitifully small amount of bombs. Each Ki-48 was capable of carrying almost 1,800 pounds of ordnance.

Warned by coastwatchers that 30 Zeros were approaching with ten Mitsubishi bombers, the Cactus Air Force was waiting for the strike when it arrived over Savo Island at 10:45 am with a dozen Marine Wildcats, six Army Lightnings, and ten Army Warhawks from no fewer than six squadrons. Every pilot, every coastwatcher, thought (or perhaps assumed) the Japanese had sent their typical Zeros. That they were facing a completely different aircraft escaped their notice, which is perhaps why the Oscar ended up with the nickname "Army Zero."

It quickly became a clash of the fighters, with the most vicious taking place directly over Henderson Field between the P-40 Warhawks of the Army Air Force's 44th Fighter Squadron and the Ki-43 Peregrine Falcons of the 1st Air Group. The 44th struggled to shoot down the Oscars, due to, as they later found out, a relative absence of incendiary rounds in their ammunition belts. The P-38s from the 339th Fighter Squadron swooped down to help, but found themselves hamstrung by the Lightning's sluggish performance at low altitudes, causing two to fall victim to the Oscars.

---

* At various points after the war, Joe Foss was the governor of South Dakota, president of the National Rifle Association, the first commissioner of the American Football League, and a television broadcaster.

While the aerial melee was at its height, the Kawasaki Ki-48s snuck in at low altitude to drop their bombs on the Henderson Field complex but in reality they only succeeded in dropping their little bombs on the Matanikau River area and did little damage. The 11th Air Squadron set up a rear guard as the rest of this weird airstrike made off. The Americans had lost two Warhawks shot down, with two upon landing found to be trashed; and a Wildcat ditching for lack of fuel, in addition to the two P-38s shot down. The 6th Air Division found itself down by seven Ki-43s – six shot down, and a seventh had to be written off.[128]

It was indecisive – a tie. In theory a tie was better for the Japanese than the tactical defeat that they had suffered two days earlier. But with the Japanese trying to regain air superiority over Guadalcanal, a tie went to the Allies.

A measure of the failure of the Japanese Army Air Force to knock out or even inconvenience the Lunga airfield complex came at 5:40 pm that afternoon when ten Dauntlesses and six Avengers from Henderson Field found the transport *Mikage Maru No. 20*, carrying elements of the 6th Kure Special Naval Landing Force, and her escorting submarine chaser *Ch-17* off the northern tip of Kolombangara, with an alleged air cover of two F1M2 floatplanes from the *Kamikawa Maru* rotating in shifts. The Americans had an escort of nine Wildcats of Marine Observation 251 and four Warhawks of the Army's 44th and 68th Fighter Squadrons. The Dauntlesses planted three bombs into the *Mikage Maru No. 20* and set her ablaze, sending off columns of black smoke. Her escort *Ch-17* allegedly sent off columns of white smoke from a near miss, but she was apparently not damaged. The Avengers made textbook torpedo runs on the transport and released their missiles from a range so close they couldn't miss. They missed – or else the torpedoes didn't detonate. Attempted interference by the Petes led to an inconclusive result. The Cactus fliers headed back, certain they had sunk the freighter. But the *Mikage Maru No. 20* survived. She put in at Vila around 9:20 pm, dropping off her troops and what remained of her cargo.[129] She had lost ten killed and 30 wounded.[130]

Even though the *Mikage Maru No. 20* survived and completed her mission, her experience could not have been encouraging to Admiral Kusaka. The Imperial Army had been assured that the Reinforcement Group was built around the finest destroyer force in the Imperial Navy, the 10th Destroyer Flotilla, with a respected veteran commander in Admiral Kimura.[131] However, Kimura was injured when the *Nautilus* torpedoed his flagship *Akizuki* and was now unavailable. Admiral Koyanagi was called back to replace Kimura as head of the 10th Destroyer Flotilla. But Koyanagi had just been recently promoted to rear admiral. It would not do interservice relations any good to have such an inexperienced commander head such an important mission. And did they really want someone so new leading these missions? No, Admiral Kusaka decided. So Hashimoto Sentaro was pulled away from a well-earned rest to lead the Reinforcement Unit again.

Admiral Hashimoto's first assignment as head of the Reinforcement Unit was to lead the seizure of the Russell Islands, just west of Guadalcanal. On January 28, Hashimoto's flagship destroyer *Tokitsukaze* led fellow destroyers *Kuroshio* and *Shirayuki* out of the

Shortlands in escorting the *Urakaze*, *Kawakaze*, and *Tanikaze* carrying Special Naval Landing Force troops to take over Baisen Island, one of the tiny islets in the Russells.

But their occupation did not go undetected. A coastwatcher on Choiseul reported the convoy passing at 2:05 pm. An hour later the destroyers were spotted passing Vella Lavella. At this point, Admiral Hashimoto's convoy got entangled with a second convoy of two unidentified ships, apparently one tanker and one transport, and an escort of the busy submarine chaser *Ch-17*.[132]

Guadalcanal sent out a 33-plane airstrike to handle both convoys. Six Avengers from Marine Scout Bombing 131 – two turned back because of engine trouble – seven Dauntlesses from Marine Scout Bombing 233 and five from Marine Scout Bombing 142, with an escort of seven Wildcats from Marine Fighting 112, six Army Warhawks, and two Lightnings – though the P-38s got caught in a cloudbank, gained altitude to get clear air, and lost track of the rest of the strike.

The Dauntlesses moved to go after the supply convoy. Four Zeros of a nine-fighter combat air patrol from the 582 Air Group, assigned to protect Admiral Hashimoto's destroyers, moved against the Dauntlesses. The Warhawks moved against the Zeros. The supply convoy already had air cover of two F1M2 floatplanes, which shows the relative difference in importance the Japanese assigned to each convoy. The Petes kept a respectful distance from the American fighters. The clash between the P-40s and the A6Ms resulted in no losses to either side.

The Avengers went after Admiral Hashimoto's destroyers. The five Zeros ostensibly providing air cover saw the TBFs too late to intervene. The Avengers made textbook torpedo runs on the destroyers and released their missiles from ranges so close they couldn't miss. They missed. Again. Master Technical Sergeant George Nasif claimed a hit on a destroyer "resulting in serious damage and subsequent sinking." An explosion and a water column were observed off the side of one of the destroyers. It must have been a premature or low order detonation, because there appears to have been no damage, though there were 17 casualties.[133] This was yet another proud moment for American torpedoes.

The supply convoy went into 45-degree turns to port under attack from the Dauntlesses, who reported two bomb hits on the transport and a plethora of near misses on the other ships, including one that killed ten and wounded 30 on the *Ch-17*. They believed they left the transport in sinking condition and the tanker damaged. A B-17 flying reconnaissance reported seeing a "burning Jap tanker and destroyer near Vella Lavella."[134] The *Ch-17* must not have been too badly damaged, however, as by 11:00 the next morning she was back in Rabaul, ready for more escort work. By the next morning, Admiral Hashimoto's destroyers were well on their way back to Shortland, having completed their mission.

Nevertheless, none of this could have been encouraging to Admiral Kusaka, either: two air raids on Guadalcanal, two defeats. No shooting down of American aircraft in large numbers had occurred. In truth, the raids accomplished nothing but had a heavy cost in pilots, planes, and fuel. The Americans were still able to defend the Lunga airfield, still able to harass convoys throughout the Solomons. The next strike in Guadalcanal was scheduled for January 29. There was nothing to indicate it would be any more effective than the first two.

With no air superiority, with barely any ability to challenge American air superiority, Admiral Kusaka asked for a postponement of Operation *Ke*. That was unacceptable to the Imperial Army. General Inamura insisted it go forward as scheduled.[135]

So it continued the next day. And added another clue about Japanese intentions to Pacific Fleet intelligence. Admiral Kusaka did postpone the January 29 attack on Guadalcanal because Base Air Force had found a much bigger, much more vulnerable, target. And they could strike when the Americans least expected it.

Delay, linger, and wait: that was Admiral King's assessment of the current state of the Guadalcanal campaign, or at least the American strategy in conducting that campaign. He certainly was not happy about it. On the last day of January, amidst discussions of the replacement of the 2nd Marine Division on Guadalcanal, Admiral King sent a signal to Admirals Nimitz and Halsey that the Guadalcanal campaign "continues in current status of delay, linger, and wait."[136] It was not a friendly message. Then again, few of King's messages were.

Admiral King was an aggressive admiral. So was Admiral Halsey. Caught between the two was Admiral Nimitz, aggressive in his own way but also a calming presence on King and Halsey. Halsey's aggressiveness was a welcome and indeed necessary change from his predecessor. But as Santa Cruz showed, Halsey did not always pair it with proper preparation.

This time Admiral Halsey was well aware of the increased Japanese activity, their new air assets, their ship movements. Like all the other top brass on the US Navy side, Halsey believed it meant another Japanese offensive. And he welcomed it. He believed he was ready for it.

Let them come, he figured, because the US Navy had assembled its largest collection of ships since the beginning of the Guadalcanal campaign. This collection of ships was focused on, strangely enough, a small convoy with the veteran transports *President Adams*, *President Hayes*, *President Jackson*, and *Crescent City*, carrying the 214th Coast Artillery and other US Army units to Guadalcanal. With an escort of destroyers *Craven*, *Gansevoort*, *Jenkins*, and *Lardner*, this convoy left Nouméa the morning of January 27, expecting to arrive at Guadalcanal the morning of January 30.[137]

The naval forces of the South Pacific Command had increased markedly since November, even since the disaster at Tassafaronga. Admiral Halsey now had fleet carriers *Saratoga* and *Enterprise*, though the Big E's flight operations were still slowed by the elevator jammed at Santa Cruz. He also had six small escort carriers. Add to that three new, fast battleships, 13 cruisers, and 45 destroyers. By the standards of 1942 Ironbottom Sound, this was unheard-of wealth. Halsey meant to make use of them for offensive action.

The South Pacific commander organized his ships into no fewer than six task forces. One was centered on the freshly repaired carrier *Saratoga*, with also freshly repaired light antiaircraft cruiser *San Juan*; and destroyers *Case*, *Maury*, *McCall*, and *Saufley*, all under Admiral Ramsey. Another carrier task force was under Rear Admiral Frederick Sherman, former skipper of the carrier *Lexington* at Coral Sea. Now he had the *Enterprise*, light antiaircraft cruiser *San Diego*, and destroyers *Ellet*, *Hughes*, *Morris*, *Mustin*, and *Russell*. There was the task force of three new fast battleships under Admiral Lee, with the *Washington*, *North Carolina*, and *Indiana*; and destroyers *Balch*, *Cummings*, *Dunlap*, and *Fanning*. There was also a task force of four old, slow battleships under Vice Admiral Herbert F. Leary, with the *New Mexico*, *Colorado*, *Mississippi*, and a freshly repaired *Maryland*; and destroyers *McCalla* and *Woodworth*.

There were now two instead of one cruiser-destroyer task forces. This would have been unheard of just one month earlier. One was under Rear Admiral Walden L. Ainsworth, with the heavy cruiser *Nashville*; light cruisers *Helena*, *Honolulu*, and *St. Louis*; and destroyers *Drayton*, *Lamson*, *O'Bannon*, and *Reid*.

When the transport convoy left Nouméa on the morning of January 27, Admiral Halsey sent in close support a second cruiser-destroyer force that consisted of three heavy cruisers (*Wichita*, *Chicago*, and *Louisville*); three light cruisers (*Montpelier*, *Cleveland*, and *Columbia*); eight destroyers (*La Vallette*, *Waller*, *Conway*, *Frazier*, *Chevalier*, *Edwards*, *Taylor*, and the veteran *Meade*); and, in an interesting wrinkle, two escort carriers (*Chenango* and *Suwannee*). It was christened "Task Force 18" and placed under the command of Rear Admiral Robert C. Giffen.

"Ike" Giffen was a veteran of the Atlantic and North Africa. He had worked the icy convoys to Murmansk, in which he had to deal with German U-boats, and Operation *Torch* in North Africa, battling the Vichy French navy, such as it was, off Casablanca as commander of Task Group 34.1. Both experiences earned Giffen the good graces of Admiral King. King had Giffen sail aboard the *Wichita* all the way from North Africa to the New Hebrides.

As Admiral Giffen was very new to the Pacific theater, Admiral Halsey wanted Giffen to "get his feet wet in the Pacific," perhaps not the best motivational phrase for someone commanding warships at sea.[138] Guadalcanal historian Richard Frank says Giffen may have had "a certain rigidity of mental processes[.]"[139] It is an example of this fine historian's gift for understatement.

The first thing the sailors of Task Force 18 noticed was that Admiral Giffen forced them to wear white uniforms. It was a major change from the khakis and dungarees that were the norm in the hot, humid, wet Solomons.[140] Rumor had it that Giffen had refused to meet the new skipper of the *Chicago*, Captain Ralph O. Davis, until Davis changed out of his khakis into his whites.[141] He even refused to step aboard Admiral Halsey's flagship *Argonne* because Halsey, the Supreme Commander in the South Pacific and Giffen's immediate superior, wore open-necked shirts and rumpled garrison caps. But every commander, even the good ones, especially the good ones, have their idiosyncrasies, and if the gruff and by-the-book Giffen restricted his to laundry, they might be okay. Historian Samuel Eliot Morison even described Giffen as "colorful."[142]

Late in the afternoon of January 27, 1943, the new admiral led his new task force out of Efate and headed for Guadalcanal. They would be looking for a fight. Admiral Giffen's orders were to rendezvous at 10:00 pm on January 30 at a point 15 miles off Cape Hunter, on Guadalcanal's southwest coast, with the destroyers *Fletcher*, *De Haven*, *Nicholas*, and *Radford*, four destroyers of the so-called "Cactus Striking Force" under Captain Robert Briscoe. Once this was completed, Giffen's newly enlarged force would screen the transports, who would then be unloading their Marine reinforcements and supplies at Lunga, by going into The Slot and sweeping for Japanese ships.

On January 29, Admiral Giffen received intelligence that the Japanese had from three to ten submarines operating in the area. Also, a large number of Japanese fighters and bombers had appeared over Guadalcanal the previous morning, suggesting an air attack was in the offing, probably part of a strong move toward Guadalcanal. Finally, and rather curiously, intelligence also warned that the Japanese might try an air attack at night.[143]

Admiral Giffen saw this information and one word stood out: "submarines." In the Atlantic theater, the biggest naval threat to all Allied shipping was German submarines. Giffen had not had to deal much with German air power but had been constantly on alert for German submarines; the dangerous component of the *Kriegsmarine*. Japan was an ally of Germany, so Japan must surely be just like Germany. So, to Giffen, just as in the Atlantic, submarines must surely be the most significant threat in the Pacific, too. Right?

There were some troubling signs, though. Throughout the day unidentified aircraft kept appearing on radar. Some were ultimately identified as American, using the new Identification Friend or Foe (IFF) transponders, which at this time did not work reliably. It was the others that were disconcerting. Fighters from the *Chenango* and the *Suwannee* attempted to intercept the uninvited intruders. But they had to blindly poke around for them. The fighter director was on the *Chicago* and could not vector the fighters in because Admiral Giffen had ordered radio silence to avoid giving the enemy a fix on the task force's position, although the presence of so many unidentified aircraft suggested his position had already been fixed. In any case, Giffen believed that aircraft were not the real threat – submarines were, as they were in the Atlantic.

At 12:44 pm, Captain Ben H. Wyatt, skipper of the *Chenango* but also serving as group commander for the escort carriers, asked permission to launch search planes to check out the area near Indispensable Reef and San Cristobal for snoopers or maybe a seaplane tender.[144] The Japanese did love their seaplanes. But Admiral Giffen was seething about his escort carriers.

Escort carriers, also called "auxiliary carriers," "jeep carriers," or "baby flattops," were usually built on the hulls of converted tankers, merchant ships, and cruise ships – basically, anything that could carry a flight deck. These civilian ships generally cannot go very fast, certainly not up to the speeds required for combat. That was not usually a problem because their mission duties mainly involved protecting slow-moving convoys from submarines and the occasional small air attack. This was not a slow-moving convoy, however, but a fighting task force of warships. And, like most task forces, its speed was limited to the speed of the slowest units, which were the *Chenango* and the *Suwannee*, whose top speed was a mere 18 knots.

As if to further drag the task force, the wind was, as usual, coming out of the southeast. So whenever the carriers were conducting flight operations, they had to turn into the wind, which was opposite the direction into which the task force was supposed to be headed.[145] Admiral Giffen's staff determined from the carriers' lack of speed that they were going to be late for their rendezvous with Captain Briscoe's destroyers. Giffen was incensed because the carriers were slowing him down, calling them his "ball and chain."[146]

This situation was hardly unforeseeable and could have, and should have, been differently handled. One potential solution would have been to have the carriers and a minimal escort leave port before the rest of the task force did, so the carriers would be in position when the other cruisers and destroyers arrived. Another potential solution would have been to have Admiral Halsey's staff make better calculations and determine a reasonable rendezvous time and place based on the slowest speed of the ships involved. Clearly, someone on Halsey's staff in Nouméa had screwed up.

Even so, there was really nothing essential about the time of the rendezvous with Captain Briscoe's destroyers.[147] But Admiral Giffen was a strict by-the-book commander. He was determined to meet the destroyers on time.

To speed up his task force to make the rendezvous, Admiral Giffen ordered the carriers to break off at 2:00 pm.[148] He did accede to Captain Wyatt's request, but he ordered the reconnaissance flight for 2:00 pm as well, in order to avoid having his cruisers and destroyers delayed – again – by the carriers' flight operations.[149]

Those flight operations continued, however, because the force's radars kept picking up bogeys. Some of the unidentified aircraft turned out to be friendly, but there were some more troubling signs. Groups of aircraft were detected circling the force at a range of 40–50 miles.[150] Even more ominously, at intervals of about half an hour, aircraft approached as close as 20 miles.[151] The covering fighters still could not catch the intruders because no one could tell them where the approaching aircraft were due to the continued radio silence.

At 3:00 pm Captain Wyatt broke off as ordered with the *Chenango* and the *Suwannee*, with destroyers *Frazier* and *Meade* – the latter his only destroyer with any Guadalcanal combat experience – as escorts. It was at that time Wyatt had the *Chenango* launch two radar-equipped Avengers and four Wildcat fighters. They were sent off toward San Cristobal.

Free at last from his "ball and chain," Admiral Giffen had the task force raise its speed to 24 knots, zigzagging on a base course of 305 degrees True, now comfortably headed for the rendezvous. He arranged his force with the cruisers in two columns. To starboard were the heavy cruiser flagship *Wichita* and fellow heavy cruisers *Chicago* and *Louisville* at 2,500-yard intervals. To port were the light cruisers *Montpelier*, *Cleveland*, and

Columbia at similar intervals. The remaining destroyers were sent some 2 miles forward in a semicircle.

It was a great formation for defense against submarines. For defense against surface ships, it was okay because everyone could quickly move into a surface combat formation. For defense against aircraft, it was utterly useless because the destroyers no longer screened the sides and rear of the task force. But that was a small price to pay, in Admiral Giffen's view, for protection against those submarines. No submarine would take down his ships.

The fighters from the two escort carriers continued to provide air cover and continued to chase unidentified specks in the sky without success. At 6:50 pm, as the sun was going down, the last of the fighters returned to their carriers – even though there were still unidentified aircraft about. By now the task force was 50 miles north of Rennell Island, almost directly south of Guadalcanal. There was some light left, but not a lot, and with darkness there was presumed to be some safety from a Japanese air attack.

Just after the air cover vacated the premises, the destroyer *Edwards* along with several other ships detected a flight of unidentified aircraft about 30 miles away on her SC radar. The flight closed and passed down the port side of the task force some 15 miles away. More groups of aircraft showed up on radar, 25–50 miles away. Some showed IFF and were friendly; others, not so much. The destroyer *La Vallette* finally got a visual on one of these groups. It had 12–18 aircraft, heading south some 12 miles off the port bow. They were "probably" friendly, but the presence of so many aircraft, especially so close to dusk, was unnerving.[152]

Things were about to get more unnerving. At 7:09 pm the *Columbia*'s radar was tracking two groups of planes that were friendly and other planes that were … not. She went to battle stations. One minute later the CXAM radar on the *Chicago* detected a large group of bogeys 25 miles to the west. They were not approaching directly, however, but were making a wide circle to the left, heading aft, closing slightly. They would pass clear of the American ships, Captain Davis thought – or hoped, to be more accurate.[153] By 7:20, this flight was 14 miles to the rear – the rear left exposed when Admiral Giffen sent all his destroyers forward. Worse, the unidentified aircraft were coming from a position in which they would be difficult to see against the darkened eastern sky, while the American ships, whose positions were already revealed by their phosphorescent wakes, were silhouetted against the dwindling light on the western horizon.

The *Chicago* discussed the incoming bogeys with the flagship *Wichita*. These were not the actions of friendly aircraft. Looking at the plot of the aircraft on the *Wichita*, Admiral Giffen thought it looked like a "disturbed hornet's nest."[154] But this did not motivate the Atlantic admiral to do anything about it, such as issue any orders, change course, request air cover, or make any preparations.[155] The ships were on their own.

Of those ships, the *Chicago* was a Pacific war veteran – with the torpedo scars from Savo Island to prove it – and was experienced with air attacks off Guadalcanal. Her skipper Captain Ralph Davis was prepared: the ship was at Condition II, darkened and conducting radar searches with all antiaircraft batteries manned. Even better, the *Chicago* and some other ships were now armed with the new and secret Mark 32 proximity fuse antiaircraft shells, which did not have to hit an attacker to explode, just come near it. Davis went to battle stations.

The *Chicago*'s radar continued tracking this large force of unfriendly aircraft as it continued its wide circle around the task force until it was off the starboard side. The formation had split into two groups, 10,000 and 17,000 yards distant.[156] The nearer one was now on an attack vector from starboard. They were coming. The time was 7:24 pm.

The destroyer *Waller*, almost directly off the starboard beam of the *Chicago*, was the unhappy recipient of a strafing run from one of the incoming intruders. The destroyer returned fire. The *Chicago* joined in with her starboard 5-inch batteries, operating under radar control, and 20mm Oerlikons. It was apparently this strafing plane that crashed in a ball of fire between the *Chicago* and the *Waller*. It was a Japanese twin-engine Mitsubishi G4M Type 1 bomber, a Betty.

The Japanese *had* been watching them. All day.

The Japanese had known about the approach of Admiral Giffen's cruisers. At least one Japanese submarine had reported the force's presence and tracked it.[157] The 751 (former Kanoya) Air Group had staged a squadron of G4Ms from Buka into the new airfield at Ballale, in the Shortlands, to perform long-range reconnaissance.[158] Its Bettys had found Task Force 18 shortly after dawn and kept it under surveillance throughout the day.[159] Two of the Bettys had been spotted in the central Solomons en route to Admiral Giffen's location at around 8:00 am by two Army Air Force P-40s out of Henderson Field. These Bettys shadowed the American ships from 9:35 until 10:40 am before heading back.[160] They were replaced by others.

Meanwhile, Guadalcanal's radio intelligence station, Station AL (locally known as "Cactus Crystal Ball"), was intercepting Japanese reports of American ships south of Guadalcanal. Those reports stopped around 6:00 pm to be replaced, ominously, by reports of large numbers of twin-engine bombers headed for the area. The radio intelligence unit on the carrier *Enterprise* picked up the messages as well, but could not forward them to Admiral Giffen because of radio silence.[161]

Admiral Kusaka had canceled Base Air Force's planned air raid on Guadalcanal to send out a large airstrike, consisting of 32 bombers, each trained in night attacks, each armed with a single aerial torpedo, launched from the Vunakanau airbase outside Rabaul under the command of 701 Flight Leader Lieutenant Commander Higai Joji.[162] After one bomber turned back because of engine trouble, Higai was leading 15 Mitsubishi G3M twin-engine bombers – the Allies called the G3M "Nell" – of his own 701 (former Mihoro) Air Group, and 16 Mitsubishi G4M Bettys of the 705 (former Misawa) Air Group in a twilight strike. It was the same combination of bombers that had sent the battleship *Prince of Wales* and the battlecruiser *Repulse* to their deaths a little more than a year earlier.

The veteran Lieutenant Commander Higai was considered one of the best torpedo strike commanders in the Japanese Naval Air Force. His cunning showed as he maneuvered the airstrike around Admiral Giffen's ships to strike from the darkened eastern sky, making them almost invisible, while the US Navy ships were backlit by the remnants of twilight. Higai split the strike into two groups, sending the Bettys of the 705 Air Group under Lieutenant Commander Nakamura Tomo in first.

Lieutenant Commander Higai had indeed positioned his airstrike perfectly. While their approach was tracked on radar, the Bettys were almost on top of the Americans before they got a visual. Two Bettys were seen approaching the *Chicago* from the starboard beam; one was seen dropping a torpedo at a range of 500–600 yards. The cruiser's lookouts could not find a wake from the torpedo, and both planes crossed in front of the *Chicago* and disappeared in the night. Hit by gunfire, a third Betty, piloted by Flight Petty Officer 1st Class Imamura Bunzaburo, crashed into the water off the port quarter.[163]

All of Admiral Giffen's ships were now swatting at Lieutenant Commander Nakamura's Bettys as the Japanese tried their best to deliver their sting. Captain Davis heard impacts in the water near the *Cleveland* and *Columbia*, but, whatever the sound was, neither ship was damaged.[164] A Betty roared low over the bow of the *Wichita*, raking the flagship with her machine guns. Another dropped a torpedo some 500 yards off the starboard quarter at a rather poor angle. It missed. Six more Bettys, some looking like their running lights were on, sped from astern down the port side.[165]

Yet another Betty was seen heading for the *Louisville*. The cruiser opened up on the bomber at a range of 1,500 yards, but the Mitsubishi dropped her torpedo and disappeared. The *Louisville*'s lookouts spotted the incoming torpedo, and after the cruiser executed a hard port turn, the torpedo crossed ahead a scant 75 feet.[166] While that torpedo missed the *Louisville*, another apparently did not, though neither did it explode; the cruiser was shaken by a "violent shock," believed to have come from a dud torpedo.[167]

And just like that, in a matter of five minutes or so, the Japanese were gone.

Admiral Giffen seemingly took stock of the situation. The Japanese had attacked them. With aircraft. At night. Can they *do* that?

To Giffen there was only one obvious solution. At 7:30 pm, he ordered his ships to stop zigzagging and to increase speed.[168] They were going to make a straight shot to that all-important rendezvous. One can only wonder what his skippers thought when they received this instruction.

By now, the last vestiges of twilight had faded and it was completely dark – but not for long. To starboard there appeared a line of blinking green float lights on the water. Another line of float lights, red ones, appeared to port, evenly spaced, having "the appearance of quick-flashing navigational lights."[169] Yellow-white parachute flares drifted down very slowly. It was like sailing down a landing strip with streetlights. Japanese seaplanes were clearly stalking Admiral Giffen's rattled cruisers, revealing their course and illuminating them in the night for the next air attack. Though Admiral Giffen seems to have forgotten about them, Lieutenant Commander Higai and his 15 Nells of the 701 Air Group were still on the radar. The Japanese air attack was, in fact, not over.

Now the malevolent Mitsubishis roared in low to aim their torpedoes. One Nell dropped a torpedo toward the back of the *Wichita*'s starboard beam. The *Louisville* sighted at least two torpedoes approaching, one from port and one from starboard. If it was an attempt at an anvil attack, it was a poorly executed one, as the *Louisville* turned hard to port and avoided both. An observer said that the torpedo coming from port was "short and fat and ran near the surface about 25 yards from the ship."[170] With his guns blinding the gunners with their flashes but seemingly not hitting anything, an exasperated *Louisville* skipper Captain Charles T. Joy ordered, "Hold fire except for positive targets."[171]

At 7:36 the *Columbia*'s guns caught a Nell coming in low and fast on the port bow, sending it plowing into the drink. Two minutes later, the *Chicago*'s starboard 5-inch battery opened on the attackers at a range of 10,000 yards – not surprisingly, under radar control. Next, "[t]he automatic weapons (20mm Oerlikons) took up the fire as the planes approached at the extreme ranges of these weapons," Captain Davis would later write.[172]

Marine Private Tom Sheble of the *Chicago* was not on duty at the time, but ran to his battle station on a 20mm Oerlikon above the bridge. Sheble later explained, "You were shooting at the blue flame that you could see coming out of the side of the engine, the exhaust."[173]

The gun crews cheered as the antiaircraft guns mauled the Mitsubishis. One Nell careened into the water off the starboard quarter of the *Waller*. Another G3M off the *Chicago*'s starboard bow – Lieutenant Commander Higai's – took a punishing barrage from the Oerlikons and burst into flames. As the *Chicago*'s air defense officer Lieutenant Edward Jarman described it, "We filled one torpedo plane so full of steel that it almost exploded on the *Chicago*. It missed our boat by 10 feet."[174] Like a comet streaking through the night, Higai's G3M trailed fire as it glided down over the *Chicago*'s bow, apparently clipped the cruiser's CXAM radar, and crashed in the water to port.

Taking out this veteran torpedo strike commander was by itself a victory for the US Navy as the long attrition of the best of Japan's prewar pilots continued, but Higai Joji, in his final moments in this world, got some measure of revenge. His pyre off the *Chicago*'s port bow left a fiery wreck and a pool of burning aviation fuel on top of the water.

Captain Davis knew what that meant: "The flames from this plane were very brilliant and hot and undoubtedly silhouetted *Chicago* for the following planes."[175] "[Lieutenant Commander Higai's wreck] burned three or four minutes, silhouetting us for the second wave," said Lieutenant Jarman. "They all concentrated on the *Chicago*, apparently mistaking her for a battleship."[176]

Indeed, they did. The remaining G3Ms made the most of the brilliant backlighting of the *Chicago*, sending a swarm of torpedoes at the cruiser. At 7:40 or so, one of the torpedoes, one her lookouts could not see, smacked the cruiser on the starboard side even with the after engine room.[177] Marine Tom Sheble remembered, "I never heard such an explosion; it was unbelievable." Two minutes later a second torpedo hit directly under the hangar near the Number 3 boiler room, sending a column of water 200 feet into the air.[178]

Still at his 20mm Oerlikon, Sheble felt the cruiser rise and fall back into the water. He heard loud noises coming from below and feared the ship was about to explode.[179]

It was not; not on its own, anyway.[180] But the torpedoes had caused damage enough. The Number 4 fireroom and after gyro room were immediately flooded, with water invading the after engine room as well. All four propeller shafts were knocked offline.[181] But her 20mm Oerlikons continued to blast away. She combined with the *Wichita* to turn one Mitsubishi into a fireball that crashed off the port bow; and combined with the *Louisville* to turn another into a flaming torch that plunged into the water off the port quarter. Even as she fought on, the *Chicago* began to list to starboard. She signaled to Admiral Giffen, "I am hit by two torpedoes and am dead in the water."[182]

Behind the *Chicago*, the *Louisville* had to veer to starboard to avoid the disabled cruiser, which served to silhouette her. She rang up 30 knots to catch up to the flagship *Wichita* and assume the *Chicago*'s former position in the formation, exactly as she was supposed to do. Meanwhile, the *Columbia* had spotted a new line of float lights, not marking the course of the cruisers but instead directly across the cruisers' path.[183] The shadowing seaplanes had dropped the float lights to point the direction back to Rabaul for the Mitsubishis.

Just before 8:00 pm, Admiral Giffen seems to have considered that perhaps the rendezvous with Captain Briscoe's four destroyers was not as important as the survival of his ships. He signaled his destroyers "Corpen 120," which meant countermarch to course 120 degrees True, back toward the east southeast and Espiritu Santo.

It was Admiral Giffen's first order for a turn during the air attack. It would fit in perfectly with the admiral's performance this night. The order required the destroyers to pass through the cruiser formation before the cruisers themselves changed course to 120 degrees True – at night. It was a recipe for collision.

Indeed, while carrying out this order, the destroyer *Conway* found herself cutting across the bow of the flagship *Wichita* from port to starboard. Only emergency maneuvers by both avoided a collision by a mere 50 feet.[184] The *Louisville* also had to maneuver wildly to avoid the destroyers now passing through on the opposite course.[185] The *Wichita* cut her speed to 15 knots, the other ships conforming; someone evidently had told the admiral that you reduce the phosphorescence of the ships' wakes by cutting speed, not stopping zigzagging while increasing speed. The cruisers reversed course to follow their destroyers.

The Japanese were still out there, stalking them like wolves and dropping flares to taunt them. A single G4M appeared out of the dark and reportedly dropped two torpedoes about 200 yards off the *Wichita*'s starboard quarter. One broached and ran parallel to the cruiser off the starboard side; the other "made [an] underwater metallic blow and scraping sounds" as the Type 91 apparently glanced off the starboard side without detonating.[186] With the number of uncharacteristic dud torpedoes that plagued the Japanese this night, maybe the fine Type 91 aerial torpedoes they normally used had been secretly replaced with the American Mark 13.

The flagship reported an attack from the port quarter that drew fire from the *Wichita* and *Louisville*, which the *Louisville* did not record; nor did she record a bomber crashing nearby, which the *Wichita* believed had been downed by the *Louisville*'s 20mm Oerlikons.[187]

At 8:30 Admiral Giffen signaled Captain Joy in the *Louisville*, "Take *Chicago* in tow."[188] It was a dangerous order because the Japanese were still about, but they had to get the *Chicago* out of the range of the Japanese bombers if she would have any chance to survive. Giffen also ordered his ships, "Do not open up unless you have a good target."[189]

This was a tactic of desperation, but a logical one. The night was exceedingly dark with no moon; the flares, float lights, and wrecks had burned out, so the only fix the Japanese pilots could get on the Americans was through the flashes of antiaircraft gunfire. The Nells tried to bait the Americans into firing by such measures as turning on their running lights and firing long bursts of tracer fire. US Navy discipline held, and the Mitsubishis started heading west for the long trip back to Vunakanau.

By 9:15 pm, the attack was finally over. The *Chicago*'s starboard list had stabilized at 11 degrees, with about 6 feet of freeboard (space between the deck and the water) remaining aft. The destroyers *La Vallette*, *Edwards*, and *Taylor* screened the *Louisville* as Captain Joy took the cruiser out of formation to prepare to tow the disabled *Chicago*.

On board the *Chicago*, the veteran crew that had survived Savo Island and saved their ship then had no intention of losing her now. Small fires in the galley and radio room II were quickly extinguished. Bulkheads were shored up to prevent further flooding. Albert Bartholomew, the ship's carpenter, led a damage control party deep into the ship to close critical hatches. The party "worked like dogs to keep us afloat," he said. "They swam 30 feet in water chin deep, dodging heavy tables and chairs as the ship rolled, to dog down hatches."[190] No pun intended.

While the *Chicago*'s veteran crew was working diligently to save their ship, an incredible bit of seamanship was being performed by Captain Joy and his crew in the *Louisville*. Imagine trying to rig a car for towing with absolutely no light whatsoever, then multiply that level of difficulty by a thousand. "The darkness of the night was a major difficulty," Captain Joy would later say with impressive understatement. "Added to this was the lack of power on the *Chicago* and the concern felt over the presence of enemy planes, a number of which were heard overhead and tracked in the close vicinity."[191] As if that was not enough, the *Chevalier* opened up on what she thought – incorrectly – was a surfaced enemy submarine just before midnight.[192]

Even so, in complete darkness, the *Louisville* maneuvered into position with its stern about 1,000 yards off the bow of the *Chicago*. The *Louisville*'s whaleboat was lowered, and crewmen groped in the gloom the more than half-mile to the immobilized cruiser. Then the towing apparatus was prepared; the thick, heavy steel cable was wrestled aboard and shackled to the anchor chain; and 60 fathoms of chain let out. With no hint as to the impressive nature of the feat, Captain Joy later commented, "The passing of the tow was accomplished without a hitch and exactly as planned, with no injury to personnel, or damage to material."[193]

With all that completed, at ten minutes after midnight, Captain Joy ordered the *Louisville*'s engines slow ahead. But there was a slight problem: the *Chicago*'s rudder was jammed 10 degrees to port.[194] That was quickly cleared, and at 12:55 am on January 30, the *Louisville* moved ahead at 4 knots, towing the *Chicago* behind her, on a course of 130 degrees True. The three destroyers screened the cruisers as they painfully, slowly headed for Espiritu Santo.[195] During the remainder of the night, the flagship *Wichita* and destroyer *Conway* maneuvered to the eastward while the light cruisers and remaining ships maneuvered to the westward, trying to keep the *Chicago* group in a protective cocoon.

Further progress was made on board the *Chicago*. The engineers managed to restart boiler Number 4 to provide additional power. With this help, pumps shifted fuel oil around the various tanks to correct the list. Captain Davis ordered most of the life rafts and floater nets be cut loose and placed on deck, just in case. He hoped for the best but wanted to be ready for the worst.

Back at Nouméa, Admiral Halsey was informed of the *Chicago*'s plight. Halsey was no doubt furious with Admiral Giffen, but taking the necessary steps to help save the cruiser required him to keep his temper in check. Mostly. First thing he did was order Admiral Fitch to send up a night-trained Black Cat PBY Catalina to cover the force; it arrived after midnight.[196] Halsey also sent the fleet tug *Navajo* to take over the tow, under escort by the old four-piper destroyer *Sands*.

Most importantly, the South Pacific commander moved to get the beleaguered *Chicago* some air cover. Halsey ordered Giffen's own carriers *Chenango* and *Suwannee* to move to a better position to provide fighter protection. More dangerously, Halsey ordered the *Enterprise* to also move into position to provide fighter protection. The *Enterprise* task force was about 350 miles south of the *Chicago*, but Admiral Sherman had it speed north at 28 knots. Sherman had been given a tricky proposition. The carrier had to be close enough to the cruiser to allow for a short flight time for his fighters, yet far enough away that Japanese planes sent to attack the *Chicago* would not be in a position to sight the *Enterprise*.

Dawn on January 30 found the *Chicago* still afloat, an accomplishment in itself. "We were settling fast and it looked touch and go whether we would sink. The next morning we were taking on more water than the books said we could and keep afloat," recalled Lieutenant Jarman, "but we kept her up."[197]

Just after 6:00 am, the *Navajo* found the *Chicago*. The tug pulled alongside the *Louisville* and the tow line was transferred by 7:40 am.[198] While this was going on, Admiral Giffen ordered Captain Davis to transfer wounded and nonessential crew to the escorting destroyers while they were stopped for the change in tow. Davis asked if they could send the wounded to land hospital in a designated destroyer at high speed. Giffen refused, saying no vessel could be spared because of the submarine danger. Davis then refused to send any of his sailors over, citing the precarious buoyancy of the cruiser and the probability of another air attack.[199] This was a curious exchange, suggesting that by this time Davis did not have full confidence in his admiral.

But hopes nonetheless rose at 8:00 am or so when six Wildcats from the *Enterprise* showed up to provide air cover. The carrier had sent up four Dauntless scouts just after 6:00 am to find the cruiser. They located her around 7:15 some 35 miles east of Rennell Island, and then the six Wildcats were vectored in as four more Wildcats circled the *Enterprise* herself.[200]

All that air cover would be needed. If there had been any doubts as to that need, they were dispelled when the sun came up to reveal a long oil slick trailing behind the *Chicago* that could lead Japanese bombers straight back to the cruiser.[201] To help direct fighter coverage for the *Chicago*, the *Wichita* and *Conway* had switched positions with the light cruisers, moving to starboard of the *Chicago* so they would be better positioned to detect aircraft approaching from Rabaul. The light cruisers and their screen had switched to the *Chicago's* port hand.[202]

The escort carriers *Chenango* and *Suwannee* were having issues protecting the *Chicago*. Pursuant to orders from Admiral Halsey, they were trying to position themselves some 60 miles southeast of the *Chicago's* position. They would launch fighter protection around dawn, then rendezvous with the *Enterprise*. But when her fighters were scheduled to take off at 5:50 am, it was dark and raining with little wind for takeoff. The pilots were, of course, from escort carriers and therefore were not trained for nighttime operations or even pre-dawn operations. But for all they knew, the *Chicago* would be attacked at dawn. So ten of the *Chenango's* pilots braved it and took off at 6:00 am, three to search for the *Chicago*, which they found an hour later, and seven to give the cruiser fighter cover. The *Suwannee* was supposed to provide air cover for the escort carriers themselves, but with conditions so bad she did not launch her fighters until dawn.[203]

With the arrival of the fighters, hopes for the *Chicago* rose further. "We were all celebrating," recalled Chief Electrician's Mate Art King. "We were celebrating because, hey, we were going to get out of here. We were thinking about getting into Sydney and all that good liberty down there. We were pretty happy."[204]

They were indeed getting out of there, but whether they took their ship with them remained an open question. At about 8:30 am, Wildcats from the *Enterprise* chased off a Japanese scout plane that was sighted about 20 miles west of the carrier. This appears to have been the aircraft that reported a battleship was under tow and trailing oil.[205] The supposed battleship was the *Chicago*. Soon radio intelligence on Guadalcanal picked up Japanese reports referencing "Chicago."[206] Ever careful about communications, the Japanese Naval Air Force was using the same code captured on the destroyer *Smith* at Santa Cruz, cold comfort for the crew of the *Chicago*.[207] They were found.

The escort carriers had joined the *Enterprise* around noon for centralized fighter direction from Admiral Sherman's crew, but the 50-mile distance between the carriers and the *Chicago* was a major handicap. Nevertheless, at 12:35 pm fighters were vectored out from the *Enterprise* to chase a bogey which had been picked up 40 miles southwest of the *Chicago*. The Wildcats pursued the scout 40 miles to the northeast, near the *Chicago's* position. The bogey was monitored on radar circling the *Chicago* task force before it "faded from the screen."[208] Whatever happened to the aircraft, it apparently reported the cruiser's position.

Admiral Sherman detached the two escort carriers around 2:00 pm, ordering them to continue providing air cover to the *Chicago* and her escorts. That was not quite enough for Admiral Halsey, who apparently lacked confidence in the air defense arrangements – he certainly lacked confidence in Admiral Giffen's ability to direct air defense – and wanted to get his undamaged cruisers out. He ordered the undamaged cruisers of Giffen's force to split off from the *Chicago* group and make for Efate at 25 knots. At around 3:00 pm, the cruisers formed on the *Wichita* with the destroyers *Chevalier* and *Taylor* as a screen. Having gotten the *Chicago* into trouble, Giffen now signaled, "Adieu and good luck" and took off, taking with him fighter direction and a lot of antiaircraft power, including the new proximity fuses.[209] The *Chicago* now had only a screen composed of the destroyers *Conway*, *Edwards*, *La Vallette*, *Sands*, and *Waller*. Captain Davis commanded this force.

The severance took place just in time to receive the long-awaited word from Guadalcanal, broadcast in plain language at 3:45 pm: "Eleven unidentified twin-engine aircraft bearing 268 degrees x distance 130 miles course 150 degrees x."[210]

Coastwatchers had spotted 11 Mitsubishi G4Ms of the 751 Air Group south of New Georgia heading for Rennell Island and alerted Guadalcanal, who in turn alerted the *Enterprise*. They calculated when the attack would arrive; they had better be ready. One big question, however: was the target the *Chicago* or the *Enterprise*, who was now about 43 miles southeast of the cruiser?

The ten *Enterprise* Wildcat fighters under Lieutenant Commander William "Killer" Kane patrolling over the *Chicago* already had their hands full. At 4:10, they had sighted a single Japanese Mitsubishi north of Rennell Island approaching at high altitude. It was a high-speed advance scout, sent to fix the position of the *Chicago* for the following airstrike. Kane sent four Wildcats to take care of it. But this Betty was particularly obnoxious and cunning. It sped south and headed around the eastern end of Rennell Island – where it could see both the *Enterprise* and the *Chicago*. That was intolerable, so the four Wildcats kept up the hot pursuit, eventually setting fire to the Betty's starboard engine and sending it tumbling toward the sea in a fiery mess. But the Betty had done its job. It had certainly reported the position of the *Chicago* and probably the *Enterprise*; it had also taken four Wildcats 40 miles out of position for defending the *Chicago*.[211]

At 4:24 the incoming Bettys finally appeared on the *Enterprise*'s radar, 67 miles away, bearing 300 degrees True. Captain Hardison ordered battle stations. Ten additional Wildcats were launched to augment the four over the carrier and the six over the *Chicago*.[212] The defending Grummans were warned and ready.

But something or, more properly, some things went seriously wrong, though precisely how is unclear. It is known that the *Chenango* and *Suwannee* were supposed to send up additional fighters to cover the *Chicago*. The little carriers launched 19 Wildcats and four Avengers, who soon found Admiral Giffen's flagship *Wichita*. They assumed she was going to meet the *Chicago*; no one had told them that Giffen's undamaged cruisers had split off. No, fighter direction was not one of Giffen's strong suits.

There was more. The *Enterprise's* radar showed the Bettys were headed straight for the *Enterprise*. That was not part of the plan. Lieutenant Commander Kane had landed to refuel, and the six fighters still over the *Chicago* were now under the command of Lieutenant MacGregor Kilpatrick. They were vectored southwest to form a line of fighters awaiting the deadly Bettys, who had fanned out and now were in a line abreast, wingtip to wingtip, only 17 miles from the *Enterprise*, gliding down past 6,000 feet. Kilpatrick, at 10,000 feet, sent four of his fighters to hit from the Bettys' right flank, while he and his wingman Bob Porter took the left.[213]

But 751 Flight Leader Lieutenant Commander Nishioka Kazuo, leading the attack, had a surprise.[214] "We dropped down to the attack. The Jap commander saw our Wildcat fighter planes and realized he could not get across the miles separating him from the task force, so he took what seemed to be the easy way out," recalled Kilpatrick in a later interview. "The torpedo planes turned sharply and headed [east] toward the *Chicago*."[215]

According to multiple American accounts, eyewitnesses visually or on radar, the 11 Mitsubishi G4Ms made a sharp turn to the left, almost reversing course away from the *Enterprise* and toward the *Chicago*.[216] The four Wildcats Lieutenant Kilpatrick had sent to the bombers' right flank were now hopelessly behind. Only Kilpatrick and Porter were in any position to intercept.

If the Japanese maneuver was a planned feint, it was brilliantly executed – except, as historian John Domagalski notes, the Japanese accounts do not mention it.[217] Nevertheless, if it is accepted that the high-speed scout reported first the *Chicago* and then the *Enterprise* before being shot down, it is not unreasonable to wonder if, when Lieutenant Commander Nishioka got the report that the *Enterprise* was so close by, he went off script to go after the much more valuable target; but when he saw he was facing opposition, he turned back toward the *Chicago* to carry out his orders.

As it was, Lieutenant Commander Nishioka had outfoxed, intentionally or otherwise, American interception efforts. There were only two fighters capable of giving him trouble. But give him trouble they did. Both Kilpatrick and Porter gave chase as the Bettys continued a power glide to hit the deck for their torpedo attack. "[B]efore the Japs had come completely around, two of their number were spinning down with dead pilots at the controls," Kilpatrick remembered.[218] On the second pass, Kilpatrick splashed a third bomber while Porter crippled one that dropped back.[219]

That left eight Mitsubishis roaring in toward the crippled *Chicago*. The cruiser and her escorts were as ready as they could be, not that that was saying much. The destroyer *La Vallette* had been tracking the incoming strike on radar. The fire control radar took over and the *La Vallette* – the only ship between the *Chicago* and the incoming bombers – opened up with her guns under radar control.

At 5:20, the *Chicago* saw 11 planes approaching from 7 miles away off the starboard bow in a flat "V" formation.[220] Now the cruiser opened up at a range of 8,000 yards with her starboard 5-inch battery under local control because her CXAM radar had been disabled by Lieutenant Commander Higai's bomber the night before. She did not sight the combat air patrol, although it was reportedly attacking the enemy about this time. Two planes approaching to starboard were seen to dive into the water when under *Chicago* fire. Another, with one engine blazing, tried to crash the cruiser but missed the stern and fell off the port quarter in flames. A fourth plane went down about 3,000 yards on the port quarter, under fire from the *Chicago's* port battery. One plane crashed on the port bow, probably shot down by the *Navajo*. The *Chicago* was now aware that Wildcats were attacking her tormentors, and she had some difficulty in keeping the antiaircraft fire off them. In desperation, the *Navajo* tried to turn the cruiser toward their attackers in an effort to comb the expected torpedoes, or at least present the narrowest possible target. But there was not enough time.[221]

Back on his antiaircraft gun, Private Sheble saw the Bettys roaring in, "flying wing to wing and coming right at us."[222] Worse, after the bombers had passed, Sheble saw five torpedoes inbound: "You could see all of these streaks coming at you."[223] Seaman 2nd Class Bill Grady wrote: "It was something when you are standing there and you see the fish leave the belly of that plane and there is nothing that you can do about it."[224] There was nothing anyone could do about it, not with the cruiser under tow at 3 knots.

At 5:24 pm came the inevitable. An aerial torpedo detonated against the *Chicago's* starboard side well forward, sending up a towering plume of water, oil, and debris that ultimately came crashing back down on the forecastle and bridge. Three more torpedoes joined the first in pummeling the helpless cruiser, leaving the *Chicago's* starboard side more hole than hull. The fifth torpedo missed astern – for all the good that did.

Misery loves company, however. Little destroyer *La Vallette*, who had stayed in the path of the bombers to help screen the *Chicago*, was mistaken for a *Honolulu*-class cruiser and was thus targeted by three of the Bettys.[225] "One of the attacking 'Bettys' dropped a fish at us and then continued straight over us, as it was hit and going down into the sea," recalled Chuck Witten, who was working in secondary battery control as a lieutenant (jg) radar officer. "The plane passed so close over our stack, almost hitting it, that I could actually see the pilot's face. Then 'bang' we were hit."[226]

With no time to twist away, the *La Vallette* had to just grin and bear it as the torpedo plowed into her port side at the forward engine room, ripping a 48-foot hole and flooding the engine room and its accompanying fire room. The keel bent upward 14 inches and even snapped.[227] Damage control officer Lieutenant Eli Roth and 20 other men were lost. The *La Vallette* was saved by some incredible work of her engineers. Perhaps the most incredible was performed by Water Tender 2nd Class Maynard W. Tollberg. Scalding steam spewing from a damaged pipe left Tollberg partially blinded with "his skin charred and dropping off in chunks," yet he still managed to climb from the boiler room onto the main deck and used his last strength to close an oil valve to his boiler room below where other crewmen were trapped. Tollberg was posthumously awarded a Navy Cross.[228] Such efforts managed to limit the damage and get the destroyer under way within two minutes to escape the area.[229]

There would be no escape for the *Chicago*. "In spite of extensive flooding, CHICAGO undoubtedly would have survived the hits on 29 January," Captain Davis later reported. "Four additional hits, however, were more than the ship could absorb without sinking."[230] And the ship was sinking fast, being almost completely disemboweled. Davis's order of the night before to bring out the life rafts, floater nets, and other floatables now seemed prescient. Captain Davis ordered the *Navajo* to cut the towline and told his crew to abandon ship. The *Edwards*, *Waller*, *Sands*, and *Navajo* moved to rescue survivors, eventually plucking 1,049 survivors from the Coral Sea. And at 5:43 pm, the *Chicago* "rolled slowly over on her starboard side and settled by the stern, with colors flying."[231] As she sank, "everyone in the water yelled, hollered, and clapped," recalled sailor Frank Dinovo. "It was a last salute. That was our salute to the *Chicago*,"[232] and to the six officers and 56 men the cruiser took with her. These were much lower figures than one would normally expect with six torpedo hits, as Davis acknowledged. "Loss of life was fortunately small, almost all casualties resulting from the direct effects of the torpedo detonations."[233]

The direct effects of the torpedo detonations, along with indirect effects, would be felt for some time. At 7:15 pm, Guadalcanal forwarded to the *Chenango* a report from coastwatchers on Vella Lavella that at 6:09 pm 11 twin-engine and eight single-engine aircraft had been sighted on a southeasterly course – likely a Japanese airstrike searching for the aircraft carrier spotted earlier that day. Captain Wyatt and his staff plotted out the course track of these 19 aircraft; he found they would arrive over the *Chenango* and *Suwannee* at about 8:30 pm, after sunset. It seems the Japanese were trying for a repeat of their success of the previous night, this time hoping to bag a carrier, and when they arrived over the *Chenango* and the *Suwannee* and found the little carriers were not the big *Enterprise* they were hoping to sink, they probably would not turn away and go home out of disappointment. Worse, while Base Air Force had suffered heavy losses among its night-trained aircrews, obviously some were still available. The *Chenango* and *Suwannee* had none. They would not be able to launch fighters to defend them after dark. So Wyatt had the carriers' aircraft recovered and then had the carriers speed to a rain squall conveniently located about 3 miles away. But the reported Japanese strike never appeared in the area, so at 9:40 pm the escort carriers headed southeast on a course of 127 degrees True.[234]

This was good for the destroyer *La Vallette*, whose own ordeal was far from over. At about 9:00 pm, the *La Vallette*, trying to make Espiritu Santo, lost feed water for her boilers and went dead in the water. The *Navajo* moved in to tow the destroyer. The other destroyers – *Conway*, *Edwards*, *Sands*, and *Waller* – remained with the *La Vallette* and *Navajo*. The *Chenango* and *Suwannee* were supposed to provide the *La Vallette*'s group with fighter protection, but no one told Captain Wyatt where the group was supposed to be or that the *La Vallette* had lost power, slowing the group down to the speed of her tow. Wyatt had to grope across the Coral Sea for the damaged destroyer in an effort to intercept her at dawn.

Unable to do so overnight, Captain Wyatt launched search planes at 7:00 am on January 31 along the *La Vallette*'s projected course track. The crippled destroyer was found

80 miles away, and the carriers changed course to close on her at 15 knots. With radio silence still in place, two more planes were sent up to make message drops to ships in the *La Vallette's* group to facilitate their control of the fighter coverage provided by the carriers. The two planes gave proper recognition signals, flying slowly along the ships' beam so the nervous ships could identify them more easily. The planes also lowered landing gear and flaps to further signal their lack of hostile intent; no matter. Each plane began a low, slow approach on a separate destroyer to drop the messages. Naturally, the destroyers' antiaircraft guns opened fire on both, damaging one and injuring the pilot. In the Solomons, no good deed goes unpunished. Not so politely rebuffed, both planes returned to the carriers, who had to come within the "Talk Between Ships" voice radio range to arrange the fighter coverage.[235]

Trying to avoid further punishment for the *Conway*, *Edwards*, *Sands*, and *Waller* after their good deeds in picking up the survivors of the *Chicago* and inching through the Coral Sea to protect the vulnerable *La Vallette*, Admiral Halsey had them leave the *La Vallette* formation and head to port to drop off the *Chicago's* survivors. The destroyer *Cummings* came from Admiral Lee's battleship group and the workhorse destroyer *O'Bannon* came from Admiral Ainsworth's force to guard the *La Vallette* and *Navajo* on their way to Espiritu Santo, where they all arrived on February 1.[236]

It was not a happy situation for anyone, this rather little-known action called the Battle of Rennell Island. The Japanese victory had ramifications out of proportion to its tactical importance. "The loss of the *Chicago* would have been a blow at any time, and just now we felt it with special severity," Admiral Halsey later wrote.[237]

However, Nimitz ordered that word of the cruiser's sinking be withheld from the public. He also vowed in a staff meeting, "If any man lets out the loss of the *Chicago*, I'll shoot him!"[238] Nimitz's report to King said the loss of *Chicago* was "especially regrettable because it might have been prevented."[239] Nimitz was probably watching his words, understanding Giffen's popularity with Admiral King – and perhaps that King would take care of the matter himself. Even so, Nimitz vented his anger on his staff. In his cover memo to Admiral Giffen's action report, Admiral Halsey took five type-written pages detailing every one of the numerous mistakes Giffen had made.[240] Nevertheless, he could not have done any better than the prominent Guadalcanal historian Richard Frank:

> A long list of errors supported this verdict, prominent among which was Giffen's obsession with keeping a rendezvous to the exclusion of other valid considerations and a very complete assortment of mismanagement of fighter direction, formations, maneuvers, and the escort carriers, together amounting to tactical ineptitude of the first order[.][241]

The Pacific War was already littered with instances of American tactical ineptitude of the first order. Admiral Giffen's was arguably the worst. Giffen was an experienced flag officer who had ample warning of what was coming. He chose to ignore it because it did not fit with what he had experienced on the other side of the world with a different enemy; he thought he knew better. "Rigidity of mental processes," indeed.

It was part of the unfairness of the politics behind the war that effective and popular Captain Hoover had his career ruined by a grudge held by Halsey's chief of staff, that Admiral Wright, who had done almost everything right and still lost his one and only battle was put on the beach, but that Admiral Giffen, whose arrogance and incompetence had got the *Chicago*'s crew's feet wet, would be back at sea in short order.

It was part of the unfairness of war that because of this one setback, there would be almost no Allied surface force standing between the Japanese and Guadalcanal.

Naval war histories usually involve relating the stories of the top brass, the submarines, the warships – aircraft carriers, battleships, cruisers, destroyers – and the men who serve thereon. Rare is the history that discusses the efforts of the oilers, the tenders, the minesweepers, the PT boats, the patrol boats, the corvettes, and other smaller units. Theirs is a thankless lot, but navies cannot function without them.

Since mid-December, four corvettes named after Maori birds – *Matai*, *Kiwi*, *Moa*, and *Tui* – had been operating out of Tulagi. They were the first members of the Royal New Zealand Navy. They mostly roamed around Ironbottom Sound listening for submarines.

This brought them into contact and sometimes conflict with those other permanent residents of Tulagi, the US Navy PT boats. One dark night veteran PT boat skipper Lieutenant (jg) Lester H. Gamble thought he saw a member of the Tokyo Express and launched a corresponding number of torpedoes at the unwanted guest – no hits, of course. Then he heard a very irritated voice growling over the radio, "Are you little bastards shooting at us?"

"Affirmative," responded Lieutenant Gamble, sheepishly.

The next day he met the mountain of a man behind the growl: Lieutenant Commander Gordon Bridson of the *Kiwi*. The two became fast friends.[242]

It was not long before New Zealand's so-called Birds got a plum assignment. The Japanese had begun using mole transportation – transporting food to their troops on Guadalcanal using submarines – again back in late December. American radio intelligence had been connecting the dots between the submarines and Guadalcanal, and predicted Japanese mole runs on the nights of January 26, 27, and 29. American intelligence was aware that most of the runs were to Kamimbo Bay, just west of Cape Esperance.[243]

While Admiral Giffen's force was disturbing a hornet's nest the night of January 29, 1943, the *Kiwi* and her sister *Moa* patrolled off Kamimbo in the midst of one of those squalls that tend to pop up in the evening in these parts. At 9:05 pm, the *Kiwi*'s Asdic officer Sub-Lieutenant D.H. Graham reported a contact 3,000 yards away, the maximum range. The *Moa* could not confirm the contact, but Lieutenant Commander Bridson was certain. The *Kiwi* went charging in.

The contact was the Japanese submarine *I-1*, under the command of Lieutenant Commander Sakamoto Eichi. The submarine had surfaced in the squall, her decks awash to facilitate the transfer ashore of her cargo: rubber containers containing two-day rations for 3,000 men. She was headed into the bay, much of her crew topside preparing the barges to carry the cargo, when one of the aft lookouts shouted a warning of two torpedo boats. Sakamoto ordered a hard turn to port to gain room and crash-dive to 100 feet, rigging for silent running.

The previous day the 6th Fleet had warned the 7th Submarine Division of enemy torpedo boats off Kamimbo. They suggested unloading the supplies only after sundown, which is exactly what Lieutenant Commander Sakamoto had done. And still he had surfaced in the crosshairs of two of the reported torpedo boats. Sakamoto could only hope to survive long enough to inform 6th Fleet of the efficacy of their advice.

The *Kiwi* continued dashing in. Lieutenant Commander Bridson's initiative was rewarded with a glowing silhouette of a submarine, thanks to the helpful bioluminescent *Noctiluca scintillans.* The *Kiwi* dropped a string of six depth charges.

The first depth charging had badly shaken the *I-1*, which sprung a leak in the aft provision room. But it was a second pattern of depth charges that truly punished the submarine. The pumps, steering engine, and port propeller shaft were all disabled. The high-pressure manifold cracked, spraying water across the control room and causing a short circuit in the main switchboard that knocked out all the lights. A second leak appeared, this one major, in the forward torpedo room.

Worst of all, the cargo had shifted during the attack, causing the *I-1*'s bow to aim downward at a 45-degree angle. The submarine nosedived all the way down to 590 feet, almost three times the submarine's rated depth of 210 feet. In desperation, Sakamoto ordered the forward main ballast tanks blown and full reverse on the remaining shaft. Blowing main ballast is a move normally used only in emergencies because it causes the submarine to ascend almost uncontrollably. This was an emergency.

The submarine's uncontrolled descent was halted and she started heading toward the surface, but yet another problem developed: seawater had flooded the cracked batteries, releasing deadly chlorine gas. The problems were piling up to unmanageable proportions. And they were about to get much, much worse.

Around 10:00 pm, the battered *I-1* burst through the surface of Ironbottom Sound, down by the bow. Now they could at least air out the submarine, but as the sailors came topside, they saw their tormentor 2,000 yards away. And their tormentor saw them, off her starboard beam.

That was it; *I-1* was finished. Lieutenant Commander Sakamoto ordered the submarine to head to the Guadalcanal shore at 11 knots on the one remaining operational propeller shaft. He was going to run her aground to deny her use to the enemy and have his crew run into the jungle to join the starving Imperial Japanese Army troops.

---

* The wakes of ships in the South Pacific will often glow. This luminescence is caused by the propellers disturbing the *Noctiluca scintillans*, a microorganism indigenous to South Pacific waters. The bioluminescence earned the species the nickname "Sea Sparkle."

But the *I-1* would have to fight just to make it to shore. The *Kiwi*'s Acting Leading Signalman Campbell Howard Buchanan turned his 10-inch signal lamp into a searchlight and pinned the *I-1*. Lieutenant Commander Bridson was ready for a fight. Behind the *Kiwi*, the *Moa* was shooting up starshells to illuminate the submarine. But there was a slight problem.

While this particular scuffle looked like a two-to-one matchup in favor of the New Zealanders, in actuality, it was the reverse. The *I-1* was one-and-a-half times bigger than the *Kiwi* and *Moa* combined. Undamaged, the I-boat could outrun them by about 5 knots. The *I-1*'s 5.5-inch deck gun outranged and outgunned the corvettes' 4-inch guns; the *I-1* still had her torpedoes as well. While submarines were unarmored, the plating of the *I-1* could withstand the gunfire of the corvettes. And Lieutenant Commander Sakamoto was trying to use those advantages, ordering that big deck gun and the 13.2mm machine gun on the conning tower manned. On the bridge, Sakamoto took the helm personally.

But Lieutenant Commander Bridson had a solution to the comparative disadvantages: ram her.

The *Kiwi* skipper ordered full speed. The engineering officer was incredulous. "Why?" he asked. "Shut up!" Bridson snarled. "There's a weekend's leave in Auckland dead ahead of us!"[244]

Now the little *Kiwi* charged at the crippled submarine with the ferocity of a Spanish bull. She roared with her 4-inch gun and her 20mm Oerlikons. Like a wounded animal, the *I-1* lashed back with her 5-inch gun, firing two shots. To the *Kiwi*'s crew, the Japanese shells sounded "like an express train going through." But the submarine's forward deck gun was partially obstructed by the conning tower and could not quite find the range.

Yet the *Kiwi* could – and quickly did. At point-blank range, her gunners sent a hailstorm of hot metal at the startled submarine. The submarine's machine gun was disabled. Most of the bridge crew and gunners were killed. Lieutenant Commander Sakamoto himself was mortally wounded and let the wheel slip from his weakening grip. The *I-1* started to drift to starboard, and the *Kiwi* adjusted her course to compensate.

Wondering why the *I-1* was now lazily turning to starboard, the submarine's navigator Lieutenant (jg) Sakai Toshimi stepped onto the bridge and found everyone either dead or crippled. He raced back below, shouting a word rarely heard in modern navies: "Swords! Swords!"[245]

Lieutenant Sakai's word was a major shock to the men below. What was going on up there? The officers got out their swords. The torpedo officer Lieutenant Koreda Sadayoshi appeared on the bridge to assume command. To him, it looked like the New Zealanders were trying to capture his boat. Koreda preferred to avoid that. The reserve gun crew was sent up, and four Arisaka Type 38 carbines carried aboard were passed out to the best shooters in the remaining crew.

Just then the *Kiwi*'s bow plowed into the *I-1*'s hull in the rear part of the conning tower. Startled crewmen were knocked overboard. The submarine's gunners attempted to train the

5.5-inch gun on their attacker, but were blocked by the conning tower. Nevertheless, the *I-1*'s gunners claimed one of the attackers was "set afire." Also set afire was the *daihatsu* barge on the submarine's afterdeck, by the corvette's guns. The corvette backed off, its 4-inch gun hammering away. It was apparently at this time that the beleaguered submarine deployed its secret weapon: the navigator Lieutenant Sakai, a Kendo 3rd *dan* (upper level) swordsman, made his reappearance on the *I-1*'s deck – with his katana.

Lieutenant Commander Bridson ordered ramming speed again. Guns blazing, profanity flying, the *Kiwi* charged back in, but the submarine had started moving and the corvette was only able to get a glancing blow near the bow, which nevertheless crushed one of the *I-1*'s foreplanes. Bridson roared, "That'll be a *week*'s leave!"[246] Machine-gun fire mortally wounded Acting Leading Signalman Buchanan, but despite the pain and bleeding, he maintained the signal lamp's lock on the *I-1*. The *Kiwi* retaliated by picking off an officer on the bridge with a 20mm Oerlikon.

Holding his katana high, Lieutenant Sakai charged at the *Kiwi*, attempting to jump onto her deck. The *Kiwi* had started backing off, though, and Sakai was only able to grab onto the upper deck rail. As the corvette continued backing, Sakai lost his grip and plopped into the water. It was somewhat anticlimactic.

Lieutenant Commander Bridson ordered ramming speed again, bellowing, "Once more for a *fortnight*!"[247] Guns blazing, profanity flying, the *Kiwi* charged one more time, now plowing into the *I-1*'s starboard side and knocking out all but one of her main ballast tanks. The corvette ran all the way up onto the *I-1*'s afterdeck, making hash of the remnants of the barge and damaging her own bow and Asdic gear in the process.

As the *Kiwi* pulled off, oil gushed from the battered *I-1*, covering the *Kiwi*'s forecastle, and the submarine took an increasing list to starboard. But as damaged as the *Kiwi* was, what forced her to pull back was her guns overheating, rendering them unable to fire. No matter; the *Moa* was standing by, her skipper Lieutenant Commander Peter Phipps eager to get his ship's shots in at the submarine. The *Moa* pinned the *I-1* with her own searchlight and opened fire. She didn't do much damage, and the splashes from her near misses actually put out the fire on the *I-1*'s afterdeck.

But the *I-1* was finished. She was too badly damaged to outrun the little corvettes and she obviously could not dive. The best Lieutenant Koreda could hope for was to run aground on Guadalcanal. And, ultimately, he could not even manage that. At 11:20 pm, bathed in the glare of the *Moa*'s searchlight, the submarine ran hard aground on Fish Reef, about 330 yards north of Kamimbo. The starboard list was increasing, and the submarine was rapidly settling by the stern. Lieutenant Koreda ordered the hulk abandoned and the *I-1* sank. The submarine's bow, resting on Fish Reef, projected 15 feet out of the water at an angle of 45 degrees. The *Kiwi* and *Moa* guarded the wreck until morning.

As incredible and bizarre as this exchange was, what happened next put even that to shame. Lieutenant Koreda was the senior officer of the 66 *I-1* survivors who reached shore and joined the Imperial Japanese Army troops; 27 sailors were killed or missing; two were captured. As he left the boat and headed ashore, Koreda took some secret materials with him, including code material. What he did with them is open to question – and interpretation.

Lieutenant Koreda later said he burned the materials. Under this version of events, the submarine's chief paymaster retrieved the current code books from the wreck; the books were then immediately destroyed on the beach.[248]

To confuse matters, Lieutenant Koreda apparently told others he had actually buried the documents.[249] *The Operational History of Japanese Naval Communications, December 1941–1945*, which was written after the war by former Japanese officers of the General Staff and the War Ministry at the direction of the Allies, says of the top secret documents:

> The responsible persons evacuated some of the military top secret documents from the craft and buried them in the coastal sands of enemy territory where there was every fear of their being dug out plus the fact that water-soluble ink had been used for only a few of these documents. The loss comprised (sic; should be "compromised") many code books for future use in addition to those in current use, totalling (sic) about 200,000 copies. This fact was reported about a month after the "accident" when the crew involved returned to Rabaul. Although the Submarine Squadron Command issued orders to dig them out and destroy them immediately, one or two of the numerous places where the documents were buried could not be located.[250]

Rabaul was actually informed on the morning of January 30 of the sinking of the *I-1* by message from the survivors at Kamimbo.[251] Both Rabaul and the 6th Fleet had to be flabbergasted by the news from Lieutenant Koreda. Koreda had been the torpedo officer, not the skipper, of *I-1*, so he may not have been fully trained in the handling of classified documents. But this episode suggests Koreda was not exactly flag-rank material.

Whether it was the current code or not – and the likelihood is that the current code book was indeed destroyed on the beach – on February 1, 63 survivors from *I-1* arrived in Rabaul where a liaison officer of the Naval General Staff's 10th Section, who had come in from Truk, was waiting for them. After questioning these survivors, the officer concluded that the entirety of the code material involved, which was the purview of the 10th Section, was in danger.[252] It was. The *Moa* had already examined the wreck and recovered the probable log of *I-1* and some charts.[253] Lieutenant Koreda was ordered to recover the classified materials and destroy them immediately.

This incident had already crossed from the unusual to the surreal. Now it crossed into the comedic. On February 2, a little after 7:00 pm, Lieutenant Koreda and two junior officers from the *I-1*, and 11 destroyermen not from the *I-1* returned to the wreck. They rigged two depth charges and four small explosive charges to the bow and lower hull. Koreda's hope was to detonate the remaining torpedoes in the submarine, thereby obliterating everything inside the wreck and probably the wreck itself. The charges exploded; naturally, the torpedoes did not. On February 7, Koreda was taken to Rabaul, where he reported his failure to destroy the *I-1*.[254]

The Japanese had other options, however. On February 10, the 582 Air Group, operating out of Buin, sent nine Val dive bombers escorted by 28 Zeros to bomb the *I-1*. Only one bomber, that of Flight Petty Officer 2nd Class Suzuki Yoshitame, was able to even find it. Suzuki did succeed in hitting the submarine near the conning tower with a bomb. It still did not destroy the wreck.[255]

Maybe the third time would be the charm. The submarine *I-2*, skippered by Lieutenant Commander Inada Hiroshi, arrived off Kamimbo on the night of February 13. Lieutenant Koreda was aboard to help Inada locate the wreck of the *I-1* so the *I-2* could destroy it with torpedoes. But they could not find the wreck. Inada reported in that they would try again on the night of February 15. But the Allies deciphered the message and had PT boats waiting for the *I-2*.[256] Now the submarine not only could not find the *I-1*, but she had to avoid depth charges, too. She kept looking, but the appearance of a subhunting aircraft after 11:20 am convinced Inada to break off and head back to Shortland.[257] The Japanese gave up trying to destroy the submarine.

It was too late in any case. The US Navy had been salvaging documents from the wreck, using the submarine rescue vessel USS *Ortolan*. Her divers recovered five code books, a list of call signs for ships and stations that dated from 1942. The documents were taken to Lunga, where they were carefully dried out before they were shipped to Pearl Harbor. It was a treasure trove of information for the Pacific Fleet's radio unit.

By the time the documents arrived at Pearl Harbor, however, they were already out of date. The 10th Section rightly concluded that their codes had been compromised and immediately issued new code books. A new additive table was also issued for the wartime code. New coding procedures were instituted as well. But these new measures were already compromised by the *I-1* documents, which gave clues as to how the Japanese structured their code. Worse for the Japanese, they did not revise their strategic code book. Arrogant, overconfident, sloppy – as they had been for much of the early part of the war.

This time, it would cost them.

While Admiral Giffen was disturbing hornets' nests and Lieutenant Commander Bridson was trying to earn leave for his crew, Allied intelligence services were busy trying to determine what all this increased Japanese activity meant.

That very day, January 29, the Pacific Fleet intelligence summary noted that a Japanese offensive "impended," and speculated on whether carriers would be involved.[258] Immediately after the sinking of the *Chicago*, Admiral Nimitz issued an all-hands warning of an enemy offensive. The intelligence bulletin that day was the first to put a timeframe on the expected attack: between January 29 and February 12. Analysis of *Magic* intercepts allowed an estimate of the strength of Base Air Force: at and around Rabaul, 142 aircraft, including 49 twin-engine bombers and 17 dive bombers; and at Kahili, 49 to 69 aircraft, including 35 to 55 dive bombers. None of this included the Japanese Army Air Force elements on hand or *Kido Butai*.[259]

But they had to consider *Kido Butai*. *Magic* revealed that Admiral Kondo's 2nd Fleet had left Truk, heading for the Solomons. With him were two aircraft carriers, two battleships, and four heavy cruisers.[260]

The stage was set, with a Pacific Fleet intelligence summary released January 31:

A major action ... is expected soon. This will probably consist of an attempt similar to the one on November 13–15 where transports attempted to land at Guadalcanal covered by fleet units. Whether or not carriers will be [i]nvolved is unknown as yet. It is known that a detached group of carrier aircraft is operating in the Shortland area.

It predicted the Japanese offensive would begin on February 3 or 4 – in three or four days.[261]

But the Allies did not have three or four days. They didn't even have one.

CHAPTER 7

TURN AROUND AND ADVANCE

Today, when most people hear the word "Casablanca," they think of a black and white movie starring Humphrey Bogart, Ingrid Bergman, Paul Henreid, and a roundup of the usual suspects. It's the same old story, a fight for love and glory, but the love is doomed. There's an air of international intrigue, with the setting a nightclub and casino in North Africa, ostensibly under Vichy French suzerainty but actually controlled by Nazi Germany. It was released in late 1942 during the timeframe of this book.

Also during the timeframe of this book, Casablanca and most of Vichy French North Africa had fallen to Operation *Torch*, the Allied invasion of Vichy French North Africa and an offensive into the rear of the famous Afrika Korps. At this point in the story Field Marshal Erwin Rommel's troops were being driven into an enclave around Tunis.

With Casablanca cleared out of Axis troops, the international intrigue and mystery of the movie *Casablanca* was no longer possible in real life. But the international intrigue and mystery of a conference of Allied leaders at Casablanca would be not only possible, but probable, and with far higher stakes than anything arising out of the interplay of a bar owner, his lost love, a Czech Resistance leader, a corrupt Vichy cop, and a Gestapo agent.

A meeting of the "Big Three" Allied leaders – Roosevelt, Churchill, and Stalin – at Casablanca was set for mid-January, 1943. The big item on the agenda would be what to do after North Africa and Guadalcanal, because there was no agreement on a course of action between the Americans and the British, or even among the Americans themselves. A suspicious Stalin ultimately backed out of the conference, claiming he was still trying to hold off the German hordes.

Ultimately it was President Roosevelt and Prime Minister Churchill who met at Casablanca and, as the various forms of that old saying, often misattributed to Otto von

Bismarck, hold, "The making of laws, like the making of sausages, is not a pretty sight." No laws were made here, but the old saying held all the same. It certainly was not a pretty sight, but it did make for drama and intrigue.

Officially, the Casablanca Conference ran from January 14 to 23, 1943. Unofficially, it started much earlier. The US Joint Chiefs and their British counterparts were well aware of major differences in their views of how the war should be conducted. The Americans, though, had to hash out among themselves their own unified strategy to present to the British.

Using boxing as an analogy, Admiral King's philosophy was that the war had four phases:

(1) Defensive phase … a boxer covering up.

(2) Defensive-offensive phase … a boxer covering up while seeking an opening to counterpunch.

(3) Offensive-defensive phase … blocking punches with one hand while hitting with the other.

(4) Offensive phase … hitting with both hands.[1]

In King's view, the Pacific War was in Phase 3, even though the Pacific War was getting, in his estimation, only 15 percent of the resources the war against Nazi Germany was getting. He wanted at least twice that amount. He believed it would allow Admiral Nimitz to advance northward from the Solomons and westward from Hawaii, and to drive across the Central Pacific toward the Philippines, which was the chokepoint in the Japanese supply connection to their "Southern Resources Area" in the East Indies and Malaya. If the Philippines could be retaken, Japan would be cut off from the Southern Resources Area and could be blockaded into submission.[2]

That said, Admiral King was supportive of the main effort being against Nazi Germany, and would provide whatever naval forces were necessary for that effort, but he was agnostic as to where the next phase of that effort should take place.[3]

This was typical of the American position before Casablanca, as there, once again, was no agreement between Admiral King and Generals Marshall and Arnold about what should be done next or how. Marshall, and to a lesser extent Arnold, had softened the utter disinterest and even contempt for the Pacific War that they had felt before, say, March 1942. They ultimately managed to slap together a three-page position paper, revealing the individual special interests of King, Marshall, and Arnold, which had nothing in common:

What King wanted: an offensive in the Pacific;

What Marshall wanted: a cross-Channel invasion in 1943;

What Arnold wanted: a strategic air offensive against Germany.[4]

After that had been agreed upon, for want of a better description, and after King and Arnold had argued over who would land first on a stopover in Puerto Rico, the Americans and British went to Casablanca.

The British came knowing what they wanted and prepared to get it. They had anchored in the harbor a 6,000-ton cruise ship, serving as their staff headquarters and communications center, which contained a "technical mechanism for presenting every quantative [sic] calculation that might be called for."[5]

It started at the very first meeting of the Combined Chiefs of Staff at Casablanca between General Marshall, General Arnold, and Admiral King for the United States and their British counterparts, Field Marshal Sir Alan Brooke, Chief of the Imperial General Staff; Admiral of the Fleet Sir Dudley Pound, First Sea Lord; and Air Chief Marshal Sir Charles F.A. Portal, Chief of the Air Staff, assisted by Field Marshal Sir John Dill, Chief of the British Joint Staff Mission in Washington. For once, the Americans came in with a unified front. General Marshall warned that sufficient resources had to be directed to the Pacific to keep the pressure on Imperial Japan, and proposed that 70 percent of the resources go to the European and Atlantic theater and 30 percent to the Pacific and East Asia. King seconded that idea vigorously, complaining that only 15 percent of the resources had gone to the Pacific War, an insufficient percentage that, he believed, had crippled operations in the Solomons.[6] It was barely enough to hold the present line, in fact.[7] King reminded the British that operations in the Solomons and New Guinea were designed to protect Australia and its lines of communication. That task could not be considered complete until Rabaul, "the key to the situation," was taken.[8]

In perhaps oversimplified terms, the British position was:

Continue offensive operations in the Mediterranean;
Delay a cross-Channel invasion until 1944; and
Minimize the war in the Pacific.[9]

Field Marshal Dill, who seems to have been a fountain of wisdom in a sea of craziness, believed Admiral King was the key to the negotiations. Dill had reported that the Americans, especially King, suspected that the British had little interest in or understanding of the war in the Pacific, and were suspicious that once Germany was defeated, the British would not fight Japan with any great enthusiasm and might even bail on the Pacific War altogether.[10] Indeed, this was King's fear.[11]

Admiral King's attitude was crucial, Dill believed, because King controlled most of the scarce Allied landing craft, without which no eventual amphibious operation could succeed. If King felt that they were critically needed in the Pacific, he might not send them to Europe. Moreover, he would never allow landing craft to remain idle in Europe if they were being detained for indefinite future operations. The British, warned Dill, would have to respect King's views. Additionally, since the Americans produced and controlled an ever larger share of the resources, so the Americans would understandably demand a proportionately greater voice in Allied strategy. Churchill shared this view, and cautioned the British chiefs to let the Americans have their say.[12]

They did. And, like making sausage, it was not pretty. The British, mostly led by Field Marshal Brooke, were adamant that the most effective way of winning the war in the shortest time possible was to concentrate everything on defeating Nazi Germany and then to devote all possible resources against Japan. Fight one enemy at a time.[13]

But General Marshall and Admiral King were just as adamant that proposed Pacific operations would not interfere with plans for the buildup in Europe or for Mediterranean operations. King stressed that the United States had often been close to the brink of disaster in the Pacific. It was not the intention of the United States to plan beyond gaining positions for the final offensive against Japan. Nevertheless, in the meantime, steps must be taken to weaken Japan.[14]

The Americans went so far as to use Pacific operations as a counterbalance to the Mediterranean operations. The Pacific and Mediterranean were analogous inasmuch as the British considered the Pacific as the theater that threatened to drain resources away from the area of primary interest, while the Americans considered the draining theater to be the Mediterranean. General Marshall was well aware of this and deliberately linked the two when he warned the British that the threat of "another Bataan" in the Pacific "would necessitate the United States regretfully withdrawing from the commitments in the European theater." It was a chilling way of serving notice on the British that proposals for further offensives in the Mediterranean would be met with similar proposals for the Pacific.

But not nearly as chilling as Admiral King finally vocalizing his suspicions that once Germany was defeated, the British would bail on the Pacific War. As the British delegation reiterated its position over and over again that until Germany was defeated the Allies should limit themselves in the Pacific to the defense of a fixed line in front of those positions that must be held, an exasperated King finally asked who would have the principal burden of defeating Japan once Germany had been knocked out of the war?[15]

It was just this suspicion, that one ally was shirking its commitments, that had wrecked many a previous wartime alliance. Field Marshal Brooke and Air Chief Marshal Portal were so taken aback that they tried to assure King of Britain's commitment to defeat Japan. But just the question and its implications were so disturbing that Churchill himself had to interject several days later. "I wish to make it clear," said Churchill, "that if and when Hitler breaks down, all of the British resources and effort will be turned toward the defeat of Japan. Not only are British interests involved, but her honor as well." Churchill even offered to enter into a formal treaty if Roosevelt thought it necessary.[16] The word of a great English gentleman, Roosevelt assured him, was enough for the American people.[17] The point had been made.

It was all frustrating and indeed perplexing for Field Marshal Brooke. He worried that nothing the British could ever say would have "much effect in weaning King away from the Pacific." The war in Europe was "just a nuisance that kept him from waging his Pacific War undisturbed." He despairingly told Field Marshal Dill, "It is no use, we shall never get agreement with them."

"You have already got agreement on most of the points," Dill responded. "It only remains to settle the rest."

"I won't budge an inch," Brooke vowed.

Dill smiled reassuringly. "Of course you will. You know you have to reach an agreement or else put the whole thing up to the Prime Minister and the President. And you know as well as I do the mess that they would make of it."[18]

The hard line taken by Field Marshal Brooke and the British chiefs is understandable. Nazi Germany was an existential threat to Great Britain. Its bombing raids against Britain were nightly. It had used and was continuing to use its Kriegsmarine, especially the U-boat arm, to strangle Britain by attacking the supply convoys it needed to survive. And until Hitler invaded the Soviet Union, Britain had stood alone. While the Soviet Union shared a common enemy with Britain, until the Japanese had attacked Pearl Harbor, Britain had had no real allies against Hitler.

But while Pearl Harbor had brought the US into the war, it came with a caveat that members of the British delegation, with the exception of Field Marshal Dill and probably Churchill, did not understand. Imperial Japan had attacked the US; Nazi Germany had not.

In this time period before the true extent of the Final Solution and Nazi war crimes and crimes against humanity was fully understood, to a good portion of the American people, Japan was the greater evil. After all, Nazi Germany had declared war on the US, but Imperial Japan had attacked Pearl Harbor before a declaration of war, before even breaking off negotiations.

What came out of Casablanca was this:

Memorandum by the Combined Chiefs of Staff

[Casablanca,] January 19, 1943.

Conduct of the War in 1943

The Combined Chiefs of Staff have agreed to submit the following recommendations for the conduct of the war in 1943.

1. Security:

The defeat of the U-boat must remain a first charge on the resources of the United Nations.

2. Assistance to Russia:

The Soviet forces must be sustained by the greatest volume of supplies that can be transported to Russia without prohibitive cost in shipping.

3. Operations in the European Theater:

Operations in the European Theater will be conducted with the object of defeating Germany in 1943 with the maximum forces that can be brought to bear upon her by the United Nations.

4. The main lines of offensive action will be:

In the Mediterranean:

(a) The occupation of Sicily with the object of:

(1) Making the Mediterranean line of communications more secure.

(2) Diverting German pressure from the Russian front.

(3) Intensifying the pressure on Italy.

(b) To create a situation in which Turkey can be enlisted as an active ally.

In the U.K.:

(c) The heaviest possible bomber offensive against the German war effort.

(d) Such limited offensive operations as may be practicable with the amphibious forces available.

(e) The assembly of the strongest possible force (subject to (a) and (b) above and paragraph 6 below) in constant readiness to reenter the Continent as soon as German resistance is weakened to the required extent.

5. In order to insure that these operations and preparations are not prejudiced by the necessity to divert forces to retrieve an adverse situation elsewhere, adequate forces shall be allocated to the Pacific and Far Eastern Theaters.

6. *Operations in the Pacific and Far East:*

(a) Operations in these theaters shall continue with the forces allocated, with the object of maintaining pressure on Japan, retaining the initiative and attaining a position of readiness for the full scale offensive against Japan by the United Nations as soon as Germany is defeated.

(b) These operations must be kept within such limits as will not, in the opinion of the Combined Chiefs of Staff, jeopardize the capacity of the United Nations to take advantage of any favorable opportunity that may present itself for the decisive defeat of Germany in 1943.

(c) Subject to the above reservation, plans and preparations shall be made for:

(1) The recapture of Burma ([Operation:] Anakim) beginning in 1943.

(2) Operations, after the capture of Rabaul, against the Marshalls and Carolines if time and resources allow without prejudice to Anakim.[19]

It was not the mess that Field Marshal Dill had feared would result once Roosevelt and Churchill got involved. Both the President and the Prime Minister accepted it almost without question. Churchill went so far as to declare, "There never has been, in all of the interallied conferences I have known, anything like the prolonged professional examination of the whole scene of the world war in its military, its armament production and its economic aspects."[20]

Yet it was a document full of vague undefined terms. The vague undefined terms merely papered over cracks in the alliance. But in the short term, the Casablanca agreement had ratified offensive operations in New Guinea and the Solomons.

The American positions west of Henderson Field had mostly stayed the same since November. General Patch's effort to take Mount Austen was intended to clear the southern flank so the drive westward could resume. The American Division's 132nd Regiment had gotten chewed up in the Gifu meatgrinder on Mount Austen and weakened by malaria and other tropical diseases, as had pretty much every unit that had ever set foot on Guadalcanal. It had exhausted itself, but had taken enough of the mountain to remove the irritating Japanese lookout post and at least secure enough of the southern flank for the westward drive to resume.

Then-Lieutenant Colonel Samuel B. Griffith of the 1st Marine Raider Battalion, which had fought earlier in the Guadalcanal campaign and been withdrawn after such engagements as the landing at Tulagi and its satellite islands, Tasimboko, and Edson's Ridge, opined, "As the thoroughly butchered Mount Austen operation dragged on into January, it became apparent that both Major General Patch and his assistant Division commander [Brigadier General Edmund Sebree] had much to unlearn, and perhaps even more to learn."[21]

General Patch and his troops were indeed learning, however – the hard way, certainly, but learning nonetheless. He had ordered the 132nd to go to the defensive while reinforcements arrived. Those reinforcements had started on December 17, 1942, when the 35th Infantry Regiment arrived. On New Year's Day, the 27th Infantry Regiment stepped off at Lunga, and three days later the 161st Infantry Regiment made its appearance. These three regiments were from the US Army's 25th Infantry Division under Major General J. Lawton Collins.[22]

Quiet, calm, intelligent, General Collins was a character, something like the American equivalent to Rommel. Admiral Halsey had been impressed with him. The 25th Infantry had originally been intended for General MacArthur's forces, but Admiral Nimitz pulled Collins aside to warn him it might be sent to Guadalcanal instead. Sure enough, the Joint Chiefs agreed on November 30 to send the 25th to Halsey's South Pacific Command instead of to MacArthur's command. When Collins reached Nouméa, Halsey invited him to dinner. Also there was General Vandegrift, on a stopover on his trip to Australia to arrange some rest for his 1st Marine Division. Vandegrift described conditions on Guadalcanal for Collins.[23]

When asked about going to Guadalcanal, General Collins said his 25th was "The finest regular division in the Army ... Give me three weeks to unload my transports and combat-load them, and I'll be ready to go anywhere ..." Collins paused, a bit puzzled. Admiral Halsey was laughing.

"Why, what are you laughing at?"

Halsey answered, "Your division is leaving for Guadalcanal tomorrow!"[24]

That was close enough for General Collins. Also entering the scene on January 4 when the 25th Infantry Division completed its arrival was the 6th Marine Regiment and the division headquarters of the 2nd Marine Division commanded by Brigadier General Alphonse De Carre, the assistant division commander.[25] They joined the 2nd and 8th Marine Regiments already on Guadalcanal. Upon their arrival, General Patch turned command of the American Division over to General Sebree, while Patch would command all US ground forces on Guadalcanal under XIV Corps, now with more than 40,000 troops.[26]

It was time to take the offensive and finish off the Japanese on Guadalcanal. General Patch's plan had the 25th Infantry Division finish clearing Mount Austen and various ridges along the upper Matanikau River, while the 2nd Marine Division would push along the coast from the lower Matanikau line westward. The exhausted Americal Division and the independent 147th Infantry Regiment would guard the Lunga perimeter.[27]

It was hardly a perfect plan, in part because of a lack of information about the Japanese strength and dispositions. The 25th Infantry Division's intelligence officer described General Patch's information as "sketchy." In truth, the intelligence information behind the plan consisted almost entirely of overhead photographs of the terrain, which was indeed "sketchy" but perhaps the best they could do at the time.[28]

General Collins' 25th Infantry Division drew the more difficult end of the offensive. Once they had relieved the Americal Division's 132nd Infantry Regiment on Mount Austen, they still had to deal with the frustrating Gifu. But there was far more than Gifu. To the northwest of Gifu was a series of ridges and hills that, when viewed on a map with north at the bottom, appears to be in the shape of a sea horse and was thus christened accordingly. Further northwest of that was another series of ridges and hills that, if you look at it on a map with north at the bottom and squint just the right way, appears to be in the shape of a galloping horse and was thus called the "Galloping Horse." The 35th Infantry was assigned to clear Gifu and the rest of Mount Austen, and capture the Sea Horse. The 27th Infantry was to move on the Galloping Horse from the north and capture it, where it would link with the 35th at the horse's head. Collins' hope was to create "three great pockets … [that] could be reduced more or less at leisure." It was probably not a good idea to use the word "leisure" in connection with anything on Guadalcanal. The 161st, a Washington State National Guard unit, was to be kept in reserve.[29]

The offensive was to start on January 10, 1943. It did, with an artillery bombardment and air attacks by the Cactus Air Force, which had little effect. As they had done to the 132nd, Colonel Oka's 40-some hidden Nambu machine guns in Gifu stopped the 35th cold. They stopped the 35th cold again on January 11. And yet again on January 12.[30]

Fortunately for the Americans, operations on the Sea Horse went a little better. Two battalions of the 35th went on a march around Mount Austen to strike at the Sea Horse from the south. Riding the Sea Horse were the 1st and 3rd Battalions of the Imperial Japanese Army's 124th Regiment, as well as Colonel Oka's headquarters. The Japanese plan for the defense was "simply for each unit to stand unflinchingly at its post."[31] This at least saves a lot of time and effort in planning a tactical defense, time that can be used for other efforts, like seemingly trying to forget that you are starving or figuring out how to shoot your rifle with no ammunition. The Japanese even planned to allow the Americans to infiltrate their positions, at which point the American and Japanese troops would become intermingled, thus preventing the American use of artillery and air attacks.

Combined with night infiltrations of their own to keep the Americans off balance, the intention seems to have been to simply hold out long enough for reinforcements to arrive. As Guadalcanal historian Richard Frank put it, "what passed for a defensive scheme appears to be an attempt to formalize sheer desperation."[32] But when you refuse to retreat, don't even have a word for retreat, and you're out of ammunition and food, what else can you do?

In any event, the attack by the 35th was almost stillborn. While trying to cross a branch of the Matanikau, the 35th was spotted by Japanese troops from Colonel Oka's command post, who quickly attacked the divided units, driving off the infantry and threatening to drive into the unit's flank. Although ordered to withdraw, Sergeant William G. Fournier and Technician 5th Grade Lewis Hall manned an unattended machine gun posted on a knoll and opened fire on the Japanese, who were then in the low stream bottom in front of and below them. As the gun on the knoll could not be depressed enough to bear on the Japanese, Fournier lifted it by its tripod to depress the muzzle sufficiently while Hall operated the trigger. Both soldiers stayed at the knoll in this very compromising physical position, pouring fire at the Japanese, and finally breaking the best chance the Japanese had to prevent their being knocked off the Sea Horse. Both Fournier and Hall were fatally wounded, and were posthumously awarded the Medal of Honor for their heroism in saving their comrades and the offensive.[33] By sundown on January 11, the Sea Horse was in the hands of the 35th. By capturing the Sea Horse, the 35th had thus cut off Gifu from the west, its last connection with Japanese units west of the Matanikau.

Next was the Galloping Horse. In the words of the eminent Guadalcanal historian Richard Frank, "The plan of the 27th Infantry to take the Galloping Horse resembled an assault by ants – crawling upward from the hooves of the front and rear legs to the head."[34] The subjects of this rather horrifying image were 600 Imperial Japanese Army troops from the 3rd Battalion, 228th Infantry Regiment under Major Nishiyama Haruka.

The key to the Japanese defense was a hill on the horse's neck, where the 27th was supposed to meet the 35th, which was defended with mortars and multiple machine guns. The men of the 27th, who had not received enough water and were suffering from heat-related illnesses, couldn't even determine from where the fire was originating. Captain Charles W. Davis, the 2nd Battalion's executive officer, went with Captain Paul K. Mellichamp and Lieutenant Weldon Sims to crawl down the east side of the ridge behind a waist-high shelf to try to locate the Japanese position. When Lieutenant Sims poked above the shelf to see the enemy position, a Japanese machine gunner shot him fatally through the chest.[35] They had located the Japanese strongpoint, not that it did Lieutenant Sims any good.

With the machine-gun and mortar fire from the Japanese position on the neck continuing to stymie efforts to take the Galloping Horse, Captain Davis and four men crawled close to the Japanese position in the hopes of neutralizing it for a final assault on the neck. But nothing worked out like it had been planned – for anyone, really. Davis's crew had gotten to within 10 yards of the strongpoint when the Japanese spotted them and threw hand grenades. Their aim was devastating, their grenades less so, as they failed to explode. The Americans countered with eight grenades, which did explode. Then they stormed the Japanese position, led by Captain Davis, whose rifle jammed after one round. He tossed it aside, drew his pistol, and then he and his party finished of the remaining Japanese. Davis's actions inspired the men of the 27th, who, once their desperate thirst was quenched by a thunderstorm, stormed the neck. Major Nishiyama and his troops were driven into a nearby ravine where they were gradually reduced. Nishiyama and survivors broke out to the west on January 19. Davis was awarded the Medal of Honor.[36] Lieutenant Sims, whose death made the success of the mission possible, didn't receive any posthumous medals, but the ridge was named after him.

That left Gifu. It was cut off and completely surrounded, its troops starving, having eaten their last rations at some point between January 10 and 17; but it stubbornly continued to hold out. On January 15, an attack by the entire 2nd Battalion of the 35th gained only 100 yards and no points.[37] The commander of the 2nd was sacked, the second such sacking caused by a lack of progress on Gifu.

The stalemate was broken by a single tank, one of three M3 light tanks left over by the Marines for use by the Army. They were taken over by the 25th Infantry Division's Cavalry Reconnaissance Troop. Tanks and trees generally do not get along, tanks and forests even less so, and tanks and jungles really, really do not get along. And they did not here. Two of the tanks broke down.[38]

But the third M3, better known by its British nickname "Stuart," got all the way up a trail improvised for Jeeps into the perimeter of Gifu. Colonel Oka's web of hidden Nambu machine guns was devastating against infantry, but useless against tanks, and the Japanese had no antitank weapons of any kind. On January 22, supported by 16 infantrymen, the Stuart nibbled away at the northeast corner of Gifu. It first destroyed three bunkers using high-explosive 37mm shells, then used canister and machine guns on the Japanese infantry. Later that day it destroyed five more bunkers. The infantry moved into the 200-yard gap and moved on the remaining bunkers from behind.[39]

On around January 14, Colonel Oka, commanding the troops on Mount Austen, and his staff left the command post on the Matanikau in the Sea Horse and made their way to Japanese lines to the west. Some called Oka's actions desertion. Whatever the case, Oka ordered the last defenders of Gifu to infiltrate through the American lines to Japanese lines to the west. But Major Inagaki and his troops in Gifu refused to follow these orders and decided to stay at their posts and fight to the end rather than abandon their sick and wounded comrades in the bunkers.[40]

In the early hours of January 23, Major Inagaki led about 100 Imperial Army troops in a suicide charge on the American lines. It was easily shattered. The next morning, the US Army troops found 85 dead bodies, including those of Inagaki, eight captains, and 15 lieutenants. Gifu was finally broken.[41] It had taken more than a month.

That left the Japanese positions along the coast west of the Matanikau, mostly between Point Cruz and Kokumbona as they had been for most of the campaign. Now it was held by the remnants of the 2nd Sendai Division under General Maruyama plus one battalion, commanded by Major Hayakawa Kikuo from the 38th Nagoya Division. Well, "held" might be a strong word. They did hold a blocking position along the coast, but their strength was in maintaining enfilading fire positions south of the coast on hills and ridges and in ravines.

The Americans were prepared for such a defense, however. The 2nd Marine Division advanced with the 8th Marine Regiment moving along the coast and the 2nd Marine Regiment moving inland to try to neutralize the flanking fire positions. They were only partially successful, however, and on January 14, the 6th Marine Regiment took over for the 2nd. The offensive resumed the next day, and moving along the Japanese inland flank much faster than they had anticipated, the 6th drove back to the coast and cut off the Sendai Division's 14th and 16th Regiments. By 2:00 pm on January 17, both regiments had been eliminated, with two captured and 643 killed.

General Patch wanted to keep the pressure on. The 161st Regiment was added to the 27th on the Galloping Horse to make a push from there westward. Japanese resistance was lighter than had been anticipated, however – much lighter, in fact, nothing like the 132nd and 35th had seen at Gifu. By January 22, the Americans were in position to capture Kokumbona, the headquarters of the Imperial Japanese 17th Army under General Hyakutake. They managed to capture Kokumbona the next day, cutting off a few Japanese units, but again, resistance was uncharacteristically light. It was very strange.

General Patch did not know what was going on or what the Japanese were planning, but he had an idea of maybe how to stop it.

We do more before 9 am than most people do all day.

This used to be a recruiting slogan for the US Army. Not calculated to attract the night owls of the world, to be sure, but it was certainly honest if the first day of February 1943 is any indication.

Shortly after dawn, the destroyer-transport *Stringham* and six tank landing craft left the Lunga roadstead. They were carrying the US Army's 2nd Battalion, 132nd Infantry Regiment under the "eccentric" Lieutenant Colonel George and four 75mm pack howitzers of the 10th Marine Regiment. In a plan General Patch had been brewing since December, he was hoping to land them beyond Cape Esperance on a beach near Verahue in a position that would flank any possible reinforcement of General Hyakutake's army or block any retreat to the southwest coast of Guadalcanal where the Japanese could make a last stand. This could throw a wrench into whatever the Japanese were planning. The plan had originally been for this little force to leave at 2:00 am but there had been a delay, though it was still well before 9 am.

Escorted by the four destroyers of Captain Briscoe's Cactus Striking Force – *Fletcher*, *Radford*, *DeHaven*, and *Nicholas* – and covered by Wildcats of Marine Fighting 112, this little flotilla crawled along at 10 knots, the fastest the barges could go. The destroyers had to herd the landing craft like ranchers herding cattle. And when one of those steers got a little wayward and steered for the Russell Islands, Briscoe had the *Fletcher* herd it back into formation.[42]

But that long delay could be a problem. Foster Hailey, war correspondent for the *New York Times*, was aboard the *Nicholas* and had a bad feeling about the delay:

> The lateness of the start forfeited any element of surprise for the expedition, as we were clearly visible from the enemy held beach of Guadalcanal. They were undoubtedly in touch by radio with their air bases on the middle and upper Solomons and the fleet units that had been reported maneuvering south of Truk.[43]

Indeed, one Imperial Japanese Army Mitsubishi Ki-46 Type 100 Command Reconnaissance Aircraft had spotted the landing force and reported it to Rabaul. It had reported wrongly, apparently calling the destroyers "cruisers." "We'll probably get the hell bombed out of us," one of the talkers on the bridge of the *Nicholas* sighed.[44] Then again, they were guarded by that flight of Wildcats, who never saw the Dinah over the shore. The flotilla continued on.

Meanwhile, while the Army was at sea about to land, the Army was also in the air. A lone Army Air Force B-17 performing reconnaissance flew over the Shortlands and at 8:20 am reported 35 Japanese ships in the anchorage.[45] Less than a half-hour later an airstrike joined the scout. This was all still before 9 am.

Nine B-17s – six from the 72nd Bombardment Group and three from the 42nd – all under Major Narce Whitaker, formed the airstrike. They had an escort of four Warhawks of the 44th Fighter Squadron under Captain Albert Johnson and four Lightnings from the 339th under Captain John Mitchell. The bombers looked over the anchorage and its unusually large assemblage of ships, picking the targets they would attack from 15,000 feet.

Bombing from high altitude is more effective when the target is not moving. Five B-17s dropped 40 500lb bombs in the vicinity of what turned out to be the seaplane tender *Kamikawa Maru*, sitting at anchor. The *Kamikawa Maru* was struck on the bow by one bomb, which is one more than the B-17s usually got from high altitude. A bomb struck the freighter *Kanagawa Maru* and set her afire as well. Whitaker's Fortresses didn't stay to admire their handiwork. The heavy antiaircraft fire and a late intercept by Zeros of the 204 Air Group convinced Whitaker to hightail it out of the Shortlands, taking the fighters with him.

Major Earl Hall, commanding officer of the 42nd, was leading four of the B-17s. Hall apparently aborted his attack on Major Whitaker's target to go after the ships in the Tonolei Harbor area of the Shortlands. It required Hall's flight to stay over the Shortlands a little bit longer. Too long.

Major Hall's Fortresses dropped 32 500lb bombs, and believed they had gotten three hits on a transport. But the Japanese got a hit on them. As they started to head away from their target, an antiaircraft shell burst under the still-open bomb bay doors of Hall's wingman, Captain Frank Houx. With an open route into the fuselage, shrapnel tore into the auxiliary fuel tank, located in the bomb bay. Houx's B-17 just exploded.

It was a freak hit, but the abrupt disappearance of Captain Houx and his crew was apparently a major shock to Major Hall and his men. The plan was to join back up with Major Whitaker's flight in order to mass the Fortresses' defensive gunfire against any pursuing fighters. However, it seems that Hall decided to take the shortest route possible out of the Shortlands and its obviously dangerous flak before doing anything else. Unfortunately, while that route put the antiaircraft fire behind them, it also took them away from Whitaker's flight. Hall could catch up to it later – unless something caught up with him first.

And something did. Ace fighter pilot Lieutenant (jg) Morisaki Takeshi led 11 Zeros of the 204 Air Group in pursuing the fleeing Flying Fortresses. Not insurmountable odds, especially given the B-17's ruggedness and defensive armament. But Major Hall could mass the gunfire of only his three B-17s; he and his men would sorely miss the additional concentrated gunfire Major Whitaker's flight offered, because the odds didn't stay 11 on 3 for long.

Lieutenant Morisaki's 11 Zeros were soon joined by 17 Zeros from the 252 Air Group, five from the 253 Air Group, and 14 from the 582 Air Group.[46] Major Hall and his men could only have watched in horror, as 47 Japanese Zeros, all square-winged A6M3 Model 32s, were now buzzing around the three Flying Fortresses. It descended beyond nightmares into the nonsensical. 47 to 3? At what point does the Rule of Diminishing Returns kick in so the Japanese simply have too many Zeros?[47]

It was indeed ludicrous, but it was even more lethal. The Zeros swirled around the bombers like a hurricane, making coordinated shooting passes to try to divide the defensive gunfire. The .50-cal gunners of Major Hall's flight apparently managed to shoot down four Zeros. The Fortresses kept their defensive formation while redlining their engines trying to escape. The terror of the antiaircraft gunfire over the Shortlands and its fatal effect on Captain Houx and his crew was now merely disconcerting compared with the horror of the horde of Zeros now after them.

In desperation, Major Harold Hensley broke formation and turned his Flying Fortress to make for Major Whitaker's flight. Hensley had barely left before his B-17 was mauled by Mitsubishis and, last anyone heard, left to ditch in The Slot. Major Hall led his lone remaining wingman Captain Jay Thomas in a race against death across Choiseul. Death nipped at one of Hall's engines, leaving it smoking. Hall and his crew were able to nurse it for a while, but the Zeros clawed at the faltering Fortress, making runs at the weak spot in the bomber's nose, pecking and pecking and pulling it back until, last anyone saw, it drifted downward off Ringana Point.

That left Captain Thomas' B-17. He had his Fortress hit the deck, diving from 13,000 to 1,200 feet, trying to eliminate at least one dimension of the Zeros' attacks. Thomas was flying on borrowed time, and he knew it. His co-pilot was wounded by 20mm shrapnel. His bombardier and waist gunner were seriously wounded. The tail gun, top turret, and ball turret were shattered. The other defensive guns were out of ammunition. The shorter-range Model 32 Zeros had to pour on the speed to engage the Flying Fortresses, forcing some to head back because of dwindling fuel. But some very persistent pilots pursued Thomas' Flying Fortress as it roared on at 250 knots, now unable to fire back. Finally, after 55 minutes of Hell, during the last 20 of which the bomber's guns were silent, the last Zeros broke off and headed back to Buin.

But they left a badly broken B-17 and crew, with everyone except the commander and pilot wounded, and with Engines 1 and 2 damaged, running at one-third their normal thrust. Captain Thomas and his wounded co-pilot had to wedge their knees against the control yokes to keep them forward while they used their hands to try to offset the torque created by the damaged engines and keep the plane level. "[T]his is how the flying sieve reached Guadalcanal," said one pair of historians. Against all odds they had made it back: "After manually cranking down the landing gear and flaps, a near-perfect landing was made on Henderson Field even though both tires were flat."[48] So 47 Zeros had taken on three B-17s and still could not shoot all of them down. That's why the B-17 is called a "Flying Fortress." It was now after 9 am. By non-Army standards, the day had just begun.

It was unusual for Base Air Force to mount so many Zeros in air defense, even over their main bases at Rabaul and the Shortlands. But they were clearly jumpy this day. At 9:50, the same reconnaissance Flying Fortress was chased away from the anchorage by perhaps six Zeros of the 253 Air Group and was thus not able to deliver follow-up reports. But they could afford to be jumpy, afford to be extravagant in their use of Zeros. Base Air Force did not have the job of bombing Guadalcanal today, not the airfields, at any rate. The Imperial Army's 6th Air Division did with its Kawasaki Ki-48 bombers.

The Japanese Army Air Force had acquired a few bad habits over the years it faced only the Chinese air force, such as it was, including a leisurely attack schedule. Richard Gallagher, intelligence analyst in the 7th Fighter Squadron, would later opine, "I personally think the Lily (Kawasaki Ki-48) has a record that has never been cited before. I now propose that the following should be put on record: 'The Lily bomber was the plane most destroyed or damaged on the ground, by enemy air action, in World War II in the Pacific Theater.'"[49]

The US Marines took advantage of that leisurely schedule by paying a breakfast visit to the Munda airfield, where the Imperial Army bombers were based. At 6:25 am, a dozen Dauntlesses from Marine Scout Bombing 233 and 234 took off from Henderson. They were later joined by four Avengers from Marine Scout Bombing 131 and a dozen Wildcats from Marine Observation 231 in making the trip up to Munda.[50]

The Japanese had coastwatchers of their own who gave warning of incoming air raids and ship movements, but on this day they failed and 16 Ki-48 bombers were caught lounging on the ground. So vulnerable and plentiful were targets that the Dauntlesses were falling all over each other to attack, literally – two Dauntlesses collided, causing one to crash. A second Dauntless was hit by flak and went down on the way back to Guadalcanal. A costly mission, but a successful one. Of the 16 Lily bombers at Munda, only six were operational after the Americans had left.[51]

On the way back, two of the Avengers saw tents and barges on one of the Russell Islands.[52] So the Japanese had occupied those islands. That was another ominous piece of information for General Patch, Admiral Nimitz, and Allied intelligence analysts. It looked like the Russells were going to be a staging area for the new Japanese offensive.

Despite having all of six Kawasaki bombers left, the 6th Air Division went ahead with its attack on Guadalcanal anyway, accompanied by 23 Nakajima Ki-43 fighters of the 11th Air Squadron. Again, this lopsided fighter-to-bomber ratio was typical of Japanese Army Air Force tactics.

As usual, Allied coastwatchers radioed Henderson Field of the incoming attack, but atmospheric interference prevented the message from getting through until 10:00 am. This was not early enough for fighters to reach altitude for interception. To make matters worse, the Japanese came in low over Ironbottom Sound and looped around Savo to come from the northwest. Henderson Field did not go to Condition Red, the warning that an attack was imminent, until the Kawasakis were already into their bombing runs. To top it off, a few Wildcats of Marine Fighting 112 were patrolling above, but were out of position.

Two divisions of Wildcats from Marine Observation 251 and Marine Fighting 112 scrambled, but were not able to engage the Lilys before they had completed their bombing runs. The Japanese claimed to have destroyed four "large aircraft" and four fighters on the ground, which was awfully productive for only six bombers in an opposed strike. The Marines said there had only been one hit on the Henderson Field runway.[53]

Marine Observation 251 was the only American air unit to tangle with the Japanese, hacking away at the Lilys as they raced toward the dubious safety of Munda. The Marines shot down two of the bombers and one of the Oscars. The Japanese bombers roared at 5,000 feet over Lieutenant Colonel George's convoy, just setting up to land at Nugu Point.[54]

"Oh, oh. What did I tell you?" the talker on the *Nicholas*'s bridge triumphantly declared as he dug out his helmet.[55]

One of the *Nicholas*'s bridge officers, Lieutenant Johnny Everett, disagreed with the talkative talker, identifying the "two-motored" aircraft as a Catalina. Skipper Lieutenant Commander Andrew J. Hill disagreed with Everett and ordered the *Nicholas* to open fire. Both forward 5-inch mounts started pounding away at the intruder. Everett kept shouting that it was an American plane, eventually getting Hill to cease fire, after a few rounds. But not the destroyer *Radford*, who unloaded her 5-inchers and machine guns at the aircraft.

Shell-bursts within 10 yards of the twin-engine aircraft sent it into a fatal dive into the drink. "My God, we've shot down one of our own planes," lamented Lieutenant Everett.

But everyone knew better when the *Nicholas* passed the wreckage. It was identified as a "Mitsubishi 01" – a Mitsubishi G4M Type 1 bomber, a Betty, which was the only bomber with which the *Nicholas* had had some experience. They didn't recognize it was really a Kawasaki Ki-43, a Lily.[56]

Over the voice radio, someone on the *Radford* yelled, "We got him! We got him!"

This prompted an indignant reaction on the *Nicholas*. Lieutenant Commander Hill coldly walked to the microphone and spoke into it.

"We got that plane," Hill said with the air of a commander. "We were the first to open fire, and we claim him as ours."

"We opened first," the *Radford* countered.

"Knock off the chatter," ordered Captain Briscoe.[57]

The argument would continue as a barrage from both the *Nicholas* and the *Radford* left a second bomber "smoking and wobbling," but it stayed aloft.[58] Then "a whole flock of Zero fighters [...] passed astern" but since they were "flying high and fast" the destroyers did not open fire. The Zeros were actually the Ki-43 Oscars.[59]

The little convoy went back to its work. Captain Briscoe had the *Radford* stop to check out the bomber's wreckage. The *Nicholas* concluded – correctly – that Briscoe was giving the *Radford* credit for the kill. The outrage on board the *Nicholas* rekindled. "You know what I think?" said a grinning young lookout on the fire control platform. "I think we ought to anchor alongside the *Radford* tonight and go over and talk this over with them, say about three hundred of us."[60] That physical debate with which the Japanese were so familiar was also present in the US Navy.

At around 11:30 am, the *Stringham* stopped at Nugu Point and began unloading troops and equipment. But a report of Japanese activity in the area convinced Lieutenant Colonel George to leave only a company at Nugu Point and drop everyone else off at Verahue, about 1.5 miles away. Perhaps anxious to separate the sniping *Nicholas* and *Radford*, Captain Briscoe had the *Fletcher* lead the *Radford* to escort this group to Verahue while ordering the *DeHaven* and *Nicholas* to remain around Nugu Point to guard the continued unloading of the landing craft. The *Stringham*, her work finished, set off all by herself.

At the same time the unloading at Nugu Point began, Admiral Hashimoto's "Reinforcement Unit" of 20 destroyers cleared the Shortlands and was heading down The Slot.[61] Hashimoto had arranged his destroyers in two sections, one for Cape Esperance and one for Kamimbo. Hashimoto himself would be in the *Makinami*.[62]

The Cape Esperance unit had the *Maikaze*, *Kawakaze*, *Suzukaze*, *Shirayuki*, and *Fumizuki* as the screen. They would guard transport destroyers from 10th Destroyer Division (*Kazegumo*, *Makigumo*, *Yugumo*, and *Akigumo*) and 17th Destroyer Division (*Tanikaze*, *Urakaze*, *Hamakaze*, and *Isokaze*). For the Kamimbo unit, the screen was the destroyers (*Satsuki* and *Nagatsuki*), escorting the destroyers of 16th Destroyer Division (*Tokitsukaze* and *Yukikaze*) and 8th Destroyer Division (*Oshio* and *Arashio*).[63] The Reinforcement Unit had a "Support Unit" of heavy cruisers *Chokai* and *Kumano* and light cruiser *Sendai* sitting at Kavieng.[64] How exactly three cruisers sitting at Kavieng were supposed to support 20 destroyers at Guadalcanal was never explained.

Admiral Hashimoto expected an attack and arranged his force for rapid dispersal, which, again, as the Allies had learned in the Java Sea Campaign, was not the way to fight off an air attack. Be that as it may, the force was arranged in two columns 2 miles apart. Each column contained three divisions – two of three ships each followed by one of four ships – 1 mile apart. There was a 300-yard interval between each destroyer within each group.[65] Base Air Force and the 6th Air Division were splitting air cover duties during the day, with 18 Zeros from the 252 Air Group out of a new airfield at Ballale providing fighter protection.[66]

The Reinforcement Unit was under almost constant surveillance. Two coastwatchers on Choiseul, Lieutenants Nick Waddell and Carden Seton, radioed at 12:22 pm that 15 light cruisers and destroyers were leaving Faisi. They later reported two heavy cruisers, two light cruisers, and 16 destroyers passing Choiseul.[67] Another report from a Kiwi No. 3 Squadron Hudson at 1:20 had the convoy north of Vella Lavella and apparently continued tracking it.[68] Henderson Field started preparing an airstrike against the convoy.

While that was going on, the unloading at Nugu Point was completed at around 1:00 pm, and the destroyers *Nicholas* and *DeHaven* had the honor of shepherding the three landing barges back to Tulagi. The *DeHaven*'s skipper Commander Charles Tolman had allowed two of his ship's four boilers to be shut down for routine maintenance.[69] They wouldn't need the additional speed guarding these crawling craft, now heading east between Savo Island and Guadalcanal. The daily air raid was done. Tojo Time had come and gone.

In theory. It was a little after 2:30 pm when Henderson Field issued a Condition Red for an approaching air raid. That was strange; two in one day. But Lieutenant Commander Hill, well aware of what Japanese air power had done to the *Chicago*, was taking no chances. The *Nicholas* was working for full speed, while the *DeHaven* had to relight those two boilers first, then bring them back on line. Five minutes after it had been issued, the red alert was cancelled – false alarm. The *Nicholas* slowed down again.

Talk came from Henderson Field at 2:43 pm, when a rather urgent-sounding voice came over the voice radio with the words, "The condition is red." Lieutenant Commander Hill on the *Nicholas* ordered full speed again. The destroyer's lookouts went on the watch for the incoming attack and were alarmed to see that the *DeHaven* was still at cruising speed.

On board the *DeHaven*, Commander Tolman had ordered enough revolutions for full speed, but he was unsure of the situation. There were a lot of friendly aircraft in the area. Indeed, barely an hour before a flight of Airacobras had flown low over the convoy heading back to Fighter 2.[70] There were aircraft circling Henderson Field, which was hardly unusual.

"Planes at three o'clock," came the call from one of the *DeHaven*'s lookouts.[71] The planes were coming from the direction of Henderson Field, still too far away and too high to identify. The destroyer kept her relatively slow speed trying to get a good visual. Commander Tolman had his signalman striker Seaman 2nd Class Albert L. Breining ask the lookouts to report as soon as they could determine what the aircraft were. The lookouts did not respond.

The unidentified aircraft were closing. When they were about 6,000 yards away, the *DeHaven*'s gunners could tell they were Japanese and asked the bridge for permission to open fire. Commander Tolman hesitated. Again, he had his signalman striker Breining ask the lookouts to report. Again there was no response.

The aircraft were getting closer. And closer. Commander Tolman asked Henderson Field for air support. After all, the destroyers were supposed to have the Wildcats of Marine Fighting 112 protecting them. But all the Wildcats of Marine Fighting 112 were over Verahue protecting the *Fletcher*, the *Radford*, and their landing craft. The *Nicholas* and the *DeHaven* were on their own.

For the third time, Commander Tolman had his signalman striker Breining ask the lookouts to report. An exasperated Tolman added, "Damn, tell them to hurry up!"

Six of the mysterious aircraft were overhead. Pushing over …

"They're Japs," reported the lookouts, "we can see the meatballs!"[72]

… into dives. On the *DeHaven*.

The *Nicholas* had already opened fire at 2:54 pm. The *DeHaven*'s propellers began churning the sea more and more, but it would take time to build up speed. Out of frustration more than anything else, some of the gunners on the *DeHaven*, without orders, opened up with the destroyer's main battery on the plunging dive bombers screaming down at them. But the bombs were already falling.

Correspondent Foster Hailey saw "the flash of an explosion between the *DeHaven*'s stacks, followed [by] a billowing cloud of black-and-brown smoke." The first bomb had hit, going deep into the ship to detonate in the engineering spaces, causing the *DeHaven* to lose power.[73] It was a very bad sign.

The second bomb hit in almost the same place, this time toppling the forward stack and lifting the 5-inch gun director off its base. Storekeeper 3rd Class William R. Stevenson later recalled "the amidships section was in a devil of a mess." He felt the first two bombs "tearing the ship almost in half."[74] With good reason: like the *Juneau*, the *DeHaven*'s keel had snapped.[75]

The *DeHaven* was a dead ship sailing. The order went out to set the depth charges on "safe," so they would not explode and kill men in the water. Torpedoman 3rd Class Leonard Elam went below to assist in that effort, which was quickly completed.[76] Then a third bomb apparently glanced off the port side and exploded in the water before a fourth made its deadly journey toward the stricken ship.

Henderson Field broadcast the bearing and distance to the attack on the *DeHaven* to all Army Air Force pilots. But then the control for Fighter 2 chimed in with "escort fighters to carry on original mission." Four Lightnings of the 339th Fighter Squadron were left totally confused as they watched eight to ten unidentified aircraft fly between Savo Island

and Cape Esperance, soon joined by flashes and splashes around a destroyer that disappeared within five minutes. In ignorance or defiance of Fighter 2's orders, Major Kermit Tyler led four Warhawks of the 44th Fighter Squadron over Savo, where they saw a flash on a destroyer. By the time they got to the site, there was only an oil slick.[77]

Captain Robert Fraser was leading two divisions of Wildcats from Marine Fighting 112 in forming up to cover the strike against the Tokyo Express when they too saw the attack on the destroyer and three bomb hits. After the third, according to Fraser, "There was a black billow of smoke that hid the destroyer. Then I saw the bow, just the bow, coming slowly out from under. It sank. Like somebody had whacked the ship with a big fist."[78]

The fourth bomb was the third hit on the *DeHaven*. It went through the Number 2 5-inch mount, only about 12 feet in front of the bridge, to explode in the 5-inch ammunition handling room – the magazine – beneath. The explosion set off the magazines under both forward 5-inch mounts, resulting in a titanic blast into which the *DeHaven* completely disappeared. The cataclysm brought comparisons to the destroyer *Shaw* in the Pearl Harbor attack, William Stevenson described:

> Like the destroyer in Pearl Harbor on December 7, our bow and forward part of the ship was literally torn asunder. Gun No. 1 completely disappeared with the entire gun crew. Gun No. 2, when the bow split open, went through the wardroom dressing station and finally stopped its downward course in the plotting room. Almost all the men in the gun crew, battle dressing station, and in the plotting room lost their lives as the gun crashed through and the magazine exploded. The explosion also moved the bridge off its base and left it upside down about fifty feet away.[79]

Leonard Elam was trying to return to the bridge after making certain the depth charges were set to "safe" when he was blown onto the main deck and landed on a pile of potatoes. The bridge was a barely recognizable wreck, with the only one left alive being a dazed, probably concussed Seaman Breining.[80] So shattered was the bridge that Breining only had to step off to get into the water. "I can remember in bootcamp how I hardly passed the swim test," Breining later recalled, "and now I'm Olympic material."[81]

Her bow blown off, completely hidden in a massive cloud of brown and black smoke, the *DeHaven* took seven minutes to sink, give or take a few more for her bow.

That morning delay had indeed been a problem. The Dinah reconnaissance plane had reported in to Rabaul, identifying Captain Briscoe's four destroyers as "cruisers." Base Air Force sent out two more reconnaissance planes, each escorted by Zeros, to keep track of the flotilla. The Wildcats covering the ships had never made contact with either scout plane. Both Admiral Kusaka and General Inamura saw the presence of Lieutenant Colonel George's convoy as a tad inconvenient. The "cruisers" could wipe out Admiral Hashimoto's approaching Reinforcement Unit of destroyers.

Reacting quickly, Admiral Kusaka ordered the Buin airbase to take out the cruisers. Base Air Force sent up 18 Aichi D3A Type 99 carrier bombers from the 582 Air Group under Lieutenant Kitamura Tensai, though three had mechanical issues and had to turn back. Escorting the dive bombers were 23 Zeros led by Lieutenant Shindo Saburo, also of the 582 Air Group, which was a mix of fighters and carrier bombers, and 19 Zeros from the *Zuikaku* led by Lieutenant Notomi Kenjiro.[82]

This Japanese airstrike found almost no aerial opposition between them and the destroyers. When word of the approaching Japanese came in, Henderson Field assumed, not unreasonably, that it was the target and positioned interceptors over the airbase. The Wildcats of Marine Fighting 112 who were covering the Cactus Striking Force destroyers were, by some mistake, vectored over Verahue, protecting only the *Fletcher* and *Radford*. To complicate matters for the Americans, the Japanese strike had gone over Tulagi then looped back to approach the destroyers from the direction of Henderson Field, which was in the process of launching an airstrike.

The 347th Fighter Group's report on the incident was not complimentary of the fighter direction from Henderson Field. "Confusion and chaos prevailed regarding instructions. Without doubt the destroyer would have been saved if logical instructions had been directed. TARFU."[83] ("TARFU" is military slang for "Things Are Really F[ouled] Up".)

It was a perfect storm of problems, starting with the lookouts' tardy response to Commander Tolman's requests for information. Tolman taking the two boilers offline was an example of a reasonable judgment call turning into a bad one through no fault of his own. A livid Albert Breining would later comment, "All the delay in identification combined with the slow speed of the ship gave the aces that dove on us a real field day. Bye-bye DD!"[84] He who hesitates to open fire for fear of hitting friendlies is lost.

Lieutenant Commander Hill on the *Nicholas* had not hesitated, but was in danger of being lost anyway. While the *Nicholas*'s guns were hammering away at the Vals diving on the *DeHaven*, one of her signalmen gave the unwelcome shout, "Plane diving on us, starboard quarter." Foster Hailey recognized it as an "Aichi."[85]

But the *Nicholas* was as ready as she could be. With the destroyer now making 32 knots, Lieutenant Commander Hill ordered, "Full right rudder," causing the *Nicholas* to swing to starboard and in the process heel far over to port.[86] The *Nicholas*, in the words of Foster Hailey, "was turning flank speed, the wake boiling high above her fantail as she squatted like a running horse and tore along through the glassy water."

All the destroyer's guns were firing. And if that was not enough, an ensign on the bridge wing grabbed a Tommy gun and started firing that, too. Then a report came in that another dive bomber was coming in off the port quarter. In fact, eight were coming in.

Nevertheless, Lieutenant Commander Hill's maneuvering held. The first bomb missed. The next seven missed. One, however, detonated so close that steering control from the bridge was temporarily lost. The rudder returned to center and helm control was moved to the steering motor room, where right full rudder was ordered again.[87] John Stone, in charge of one of the *Nicholas*'s 1.1-inch batteries, said none of the eight bombs missed the ship by more than 20 or 30 feet. "It was almost miraculous to see our stern swinging just far enough to get out of the way."[88] The only damage the *Nicholas* suffered was ruptured hull plates, causing some leakage in the engine room. That damage was plugged up.

Lieutenant Commander Hill took stock of his casualties: three killed, 16 hurt. The *Nicholas* joined landing barges *LCT-63* and *LCT-181* in searching for survivors of the *DeHaven*, whose grave was now a smoke plume over an oil slick. The haul – 38 wounded and 108 other survivors – was pitiful, though perhaps miraculous considering the circumstances. Dying with the *DeHaven* were 167 of her crew, including Commander Tolman.[89]

Angry that the botched handling by Cactus fighter control had cost them a chance to save their comrades, Captain Fraser's vengeful Wildcats of Marine Fighting 112 tore after the killers of the *DeHaven* and, 3 miles west of Savo Island, ran into the escort of an estimated 30 Zeros from the *Zuikaku* and the 582 Air Group that was ready for them. The result was a particularly savage melee over Ironbottom Sound. Despite being badly outnumbered, the Marines gave more than they got, Fraser and several others actually punching through the Zeros to slash at the retreating Val dive bombers.

An example of the viciousness of this fight was the experience of Lieutenant John Moran. Moran was lining up a Val when he was in turn lined up by four Zeros led by future ace Chief Petty Officer Saito Saburo of the *Zuikaku*. They left Moran's engine smoking profusely and about to quit over Savo, but that was not enough for one unidentified Zero pilot, who put down his flaps so he could continue inundating Moran's dying Grumman with machine-gun and 20mm cannon fire. Moran was compelled to ditch, and was rescued the next day. Saito shared in his first aerial victory.

The Japanese had sunk a destroyer, but the aerial cost was again high. One Aichi was shot down, while four more were "missing" and three damaged. The *Zuikaku* lost one promising Zero pilot, Petty Officer 2nd Class Tanaka Sakuji, while the 582 Air Group lost five Zeros, with one pilot recovered, and had five other Zeros damaged.

Even so, they had accomplished their mission, in more ways than one. The *DeHaven* was sunk and the *Nicholas* damaged, and the attack had also fouled American efforts to send an airstrike against the convoy. Henderson Field had sent up 18 Dauntlesses of Marine Scout Bombing 234 (one had to land with mechanical issues) and seven Avengers from Marine Scout Bombing 131 when the Japanese strike on the *DeHaven* arrived. At 3:05 pm, Henderson ordered the partial strike to circle east of the airfield to keep clear of the attack. It was not until 3:30 when the red alert was canceled. By that time, the Dauntlesses and Avengers had used so much fuel they had to land again to top off their fuel tanks beginning at 3:45.

It was almost 5:00 pm before the strike was finally on its way. Now up went 17 Dauntlesses of Marine Scout Bombing 234 and seven Avengers from Marine Scout Bombing 131, with 17 Wildcats of Marine Fighting 112 and Observation 251. Joining them were four Airacobras from the 67th, four Warhawks from the 44th, and four Lightnings from the 339th Fighter Squadrons.[90]

After having such a miserable time getting off the ground, the strike had an easy time finding the convoy. As the Americans approached at 6:20 pm, the 20 destroyers stood out rather obviously in The Slot northeast of Vangunu Island only 135 miles from Guadalcanal.

The 17 SBD Dauntless dive bombers under Captain Dick Blain moved in first, diving on what from the Japanese view was the first division of the left column. In fact, Blain ended up leading five other Dauntlesses in dives on the lead destroyer in that column, Admiral Hashimoto's flagship *Makinami*, completed after the Guadalcanal campaign had begun. As Blain's SBD screamed downward and his bomb whistled downward, the *Makinami*'s skipper Commander Hitomi Toyoji swung hard to starboard. Blain reported his 1,000lb bomb hit amidships. Behind him, Lieutenant Don Russell saw an explosion amidships where his bomb should have hit, while Lieutenant John Beebe glimpsed his bomb explode on the *Makinami*'s stern.[91]

The destroyer behind the *Makinami* swung hard to port to successfully avoid attacks by three Dauntlesses. The destroyer behind her ended up doing a complete 180 to starboard as she was able to avoid bombs from six Dauntlesses, though Captain George Wilcox reported a near miss off the ship's stern. Faulty releases meant two other SBDs were unable to drop their bombs. It was not the best day for Marine Scout Bombing 234. Worse, the Dauntless of Lieutenant I.J. Williams and gunner Sergeant Amos Hawkes was flamed by antiaircraft fire and crashed with no survivors.[92]

The Dauntlesses of Marine Scout Bombing 234 made dives unimpeded by defending fighters because the 18 Zeros of the 252 Air Group saw the 17 Wildcat fighters protecting the SBDs and decided to keep a respectful distance. Japanese Zeros didn't used to be intimidated by Grumman F4F Wildcats in an even fight. Japanese Zeros of the Genzan Air Group, who had been reorganized into the 252, didn't used to be intimidated by much anybody. How times had changed.

Japanese Zeros were still not intimidated by Bell P-39 Airacobras or Curtiss P-40 Warhawks, and four Airacobras and four Warhawks were defending the seven Grumman TBF Avengers. The Zeros moved to intercept the torpedo planes.

Seeing the danger developing below, the four Lightnings at high altitude dove to try to bait some of the Zeros into climbing to engage, but the Japanese pilots did not take the bait. Instead they slashed through the Warhawks.

Next up were the four Airacobras. During the early part of the Guadalcanal campaign, Army pilots of the 67th Fighter Squadron had been frustrated by the utter inability of the Bell P-39/P-400 Airacobra to even hold its own against the Zero. Ever since, the P-400 was derided as nothing but a P-40 with a Zero on its tail.[93] It hadn't improved much since then. At one point, Captain Jerry Sawyer found himself surrounded by at least eight Zeros. One Airacobra, that of Lieutenant Bob Bauer, was shot down; the remainder were scattered.[94]

The Grumman Avengers were setting up their attack runs on a much-changed Japanese formation. The left column had swollen to 11 ships, while five destroyers from the right column had moved to port to form a center column and add their antiaircraft power to the *Makinami* and the besieged left column. The TBFs' time was cut short when about a dozen Zeros broke through to harass them, shooting down two, and fouling all of their attack runs. Upon their return to Henderson Field, two more were written off. The Avenger pilots were furious at what they believed was the lack of effort by their fighter escort. The Marine Scout Bombing 131 after action report included this charming bit: "None of our fighters made any effort to beat off Zeros which made attacks before runs could be made."[95] Lieutenant Bauer was unavailable for comment.

The plight of the Avengers topped off a miserable day for American striking power. The SBD pilots reported only three hits out of 16 bombing runs – all on one destroyer, leaving it burning and dead in the water. But even the silver lining to this dark cloud was not what it appeared to be, as they would find out much later. The Dauntlesses had not actually achieved any direct hits. They had, however, gotten enough near misses on the *Makinami* to rupture her hull plating and flood her engineering spaces, causing her to lose power.

By pure chance they had succeeded in disabling Admiral Hashimoto's flagship. Hashimoto could not command the convoy like this. Fortunately, Admiral Koyanagi Tomiji was able to take over command while Hashimoto was getting himself sorted out. Koyanagi detached the *Fumizuki* and *Shirayuki* to stand by the *Makinami*. Hashimoto moved to the *Shirayuki* while the *Fumizuki* was ordered to tow the *Makinami* back to Shortland. Hashimoto then had the *Shirayuki* hurry to catch up with the rest of the Reinforcement Group.

Meanwhile the Americans faced a quandary. With Admiral Giffen's force having withdrawn, there were only three combat units left to intercept the incoming Japanese. There were some night-trained dive-bomber pilots with SBD Dauntlesses. There were those PT boats that everyone – Japanese and Allied – found so annoying, there were some minelayers, and there were the three remaining destroyers of Captain Briscoe's Cactus Striking Force.

Briscoe was ordered to attack the incoming Japanese convoy. He wasn't happy about it, no doubt wondering what good three destroyers could do against 20 – now actually 18 with the retirement of the *Makinami* and *Fumizuki*. The commodore worked out an arrangement with Lieutenant Commander Alan Calvert, who was heading the PT boats. The destroyers would sweep the western approaches to Guadalcanal west of Savo Island, while the PTs would handle the gap between Savo and Cape Esperance.

With those arrangements concluded, Captain Briscoe had the *Fletcher*, *Radford*, and *Nicholas* make for the Russell Islands, which he hoped to use to help mask their movements in the dark and ambush the Japanese. Their only chance against 20 destroyers was surprise. To motivate his crews Briscoe gave a speech that if anything overstated his level of confidence in the mission: "This is the Commodore speaking. It is our duty to inflict as much damage as we can with our small force. We will attack the enemy with torpedoes and gunfire and we will attempt to escape under a smoke screen."[96]

With such an uplifting polemic firing up the crews, the three American destroyers tried to hide themselves near the Russells – where they heard the almost constant drone of enemy airplane engines. Base Air Force had sent another laundromat of eight Washing Machine Charlies to harass the Lunga perimeter that night, but this wasn't what they could hear.

The Japanese convoy was not sighted until it was almost past Savo Island. Briscoe ordered his destroyers to close in for the surprise. Then he found out what those airplane engine noises were: an F1M2 floatplane, a Type 0 Observation Seaplane, a "Pete." Or, more, precisely, a few Petes from the R-Area Air Force. They were running interference for tonight's Tokyo Express.

The Petes had seen the phosphorescent wakes, due to the luminescent *Noctiluca scintillans*, of Captain Briscoe's destroyers and decided to shine some light on these subjects, with flares marking the destroyers' positions and floatlights marking their course. So much for the surprise. Briscoe had to hold his destroyers back while he looked in vain for an opportunity to strike at the Tokyo Express.[97]

The Petes were very busy that night. They also took to harassing the PT boats, who were deployed in four groups of two and one group of three between Cape Esperance and Savo Island.[98] The first to encounter the Japanese were the *PT 48* commanded by Lieutenant Lester H. Gamble, and *PT 111* under Lieutenant John H. Clagett, both operating southwest of Savo. The Petes harassed them with machine-gun fire and bombs right out of the gate, but inflicted no damage. Clagett sighted one destroyer, believed to be the *Kawakaze*, who sighted him back. Braving a tempest of gunfire from the destroyer, Clagett got to within 500 yards, launched all four of his torpedoes, then beat a hasty retreat. It was not hasty enough, as at 10:54 pm a shell set the boat on fire and forced everyone to bail out into shark-infested waters. Two crewmen died, but the rest were rescued. All four torpedoes missed.[99]

Not to be outdone, Lieutenant Gamble went after two destroyers, one of which seems to have been the *Nagatsuki*. Also subject to withering gunfire, Gamble's *PT-48* got to within 900 yards, then spit out two torpedoes at each destroyer and retreated behind a smoke screen. All the torpedoes missed. The heavy gunfire compelled him to beach his boat on Savo Island and abandon it. *PT-48* was recovered the next morning.[100]

So far, the PT boats were not having a good night. And it was about to get worse. The one group of three PT boats – *-37* under Ensign J.J. Kelly, *-59* under Lieutenant John M. Searles, and *-115* under Ensign Bartholomew J. Connolly III – was also harassed without damage by the Petes. The trio of boats then found themselves amidst what appeared to be a dozen dark shapes of destroyers on three sides and Japanese-occupied Guadalcanal on the fourth. Connolly fired two torpedoes at each of two destroyers, then retreated under a lashing counterattack from the *Nagatsuki* and *Satsuki* that compelled him to reduce his speed so his wake was less apparent, hide in a convenient rain squall, and, ultimately, beach his boat on Savo and hide, recovering it the next morning. Searles also hid in the squall and moved north of Savo until dawn. Kelly was not as fortunate. As he was putting on the speed after launching four torpedoes, a shell found *PT-37*'s fuel tank. "The brilliant, blinding flash lighted the whole sky in the vicinity of Cape Esperance[,]" leaving "a burning inferno of gasoline-soaked mahogany." Only one crewman, badly burned, survived.[101] All of their torpedoes missed.

But if at first, second, and third you don't succeed, try, try again. Now came *PT-123* under Ensign Ralph L. Richards following behind *PT-124* under Lieutenant Clark W. Faulkner. Like all the other PTs, both had been harassed by the Petes. Now the two boats were stalking a single destroyer between Cape Esperance and Savo Island. It was Commander Fujita Isamu's *Makigumo*, which had apparently chased some of the PT boats almost to Tulagi before Admiral Koyanagi ordered her back. Faulkner closed to within 1,000 yards and fired three torpedoes, then gunned his engine to clear the area. Richards was also about to launch when his *PT-123* exploded, courtesy of a bomb from an unseen Pete that hit her fantail. The crew bailed out, only to have Petes bomb and strafe them in the water. One was killed, three were missing, and three others suffered serious injuries from shrapnel wounds, burns, or fractures. It was very fortunate the casualties were not much, much worse.[102]

Even so, one of the *PT-123*'s survivors in the water watched the *Makigumo* turn to avoid the *PT-124*'s torpedoes, only to suffer an underwater explosion aft. She lost power and came to a halt. The blast flooded the Numbers 5 and 6 crew spaces aft of Mount 3 on the lower deck as well as the auxiliary engine room. It looked like a torpedo hit, but it apparently was not; it was a mine. At least one and possibly more of the spiked spheres had struck the *Makigumo*. They were among the 300 or so laid by the former four-piper-turned-minelayers *Montgomery*, *Preble*, and *Tracey*. They had spent three days racing up from Nouméa at top speed to lay their mines between Doma and Cape Esperance, leaving only when the Japanese destroyers came into sight.[103]

This concluded a lousy night for the PT boats, and not a particularly good one for the US Navy. Of the 11 PTs that went out to meet the enemy, five had fired 19 torpedoes, and three had been lost. Six men were killed, three officers and six men were missing, and one officer and five men were seriously injured – for no hits.[104]

It was not a good night for the Cactus Air Force, either. A Black Cat was supposed to drop flares to illuminate targets for six night-trained Dauntlesses of Marine Scout Bombing 234. But they could not coordinate the flares and thus the bombing by the Dauntlesses was ineffective.[105]

But it had also not been a good night for the destroyer *Makigumo*. The destroyer *Yugumo* was ordered to tow the unnavigable destroyer. The *Yugumo* moved alongside to commence the tow and eventually they got up to 5 knots. However, the flooding continued in the *Makigumo*, causing her to settle aft. When it reached Crew Space Number 4, Commander Fujita had to admit defeat and ordered the ship abandoned. At 2:50 am, the *Yugumo* launched one torpedo. It detonated against *Makigumo*'s cracked hull, sending her to the depths 6.7 miles southwest of Savo Island. Casualties were one dead, two missing, one seriously injured, and six slightly injured.[106]

Admiral Hashimoto's destroyers headed back up the Center Route, one of the Imperial Navy's alternative terms for The Slot, followed by Captain Briscoe's destroyers for a bit, in a futile attempt to pick off a straggler.[107] Brigadier General Francis P. Mulcahy, commander of the 2nd Marine Air Wing, had taken over as commander of the Cactus Air Force on December 26, 1942. He ordered his flyers to strike back at Hashimoto's fleeing tin cans. Up before first light were six Royal New Zealand Air Force Hudsons from No. 3 Squadron to scout the central Solomons for signs of the destroyers. Next at 5:40 am came eight Airacobras from the 70th Fighter Squadron armed with 500lb bombs escorted by four Lightnings from the 339th Fighter Squadron. There had been no time to attach drop tanks to the Airacobras and they were forced to abort and turn back for lack of fuel, but the Lightnings kept going and found one of the Hudsons, who had caught up with Hashimoto's destroyers at 6:25 am. The Hudson loitered over the destroyers for some two hours, radioing updates, not realizing that its radio had malfunctioned and was not transmitting.[108]

But Guadalcanal received the Hudson's first report, and at 6:30 Mulcahy sent up ten Dauntlesses from Marine Scout Bombing 233, three Avengers of Marine Scout Bombing 131, and seven Navy Avengers, escorted by 21 Wildcats.[109]

This airstrike caught up with Admiral Hashimoto at 8:10 am, 210 miles from Guadalcanal, 10 miles off Vella Lavella, and within range of Japanese Zeros from Buin. Hashimoto had his ships in their typical antiaircraft formation, albeit a little ragged: a right column of six ships, and a left column of five, with another destroyer stationed off the port bow of the flotilla while two more straggled behind the left column. Far behind and out of view was the *Yugumo* and two other destroyers.[110]

The US Navy would not consider it an effective antiaircraft formation. But it was effective enough. Between them, the two Marine Corps squadrons dumped ten 1,000lb bombs, eight 500lb bombs, and one torpedo on the Tokyo Express, netting a possible pair of bomb hits. The seven Navy TBFs reportedly all missed, expending up to four 500lb bombs each. They hit nothing and that was before a dozen Zeros from the 204 Air Group arrived from Buin.[111] One destroyer sunk and one destroyer damaged was not a good return for the effort expended.

Consequently, Admiral Hashimoto's destroyers entered the Shortlands anchorage at 11:00 am, according to coastwatcher Nick Waddell. About a half-hour later the *Fumizuki* towed in the disabled *Makinami*.[112] This latest mission for the Reinforcement Unit was complete.

Meanwhile, on Guadalcanal, the capture of Kokumbona spurred General Patch to slap together a new division. He threw the US Army's independent 147th Regiment and 182nd Regiment and the US Marines' 6th Regiment into a pot and called them the Composite Army-Marine Division, or CAM Division for short. The CAM Division linked up with the 27th Infantry Division moving from the Galloping Horse, but that left the Americans with a reduced front of only 300–600 yards that minimized their firepower advantage. The 300–600 yards was the space between the coast and the inland ridges that run perpendicular to the coast, "a narrow defile with the sea on one side and on the other a close series of ridges and woods."[113] Streams cut this defile with "washboard regularity."[114] It was great territory for a defender.

The 27th Infantry Division's cautious advance on January 24–25 encountered pockets of Japanese resistance just before the Poha River. The 27th held up and the CAM Division renewed the advance on January 26, but the Japanese gave ground only grudgingly. It was only after a bombardment of Japanese positions by the destroyer *Wilson* that the 147th, taking point for the CAM Division, was able to cross the Bonegi River on February 1.[115]

But there were other strange developments. A complete Japanese radio station was captured – undamaged; it had just been abandoned. Lieutenant Commander Daniel J. McCallum, head of radio intelligence at Henderson Field, and his staff were aware that an enemy radio station at Tassafaronga had gone off the air a week earlier. Petty Officer Jim Perkins, radioman Phil Jacobsen, and a Marine intercept operator came out to recover the equipment. What they found was indeed "strange": the Japanese radio and a generator were completely functional. The only document was a radio frequency list that the US already had. No codes, no playlist. The Japanese had clearly taken the trouble to secure their documents but had done nothing to destroy the equipment. McCallum passed the information up the intelligence food chain.[116]

In the meantime, 20 destroyers were gathering at Shortland. Again under Admiral Hashimoto and again under the auspices of the Reinforcement Unit, they sailed at around 11:30 am on February 4. This time the Cape Esperance unit consisted of the *Asagumo*, *Kawakaze*, *Kuroshio*, *Maikaze*, *Samidare*, and *Shirayuki*, flying Admiral Hashimoto's flag, guarding transport destroyers from the remnants of 10th Destroyer Division (*Kazegumo*, *Yugumo*, and *Akigumo*) and 17th Destroyer Division (*Tanikaze*, *Urakaze*, *Hamakaze*, and *Isokaze*). For the Kamimbo unit, the screen was the destroyers (*Fumizuki*, *Satsuki*, and *Nagatsuki*), escorting the destroyers of 16th Destroyer Division (*Tokitsukaze* and *Yukikaze*) and 8th Destroyer Division (*Oshio* and *Arashio*).[117]

Assigned to fly protective cover over them starting at 3:00 pm were 16 Army Type 1 Fighters from the 1st Squadron of the 11th Air Group, but just to be safe, 16 Zeros from the Imperial Navy's 582 Air Group conducted a sweep over the Center Route looking for enemy aircraft or ships. They passed to within 100 miles of Henderson Field, but found nothing and thus turned back. At about 3:30, 15 Zeros from the *Zuikaku* joined the protective aerial umbrella over Admiral Hashimoto's ships.[118]

They would be needed, because General Mulcahy had received reports on the convoy from coastwatchers on Choiseul and Vella Lavella, and he prepared a reception: 11 Dauntlesses from Marine Scout Bombing 233 and 234, escorted by 16 Wildcats from Navy Escort Scouting Squadrons 11, 12, and 16. Fourteen Navy Avengers were guarded by eight Airacobras from the 67th and 70th Fighter Squadrons. Four P-38 Lightnings from the 339th Fighter Squadron flew high cover over them all. They left the Lunga area at 2:40 pm.[119]

But nine Dauntlesses were compelled to return to Henderson Field as a result of mechanical issues, ranging from jammed machine guns to engine problems. The remainder of the strike continued on and at around 4:00 found Admiral Hashimoto's ships northwest of Kolombangara crossing the entrance to Vella Gulf. Once again, the destroyers were in two parallel columns, this time of ten ships each. Upon sighting the American airstrike, Hashimoto had his ships disperse again, this time by 90-degree turns, the north column to port, the south to starboard.[120] They also found about 30 Zeros at high altitude, ready to pounce. And if they were not pouncing, the at-least-16 Oscars at lower altitude were.

It made for a wild and very complicated aerial melee around not particularly effective bombing attacks. American light-bomber pilots dropped four 1,000lb bombs, 21 500lb bombs, four 100lb bombs, and two torpedoes. They got all of one near miss on the destroyer *Maikaze* that started a deck fire and flooded an engine room. Five Zeros circled overhead as the *Nagatsuki* rigged a line to tow the destroyer back to the Shortlands, with the destroyer *Yugiri* meeting them en route as an additional escort.[121]

The first ineffective strike force had been gone about an hour when General Mulcahy slapped together another strike, this one of 15 Dauntlesses from Marine Scout Bombing 233 and 234, escorted by a dozen Wildcats from the Fighting 72, four Warhawks from the 44th Fighter Squadron, and another four Lightnings from the 339th.[122]

Just like the first strike, a number of the Dauntlesses had to drop out. In this case, three, all due to engine trouble. Just like the first strike, the rest of the aircraft continued onward, and at 5:05 pm, with the burning *Maikaze* in view on the horizon, found Admiral Hashimoto's destroyers, now in two columns of nine each, "north at the tip of New Georgia." Just like the first strike, the columns split off.[123]

And just like the first strike, this second strike, in the midst of another aerial melee, was also ineffective. "[Zeros] were thick," reported the Dauntless crews. "Attacked SBDs in sections of 3 and seemed to be all over the sky."[124] The SBDs mostly focused on the destroyer *Kuroshio* and at one point the destroyer was reportedly seen burning and listing to port. Her magazines were reportedly flooded as well, but she continued on with "minor damage" from near misses.[125]

Also targeted was the *Kawakaze*, who narrowly avoided two 1,000lb bombs off her fantail and starboard bow. She supposedly suffered split seams that caused flooding in five of her compartments. Admiral Hashimoto reportedly ordered her to return to Shortland, but rescinded the order when the *Kawakaze*'s skipper Lieutenant Commander Yanase Yoshio reassured him that the destroyer could continue on the mission.[126]

This was a good thing for Admiral Hashimoto. His flagship *Shirayuki* just managed to avoid a bomb off her port bow. But the near miss's concussion may have jarred her drivetrain, for at 5:25 pm her engines sputtered out and the *Shirayuki* coasted to a stop. Hashimoto had to be getting frustrated with his flagships always having trouble. He shifted his flag to the allegedly damaged *Kawakaze* and continued on. The *Shirayuki*'s engineers worked on her and made temporary repairs that allowed her to continue onward by 6:30.[127]

It was not a productive day for the US Navy. This second strike dropped a total of nine 1,000lb bombs, one 500lb bomb, and two 100lb bombs. They got a total of maybe three near misses. For the day, they had damaged three, maybe four destroyers, one of which had to be towed back to base. This came at a cost of 11 aircraft – four Avengers, three Dauntlesses, three Wildcats, and one Warhawk. How many Japanese fighters were downed is unclear. The numbers range from one that "failed to return" and one that "force-landed" to 20 shot down. Given that the *Zuikaku* air group alone reported two shot down, but only two, the truth is likely closer to the former.[128]

It would be another sleepless night for the inhabitants of Henderson Field, thanks to a laundromat of Washing Machine Charlies, this time Nells from the 701 Air Group. One showed up at about 7:30 pm to make a bombing run. Another came at 9:35 pm, a third at 10:30, then finally four at 2:40 am, who each dumped ten bombs on the airbase. Henderson Field collected 75 133lb bombs that night.[129] If Washing Machine Charlie had hoped to keep the men of the Cactus Air Force sleepless, he succeeded.

But if Washing Machine Charlie hoped to keep the Cactus Air Force suppressed, he most certainly failed. At 10:45 pm a Black Cat had detected ten of Admiral Hashimoto's destroyers on its radar about 40 miles west of Guadalcanal. The PBY tracked the first four until they arrived in the vicinity of Coughlin Harbor, then found the other six near the mouth of the Aruligo River. Five Marine Dauntlesses took off for Aruligo. In the light of the Black Cat's flares, they made their dive-bombing runs. All their 1,000lb bombs missed. Then at 12:30 am the PBY itself made its bombing run with four 500lb bombs and missed as well.[130]

It marked the end of a very frustrating day. The Americans had shot their bolt and not stopped the Tokyo Express, not really even slowed it down, or even inconvenienced it much. The PT boats were too shot up from the night of February 1–2 to go out, while Captain Briscoe's Striking Force had been withdrawn at his request by Admiral Halsey, as it was down to two undamaged destroyers and would not be of much use against 20 enemy destroyers. It would arrive at Espiritu Santo on February 5.[131]

So Admiral Hashimoto's Reinforcement Unit completed its work and left at around 1:00 am, dutifully reported by the Black Cat. The PBY followed them up The Slot until it lost contact at around 3:25 am.[132]

Again, General Mulcahy sent a strike out to hammer at Admiral Hashimoto's fleeing ships. This time Dauntlesses and Avengers, escorted by a dozen US Navy Wildcats, took off at 6:45 am. They roared up The Slot to 220 miles out but did not find any Japanese destroyers. So, they relied on a piece of wisdom from Allied air operations of late: *when all else fails bomb Munda*. They did, to little effect, then they returned to Henderson.[133] Still determined to find those destroyers, Mulcahy sent up four B-17s from the 72nd Bombardment Group and some Royal New Zealand Air Force Hudsons from the hard-working No. 3 Squadron. They scoured The Slot. Again, they had no luck finding the Japanese destroyers. They had just disappeared.[134]

But coastwatchers on Vella Lavella found them at 9:40 am, heading north-northwest toward Shortland. They had fighter cover provided by the 253 Air Group. Admiral Hashimoto had been happy to let the Black Cat tag along for a bit. As soon as it lost contact, Hashimoto sprinted southwest out of The Slot, moving well south of New Georgia and Kolombangara. That was why all the searches and airstrikes running up and down The Slot had failed to find them. They weren't in The Slot. The Reinforcement Unit arrived at the south entrance to Shortland just after 10:00 am.[135]

Two massive Tokyo Express runs had succeeded within a week. Admiral Kondo's fleet was still north of the Solomons near Ontong Java Atoll, just as it had been during the last major Japanese attacks. It meant a new Japanese offensive was imminent. Admiral King had issued a warning to Admirals Nimitz and Halsey, and General MacArthur on February 1: "Indications are that Jap offensive operation now in full swing on major scale primarily directed against southern Solomons."[136]

Pearl Harbor intelligence reiterated its prediction of a Japanese offensive, advising that it appeared more and more probable.[137] Admiral Halsey moved the *Saratoga* and *Enterprise* carrier groups closer to Guadalcanal.[138] Concluding the Japanese had landed the equivalent of a regiment of troops, General Patch had his troops advancing westward move cautiously.[139]

But, if the Japanese had landed a regiment of troops, where were they? That was only one of a series of questions the Americans had. The morning of February 5, American patrols found about 30 abandoned barges drifting off Cape Esperance.[140] What was going on here? And what about the abandoned radio station found a few days earlier?

On February 6 a few dissenting voices within Naval Intelligence in Washington sent out a query to their compatriots at Pearl Harbor and in the South Pacific:

"Are there any indications that recent Tokyo Expresses may have been for the purpose of evacuating Nip forces from Guadalcanal?"[141]

Back on December 8, 1942, General Inamura of the 8th Area Army had met with officers from the Imperial Navy in the South Pacific area – the 11th Air Fleet (Base Air Force) and 8th Fleet – and Combined Fleet in Rabaul.[142] It had the air of an international treaty negotiation. In most countries the army and navy are not friends, but in Imperial Japan they hated each other almost as much as they hated the Americans.

They would hate each other more after this conference. The representatives of the Imperial Navy told General Inamura they had to stop all destroyer runs to Guadalcanal. The Navy had lost ten destroyers since October and were expecting only 11 to be constructed in 1943.[143] "Sustainability" was the Navy's issue. These losses were not sustainable, because if they continued, the Navy would be unable to fight the "great decisive battle," which is what Guadalcanal was – sometimes, during Combined Fleet's more lucid moments. But now, it wasn't; it was just an excuse.

Combined Fleet and 8th Fleet agreed to two more destroyer runs, one to Buna and one to Guadalcanal. The latter failed, at the cost of yet another destroyer, *Teruzuki*, and Admiral Tanaka's career. Base Air Force was busy retooling and could not adequately cover such runs at the moment. It had exactly 100 aircraft – 41 Zeros, 36 Type 1 land attack planes, and 23 Type 99 carrier bombers. It was a nice round number, but too low for sustained operations. However, they hoped to have 168 Zeros and 100 G4Ms available by the end of December. The Japanese Army Air Force's 6th Air Division, with 110 aircraft, would start to arrive on December 18.[144]

But numbers of aircraft were only part of the problem, and not even the greater part. Too late had the Japanese started to work on intermediate airfields between Rabaul and Guadalcanal. The latest one, at Munda, would have been the most useful, being about halfway between Shortland and Guadalcanal. On November 13, the old destroyer *Hakaze* had dropped off airfield surveyors and three companies of the 6th Sasebo Special Naval Landing Force to secure and assess the Cape Munda site.[145] A week later the *Kamo Maru* had dropped off a battalion of Army troops. More small convoys had dropped off infantry and construction workers.

Then there were larger convoys. On November 27, a sizable convoy consisting of the auxiliary repair ship *Yamashimo Maru* and cargo ship *Chihaya Maru*, escorted by destroyers *Kuroshio* and *Hakaze*; and *Patrol Boat No. 2* (the former destroyer *Nadakaze*) had left Shortland and arrived at Munda to disembark troops and supplies. They left the next day, only to stumble across a flight of B-17s that dropped a bomb on the port rear bridge of the *Chihaya Maru*, causing her to lose power and compelling the *Yamashimo Maru* to tow her back to Shortland.[146]

Command of the new Munda airbase was turned over to the former skipper of the *Kirishima*, Captain Iwabuchi, still not over the loss of his battleship. He arrived in late November to find 2,500 construction troops who were using hand tools to build the airstrip. They apparently thought the ample earth-moving equipment available nearby was merely decorative in nature; it had not occurred to anyone to actually use the bulldozers for building the airfield, so the earthmovers just sat around like topiary while hard-pressed workers shoveled and pushed.[147] It did carry an advantage, however; the Japanese were able to build the runway mainly at night and under a camouflage of palm fronds strung by wires. The camouflage might have made the site more photogenic, but no less photographic, and a December 5 mission by PB4Y Privateers, the US Navy's version of the B-24 Liberator, of Marine Photographic Squadron 154, confirmed reports from coastwatchers that the Japanese were indeed building an airstrip.[148]

From the very next day, the Allies started regularly visiting the new Munda airfield to add their own twist to the Japanese construction efforts. On December 6, it was P-39 Airacobras making strafing runs, through which the work crews stayed at work. On December 9, it was 18 B-17s.[149] Two days later came another attack by B-17s, followed on December 12 by seven B-17s and nine SBDs of Marine Scout Bombing 142.[150] On the night of December 13 it was a Consolidated PBY Catalina playing the role of Louie the

Louse, harassing the base by night.[151] So many bombs hit Kokenggolo Hill near the site that the Japanese took to calling it Bomb Hill.[152] Nevertheless, by December 15, the Munda airfield was operational. The next night, transports landed base personnel and elements of the 15th Field Antiaircraft Regiment.[153] Now the Japanese had to get it some aircraft.

But their biggest and most intractable problem remained new pilots. To replace combat losses, new pilots were being sent to Base Air Force quickly – too quickly, in the eyes of Admiral Kusaka. These new Sea Eagles were being pushed out of the nest and instead of flying were crashing to the ground, figuratively speaking – mostly. Kusaka had been compelled to send half his G4M crews to Tinian for remedial training. Kusaka also directed a large percentage of his replacement fighter pilots – most of whom had been trained on the Mitsubishi A5M Type 96 ("Claude") fighter and had never flown a Zero – to Kavieng for remedial training as well. Chief of Staff Rear Admiral Sakamaki Munetaka estimated that the new pilots were only a third as proficient as the pilots they had replaced.[154] By the end of 1942, the proportion of Japanese Naval Air Force pilots with at least 500 hours of flight time was down to 15 percent.[155]

All of this weighed heavily on the Navy representatives at Rabaul, but not General Inamura. After what Inamura called the Navy's "bombshell" in cutting off destroyer supply runs, he appealed to Imperial General Headquarters for help in convincing the Navy to supply Guadalcanal.[156] The question of supplying Guadalcanal brought up the question of what to do about Guadalcanal. That larger question was weaving its tendrils throughout the Imperial Navy, Imperial Army, Imperial General Headquarters, and the War Ministry.

And as usual one of those tendrils was Colonel Tsuji. The proud war criminal admitted he deserved "a sentence of ten thousand deaths" for his mistakes on Guadalcanal.[157] He was half right. The grim reality Tsuji had experienced on the island – he reported seeing bloated corpses covered with flies all along the army's path – seems to have moved him toward a smidgen of sympathy for the suffering Japanese troops on Guadalcanal.[158]

When Tsuji returned to Imperial General Headquarters in Tokyo, however, he had a new plan for saving Guadalcanal. He convinced the Army General Staff to send Lieutenant Colonel Imoto Kumao to organize a new offensive on the island.[159]

The only problem was that Lieutenant Colonel Imoto thought Guadalcanal should be abandoned. Whether this was what the duplicitous Tsuji had in mind is unclear. He himself had doubts about the viability of the battle for the lower Solomons, doubts he had discreetly expressed to staffers, and may have wanted Imoto to coordinate the recognition of that truth by the responsible commands, such as Combined Fleet at Truk, where Imoto went to confer and found an ally in Admiral Ugaki, who had been Imoto's instructor at the War College. Ugaki was fearful that the Army's new obsession with Guadalcanal was going to drag the Navy into the proverbial quagmire. "This is a most difficult situation," Ugaki told him. "Let's not worry about who should take the initiative in solving the problem. Our sole concern should be to decide what ought to be done at the present moment."[160]

As eminent historian John Toland put it, Admiral Ugaki's statement was "an abstruse way – understandable only to one used to Navy subtlety – of advising Imoto that withdrawal from Guadalcanal was the only alternative."[161] There is subtle, and there is subtle. "I understand what you mean," Imoto responded.[162]

When Lieutenant Colonel Imoto reached Rabaul, the assumption was that he carried an order from Tokyo for a new offensive, which left General Inamura and his staff completely exasperated. As Imoto supervised map games to simulate the new offensive, one of the staff officers exclaimed, "The people in Tokyo are insane! Do you honestly think there is the slightest chance of success in another attack?"[163]

Not really, in the case of Lieutenant Colonel Imoto, but they played the games out all the same, discovering what issues they had to address in the offensive. The games kept coming out the same way: no matter what they tried, few if any of the transports carrying troops and supplies reached Guadalcanal.[164] At best, barely a quarter of the transports got through.[165] General Inamura declared he would do everything possible to get his troops out, and insisted on gaming a possible evacuation. The results showed it was dangerous, but feasible.[166]

Transports were becoming an issue in Tokyo as well. Back in October, Imperial General Headquarters had agreed to transfer 220,000 tons of shipping back to transporting raw materials from the Southern Resources Area to the Home Islands after completion of operations in the Solomons. But then the October offensive failed and the subsequent effort to reinforce and resupply the island had cost almost 70,000 tons of transport.[167]

As a result, far from returning 220,000 tons of shipping, Imperial General Headquarters demanded another 620,000 tons – "another," as in, "in addition to what it already had." This demand rang alarm bells in the War Ministry, and brought mention of the dreaded "w-word" – withdrawal. Well, strictly speaking a word for "withdrawal" was literally not in the vocabulary of the Imperial Japanese Army. Imperial General Headquarters had coined the term *tenshin* – meaning "turn around and advance" – and this was the term the Army preferred.[168] Major General Sato Kenryo, chief of the military affairs bureau of the War Ministry and one of General Tojo's closest confidants, told the prime minister they should "give up the idea of retaking Guadalcanal."[169]

Tojo seemed indignant but it was soon made clear to him that the alternative was a battle of attrition for Japanese transports, which would be a disaster – as if it was not a disaster already. Japan's minimum requirements for the production of steel in 1943 was estimated at 3.5 million tons. The diversion of 620,000 tons of shipping to the military and away from transporting raw materials back to Japan for production of steel would reduce that figure to only 2 million.[170] They could not continue to fight the war with so little steel.

Tojo asked Sato if a reduction in the tonnage allowed would force withdrawal from Guadalcanal. "Not immediately," Sato answered. The Army could not retake or even hold its position on Guadalcanal without more shipping. Well, there, it seemed, was the solution. Sato suggested the prime minister give the Army only its normal share of shipping without any mention of the dreaded w-word. It was devious, dishonest, and underhanded, in a way which only politicians and bureaucrats could concoct, but a solution nonetheless.

So Prime Minister Tojo allotted the Army and Navy 290,000 tons of shipping. General Sato explained the reasoning to an Army General Staff that remained unconvinced, to put it mildly. The officers brought howls of outrage at Sato's implication that the Guadalcanal campaign would have to be "suspended."[171]

The controversy compelled Tojo to call another cabinet meeting for December 5, where it was agreed to give another 95,000 tons of shipping. That still was not good enough for the Army. It was suggested to General Sato that he explain the decision in person to the Army General Staff. Since it was after 10:00 pm, Sato demurred, saying he would do it in the morning. But once again, that was not good enough for the Army. The Vice Chief of Staff, Lieutenant General Tanabe Moritake, asked Sato to come to his residence to explain the decision.

Dutifully, General Sato presented himself at General Tanabe's residence. But when he arrived outside the door, Sato heard angry voices from the inside. One voice, Sato recognized, was that of Lieutenant General Tanaka Shinichi. Sato knew him well. Tanaka was short-tempered and impulsive; naturally, he was also the Chief of Operations. When Sato came inside, he was greeted by more than a half-dozen General Staff officers.

"*Bakayaro!*" came the welcome from General Tanaka, filled with the liquid courage of *sake*, none of which he offered General Sato. Tanaka reached for his sword. This was too much even for the other members of the General Staff, who tried to restrain Tanaka. And failed. Tanaka lunged for Sato and punched him in the face. Sato punched back.

And thus the skills of physical debate became the means by which this difference of opinion between the Army General Staff and the War Ministry was discussed. The General Staff officers egged on General Tanaka, whose physical debating prowess seemed much improved by the "power of *sake*." Badly outnumbered, General Sato managed to break free and push his way out of the house.

But General Tanaka was not finished. After midnight Tanaka forced his way into the home of Tojo's deputy in the War Ministry, Kimura Heitaro. Almost the opposite of Tanaka, Kimura was quiet and demure, and apologized to Tanaka for the "insufficiency of my efforts" to secure the Army's shipping. Eventually, Kimura convinced Tanaka, who by this time must have been running out of energy, to go home.

But the next day General Tanaka went after General Suzuki Teiichi of the Cabinet Planning Board. Tanaka's rampage was starting to get back to Tojo, who, thoroughly disgusted by Tanaka's conduct, decided that "come what may" the Army was to get only the shipping the Cabinet had decided to release and not a kilogram more.

This clearly meant withdrawal from Guadalcanal – and a loss of face. This was unthinkable. The division chiefs of the Army General Staff stormed over to the prime minister's official residence late at night and uninvited. General Sato and a few staffers were waiting for them. Sato and Tanaka eyed each other warily, both spoiling to renew their physical debate.

Prime Minister Tojo came out just before midnight, wearing a kimono. For reasons known only to the Army General Staff, General Tanaka was selected to present their case to Tojo. The hot-tempered general kept his composure long enough to beg the prime minister for more shipping. "Calmly, without a trace of emotion," Tojo refused. The discussion continued for a half-hour.

Finally came the much expected eruption of Mount Tanaka. "What are you doing about the war?" Tanaka shouted. "We'll lose it this way! *Kono bakayaro* [You stupid bastard]!"

General Tanaka was reprimanded for insulting a superior officer and eventually, like Admiral Tanaka, shipped off to win glory in Burma. But the next night Tojo gave the Army additional shipping – 115,000 tons.[172] It was an example of why insubordinate conduct was so prevalent in the Imperial Japanese Army – it worked.

Aside from the physical debates, this was typical of Japanese policy discussions. Circumlocution: avoiding the elephant in the room, right up until and even after the elephant starts trampling the furniture and fouling the carpet. Don't explicitly say withdraw from Guadalcanal – not yet anyway – just make it impossible to stay there.

But the unthinkable began to seem all too thinkable after the resupply efforts of December were only partially successful. The next hint that Imperial General Headquarters was thinking the unthinkable came on December 12, when the Army General Staff ordered General Inamura to deploy the newly arriving 51st Division to New Guinea instead of Guadalcanal.[173] Finally, the leaders of the Imperial Army and Navy met on Christmas Day to determine who would suggest to the emperor withdrawal from Guadalcanal. Representing the Navy were Chief of Naval General Staff Admiral Nagano Osami, his assistant Vice Admiral Ito Seiichi, Chief of Operations Admiral Fukudome Shigeru, and Captain Baron Tomioka Sadatoshi of the Operations Section. The Army was represented by Chief of Army General Staff General Sugiyama Hajime and the ubiquitous Colonel Tsuji.[174]

Admiral Fukudome was in favor of withdrawing from Guadalcanal, but, like any good bureaucrat, punted. "What do you think of joint tactical map games before we decide?" This was the equivalent of a legislature sending an issue to a study committee.

Now came the eruption of Tsuji-yama, who started shouting and waving his arms:

You are all very well posted on the battle situation and yet you can't even reach a decision. You had better all resign! I've often been on destroyers and undergone heavy air raids. The naval commanders I met there all told me, "The big shots at the Tokyo Hotel and the Yamato Hotel should come out here and see what we have to take and then they might understand!"

This was too much for Captain Tomioka, a brilliant staff officer close to Admiral Ugaki, who had taught him strategy at the Navy War College. Tomioka actually agreed with withdrawal from Guadalcanal but the baron was third-generation Imperial Navy and one of its few noblemen. Tomioka would not let the insult to the Navy – by Colonel Tsuji, of all people – stand.[175] "What are you trying to say? That destroyer commanders are all faint of heart? Take that back!"

"Have you ever been to the fighting front?" Tsuji shot back. "Do you understand what's going on out there today?" Enraged, Tomioka lunged at Tsuji, but another instance of physical debate was short-circuited by Admiral Fukudome, who restrained the captain. "I am sorry, Tsuji-kun. What you say is true."

They gamed the reinforcements all the same. And, again, less than a quarter got through.[176] The finger pointing began anew. The Imperial Army wanted to know how it could fight without food and ammunition. "You landed the Army without arms and food and then cut off the supply. It's like sending someone on a roof and taking away the ladder."[177] The Navy, based on Admiral Ugaki's fear of a bottomless quagmire, wanted to know how long it would have to sacrifice ships to support the Army. The Army responded that if it had half the Americans' supplies it could win. "Up till now we've only received one percent."[178]

It was not a friendly conversation, not a friendly debate. But a new solution did appear later that Christmas Day: Colonel Sanada Joichiro of the Imperial Japanese Army. Sanada was the latest officer to have been sent on a fact-finding visit to Rabaul; staff officers had been conducting such visits and studies as far back as Colonel Tsuji's arrival in September. Back on November 26, Army Major Sejima Ryuzo had reported that the decline in effectiveness of the 17th Army threatened the viability of the proposed Guadalcanal offensive.[179] Then two staff officers, Navy Commander Yamamoto Yuji and 17th Army Major Hayashi Takahiko returned to Tokyo from a visit to Rabaul and confirmed Sejima's bleak assessment, adding that none of the local commands in Rabaul had any confidence in the operation.[180]

At the behest of his boss, Major General Ayabe Kitsuju, who had replaced General Tanaka as Chief of the Army Operations Division at Imperial General Headquarters, Colonel Sanada headed to Rabaul, where he arrived on December 19. The opinions he received can be easily summarized. Admiral Kusaka was blunt, saying Guadalcanal should be abandoned in favor of New Guinea. General Inamura demurred, merely describing the problems inherent in continuing operations on Guadalcanal. Inamura also stated that any decision to withdraw should include plans to evacuate as many of his soldiers as possible. However, the general cautioned, news of the order to withdraw had to be kept secret until after it was executed, because if the troops on Guadalcanal got wind of it beforehand, they would all commit suicide.[181]

Colonel Sanada returned to Tokyo on Christmas Day. He carried with him a report he had drafted with the help of Major Sejima. Guadalcanal could be retaken "only by a miracle," Sanada said. He went on to warn that future operations "must not, out of eagerness to regain *Gadarukanaru*, be jeopardized by following previous plans and by continuing a campaign in which neither the [17th Army] nor the frontline commanders have any confidence."[182] In Sanada's informed opinion, Guadalcanal should be abandoned immediately and all priority given to New Guinea. Much to his surprise, his report drew no objections. General Sugiyama even seemed "rather relieved."[183]

It remained to inform the emperor of the decision. The emperor had been aware of bad tidings in the Solomons. His Annual New Year's Rescript – issued, naturally, on December 26 – was not without a hint of pessimism. "The Emperor is troubled by the great difficulties of the present war situation," he said. "The darkness is very deep but dawn is about to break in the Eastern Sky. Today the finest of the Japanese Army, Navy, and Air units are gathering. Sooner or later they will head toward the Solomon Islands where a decisive battle is being fought between Japan and America."[184]

General Sugiyama and Admiral Nagano had some explaining to do. On December 28, the two chiefs of staff personally informed the emperor of the decision to withdraw from Guadalcanal. They suggested returning on January 4 to brief him on the completed plans. That was not good enough for the emperor. He wanted to know not only about the withdrawal but about what Imperial General Headquarters planned to do next. And he wanted it before January 4.[185]

Two very uncomfortable chiefs of staff returned to the Imperial Palace at 2:00 pm on December 31 for an imperial conference that included the emperor and Prime Minister Tojo. They were made even more uncomfortable by some two hours of pointed questions from the emperor as they tried to explain what had happened, what the next steps would be, and how they would halt the combat losses. The emperor explicitly declared that any withdrawal from Guadalcanal must be matched by offensive action elsewhere.[186] Finally, in his high-pitched voice, the emperor announced, "Well, the Army and the Navy should do their best as they have just explained."[187] He formally endorsed the decision. All they had to do was carry it out.

It had to be done, but it certainly was not a happy time. That night, aboard the *Yamato* at Truk, Admiral Ugaki lamented in his diary, "How brilliant was the first-stage operation up to April! And what miserable setbacks since Midway in June!"[188]

Despite the gloom surrounding the Guadalcanal situation, the staff of the Combined Fleet set about celebrating the arrival of the New Year, 1943. Omi Heijiro, Admiral Yamamoto's steward, placed the ceremonial meal – broiled sea bream, head and all, and salt – at the admiral's table. Yamamoto sat down to begin the dinner and found it was off. The fish head was facing left. It was a major breach of etiquette and, in Japanese culture, an ill omen.

Admiral Yamamoto shrugged it off with a smile.[189]

"During the period from about the latter part of January to the early part of February, the Army and Navy will, by every possible means, evacuate the units on Guadalcanal."[190]

So read Imperial Japanese Navy Directive No. 184, issued January 4, 1943. It resulted in a plan finalized on January 9, 1943 between the Imperial Japanese Army's 8th Area Army under General Inamura, and the Imperial Japanese Navy's Combined Fleet under Admiral Yamamoto and Southeast Area Fleet, a new overarching navy organization analogous to Halsey's South Pacific Command or MacArthur's Southwest Pacific Command, under Base Air Force's Vice Admiral Kusaka. As most Japanese plans tended to be, this one was complicated and full of deception, which in fairness may have been a necessity. It was called "Ke."

That deception was intended to convince the Allies of what the Japanese had originally been planning throughout November and part of December, which was that the Japanese were planning a new offensive on Guadalcanal. Every time the Japanese had started a major offensive on Guadalcanal, Admiral Kondo's 2nd Fleet had sortied from Truk and loitered north of the Solomons near Ontong Java Atoll. So Kondo would do that again on January 31. In the Marshall Islands, the Japanese sent an air flotilla to make it appear that forces were gathering, had the heavy-cruiser-seaplane-carrier hybrid *Tone* use its communications facilities to mimic the activities of a large naval force, and had a submarine shell Canton Island. The Japanese Naval Air Force also bombed Darwin, Australia, again. What Darwin had to do with Guadalcanal was never made clear, but why not?

In the meantime, Japanese air assets in the Solomons were significantly strengthened. About 60 aircraft from the *Zuikaku* staged into Buin. Two Japanese Naval Air Force units trained in night attacks, the 701 and 705 Air Groups, staged into Rabaul as well. With an additional 100 or so aircraft from the Japanese Army Air Force and 60 from the Navy's R-Area Air Force, Base Air Force would be up to about 436 aircraft.[191]

Admiral Mikawa gathered as many destroyers as he could find, 21, into the Shortlands to serve as the new Reinforcement Unit.[192] They'd keep the old name for it; it would fit with the deception that way. They would be the key to *Ke*. The Army troops on Guadalcanal would be removed in three "rat transportation" destroyer convoys, with some 600 troops comfortably crammed into each destroyer upon embarking at Cape Esperance. Base Air Force would provide air cover and attempt to suppress American air power, but if American air and naval forces drove off or sunk the destroyers, barges were to carry the troops to the Russell Islands, where the Japanese would establish a temporary base for the troops to wait until destroyers or submarines could pick them up for the trip to Shortland. Submarines would try to bring some supplies to Guadalcanal in the interim. The entire operation was to be completed by February 10.[193]

But Operation *Ke* began under a dark cloud. Army war games at Rabaul evaluated the concept of lifting out the troops in several rat transportation convoys. General Inamura estimated half the destroyers might be lost, and worried that the Navy's extraction of a few men by submarine or barge would be used to excuse cancellation of *Ke*. It was typical of the historical and institutional lack of trust between the two services, but here it was baseless. Admiral Yamamoto feared forfeiting half the destroyers in *Ke* while saving only a third of the remaining troops of the 17th Army, but he ordered the use of the destroyers anyway. Commander Watanabe Yasuji, Yamamoto's operations officer, believed that 80 percent of those on Guadalcanal could be saved.[194]

And so *Ke* went into motion. On January 14, the Japanese had sent an actual reinforcement convoy, under Admiral Kimura, to Guadalcanal to genuinely reinforce it, which helped even more with the deception. The reinforcement was 750 men of the newly formed Yano Battalion under Major Yano Keiji, and 100 men with a battery of 75mm guns from the 8th Mountain Gun Company, 38th Howitzer Regiment.[195] Yano was considered an expert in delaying tactics, and his job here would be to form a rear guard for the retreating Imperial Army troops of the 2nd and 38th Divisions to evacuate. His men, however, were mostly reservists intended as replacements for the 230th Regiment of the 38th Division.[196] How they would perform under the circumstances was a major question.

With Major Yano's troops was the redoubtable Colonel Imoto. His job was to inform General Hyakutake and 17th Army Headquarters of the withdrawal – *tenshin* – order and help implement it. Colonel Imoto and a party from the operations division of the 8th Area Army headquarters stepped off onto Cape Esperance the night of January 14 and were greeted on the beach by a dead body; welcome to Guadalcanal, Colonel Imoto. Each member of the party was carrying a pack of almost 100lb containing "consolation prizes" – small flasks of whiskey, sweet cakes, dried fish, and cigarettes – perhaps more accurately described as bribes. Imoto and his men needed little direction to 17th Army headquarters; Imoto simply followed the corpses of "many soldiers who had died from hunger and disease" and saw the medical facilities were "deplorable." Proceeding gingerly through the jungle and stopping frequently to avoid American air attacks, it took some 18 hours to get to Hyakutake's camp, a collection of tents and ramshackle shelters near Tassafaronga, finally arriving at around midnight in a driving rain.[197]

Colonel Imoto managed to locate an old friend, Major Suginoo Mitsuo, in a leaky tent that he was sharing with several staff officers, who at that time were trying to sleep on beds made from coconut leaves and covered with mosquito netting. Not Suginoo; he was shaving by candlelight. "I'm preparing to die tomorrow," Suginoo said. It was a joke, sort of.

"That's an admirable attitude," Imoto replied. The senior staff officer Colonel Konuma Haruo led Imoto to the next tent to meet the chief of staff Major General Shuichi Miyazaki.

Colonel Imoto sat down stiffly in front of the general and announced, "I have brought General Inamura's order for the 17th Army to turn around and advance from Guadalcanal."

The immediate response was silence: a pregnant pause, it would seem. They had expected to be ordered to resume the counteroffensive. They were shocked. The order would start a conversation and not a pleasant one. General Miyazaki was stunned. "The army cannot withdraw under the present circumstances regardless of the order," he replied.

Colonel Konuma was aghast. "How could we go home after losing so many men?" he chimed in. He had ordered the men to die in their foxholes.

"If we take the offensive after we have been strengthened and sufficiently supplied, that would alter the situation," Miyazaki said. Of course, they had tried that and failed in November. "But if the army cannot be strengthened and sufficiently supplied, then we have no choice but to cut our way into the enemy lines and bring our own one last bit of glory." This was the decision General Hyakutake and his staff had reached.

"In a situation like this, to consider such an operation would be unthinkable even in a dream!" General Miyazaki angrily declared. "We don't mean to disobey the order but we cannot execute it. Therefore we must attack and die, and give everyone an example of Japanese Army tradition."

In the face of such dubious logic, Imoto's rational arguments had no effect. Colonel Konuma at least had a practical complaint in that he doubted that any withdrawal was feasible; the men out front were too entangled with the enemy. "To withdraw," Miyazaki concluded, would be more difficult than to pass over the raging seas." On that note, Konuma added, given how the November convoy turned out, if any of them did manage to get on ships they would drown.

"It's impossible, so leave us alone!"

Since reason had failed, as he suspected it would, Colonel Imoto drew his trump card: the order from General Inamura.

"Don't you realize that this is an order of withdrawal from the commander of the Army Group," Imoto said, "based on the emperor's order!" They had no right to oppose it.

After what must have been a moment of consideration and calming down, Miyazaki finally replied, "You are correct," he said. "This is not our decision. The Army commander must make it."

The discussion, such as it was, took until dawn. Then Colonel Imoto was brought before General Hyakutake. The general was in his tent, hidden in a cave dug at the roots of a huge tree, sitting on a blanket, meditating with his eyes closed before a biscuit box pressed into service as a table. He opened his eyes.

The colonel explained why he was there, detailing the order. Hyakutake stared silently at him for a moment and closed his eyes again. After another moment, the general said quietly, "This is a most difficult order to receive. I cannot make up my mind right now. Give me a little time."

The morning lull was broken by a rumble of explosions; the Americans were resuming their daily bombardment. It was almost noon before Imoto was summoned to Hyakutake's tent. "I will obey the order," the general stated with dignity, "but it is very difficult and I can't say if the operation will succeed. At least I will do my best."

Colonel Konuma knew the men in the front lines felt even more strongly about retreat than those at headquarters. They would find it unbearable to leave dead comrades behind. He volunteered to go up front. Both General Maruyama, the commander of the 2nd Sendai Division, and General Sano, commander of the 38th Nagoya Division, "had decided to abide by the decision of the Commanding General, 17th Army." They did have one caveat, saying it would be necessary to tell their men it was simply a strategic withdrawal, not that they were being taken off the island. Readers may be forgiven for thinking that, in the Imperial Japanese Army, orders were treated more like what you'd call suggestions than actual directives.

So began two weeks of leapfrogging. The 38th Nagoya Division, defending the inland ridges and passes, was to withdraw first toward Cape Esperance, screened by the 2nd Sendai Division and the Yano Battalion. The Yano Battalion put up a surprisingly resolute defense, especially for reservists. Base Air Force renewed daytime fighter sweeps and a few nighttime attacks on Henderson Field, with an exception for the night of January 29 when, concerned about the potential for Admiral Giffen's cruisers to disrupt the evacuation, Admiral Kusaka directed the 701 and 705 air groups to make the twilight attack that would lead to the sinking of the *Chicago*. It was devastating to both air groups, but it worked better for *Ke* than Kusaka could have hoped, as it spooked Admiral Halsey from sending anything larger than Captain Briscoe's Cactus Striking Force of four destroyers into Ironbottom Sound.

The Japanese had indeed noticed Captain Briscoe's Cactus Striking Force. When his four destroyers moved out on February 1, 1943, it provoked a strong reaction from Base Air Force and, ultimately, the sinking of the destroyer *DeHaven* because of its potential to disrupt the first evacuation convoy, scheduled to run that very night.

Despite air and PT boat attacks leading to the disabling of the *Makinami* and the necessity of the *Fumizuki* towing her back to Shortland, the convoy did run that very night. Admiral Hashimoto's deceptively misnamed Reinforcement Unit arrived off Cape Esperance and Kamimbo Bay with destroyers *Kazegumo*, *Makigumo*, *Yugumo*, *Akigumo*, *Tanikaze*, *Urakaze*, *Hamakaze*, *Isokaze*, *Tokitsukaze*, *Yukikaze*, *Oshio*, and *Arashio*. They picked up 4,935 men, mostly from the 38th Nagoya Division, including General Sano.

Although this was nothing short of a rescue, these did not look like happy, grateful troops coming on board. Admiral Koyanagi was horrified by what he saw:

> [They] wore only the remains of clothes [that were] so soiled their physical deterioration was extreme. Probably they were happy but [they] showed no expression. All had dengue or malaria and their diarrhea sent them to the heads. Their digestive organs were so completely destroyed, [we] couldn't give them good food, only porridge.[198]

Their condition was reported to Admiral Yamamoto:

> When finally rescued, the troops were so undernourished that their beards, hair, and nails had all but stopped growing, and their joints looked pitifully large. Their buttocks were so emaciated that their anuses were completely exposed, and on the destroyers that picked them up they suffered from constant and uncontrollable diarrhoea.[199]

Except for the destroyer *Makigumo*, sunk by that mine, this rat transportation run made Shortland safely.

On February 2 a G4M from the 705 Air Group on a reconnaissance mission found a US Navy carrier task force south of Guadalcanal. It radioed a contact report before it was shot down by American fighters. Base Air Force now knew the location of one carrier. It sent up 14 G4Ms but they found no carrier that day. The following day another airstrike was sent to the same area. The problem was that they flew into a storm that cost the Japanese no fewer than six aircraft and most of each of five crews. The biggest tragedy was Lieutenant Commander Mihara Gen'ichi, leader of the 705, was killed in a midair collision with his wingman.[200] There went another veteran pilot and flight leader.

Admiral Yamamoto may have been an inveterate gambler, but he was trying to minimize the chances his fleet was taking here. On his orders, 16 Zeros from the *Zuikaku* and 11 Zeros and 17 Type 99 carrier bombers from the *Zuiho* staged into Rabaul on January 29. Yamamoto also ordered Admiral Kondo to take his fleet to within 550 miles of Guadalcanal and distract the Americans with it. This would firm up the charade that the Japanese were about to launch another offensive. If that didn't work, Kondo would be in a position to support the convoys.[201]

On February 3, a conference between General Inamura and Admiral Kusaka and their staffs approved the second evacuation run, set for the night of February 4–5.[202] Admiral Kondo had lent two of his destroyers, *Asagumo* and *Samidare*, to replace the sunken *Makigumo* and damaged *Makinami*. Thus Admiral Hashimoto arrived off Cape Esperance with the unit consisting of the *Asagumo, Kawakaze, Kuroshio, Samidare,* and *Shirayuki,* flying Admiral Hashimoto's flag, guarding transport destroyers *Kazegumo, Yugumo, Akigumo, Tanikaze, Urakaze, Hamakaze,* and *Isokaze.* For the Kamimbo unit, the screen was the destroyers *Fumizuki,* and *Satsuki* escorting transport destroyers *Tokitsukaze, Yukikaze, Oshio,* and *Arashio.* They picked up 3,921 men, mostly of the 2nd Sendai Division, including its commander General Maruyama, who boarded the *Hamakaze,* and the 17th Army headquarters, including General Hyakutake, who boarded the *Isokaze.* They, too, made Shortland.

Admiral Koyanagi attributed success of the *Ke* convoys so far largely to "heavenly assistance," but he feared the third and last convoy would meet with disaster.[203] So did Admiral Yamamoto.[204] The Americans were sure to catch on.

On February 5 at 10:37 am, a PB4Y Privateer found 16 warships about 200 miles north of Choiseul, heading southwest. Fifteen minutes later came an update that identified the ships as two carriers, four battleships, six heavy and two light cruisers, plus 12 destroyers. Another update came just after noon: the ships were one fleet carrier, one smaller carrier, a battleship, four cruisers, and an escort of 12 destroyers. Two hours later, a B-17 from the 26th Bombardment Squadron also found Japanese ships: one large and one small carrier, six heavy and six light cruisers, plus 14 destroyers, moving northwest at 18 knots. But the presence of the American reconnaissance plane convinced Admiral Kondo to turn around and head back to the southeast – toward the lower Solomons and any American forces there. At 6:00 am on February 6, Allied intelligence radio direction finders pinned Kondo's fleet as some 350 miles east of Ontong Java Atoll.[205] Admiral Yamamoto wanted him within 500 miles of Guadalcanal, again to support the evacuation if necessary.

That last *Ke* convoy was set for the night of February 7–8. It was different from the first two. The *Arashio* and *Oshio* would escort transport destroyers *Fumizuki*, *Satsuki*, *Tokitsukaze*, and *Yukikaze* to Kamimbo. The *Akigumo* and *Yugumo* were transport destroyers directed not to Cape Esperance, but to the Russells to pick up the personnel of that temporary base. They would have a close escort of *Hamakaze*, *Isokaze*, *Tanikaze*, and *Urakaze*. Admiral Hashimoto expected trouble, so he had a lot more escort destroyers this time: flagship *Shirayuki*, *Asagumo*, *Kuroshio*, *Samidare*, *Kazegumo*, and *Nagatsuki*.[206]

Admiral Hashimoto would not be disappointed. He tried to use the same southerly route that flummoxed the Cactus Air Force on February 5. But at 12:20 pm he was spotted by one of those F5A reconnaissance variants of the P-38 Lightning, this one from the 17th Photographic Squadron (Light).[207] It reported seeing "15 ships, probable DD [destroyer]" 4 miles southeast of the Shortlands. It then invited itself along. About 90 minutes later, the Vella Lavella coastwatchers reported "nineteen" destroyers bearing 293 degrees True, headed south-southeast at 30 knots about 250 miles from Guadalcanal. And a half-hour after that, the F5A Lightning updated its report as "twenty" enemy ships bearing 286 degrees True and closing a half-hour on Guadalcanal. Sadly, the Lightning and its pilot were never heard from again.[208]

At Henderson Field, the Cactus Air Force undoubtedly wanted to be heard from, loudly. Eighteen Dauntlesses from Marine Scout Bombing 234 and Marine Scout Bombing 144, who had arrived two days before, were readied to go after the destroyers. But they took off under a dark cloud, both literally – it was "moderate[ly] overcast" – and figuratively. One SBD plowed into a bomb cart that, bizarrely, had been left on the taxiway. Another was delayed by the accident and never caught up with the main group, and a third had mechanical issues and had to abort. But the remaining 15 were up by 4:30 pm and rendezvoused with their escort of 20 Navy Wildcats.[209]

Their luck did not get much better. It was just after 5:30 pm when they found the convoy some 5 miles off the southern tip of Rendova. The rear of the convoy was hidden by a squall, particularly the last destroyer.[210] Captain Blain had ordered his pilots to split into three six-plane divisions for an attack on the three leading destroyers of the left column of what they suspected would be a twin-column convoy. Sure enough, it was, and when the Dauntlesses approached, the two columns split off in opposite directions – except for the first destroyer in the left column, who did an about-face and steamed back between the separating columns. This threw Blain's plan off. He had his lead division target the second destroyer in the left column.[211]

That was not the only thing throwing off Captain Blain's plan. Admiral Hashimoto's destroyers were putting up an impressive amount of antiaircraft fire for destroyers. Several pilots remarked that the dense barrage put up by these destroyers was heavier than even what one would expect from the *Akizuki*-class antiaircraft destroyers.[212] Worse still, the squall had hidden more than just that rear destroyer. It hid no fewer than 17 "Zeros" – actually Army Oscars – and 15 actual Zeros of the 582 Air Group, who now charged at the Dauntlesses.[213]

Adjusting on the fly, Captain Blain decided to go after the last two destroyers in the left column. But his bomb would not drop, and everyone behind him seemed to miss. The destroyer kept swinging around, frustrating the best efforts of the Marine pilots, until Lieutenant Bob Ayers, recovering from being inverted by a blast of flak, put a 1,000lb bomb on the destroyer's bow forward gun mount. Technical Sergeant Abraham Daniels, very new to piloting, pulled out of his dive only about 100 feet above the water. Daniels had to pull his stick all the way back into his groin, rather uncomfortably, just skimming the sea before he had to gain altitude to barely clear the destroyer. His bomb landed on the forward 5-inch mount toward the bridge, starting a large fire that engulfed the bow area. But, burning though she was, her skipper Commander Uwai Hiroshi radioed that his ship, the *Hamakaze*, had received direct hits on her Number 1 turret "and other parts of the ship," and a near miss on her starboard side that flooded one of her boiler rooms. Nevertheless, her engines were functional and she continued onward.[214]

Not continuing onward was, apparently, the destroyer *Isokaze*. It is not clear what exactly happened to her, but some *thing* definitely hurt the destroyer, killing ten and wounding 14.[215] The prevalent theory is that her Number 1 mount was bracketed by near misses. The destroyer came to a stop and ultimately had to be assisted back to Shortland by the *Kawakaze*, who had to be wondering why it was always she who had to escort damaged ships back.[216]

With that, the Dauntlesses and Wildcats started back, only for the Japanese to spring an ambush with the 17 Army Oscars and 15 Zeros from the 582 Air Group, plus 15 Zeros from the 204 Air Group, and 15 from the 252 Air Group. The Japanese, however, did a terrible job springing the trap; the Zeros from the 204 and 252 air groups were nowhere to be seen. The Americans were able to claw their way out, with no losses, claiming three Zeros shot down. For its part, the Japanese Naval Air Force acknowledged the loss of one pilot, Chief Petty Officer Takemoto Masami Takemoto of the 582 Air Group. And thus the Sea Eagles lost another veteran.[217]

Except for the *Isokaze* and *Kawakaze*, Admiral Hashimoto's destroyers continued onward. The *Akigumo* and *Yugumo* split off for the Russell Islands to collect their troops from the temporary base and anyone who had made their way there from Guadalcanal. The remaining 14 destroyers stopped at Kamimbo, and weary, sick, starved Japanese troops climbed and crawled into barges and on board the destroyers. At three minutes past midnight on February 8, 1943, the boarding was complete. But Admiral Hashimoto stayed for another 90 minutes, sending sailors out in boats to search the shore for Japanese left behind on the beach. Satisfied that everyone who could board – all 1,796 – had done so, Hashimoto got the engines going and his destroyers sped up The Slot.[218]

The Cactus Air Force had no intention of letting the Japanese get away with … whatever it was they wanted to get away with. The next morning the entire Marine Scout Bombing 144 went up The Slot and loitered there with fighter protection from 15 Navy Wildcats and three Lightnings from the 339th Fighter Squadron. But Admiral Hashimoto and his ships were long gone, past Vella Lavella, and with a wall of Oscars from the 6th Air Division and Zeros from the 204 Air Group in between. So the Marine Dauntless pilots went back to that new piece of American wisdom: *when all else fails, bomb Munda*, which they did, just not very well.[219]

Admiral Hashimoto's ships made it into the Shortlands anchorage at 10:00 am.[220] The evacuees were divided into two groups. The very sick soldiers were immediately transported to a hospital in Rabaul; all others were sent to Erventa, Bougainville.[221] But whether they needed to be hospitalized or not, Imperial General Headquarters was warned that it would take a long time and a lot of effort to make the evacuees fit for duty again, because "the months of bitter fighting and loss of many friends has been agony that is very difficult to wipe away."[222]

Twenty-nine minutes after Admiral Hashimoto's last Tokyo Express run to Guadalcanal had concluded with the successful evacuation of the last of the reasonably ambulatory elements of the 17th Army, Admiral Halsey responded to Washington's question about whether these latest Tokyo Express runs were for the purposes of evacuation:

"As yet nothing definite."[223]

CHAPTER 8

PAPPY'S FOLLY

The beginning of February had been more than a little interesting and more than a little too exciting for Lieutenant George of the 2nd Battalion, 132nd Infantry Regiment. He was part of the group that had been dropped off in Verahue to attempt a flanking movement around the Japanese forces near Cape Esperance and Kamimbo – the same landing that had brought Base Air Force down on the destroyer *DeHaven* with fatal results.

Lieutenant George's company was part of an effort to trap a group of Japanese soldiers in the area. The action was getting hot on his left when he heard a gunshot that quickly became a "*Snap!*" louder than anything George had ever heard. George tumbled to the ground in pain, holding his left ear. The bullet had not hit him but had just passed within a hair of his ear.

With the combat to his left now getting even hotter, Lieutenant George gathered himself and got up to look for the sniper who had almost killed him. He found him some 60 yards away by a palm tree, watching the fighting and looking for an opening, oblivious to his original target now targeting him back. More angry than hurt, George resolved to shoot him in the stomach, for a long, slow, agonizing death. He aimed, fired, and watched his would-be killer "lurch forward as though struck from behind with a sledge hammer."[1] Like the sniper, the other trapped Japanese troops were soon cut down.

At twilight, a Nambu machine gun across the bay emptied a magazine at them. They went to look for it – and found three camouflaged Japanese barges. What were they doing here? A few rounds of artillery took care of them. That night, the Americans had no combat with the Japanese but had to deal with an invading army nonetheless – land crabs. Moving like barbarians storming late Roman Gaul, hundreds of land crabs skittered across the camp, crawling across sleeping soldiers.[2] It could have been worse. It could have been crocodiles.

The next morning the Americans resumed their advance, against no opposition whatsoever. It was strange. After a long trudge through the jungle, they set up camp on a high spur jutting out from the interior mountains. It had a dominating view of Kamimbo Bay.[3] They dug in as much as they could before dusk and then set up for "the most interesting and eerie night that [Lieutenant George] spent on Guadalcanal":

A Japanese destroyer or submarine pulled into the bay just after dusk and took on a number of evacuees. All sorts of craft: boats powered by outboard motors, row boats, life rafts, landing barges – all were used that night in effecting the escape of several hundreds of Japs. One of the principal embarkation points for the operation was within spitting distance of us – less than 300 yards below and to our front.

Yet we could do nothing. We did not have ammunition to fire blindly – we had only a few rounds of 60mm mortar stuff. No machine gun or rifle ammunition to blaze away with at area targets. But we were sitting and watching hundreds of Japs leaving an island that rightly should have become their last resting place!

The most tantalizing factor involved was that we had our artillery in position, in readiness to bring deadly fire to bear on a closely observed enemy. We could have engineered a wonderful slaughter with a few rounds of high-explosive. But it was the ancient and honorable military problem of communication. The damned radio always weakened as night set in. Just a characteristic of that particular set – the M511. [Capt. Raymond A.] Geisel struggled heroically all night in an effort to make contact with Force, but luck was not with him. He climbed a tree to gain height for the antenna; he yelled into the mouthpiece at intervals all through the night; but to no avail! The guns of our Marine battery, which had displaced forward during the day in order to keep fire ahead of us, remained silent. The Japs loaded and escaped under our noses. That is, all that the vessel could carry escaped. Many wounded and sick were left behind. Many able bodied Japs were left behind while officers pulled their rank and lived to fight another day. That we learned later on when we killed or captured those who remained.

I moved over with Geisel and together we watched the activity below. Geisel was beside himself, angry beyond words that the Nips were making their escape. When one of our Navy patrol planes came over and dropped a flare on the scene we took up hope that perhaps some action would be taken. We anxiously waited for a cloud of bombers to come over from Henderson Field – even made plans to pull our people back on the south side of the hill during the bombing, but nothing came of it.

I went to sleep shortly after the plane came over. The last thing I remembered were the few words that Geisel uttered, expressing measureless disgust: "Isn't this the Goddamnest foul up you ever saw?" With that pathetic question he threw down the useless radio and lay down on the ground, pulling his poncho over his head.[4]

That was the closest any of the American soldiers and Marines came to interfering with the Operation *Ke* evacuation.

At 4:25 pm on February 9, the 2nd Battalion of the 132nd Regiment with Lieutenant George marched into the village of Tenaro where they linked up with the 1st Battalion of the 161st Infantry Regiment. This marked the end of organized combat on Guadalcanal. Only isolated stragglers from the 17th Army remained.[5]

This was victory on Guadalcanal. The first piece of Japanese-conquered territory had been finally wrestled back. General Patch sent a rather historic message to Admiral Halsey: "Total and complete defeat of Japanese forces on Guadalcanal effected 1625 today … Am happy to report this kind of compliance with your orders … because Tokyo Express no longer has terminus on Guadalcanal."[6]

Admiral Halsey's mercurial chief of staff Captain Browning responded over Admiral Halsey's signature: "When I sent a Patch to act as tailor for Guadalcanal, I did not expect him to remove the enemy's pants and sew it on so quickly. Thanks and congratulations."[7] No one, to this day, is quite sure what that means exactly, but presumably it is supposed to be good.

Yet the victory came with something of a bitter aftertaste. They had let so many Japanese troops escape. Admiral Halsey had held back his major forces, and General Patch had moved so cautiously, both expecting a major Japanese attack, when the Japanese were in fact planning exactly the opposite. Admiral Nimitz explained:

> The end was as abrupt as the beginning of the struggle for Guadalcanal. Until the last moment it appeared that the Japanese were attempting a major reinforcement effort. Only skill in keeping their plans disguised and bold celerity in carrying them out enabled the Japanese to withdraw the remnants of the Guadalcanal garrison. Not until all organized forces had been evacuated on February 8 [East Zone date – at Pearl Harbor] did we realize the purpose of their air and naval dispositions. Otherwise, with the strong forces available to us … and our powerful fleet in the South Pacific we might have converted the withdrawal into a disastrous rout.[8]

Operation *Ke* was, arguably, the best planned and executed Japanese operation of the war. Some 10,000–13,000 troops were saved in the face of enemy air superiority at a cost of one destroyer sunk and a few others damaged. To call it a success is an understatement.

At Truk, Admiral Yamamoto, architect of another candidate for the best planned and executed Japanese operation of the war, sat on his new flagship, the new superbattleship *Musashi*, where he received Admiral Koyanagi. The Combined Fleet head confessed that he too had feared the withdrawal would be a disaster when he heard, early on, that Admiral Hashimoto had lost a destroyer to damage, but that he had consoled himself with the thought that Koyanagi Tomiji was on the scene. Yamamoto congratulated Koyanagi on a job well done.[9]

Nevertheless, it was a Japanese tactical victory in an operation that signaled a Japanese strategic defeat. As the February 9 intelligence summary from Pearl Harbor reasoned:

> The return of the Advance Force to Truk along with the comparatively rapid advance of U.S. Army forces as far as Visale from the southwest and the Doma Cove area from the east may

indicate that the enemy is indeed evacuating from Guadalcanal and that the major operational stage [for] the present … is completed. If this be true it shows that the tide of war in the Pacific has changed and that the Nip is on the defensive at last.[10]

Perhaps. The problem was, the Japanese did not see it entirely the same way.

With Buna and Guadalcanal now in Allied hands, the Japanese decided to fortify a defense triangle of Munda-Rabaul-Lae. Actually, it was more like a "V" than a triangle because the defense of Rabaul depended on both, but not vice versa. Munda held a blocking position in the Solomons, while Lae held an even more important blocking position on New Guinea. If Lae fell, the fortress at Rabaul would be threatened, and not just by its resident volcanoes. Moving northwest from Buna on the north coast of New Guinea, the next positions were Lae and Salamaua.

Lieutenant General Nakano Hidemitsu, commander of the 51st Division, believed the "whole fate of the Japanese Empire [now] depends upon the decision of the struggle for Lae-Salamaua."[11] It was an exaggeration, but not by much. If Lae and Salamaua fell, the Huon Peninsula and its tiny port of Finschhafen would be outflanked. And once Finschhafen fell, it would be a short jump across the strait to Cape Gloucester, which meant there would be enemy troops on New Britain with the possibility of taking Rabaul. That was just intolerable.

But the Japanese held one important advantage: they were working with interior lines. They had been preparing for this possibility for some time, which was why General Inamura had ordered General Adachi's 18th Army to secure Madang and Wewak in northern and western New Guinea. The 102nd Regiment and other infantry units from General Nakano's 51st Division, already moving to Lae, were to move inland and secure Wau. By the end of January, Imperial General Headquarters decided to also divert the 20th and 41st Divisions to seize Wewak.

On January 5, in what the Japanese called "Operation *18*," five transports – *Brazil Maru*, *Nichiryu Maru*, *Clyde Maru*, *Chifuku Maru*, and *Myoko Maru* – carrying the 102nd Regiment left Simpson Harbor for Lae. They were escorted by the destroyer *Maikaze* and the 17th Destroyer Division with *Isokaze*, *Urakaze*, *Tanikaze*, and *Hamakaze*.[12]

Despite the Japanese having changed their codes on January 1, *Magic* was able to identify the convoy on January 9. The submarine command at the new base in Brisbane, Australia, led by US Navy Captain James Fife, vectored the submarines *Grampus* and *Argonaut* to intercept. Lieutenant General George Kenney, head of General MacArthur's 5th Air Force, had already found the convoy and mustered American Flying Fortresses, Liberators, and Marauders, joined by Australian and Kiwi Catalinas and Hudsons and supported by Lightnings and the venerable Warhawks, which included Australian Kittyhawks who were simply renamed Warhawks, to hammer away at this convoy.

His first effort occurred on January 5. General Kenney wanted "to try to see if we could break the movement up at the source." He ordered the commander of 5th Bomber Command, Brigadier General Kenneth Walker, to conduct a "full-scale bomber attack" on Simpson Harbor at dawn on January 5, before the convoy had left. Walker counter-proposed a noon attack, saying a dawn attack would have his bombers leaving in the pre-dawn darkness and make it too difficult for them to rendezvous. Moreover, Walker believed a noon attack would enable better concentration of defensive firepower and also yield a tighter bombardment pattern. Kenney said he understood Walker's concerns, but Kenney was more concerned about his bombers being shot down than he was their staying in formation. As Kenney saw it, the Japanese fighters "were never up at dawn but at noon they would not only shoot up our bombers but would ruin our bombing accuracy. I would rather have the bombers not in formation for a dawn attack than in formation for a show at noon which was certain to be intercepted."[13]

With that, a massive spider web of intrigue and politics took on explosive qualities. It centered on prevailing air combat theory. It was something of an article of faith in the US Army Air Force that you were supposed to bomb targets from high altitude, beyond the reach of enemy antiaircraft fire. The Army Air Force used this tactic whether the target was on land, such as factories in Nazi Germany, or on the sea, such as Japanese task forces and convoys.[14] It was out of this philosophy that the Boeing B-17 Flying Fortress was developed. The idea was enunciated in the design in which the B-17 could "hit a pickle barrel from 20,000 feet." Leaving aside the question of why anyone would want to bomb a pickle barrel, let alone bomb a pickle barrel from 20,000 feet, what if that pickle barrel was moving?[15]

This was the crux of the problem. As already noted, against moving ships at sea, bombing from high altitude simply didn't work. Bomber formations at high and even medium altitude would drop lots of bombs, but the results in terms of actual hits on the target were, in the words of one Army Air Force study, "less than satisfactory."[16] The Army Air Force seemingly had an answer to the problem of not hitting the target: add more bombers. If you have more bombers, you can essentially carpet bomb the target. Unfortunately, General Kenney and his men were at the end of a very long supply line in a theater of war being starved for resources. There were simply not enough B-17s for the massed bombing Army Air Force doctrine demanded.

Moreover, as much as the Boeing B-17 Flying Fortress has become a symbol of Allied power in World War II, its performance in the early months was less than satisfactory. The 19th Bombardment Group is but one example.

When the 19th Bombardment Group arrived in Australia in March 1942 after withdrawing from the Philippines, they continued to bomb from altitudes above 25,000 feet. According to one member of the 19th's 93rd Bombardment Squadron, "Most of our bombing during this period was done from 20,000 to 30,000 feet and we usually carried eight 600 pound demolition bombs."[17] The percentage of hits on Japanese shipping was less than one percent.[18]

Likely remembering the disastrous performance of his air forces in the Philippines in the early days of the war – and his own contributions to that disastrous performance – and determined to learn from his mistakes, General MacArthur was understandably not happy about the ineffectiveness of his Army Air Forces. That was why he brought in General Kenney. According to Kenney:

[F]rom these altitudes everyone thought that was the thing to do – get up around 25 to 30,000 feet and do your bombing. Well, it didn't make any difference whether you had this marvelous Norden sight or what sight you had – you don't hit from that altitude. You don't hit moving targets or maneuvering targets like a ship, and so then everybody says, "Oh, let's go to pattern bombing. We'll get a whole formation and bunch them up together, and maybe out of all those bombs we drop, one of them will get on the deck." Well, I didn't have enough airplanes to do that kind of stuff. If I put 20 bombers over a target – why, that was a maximum effort there for almost the first year in the Pacific.[19]

And that ineffectiveness was obvious to the Japanese, as indicated by how they handled the placement of their ships and aircraft at Rabaul. "The placement of the vast number of ships also indicated little fear of bombing raids," Kenney believed. "They were lined up so that accurate bombing would have created many losses. I now understood perfectly what it meant to have air, sea, and ground superiority."[20]

Kenney was one of the few Army Air officers who was willing to buck the prevailing philosophy. He didn't care about doctrine. He cared about results, particularly given the limited resources at his disposal. High-altitude bombing did not get results. Kenney was looking for something that did. He needed creativity, innovation.

If high-altitude bombing was ineffective, what about low-altitude bombing? Or really low-altitude bombing? Like 500 feet or even ridiculously low like 100 feet? It seemed an obvious option, except to the Army Air Force brass, who refused to even acknowledge a problem with their philosophy. General Kenney discussed the issue with his aide Major William Benn. Then he fired Benn. But only so that Benn could take over the 63rd Bombardment Squadron and experiment with new low-level tactics.

However, likely out of concern for his crews, General Walker did not agree with trying low-level tactics. General Kenney said of Walker, "He was stubborn, oversensitive, and a prima donna, but he worked like a dog all the time."[21] Walker flew some 17 combat missions to gain experience of the problems facing the crews, which made him popular and respected by his men, though Kenney later grounded him to protect him from possible capture by the Japanese. Walker was good at talking with and listening to his men, regardless of rank. But Walker had a blind spot. He was a firm believer in existing Army Air Force doctrine and bombing from high altitude. In fact, he had written the book on strategic bombing tactics, which formed the very basis of the doctrine. Walker and Kenney clashed over Walker's refusal to consider the evidence that high-level bombing was ineffective and Walker's insistence on continuing with high-level bombing until it worked.

Walker did not appreciate General Kenney's objections to the prevailing Army Air Force wisdom, such as it was. He really did not appreciate Major Benn in the 63rd Squadron trying to give those objections form.[22]

So, for this January 5 "full-scale bomber attack" on Rabaul's Simpson Harbor, General Walker treated General Kenney's orders as what might be called "suggestions." Walker violated not one, not two, but three of General Kenney's orders. First, without telling Kenney, Walker ordered the takeoff time delayed until after dawn so the bombers would arrive over Rabaul at noon. When Walker revealed his intention to bomb Rabaul at midday to the squadron leaders, Major Benn objected. "You're going to lose two airplanes," he said. "You shouldn't try going into Rabaul at high noon. It's best to keep bombing it at night."[23]

General Walker already didn't like Major Benn, and he really did not like Benn's objection. The general responded, "Fine, we just won't take your squadron," or words to that effect. So, though General Kenney had ordered Walker to conduct a "full-scale bomber attack," it would now take place without one full squadron, the 63rd.[24] No one would be trying extremely low-altitude bombing on this mission.

Major Benn was hardly the only one who thought attacking in broad daylight was a bad idea. Lieutenant Jean Jack, assistant operations officer of the 403rd Squadron, assigned to fly ahead and suppress Lakunai where most of the Japanese fighters were based, "blanched" when he saw General Walker's order and requested confirmation. Lieutenant Frederick Wesche III of the 64th Squadron recalled: "When this was announced [that the attack] was going to be done in broad daylight at noontime, as a matter of fact at low altitude, something like 5,000 feet over the most heavily defended target in the Pacific … most of us went away shaking our heads. Many of us believed that we wouldn't come back from it." This would be the first daylight air attack on Rabaul since October 5, 1942, and during that time period, Rabaul had strengthened its antiaircraft defenses to almost 400 guns.[25]

To top it off, General Kenney had a standing order for both General Walker and 5th Fighter Command head Brigadier General Ennis "The Menace" Whitehead that they not accompany combat missions. Walker was a valuable and popular officer and Kenney did not want him to take unnecessary risks. But Walker accompanied the mission anyway, riding in a B-17 with Major Allan Lindbergh, head of the 64th Squadron; Lieutenant Colonel Jack Bleasdale, executive officer of the 43rd Bombardment Group, and Captain Benton Daniel. It's not clear if it was Lindbergh, Bleasdale, or Daniel who flew the plane.[26]

After such a stellar period of preparation, it might be hard to believe the mission was less than a complete success. Three B-17s of the 403rd took off ahead of the main strike in order to suppress the Lakunai airfield. One had to turn back. The remaining two, including that of Lieutenant Jack, got to Rabaul at around 9:00 am, but succeeded only in rousing the clipped-wing Zeros of the Navy's 582 Air Group and Oscars of the Army's 11th Air Group. The B-17s ended up dumping their bombs over Vunakanau. The Zeros and Oscars, which the crews mistook for German Messerschmitts, swarmed around Jack's

Fortress, shredding it and compelling him to ditch off Urasi Island, east of Goodenough Island. He and his crew were rescued a few days later.[27]

The main strike, such as it was, took off around 8:00 am. It would be six B-17s from the 64th Squadron and six B-24s. Another nine B-24s were supposed to join them, but their airfield at Iron Range on Australia's York Peninsula was pummeled by bad weather and they never took off. So, this "full-scale bomber attack" consisted of a dozen unescorted bombers.

Then, for all of General Walker's desire that his bombers stay in formation, his formation broke up, with the Liberators moving ahead of the Fortresses and conducting their attacks ten minutes apart. The two groups ended up dropping 40 500lb demolition bombs and 24 1,000lb bombs from 8,500 feet. "The official report indicated that nine vessels of an estimated total tonnage of over 50,000, including one destroyer tender hit with destroyer alongside, had been sunk or left burning."[28] That report was not entirely accurate. The 5,857-ton Imperial Army transport *Keifuku Maru* was indeed sunk, but the Japanese reported light damage to transports *Kagu* and *Seia Maru*s and destroyer *Tachikaze*.[29] Out of as many as 87 Japanese ships in Simpson Harbor. Only ten ships were involved in the convoy – and they had already moved out of Simpson Harbor two hours earlier.[30] It was, as one historian put it, "a total bust."[31]

And it got worse. The attack drew more swarms of fighters, mostly Oscars from the Imperial Army's 11th Air Group with a few clipped-wing Zeros from the Imperial Navy's 582, 252, and 253 air groups.[32] Antiaircraft fire hit the Number 1 engine on one B-17; it was that in which General Walker was a passenger. It was last seen flying south of Vunakanau at about 5,000 feet, with ten to 20 Zeros on its tail as it tried to escape into a cloud. Two Japanese Army Air Force pilots reported finally shooting it down over water near Wide Bay. It is believed that Lieutenant Colonel Bleasdale and Captain Daniel bailed out over land and were captured and taken to a Japanese POW camp from which they ultimately disappeared. Neither the plane, nor the rest of its crew, nor its passengers were ever seen again.[33]

The search for General Walker and his crew produced a new tragedy. On January 6, a Liberator flown by Lieutenant George M. Rose took off from Port Moresby on a dedicated search for the general. It was never seen again. The 582 Air Group later reported that it intercepted and shot down a lone Liberator over Wide Bay, near where Walker's Liberator was believed to have gone down, which would seem to explain the B-24's disappearance.[34] General Kenney had been furious with Walker for violating his orders, though he attributed it to stress. Kenney was planning on reprimanding him and sending him to Australia for some leave that was probably badly needed, but General MacArthur had said if Walker did not return he would put him in for the Medal of Honor. MacArthur was true to his word, with Kenney's whole-hearted support.[35]

Meanwhile, on January 6, Allied reconnaissance planes had found the convoy at sea headed for Lae. One of the scouts was a Liberator piloted by Lieutenant Walter E. Higgins, who decided to make a solo bomb run. But his B-24 was damaged by antiaircraft fire and then a flight of Zeros ganged up on his limping Liberator. Higgins had to ditch south of New Britain near the bizarrely named Islet Island. When it hit the water, the bomb bay caved in, a common problem for Liberators when they ditched, and killed two of his crewmen. Higgins and the rest of the crew were rescued by an Australian Catalina from No. 11 Squadron.[36]

General Kenney's bomber crews began their usual high- and medium-altitude bombing attacks on the convoy, but with little effect. An exception occurred in the early hours of January 7. A Royal Australian Air Force PBY flown by Flight Lieutenant David Vernon of No. 11 Squadron followed flares dropped by the B-17 of 2nd Lieutenant Guyton Christopher of the 65th Bombardment Squadron, 43rd Bombardment Group, who had been assigned to shadow the convoy to guide an air attack that was scrubbed. Nevertheless, the flares drew Vernon to the convoy, and from 4,000 feet he dropped four 250lb bombs. Vernon's crew "saw flames rise from the third ship in the line and then a heavy explosion amidships." Two of Vernon's bombs had hit the *Nichiryu Maru*. Vernon sent the somewhat laconic signal, "Bombed transport. Burning fiercely. It's had it." And it had. A destroyer, probably the *Maikaze*, turned her searchlights on the dying *Nichiryu Maru*. Likely whispering thanks, the opportunistic Vernon took his Catalina to low altitude to strafe the packed transport. The destroyer turned off her searchlight. This was a smart move on her part. *Maikaze* rescued 739 of the 1,100 troops on board, but could do nothing to save their supplies as the transport sank. Christopher and his crew had accomplished their mission, if not in quite the way they had planned, but, sadly, what happened on their return was not according to plan at all. Bad weather kept Christopher from finding his Port Moresby airfield, and he ran out of fuel and ditched in the Gulf of Papua, killing all but three of his crew.[37] It was not the reward Christopher and his crew deserved after a job well done.

Vernon, Christopher, and their crews had pretty much the only jobs well done. General Kenney made a last-ditch effort to stop the convoy from reaching Lae. Five Royal Australian Air Force Douglas A-20 Bostons, what the Australians called the A-20 Havoc, attacked the runways at the Lae airfield to suppress fighter cover, while as many Flying Fortresses, Liberators, Mitchells, Marauders, and Havocs as Kenney could scrounge up went after the convoy as their escorting fighters tried to hold off defending Japanese fighters. The 9th Fighter Squadron's Lieutenant Richard I. Bong claimed three from the cockpit of his P-38. The bombers managed a few hits on the *Myoko Maru*, which had to be beached near Malahang outside of Lae; the other three successfully made port. General Kenney then tried to bomb them all the next day as they were unloading. He succeeded in hitting the beached carcass of the *Myoko Maru*, but by then she had disembarked all her troops and much of her cargo.[38]

After losing 40 percent of their transports, the Tokyo Express managed to land some 4,000 troops at Lae with most of their supplies. The 5th, Royal Australian, and Royal New Zealand Air Forces were left bombing the supply dumps left behind and striking the empty retreating ships of the convoy on their way back to Rabaul, damaging the *Brazil Maru*.[39] One of the US Army Air Force bombers, its bomb racks empty, was over the convoy on January 10 when it saw a flash and a column of water burst up next to one of the destroyers. It had to be a torpedo from a submarine.

But the Japanese were way ahead of the Army aircrew. An aircraft attached to the 582 Air Group had spotted the submerged boat and dropped bombs to call the escorting destroyers' attention to its position.[40] One of them, *Maikaze*, raced out to the spot and dropped several depth charges. The American aviators saw an unusually large submarine bow break the surface of the water at a steep angle and hang there, like an accusing finger pointed at the heavens. There was nothing the aircrew could do except watch in horror as *Maikaze*, now joined by the *Isokaze*, circled the helpless boat like sharks, mercilessly blasting her with 5-inch gunfire. The submarine was evidently shattered, as the bow slid back into the sea from whence it had come, leaving some gruesome debris. According to the Japanese, the "destroyed top of the sub floated."[41]

The Army bomber crew headed back to report they had seen a crew of US Navy sailors die with their submarine. It would be more than a month before the Navy would identify the submarine as the *Argonaut* under Lieutenant Commander John R. Pierce. "Ancient and clumsy" was how noted submarine historian Clay Blair described the *Argonaut*, the largest submarine in the US Navy inventory and extensively refitted to serve as a Marine transport, the only one in the South Pacific.[42] But the same size that made her useful as an undersea transport made her unsuitable for major combat. Commander Richard H. O'Kane, who had served aboard the *Argonaut* for four years before becoming skipper of the *Tang*, said of her fighting capability, "If a fleet boat were stripped of one battery, two engines, six torpedo tubes, and could use no more than 15 degrees of rudder, she would still have greater torpedo attack and evasion ability than *Argonaut*."[43] For reasons known only to Captain Fife, this cumbersome and lightly armed boat was sent to intercept a heavily defended but empty convoy on her first and last war patrol. To add insult to expiry, the *Argonaut*'s torpedo had apparently exploded prematurely and hit nothing.

The arrival of most of the Japanese troops and supplies in Lae was a major embarrassment to General Kenney, his 5th Air Force, and his Royal Australian Air Force units.[44] General MacArthur was not happy with the news that only one transport had been sunk. The failure to stop the convoy was more than an embarrassment for the Southwest Pacific flyers; it meant much more work ahead of them. Because the passengers on that convoy, the 102nd Regiment under Major General Okabe Toru, were slated to help secure the Lae-Salamaua area by expanding the defense perimeter and moving southwest to capture the strategically important town of Wau.

The site of a gold rush in the 1920s and 1930s, Wau was at the south end of an almost completely isolated valley, accessible only by primitive tracks "through some of the wildest and most rugged country in the world – massive mountain ranges with peaks rising to 8,000 feet, more frequently than not covered in swirling cloud; precipitous gorges torn by rushing torrents, and dense rain forest, the whole drenched at frequent intervals by heavy tropical storms."[45]

Wau's airfield consisted of one rough 3,100-foot runway with a 10 percent slope heading directly for a mountain. Aircraft could approach only from the northeast – that is, from the direction of the Japanese – landing uphill and taking off downhill.

The mountain prevented second attempts at landing as well as extension of the runway.[46]

Wau was a major problem, because there were only some 400 Australian troops there, while General Okabe was approaching from Salamaua, much closer than Port Moresby, with some 4,000 troops. And it was almost impossible to rush in reinforcements – that is, until General Kenney arranged an air transport service. Three squadrons of the US 347th Troop Carrier Group offered a non-stop service to Wau. A total of 244 sorties were flown in the four days between January 29 and February 1, bringing in supplies and reinforcements to bolster the Australian defenders. In some instances, C-47 transports had to circle the airfield while Australian troops drove back Japanese forces firing on the runway so the transports could land. The defenders of Wau soon numbered 3,166, with arms, equipment, ammunition, food, and other requirements all delivered by air.[47] General Okabe's attack was defeated, for now.

But Japanese reinforcements were coming so they could try again. Eight transports, escorted by two light cruisers and five destroyers, landed 9,400 troops of the 20th Division at Wewak, which was quickly seized.[48] On February 12, the 41st Division joined them, arriving in a three-ship convoy.[49] Those were not the tough missions, however, inasmuch as they were further from the Allied bases at Buna and Port Moresby.

The tough mission was to reinforce Lae itself, at this time garrisoned by only 3,500 troops. Admiral Mikawa and General Inamura devised a plan to move 6,900 troops from the 51st Division to Lae. It would involve moving slow transports into the teeth of Allied air power at Buna, Port Moresby, and Milne Bay. The staff of the 18th Army war-gamed the scenario, concluding the operation could lose 40 percent of the transports and between 30 and 40 aircraft. The alternative to a convoy on slow transports to Lae was to land the troops at Madang and march them some 140 miles to Lae through jungle, swamps, and even mountains. To be sure, Admiral Mikawa's staff favored this option, but it was rejected.[50] Convoying, it was.

The operation, Operation *81*, would be conducted according to the following principles:

1. The Transport Commander would exercise complete control of all units and detachments aboard ships from beginning to end of the voyage;
2. Shipment of nonessential articles or luxuries "will on no account be permitted";
3. All cargo loading was to be done from consideration of the unloading operation, and position of cargo was to be made with unloading as the first essential;
4. All personnel of units and detachments "must therefore apply themselves to the task and make best use of the unloading craft. Organization and distribution must be perfected in order to eliminate all idle time"; and
5. Order of unloading was to be personnel and necessary equipment first, then munitions, rations and anti-malaria medicines, then the most important equipment of each unit, then baggage.[51]

The major concern seems to have been unloading the convoy; it should be noted that the January convoy made it to its destination, but once its supplies were offloaded, they were bombed before they could be moved to interior caches. The convoy was scheduled to reach Lae by 4:30 pm March 3, a time that was later changed to 11:00 pm. Upon arrival, the transports would spread out, anchoring 600 meters apart some 500 meters from shore. They wanted the helpless ships and their cargo (living and otherwise) dispersed as much as possible to limit damage from air attacks. Smoke screens would be employed to obscure the ships in the anchorage.[52]

To avoid a repeat of the November convoy of Admiral Tanaka the convoy would need massive air support. At and around Rabaul, Base Air Force had the 204 Air Group, with about 30 Zero fighters; the 253 Air Group, with 25–30 Zeros, 11 fighters from the 252 Air Group, and 19 from the *Zuiho*, now an honored member of *Kido Butai*.[53] These Zeros, which except for those from the *Zuiho* were all A6M3 Model 32 "clipped wing" models, would operate from and stage between Rabaul, Gasmata, and Kavieng. How fighters in Kavieng were supposed to protect transports off New Guinea was never explained. The Japanese Army Air Force contributed its 1st and 11th Air Groups, each with 26–28 Nakajima Ki-43 Type 1 fighters, operating from and staging between Rabaul and Lae itself.[54] In total, these units had maybe 100 fighters.

The elements of the convoy assembled in Rabaul's Simpson Harbor, destroyers of the 3rd Destroyer Flotilla under Rear Admiral Kimura Masatomi – not, it is worth noting, Rear Admiral Kimura Susumu, the respected navigator who commanded the 10th Destroyer Flotilla, most famously at the naval battle of Guadalcanal. This was the other Admiral Kimura. Kimura Masatomi was a new rear admiral, just promoted at the beginning of November. He had been commander of the 3rd Destroyer Flotilla for about two weeks, and he spent the most recent three days of that in the hospital with dysentery.[55] He had a big handlebar mustache that made him look like a Japanese Wyatt Earp. Kimura would be the "Transport Commander," flying his flag from the destroyer *Shirayuki*, from 11th Destroyer Division.

Joining her would be a force of destroyers with veteran crews: 16th Destroyer Division, with the *Tokitsukaze*, carrying the commander of the 18th Army, Lieutenant General Adachi; the *Yukikaze*, the means of transport for the commander of the 51st Division, Lieutenant General Nakano Hidemitsu and his staff; and five other destroyers – the *Arashio* and *Asashio* from 8th Destroyer Division; *Asagumo* from 9th Destroyer Division; and *Shikinami* and *Uranami* from 19th Destroyer Division. Just as on the rat transportation convoys to Guadalcanal, the destroyers would be carrying troops – 150 men on each of *Tokitsukaze*, *Arashio*, *Yukikaze*, *Asashio*, *Uranami*, and *Shikinami*, while the *Shirayuki* and *Asagumo* carried 29 each, for a total of 958.[56]

These eight destroyers would be escorting eight transports and cargo ships carrying 6,004 troops and 750 drums of fuel. Six were Army transports: the 6,870-ton *Teiyo Maru*, carrying 1,923 soldiers; the 6,494-ton *Oigawa Maru*; the 5,493-ton *Kyokusei Maru*, a one-time POW "hell ship"; the 3,793-ton *Shinai Maru*; the 2,883-ton *Taimei Maru*; and the 2,716-ton *Aiyo Maru*. One was a "sea truck": the 950-ton *Kembu Maru*, who carried 50 men from the 51st Division and the 221st Airfield Battalion, but was mostly carrying 1,000 drums of high-octane aviation fuel and 650 drums of gasoline.[57] One was a Navy special service ship: the 8,125-ton *Nojima* carried 400 Special Naval Landing Force troops and was filled with provisions, always a necessity, and even more of a necessity after what starvation had done to the Sendai and Nagoya divisions on Guadalanal.[58] These were veteran ships with veteran crews; in fact, the *Oigawa*, *Kyokusei*, and *Shinai Marus* were veterans of the recently mostly completed "No. 6 Go Transportation Operation: Convoy No. 35."

The loadout for the convoy was precisely detailed; it had to be. Loading cargo began on February 22 with munitions loaded first, followed by materials belonging to the units which would embark, then more munitions, unit baggage, and, finally, on February 28, personnel.[59] The troops and their equipment and supplies were distributed across the ships in such a way that if one ship was lost, any unit would lose only a fraction of its men and equipment.[60] If even half of the ships were lost, a balanced force could still be landed.[61] It was combat loading at its finest.

With the troops being embarked last, instructions concerning conduct aboard ship were issued to all units. Given the nature of the mission, normal cruise activities such as shuffleboard and karaoke were not permitted, although officers were to take turns leading a daily half-hour of singing war-songs. And, just like a cruise ship, after boarding and settling into their quarters – or in the case of the soldiers, tiny sleeping platforms, all units carried out an evacuation practice at 5:00 pm. With the threat of Allied air attack and the resignation to losing at least a ship or two on this mission, abandoning ship quickly and efficiently was of paramount importance, for which specific orders were given.[62]

With regards to the threat of Allied air attack: for air cover, the Army and Navy would take turns providing fighter protection, generally switching after each half day, although directing that fighter protection would be, at best, a challenge. Once again, the large air combat unit that called itself Base Air Force had no large bases available that were reasonably close for the conduct of a major operation. The Navy fighters were based primarily in the Rabaul area, the Army's at Lae; in other words, at the beginning and end points of the convoy. This meant that fighters from at least one base and often both bases would be practicing long-range air cover, with which, it will be recalled, the Japanese struggled during the disastrous November convoy; even the US carrier *Enterprise* struggled when it tried to protect the *Chicago* at a range of just 40 miles. The airbase at Kavieng, where the fighters from the *Zuiho* were based, was close to no one. The closest airfield for purposes of Operation *81* was at Gasmata, on the south coast of New Britain, but it was too small to handle the large groups of aircraft needed for this mission.[63] In practice, what the Japanese seem to have tried here was, for example, having the *Zuiho* fighters launch from Kavieng, patrol over the convoy on its trip west, then land at Lae. For their next patrol, the *Zuiho* group would reverse it. There were instances of Army and Navy fighters switching between Rabaul and Lae during the convoy.

The normal difficulties of providing long-range fighter protection were compounded by several self-inflicted factors. One was that the Army's Nakajima Ki-43s did not have the endurance of the Navy's Zeros. Second and far war worse was the recurring issue of communications. The Army fighters did not have radios compatible with those of the Navy air units or the ships, while the Navy's Zero fighters typically did not have radios at all. How the Japanese planned to conduct this long-range fighter protection over these important ships without radios is unclear, but the Japanese air forces had always done it that way, so why change now? Japanese Naval Air Force units also planned to attack Port Moresby and Milne Bay, while Army Air Force units would attack Wau and Buna, hoping to suppress enemy air operations or at least keep them defensive.[64]

The Army and Navy both providing air cover is a hint of the importance attached to this convoy, although apparently not important enough to get radios for their fighter aircraft.* Another hint is a series of orders from the 51st Division's commander General Nakano. One, Order A-59, stated that with the Navy's cooperation it would "make a vigorous landing in the vicinity of Lae." Order A-60 stated that "the division will make a landing at all costs in the vicinity of Lae on the night of 3 March."[65]

Not to be outdone by his own general, the 115th Regiment's commander, Colonel Endo Torahei, issued a mimeographed speech to his men on February 25:

Our regiment is about to enter the decisive battle area of the Great Asia War. From the first, this has been the inspiring deed for all officers and men. There is no greater feat than this. It has been observed that this task is extremely serious and at the same time important. It is our objective to bring the Great East Asia War to a close by suppressing New Guinea and then subjugating Australia, which is our appointed task, thus sealing the fate of our enemy. One cannot refrain from saying that the result of this decisive battle will decide the destiny of the Great East Asia War. Therefore, all officers and men, advance vigorously, fight bravely, and plunge into the jaws of death. Exalt the brilliancy of our regimental colors. Display the traditional spirit of Joshu boys. You must be determined to accomplish this important task. Study the following poem by Nanko:

"Divorce yourself from life and death and let Heaven guide your sword"

Give your special attention to the following instructions. I want brave and prompt action. Always be loyal. Display your aggressive spirit and annihilate the strong stubborn enemy. Display the power of unity and collaboration. Advance vigorously with the Company Commander as the backbone of a strong impetuous charge. Staff must always have absolute control over men. No matter what difficulties you face, don't be terrified. Lead your men boldly, fight wisely and bravely.[66]

---

* It was said that the pilots themselves removed the radios because they were so unreliable and went so far as to saw the Zero's wooden antenna off to gain an extra knot of speed. (Davis, *Lightning Strike*, 3830.) The fact that the antenna was wooden might help explain why their radios were so unreliable.

It probably sounded better in Colonel Endo's head than it read on paper. How one could win the Great East Asia War by "suppressing New Guinea and then subjugating Australia," which are on a separate continent, Endo never explained. But that was his story and he was sticking to it.

So, with this attitude of "Lae or bust," the convoy slipped out of Simpson Harbor a half-hour before midnight on March 1. Entering St. George's Channel, the convoy turned northwest. It would loop around Rabaul and move along the north coast of New Britain before heading southwest. This counterclockwise course around New Britain had two purposes. It was hoped that by going north of New Britain, Allied scout planes would be misled into believing the convoy was headed for Madang. The Allies did not care much about Madang at that time. Second, any Allied air attack would have to pass by the Japanese airbase at Lae and practically fly over Gasmata, so interception of Allied air attacks would be easier and more effective. Finally, they wanted to take advantage of a large and violent storm front north of New Britain. It was hoped that the convoy could hide behind that front for much of its journey. The drawback was that the route had several chokepoints, the most dangerous of which was the Vitiaz Strait between New Britain and the Huon Peninsula of New Guinea. It was very close to their destination at Lae, but it was also within range of multiple enemy airbases. It was where they would need their air cover the most.

At dawn, the convoy moved into its daylight cruising formation. Screening the convoy on the starboard side would be the destroyers *Tokitsukaze* and *Yukikaze*. On their port hand would be a column of the Number 1 Division of the convoy's transport ships: the *Shinai*, *Teiyo*, *Aiyo*, and *Kembu Maru*s, at 800-meter intervals, forming the convoy's starboard column. The Number 1 Division would be led by the destroyer *Uranami*, while bringing up the rear was the destroyer *Asagumo*, who was also ordered to rescue any downed Japanese pilots.[67]

In another column to port of the Number 1 Division was the Number 2 Division, consisting of the *Kyokusei*, *Oigawa*, and *Taimei Maru*s, and, last and apparently least, the *Nojima*, also at 800-meter intervals. This division would be led by the destroyer *Shikinami* and tailed by the flagship *Shirayuki*. Finally, screening the convoy on its port side were the destroyers *Arashio* and *Asashio*, together, as they usually were. The destroyers were generally 2 kilometers from the transport ships.[68]

With that, the convoy settled in, moving at 7 knots. Despite or perhaps because of the weather – storms, gale-force winds, mist, and rain – Japanese Army Air Force Nakajima fighters flying out of Rabaul arrived over the convoy and assumed air coverage for the day. The day of March 1 was boring and uneventful until around 4:00 pm. That was when a Consolidated B-24 Liberator of the Army Air Force's 321st Squadron, 90th Bombardment Group emerged from dark clouds over the convoy.[69] There was a momentary pause of mutual surprise as both the bomber and the convoy saw each other. About the only ones not to see the B-24 were the Army Nakajima fighters whose job it was to keep such snoopers away from the convoy.[70]

The Liberator was commanded by Lieutenant Higgins, who had gotten himself another rig after being forced to ditch his former one. Higgins had been compelled to truncate his planned course, a counterclockwise rough circle around New Britain, by the stormy weather. He came out over the north coast some 150 miles west of Rabaul, expecting to find nothing and with no aerial radar to guide him. The navigator 2nd Lieutenant George Sellmer first detected the ships with his Mark 1 eyeball, exclaiming, "My God! Look at the ships!"[71] Higgins radioed a sighting report of a "14-ship convoy" off Cape Hollman, New Britain, with "six destroyers, one 7,000-ton AK (freighter), one 5,000-ton AK, and the remainder of 1,500 to 2,000-tons." Higgins' transmission and Port Moresby's acknowledgment of it were intercepted by the destroyer *Tokitsukaze*, who radioed Admiral Kimura and Rabaul that the enemy had found the convoy. General Adachi passed word to the Army units embarked.[72] A sense of foreboding spread throughout the convoy. Yamazaki Yasuhira, an Imperial Army soldier on the *Oigawa Maru*, remembered: "Security and black-out orders were more rigid. All individuals arranged their belongings in order."[73] Privately, the senior officers believed they were lucky to have gotten this far before they were found.[74]

They were still hopeful, however. That storm could still prevent enemy attacks on the convoy, just as it was preventing airstrikes the Japanese had planned to make on the Allied airdromes in New Guinea, from which such attacks could originate.

Except the weather was not preventing enemy attacks. At around 8:30 pm, the Japanese ships sighted flares falling in the distance to starboard. They were from another B-24 Liberator, this one flown by Lieutenant George Shaffer, also from Army Air Force's 321st Squadron, 90th Bombardment Group. He was hoping to shadow the convoy with his radar-equipped Liberator, but the weather was closing in again and he never found it. He dropped four bombs and a dozen flares and still could not find it, so he headed back.[75] Given how often they themselves used flare-dropping seaplanes at night, sighting the flares dropped by enemy aircraft at night was disconcerting to the Japanese. One of the soldiers on board wrote in his diary, "The moon has already dropped below the horizon and we sailed on with uneasiness in the darkness."[76]

The darkness and storms were not stopping the Flying Fortresses of the 43rd Bombardment Group. Upon receipt of Lieutenant Higgins' report, seven B-17s from the 63rd Bombardment Squadron led by Captain Tommy Thompson took off from Port Moresby's Jackson Field (also known as "7-Mile Drome") to find the convoy.[77] According to pilot 2nd Lieutenant James T. Murphy, "The ceiling and visibility were so limited that they had to search at 50 to 100 feet off the water." Maybe they could have overcome that height restriction if they had been given the correct coordinates, but they had not and thus did not find the convoy.[78] Thompson's flight headed home, but on the way took a detour to drop 16 500lb demolition bombs on the runway at Gasmata shortly after 9:40 pm.[79]

Not wanting to leave the convoy unwatched for the night, another B-17 of the 63rd, this one piloted by Lieutenant Herbert O. Derr, was packed with two extra fuel tanks in the bomb bay in place of the usual bombs and took off from Port Moresby into the storm to find the convoy again. Despite the bad weather, Derr somehow managed to track down the Japanese ships. And, with those two extra fuel tanks in his bomb bay, Derr began a marathon 11-hour-20-minute game of hide-and-seek in the thunderheads with Oscars and antiaircraft fire in an effort to keep the convoy in sight. Every half-hour Derr sent in "a beautiful report on composition, speed, and course of the convoy, plus strength of enemy fighter cover." It was textbook shadowing, with messages like "Enemy convoy now at 0.500 South, 147.50 East, heading 270 degrees, speed eight knots, 25 Zeros circling convoy. Weather fair, ceiling ragged at 5,000 feet, visibility 15 miles plus."[80] Though Derr took some hits from the Oscars, which threatened to detonate those extra fuel tanks in the Fortress, he was able to stay up until Captain William Crawford, Jr. of the 65th Bombardment Squadron arrived to take over the surveillance around 2:00 am. Derr and his crew were able to return safely to Port Moresby.[81]

Nor did the weather stop the Allies the next day. The Imperial Army airbase at Lae got a 6:30-am wake-up call from six Royal Australian Air Force Douglas A-20s – called "Bostons" in Australia but "Havocs" in the US – from No. 22 Squadron. Led by Wing Commander Keith Hampshire, the Bostons served breakfast in the form of a dozen each of 250lb and 500lb bombs, fitted with instantaneous and 11-second-delay fuses. The Australians claimed 15 hits on the runway itself, with the rest raising havoc into dispersal areas on either side. They then proceeded to strafe antiaircraft positions. This suppression mission appears to have caught the Japanese by surprise and claimed several aircraft destroyed on the ground.[82]

Meanwhile, Captain Crawford had been struggling to shadow the convoy. "The weather was thick and it was raining hard," Crawford later wrote. "It was a grueling job tailing those ships through the night. The difference in speed between a Flying Fortress and a slow cargo or warship ship is tremendous, but I was determined not to let that convoy get out of my sight." And it did not, for almost four hours. "As the skies grayed into morning, the weather cleared enough for us to distinguish our quarry ... They were rounding the northwestern tip of New Britain from the Bismarck Archipelago and heading southward towards Lae." That was good enough for Port Moresby, apparently. For reasons known only to 5th Bomber Command, at around 6:00 am Crawford was ordered to return to base.[83] Now no one was watching the convoy.

So no one saw the convoy transitioning into its daytime formation until 8:15 am, when another B-24 Liberator from 320th Squadron found the convoy, reporting seven warships and seven merchantmen about 50 miles north of Cape Gloucester. About 15 minutes later, nine Zeros from the 253 Air Group arrived over the convoy, joined by another nine from the 253 another half-hour after that. The B-24 had to play another game of hide-and-seek against the Zeros of the 253 Air Group but was able to circle the convoy until friends arrived.[84]

Although, to be fair, some of the 253 Air Group Zeros may have been preoccupied. Sixteen Lockheed Lightnings of the 39th Fighter Squadron were supposed to rendezvous with a flight of eight B-17s from the 63rd Squadron, but missed the rendezvous, leaving the B-17s on their own. Trying to poke their way through the dark clouds, the P-38s seem to have gotten completely lost, because they never did find the convoy, but eight of them did run into three fighters they specifically identified as Japanese Army Oscars some 50 miles north-northwest of Arawe, where the *Myoko Maru* had met her doom. These alleged Oscars were following a flight of B-17s from the 65th Squadron.[85] There were no Oscars up at this time, as it was the Navy's turn to provide fighter coverage, so the fighters they saw were Zeros from the 253 Air Group, probably from the first flight that had arrived at 7:30.

The P-38s, led by Captain Tommy Lynch, had surprise and numbers on their side. Lynch himself opened fire and convinced the Zeros to turn away from the Flying Fortresses to face their new tormentors. It was no contest. Second Lieutenant Wilmot "Wil" Marlatt quickly fired on one from the left front, sending it down out of control with heavy smoke streaming behind. Captain Charles W. King dove on another from behind and caught it, as the Zero was climbing too fast to the point it had practically stalled, and shot it down, last seen spinning on fire into the clouds. It was King's first confirmed kill.[86] Captain Curran "Jack" Jones claimed a third, but Japanese records do not confirm it.[87] The two Japanese pilots killed were Petty Officer 2nd Class Nishiyama Shizuki and Chief Flyer Yagashira Gansuke.[88]

The flights those P-38s were theoretically supposed to be escorting, eight B-17s from the 63rd Bombardment Squadron under Major Edward W. Scott, Jr., arrived on scene at 9:50 am. They were not exactly in the ideal formation, however. The turbocharger of Captain Harry Staley's Flying Fortress went out over the imposing Owen Stanley Mountains, so Scott and another B-17 flown by Lieutenant Frank Denault moved in to protect it while the other five B-17s moved on ahead, not that it mattered much. "The other Fortresses went ahead and we stayed behind," recalled Scott, "but we hit the convoy first."[89] As they say, the last shall be first and the first shall be last.

Major Scott explained how it happened. "The weather was the thickest I ever saw. I could hear the other bombers on the radio but I couldn't see them," Scott told a reporter. "Suddenly, the clouds cleared slightly and though it was still raining like hell we could see the ships below us." Staying together in formation, the three B-17s moved to cross diagonally over the line of ships at 6,500 feet, rather low for a Flying Fortress, from right rear to left front. They were targeting what they estimated to be a 10,000-ton transport, which would indeed be huge.[90]

Admiral Kimura's flagship *Shirayuki* opened fire to port, quickly followed by the other destroyers. "Then the Zeros hit us," Scott went on. "There were eight of them. They made a double coordinated attack both high and low."[91] More Zeros from the 253 Air Group, this time making specially designed attacks that involved two attacking from the front, a third attacking from a 45-degree angle below the bomber, and a fourth attacking from 45 degrees above. Of course, that's what gunners are for, but this attack targeted the areas least protected by the gunners – the nose section, cockpit, and belly.[92] As the gunners got to work, so did the pilots, holding formation as they arrived over the target. Each bomber dropped its four 1,000lb demolition bombs simultaneously, because if the wing planes dropped simultaneously with the leader this gave better bombing results.[93]

Major Scott's bombs were reported to hit across the ship – three amidships and the fourth in the water; Captain Staley got a hit on the bow, and Lieutenant Denault put one on the stern – as best as they could tell, anyway. The bombs "completely envelop[ed] the vessel with smoke and water." The pilots thought they saw secondary explosions, too. "These were all 1,000-pound bombs," Scott remembered, "and the big transport went up in one huge puff of smoke."[94]

The big transport in question was the 5,493-ton *Kyokusei Maru*. Officially, the ship was hit twice, but the Japanese on board described five hits. First there was a group of three, followed by two hits each on the Number 1 and Number 2 holds. The hits on the holds started a fire, and the transport began dropping out of formation. The *Kyokusei Maru*, a hell ship that had transported Allied (mostly Dutch) prisoners of war to slave labor camps in Burma, was now carrying 1,203 troops of the 3rd Battalion, 15th Regiment, under what were, to be fair, conditions not that much better than those endured by the POWs. The hell ship also carried four large motorized landing craft, ten smaller collapsible boats, eight rowing boats, three antiaircraft guns, six field guns, 500 sealed supply drums, and 2,000 cubic meters of ammunition. Efforts to contain the fire proved ineffective, and it soon reached the ammunition and the drums of gasoline. The resulting explosions caused the inferno to spread, as it now engulfed the bridge. At 10:30, Admiral Kimura ordered the blazing *Kyokusei Maru* abandoned.[95] Destroyers *Yukikaze* and *Asagumo* came alongside to assist the stricken vessel and evacuate her passengers and crew.

While they did so, the attack continued, and the defending Zeros tried to exact vengeance. Lieutenant Denault's Fortress took two 20mm cannon shells, one piercing the windshield between Denault and his co-pilot and sending fragments throughout the cockpit. Denault said his eyes could have been injured if not for his Ray-Ban sunglasses.[96] How this did not end up in a commercial is perhaps the biggest mystery of this action.

Watching without Ray-Ban sunglasses the B-17s rumbling through the dark and rainy skies from the *Aiyo Maru*, Superior Private Okamoto Juichi, a 23-year-old from Wakayama Prefecture who was in the Koike Independent Motor Transport Unit, called the Flying Fortresses "terrible, fearful."[97] The 63rd Squadron's Lieutenant Murphy called his Flying Fortress *Panama Hattie*. He joined with Captain Folmer J. Sogaard to target one of the escorting destroyers. He dropped two 1,000lb bombs but missed.

Lieutenant Murphy circled around to about 1,000 feet to make a run at one of the convoy ships. "With the warships and Zeros firing at me, I had to drop our remaining bombs and get away quickly," Murphy explained. Dropping to masthead height, Murphy came in on the ship's broadside and dropped his last two bombs. "I quickly dove for the water," he wrote, "and headed for the nearest weather to get away from all the guns." He heard cheers from his crewmen, who had seen their target explode. "I turned the plane around, dropped closer to the water, and saw one end of the transport pointed toward the sky," he said. "The ship had been split apart and was sinking."[98] Not exactly. Not yet, anyway.

But the attack wasn't over. Not to be outdone, Captain Sogaard had split off from Lieutenant Murphy to target what he determined was a 5,000-ton transport. He dropped two bombs, reportedly causing smoke and flame to shoot out of the ship's hold and stopping the ship dead in the water.[99] Sogaard tried other bombing runs, but his bomb sight "failed," and he had to return to Port Moresby with two bombs remaining.[100]

Captain Sogaard was not the only one having mechanical troubles. Captain James DeWolf attacked two ships, but bomb-rack malfunctions caused his bombs to miss. Lieutenant Woodrow Moore had no malfunctions, but all four of his bombs missed all the same.[101]

None of these issues compared with those of Lieutenant Jim Dieffenderfer. He made two bombing runs on the same ship, but all four of his bombs missed, though his bombardier Lieutenant Fred Blair thought he saw the ship slowing as a result of the concussions. In the midst of Dieffenderfer's second run he found his Fortress the target of several Zeros, so put his bomber into a steep dive to enter a convenient cloud. In the course of the dive, his speed increased to 280mph – and tore the fabric of the plane's elevators. Dieffenderfer and co-pilot 2nd Lieutenant Jack Campbell braced themselves with feet on the crossbars under the instrument panel and, using all of their strength, hauled back on the wheel, dragging the big bomber out of the dive and into level flight at about 1,000 feet – well, as level as they could make it. The slightest turbulence caused the plane to shoot straight up or dive straight down. For nearly three hours the two pilots struggled to keep the plane level while also trying to gain altitude to get over the Owen Stanley Mountains. Somehow, Dieffenderfer and Campbell made it back to Port Moresby, where they were greeted by a Boeing representative. He congratulated the pilots and told them he was surprised the B-17 had been able to stay in the air, let alone cross the towering Owen Stanleys.[102]

So ended the first attack of the day. Major Scott and Lieutenant Murphy were each given credit for sinking an enemy merchant ship.[103] In reality, it was only Scott and his wingmen who got bomb hits. Murphy's crew seems to have seen the explosion on the *Kyokusei Maru* and believed that was their bomb striking their target. That was not the case. When the 63rd headed for home, the *Kyokusei Maru* was still afloat. No other ship was hit.

Historian Lex McAulay's gives an excellent explaination of the difficulties these aviators faced which led to erroneous battle damage reports:

Crew members attempted to compile an accurate record of observations while watching for fighters, peering through fat towering rain clouds and anti-aircraft bursts at distant manoeuvring ships with decks sparkling with gunfire wheeling among bomb explosions and rain showers. The problems of the Operations and Intelligence staffs at Port Moresby trying to produce accurate reports were compounded. Imposed on all this was the desire for victorious communiqués by Kenney and MacArthur.[104]

And the day was still young. Coming in at 10:20 am was a flight of 20 Flying Fortresses – 11 from the 64th Bombardment Squadron, five from the 65th, and four from the 403rd, all with the 43rd Bombardment Group – under the 64th's Major Ken McCullar.[105]

The B-17s split up by squadron. Captain Charles Giddings led a three-plane group, but he couldn't catch a break. First, Japanese Zeros of the 253 Air Group pounced on his formation. Then his bombardier announced that his bomb sight had malfunctioned; the glass had been broken by an empty cartridge case from the forward machine gun. Giddings had Captain Marshall Nelson, flying the Fortress on his right, took the lead. But they had taken too long for a good bombing run and were now over the target. They dropped their bombs but all missed. The trio flew into a cloud and escaped.[106]

The Fortresses from the 65th, whom those three Zeros had been stalking before the Zeros were ambushed by the Lightnings, and the 403rd joined to make one pass. Captains Daniel Cromer and Arthur Fletcher of the 65th each managed to hit a cargo ship and set it on fire. The 65th's Lieutenant James L. Easter got a near miss on a destroyer, while Captain James Harcrow got one direct hit and two near misses on a transport – or so they all claimed. Easter and Harcrow were attacked by a dozen Zeros but Harcrow's gunners shot down one of the fighters.[107]

At about the same time, two B-24 Liberators from the 321st Squadron, 90th Bombardment Group entered the area. Their job was to observe the bombing attack by the 43rd Bombardment Group squadrons, and to make a bombing attack of their own, if they chose. They chose, trying to drop their 12 bombs on what they called a "cruiser" and a "4,000-ton" ship, but got not even a near miss. Then some 15 Zeros of the 253 Air Group came at them but were held at bay by the P-38s as the Liberators made their escape.[108] Fourteen additional fighters from the 204 Air Group arrived around 9:40 but, despite the 253 Air Group's struggling all around them to defend the convoy, the 204 saw no enemy to fight, hampered once again by their lack of radios.[109]

That was it for the airstrikes. For now. Allied intelligence had to try to put together an accurate picture from the various reports. The 63rd Squadron stated they had attacked "a light cruiser, five destroyers and eight transports." The 64th reported, "Three destroyers, two light cruisers, and eight or nine cargo vessels of various sizes." The Liberator crews reported five warships and nine transports, and claimed the B-17 attacks had sunk one transport and set another on fire.[110] According to the 43rd Bombardment Group's pilots, the tally for the two morning strikes was a 6,000-ton transport "burning and exploding," a 5,000-ton ship "burning," a large cargo vessel "smoking and burning amidships," a 6,000- to 7,000-ton vessel "seen to explode," and a somewhat larger one "in a sinking condition."[111]

The official Army Air Force history warns that estimates of damage inflicted on the Japanese convoy were reported "no doubt with some duplication[.]"[112] That would be an understatement. It was all the same ship: the *Kyokusei Maru*. The hell ship was a blazing wreck, but she was still not sinking.

She was hanging on, so the *Yukikaze* and *Asagumo* were being thorough in picking up survivors. The fires seem to have consumed all but four of the *Kyokusei Maru*'s boats and rafts, so the destroyers had to pick up everyone either from the water or from the ship itself. What seems to have gotten an inordinate amount of effort is described by an officer in the 14th Artillery Regiment:

> Working with all our might, we were able to salvage two mountain artillery guns from the burning transport *Kyokusei-Maru* and successfully set them afloat on the sea. The evidence of the spirit of the artillerymen greatly moved the captain and men of the destroyer *Asagumo*. Regardless of the effort, the destroyer made every effort to raise the guns. The guns were rusted and some parts lost, but they could be fired.[113]

It was 11:27 am when the *Kyokusei Maru* exploded one last time and, conveniently "after all the survivors had abandoned ship," slipped under the waves to the maritime hell she so richly deserved.[114] The attack had killed 464 soldiers, 21 ship's gunners, and one crew member. The *Yukikaze* and *Asagumo* stayed until a little before 1:00 pm picking up more survivors, saving a total of 819 men and even salvaging 110 drums – a remarkable haul considering the circumstances.[115]

So now what? Watching from the *Tokitsukaze*, Lieutenant General Yoshihara Kane, the Chief of Staff of the 18th Army, noticed a problem. The *Kyokusei Maru* survivors "were immediately crowded aboard the destroyer in which Divisional Commander Nakano was traveling, making it a case of House full."[116] Not quite, because there were two destroyers, but Yoshihara had the right idea. The *Asagumo* had been transporting 29 passengers and had just taken on maybe another 410. The *Yukikaze*, on whom the divisional commander General Nakano sailed, also took on maybe 410, but she had already been carrying 150 troops. She was now top heavy as a result. Neither destroyer could be an effective combatant with so many people on deck. As a result, Admiral Kimura ordered the destroyers to speed to Lae and drop off General Nakano and his troops and the survivors, then speed back and rejoin the convoy.[117]

Meanwhile, at 10:42, Lieutenant Archie Browning of the 320th Squadron popped out of the clouds so the crew of his Liberator could count the Japanese ships. They reported by radio to Port Moresby: three cruisers, four destroyers, and seven transports.[118] Browning started winging his way back. But at 2:00 pm, the 63rd Squadron's indefatigable Lieutenant Derr arrived in his B-17 to keep the Japanese convoy company for the next six hours.[119]

As he did so, he was perhaps witness to some rather curious events. For reasons known only to Admiral Kimura, at around 2:30 pm when the convoy was northeast of Long Island, he ordered his ships to circle, basically marking time. At that point, the convoy was set to arrive at Lae just after dawn, but Kimura's order would delay that arrival until midmorning. It has been suggested that he was trying to give the *Asagumo* and *Yukikaze* a cushion of time for rejoining. It has also been argued that delaying the convoy's arrival was the idea behind the order, but why he would want to delay the arrival, what possible benefit it would have had, is unclear at best. Other possibilities include trying to deceive the Allied aircraft he knew were shadowing him, or to perhaps arrange for the convoy to stop in Finschhafen instead of Lae. Why exactly Kimura chose to have the convoy circle and mark time in broad daylight is unclear, but choose it he did. He chose poorly. Be that as it may, at about 4:00 pm Kimura ordered the convoy to resume its trudge southward.[120]

Probably misinterpreting the convoy's activities in circling and uncircling, Lieutenant Derr radioed that two unidentified vessels had joined the convoy between 3:30 and 4:30 pm. And at 5:30, he reported that "two possible CL's [light cruisers] left convoy."[121] Derr had to wait only ten minutes after that report for the next attack, at 5:40 p.m. A lone Fortress from the 403rd Squadron appeared over the convoy and dropped two 1,000lb bombs from 7,500 feet. Both missed. The dozen "Zekes" – actually Japanese Army Air Force Oscars from the 11th Air Group – who swarmed him afterwards did not, riddling the bomber but not shooting it down, and it escaped.[122] It had probably missed the rendezvous for the next massed air attack – five B-17s from the 64th Bombardment Squadron and three from the 403rd, all led by Major McCullar, who arrived about 40 minutes later.[123] They counted 16 ships, two of which were on fire – six warships and ten transports, now off Rooke Island at the northern entrance to the Vitiaz Strait. Into the teeth of heavy antiaircraft fire and 18 grouchy Oscars, the Flying Fortresses pressed home their attacks.

Just not very well. Dropping 43 bombs from altitudes between 4,500 and 7,800 feet, the crews claimed two direct hits amidships on a "6,000-ton" ship, which was "left sinking"; two near misses on another ship that stopped, and two more near the stern of a third, "5,000-ton" ship, which lifted its stern out of the water. In actuality, the big *Teiyo Maru* had suffered buckled plates from a near miss off the bow, probably from a bomb dropped by the 64th's Captain Robert L. Schultz. The ship also suffered some 50 men killed, it would seem from two near misses near the stern.[124] The *Shinai Maru* took two near misses off the starboard beam, but suffered no damage, while the *Oigawa Maru* watched two bombs plunge into the water off the stern, also doing no damage – not to the *Oigawa Maru*, at least. The two bombs had come from Captain Raymond E. "Ray" Holsey's flaming Flying Fortress of the 64th Squadron. What was apparently a flak burst in the open bomb bay had ruptured a hydraulic line, igniting the fluid, and spewing the flaming liquid on the bottom of the Fortress's fuselage and all over the bomb bay, injuring five of Holsey's crew. This was a bad thing. Oscars began to swarm the stricken B-17. His hydraulics failing for obvious reasons, Holsey struggled to control the Boeing, and it slowly lost altitude. He shouted into his command radio, "They've got us … we're falling … so long" before adding a resigned "Farewell."[125]

"Hold on Ray, I'll be right down," replied Captain Giddings. His instantaneous response in his slow Texas drawl became a legend for the squadron, who came to believe, *Have no fear. Captain Giddings is here.* Giddings pushed his own B-17 into a steep dive to close in and provide additional firepower against the Oscars trying to trash the faltering Fortress. Captain Holsey's co-pilot, Lieutenant Vernon Reeves, grabbed a fire extinguisher and ran back to the bomb bay, where two crewmen, engineer Technical Sergeants J.B. Young and John W. Rosenberger, soaked the aircraft's stash of heavy flying coats with fire extinguisher fluid and worked hard to smother the flames.

"It's sure hot in here," Holsey commented over the radio. But it was a dry heat.

"Yeah, Ray," Giddings answered. "Does look kind of warm. Y' look like a kettle on a stove."

A Japanese voice intruded into their radio conversation with "You're a gone, Yank!" Holsey's response was "not printable."

Captain Holsey was down to 300 feet altitude and resigned to trying to crash land on a small island when the fire was finally put out. Both Lieutenant Reeves and Sergeant Rosenberger suffered 2nd degree burns, as did the B-17, the metal plates of its belly fuselage burned away, leaving only the naked supporting spars. But all three held together, and Holsey got them all over the Owen Stanleys and back to Port Moresby safely – yet another example of why they called the Boeing B-17 the "Flying Fortress."

Major McCullar's flight headed home at 6:45 pm, with the convoy at 05.40 degrees South, 147.30 degrees East. The Oscars continued lashing at the B-17s as they exited the scene. They damaged four, wounding seven crewmen. One Oscar was shot down, and a second was listed as probably shot down.[126] It ended a long and frustrating day for both Allies and Japanese. In the day-long series of attacks, the Japanese had lost one ship with some 400 men; the Allies believed they had sunk more and should have sunk still more.

Major McCullar's was the last sighting of the convoy for a while. At 4:30 pm a 65th Squadron B-17 piloted by Lieutenant Jose Holguin was sent up to observe McCullar's attack and shadow the convoy, but although it searched the Dampier and Vitiaz Straits for some nine hours, it sighted nothing.[127] Even so, there would be other scout planes.

One of these was a Consolidated PBY Catalina from the Royal Australian Air Force's No. 11 Squadron. Not quite a Black Cat, this one was piloted by Flight Lieutenant Terence Lawless "Terry" Duigan with Squadron Leader Geoff Coventry as co-pilot.[128] Though 11 Squadron was based in Cairns, this Catalina had been flown off to Milne Bay to refuel before starting off on its mission after dark. While passing the time, Duigan had to go to the latrine. A US Army Air Force officer was there, and asked Duigan if he was with the PBY parked offshore. When Duigan answered in the affirmative, the American introduced himself as Lieutenant Higgins. Higgins explained that he and his B-24 crew had spotted the convoy the previous day off the northwest coast of New Britain. Comparing notes on the crapper might be socially taboo, but in war it could be a necessity, as it was in this instance.

Though Coventry may have been squadron leader, Flight Lieutenant Duigan commanded this flight because he was by far the more experienced pilot, with 1,872 hours flying time in a Catalina, including 453 at night. Coventry was along to get experience himself.[129] When the mission started, Duigan took the Catalina north into the location he had learned of in the latrine. Duigan's radar easily picked up the convoy around 10:00 pm, in an area of small islets south of Rooke Island.

Flight Lieutenant Duigan swung the PBY across the convoy to drop a flare and get a count of the ships. When his crewman prepared the flare, however, it prematurely started and he had to dump it out the blister hatch before it fully ignited. The flare ended up illuminating the Catalina more than it illuminated the Japanese. It seemed that, like the Americans, the Australians just could not get the hang of how to use seaplanes at night.[130]

Nevertheless, the flare illuminated enough of the Japanese convoy to pick out a ship's wake, heading southeast. Then they saw six more, with what Duigan described as "hints of more beyond the illumination, all quickly adopting a disturbed ants' nest configuration" – whatever that means. Duigan circled the Japanese ships to get a head count, and at 10:40 pm reported five ships, including one cruiser, and a transport he estimated at 10–12,000 tons between Umboi Island and the coast of New Guinea on a course of 180 degrees. The Japanese intercepted this report.

Port Moresby told Duigan to remain with the ships "until dawn." Duigan understood he was to harass the convoy as much as he could. But what could one slow Catalina do?

The convoy re-formed and started to resume its course. The ships were difficult to see, visible only from 2,000 feet directly overhead as black blobs trailing white wakes. Duigan dropped another flare. This one ignited properly, and the Japanese ships immediately scattered again – like cockroaches, in more ways than one, given the filth of the transport ships. The convoy re-formed yet again.

Duigan and his crew had great fun amusing themselves with this game, dropping a few bombs along the way, until the Japanese stopped scattering. Port Moresby ordered Duigan to remain with the ships as a beacon for a morning airstrike. He had no idea how to do this, so he ignored the order. Nor did he want to stay until dawn as ordered because, he guessed, that was when the Zeros and Oscars would show up. For that reason, Duigan decided to head back, but just before he did so, he lined up a Japanese destroyer from stern to stem and dropped his load. All the bombs missed, in part because the exhausted bombardier had not set the bomb sight properly. The destroyer was the *Asashio*. Duigan finally left the convoy at 2:40 am, reporting it was heading south at position 06.13 South, 148.02 East; that is, well south of Umboi Island, northeast of Finschhafen on the Huon Peninsula. The Japanese also picked up this message. Radio security was always a problem, albeit not nearly as much for the Allies as it was for the Japanese.

As Duigan flew his Catalina back to Cairns, he passed over another aircraft with navigation lights that passed under them, flying west. They could not identify it; it was likely the B-17 of Lieutenant William Trigg of the 63rd Bombing Squadron, who was coming to relieve Duigan on surveillance of the convoy.[131] Duigan and his crew landed safely at Cairns after an exhausting 15.5 hours in the air. Duigan, Coventry, and their crewmates had done their job and done it very well.

At 4:00 am, Japanese radio monitors picked up another report from an enemy snooper shadowing the convoy, giving the position as almost due east of Finschhafen.[132] This would have been Lieutenant Trigg's B-17 from the 63rd Squadron.[133] Trigg and his crew were indeed watching the convoy.

At some point during the early morning Admiral Kimura radioed Rabaul for instructions. It is not clear what he wanted, maybe permission to put in at Finschhafen. But he got no response from Admiral Mikawa or Admiral Kusaka.[134] In fact, he had received no guidance from them at all during the voyage. Kimura was on his own – and Imperial Japanese officers were not prone to aborting missions even in the most dire of circumstances without permission from above.

And directly above, at 6:15 am, was one Bristol Beaufort bomber flown by Squadron Leader J.A. Smibert of the Royal Australian Air Force's No. 100 Squadron. He promptly dropped some flares, which ten minutes later attracted the Beaufort of Pilot Officer Ken Waters. They were the only ones from a flight of eight torpedo-carrying Beauforts that had left Milne Bay around 3:30 am who had been able to work through stormy weather to find the convoy.

Waters maneuvered to attack from 45 degrees on the bow of what he thought to be a cruiser. He watched the torpedo run to within 100 yards of the ship, but saw no results before he had to turn to avoid any antiaircraft fire and head for home. The torpedo missed its target, which is believed to have been the destroyer *Asashio*, a very popular destroyer this morning. At around 7:00 am, Pilot Officer Lew Hall managed to find the convoy himself and made a torpedo run on an "8,000-ton ship" but his torpedo would not release. The Bristol Beaufort was designed to carry British torpedoes, not the American torpedo that he was carrying,

That was it for a while. Except for the *Kyokusei Maru*, Admiral Kimura's convoy had beaten back every Allied air attack and the damage from the loss of the *Kyokusei Maru* was limited inasmuch as two-thirds of her passengers were saved and run to Lae by the *Asagumo* and *Yukikaze*, who had since returned. This was supposed to be the big day, however, when they finally reached Lae. At dawn, General Yoshihara, the 18th Army Chief of Staff, went up on the *Tokitsukaze*'s deck for a breath of fresh air and a look around.

The convoy had cleared the Vitiaz Strait and turned southwest to start the final run to Lae. Yoshihara saw the coast of New Guinea, still dark in the distance. Then he saw an enemy plane coming from the south. It flew away to the north and disappeared into the morning mist.

"On seeing this plane, I was assailed by a premonition of evil," Yoshihara later wrote. "I surmised that the enemy's attention had been focussed [sic] on our landing place, wondering whether, as we passed north of Umboi Island and [sic] we would head for Madang or veer southwards to land at Lae."

The thought chilled the 18th Army Chief of Staff:

> Now was just the very moment when the convoy would diverge and definitely take its course. This was not the observation plane of time-honoured custom. Undoubtedly it must be a reconnaissance plane with the special mission of concentrating on our convoy. If this

were the case then it was necessary to give sufficient warning. But in the next instant I thought of our skill when attacked by enemy planes off Talasea the day before. And our evading movement continued all day. Even though a thousand enemy planes came, we would be able to land without big losses, I judged.[135]

General Yoshihara went back down below for breakfast and then returned to the main deck. He could see the ships in their new daytime formation, adjusted with the loss of the *Kyokusei Maru*. As best as can be determined, the general's own *Tokitsukaze* was leading a column screening the convoy on the port side. It was followed by the *Arashio* and the recently returned *Yukikaze* bringing up the rear. A similar column screened the starboard side led by the destroyer *Uranami*, followed by the *Asashio*, with the *Asagumo* bringing up the rear.

The Number 1 Division was in its familiar position as the starboard column. Admiral Kimura's flagship *Shirayuki* led the *Shinai*, *Teiyo*, and *Aiyo Marus*. The Number 2 Division was also in its familiar position as the port column. The destroyer *Shikinami* led the *Oigawa* and *Taimei Marus*, with the *Nojima* in column behind them. It is not clear where the sea truck *Kembu Maru* was at this time, but she was supposed to be in the back of the Number 1 Division.[136]

The sun was now fully up, shining without a cloud in the sky. That wasn't good. The weather seems to have cleared as they passed the Huon Peninsula. They no longer had the storm front to protect them. Yet General Yoshihara saw no sign of enemy planes. There were friendly planes, however, as this morning it was the Navy's turn to provide the fighter protection. At 7:00 am, 14 Zeros of the 253 Air Group arrived overhead from Gasmata. An hour later they were joined by a dozen from the 204 Air Group, followed a little over an hour later by 18 from the *Zuiho* out of Kavieng. Why they had not staged into Gasmata is anyone's guess. Maybe Gasmata wasn't nice enough for the Sea Eagles of *Kido Butai*, who at the insistence of flight leader Lieutenant Sato Masao arrived on station a half-hour early. By this time, the Zeros from the 204 and 253 air groups, the "square wing" Model 32s, were patrolling at 6,000 meters, circling the convoy like vultures.[137]

They had passed through the narrowest part of the Vitiaz Strait without enemy air attack. It was the most logical place for the enemy to make their big attack, and now the convoy had passed it. General Yoshihara concluded they were safe and went back down below to discuss the unloading procedures with his colleagues.[138] It was 9:45 am.[139] Lae was only 80 miles away.

The 18th Army Chief of Staff was hardly alone. Throughout the convoy, everyone was getting ready for landing and unloading, hoping to complete it as quickly as possible. The 51st Division troops assembled, almost entirely on deck, to receive their orders as to what to do when they arrived in Lae. One of those decks was that of the *Oigawa Maru*.[140]

Superior Private Machida Tatsue, with the 115th Regiment's headquarters, had just joined Superior Private Yamada Noburo and his group on deck. The briefing officer, a Lieutenant Hashimoto, stood facing the troops with his back to the New Guinea coast.

He proudly told them that the Japanese had conducted a massed airstrike on the Port Moresby airbases. The strike was successful, eliminating the threat from Allied aircraft. Hashimoto triumphantly announced there would be no air attacks today.

The lieutenant continued speaking. Japanese discipline was exceptional. The troops stood and listened. Hashimoto apparently did not notice the uncomfortable looks he was probably getting about now, or that many of his men were looking not so much at him as behind him, their eyes getting wider and wider. In the Imperial Japanese Army, you didn't interrupt a superior, ever, no matter what.[141] Private Machida silently wished the lieutenant would shut up and look behind him.

As Private Yamada later remembered, as soon as Lieutenant Hashimoto announced there was no fear of Allied air attacks, two groups of Allied aircraft emerged from the clouds behind him. While Hashimoto continued to enjoy the sound of his own voice, the troops watched the planes getting closer and closer, revealing themselves to be B-17 Flying Fortresses at high altitude and twin-engine bombers, maybe B-25 Mitchells, at a much lower altitude.

Army bugles sounded the air attack alert. Lieutenant Hashimoto shut up; his reaction was not recorded. The troops headed below decks except for those manning the antiaircraft guns, of which the *Oigawa Maru* had two, plus a field gun. They would be manned by members of the 50th Antiaircraft Battalion.[142] On the *Tokitsukaze*, the siren sounded an air raid alarm, and General Yoshihara headed for the bridge.[143] Similar scenes played out on all the ships of the convoy.

The gunners watched the Americans and Australians coming from the port side. The Japanese saw the approaching squadrons to port and watched the formations fan out. The B-17s tried a pincer approach from both the east and west. Some of the B-25s moved east; others came directly at the ships of the convoy. The four-engine bombers stayed at high altitude while the twin-engine bombers stayed at much lower altitudes, maybe 1,000 to 2,000 meters from the target. Must be planning torpedo attacks, the Japanese thought. Unusual for the Americans, but nothing the Japanese hadn't seen before.[144]

The scary part was that these Americans and Australians were positioning themselves to attack from all sides. There were so many of them. And the Japanese could see ever more aircraft approaching in the distance.

Lieutenant Hashimoto had gotten one thing right: this was not really an attack. This was an ambush, the likes of which the Japanese had never seen before.

It was *Magic*.

On February 25, General Kenney walked into General MacArthur's office, where he was handed a message. It was not a message for him, however, or for anyone in the US Army Air Force, the US Army, or even anyone in the US or Australia. Rather, it was a

Japanese message from February 21. It had been intercepted, decoded, and forwarded by the US Navy.

Recall that *Magic* was the term adopted by the Allies to reference signals intelligence obtained by breaking encrypted Japanese radio and wireless telegraph communications. The major breakthrough had come in decrypting the Japanese naval high-level command and control communications code the Allies called "JN-25." With the Japanese unaware of the breach, *Magic* and signals intelligence would be the gift that kept on giving, most of the time; the Japanese did change their codes every now and then, usually at the most inconvenient times, like August 1942 and January 1943. And the system did not always work perfectly. The Allies could not and did not read and decrypt every single Japanese message as if it were a tap on a phone, but often enough to get a general picture of what the Japanese were intending. Decrypts of Japanese messages had allowed the Americans to challenge the Japanese at Coral Sea and, most famously, ambush the Japanese at Midway.

Now, here was another Japanese decrypt. The decoding was performed by the US Navy analysts at Pearl Harbor, but in other locations as well, such as in Melbourne. In this particular case, it was passed up the food chain to Washington and took three days to decrypt.[145] This was how General MacArthur's people got a hold of the message and how General Kenney saw it. Without taking it out of MacArthur's office. *Ultra* and its subset *Magic* were two of the Allies' biggest and most closely guarded secrets in the war.[146]

The message was from Base Air Force (11th Air Fleet) about a six-ship convoy intended to land the 51st Division on New Guinea around March 5.[147] As General Kenney explained:

> [It] indicat[ed] that a big Jap convoy was scheduled to arrive in Lae sometime early in March. Several cargo and transport vessels escorted by destroyers appeared to be coming from Rabaul and some others were coming from Palau. There might even be another increment from Truk. Both Madang and Lae were possibilities as unloading points for all or part of the convoy. The information was rather sketchy, but this was definitely to be on a much bigger scale than the convoy run into Lae on January 7th, which had consisted of five destroyers and five merchant ships. This looked as though it would be at least twice as large.

This was a major crisis. General MacArthur had just captured Buna and was planning to roll up Japanese strongpoints along the north coast of New Guinea, but the units he had used to take Buna, Gona, and Sanananda were pretty much exhausted and needed time to recover before undertaking any other major combat operations. A lot of Japanese troops running into Lae would complicate that tremendously. MacArthur had actually predicted such a Japanese move after he captured Buna. His own intelligence analyst General Willoughby warned on February 19 of "further troop movements to the Lae area."[148] MacArthur had been proven right. He believed that the Japanese planned to reinforce Lae with a full division, which would allow them to take the offensive in New Guinea. This convoy or convoys,

MacArthur predicted, or convoys, would be composed of both troop and supply vessels, heavily escorted by surface craft and airplanes. He was mostly right.[149]

It was going to be a huge convoy. It had to be stopped. The general did not have the naval forces to stop it, and his troops were too worn out to stand up to it on land. He did have heavy air forces. General Kenney sent a fast courier to General Whitehead, the deputy commander of the 5th Air Force, who not only ran the fighters of the 5th Fighter Command, but basically ran operations in New Guinea from what was known as the 5th Air Force, Advanced Echelon (with a painkiller-sounding acronym of "ADVON") in Port Moresby. Kenney passed along the information, if not the source, and ordered Whitehead to heavily patrol the Wewak-Admiralties-Kavieng-Rabaul area so they could locate the convoy early in its voyage. Kenney planned to pound the convoy relentlessly until it was sunk.[150]

But therein lay a few major problems. One was the weather. The forecasts indicated bad weather for the first three or four days of March along the north coast of New Britain. The storm front would be the perfect cover for a troop convoy. General Kenney told General MacArthur he planned to find the enemy convoy as soon as possible and attack it with heavy bombers until it came into range of his medium and light bombers. And therein lay a second major problem, rearing its ugly head once again: the ineffectiveness of bombing ships at sea from high altitudes. Major Benn had been working with the 63rd Bombardment Squadron on a solution, which was, basically, bombing ships at sea from low altitude. Unfortunately, on January 18 he and his B-25 Mitchell had not returned from a reconnaissance mission.[151] But the results of his experiments had been passed on.

The first idea Major Benn had tried was a tactic previously tried by the British, in particular in an attack on *Kriegsmarine* ships at Wilhelmshaven in 1939, known as skip bombing.[152] Skip bombing involved the same concepts one uses when throwing a small rock across a lake and watching it bounce or skip across until its horizontal momentum and the upward pressure of the water are overcome by the rock's weight – except instead of using a rock, you use a bomb.

The idea was for a B-17 or similar bomber to not just go to low altitude, but at an incredibly low altitude, as in between 200 and 250 feet. Speed would be about 200 knots. The bomber would release the bomb so it bounced 60 to 100 feet short of the ship. A perfect skip would take the bomb the rest of the way to the ship.

As initially tried, this idea needed fine tuning. First, when the bomber dropped the bomb, instead of bouncing ahead to the ship, it bounced back up at the bomber. In combat, that would be, at best, embarrassing. The weight of the bomb was adjusted to put more of it forward so it hit the water at a slightly downward angle. One problem solved.[153]

A second issue was that the bomb could detonate when it hit the water, both before it hit the ship and before the bomber could get clear of the explosion. The solution was to have a 4- to 5-second delay on the fuse. Another problem solved. And this is why you test things before you try them. Just because something works in theory does not mean it will work in practice.

A second tactic tested was low-altitude bombing. In fact, low-altitude bombing, also called masthead bombing because the bombers were often at the height of the top of the target's masts, evolved out of skip bombing. Instead of trying to get the bomb to skip, they would simply aim for the hull of the target ship. The attack run would still be at low altitude – 2,000 feet or so – but not as low as in skip bombing. Again, speed would be about 200 knots. At the end of a bombing run of about 20 seconds, the bomber or bombers, since it often worked better with two, but no more than that, would drop two to four bombs each, aimed at a reference point on the front of the aircraft used as a bomb sight. If anything, low-altitude bombing was even more effective than skip bombing.

Of course, low-altitude bombing is dangerous, as pilots attempting to aim torpedoes at enemy ships had learned. There seems to have been a lot of animosity in the American military establishment, whether Navy or Army Air Force, to torpedoes. Part of it was undoubtedly because American torpedoes at that time simply didn't work, which brings up the question of whether American torpedoes didn't work because that animosity prevented sufficient effort and development being put into them. Skip bombing and low-level bombing could be decent substitutes, however. Unlike complicated and temperamental torpedoes, bombs were relatively straightforward. And cheap.

But the dangers of low-level attacks remained. Being close to the water runs the risk of a turn going wrong, causing the wing to dip into the water and the plane to cartwheel spectacularly into a final, fatal crash. But the big danger is from enemy antiaircraft fire. That was one reason the Army Air Force kept the high-altitude bombing theory, because it was well above antiaircraft fire. Low-level bombing and skip bombing added that variable back into the equation. As the head of the 43rd Bombardment Group warned:

Skip bombing with heavy bombardment aircraft must be considered an attack of opportunity. An attempt to skip bomb a war vessel in the daylight, unsupported, would be hazardous, because of lack of speed, maneuverability, and small amount of forward fire. Successful daylight attacks have been made on unescorted merchant vessels by heavy bombers. Repeated skip bombing attacks in the same area would result in some form of protection to defeat it.[154]

That was with reference to the B-17, a four-engine heavy bomber. But what about something smaller, faster, more maneuverable? Like a twin-engine bomber, say, the A-20 Havoc or the B-25 Mitchell, something not as expensive or as rare as a B-17? That was part of it – but no risk, no reward.

There had to be some way of minimizing that risk, however. One way was to suppress enemy antiaircraft fire by strafing the decks of the target ship, forcing the gunners to seek cover away from their guns. But that was a problem, too. The B-17s were infamous for having their weakest spot in front of the cockpit, because there was very little in the way of guns up front. The assumption in the design was that the B-17 would be targeted from behind, above, below, or the sides, not the front. Once the Japanese had learned about this weak spot, the B-17s suffered. A lot of the bombers the Army Air Force used suffered from this same weakness.

Enter one Paul Irvin Gunn. Known as "Pappy" due to what was considered to be his advanced age, he had been made a major in July 1942 despite the beliefs among many in his unit – including him – that he was sure to be court martialed, not that anyone in his unit wanted him court martialed. Gunn was very popular – except with staff inspectors.

Born in 1899, Major Gunn was a pilot, but when General Kenney met him in August, he was serving as group engineering and maintenance officer for the 3rd Attack Group – a sort of composite combat group that consisted of the 8th, 13th, 89th, and 90th Bombardment Squadrons – not that that was saying much. The 8th had no airplanes at all. The 13th had a few Douglas A-24 Banshees, the Army Air Force's version of the Navy's SBD Dauntless dive bomber, which was unpopular with the Army Air Force in general and Kenney in particular. The 89th was equipped with about 12 North American B-25 Mitchell medium bombers, which had only one 30-caliber front gun, once again showing that lack of forward firepower. The 90th had 16 Douglas A-20 Havoc light bombers, which had arrived in Australia with no guns and no bomb racks.[155]

When the Havocs had arrived, Gunn let anyone know "in definite and highly profane terms what he thought of everyone from Washington to Australia who had anything to do with sending airplanes to 'his' outfit without guns or bomb racks to fight a war."[156] Gunn built a package mount for four 50-cal machine guns and rebuilt the nose of the Havoc with them. Gunn tested the design himself by flying a one-man attack at treetop level on a Japanese airbase on the north coast of New Guinea. He managed to destroy several aircraft, set fire to a gasoline dump, and detonate parts of an ammunition dump – not a bad job at all. The only problem was that he had not received permission for the aforementioned modifications. He rarely did, which would get him into trouble with the staff inspectors and the threat of court martial.[157] That's military bureaucracy for you. Find something that works and it crucifies you for not having your i's crossed and t's dotted.

But the threat of a court martial ended when General Kenney found him. Kenney considered Gunn's style as unorthodox as his own, perhaps more so. Gunn's energy and enthusiasm was infectious. From the way Gunn talked, Kenney could tell he was highly intelligent, and his work showed he was creative, resourceful, and mechanically inclined. Kenney ordered him to report to Brisbane and put him in charge of "special projects."

Major Gunn's first "special project" was to take the 170-odd wrecked fighter planes sitting at an airfield west of Brisbane and get as many of them flying as possible because General Kenney knew he was not going to be getting more in the way of aircraft from the US for a while. Gunn got more than 100 of them up and running. They were forwarded to New Guinea where they played a "vital part" in holding off the Japanese from taking the entire island.[158] Then came the next project for Major Gunn: skip bombing.

General Kenney was an advocate of skip bombing. Indeed he had been an advocate of low-level bombing since at least the 1930s. By November 1942, under his direction,

Major Benn was experimenting with skip bombing. But they faced the old problem of trying to suppress enemy antiaircraft fire. The forward guns of the B-17s just didn't do it. Kenney had been impressed with Major Gunn's work on those A-20s, but most of the A-20s were going to the Soviets these days. They needed to try that on a different airframe.

According to General Kenney:

> I sent word to Pappy at Brisbane to pull the bomb sight, the bombardier, and the one 30-caliber gun out of the nose of a B-25 and fill the place full of as many 50-caliber guns as he could squeeze in there, with five hundred rounds of ammunition per gun. I suggested that he also strap a couple more guns on each side of the fuselage and about three more underneath. If, when he had made the installation, the airplane would still fly and the guns would shoot without tearing the airplane apart, I figured I'd have a skip bomber that could overwhelm the deck defences of a Jap vessel as the plane came in for the kill with its bombs.[159]

Within a few weeks, Gunn had made progress on the B-25. There had been a few teething problems with adjusting the weight and the position of the guns, but eventually Gunn managed to put eight .50-cal machine guns in the nose of the B-25 Mitchell – four in the nose itself, and four more in blisters on either side.

By mid-December 1942, Pappy Gunn was ready to try his prototype modified B-25, which on the left side of the fuselage just below the pilot's window bore the words in 8-inch-high letters: "PAPPY'S FOLLY." Next to it was painted a two-gun cowboy with both guns drawn, a determined look on his face, and the message preceded by stars, crosses, and exclamation points, "And that's Plain English."[160] Gunn flew *Pappy's Folly* up to the Charters Towers airbase some 80 miles southwest of Townsville in northern Australia to demonstrate it to the 3rd Attack Group. The next day Gunn took off from Charters Towers followed by five other Mitchells, whose crews were watching how he handled a low-altitude strafing attack and the results of said attack. The Mitchell pilots were suitably impressed with the volume of fire. Less impressed was a farmer whose cow had wandered into Gunn's field of fire and was turned by *Pappy's Folly* into hamburger. General Kenney had the farmer reimbursed.[161]

The cost was immaterial. *Pappy's Folly* had been a rousing success. Pappy Gunn had turned the previously mediocre North American B-25 Mitchell medium bomber (the Doolittle Raid notwithstanding) into a strafing machine, a type of early gunship, or, what General Kenney preferred to call it, a "commerce destroyer."[162]

And thus strafing became an essential part of skip bombing and low-level bombing:

> The added ability to strafe proved crucial to the success of the low-level mission against shipping. The firepower-laden aircraft negated the enemy's defensive fire: "The strafing attack is an essential element in minimum-altitude bombing of enemy vessels. To minimize losses from antiaircraft fire it is necessary to cover the enemy's decks with .50-caliber fire

which will keep gunners away from their positions and greatly hamper the efforts of any gunners who do remain at their posts." These strafing attacks were carried out simply "by ruddering slightly during the bombing approach … [making] it possible to sweep the entire deck of an enemy vessel with machine-gun fire."[163]

By early February 1943 Pappy Gunn had modified enough B-25s to equip a squadron. From the 89th Bombardment Squadron, General Kenney plucked Ed Larner, a "fireball" who had a reputation for taking his A-20 Havoc so low on strafing runs that he once tore through about a hundred yards of palm trees. This was exactly the type of aggressive pilot Kenney wanted. He told Larner to "help Pappy with testing, and learn to like the airplane." Two weeks later, Larner returned from the temporary assignment, at which time Kenney gave him another promotion, placing him in command of the 90th Bombardment Squadron, and told him to train the squadron in the art of low-level attack with Pappy Gunn's new "commerce destroyers."[164]

There was a major learning curve. The newly promoted Major Larner's men trained by skipping bombs into the side of what was known as the "Moresby Wreck," the beached hulk of the 4,700-ton British cruise liner SS *Pruth* that had run aground on Nateara Reef in 1923.[165] It wasn't easy and it was dangerous, even without an enemy shooting back at them. One B-25 crew was lost during training when the tail of the aircraft hit the mast of the wreck; at that height and speed the plane went into the water in seconds. Another B-25's bomb exploded instantaneously on impact, badly damaging the aircraft and forcing the pilot to land on a reef, while a third aircraft was peppered with rust and small fragments when the bomb exploded almost instantaneously but inside the wreck.[166]

But they learned. As General Kenney later explained, "I saw a couple of them practicing on the old wreck on the reef outside Port Moresby. They didn't miss. It was pretty shooting and pretty skip-bombing."[167] Also instructed in "the art of low-level attack" were the A-20 Havoc crews of the 89th Bombardment Squadron with their six .50-cal guns, and the Beaufighter crews of the Royal Australian Air Force's No. 30 Squadron with four 20mm cannons and six .303-cal machine guns.[168]

There is practice and there is putting it together. A "dress rehearsal" was held on February 28, with all three elements of a coordinated attack targeting the Moresby Wreck. B-17s opened the bombing from 8,000 feet, then regular B-25s at 5,000 feet. After the high- and medium-level bombing came strafing by the Beaufighters of No. 30 Squadron, followed by the low-level bombing by Major Larner's B-25 commerce destroyers, each armed with 500lb bombs. P-38 Lightnings were also on hand, each one representing a flight of fighters.[169] No one explained to the fighter pilots, or really anyone, why they were doing this "dress rehearsal" right now. They did not know how soon the stage curtain would go up and the spotlights would come on.

Not even General Kenney knew. He went to Port Moresby to analyze the information they had with General Whitehead, including the routes and patterns of previous Japanese convoys, both around the north coast of New Britain and around the south coast, and the weather forecasts. The meteorologists were predicting storms along the north coast of New Britain and sunny weather to the south. Kenney guessed the Japanese would take the northern route to try to hide behind the storm.[170]

That was why Lieutenant Higgins' report had put a lot of wheels in motion in Port Moresby. He returned to the Port Moresby base complex and headed in for debriefing. He wasn't expecting the Spanish Inquisition. Nobody does.

Higgins' mission may have been routine to him, but it was anything but to his superiors. A naval officer was present, as were several journalists, all of whom could ask questions. The debriefing was much more extensive than after previous routine flights. There were quite a few questions about the ships. Lots of important people wanted information about the convoy.[171] General Kenney had guessed right.

Of course, the downside to his guessing right was that the Japanese would not come into range of Kenney's newly upgraded medium and light bombers until March 3. Until then, the 5th Air Force could only attack with the Fortresses and Liberators, and on March 3, the Japanese convoy would be close to Lae. This meant that the commerce destroyers would get only one shot at this.

That was fine with Major Larner. According to General Kenney:

Major Ed Larner promised me that his squadron of B-25 commerce destroyers "wouldn't miss." […] I told Ed to warn that cocky gang of his that they were not taking on any high-school team this time. They were playing Notre Dame. Ed grinned and said he would give them my message. We really had something, I was sure. I had a hunch that the Japs were going to get the surprise of their lives.[172]

Or maybe General Kenney was going to get the surprise of his life because, it seems, General Whitehead was not completely sold on this skip-bombing thing. The story goes that Pappy Gunn heard that Whitehead was reluctant to send out the low-level bombers because the tactic "was unproved and certainly not safe." Whitehead also seems to have been put off by Gunn's "unorthodox methods" and "wild ideas." Some officers are about style more than substance, like Admiral Giffen.[173]

Major Gunn flew up to Port Moresby to have it out with the general, determined to take a commerce destroyer out there himself and prove the efficacy of the tactic. But the pilots had been ordered to not allow him to borrow their aircraft. Pappy Gunn fumed.[174]

But General Whitehead relented. Perhaps it was out of desperation, with the high-level attacks' relative ineffectiveness and the convoy so close to Lae. Or perhaps he had run the idea past his men first, as another story suggests:

That night [March 2], B-25 and A-20 crews prepared to put practice into action: "Colonel [Robert] Strickland [commander of the 3rd Attack Group] assembled the airmen of his

90th and 89th Squadrons. He told them he planned to hit the Japanese convoy with skip bombs in the morning. "However, we're only asking for volunteers. Nobody has to fly on a skip bomb [mast-height] run if he doesn't want to." Nobody declined.[175]

March 3 arrived. It was 8:03 am when the order for the mass attack was finally given:

Enemy convoy consisting of one cruiser, six destroyers, two transports, four cargo approaching New Guinea; probable destination Lae last reported position latitude 0654s longitude 14805e, course 270 speed 10 time 0615/l convoy protected by enemy fighters during daylight hours ... v bom com with maximum striking force of medium, heavy, and light bombardment supported by P-38's will attack enemy convoy when in range of light bombardment. The attack will be made by one squadron B-17's (12 airplanes) four squadrons B-25's one squadron Beaufighters, one squadron A-20's escorted by two squadrons P-38's.[176]

In preparation for the strike on the convoy, 12 B-25s of the 38th Bombardment Group and 20 A-20 Bostons from No. 22 Squadron were performing a low-level attack with frag clusters and napalm to suppress the Japanese Army Air Force's Lae airbases. For some reason, the Japanese were caught by surprise again and there was no fighter opposition or even antiaircraft fire. Afterwards, Warhawks of the 7th and 8th Fighter Squadrons as well as Beaufighters patrolled the skies over Lae and occasionally strafed the runways to try to keep the Japanese fighters down, rendering the airfields useless for much of the morning.[177]

The orders for conduct of the attack went out:

Order of assembly and approach to target one squadron of B 17's at 9000 feet, one squadron of B25's 8000 feet, one squadron B25's 7000 feet, one squadron Beaufighters 6000 feet, one squadron B25's 5500 feet, one squadron B25-C l's 5000 feet, one squadron A20's 4500 feet, one squadron of Bostons [Australian A-20s] 4000 feet[.]

Order of attack[.] First Beaufighters strafing, the B25's, then B25's-C1, followed by A20's and Bostons all mast head-then B17's from 7000 feet to 10,000 feet, followed by one squadron B25's 3000 to 6000 feet[.] Bombs medium bombers 1000 lb. demolition and instantaneous fuse, high bombers 1000 lb. demolition instantaneous fuse, mast head attack 500 and 250 lb. 5 second delay[.][178]

Leading off were 13 Bristol Beaufighters led by Squadron leader Ross Little of the Royal Australian Air Force's 30 Squadron. The Beaufighters' job was to strafe the decks of the Japanese ships. When 30 Squadron skipper Wing Commander Brian "Blackjack" Walker briefed his aircrews, he reminded them that their mission was to force the Japanese gunners to take cover. It might be just a few seconds, but those few seconds could be used by the following aircraft attacking at low altitude. Additionally, Walker told them to attack the ships' bridges and thus cause maximum destruction and confusion in the ships' nerve centers. It was an idea he got from Group Captain William "Bill" Garing, commander of Australian air forces in New Guinea. Garing believed ships' bridges were far more vulnerable than generally believed. Now, they would find out. In fact, Garing supplied a lot of the ideas used on this attack, including the rendezvous point for the airstrike at Cape Ward Hunt.[179] After the Australians and Americans were all together, they'd head off to the convoy. First priority for this attack was the transports carrying Imperial Army troops. Warships were second priority, and the Lae airfield a rather distant third.[180]

Major Larner gave his crews a short briefing. They knew what was at stake. It was five minutes to 9 o'clock when Larner was (finally) informed the rendezvous point was Cape Ward Hunt, on the far coast of New Guinea, at 9:30. He shouted, "Cape Ward Hunt! Let's go!" and led everyone out to the commerce destroyers.[181]

Arriving at Cape Ward Hunt first at 9:25 were B-25s of the 71st Squadron, 38th Bombardment Group, circling at 5,300 feet. Captain W.S. Royalty watched in awe as the procession of aircraft for the strike at the convoy assembled. Twenty-eight P-38 Lightnings of the 9th and 39th Fighter Squadrons were at the highest altitude. Below them were 13 B-17 Flying Fortresses of the 64th and 403rd Bombardment Squadrons. Two squadrons of B-25 Mitchells – one of 13, the other of 12 – 12 A-20 Havocs of 89th Squadron, plus the 13 Beaufighters, circled at 6,000 feet. Royalty described it as "an almost unbelievable number of planes."[182]

"The weather was near to perfect with only scattered clouds over the water," said the 39th Fighter Squadron's Captain King. "It was quite a sight for pilots who were accustomed to only small operations and who were almost constantly outnumbered in the air." It was a veritable layer cake of death, an aerial armada larger than anything the Allies had previously assembled in New Guinea, or, for that matter, the Pacific War.[183]

One big circle and they all headed for a point in the Huon Gulf 50 miles southeast of Finschhafen.[184] Lieutenant Trigg had been keeping the convoy in sight despite constant harassment by eight to ten Zeros so the airstrike would know exactly where to go.[185] It was about 10:00 when a crewman in a 90th Squadron B-25, Royal Australian Air Force Sergeant Bob Guthrie, heard a radio call, "that the convoy was in sight; and the game was on."[186] When the 71st's Captain Royalty first saw the convoy:

> Nearest to us, as we came closer, were what seemed to be two cruisers and three destroyers. These ships were making violent maneuvers and wakes were streaming out ten or twelve times their lengths. I counted six transports and cargo vessels on the other side of these warships, and at least two warships further on. The warships were moving fast, but the cargo ships seemed to be almost at a standstill.[187]

On the Japanese ships down below, the bugles and klaxons blared, but any shock at the sudden appearance of so many enemy aircraft had given way to the practiced routine of responding to air attack. The ships, the crews, the soldiers were all veterans; they instinctively knew what to do. But some of the gunners despaired at the sight of so many enemy aircraft: "Together they numbered fifty planes and swarmed over our heads. Everyone had a feeling of helplessness. There were none of our planes."[188]

That wasn't quite true. Base Air Force was indeed here. Those 12 Zeros of the 204 Air Group and 14 Zeros of the 253 Air Group were now at about 6,000 meters. Below them were the *Zuiho*'s 18 Zeros.[189] Of course, someone had to tell them where the enemy attack planes were, which was rather difficult since most of the Zeros did not have radios. Anyway, the Zeros from the *Zuiho* seem to have been close to the approach of the B-17s and moved in to intercept.[190]

The Beaufighters of 30 Squadron had descended to about 500 feet. They fanned out, like a cavalry charge of old. As they did so, the Beaufighters "lost height rapidly and using rated power attacked in line abreast at a speed of 220 knots." Their course would have taken them from south to north over the leading four destroyers: *Tokitsukaze, Shikinami, Shirayuki,* and *Uranami*. To Admiral Kimura and his skippers, it looked like a torpedo attack, similar to what those Beauforts from 100 Squadron had attempted earlier. But these pilots had committed too soon. Consistent with orders for evasion issued before sailing, the ships turned into the Beaufighters' attack to present a narrow bow profile.

At about the same time, the 13 B-17s had maneuvered into position above to drop their bombs – after a fashion. They had fallen foul of the Zeros from the *Zuiho*.[191] Major George Prentice had a plan for dealing with the Zeros – just plunge into their midst – except the Zeros of the 204 and 253 air groups were there, too. The Lightnings of the 39th Squadron did not have the height advantage they usually had, and they got tied up in a series of dogfights with the "clipped-wing" Zeros.

The *Zuiho*'s fighters slashed viciously at the Fortresses. The B-17 of the 403rd's Captain Easlon S. Halcutt was riddled by 20mm cannon fire from the Zeros, wounding Halcutt in the head. His co-pilot took control and headed back to Port Moresby in time to save Halcutt's life. The 403rd's Captain Crawford endured his Fortress being shredded by Zeros, but he did drop his bombs, ineffectually, and somehow made it back to Port Moresby.

Not making it back to Port Moresby was the B-17 of the 65th's Lieutenant Moore. A Zero came in under the wing and fired a burst of 20mm cannon upward into the fuselage. Moore's Fortress-mates saw an explosion in the cockpit and flames coming out the bomb bay. Soon, flames were seen "spouting from the windows and tail." Moore's B-17 began to lose altitude, its Number 3 engine and radio compartment ablaze. Its bombs tumbled out of the partially open bomb bay, followed by seven crewmen. Moore may have been trying to ditch the burning bomber, but just before it was to hit the water, the tail fell off and the plane disintegrated.[192]

Japanese sources, especially one Flight Petty Officer Iwai Tsutomi, claim a *Zuiho* Zero flown by Chief Flight Petty Officer Maki Masanao actually rammed the Flying Fortress. Why Maki would ram his perfectly good and undamaged Zero into an enemy bomber and kill one of the relatively few trained fighter pilots in the Japanese Naval Air Force is anybody's guess; he may have simply been overcome with emotion at the attack on the convoy. In any event, none of the Americans around it recalled seeing a Japanese Zero ram the Fortress, but the Japanese are insistent on the story; Iwai claims to have witnessed it. In fairness, many of the Fortress crews saw the Japanese fighters cutting it very close in their firing passes, making the pilots fearful of a midair collision and creating a deadly game of chicken in the air. So a midair collision, if not an intentional ram, is possible. Furthermore, many are skeptical of the idea of a Flying Fortress's tail falling off due solely to gunfire. Of the seven crew who bailed out, one man was seen to fall out of his harness and plunge to his death. The remaining six opened their parachutes just long enough for three Zeros, from either the 204 or 253 air groups, to strafe them and riddle their canopies. Neither Moore nor any of the other crew was ever seen again.[193]

While the crews of the Flying Fortresses seethed over what they considered a war crime, their bombs were busy splashing in the water. All missed, it was later determined. Nevertheless, the B-17s had done their job and done it very well. Many of the antiaircraft guns on Admiral Kimura's ships were now trained upward and the Zeros were led to high altitude. Not too many eyes were focused on low altitude.

But those that were knew what they were doing. Destroyer *Tokitsukaze* was the first to open fire, with her main battery to boot. She was quickly followed by the *Arashio* and other destroyers. These Japanese sailors were veterans, and they knew air defense. They did not open fire until they had targets in a crossfire, and then they used a stepped fire pattern that was especially effective against torpedo bombers.[194] The Allied aviators agreed that the Japanese fire control was excellent.[195]

Even so, the Japanese were getting it wrong, as the Beaufighters were about to prove. Admiral Kimura's turn into their course was the proper maneuver for countering a torpedo attack, presenting with only a narrow bow profile. Unfortunately for him, these Beaufighters were not making a torpedo attack. And Kimura's turn had the effect of taking the destroyers out of position for protecting the transports. The Beaufighters mostly ignored the destroyers and turned to go at the vulnerable convoy ships, dodging falling drop tanks from the P-38s in the process. The transports themselves had also tried to turn into the alleged torpedo attack, improving the targets for the Beaufighters, who could now make stem-to-stern strafing runs.

Flight Lieutenant George Drury of 30 Squadron managed to get his Beaufighter lined up with the *Taimei Maru*. He put his targeting reticle over the merchant ship's bridge, where they were changing the watch at this rather inopportune time. Drury then "pressed that firing button with gay abandon. Left the pull out a little bit late and had to bank to go between the masts."[196] The 20mm cannons scythed through the *Taimei Maru's* overcrowded bridge, leaving it wrecked and burning.[197]

Similar scenes occurred throughout the convoy. With their four 20mm cannons in the nose and six .303-cal machine guns in the wings, the Beaufighters delivered a storm of white-hot metal to anyone on deck, in particular the men manning the antiaircraft guns. According to the Royal Australian Air Force official history, "The attack had its intended effect of silencing many of the anti-aircraft gun crews, among whom the casualties, as torn and burning superstructure indicated, must have been considerable[.]"[198]

Among those casualties was Admiral Kimura. A Beaufighter strafing run over the *Shirayuki* cut down most on the destroyer's bridge and left the admiral with wounds from .303-cal rounds in his left thigh, right shoulder, and stomach. Remarkably, Kimura just walked it off and continued to command. Signal flags were raised to advise the other destroyers of his condition, but initially the wrong flags were raised, flags that signaled the admiral was dead. Morale tanked throughout the convoy until the flags were corrected.[199]

After the brutal beating by the Beaufighters, the next attack by 13 B-25s from the 71st Squadron, bombing from medium altitude, was almost a respite. None of their bombs was believed to have hit. But more B-25s were coming – in particular, Major Ed Larner's 12 B-25s of the 90th Bombardment Squadron. Each was carrying three or four 500lb bombs. The squadron split into three sections, then it split up some more. Larner split off to port to attack a large destroyer at the head of the convoy. Three other Mitchells followed him. "Dammit," he growled on the radio, "get the hell off my wing and get your own boat."[200] That was one way to avoid overconcentration of fire. Approaching from the bow at an altitude of 500 feet, into the teeth of antiaircraft fire, Larner unleashed his eight .50-cal machine guns on the destroyer. The antiaircraft fire stopped. Larner then executed a textbook masthead bombing attack, going below mast height and releasing two bombs before pulling up, up, and away.

Major Larner scored one hit near the stern at 10:03 am and a near miss, which, as it developed, was exactly the result the pilots would want. The near miss would be so close as to cause mining damage to the hull, the concussion rupturing seams and hull plates. In this case, the bomb hit the aft 5-inch mount and apparently started a fire in the mount's handling room below. The destroyer rolled onto her side, then righted herself. The handling room then detonated and, in the words of one observer, "blew the arse right off" the enemy ship, which turned out to be Admiral Kimura's flagship *Shirayuki*.[201] Her stern gone, her hull flooding, the *Shirayuki* held on for only another 90 minutes, during which time the *Shikinami* bravely came alongside and stopped to take off Kimura and his staff and some of the wounded. The *Shirayuki* plunged to the depths at 11:35 am with 32 of her crew. Survivors included Admiral Kimura; Captain Sugino Shuichi, commander of 11th Destroyer Division; and skipper Commander Sugawara Rokorou.[202]

The skip and low-level bombings were being finely tuned in their first major mission. The typical attack would involve two aircraft, one to strafe the target ship from stem to stern, or vice versa, to suppress antiaircraft fire, and one to drop the bombs on the ship's beam.[203] And, again, the pilots would try for one direct hit and one near miss.[204]

Captain John "Jock" Henebry dove toward what was probably the *Oigawa Maru* and machine-gunned her decks, noticing as he did so that there were already fires there courtesy of the Beaufighters. He dropped two bombs: one hit the waterline amidships and the other missed by 15 feet. He then turned to the *Shinai Maru*, strafed her, and started a fire on her deck before getting a near miss with his bomb. Then he headed for home.[205]

The *Shinai Maru* was rapidly becoming popular. Lieutenant Gordon McCoun zoomed in so low that the Japanese troops on board thought he would hit the bridge, while

McCoun could see the individual Japanese soldiers on deck. The Mitchell put two bombs into the *Shinai Maru*. The merchant ship would suffer a total of four bomb hits and six near misses. One bomb hit the Number 3 hatch while another exploded on the bridge, killing her skipper. Her steam pipes were ruptured and the *Shinai Maru* lost power and staggered to a stop. At 10:20, her crew was ordered to evacuate.[206]

The mayhem multiplied. Lieutenant Charles "Chuck" Howe was caught between two destroyers whose antiaircraft fire forced him into evasive maneuvers "to a degree (Howe) never contemplated." He turned his machine guns on what is believed to have been the *Teiyo Maru* and raked the merchant ship for 260 yards before releasing two bombs and vaulting over the ship. No one saw what happened to these bombs.

But they saw what happened to the next ones. Lieutenant Howe swung to starboard to take a crack at the *Aiyo Maru*. He opened up the Mitchell's guns at a range of 500 yards, then dropped two bombs. His gunner told him what the bombs did. One had just missed, as it was intended to do, but the other had been a direct hit amidships. Not just a direct hit, but one that set off "a terrific explosion which all but cut the vessel in two. This vessel was left obviously in a sinking condition."[207] Howe went on to strafe one more ship before turning for home at an altitude of 20 feet.

Like Lieutenant Howe, Lieutenant John William "Bill" Smallwood was caught between two destroyers – the *Shirayuki*, who would not be around much longer, and the *Shikinami* – as he made a run at the big *Teiyo Maru*. Sergeant Richard Martin, manning the top turret, climbed down and excitedly shouted, "You ought to see what's going on out there!" Radioman Bill Blewett of the Royal Australian Air Force shouted back, "Get back in that [expletive deleted] turret!" Lots of Royal Australian Air Force aviators were peppered throughout the 13th and 90th Squadrons especially, and throughout the 5th Air Force generally, due to a shortage of trained American crewmen in the theater. As they usually did, the Australians acquitted themselves very well.[208]

The destroyers' gunfire knocked out the Mitchell's hydraulics, but Lieutenant Smallwood pressed on, dropping two bombs on the big transport and roaring on to drop a third that near-missed the bow of the *Aiyo Maru*, sending up a towering column of water.

Below him, the *Aiyo Maru* reeled from the explosion off the bow, in mortal agony. Survivors reported a bomb, apparently that of Lieutenant Howe, hit between the bridge and the stack. Another bomb hit aft and caused an explosion in the boiler, while a third bomb hit the top of the Number 3 hold, setting afire the ammunition and drums of fuel inside.[209]

The *Teiyo Maru* was little better off. One Japanese solder on board watched the attacks, later writing, "They seemed to skim the water and climbed just before releasing bombs." The *Teiyo Maru* was hit by four bombs and two of what were called "aerial torpedoes" but were actually skipped bombs on the port bow, plus an incredible 11 near misses. Survivors claimed it was the second bomb that spelled the end for the ship. It stopped the engines, while another bomb had set fire to those fuel drums on deck. The *Teiyo Maru* soon began heeling over and Admiral Kimura ordered her abandoned at 11:00. With the help of the destroyer *Uranami*, the evacuation was complete in a half-hour and the derelict lingered on, though for how long is disputed, to sink either at around 2:00 pm or 5:30 pm. She took with her skipper Captain Ishisaka Takezo, 17 crew, 15 shipboard gunners, and a nightmarish 1,882 troops.[210]

Admiral Kimura and the Japanese, veterans all, had never experienced an attack like this – had never even heard of an attack like this. The enemy attacked from all sides, from every possible angle, and even a few that were impossible, such as below the ship. They were skimming on the water. What devil tactics were the hated Westerners using? Where did they come up with this? Sub-Lieutenant Masuda Reiji of the destroyer *Arashio* recalled:

> They would come in on you at low altitude, and they'd skip bombs across the water like you'd throw a stone. That's how they bombed us. All seven of the remaining transports were enveloped in flames. Their masts tumbled down, their bridges flew to pieces, the ammunition they were carrying was hit, and whole ships blew up. [...]
>
> They hit us amidships. B-17s, fighters, skip bombers, and torpedo bombers. On our side, we were madly firing, but we had no chance to beat them off.[211]

Indeed, Sub-Lieutenant Masuda's ship was next, the 90th's Captain Robert Chatt and Royal Australian Air Force co-pilot Maurice Carse taking on the destroyer. Chatt moved to skim the water at 3 miles out, then began strafing the destroyer at a range of 1,500 meters. Their target's skipper Commander Kuboki Hideo believed he was facing a torpedo attack and turned his *Arashio* to face her tormentor. It was a major mistake. While the narrow bow profile made a difficult target for torpedoes, Kuboki had actually made his ship a larger target for bombing, and allowed the approaching Mitchell to strafe the length of the ship. Chatt dropped four bombs and, sure enough, all four hit – one on the bow, two on the bridge, and one aft on the Number 2 5-inch mount.[212]

In the engine room at the time of the attack, Sub-Lieutenant Masuda felt large shocks through the hull and the ship seemed to jump several times. Then the lights went out as the power died. Masuda called to the bridge and got no answer. A messenger he sent to the bridge returned with the discouraging news that the bridge was gone and the forward part of the ship was in flames. Masuda ran up to see for himself, and was presented with a horror:

> Our bridge was hit by two five-hundred-pound bombs. Nobody could have survived. The captain, the chief navigator, the gunnery and torpedo chiefs, and the chief medical officer were all killed in action. The chief navigator's blackened body was hanging there, all alone. We were carrying about fifty men from the landing force, one hundred and sixty armed men, and three special newspaper correspondents. They, too, were all killed. Somehow, those of us down in the engine room were spared.[213]

Assuming command, the chief engineer joined Sub-Lieutenant Masuda on what was left of the bridge, where they were faced with an immediate crisis. The bomb that hit the Number 2 5-inch mount had gone into the aft machinery room and disabled the *Arashio*'s steering. The ship was still moving – fast – but was out of control.

The Imperial Navy's *Nojima* (not the *Maru*) was moving to assist the stricken destroyer. But no good deed goes unpunished in this part of the world. Out of control, the *Arashio* swung out at high speed and plowed into the *Nojima*. The impact cost the destroyer about four meters of her bow.

But it was far worse for the *Nojima*. While the ships were locked, or shortly thereafter, the *Nojima*, up until now largely unscathed, attracted unwanted attention from the malevolent Mitchells. The B-25 of Lieutenant Harlan Reid made the first run, raking the decks with the devastating bunch of .50-cal machine guns, then released four bombs. He got one hit and three near misses, two of which he had accidentally tossed over the ship as he vaulted his plane upward and over it.

Next was Lieutenant Robert Reed. He started continuously firing his .50-cals at 1,000 yards, and stopped at 400. He dropped three 500lb bombs and got two hits. "We were able to see the result," said Reed's Royal Australian Air Force co-pilot Royce Johnco. "Most satisfactory. A badly crippled ship."[214] With an assist from the *Arashio*.

The 90th Squadron was just finishing its attack when the 89th Squadron with its A-20 Havocs, hot on the heels of the 90th, started its own attack. The 90th's Lieutenant John Sbisa lined up the *Taimei Maru* and unloaded his mass of .50-cals that "blasted well and truly into the superstructure[.]"[215] Sergeant Guthrie pulled the release switch, and the Mitchell roared over the shredded superstructure and away. Behind them, the ship was "going up in smoke, big black puffs of smoke[,]" according to Guthrie. But not from their bombs. "[A]n A-20 had come lengthways down the ship and hit it!" Sbisa's own release mechanism had malfunctioned, and his bombs remained in the bay.[216]

Sure enough, on Lieutenant Sbisa's tail was the A-20 Havoc of the 89th's Captain Glen "Gee-dub" Clark, on whose tail was the A-20 of the 89th's Captain Ed Chudoba. Clark had intended for each two-plane element of his six-plane formation to attack a different ship. But four Havocs were targeting the same ship, and, in sorting themselves out on the fly, they ended up breaking up the two-plane elements. Chudoba swooped on the *Taimei Maru*, only to have Clark and Clark's wingman, Lieutenant Ed Richardson, pass him. Clark raked the ship with his .50-cals then dropped his bombs. One was a near miss, the other a direct hit. This is exactly what low-level attack theory wanted – except the explosion of his bomb caught the tail of Chudoba's Havoc as he was releasing his own bombs. Taking damage from friendly bombs was a danger of these low-level attacks.

But it was hard to argue with the results. Captain Chudoba's bombs skipped into the hull amidships and just off the bow. Lieutenant Richardson also claimed one hit and one near miss. All three Havocs banked away for home.

The *Taimei Maru* shook and wobbled from side to side. As far as her survivors could tell, she took five bomb hits – twice in the Number 2 hold, once in the Number 3 hold, and twice on the bridge – and six near misses. The bombs smashed all the lifeboats and rafts on deck. The near misses apparently ruptured the hull near the engine room, which flooded. The power went out, and with it the lights. And at 10:05 am the *Taimei Maru* staggered to a halt.[217]

Lex McAulay, who had done more than anyone to piece together this action, gives probably the most vivid description of the *Taimei Maru*:

> The rapid succession of hits and near misses rocked the hull wildly from side to side. Inside
> *Taimei-Maru*, the intermingled dead and wounded were were (sic) rolling back and forth,
> flung around by tremendous explosions. Waves of blood were said to literally slosh across
> the decks, while panic-stricken crew members and passengers ran screaming to and fro in
> the shambles. A witness described the scene as "a painting from hell."[218]

The *Taimei Maru* was ordered abandoned a little before 10:30.

So fast, so large, so chaotic was the Allied attack that it is not clear who attacked the *Oigawa Maru*. But she was indeed attacked. Second Lieutenant Kiyoshi Nishio watched as "a cloud of aircraft appeared."[219] As the aircraft arrived, the transport sped up, relatively speaking, but it did no good. A bomb hit amidships, possibly one from Captain Henebry, smashing the lifeboats and rafts, a common theme this day. A second bomb, possibly dropped by Lieutenant Turner Messick, detonated in the engine room, wrecking the machinery and knocking out all power. Fire broke out in the Number 3 and Number 4 holds. All in all, the *Oigawa Maru* was hit by eight bombs, including at least two that skipped.[220] She went dead in the water.

In the interim, the 89th's Captain Roger "Dixie" Dunbar and his wingman Lieutenant Jack Taylor were getting frustrated at a lack of targets – more accurately, a lack of targets not already being attacked by someone else. Until they "finally spotted who must have been the smallest ship in the convoy, later estimated at about 800 to 1,000 tons. One of our 'buddies' claimed it had outriggers on it, a blatant lie if ever I heard one." That's war for you. The first casualty is always truth.

This little ship seemed rather unharmed, as if no one had noticed it yet. Captain Dunbar and Lieutenant Taylor would fix that oversight. With the ship passing in front of them from right to left, Dunbar aimed for amidships and Clark aimed for the stern. They both dropped their bombs, then pulled up and banked to the left. "We both wanted to see the damage we had done," Taylor later said. "As she came into view over our left shoulders, her entire stem blew off, lifting her out of the water by the aft section. She sank almost immediately."[221]

Captain Dunbar would say both of his bombs were near misses. It didn't matter. The ship was the little *Kembu Maru*, packed with high-octane aviation fuel and gasoline. Any air attack that connected with her was a veritable death sentence. And it was here. One or two bombs hit, causing multiple explosions that blew the "sea truck" apart. She disappeared from the sea at 10:10. The Japanese believe she was the first ship to be sunk.

Following her was the *Nojima*, whose engines were disabled by at least one of the bomb hits. Now, she no longer had power to pump out the water flooding in from the *Arashio's* collision. The *Nojima* too began to sink.[222]

On the *Tokitsukaze*, General Yoshihara's run to the bridge was delayed by a "'Blim, blim' like a hail of parched beans," of machine-gun fire that pinned him in his cabin.[223] He later counted 122 bullet holes and dents in the bulkhead. The *Tokitsukaze* was running at high speed and making evasive maneuvers, creating vibrations and groans that the general could feel inside his cabin. Then he felt "a big shock, with a bump, as though the ship had struck a rock." There was no explosion, but Yoshihara noticed the vibration from the engines had stopped; "it was just as though we were on a millpond." That wasn't good. He finally was able to make his way to the bridge where he met General Adachi and skipper Commander Motokura Masayoshi.

Seeking to first satisfy his curiosity, General Yoshihara asked, "What was that shock?"

"We've had it," Commander Motokura replied, which did not exactly answer the question.

But the skipper then proceeded to state that the *Tokitsukaze* had been torpedoed and the engines had stopped. General Yoshihara was surprised. He commented, "If we were torpedoed it is miraculous that there was no explosion." Motokura said the torpedo had passed completely through the ship and exploded on the other side, but was at a loss as to why.

In actuality, at 10:09 am, the *Tokitsukaze* had been struck by a skipped bomb, possibly dropped by a B-25 of the 90th's Lieutenant Don McNutt, on the starboard side that exploded. It flooded the starboard engine room, and the port engine room as well, killing 19. Commander Motokura's explanation may have been correct, or the bomb had just breached the centerline bulkhead. Sailors on deck were horrified to see blood flowing from the holes in the hull. With the engine rooms flooded, she went dead in the water, but she was in no imminent danger of sinking.[224]

But General Yoshihara was practical and kept his eye on the ball, observing, "There is no future in being in a ship that cannot move. Shouldn't we quickly change ships to one that hasn't been damaged?"

Yoshihara looked around and saw the devastation around him. The chief of staff pointed to a destroyer beneath his gaze and said, "Let's change to that one."

That would be the *Yukikaze*. She took off Generals Yoshihara and Adachi, and the entire crew of the *Tokitsukaze*. The evacuation was completed by 11:00 am, and the *Tokitsukaze* was left to drift, a derelict destroyer.[225]

General Yoshihara was stunned at the view around him. "Already the ships had been reduced by half their number, it seemed. And of those ships that were still on the surface, more than half were sending up smoke and flames. I was speechless with amazement because our losses were greater than I could possibly have expected."

Sub-Lieutenant Masuda was watching the *Nojima*. Her bridge was ablaze and burning ammunition on her deck was going off. That was hardly the worst of it. Masuda looked around and saw all seven transports burning.[226] It was 10:15 am, and it was an abject catastrophe.

So far, the new low-level bombing tactics had been an unqualified success, though much of it was due to the coordinated nature of the attacks:

> Despite the phenomenal success of the mast-height attacks, it was clear to the aircrews who made them that "the success of the mission was due to the carefully planned coordinated attack. The high level bombers dispersed the convoy and attracted most of the anti-aircraft fire. Their hits and near misses prevented accurate fire from heavy guns while the Beaufighters must have knocked out a lot of the small caliber fire."[227]

Losses had, so far, been relatively light: three P-38s and one B-17.

Nevertheless, as the bomber crews returned to the airfields around Port Moresby, the mood was one of rage. Everyone focused on that one lost B-17, that of Lieutenant Moore, and how the Japanese had machine-gunned the crewmen in their parachutes. Word of what was perceived as a war crime spread very, very quickly. Men who had never met Lieutenant Moore or any of the crew were suddenly gripped by a seething hatred for the Japanese, a blood rage similar to what the Marines on Guadalcanal felt after the Japanese had massacred the Goettge Patrol the previous August. As it was, the returning crews were already aware of stories from around Buna and Kokoda of war crimes and even cannibalism. Vengeance was on everyone's minds. Sergeant Gordon R. Manuel, a bombardier in the 43rd Bombardment Group, explained, "We got back to the base and everybody knew what had happened to the six boys from the 63rd Squadron. We ate dinner and nobody said much. We were all burning. We couldn't wait until the next day when we might have another crack at those rats."[228]

For those that had known Lieutenant Moore and his crew, the anger was even hotter. Lieutenant Hal Winfrey had been a good friend of Moore and recorded in his diary that the Japanese would "pay more and more for this. We're all seeking revenge."[229] Navigator 1st Lieutenant William M. Ahl recorded in his diary, "I wanted revenge for Moore's death. The other three officers were my closest buddies [...] I wanted to make the Japs pay dearly for this."[230]

Lieutenant Murphy became a part of it upon his return as well:

> We all needed a rest, but no one was willing or ready to stop. We were mad now. The Japanese had violated every rule including the unwritten rule of combat in the air. "One never shoots at people when they eject from an aircraft." The Japanese did it – in spades.[231]

Of course, unwritten rules are not worth the paper they're written on. The Japanese, both Navy and Army pilots, had been known to machine-gun parachuting airmen.[232] Sometimes there is a sense even among warring organizations of a certain shared brotherhood and mutual respect that crosses the lines of war. This is true especially among pilots. By machine-gunning the survivors of Lieutenant Moore's crew, the Japanese – or at least these particular Japanese pilots – were saying they themselves were not a part of that brotherhood.

The new bloodlust of many members of the 5th Bomber Command would be satiated this day; for others it would not. What became known as "The Battle of the Bismarck Sea" – which, technically, did not take place in the Bismarck Sea at all – was for all intents and purposes over. All the transports were either sunk or in sinking condition. All that remained was mopping up, making sure the crippled ships were sunk – and machine-gunning the survivors in the water.

Lex McAulay described the foundation of the bloodlust:

Only a year before it had been Japanese air forces which swept Pacific seas, beginning with the devastating attack on Pearl Harbor on a Sunday morning while their envoys supposedly held peace negotiations in Washington DC. [...] Then the Japanese rampaged southwards towards Australia, with aircraft ruthlessly sinking and strafing the ships fleeing Malaya, Singapore, Java, Sumatra and the Philippines. Stories from survivors of the ships had been preceded by others of Japanese behaviour in the war in Manchuria and China; tales of the Bataan Death March had leaked out; the Japanese caused many civilian casualties in bombing raids on Darwin and Broome.

[...] In the fighting across the Kokoda Track, and at Milne Bay, Buna, Gona, Guadalcanal, and other places in the Solomons, the Allies found evidence of what happened to prisoners taken by the Japanese: torture, brutality, beheadings, used for bayonet practice. A diary captured on Guadalcanal described experimental surgery (vivisection) carried out on two living Americans, who had been shot in the feet to prevent their escape. [...]

And added to that was Lieutenant Moore and his crew.

"Now the Japanese in the Bismarck Sea were to pay for all that."[233]

Many of these atrocities had been committed by Imperial Japanese Army soldiers who made up the bulk of the survivors now treading water. No mercy would be shown to them.

Certainly good fortune had not been with Imperial Japan or its flyers this day. The Zeros of the 204, 253, and *Zuiho* air groups had held their own against the deadly P-38 Lightnings. But their job had not been to stop the P-38s. It had been to stop the attacking bombers, and with the exception of Lieutenant Moore's bomber, they had not. They had been badly fooled. The frustration of the pilots in their failure and their anger at the carnage in the convoy below them is one possible explanation, not by any means an excuse, for their machine-gunning the survivors of Moore's B-17.

The Japanese fighters were about to make another crucial mistake. Imperial Army Major Taniguchi Masayoshi, executive officer of the 11th Air Group, had led 13 other Ki-43s out of Rabaul for afternoon convoy escort duty. As they neared the convoy, Taniguchi saw four destroyers hightailing it northward. Taniguchi eventually found the convoy, or what was left of it. By this time, the *Aiyo* and *Kembu Maru*s and the *Nojima* had sunk. Scattered in a 15-mile-long swath roughly east-to-west were the *Oigawa*, *Shinai*, *Taiyo*, and *Taimei Maru*s, not necessarily in that order, all burning. At the western end of this group was the crippled destroyer *Arashio*, barely moving, if at all. Furthest north and west was the abandoned, derelict *Tokitsukaze*, pointed east, leaking a lot of oil.

As Lex McAulay put it, "Around the burning hulks and patches of wreckage were several thousand Japanese soldiers and sailors of all ranks up to admiral who had just received a lesson in the use of air power."[234] Picking her way through those several thousand Japanese soldiers and sailors was the destroyer *Asashio*, not damaged, just trying to fish as many survivors, especially those of the *Nojima*, out of the water as she could.[235]

Those four destroyers Major Taniguchi had seen racing away were the *Shikinami*, *Uranami*, *Asagumo*, and *Yukikaze* of the injured other Admiral Kimura. They were not picking up survivors but running away. Kimura had learned his lesson in the use of air power. McAulay would call Kimura's actions here "prudent."[236]

Major Taniguchi was aghast. He wanted to report the convoy's status, such as it was, to his superiors in the 11th Air Group and 12th Air Brigade. Of course, he had no radio, so, taking two other Nakajimas for escort, he sped off to Lae, thereby reducing the air cover for what was left of the convoy by three fighters.[237]

The 5th Bomber Command issued new strike orders shortly after noon. However, bad weather closed in on the Owen Stanleys and blocked most of the air groups from Port Moresby save for the 39th Fighter Squadron of P-38s. Aircraft based north of the Owen Stanleys, on the Dobodura airfield, waited for the Port Moresby squadrons to join them, and then returned to the convoy. They left the rendezvous area in the following sequence: 65th Squadron B-17s, 90th, 71st, and 405th Squadron B-25s, 64th Squadron B-17s, and 22 Squadron in A-20 Bostons, all escorted by ten Lightnings of the 39th Fighter Squadron. They went out "with blood in their eyes and revenge in their hearts."[238] Their orders were to bomb anything afloat. The gunners were to destroy any lifeboats or landing barges they saw. Now the slaughter truly began.

At 3:05 pm, an observer from the 63rd Squadron at 8,000 feet counted five burning ships and two destroyers, both warships steaming north. Six B-17s of the 64th Squadron were seen to go for one of the destroyers. Ten minutes later, the 65th Squadron reported that a transport had sunk, probably *Teiyo Maru*, which Australian Boston crews reported had just exploded.

One of the destroyers that was moving was the *Asashio*. The story goes that Captain Sato Yasuo, commander of 8th Destroyer Division, had made a promise to the skipper of the *Nojima*, Captain Matsumoto Kametaro, that he would protect the *Nojima*. Sato was less than successful in that endeavor, but he did have his command ship *Asashio* move to pick up the *Nojima*'s survivors.[239] Now the *Asashio* was packed with them, along with survivors of the *Arashio*. Plucked from burning sinking ships or shark-infested waters, they thought they were lucky. They were wrong.

At 3:12 pm, the 63rd Squadron's Major Scott led two B-17s from the 65th on a run at the destroyer from 7,000 feet. They apparently made their attack at the same time a Mitchell, possibly that of the 90th's 2nd Lieutenant Edward Solomon, at low altitude was skip bombing her. The destroyer swung to port and got that bomb to miss, at the same time fouling up the targeting by Scott's group. It may have been this attack that killed the *Asashio*'s skipper Lieutenant Commander Yoshii Goro, who is known to have been killed early on.[240]

Major Scott dropped two 1,000lb bombs while each of his wingmen dropped four 1,000lb bombs. Scott thought he had hit her on the stern; one of the wingmen, Captain Arthur Fletcher, admitted all eight of the 65th's bombs had missed. However, "they came so damned close I'm sure [they] buckled her plates. Anyway she never moved after that and a large fire broke out on her bow."[241]

After this bombing run, Captain Fletcher and Lieutenant Glen Lewis, as angry as anyone over the machine-gunning of the survivors of Lieutenant Moore's B-17, went down to 200 feet and fired off 2,000 rounds in strafing lifeboats, barges, and Japanese survivors in the water. Then they were chased off by Zeros and Oscars.[242] At around this time, Admiral Kimura's remaining destroyers running away to the north received a message from the *Asashio* saying she was under attack by some 30 aircraft. The transmission ended abruptly.[243]

If the *Asashio* was still functional and navigable after Major Scott's run, she would not be much longer. A trio of B-25s from the 90th Squadron had the destroyer in her sights and scored multiple hits on her. First Lieutenant Melville Fisher's B-25 got two hits amidships. At some point 2nd Lieutenant Solomon, who had had to break off his attacks because of high-level bombers, returned and attacked the destroyer from the stern, scoring a bomb hit that wrecked the after 5-inch mount. Then Solomon strafed the destroyer's decks, packed with survivors of the *Arashio* and the *Nojima*.[244]

Lieutenant Solomon's bomb may have been the kill shot. It was hell for the *Asashio*, but at least it was a quick hell. Hit by at least four and possibly six or more bombs, not counting near misses and strafing, the *Asashio* sank at 3:15 pm. She took with her Captain Sato, who chose to go down with his ship, and 299 souls, including almost all of her crew.[245]

Meanwhile, no one had forgotten *Asashio*'s sister ship, *Arashio*, with whom she was often confused because their names were too much alike. The destroyer was crippled, but she could still make 5 or 6 knots. First Lieutenant James Criswell of the 90th Squadron part of a two-Mitchell formation, saw the *Arashio* moving, and he and his partner split up to attack. Criswell came from the stern at mast height. The other Mitchell hit the destroyer, which then swung to port, giving him the beam as a target. He strafed the *Arashio*, then skipped a bomb into her side. Then he went to strafe other Japanese survivors.[246]

The *Arashio* had been decapitated by the morning attacks. Now the attacks were hacking at her neck and shoulders. Lieutenant Masuda was still trying to steer the ship, but Lieutenant Criswell's attack finished off that idea:

> The ship shook violently. Bullet fragments and shrapnel made it look like a beehive. All the steam pipers burst. The ship became boiling hot. We tried to abandon ship, but planes flying almost as low as the masts sprayed us with machine-guns. Hands were shot off, stomachs blown open. Most of the crew were murdered or wounded there. Hundreds were swimming in the ocean. Nobody was there to rescue them. They were wiped out [...][247]

The bombers of the 5th Air Force spent the rest of the afternoon crisscrossing the oil- and debris-covered sea, dropping bombs on anything afloat, strafing any living thing they saw in the water. According to the 63rd Squadron's war diary, "Every man in the squadron would have given two months' pay to be in on the strafing." The aircrews in Australia's No. 30 Squadron were allegedly among those who found it "distasteful," but they nevertheless participated.[248]

Historian Bruce Gamble captured what had to be the surreal feeling of the Japanese:

> For thousands of once-proud soldiers and sailors of the Rising Sun, the turn of events was incomprehensible. A few hours earlier the convoy had seemed mighty, but now several ships were underwater and most of the remainder drifted lifelessly, smoke pouring from their hulls and superstructures. Although the sea was warm, it was both alien and immense, a frightening, shark-infested atmosphere for the Japanese who found themselves struggling to stay afloat. And if the sudden reversal of fortune was not shocking enough, gigantic enemy bombers now roared just above their heads, spitting ribbons of fire in all directions. The apocalypse had come.
>
> While the B-17s strafed men in the water, the A-20s and B-25s continued their low-level attacks. Some bombs inevitably overshot their intended targets and exploded among clusters of survivors, obliterating everyone within the blast radius. The sea literally turned red in places, attracting sharks to the blood and gore.[249]

Lex McAulay captured the Hobson's choice faced by the Japanese survivors:

> It must have been frightening for a man on the deck of a burning ship, out of sight of land, confronted in all directions with other stricken naval and merchant vessels, the surface of the sea littered with small boats, barges, wreckage and survivors, columns of smoke drifting over the scene, to see huge four-engined olive-drab bombers, engines roaring, machineguns hammering from nose, belly, sides and tail, relentlessly circling. Hurtling past at twice the speed of the B-17s were B-25s, often preceded by the frightening wall of water and debris flung up by massed fire from the eight .50-calibre machineguns in the nose.

Many Japanese realised the only protection against bullets was in the water. As the strafers approached, men would jump off the rafts and out of the boats until the aircraft passed, then try to climb back again. This was repeated and each time used valuable strength.[250]

Japanese would later ask, what was the difference between their machine-gunning the parachuting survivors of Lieutenant Moore's crew, which the men of the 5th Bomber Command considered such a crime, and those same men of the 5th machine-gunning Japanese survivors in the water? It is not an unfair question by any means. A distinction can be drawn inasmuch as once the Imperial Japanese Army survivors reached land, they would be combatants who would have to be fought. Aviators are not combatants without their aircraft. Moreover, Japanese survivors of sunken ships or downed aircraft had shown a penchant for either refusing to be rescued by Allied units or, once rescued, turning on their rescuers with hidden grenades or guns. It is a distinction with which not all will agree, but one made by the 5th Air Force when they ordered all lifeboats, barges, indeed anyone alive in the water, to be attacked. Some of the aircrews were appalled and disgusted by the order. Some saw it as necessary but unpleasant.

Some, like the 63rd Squadron's Captain James DeWolfe, relished it as just vengeance. DeWolfe had watched Lieutenant Moore's B-17 suffer damage, his men machine-gunned in their parachutes, and he was out for blood. He returned at 3:25 pm for a four-and-a-half-hour sortie that consisted almost entirely of strafing survivors in the water. His men expended 4,500 rounds of .50-cal ammunition and 500 rounds of .30-cal.[251] Nonetheless, as Pappy Gunn's son Nathaniel put it, "Very few men get a kick out of hitting unarmed men in the water, or anywhere for that matter."[252]

A 321st Squadron B-24 circled the scene and at 3:19 reported there were four transports smoking and a destroyer stationary. Three hours later, it reported three "4,000-tonners" on fire, a large destroyer stationary in an oil slick, and another destroyer riding very low in the water. The destroyers were the derelict *Tokitsukaze* and the disabled *Arashio*. The *Shinai Maru* had sunk.[253] And the day's end that could not have come soon enough for the Japanese finally came.

Also coming during the night was Admiral Kimura, not nearly as callous or as cowardly as he had appeared, just "prudent." He had transferred all of the survivors to the *Hatsuyuki* and refueled from her, then in the *Shikinami* led the *Asagumo* and the *Yukikaze* back to try to rescue – salvage – what they could of the 51st Division. Lieutenant Masuda and the few survivors on the *Arashio* were picked up around midnight by the *Yukikaze*.[254] Another 170 of the *Arashio*'s crew were found in the water and rescued. Another 20 were even plucked off the derelict *Tokitsukaze*, but the *Yukikaze* was so packed with survivors that she could neither tow the destroyer nor scuttle her, so the *Tokitsukaze* was left to drift in her giant oil slick. At 2:30 the Japanese destroyers sped back to Rabaul.[255] They did not want to get caught in daylight by Allied aircraft again.

The hundreds, maybe thousands of survivors in the water did not have that option. But they would first have to survive the night, when ten PT boats under Lieutenant

Commander Barry Atkins came out. They put two torpedoes into the hulk of the *Oigawa Maru*, finally putting her under. They somehow managed to miss both Admiral Kimura's ambulatory destroyers and the two derelicts.

The next day they were hunted as the 5th Bomber Command sent out its engines of death to scour the Huon Golf for anything that moved. According to bombardier Lieutenant Frederick O. Blair, "We were directly ordered to sink and machine gun everything we located that looked like being alive or floating."[256]

Not floating was the destroyer *Arashio*, who was nowhere to be seen, having apparently foundered alone and unwitnessed during the night. Floating still was the *Tokitsukaze* and, in the unique position of both foe and ostensible friend, wishing she wasn't.

The first to try to do something about it this day was Captain Fred P. Dollenberg of the 65th Bombardment Squadron. At 9:10 am, he found the derelict and dropped four 500lb bombs. Two hit the destroyer, one near the bridge. But though she was settling by the stern, the *Tokitsukaze* refused to sink.[257]

Next up was the 582 Air Group. A Zero of the 253 Air Group looking for survivors reported the *Tokitsukaze* still afloat but "listing to starboard." Around noon nine Aichi D3As from the 582 Air Group arrived, escorted by 14 Zeros. The Aichis dropped bombs on the derelict, but they all missed. No, the Sea Eagles were not what they once were.[258]

It was near dusk when nine B-25 Mitchells found the *Tokitsukaze*, her stern awash, listing to starboard, some 55 miles southeast of Finschhafen. A few runs from starboard to port scored hits that finally put her under.[259]

The *Tokitsukaze* might have been the last ship lost of the Operation *81* convoy, but she would not be the last loss. In fact, arguably the biggest loss from the convoy came not in the Bismarck Sea or the Huon Gulf, but on Goodenough Island, where numerous Imperial Army survivors from the convoy had taken refuge. One Australian patrol found eight Japanese soldiers who had landed in two boats. The Japanese were killed and their boats examined, which were found to contain a lot of important-looking documents in sealed tins.

The documents were sent to General MacArthur's intelligence group in Brisbane, where even General Willoughby could see what they were. They included a list showing the names of all Japanese army officers and their units. Allied intelligence now had a complete and detailed picture of the order of battle of the Imperial Japanese Army. The list was disseminated to all Allied intelligence units in the war against Japan.[260]

At Port Moresby, General Whitehead was big enough to admit that he had been wrong. As he told Pappy Gunn:

Pappy, you have had a huge victory these last two days and I wanted to congratulate you on that. The performance of the skip bombers will revolutionize the way we use air power against shipping from now on. I admit I didn't like your methods but by God you were right and I want you to know that. If that convoy reached Lae, we would have probably ended up fighting on the beaches of Australia. Now we can push ahead, because we have the Japs on the ropes, thanks in a great part to you and your tenacity.[261]

Pappy's Folly had become Pappy's Victory: a victory for the Allies; a victory for the good guys; a victory for ingenuity and creativity.

It was 3:00 am on March 4 when General Kenney woke up General MacArthur to give him the "final score" that had just come in from General Whitehead. "I had never seen him so jubilant," Kenney later wrote. MacArthur told Kenney to pass along a radio message to his men: "Please extend to all ranks my gratitude and felicitations on the magnificent victory which has been achieved. It cannot fail to go down in history as one of the most complete and annihilating combats of all time. My pride and satisfaction in you all is boundless."

Kenney dutifully forwarded the message with one of his own: "Congratulations on that stupendous success. Air Power has written some important history in the past three days. Tell the whole gang that I am so proud of them I am about to blow a fuze."[262]

General Kenney was not the only one about to blow a fuse, or "fuze." So was Emperor Hirohito. While "the score" was not nearly what Generals MacArthur and Kenney claimed it was, it was appalling enough. Only some 900 Imperial Army troops of the 51st Division got to Lae. About 2,700 had been rescued by Admiral Kimura's destroyers. Some 3,000 men were missing.

Emperor Hirohito immediately asked the obvious question: Why had the Navy not immediately shifted gears and landed the troops elsewhere than Lae? He knew the answer: Imperial General Headquarters had failed to learn the lessons of the Guadalcanal convoy battles.[263] Yamamoto, who had been reluctant to commit eight destroyers to the convoy in the first place, "was greatly incensed."[264]

But their anger did not change the facts or lessen the impact of the catastrophe that had just befallen the Imperial Army and Navy – and their men. An Imperial Army lieutenant watched a group of Japanese survivors come ashore at Tuluvu on the western coast of New Britain:

One group was made up of seriously injured men whose faces were covered black with oil. Their eyes were all glassy and deeply sunk into their faces. All were jittery and full of fear as if they were seeing a horrible dream. They were all worn out and their tired water soaked bodies could be seen from beneath their torn and tattered uniforms. They were just a bunch of men with their fighting spirit completely lost. A pitiful scene of a vanquished and defeated army.[265]

Unfortunately for the Japanese, the catastrophe of the Battle of the Bismarck Sea and the loss of the top secret documents was but one domino. The toppling of this one domino would start others toppling that would lead to an even worse catastrophe in the months ahead.

EPILOGUE:

PREVIEWS

Despite the successful culmination of Operation *Ke* with the Japanese withdrawal from Guadalcanal and the American victory at the Battle of the Bismarck Sea, the months of February and March were largely times of rest, recuperation, and consolidation of recent gains by the Allies on Guadalcanal and in New Guinea.

It was also a time of major changes. On February 12, a dozen members of Marine Fighting 124 under Major William E. Gise flew up from Espiritu Santo to Henderson Field's Fighter 1, but not in what had been their usual Grumman F4F Wildcats – not today, in fact not ever again. They flew a new, very distinctive aircraft which had gull wings. It was fast, faster than any aircraft the Japanese had; it could climb almost 3,000 feet a minute, and it had twice the range of the Wildcat. Marine Fighting 124 was the first squadron to have this new fighter: the Chance Vought F4U Corsair.[1]

It was the promise of a new day for Marine fighter pilots, although for now the F4U Corsair had some teething problems, including leaks of hydraulics, oil, and fuel; and a temperamental ignition. The Corsair was a demanding aircraft, and it took time for pilots to adjust to it. Some took to calling it the "Bent Wing Widow Maker."[2]

But their mission this February 12 was to make certain someone did not become a widow. Only an hour after landing at Fighter 1, the Corsairs were back in the air escorting a "Dumbo" PBY Catalina to Sandfly Bay, Vella Lavella, to rescue two Wildcat pilots who had been shot down January 31. Catalinas had always been the primary aerial platform for air-sea rescue. When the US Navy added more resources specific to such rescue efforts, some individual whose name has been lost to history decided to call an air-sea rescue Catalina a "Dumbo," after the flying elephant in the Walt Disney cartoon. The name not only stuck, but came to be applied to all such missions. Almost always carrying a doctor and pharmacist's mate to treat injured airmen immediately, as well as extra medical and emergency supplies and lifeboats, Dumbos would often rescue downed airmen in bad weather or under enemy fire, and quickly became beloved creatures. On this day, the Corsairs orbited overhead to protect the Dumbo from air attack and gunfire from Japanese troops on Kolombangara. The rescue at Sandfly Bay was completed without incident and everyone returned to Guadalcanal.[3]

Also arriving on February 12 were about 20 Consolidated Liberator bombers. Half were PB4Ys, the Navy's version of the Liberator, and assigned to the Navy's Bombing Squadron 101. The other half were the more traditional B-24 Liberators assigned to the 370th and 424th Squadrons of the 307th Bombardment Group.[4] The Liberators were slowly replacing the B-17 Flying Fortresses in the Pacific, but they, too, would have some teething problems.

And then there was combat. At 9:30 am on February 13, nine VB-101 Navy PB4Y Liberator bombers of Bombing 101 headed for Kahili and the Shortlands anchorage, with 11 Corsairs from Marine Fighting 124 and four Lightnings from the Army Air Force's 339th Squadron. They faced no opposition, though one Japanese Zero pilot came down and "looked over the new planes with what amounted to undisguised curiosity." All the American aircraft returned safely.[5]

About an hour later, six B-24s of the 424th Squadron took off, with 12 P-40s of the 347th Fighter Group and four P-38s of the 339th Fighter Squadron headed for the Shortlands. Their target appears to have been the 6,540-ton ammunition ship *Hitachi Maru*.[6] But the strike was star-crossed. All but six of the fighters had been forced to turn back before reaching the target. Base Air Force was ready with nine Zeros from the 204 Air Group and 20 from the 252 Air Group, a squadron of which was temporarily at Ballale. The R-Area Air Force chipped in with 11 A6M2N float Zeros – the Nakajima A6M2-N Navy Type 2 Interceptor-Fighter-Bomber that the Allies called "Rufe" and "float Zero" – from the 802 Air Group. Two Zeros were shot down and three were badly damaged. The target was not hit. For their troubles, the Americans lost two Liberators to antiaircraft fire and a third to Zeros, along with three fighters, their pilots killed.[7]

If at first you don't succeed, try, try, and try again. The next day, February 14, nine US Navy PB4Y Liberators from Bombing 101 were escorted by the 12 Fighting 124 Corsairs and ten Lightnings from the 339th Squadron flying high-altitude top cover, as they usually did, and several P-40 Warhawks flying low cover, again headed for the Shortlands anchorage, where the target again was the *Hitachi Maru*. Base Air Force had had plenty of warning, however, and the attack was met by some 50 Zeros and ten single-crew floatplane Rufes from the 204, 253, and 802 air groups. It rapidly turned ugly. The Japanese fighters swarmed the Americans, attacking from "around the clock." The Zeros shot down four Lightnings, two of the Warhawks, and then went after the new Corsairs.[8]

The numbers were simply overwhelming. The Japanese managed to take out two Corsairs, though one was from a collision with a Zero. One of the Marine pilots, Lieutenant Harold Stewart, was strafed to death in the water. To add injury to injury, two of the Liberators were shot down as well. But when combined with a later attack by B-17s, the mission was accomplished. It's not clear who hit the *Hitachi Maru* when, but she took from two to four bomb hits, flooded, and sank.[9]

The mission may have been a success, but it was also a disaster. It entered lore as "The Saint Valentine's Day Massacre."[10] But there was no rest for the weary. Another mission was scheduled for February 15. According to Marine Fighting 124's Lieutenant Kenneth Walsh, the mood for the mission was one of foreboding. "We were all rather apprehensive. There was little conversation among the pilots – all of us sensed what it would be like in the target area."[11]

As the Marine gentlemen were starting their engines, however, the mission was canceled. Admiral Fitch had had enough. Five Liberators lost in two days was simply not sustainable. They needed more fighters to deliver better protection before they tried any more daylight raids. So they switched to nighttime attacks, the first such mission being that very night. But the night was no better: two more Liberators from the 307th were lost to bad weather, though their crews were rescued. That was a third of the Liberators on Guadalcanal gone in just three days.[12] That was it for the attacks on the Buin-Shortlands complex for a while.

That was also it for the Cactus Air Force, because it was the next day, February 16, when the Cactus Air Force, who had defended Guadalcanal from all manner of Japanese attacks in the toughest of environments with on many occasions only the slimmest of resources, passed into history. Rear Admiral Charles P. Mason, the former skipper of the *Hornet*, now promoted, arrived on Guadalcanal to take charge of a new organization incorporating the old Cactus Air Force. It would be called Air Command, Solomons, but would become better known by its disinfectant-sounding acronym "AirSols."

In the South Pacific chain of command AirSols still resided under Admiral Fitch's South Pacific Air Command, but the job of AirSols was to oversee all land-based aircraft in the Solomons, regardless of service or nationality. Formal commands, such as the Army's newly activated 13th Air Force and the Navy's 2nd Marine Air Wing, would not have operational authority in the Solomons, but would maintain administrative, training, and logistical responsibilities for aircraft, personnel, and materiel assigned to them.[13]

AirSols had to be overarching, because when it was established, it commanded an eclectic array of air units. It would be difficult to mesh all these different air services and aircraft together into a coherent unit, but the Cactus Air Force had always done so. AirSols could be considered the Cactus Air Force writ large, a natural evolution from an informal to a formal organization.

To handle this eclectic array, AirSols would be divided into several component commands:

Fighter Command: The Army Air Force's 347th Fighter Group, composed of the 67th (Airacobras), 68th (Airacobras and Warhawks), 70th, (Airacobras), and 339th (Lightnings) Fighter Squadrons, with detachments of the 12th (Airacobras) and 44th (Warhawks) Fighter Squadrons; US Navy's 2nd Marine Aircraft Wing (Wildcats and Corsairs), Marine Fighting 123 (Wildcats), and Fighting 72 (Wildcats). Fighter Command would handle air defense, ground support, and escort for air, naval, and some Command operations.

Bomber Command: Included the Army Air Force's 5th and 11th Bombardment Groups (Flying Fortresses) and the 69th and 70th Bombardment Squadrons (Marauders). Bomber Command would attack Japanese air, naval, and ground forces and bases.

Strike Command: US Navy's Marine Scout Bombing 131, 144, and 234 (all Dauntlesses); and Torpedo 11, 12, and 16 (all Avengers), who would attack Japanese surface units and airfields.

Search Command: Included the US Navy's Patrol Squadrons 12 and 51 (Catalinas); and the Royal New Zealand Air Force's No. 3 Squadron (Hudson), plus elements of Marine Scout Bombing 131, 144, and 234 when appropriate. Search Command's primary mission would be, oddly enough, searching, but would include both Dumbos and Black Cats.[14]

Admiral Halsey was looking for a way to "Keep pushing the Japs around," as he put it.[15] His goal, for this next phase of Allied operations was the capture of Munda. He did not have a lot with which to push, however. His infantry was exhausted after the Guadalcanal campaign, with only the 43rd Infantry Division, assembled from various loose regiments lying around, available. It was green and lacking in experience.

From a naval standpoint, the US Navy would not have anywhere close to superiority over the Japanese until the middle of 1943. Admiral Halsey had the carrier *Saratoga*, but the *Enterprise* was still dealing with the damage sustained at Santa Cruz, including that troublesome forward elevator. But Admiral Nimitz's plea to the Royal Navy for help was answered in the affirmative, in the form of the carrier HMS *Victorious* under the command of Captain L.D. MacIntosh; however, she wasn't quite ready yet. Royal Navy carriers were (and are) very different from US Navy carriers, so she was being refitted at Norfolk. It would still be a little while before she arrived in the Pacific.

Admiral Halsey had air power in the form of the newly created AirSols, and that was pretty much it. With air power you can attack, you can defend, and you can deny, but you cannot take. That ruled out Munda for the immediate future. There was some proverbial low-hanging fruit, however, and Halsey decided to take it.

So at 11:00 pm on February 20 came the start of Operation *Cleanslate*: the capture of the Russell Islands, as amphibious forces left Guadalcanal. The combat portion of *Cleanslate* began at 6:00 am on February 21, when the 43rd Infantry Division under Major General John Hester landed at Banika Island of the Russell group, while the 3rd Marine Raider Battalion landed on Pavuvu Island. It had been assumed that the Japanese would fight bitterly for the islands, like they had at Gifu, but this time including air and naval elements. There was very little combat, however, as the Japanese had recently abandoned the islands. By February 26, the 579th Signal Company had set up an SCR 270 radar on the Lingata Peninsula of Banika Island, giving AirSols even more warning of approaching enemy aircraft. A PT boat base was quickly set up at Wernham Cove.

The 33rd Seabees and the 118th Engineering Battalion immediately began construction of an airstrip.[16]

It would be a few weeks before the Japanese even noticed the occupation of the Russells. They were too busy having problems of their own.

It will be recalled that the Japanese had built that airfield at Munda on New Georgia, declaring it operational on December 15, 1942. Admiral Halsey wanted Munda as his next target for occupation. For the Allies, Munda was both a danger and an opportunity.

Munda was a danger inasmuch as the Japanese had finally established the airbase in the central Solomons that they should have built before Guadalcanal. The base would serve as a front-line bastion blocking access to the Shortlands and Bougainville. It was an opportunity inasmuch as if the Allies could capture it, then they could use it like they were using Henderson Field on Guadalcanal.

There were several complications to Allied capture, however. One was that the Japanese had completed the airfield before the Allies could capture it. So the Allies began a campaign of harassment of Munda to make it untenable as a base and they had some success doing so.

The Japanese first attempted to house the Zeros of the 252 Air Group at Munda. At 8:00 am on December 23, 20 Zeros of the 252 Air Group under the command of Lieutenant Suho Monitari, escorted by nine Zeros of the 204 Air Group, took off from Lakunai headed for Munda, where they landed at 10:45. Not even 90 minutes later an Allied housewarming party arrived, with Wildcats from Marine Fighting 121 and Marine Observation 251 escorting a dozen Dauntlesses. Fifteen Zeros were ready to greet them. The ensuing air battle cost the Americans two Wildcats, with one pilot recovered. The Dauntlesses bombed the airfield.[17]

Arriving fashionably late to this particular housewarming party were five B-17s, escorted by five Airacobras from the 12th and four Lightnings from the 339th Fighter Squadrons. One Fortress and two Airacobras had to abort en route because of mechanical issues, while another Airacobra got lost in a cloud. This attack seems to have hoped to catch the Zeros refueling after the first attack, but they showed up at 12:22, not even 15 minutes after that attack, and many of the Zeros were still airborne. The B-17s left 86 100lb and eight 1,000lb housewarming presents. There seem to have been no losses for the Americans. Japanese losses for the day were one Zero shot down and seven damaged.[18] So the 252 Air Group was already down to 19 Zeros and they had been on the Munda airfield barely a day.

That night a B-17 circled over Munda, playing the role of Washing Machine Charlie, dropping flares and the occasional bomb to keep the Japanese awake. The Japanese were bleary-eyed when at 8:00 am on the morning of Christmas Eve, 1942, Wildcats of Marine

Fighting 121 and Marine Observation 251, and eight 12th Fighter Squadron Airacobras, led a dozen Dauntlesses of Marine Scout Bombing 142, except for three Dauntlesses that had aborted, over Munda. The Dauntlesses saw a dozen Zeros at the eastern end of the airfield, and the pilots' mouths watered. The "bomber pilots dove immediately on this spectacular target," destroying five planes on the ground. The Wildcats dove on the Zeros trying to take off; why the Wildcats did this instead of the Airacobras, which were much better ground attack planes but much worse fighters, is another one of those bizarre mysteries. Lieutenant Suho reported two Zeros shot down, their pilots killed, and six damaged in the air, with three pilots wounded, in addition to the five destroyed on the ground.[19] A second air attack at around noon could add only very little to the destruction, and three Zeros flown in that day could make up for some of the losses.

The 252 Air Group never recovered from Christmas Eve morning. By December 28, only three of the original 20 Zeros, plus four or five replacements, were flyable. Admiral Kusaka gave up on using Munda as a full-time base and sent three Mitsubishi G3M medium bombers to evacuate the pilots. That three became two when an Airacobra shot one down as it tried to land at Munda, but the other two embarked the pilots and, along with the three remaining flyable Zeros, returned to Rabaul.[20]

The ground crews and antiaircraft crews were left behind, however. From this point forward, the Munda airbase would serve as just a stopping off point for refueling and an emergency landing spot, like a rest area for aircraft. Even so, the Cactus Air Force and later AirSols would continue to bomb Munda on a regular basis. Even when the mission involved bombing another target, if they had to abort or could not find the target, they would drop their bombs on Munda. It was just the principle of the thing: *When in doubt, bomb Munda.*

Admiral Halsey decided to change that to *When in doubt, bombard Munda.* Halsey had been paid a visit by the chief of the Pacific Fleet's destroyers, Rear Admiral Walden L. "Pug" Ainsworth. Halsey used the opportunity to put Ainsworth himself in charge of rebuilding Task Force 67, the cruiser-destroyer force so indelicately handled at Tassafaronga.[21] Ainsworth was an intelligent and respected officer, considered "one of the best fighting admirals of the surface fleet."[22] Halsey decided to cover the arrival of the convoy to Guadalcanal by putting Ainsworth's ships to work bombarding Munda.

The convoy had a large covering force, consisting of heavy cruiser *Louisville*, light cruisers *Nashville*, *St. Louis*, *Helena*, *Honolulu*, *Columbia*, and the Royal New Zealand Navy's *Achilles*; and destroyers *Fletcher*, *O'Bannon*, *Drayton*, *Lamson*, and *Nicholas*. This would be a bit of a complicated operation. The submarine *Grayback* was to serve as a navigational aid. Two PBY Black Cats would scout ahead and serve as gunnery spotters. This would be the first plan to use and coordinate surface, submarine, and air units. Four divisions of Marine Fighting 121 under Major Don Yost covered the force until dusk.

Admiral Ainsworth set up the Bombardment Force with his flagship *Nashville*, followed by the *St. Louis* and *Helena*; and destroyers *Fletcher* and *O'Bannon*. They broke away from the rest of the force, which would be commanded by Admiral Tisdale and protect the Bombardment Unit from interference by Japanese surface forces. The Catalinas had played the role of "Washing Machine Charlie" the last two nights on Munda, dropping flares and bombs, so the Japanese would not suspect what was coming.

At 1:02 am on January 5, the *Nashville* opened fire on the Munda airfield. It started a 48-minute show that lobbed 3,000 6-inch and nearly 1,500 5-inch shells on the little Munda field. Then Ainsworth turned away and joined Admiral Tisdale's force to head for home. It certainly looked impressive. The bombardment demolished some buildings, set some fires, leveled some palm trees, and cratered the runway.[23]

But now the Americans and Kiwis learned the hard way what the Japanese had learned the hard way at Guadalcanal: you can shell a dirt runway, but once you leave, all they have to do is put the dirt back in the holes you made. Simple stuff, even though Munda was not so much dirt as it was crushed coral. Low tech means easy maintenance. The bombardment "did not do much damage," and the runway was made operable within 18 hours.[24] No real damage had been done except to the coral.

Now the Japanese added injury to insult. Base Air Force sent up four Aichi D3As from the composite 582 Air Group and six from the 956 Air Group, escorted by 14 Zeros from the 204 Air Group. They chased Admiral Ainsworth's cruisers all the way to south of Guadalcanal, 12 miles off Cape Hunter. Both the cruisers and their fighter protection – two divisions of Wildcats from Marine Fighting 121 under Captains Greg Loesch and Bill Marontate – were caught at an awkward time. The *Nashville*, *St. Louis*, and *Helena* were getting set to recover their seaplanes, which had been flown off to Tulagi, while the *Honolulu*'s seaplanes were involved in a simulated air attack drill. To complicate matters further, a Catalina was flying by. There were a lot of friendly aircraft around, of which everyone had to be aware, which should explain how the Japanese dive bombers reached their pushover points without anyone trying to stop them. All but four D3As from the 582 were able to drop their bombs. The *Honolulu* had to perform some evasive maneuvers to avoid the bombs of the first two Vals. Behind her in formation was the Kiwi *Achilles*. The *Achilles* had been famously involved with the heavy cruiser HMS *Exeter* in sinking the German pocket battleship *Admiral Graf Spee* off the Rio de la Plata in 1939. But the Pacific War had not been kind to the *Graf Spee*'s conquerors: the *Exeter* had been sunk by Japanese cruisers in the Java Sea on March 1, 1942. Now the *Achilles* took a 551lb bomb on her Number 3 turret, wrecking it and killing 11 men and wounding at least eight others.

It was now that the Wildcats managed to get among "eight to ten" Vals. The 582 Air Group lost two D3As, with the other two damaged. It is not clear how many the 956 lost, but the Allies claimed to have shot down three.[25] It was then that the D3As' escort, the 14 Zeros, showed up to harass the Wildcats, chasing them to Henderson Field before breaking off. None of the Wildcats were shot down.[26] But the veteran light cruiser *Achilles* would have to go to a shipyard.

That would be the last of the bombardments of Munda for a while but the air attacks would continue and follow the same pattern: AirSols would send bombers over to Munda;

they would put craters in the dirt and coral runway; the Japanese would fill the craters with more dirt and coral and smooth them out and the runway would be operational again. Repeat ad infinitum.

It was shortly thereafter, January 8, when the Japanese began work on a complex to support Munda on Kolombangara, a roughly conical volcanic island some 15 miles northwest of Munda, the next island to the northwest of New Georgia in the Solomons chain across the Kula Gulf. The island would be perfectly round except for Vila Point, which juts out into the Blackett Strait "like the tab on a can lid."[27] Blackett Strait narrows to 1,200 yards at Vila before connecting to Kula Gulf, which separates Kolombangara from New Georgia, but the strait is deep, and transports and destroyers could unload into barges 300 to 400 yards from shore.[28] The largest locations of flat terrain on the island run north and south along both sides of the Vila River. Here, the Lever Brothers had operated three plantations: Stanmore on the north side, and Vila and Lady Lever on the south. With not even a pretense of stealth, the Japanese built an airstrip at Vila Plantation and set up shipping facilities at Stanmore Plantation near a lagoon that carried the encouraging name "Disappointment Cove."[29] The entire site was called "Vila-Stanmore" or sometimes just "Vila."

The destroyer *Mochizuki* and torpedo boat *Otori* showed up on January 8, 1943, with the 6,658-ton ammunition ship *Seia Maru*, who dropped off a group of construction workers.[30] Eight days later it was the torpedo boat *Hiyodori* escorting the 6,777-ton cargo ship *Yamashimo Maru*, who dropped off antiaircraft guns and personnel. She was damaged on the way back to Buin by air attack, but not seriously.[31] The attack, however, was a sign that the Allies were on to Vila. The following evening the *Giyu Maru* stopped in at Vila under cover of some 958 Air Group F1M Type 0 observation seaplanes to drop off 200 barrels of foodstuffs and 20 barges. The next night, January 18, the 6,705-ton *Kaku Maru* stopped off, dropped off her cargo at 2:18 am, then sped off before enemy aircraft could find her.[32]

To Admiral Halsey, this was getting ridiculous. The Japanese were making no pretense of hiding the construction of the airfield; it was almost insulting. The runway itself was almost complete. It was time to call in Admiral Ainsworth for another bombardment. The admiral left on January 22 with the light cruisers *Nashville*, *St. Louis*, *Helena*, and *Honolulu*; and destroyers *O'Bannon*, *DeHaven*, *Lamson*, *Drayton*, *Radford*, *Hughes*, and *Nicholas*. Once again, Ainsworth divided his force, with the *Nashville*, *Helena*, *DeHaven*, *Nicholas*, *O'Bannon*, and *Radford* bombarding the airfield, while the remainder of the ships provided cover from interference by Japanese ships. Once again, this operation involved gunnery spotting by Black Cats.[33]

But it would be a little more complicated than last time. The Japanese discovered Admiral Ainsworth's force southeast of Guadalcanal, and concluded he was going to Munda. Admiral Halsey had anticipated the Japanese would be on to them and had arranged for more air cover. This time, the *Saratoga*'s air group staged in to Henderson Field.

While Navy and Marine Wildcats stood watch over Admiral Ainsworth's ships, Guadalcanal launched four air attacks on Munda during the day of January 23. First, it was 12 Airacobras escorting six Marauders, who dumped 8,400 pounds of explosives on the airbase. Then it was eight Marine SBD Dauntlesses dropping five 1,000lb bombs and 2,000 pounds of smaller bombs. Two hours later a dozen Wildcats and another dozen Airacobras arrived with eight Flying Fortresses in tow. The B-17s dropped another 8,400 pounds of explosives. The six B-26s returned for an encore at 5:30, dropping another 8,400 pounds of explosives.[34] Obviously the American aircrews had some weird fixation on the number 8,400 today.

Meanwhile, coming in the direction opposite from Admiral Ainsworth was a small Japanese convoy consisting of the torpedo boat *Hiyodori* and submarine chaser *Ch-23* escorting the transport *Toa Maru No. 2*, carrying part of the 19th Naval Construction Unit to Vila, with plans to drop them off and embark the 4th Engineer Detachment, who had just completed most of the work on the runway. Above them were nine Zeros of the 204 Air Group and two F1Ms from the 958 Air Group of the R-Area Air Force.[35] The Japanese seemed to have boundless confidence in the fighting abilities of their float biplanes.

Coastwatchers on Choiseul reported this little convoy going by at 1:50 pm on January 23. From Guadalcanal came a dozen Marine Fighting 122 Dauntlesses and four Marine Scout Bombing 131 Avengers, escorted by some 20 Wildcats. It was 6:15 when the Americans arrived over the Japanese ships. The Wildcats held off the Zeros successfully, while the Dauntlesses and Avengers made their attacks not as successfully. They got no hits on the convoy, losing one Dauntless and its crew to antiaircraft fire for their trouble. Two Wildcats were shot down, with one of the pilots recovered, while two Zeros were shot down, with one pilot killed in the crash and the other killed by Melanesian locals after he bailed out.[36]

All the while, Admiral Ainsworth's ships continued their approach. Their fighter protection left at 6:40 pm, to be followed within five minutes by a Mitsubishi G4M flown by Chief Petty Officer Toyota Sandai. Toyota was to serve as a pair of eyes for a nocturnal torpedo attack by the 705 Air Group in a sneak preview of their attack on the USS *Chicago* a week later. But Ainsworth turned toward Munda to throw him off. Then Black Cats arrived, as did a helpful squall, and Ainsworth was actually, for once, able to get rid of a snooper.

Or did he? The *O'Bannon* reported later on that she faced "three planes" that she identified as Bettys, but they never attacked. A flight of floatplanes from the *Kunikawa Maru* did arrive at 12:14 am on January 24, and stayed over for about an hour. Admiral Ainsworth started his bombardment of Vila around a half-hour later, at 2:00 am. His ships spent another half-hour tossing 2,000 6-inch shells and 1,500 5-inch shells at the airstrip, while one of the Black Cats dropped two 500lb bombs and six of what they called "mortar shells." Numerous fires were observed throughout the base area, yet not observed was the *Toa Maru No. 2*, who was still docked. She managed to escape through the Blackett Strait.

The damage to the airstrip was easily reparable, as usual, but the damage to the supplies was not. Vila reported that nearly all its supplies, including those for its maintenance crews and those for the Army's 45th Air Group, who were supposed to stage into Vila for operations against Guadalcanal, had been destroyed. The 45th had to stage into far less convenient Ballale.[37]

The Japanese were determined that this annoying cruiser force would not get off scot-free. At some point a Kawanishi H8K Type 2 Flying Boat – "Emily" – from the 851 Air Group found Admiral Ainsworth's cruisers and began shadowing them, as did several Aichi E13A Type 0 Reconnaissance Seaplanes from the *Kamikawa Maru*. Now the 705 Air Group had a definite target for its midnight Mitsubishis, and Base Air Force sent up 18 of them. But overcast skies foiled the efforts of 12 of them to find the cruisers. The remaining six did locate Ainsworth's ships at 4:34 am, but an attack by at least two of them was foiled by heavy antiaircraft fire. For their trouble, the Japanese lost a Jake to the guns of the destroyer *Radford*, while, to top off a very eventful night, Ainsworth's ships managed to evade the Japanese submarine *I-9*. The force's fighter protection returned with daylight, and they were able to make it home without incident.

It was a veritable parade of ships stopping in at Vila-Stanmore. January 25 saw the destroyer *Isokaze* and subchaser *Ch-26* each bring in a freighter, one of which was the big 7,189-ton *Noshiro Maru*. Even though she had been damaged by the 5th Bomber Command in Simpson Harbor, she was still loaded with eight field guns, food and ammunition, fuel, and 174 troops that she proceeded to drop off at Vila in exchange for the remainder of the 4th Engineer Detachment. A tanker also came in. This parade was just getting ridiculous, but an air attack from Guadalcanal intended to stop it that day was aborted due to bad weather.[38]

The next day it was the destroyer *Arashio* shepherding a freighter filled with coastal defense artillery and antiaircraft guns.[39] Someone had to put a stop to this. The air attacks were not working. Then again, the Americans were a bit distracted, as during this time, the Japanese were starting up Operation *Ke* and the Americans were wondering what was going on with regards to the much wider strategic situation. But the air assets on Guadalcanal were capable of multitasking.

But multitasking was presumably a step too far for the *Toa Maru No. 2*. The evening of January 28, she had left Simpson Harbor with Rear Admiral Ota Minoru, commander of the 8th Combined Special Naval Landing Force. With Ota was his staff, 107 of his naval infantry, two light tanks, a motorcycle with sidecar, ammunition, and cement, all headed for Vila-Stanmore. Keeping the transport company was the torpedo boat *Hyodori*, subchaser *Ch-23*, and the minelayer *Kamome*.[40] The next day she received some air cover in the form of four F1M floatplanes from the R-Area Air Force's 958 Air Group. Perhaps more realistic in terms of providing aerial protection were four to eight Ki-43 fighters from the Imperial Army's 11th Air Group, operating from Munda. At some point, the *Kamome* was detached, which is just as well since mines are not particularly effective against aircraft.[41]

On January 31 coastwatchers on Choiseul spotted "an unprotected and unescorted merchantman" off Faisi heading down The Slot at 7:45 am. Seven hours later a Catalina flying boat spotted the same freighter as it entered Vella Gulf from the north. The PBY dropped two 500lb bombs and two depth charges. All missed. The pilot described the transport as weaving like it was "out of control."[42] Not that out of control, it would seem. It made all the bombs miss. But the Catalina does seem to have spooked the Japanese, as it should have. At 4:45 pm, Combined Fleet requested Buin airbase send Zeros to protect the *Toa Maru No. 2*.[43]

It was a prescient request. A Kiwi Hudson had gotten a look-see at the little convoy. Royal Australian Navy Sub-lieutenant A.N.C. "Nick" Waddell, a coastwatcher on Choiseul, reported the *Toa Maru No. 2* leaving the Shortlands area at 2:45 pm, noting the ships' passage with two Petes overhead. Some 45 minutes later coastwatcher Henry Josselyn reported the convoy off the north coast of Vella Lavella heading southeast. They guessed she was going through the Vella Gulf through the Blackett Strait to Vila-Stanmore, which she was.[44]

On board the *Toa Maru No. 2*, Lieutenant Commander Imai Akijiro, chief of staff of the 8th Combined, was concerned when he saw the Hudson turn away to the south. "Commander," one of the other officers said to him, "the sunset is coming soon, so we won't have to worry about an enemy attack."

"Yes," Imai replied, "it seems we are going well." But as Imai continued to watch the eastern sky, he "saw something like a grain of millet on the horizon." The grain of millet gradually grew bigger; it was a number of enemy planes.[45]

The number was a dozen Marine Scouting 233 and 234 Dauntless dive bombers and nine Marine Scouting 131 Avengers escorted by six Army Airacobras and eight Marine Fighting 112 Wildcats under 1st Lieutenant Jefferson J. DeBlanc. Two Wildcats and two Avengers had to abort due to mechanical issues. The remaining 31 found the *Toa Maru No. 2* and her escorts just after 6:00 pm.[46]

The Pete floatplanes did not put up a fight and simply got out of the way – for now. The *Toa Maru No. 2* swung hard to starboard as her escorts swung hard to port, which seems like a dangerous and stupid maneuver. The Dauntlesses dropped seven 1,000lb bombs, three 500lb bombs, and six 100lb bombs. At least one bomb (exactly whose is unclear) hit the transport port side amidships. As the Dauntlesses pulled out of their dives and headed out, the Petes took the opportunity to pounce. The SBDs called for help, and Lieutenant DeBlanc took the opportunity to pounce on the Petes, quickly shooting down two of them.

While this was going on, three torpedo-carrying Avengers made their runs on the *Toa Maru No. 2*. All three claimed hits – wrongly, as it turned out. The other four TBFs carried four 500lb bombs each. Lieutenant Joe Conrad made his bombing run on the transport and witnesses saw at least one bomb strike amidships. Other bombing Avengers went after the *Hiyodori* and the *Ch-23* but scored no hits.[47]

Just as the Avengers were finishing their attack, the pilots' headsets carried the shout of "Zeros!" Lieutenant Tom Hughes had spotted nine "Army Zeros," actually Ki-43 Oscars from the 11th Air Group under Lieutenant Kimura Toshio. The Americans were mostly leaving the area by now, except for Lieutenant DeBlanc and three others who stayed to strafe the Japanese ships.

Now a "hell of a scrap" started, as Lieutenant DeBlanc ambushed from below and shot down Lieutenant Kimura, who survived and returned to base. DeBlanc chose to stay behind and tie up the Oscars so they would not bother the withdrawing Dauntlesses, Avengers, and Airacobras. Ultimately, two Wildcats were shot down, including DeBlanc, both pilots eventually recovered. Five of the Oscars were shot down, including Kimura, with two pilots recovered.[48]

The F1M remained behind to watch the *Toa Maru No. 2*. She had taken at least one bomb hit, amidships port side, that flooded holds Numbers 1 and 2. Several near misses did not help matters, and fires were raging on her main deck. But the big problem was the flooding, exacerbated by the bags of cement she was carrying in her Number 1 hold, which the flooding turned into solid concrete that weighed the ship down like a stone – literally. Efforts to control the flooding failed and at 10:50 pm the ship was ordered abandoned. Almost all of the *Toa Maru No. 2*'s passengers and crew were rescued, with only one crewman and two soldiers killed, though perhaps as many as 40 were injured. The surviving naval infantry were all taken to Vila, and subsequently to Munda, where Admiral Ota got off to a great start taking over from the neurotic Captain Iwabuchi and his nightmares of the *Kirishima*.[49] None of their vehicles or supplies could be salvaged,[50] especially the cement, which was now concrete.

The Japanese did not scuttle the transport, however, and the formerly lucky *Toa Maru No. 2* decided she was not quite ready to take the plunge to the bottom. The concrete may have shifted and plugged some of the openings in her hull near the bow. The abandoned transport refused to sink, and instead she drifted for three days, still burning in places, toward the southern end of Vella Gulf.

With her bow nearly awash from the weight of the concrete, the derelict ran aground in Kololuka Bay north of Gizo Island, stuck some 300 yards from shore. The coastwatcher Josselyn's scouts soon boarded her and salvaged her log, considerable military equipment, and the ship's supply of cutlery and linen, which they put to good use to enjoy a dining elegance not normally seen in the Solomons. The wreck was later spotted by TBF Avengers returning from an attack on Munda and a patrolling Catalina. It was in the wee hours of February 4 when a Black Cat saw the glow from the still-burning *Toa Maru No. 2*. The PBY headed over to her and dropped a 500lb bomb – which missed, of course. Her luck had not quite completely abandoned her. But the shockwave seems to have been enough to send her sliding back into the sea.[51]

Admiral Kusaka's hands were getting full. He had reorganized Base Air Force, somewhat mirroring divisions among the Allied forces. Rear Admiral Ichimaru Toshinosuke's 1st Air Attack Force, the operational title of the 21st Air Flotilla, was based at Kavieng and given the responsibility for New Guinea. It would have the fighters of the 253 Air Group and the G4Ms of the 705 and 751 air groups. Rear Admiral Kosaka Kanae had the 6th Air

Attack Force – the 26th Air Flotilla – based primarily at Lakunai, but also operating from Buin and Ballale, and was responsible for the Solomons. It had the 204 and 252 air groups, which were entirely fighters, and the composite 582 Air Group, which had both Zeros and Aichi D3A dive bombers.

Admirals Ichimaru and Kosaka and their superior Admiral Kusaka had to juggle a lot of aircraft, depending on whether there was a need for fighter protection for, say, a convoy to New Guinea or an attack on Guadalcanal. Base Air Force needed flexibility to shift fighters from Buin to Rabaul to Kavieng to Gasmata to Lae and back again. They had that flexibility to some extent because the Japanese at Rabaul were operating on interior lines. Nevertheless, Base Air Force was spread thin trying to cover two divergent – more precisely, convergent – fronts. Kosaka generally tried to keep some 30 fighters at Buin and Ballale. He usually could do nothing for the Munda base on New Georgia except maybe send a patrol over it for a few hours once or twice a month and hope they got lucky and were in the path of one of the frequent attacks on Munda.[52]

Those frequent attacks on Munda and now Vila were causing problems beyond an inability to permanently base aircraft there. The Japanese were struggling to find a way to keep Munda and Vila-Stanmore supplied. The losses of transport shipping were adding up. They tried to shift their schedule to avoid air attacks: supply and reinforcement ships would leave the Shortlands and make the run so they could unload under cover of darkness, then be off by daylight.

This is what the Japanese tried with the *Kirikawa Maru*, a 3,829-ton cargo ship. She was her own one-ship convoy on February 27. And she was a busy convoy. At 4:00 am, she had left Shortland for Buin. She arrived two hours later. Then, at 9:00 am, she left Buin, packed with elements of the 7th Yokosuka Special Naval Landing Force, two 140mm guns, four 80mm guns, and 600 tons of supplies. Escorted by the subchaser *Ch-26* and minesweeper *W-22*, the *Kirikawa Maru* started on a reinforcement run for Kolombangara.

She almost made it. As he had done with the *Toa Maru No.* 2, Royal Australian Navy Sub-lieutenant Waddell on Choiseul reported the sortie of the *Kirikawa Maru*. Northeast of Vella Lavella, she was ambushed by AirSols SBD Dauntless dive-bombers of Marine Scout Bombing 144 and F4U Corsair fighter-bombers, escorted by Lightnings and Warhawks. The Dauntlesses heavily damaged the *Kirikawa Maru*, setting her ammunition stores afire. A surviving Japanese medical officer described the Dauntlesses' bombs exploding in the ship like a fireworks exhibition at Ryogoku Bridge in Tokyo. Waddell reported, "we had the satisfaction of seeing the cargo vessel burning from stem to stern – this was the first occasion we had seen the results of our reporting."[53]

The cargo ship was scuttled with three shots from one of the escorts, but the record is not clear as to whether it was the *Ch-26* or the *W-22*.[54] The *Imperial Japanese Navy Page* suggests *Kirikawa Maru* was sunk "probably with all hands."[55] This would be curious by itself. It would mean either the *Kirikawa Maru* was scuttled by friendly ships with men still on board, or all the men aboard the *Kirikawa Maru* were killed by the air attack but the ship was left afloat.

In any event, later that day the *W-22* found herself off Kolombangara, apparently by herself. Putting together the pieces of this incomplete puzzle, it sounds as though, after the air attack, the *Ch-26* headed back to Shortland, while the larger *W-22* was left to rescue survivors of the *Kirikawa Maru* and probably to scuttle the ship as well. It was during this time that the minesweeper was the recipient of a submarine attack – not a very good submarine attack, as the minesweeper was not sunk and is usually listed as "possibly" damaged.[56] Since she went back to Shortland and was immediately sent out again, whatever damage was inflicted seems to have been minor, though she was down for ten days at the end of March for repairs in Rabaul.[57] It sounds like an approaching torpedo prematurely exploded just before hitting her.

But the loss of yet another big cargo ship had a negative effect on the Japanese. Admiral Kusaka had moved from the small, cheap sea trucks and gotten burned. Now he would go back to Admiral Tanaka's tried and true method of using destroyer runs at night. The old Reinforcement Unit was called back, and 2nd Destroyer Division's commodore Captain Tachibana Masao came from Rabaul with the destroyers *Murasame* and *Minegumo* to make a run to Vila the night of March 5–6. After all, it is not like it was Guadalcanal; Kolombangara was much closer. How hard could it be? On the way out of the harbor, his two destroyers passed *Uranami* and *Hatsuyuki* coming in with survivors of the Bismarck Sea.[58] That evidence of an enemy ambush could not have been encouraging.

They were, in fact, about to run into another enemy ambush, albeit one that was unplanned. Admiral Halsey was growing alarmed with all the ships and aircraft running into Munda and Vila-Stanmore. He had used Admiral Ainsworth's force of cruisers and destroyers to bombard Munda and Vila in the past. But Halsey now had a second force of cruisers and destroyers to play with, this second one called Task Force 68 under Rear Admiral Aaron S. "Tip" Merrill. The plan was for this force to bombard both Munda and Vila at the same time on the night of March 5–6.[59]

This was a meticulously planned operation, albeit almost identical to the ones before under Admiral Ainsworth. Admiral Merrill would leave Espiritu Santo with three light cruisers *Montpelier*, *Cleveland*, and *Denver*; and seven destroyers *Waller*, *Conway*, *Cony*, *Fletcher*, *Nicholas*, *Radford*, and *O'Bannon*. Near the Russells, Captain Briscoe would split off destroyers *Fletcher*, *Nicholas*, *Radford*, and *O'Bannon* to bombard Munda just after midnight on March 6. The remaining ships would go through The Slot to Kula Gulf and bombard Vila at the same time.

For any Japanese who tried to escape through the back door of the Blackett Strait south of Kolombangara, between it and Arundel Island, the Americans had prepared a surprise: the submarines *Grayback* and *Grampus*. On March 2 both submarines were ordered to patrol separate areas of the Vella Gulf at the other end of the Blackett Strait from the Kula Gulf to ambush any fleeing ships – assuming, of course, the submarines themselves were not ambushed.

Late in the evening of March 5, Guadalcanal broadcast a warning that two Japanese light cruisers or destroyers had left Faisi, in the Shortlands, at 7:10 pm and were heading southeast at high speed.[60] At 11:30 pm on March 5, a PBY Black Cat radioed news that it had passed over two destroyers, undoubtedly the same ships, that were headed toward Wilson Strait, between Vella Lavella and Cannongga.[61] If the destroyers were on their way to Vila-Stanmore, they could skirt the southern edge of the Vella Gulf. They were both a threat and an opportunity. Both submarines were to be on the lookout.

The *Grayback* certainly was. Having finally arrived in the Vella Gulf the night of March 5, her skipper Lieutenant Commander Edward C. Stephan was cautiously moving the submarine on the surface when at 9:55 pm her sonar picked up the sound of propellers. A look around the gulf revealed a dark silhouette seemingly creeping around all by itself. It was in the part of the Vella Gulf assigned to the *Grampus*.[62] Must be the *Grampus*, Stephan decided, right where she was supposed to be.[63] The *Grayback* was not able to exchange recognition signals with her, though, because her SJ radar, by which those signals would be transmitted, was malfunctioning, which also prevented her from tracking the *Grampus*. Unable to establish his boat's bona fides, Stephan decided to give the *Grampus* some space to avoid a case of mistaken identity. The *Grayback* passed a relatively uneventful night.

But this was not the case for the two destroyers, the *Murasame* and *Minegumo*, who, despite the Black Cat PBY passing only 700 feet overhead, seem to have been unaware of its presence or the implications therefrom. Operating under Captain Tachibana, the *Murasame* and *Minegumo* were on their quick-supply run to the airbase at Vila. While the Black Cat was sending out its warning, the two destroyers were stopped at Disappointment Cove offloading supplies for the garrison onto waiting barges.

The barge-loading did not take long and the two Japanese destroyers were ready to leave before midnight. Captain Tachibana's ships had arrived by the Blackett Strait, but the commodore was apparently uncomfortable with the strait – maybe something he saw, maybe something he encountered. The Blackett Strait was narrow, treacherous, and a great chokepoint for submarine attack. For all he knew, submarines were already waiting in ambush off the strait for his return. No, Tachibana would not play that game. He would go through the Kula Gulf into The Slot to head back to the Shortlands.

As March 6, 1943, got under way, the *Murasame*, with Captain Tachibana on board, led the *Minegumo* slowly northeast into the widening Kula Gulf. On the *Murasame*'s bridge, gunnery officer Lieutenant Kayama Homare was keeping watch while the destroyers slowly built up speed. Kayama turned to snack on a rice ball, only to find it being consumed by the destroyer's resident rodents. Before his frustration could take hold, something outside off the starboard bow caught his eye: flashes, like lightning, he thought.[64] Not uncommon in these parts, but these flashes were low, against the dark backdrop of New Georgia. What could they be?

Lieutenant Kayama did not know – could not have known – that he and his shipmates had barely 16 seconds to figure it out,[65] because when those 16.15 seconds concluded, the *Murasame* was surrounded by towering shell splashes as 36 6-inch shells plunged around and onto the lead destroyer. Six dozen more 6-inch shells were already in the air. Captain

Tachibana's destroyer was simply pummeled. A lookout on destroyer USS *Cony* said it was "like a complete bridge of fire, looking as though you could walk on it, and every one of the three branches ending right in that Jap ship."[66]

The *Cony* was one of three destroyers, the others being the *Waller* and *Conway* – of 43rd Destroyer Division under Commander Arleigh Burke. They were screening the three light cruisers – *Montpelier, Cleveland,* and *Denver* – of Admiral Merrill's 12th Cruiser Division. By trying to avoid the Blackett Strait, Captain Tachibana had blundered into Merrill's bombardment force headed for the Vila airfield.

For one of the few times in the Pacific War, the Japanese had been caught completely by surprise at night, while the Americans were almost completely prepared. From the earliest report that evening of the "two light cruisers or destroyers" leaving Faisi, Admiral Merrill had had an idea that the enemy was coming, and could be there as early as 11:00 pm on March 5.[67] Reports kept coming in from Black Cats on the approach of Captain Tachibana's little relief force as, at 12:13 am on March 6, Merrill's ships rounded Visuvisu Point, the northern tip of New Georgia, to make the dash into the "Horseshoe" of Kula Gulf at 20 knots.[68]

Admiral Merrill had arranged his ships in something of a strange formation. The destroyer leader *Waller*, with Commander Burke on board, was scouting 4,000 yards ahead of the next destroyer, *Conway*. About 2,000 yards behind the *Conway* were the light cruisers, flagship *Montpelier* leading the *Cleveland* and *Denver* at 1,000-yard intervals. The remaining destroyer, *Cony*, was 2,000 yards off the *Denver*'s port quarter.[69] All the American ships were new, having been completed since the beginning of the Pacific War. Each light cruiser carried a dozen rapid-firing 6-inch guns in four triple turrets. Unlike Admirals Callaghan and Scott, Admiral Merrill had access to the newest SG radar on board his flagship and he was very happy to use it.

So was the *Montpelier*'s navigator Lieutenant Commander Paul Whitefield Hord, in fixing their location inside Kula Gulf. At 12:53 am, Hord asked for a radar range and bearing on Sasamboki Island, a tiny islet just a few miles southeast of Vila, as a point of reference for their approach. The radar operator checked the scope, and came back with, "Sir, a part of the island seems to be moving slowly."[70]

As the *Montpelier*'s SG radar operator watched, the blip he thought was Sasamboki split into two blips. The *Waller*'s radar detected the same thing some 8 miles off the starboard bow and reported it in at 12:57 am. Within three more minutes, that new blip would divide itself further into two more blips.[71] Either they were witnessing a major geological event or they were detecting Sasamboki Island and two ships emerging from its radar shadow. While he was no geologist, Admiral Merrill guessed it was the latter.

The Japanese destroyers were now showing on radar on all the ships. The fire control radars had locked onto the nearer ship; the guns were following accordingly, ready to fire. At 1:01 am, the order came over the voice radio: "Stand by to commence firing."[72] One minute later, the lead destroyer *Waller* unleashed five Mark 15 torpedoes at the nearer target, range 7,000 yards and a speed of 24 knots. There was no hesitation, no need to worry about friendly fire, no need to worry about ranges. Another minute and Admiral Merrill came back, "Commence firing."[73]

The flagship *Montpelier* was the first to fire her 12 6-inch guns, but the *Cleveland* and *Denver* quickly followed. "Spotting [was] impossible due to the large number of splashes arising almost simultaneously around the closer target, which radar [showed] to be straddled, and to the naked eye [was] definitely exploding with flames."[74]

That "closer target" was the *Murasame*, whose bridge was abject confusion. Captain Tachibana ordered antiaircraft action; where he got the idea they were under air attack is anybody's guess. The commodore's misconception may have preempted other considerations. When Admiral Tanaka and his destroyers were ambushed at Tassafaronga, the first response was evasive maneuvers by his ships. The second was that ancient Japanese credo: *When in doubt, launch torpedoes.* Tanaka was able to eke out a victory by doing both. Tachibana did neither.

He quickly paid for his lack of vision. The *Murasame* was shattered by an "extremely violent" explosion.[75] At least one of the Mark 15 torpedoes launched by the *Waller* had poked through the *Murasame*'s starboard side into one of the aft magazines.[76] For once it had actually detonated, taking with it both magazines and blowing off most of the destroyer's stern in a blast so loud Captain Briscoe's destroyers heard it 25 miles away off Munda. The engine rooms quickly flooded and the *Murasame* lost power.[77]

As the *Murasame* staggered to a halt, Lieutenant Commander Uesugi Yoshitake had his *Minegumo* veer to starboard both to avoid ramming the rapidly slowing *Murasame* and to evade the torpedoes and gunfire directed at the tiny-and-getting-tinier flotilla. It was a necessary maneuver, but it allowed the burning *Murasame* to backlight his ship – not that it mattered, since Admiral Merrill's ships were firing by radar control. With the *Murasame* clearly in mortal agony, the recipient of that gunfire now shifted to the *Minegumo*. Uesugi's destroyer was now subject to a deluge of 6-inch shells from the rapid-firing American cruisers. The *Minegumo*'s gunnery officer Lieutenant Tokuno Hiroshi tried to have his men use the gun flashes of the American ships as points of aim, but, he later said, "We were hit so quickly that we were able to return only a few shots."[78] She did not have a visually impressive explosion like the *Murasame* did, but the *Minegumo* was reduced to a blazing wreck all the same.

Admiral Merrill's ships resumed their trip to Vila, passing the rapidly sinking *Murasame*. Lieutenant Kayama had time only to run to his cabin and get his sword and a book, not considering how the book was going to hold up in the water.[79] By 1:15, the remnants of the *Murasame* had slipped beneath the waters of the Kula Gulf. The *Minegumo* survived her by 15 minutes or so.

Admiral Merrill continued on to his main mission, shelling the airbase at Vila. At 1:25 am the guns of his cruisers and destroyers roared into the night once again. It was short – eight minutes, with 1,635 6-inch and 1,123 5-inch rounds lobbed at the airfield. It certainly looked impressive: "There were many big explosions from the shore as our guns hit their targets … We did an awful job on the Japs, we left the place in shambles, we hit troop barracks, ammunition dumps, radio towers, airfield planes, and broken bodies were everywhere."[80] The Japanese described the effects as "none in particular."[81]At Munda, Captain Briscoe's destroyers tossed 1,700 5-inch rounds at the base, detonating an ammunition dump containing 1,000 3-inch shells. And with that, the US Navy ships headed for home and got back safely.[82]

The next morning, Lieutenant Tokuno stumbled onto Kolombangara after a seven-hour swim from the wreck of the *Minegumo*.[83] There he joined 121 other survivors, none of whom was Lieutenant Commander Uesugi. From the *Murasame*, 53 made it to shore, including Captain Tachibana, Lieutenant Kayama, and skipper Lieutenant Commander Tanegashima Youji. The *Murasame* took 128 down with her and the *Minegumo* lost 46.[84]

That afternoon a reconnaissance plane from Guadalcanal flew over the area. It reported an oil slick "(southeast of) Kolombangara," its origin a mystery.[85] Maybe it was from Captain Tachibana's sunken destroyers, but at around this time it was also noticed that the submarine *Grampus* had not checked in.

As Hara Tameichi would point out, "Admiral Tanaka carried out a series of brilliant transport operations to Guadalcanal in November and December 1942. When other destroyer groups, led by officers of lesser ability, tried the same kind of operation it frequently led to such debacles as the March 5 massacre in Kula Gulf."[86] This engagement, variously called the Battle of the Blackett Strait, even though none of it took place in Blackett Strait, or the Battle of Vila-Stanmore, was small by Pacific War standards, involving only eight warships. It was the smallest engagement involving warships on both sides since the sinking of the destroyer USS *Blue* off Guadalcanal in August 1942, which had involved only three.

The Battle of Vila-Stanmore would be a sign of things to come. Midway may have changed everything in the Pacific War but the liberation of Guadalcanal, after the long, proverbial toe-to-toe slugging match, started a whole new campaign – the campaign for the Solomon Islands.

The campaign would come with a whole new set of rules. The massive surface battles off Guadalcanal that involved heavy cruisers and even battleships were, for the most part, over. The US Navy had decided that the restricted waters of the Solomon Islands were too dangerous for such heavy surface units, since they allowed lighter units to get in close with damaging shots, the *San Francisco*'s ultimately disabling hit on the *Hiei* and the *South Dakota*'s pounding at the hands of Admiral Kondo's cruisers being cases in point. From now on, the preference would be for smaller – and cheaper – ships like destroyers and light cruisers, operating in smaller, less unwieldy groups like Admiral Merrill's.

Vila-Stanmore also showed that the Japanese superiority in night engagements had substantially eroded. At a time when the US Navy was finally jettisoning the prewar bureaucrats in the officer corps, allowing the wartime performers to rise to the top, the Imperial Japanese Navy was facing the opposite problem – it was running out of its talented, veteran officers. Fewer and fewer Tanaka Raizos were coming up through the ranks. Could these new commanders hold up? Or would they just be "officers of lesser ability" like Captain Tachibana?

"Lesser ability" was becoming a theme in the Imperial Japanese Navy. Not just surface officers, but pilots too. The 11th Air Fleet's Base Air Force, the force which had destroyed Douglas MacArthur's Far East Air Force at Clark Field, destroyed Cavite Navy Yard, and sunk the *Prince of Wales* and *Repulse*, had been beaten by a tiny Cactus Air Force operating from a dirt airfield on Guadalcanal. The Cactus Air Force was rejuvenated, enlarged, now operating as AirSols. Base Air Force was facing its own two front war, threatened by AirSols in the Solomons and General MacArthur's 5th Air Force in New Guinea. How would, how could, Base Air Force continue to keep them at bay when it was running out of trained aviators?

It seemed the Japanese were running out of everything. Vila-Stanmore was the first engagement in which the US Navy had fought with only warships launched after the US had entered the war.[87] The Imperial Japanese Navy could not match such production, not with so much of its shipbuilding capacity tied up in the *Yamato* and *Musashi* superbattleships. Not with ships, not with aircraft.

Nevertheless, the Japanese, especially the Imperial Army, had demonstrated one important advantage: they were masters of defensive preparation. The Gifu positions on Guadalcanal had enabled the Japanese to contest every inch of ground, even when outnumbered, outgunned, and largely cut off, making the Americans pay dearly to root them out. Could the Japanese continue to design such defenses? Could the Allies afford to dig the Japanese out?

Because everyone knew exactly where the next Guadalcanal would be: on and around New Georgia, with the objective being a little place called Munda.

NOTES

Prologue

1 Richard B. Frank, *Guadalcanal: The Definitive Account of the Landmark Battle* (New York: Penguin, 1992), 6.

2 "Foreign Relations of the United States, The Conferences at Washington, 1941–1942, and Casablanca, 1943 Document 114," Office of the Historian, United States Department of State, https://history.state.gov/historicaldocuments/frus1941–43/d114.

3 Ibid.

4 Vice Admiral George Carroll, Dyer, USN (Ret.), *The Amphibians Came to Conquer: The Story of Admiral Richmond Kelly Turner* (Washington, DC: US Government Printing Office, 1971), 238.

5 Brigadier General Samuel B. Griffith, USMC (Ret.), *The Battle for Guadalcanal* (Toronto; New York; London; Sydney: Bantam, 1980), 9–10.

6 Dyer, *Amphibians*, 243.

7 Williamson Murray and Allan R. Millett, *A War To Be Won: Fighting the Second World War* (Cambridge, MA; London: Belknap Press of Harvard University Press, 2000), Kindle edition, 2606.

8 William Manchester, *American Caesar: Douglas MacArthur, 1880–1964* (New York: Back Bay Books, 1978), Kindle edition, 5591; Thomas B. Buell, *Master of Seapower: A Biography of Fleet Admiral Ernest J. King* (Annapolis: Naval Institute Press, 1980), Kindle edition, 3949.

9 Walter R. Borneman, *The Admirals: Nimitz, Halsey, Leahy, and King – The Five-Star Admirals Who Won the War at Sea* (New York; Boston; London: Little, Brown, and Company, 2012), 280.

10 Admiral Nimitz's first suggestion to head the South Pacific Command was Vice Admiral William S. Pye, whose main claim to fame was, in a meeting on December 6, 1941, loudly declaring, "The Japanese will not go to war with the United States. We are too big, too powerful, and too strong." Gordon Prange, *At Dawn We Slept: The Untold Story of Pearl Harbor* (New York: Penguin, 1981), 470.

11 Griffith, *Guadalcanal*, 11.

12 General Alexander A. Vandegrift, USMC, and Robert B. Asprey, *Once A Marine: The Memoirs of General A.A. Vandegrift, USMC* (New York: W.W. Norton & Co., 1964), 104; Buell, *Master of Seapower*, 4106.

13 Griffith, *Guadalcanal*, 11.

14 James D. Hornfischer, *Neptune's Inferno: The US Navy at Guadalcanal* (New York: Bantam, 2011), 24.

15 Dyer, *Amphibians*, 252–3.

16 William Tuohy, *America's Fighting Admirals: Winning the War at Sea in World War II* (St. Paul, MN: Zenith Press, 2007), Kindle edition, 1156–64.

17 John Prados, *Islands of Destiny: The Solomons Campaign and the Eclipse of the Rising Sun* (New York: NAL Caliber, 2012), Kindle edition, 36.

18 John B. Lundstrom, *Black Shoe Carrier Admiral: Frank Jack Fletcher at Coral Sea, Midway, and Guadalcanal* (Annapolis: Naval Institute Press, 2006), 311.

19 Tuohy, *America's Fighting Admirals*, 1156.

20 Frank, *Guadalcanal*, 46–7. As Robert Leckie (*Challenge for the Pacific – Guadalcanal: The Turning Point of the War* (New York: Bantam, 1965), Kindle edition, 632 note) states, in traditional practice, "The word 'Marines' is interchangeable with 'regiment' … thus, to say First Marines is to mean First Marine Regiment[.]" Frank (*Guadalcanal*, 46, n. 5) describes it as American custom to refer to Marine regiments without using the word "Regiment." By this practice, the "7th Marine Regiment" is normally referenced as the "7th Marines." While acknowledging that this is the preferred and long-standing habit in the military and among military historians, it may become confusing for the non-military reader. For that reason, the American custom will not be used here.

21 Frank, *Guadalcanal*, 17.

22 Ibid., 35.

23 Dyer, *Amphibians*, 272.

24 Ibid., 272.

25 John Prados, *Combined Fleet Decoded: The Secret History of American Intelligence and the Japanese Navy in World War II* (Annapolis: Naval Institute Press, 1995), 235–6.

26 Dyer, *Amphibians*, 274.

27 Ibid., 274. For clarification, Dyer says the version of events proffered by Samuel Eliot Morison, (*History of United States Naval Operations in World War II, Vol V: The Struggle for Guadalcanal August 1942–February 1943* [Edison, NJ: Castle, 1949], 12–14), in which an Allied reconnaissance plane spotted the airfield on July 4, was actually the work of *Magic*.

28 Hornfischer, *Neptune's Inferno*, 588; Tuohy, *America's Fighting Admirals*, 1150.

29 Frank, *Guadalcanal*, 36; Lundstrom, *Black Shoe*, 321.

30 Lundstrom, *Black Shoe*, 321.

31 Vandegrift and Asprey, *Once A Marine*, 120; John Toland, *The Rising Sun: The Decline and Fall of the Japanese Empire 1936–1945* (New York: Random House, 1970), Kindle edition, 7793.

32 Lieutenant General Merrill B. Twining, USMC (Ret.), *No Bended Knee: The Battle for Guadalcanal* (New York: Presidio, 1996), Kindle edition, 52; Frank, *Guadalcanal*, 57.

33 Lieutenant Colonel Frank O. Hough, USMCR; Ludwig, Major Verle E., USMC; Shaw, Henry I., Jr., *History of U.S. Marine Corps Operations in World War II, Volume I: Pearl Harbor to Guadalcanal* (Washington, DC: Historical Branch, G-3 Division, Headquarters, U.S. Marine Corps; 1958), 248.

34 Twining, *No Bended Knee*, 55.

35 Prados, *Islands of Destiny*, 888–92.

36 William Bruce Johnson, *The Pacific Campaign in World War II: From Pearl Harbor to Guadalcanal* (London; New York: Routledge, 2006), Kindle edition, 167.

37 Dyer, *Amphibians*, 328.

38 Ibid., 328.

39 Samuel Eliot Morison, *The Two-Ocean War: A Short History of the United States Navy in the Second World War* (Boston; Toronto; London: Little, Brown, and Company, 1963), 166–7.

40 Twining, *No Bended Knee*, 62–3.

41 Ibid., 88.

42 Ibid., 85.

43 Johnson, *Pacific Campaign*, 200.

44 William Manchester, *Goodbye, Darkness: A Memoir of the Pacific War* (New York: Back Bay Books, 1979), Kindle edition, 2372.

45 Johnson, *Pacific Campaign*, 201.

46 Ibid., 204.

47 Col. Joe Foss, USMC (Ret.), *Joe Foss: Flying Marine* (Pickle Partners Publishing, 2013), Kindle edition, 676.

48 "Ichiki" is sometimes rendered "Ikki."

49 USS *Southard* "Action Report 8–11 September 1942" (September 12, 1942), 1l; USS *Southard* War Diary 1 September 1942–30 September 1942, 4–5.

50 USS *Southard* "Action Report 8–11 September 1942" (September 12, 1942), 2. During this period, a lot of antisubmarine attacks were described as "embarrassing." While it is quite possible that surface units were, at the very least, self-conscious about such attacks, generally speaking, in this context "embarrassing" was a term-of-art, a synonym for "urgent." An "embarrassing" barrage, usually a few depth charges dropped at once (hence the older meaning of the word "embarrassing"), was intended "to frighten the submarine crew and prevent it from pressing home its attack [...I]ts value is largely psychological and cannot readily be evaluated in quantitative terms." Charles M. Sternhell and Alan M. Thorndike, *OEG Report No. 51: Antisubmarine Warfare in World War II* (Washington, DC: Operations Evaluation Group, Office of the Chief of Naval Operations, Navy Department, 1946), 114.

51 USS *Southard* "Action Report 8–11 September 1942" (September 12, 1942), 2–3.

52 USS *Southard* War Diary 1 September 1942–30 September 1942, 6.

53 Michael R. Smith, *Bloody Ridge The Battle That Saved Guadalcanal* (Novato, CA: Presidio, 2000), Kindle edition, 2667–84.

54 Ibid., 2752.

55 Ibid., 2756.

56 The conversation between Lieutenant Colonel Edson and headquarters is an amalgamation of Smith, *Bloody Ridge*, 2756; George W. Smith, *The Do-Or-Die Men: The 1st Marine Raider Battalion at Guadalcanal* (New York: Pocket Books, 2003), Kindle edition, 273; and Griffith, *Guadalcanal*, 133–4.

57 Griffith, *Guadalcanal*, 155.

58 Thomas G. Miller, *The Cactus Air Force* (New York: Bantam, 1981), 122–3.

59 Frank, *Guadalcanal*, 266.

60 Leckie, *Challenge*, 3604.

61 Hanson W. Baldwin, "US Hold in Solomons Bolstered," *New York Times*, 11/3/1942, 4.

62 John Wukovits, *Admiral "Bull" Halsey: The Life and Wars of the Navy's Most Controversial Commander* (New York: St. Martin's Press; 2010), Kindle edition, 33.

63 Wukovits, *Halsey*, 33.

64 Ibid., 33.

65 John B. Lundstrom, *The First Team and the Guadalcanal Campaign: Naval Fighter Combat from August to November 1942* (Annapolis: Naval Institute Press, 1994), Kindle edition, 7183.

66 Edwin P. Hoyt, *How They Won the War in the Pacific: Nimitz and His Admirals* (Guilford, CN: Lyons Press, 2012), Kindle edition, 2428–44.

67 Frank, *Guadalcanal*, 216–7.

68 Hornfischer, *Neptune's Inferno*, 2912.

69 Eric Hammel, *Carrier Strike: The Battle of the Santa Cruz Islands October 1942* (Pacifica, CA: Pacifica Military History, 1999), Kindle edition, 1713.

70 E.B. Potter, *Nimitz* (Annapolis: Naval Institute Press, 1976), Kindle edition, 192.

71 Robert Sherrod, *History of Marine Corps Aviation in World War II* (Washington, DC: Combat Forces Press, 1952), 82.

72 Frank, *Guadalcanal*, 209.

73 Potter, *Nimitz*, 193.

74 Unless specified otherwise, details of the October 2 meeting come from Hoyt, *How They Won*, 2492–591.

75 Miller, *Cactus*, 84.

76 *Nisshin* TROM (Tabular Records of Movement); Frank, *Guadalcanal*, 280.

77 *Chitose* TROM; Frank, *Guadalcanal*, 294; Morison, *Struggle*, 151.

78 Frank, *Guadalcanal*, 216–7.

79 Hornfischer, *Neptune's Inferno*, 2607.

80 Ibid., 2607–23.

81 Ibid., 2639.

82 Ibid., 2639.

83 Ibid., 2639.

84 Ibid., 2698.

85 Eric Hammel, *Guadalcanal: Starvation Island* (Pacifica, CA: Pacifica Military History, 1987), Kindle edition, 5203.

86 Sherrod, *History*, 99; Miller, *Cactus*, 121.

87 Hammel, *Starvation*, 5203.

88 Hornfischer, *Neptune's Inferno*, 3642.

89 Vandegrift and Asprey, *Once A Marine*, 174.

90 T. Grady Gallant, *On Valor's Side: A Marine's Own Story of Parris Island and Guadalcanal* (New York: Doubleday, 1963), Kindle edition, 5656–75.

91 Twining, *No Bended Knee*, 151.

92 Martin Clemens, *Alone on Guadalcanal: A Coastwatcher's Story* (Annapolis: Naval Institute Press, 1998), Kindle edition, 256.

93 Foss, *Flying Marine*, 459.

94 Leckie, *Challenge*, 4384.

95 Prados, *Islands of Destiny*, 117.

96 Foss, *Flying Marine*, 466.

97 Vandegrift and Asprey, *Once A Marine*, 175.

98 Hornfischer, *Neptune's Inferno*, 3691.

99 Frank, *Guadalcanal*, 318; Robert J. Cressman, *The Official Chronology of the U.S. Navy in World War II* (Washington, DC: Contemporary History Branch, Naval Historical Center, 1999).

100 Lundstrom, *First Team*, 8345; Frank, *Guadalcanal*, 318–9.

101 Lundstrom, *First Team*, 8370.

102 Ibid., 8345.

103 Vandegrift and Asprey, *Once A Marine*, 177.

104 Frank, *Guadalcanal*, 320.

105 Lundstrom, *First Team*, 8375–91. Only one of the coastwatcher station's three masts was still standing. The teleradio aerial had caught in a palm tree. When the crew radioed out to make a test of signal strength and

readability, the answer came back at once: "Seems much improved. Have you been making adjustments?" (Hornfischer, *Neptune's Inferno*, 3674).

106 Frank, *Guadalcanal*, 320.
107 Cressman, *Official Chronology*.
108 Frank, *Guadalcanal*, 325.
109 *Southard* War Diary.
110 Miller, *Cactus*, 125.
111 Lundstrom, *First Team*, 8430.
112 Ibid., 8464.
113 Hoyt, *How They Won*, 163.
114 Frank, *Guadalcanal*, 322.
115 *Southard* War Diary.
116 Prados, *Islands of Destiny*, 121; Lundstrom, *First Team*, 8560.
117 *Kyushu Maru* TROM.
118 Lundstrom, *First Team*, 8533; *Azumasan Maru* TROM.
119 *Maya* TROM; Frank, *Guadalcanal*, 326.
120 Eric Hammel, *Air War Pacific Chronology: America's Air War Against Japan in East Asia and the Pacific 1941–1945* (Pacifica, CA: Pacifica Military History, 1998), Kindle edition, 3197.
121 Miller, *Cactus*, 136.
122 Lundstrom, *First Team*, 9056.
123 Barrett Tillman, *US Marine Corps Fighter Squadrons of World War II* (Oxford, Osprey, 2014), Kindle edition, 650; Lundstrom, *First Team*, 9063.
124 Lundstrom, *First Team*, 9095.
125 Toland, *Rising Sun*, 8796.
126 Hornfischer, *Neptune's Inferno*, 3825.
127 Lundstrom, *First Team*, 8794.
128 Potter, *Nimitz*, 196.
129 Hornfischer, *Neptune's Inferno*, 3859; Potter, *Nimitz*, 197.
130 Fleet Admiral William F. Halsey, USN, *Admiral Halsey's Story* (Pickle Partners Publishing, 2013), Kindle edition, 2362.
131 Hornfischer, *Neptune's Inferno*, 3930.
132 Ibid., 3930.
133 Halsey, *Story*, 2498.
134 Ibid., 2498.
135 Hornfischer, *Neptune's Inferno*, 3964.
136 Halsey, *Story*, 2502.
137 Toland, *Rising Sun*, 8834.
138 Eric Hammel, *Carrier Strike*, 1899.
139 Halsey, *Story*, 2502–20.
140 *Southard* War Diary.
141 Lundstrom, *First Team*, 9008.
142 Ibid., 9055.
143 Ibid., 9002.
144 Ibid., 9033.
145 Hammel, *Carrier Strike*, 1990; Lundstrom, *First Team*, 9378–95; *Akatsuki* TROM.
146 *Akatsuki* TROM.
147 Frank, *Guadalcanal*, 359.
148 Hammel, *Carrier Strike*, 2091.
149 Ibid., 2089; *Yura* TROM; *Akizuki* TROM.
150 *Akizuki* TROM.
151 *Yura* TROM.
152 Hammel, *Carrier Strike*, 2127; *Yura* TROM.
153 Halsey, *Story*, 2577.
154 Ibid., 2578.
155 Ibid., 2577.
156 Lundstrom, *First Team*, 9234.

157 Frank, *Guadalcanal*, 371.

158 Halsey, *Story*, 2577.

159 Lundstrom, *First Team*, 9250.

160 Ibid., 9519–40.

161 Ibid., 9552. There are two commonly held myths regarding this order. The first is that it read "Attack, Repeat, Attack," which comes from Admiral Halsey himself (*Story*, 2593) paraphrasing the order. The second is the timing of the order, which, again thanks in part to Admiral Halsey (*Story*, 2593), is commonly believed to have been the early morning hours of October 26. In fact, official ComSoPac records (CTF 61 242350) show the order as going out early afternoon on October 25.

162 Hammel, *Carrier Strike*, 3675.

163 Ibid., 3675.

164 *Shokaku* TROM.

165 Lundstrom, *First Team*, 10417.

166 Ibid., 10718.

167 *Hornet* Report, 7; Lundstrom, *First Team*, 10816.

168 Lundstrom, *First Team*, 10839.

169 Ibid., 10945.

170 Ibid., 10945.

171 Ibid., 11153.

172 Ibid., 11057.

173 Hammel, *Carrier Strike*, 5700.

174 Henry V. Poor, Henry A. Mustin, and Colin G. Jameson, *United States Navy Combat Narrative: The Battles of Cape Esperance, 11 October 1942 and Santa Cruz Islands, 26 October 1942* (Washington, DC: Publications Branch, Office of Naval Intelligence, United States Navy, 1943), 64; Lundstrom, *First Team*, 11082.

175 Hammel, *Carrier Strike*, 5739.

176 Poor, Mustin, and Jameson, *Combat Narrative*, 64; Lundstrom, *First Team*, 11098; Hammel, *Carrier Strike*, 5739–75.

177 Poor, Mustin, and Jameson, *Combat Narrative*, 64; Lundstrom, *First Team*, 11135.

178 Lundstrom, *First Team*, 11747.

179 Ibid., 11870.

180 Halsey, *Story*, 2610–29.

181 Prados, *Islands of Destiny*, 149–50.

182 Ibid., 150.

183 See, e.g., John Prados, "Solving the Mysteries of Santa Cruz," *Naval History Magazine*, October 2011, Volume 25, Number 5.

184 Thomas Alexander Hughes, *Admiral Bill Halsey: A Naval Life* (Cambridge, MA: Harvard University Press, 2016). Kindle edition, 3431–447.

185 Wukovits, *Halsey*, 103.

186 *Southard* and *Conyngham* war diaries.

187 *I-172* TROM.

188 *I-21* TROM.

189 Eric Hammel, *Guadalcanal: Decision at Sea: The Naval Battle of Guadalcanal November 13–15, 1942* (Pacifica, CA: Pacifica Military History, 1988), Kindle edition, 911–53.

190 *I-172* TROM.

191 *I-15* TROM.

Chapter 1

1 Due to reader familiarity, the term "destroyer flotilla" will be used for a squadron of multiple divisions of Japanese destroyers led by, usually, a light cruiser such as the *Jintsu*. Nevertheless, that is a rough English translation of the Imperial Japanese Navy term *Suirai Sentai*, which means "Torpedo Squadron." What here is being called the 2nd Destroyer Flotilla was known in the Imperial Navy as the 2nd Torpedo Squadron. Similarly, the term the Japanese would use to describe what in English is usually called the 5th Cruiser Division was *Sentai* 5 or "5th Squadron." In Imperial Navy parlance, *Sentai*, by itself, refers to a division of cruisers or battleships, with each sentai organized according to type of warship but the unit designations themselves making no such distinction. Thus, the numerical designation references not the number of cruiser or battleship divisions, but the

number of sentai. Not surprisingly, the use of sentai often results in confusion, so the traditional English-language practice of referencing the "cruiser division" or "battleship division" will be used here.

2   Evans, David C. (ed.), *The Japanese Navy in World War II in the Words of Former Japanese Naval Officers* (2nd ed.) Annapolis: Naval Institute Press, 1986. Kindle edition, 2654–61.

3   Leckie, *Challenge*, 2485–501.

4   Lundstrom, *First Team*, 4620; Tanaka, "Struggle for Guadalcanal," 169; *Jintsu* TROM.

5   Hammel, *Starvation Island*, 4109.

6   H.P. Willmott, *Empires in the Balance: Japanese and Allied Pacific Strategies to April 1942* (Annapolis: Naval Institute Press, 1982), 242.

7   Willmott, *Empires*, 242.

8   Willmott, *Empires*, 242.

9   Lundstrom, *First Team*, 8118.

10 Bruce Gamble, *Fortress Rabaul: The Battle for the Southwest Pacific, January 1942–April 1943* (Minneapolis, MN: Zenith Press, 2013), 317.

11 Prange, *At Dawn We Slept*, 265.

12 Tameichi Hara, Fred Saito, and Roger Pineau, *Japanese Destroyer Captain: Pearl Harbor, Guadalcanal, Midway – The Great Naval Battles as Seen Through Japanese Eyes* (Annapolis: Naval Institute Press, 1967), Kindle edition, 126–7.

13 Tanaka, "Struggle for Guadalcanal," 181.

14 Griffith, *Guadalcanal*, 179.

15 Prados, *Islands of Destiny*, 116; Frank, *Guadalcanal*, 317.

16 Toland, *Rising Sun*, 8767.

17 Frank, *Guadalcanal*, 319; Lundstrom, *First Team*, 8370.

18 Lundstrom, *First Team*, 8370.

19 Frank, *Guadalcanal*, 347. For more detailed explanations of the replacement of General Kawaguchi, see Toland, *Rising Sun*, 8866–83, and Frank, *Guadalcanal*, 346–7. The general story is that during the early Japanese occupation of the Philippines, Tsuji wanted to have American prisoners of war and Philippine government officials executed and Kawaguchi not only refused to do so, but fought against it. Nevertheless, the reader should be aware of the caveat provided by Frank: "The murkiness of Japanese command relationships and the absence of documentation of the 2d Division Headquarters for October 23 makes segments of this day's events misty."

20 Toland, *Rising Sun*, 8910.

21 Hornfischer, *Neptune's Inferno*, 4104.

22 Frank, *Guadalcanal*, 370.

23 Lundstrom, *First Team*, 9384.

24 Toland, *Rising Sun*, 8902–19.

25 Toland, *Rising Sun*, 8947.

26 Masatake Okumiya, Jiro Horikoshi, and Martin Caidin, *Zero!* (Pickle Partners Publishing, 2014), Kindle edition, 4034; Lundstrom, *First Team*, 10682.

27 *Shokaku* TROM.

28 Hammel, *Carrier Strike*, 7147; Matome Ugaki, Donald M. Goldstein (ed.), and Katherine V. Dillon (ed.), *Fading Victory: The Diary of Admiral Matome Ugaki* (Pittsburgh: University of Pittsburgh Press, 1991), 251.

29 Lundstrom, *First Team*, 12117.

30 Morison, *Struggle*, 224.

31 Lundstrom, *First Team*, 12138.

32 Frank, *Guadalcanal*, 400–1; Lundstrom, *First Team*, 12134.

33 Hughes, *Admiral Bill Halsey*, 3431; Murray and Millett, *A War to be Won*, 591.

34 Hughes, *Admiral Bill Halsey*, 3431–47.

35 Hara, Saito, and Pineau, *Destroyer Captain*.

36 Toland, *Rising Sun*, 9161.

37 Hiroyuki Agawa, *The Reluctant Admiral: Yamamoto and the Imperial Navy* (Tokyo; New York: Kodansha, 1979). Whether or not Admiral Yamamoto actually made this promise is uncertain, as the man to whom he allegedly made that promise, Colonel Tsuji Masanobu, has been known to take liberties with the truth from time to time. But it seems he was prohibited from taking the *Yamato* to Guadalcanal by a formal imperial command from the Naval General Staff in Tokyo. Yamamoto biographer Agawa Hiroyuki would later comment, "[I]t still seems rather odd that the commander in chief of the Combined Fleet should have had to stay put, cooped up in that great battleship (*Yamato*), poised for action but doing nothing."

38   Japanese order of battle comes from Frank, *Guadalcanal*, 428–9.

39   Hammel, *Guadalcanal*, 852–72.

40   Tanaka, "Struggle for Guadalcanal," 3031.

41   Ibid., 3067.

42   Ibid., 3067.

43   Morison, *Struggle*, 226.

44   *I-20* TROM; Morison, *Struggle*, 226–7.

45   Prados, *Islands of Destiny*, 390.

46   Ibid., 391.

47   Lundstrom, *First Team*, 12378.

48   Halsey, *Story*, 2650.

49   Ibid., 2650.

50   Hammel, *Starvation*, 6636.

51   Hammel, *Guadalcanal*, 988. What the hell are "organizational weapons"?

52   Lundstrom, *First Team*, 12549.

53   The sources are vague as to how many Wildcats were scrambled to face the Zeroes. Hammel (*Guadalcanal*, 1023), says, "There were at least eight Marine F4F Wildcat fighters over the channel when the first air raid alert was sounded" and, in the following paragraph, describes how eight Wildcats scrambled from Fighter 1. Frank (*Guadalcanal*, 425), says the interception involved 21 Wildcats. Morison (*Struggle*, 229) does not give a figure but says that it was "a vigorous antiaircraft reception."

54   Lundstrom, *First Team*, 12549.

55   Hammel, *Guadalcanal*, 1060.

56   Lundstrom, *First Team*, 12549; Hammel, *Guadalcanal*, 1081.

57   Hammel, *Guadalcanal*, 1126.

58   Lundstrom, *First Team*, 12586.

59   Hammel, *Guadalcanal*, 1165.

60   Ibid., 1237.

61   Lundstrom, *First Team*, 12586.

62   Hammel, *Guadalcanal*, 1301.

63   Lundstrom, *First Team*, 12586.

64   Hammel, *Guadalcanal*, 1302.

65   Ibid., 1302.

66   Ibid., 1302.

67   ONI (Office of Naval Intelligence) Narrative, Guadalcanal, 12.

68   Hammel, *Guadalcanal*, 1457.

69   Ibid., 1457; Lundstrom, *First Team*, 12606.

70   Hammel, *Guadalcanal*, 1324.

71   Ibid., 1360.

72   Lundstrom, *First Team*, 12622; Hammel, *Guadalcanal*, 1697.

73   Hammel, *Guadalcanal*, 1697.

74   Ibid., 1513.

75   Frank, *Guadalcanal*, 432; Hammel, *Guadalcanal*, 1734.

76   Hammel, *Guadalcanal*, 1660.

77   Lundstrom, *First Team*, 12606.

78   Ibid., 12606.

79   Ibid., 12622.

80   Frank, *Guadalcanal*, 432.

81   Lundstrom, *First Team*, 12622.

82   Ibid., 12622; Hammel, *Guadalcanal*, 1773.

83   Hammel, *Guadalcanal*, 1773; Frank, *Guadalcanal*, 432; Morison, *Struggle*, 235.

84   Morison, *Struggle*, 235–6.

85   Hara, Saito, and Pineau, *Destroyer Captain*, 126.

86   Ibid., 126.

87   Hammel, *Guadalcanal*, 1817.

88   Hammel, *Starvation*, 6667.

89 Lundstrom, *First Team*, 12586. Frank (*Guadalcanal*, 431) states that the report came from Lieutenant Commander Mitsui Kenji, calling him "Mitzi." Lundstrom is explicit that Emura had replaced Mitsui by this time.

90 Frank, *Guadalcanal*, 431.

91 Hara, Saito, and Pineau, *Destroyer Captain*, 127.

92 Ibid., 127.

93 Ibid., 128.

94 Ibid., 127.

95 Ibid., 128.

96 Ibid., 128.

97 Ibid., 128.

98 Ibid., 128.

99 Ibid., 128.

100 Ibid., 128.

101 Ibid., 129.

102 Hammel, *Guadalcanal*, 2327.

103 Hara, Saito, and Pineau, *Destroyer Captain*, 129. Stephen Howarth (*The Fighting Ships of the Rising Sun: The Drama of the Imperial Japanese Navy 1895–1945* (New York: Atheneum, 1983), 312) says Admiral Abe ordered the course reversal because they had missed Savo Island in the storm, had sailed past the spot where they were supposed to turn to the southeast to head toward Lunga, and were steaming beyond it into the Coral Sea. I have found no corroboration for this claim. Hara, who as skipper of the *Amatsukaze* was present for and actually took part in these maneuvers, makes no mention of it and appears to contradict it in several respects. First, Hara (128) states that the reason for the reversal was getting out of the storm. Second, Hara says that after both course reversals, his lookouts spotted Savo Island "60 degrees to port," which indicates they were approaching from the north or west, though Hara does not mention a course change after this time. Third, Hara (128) also states that Rear Admiral Kimura on the *Nagara* was "one of Japan's top navigators."

104 Frank, *Guadalcanal*, 437.

105 Hara, Saito, and Pineau, *Destroyer Captain*, 129–30.

106 Frank, *Guadalcanal*, 437.

107 Hara, Saito, and Pineau, *Destroyer Captain*, 129.

108 Howarth, *Fighting Ships*, 313. Howarth identifies the officer with whom Commander Chihaya argued only as "senior staff officer of the battleship division." Howarth later says that officer was with Chihaya when shells hit the *Hiei*'s bridge, wounding Chihaya and killing the officer. James W. Grace (*The Naval Battle of Guadalcanal: Night Action 13 November 1942* [Annapolis: Naval Institute Press, 1999], 85–6) identifies the officer killed as Admiral Abe's chief of staff Commander Suzuki Masakane.

109 Hara, Saito, and Pineau, *Destroyer Captain*, 129–30.

110 Howarth, *Fighting Ships*, 313; Hara, Saito, and Pineau, *Destroyer Captain*, 130.

111 Morison, *Struggle*, 235–6.

112 Lundstrom, *First Team*, 12622.

113 Francis X. Murphy, *Fighting Admiral: The Story of Dan Callaghan* (New York: Vantage Press, 1952), 186.

114 Historian Eric Hammel (*Guadalcanal*, 1846) called Admiral Scott "an authentic tiger."

115 Frank, *Guadalcanal*, 433.

116 Ibid., 433 n. 2.

117 Murphy, *Fighting Admiral*, 186.

118 Ibid., 176–7.

119 Ibid., 177.

120 Hammel, *Guadalcanal*, 1863.

121 Hornfischer, *Neptune's Inferno*, 254.

122 Ibid., 254; J.E. Bennett, "Callaghan Was Calm and Collected at Guadalcanal," *Shipmate 59* (April 1996), 18.

123 Hornfischer, *Neptune's Inferno*, 254.

124 Murphy, *Fighting Admiral*, 187.

125 Ibid., 186–7.

126 *Portland* historian William Thomas Generous, Jr. (*Sweet Pea at War: A History of USS Portland* [Lexington, KY: University Press of Kentucky, 2003], 78) said of the formation, "It was symmetrical, but stupid." And he should know.

127 Murphy, *Fighting Admiral*, 186–7.

128 Anthony Newpower, *Iron Men and Tin Fish: The Race to Build a Better Torpedo During World War II* (Annapolis: Naval Institute Press, 2006), 106–7.

129 Newpower, *Iron Men*, 110.

130 *Hornet* Report, 3.

131 Poor, Mustin, and Jameson, *Combat Narrative*, 72.

132 Ibid., 73.

133 Ibid., 74.

134 Murphy, *Fighting Admiral*, 189–90.

135 There is disagreement as to which ships in Admiral Callaghan's force had the new SG radar. Everyone agrees that the *Helena*, *O'Bannon*, and *Fletcher* had it. Frank (*Guadalcanal*, 436) says both the *Portland* and *Juneau* had SG radar as well. Generous (*Sweet Pea*, 116) specifically says that the *Portland* had her SC radar replaced with an SC-1 radar during her repairs at Mare Island in 1943. Grace does not specifically mention the type of radar, but (*Night Action*, 48) says the only differences between the *Juneau* and the *Atlanta*, which had only SC radar, was the paint scheme and the positioning of the *Juneau*'s radar on the mainmast instead of the foremast. In fact, according to her war diary (http://www.ussatlanta.com/juneauwardiary.htm, retrieved 4/2/2016), the *Juneau* had SG radar installed in June 1942 and used it regularly thereafter.

136 Murphy, *Fighting Admiral*, 177.

137 Hammel, *Guadalcanal*, 2177–213.

138 Dan Kurzman, *Left to Die: The Tragedy of the USS* Juneau (New York: Pocket Books, 1994), 112.

139 Rear Admiral Bruce McCandless, "The San Francisco Story," *Proceedings*, Vol. 84/11/669 (Nov. 1958).

140 Hammel, *Guadalcanal*, 2210.

141 C. Raymond Calhoun, *Tin Can Sailor: Life Aboard the USS Sterett, 1939–1945* (Annapolis: Naval Institute Press, 1993), 1638.

142 Calhoun, *Tin Can Sailor*, 1638.

143 McCandless, "San Francisco"; Hammel, *Guadalcanal*, 2188.

144 Calhoun, *Tin Can Sailor*, 1638.

145 Hammel, *Guadalcanal*, 2259.

146 Ibid., 2259.

147 Ibid., 2199.

148 ONI Narrative, Guadalcanal, 17; McCandless, "San Francisco."

149 C.W. Kilpatrick, *The Night Naval Battles in the Solomons* (Pompano Beach, FL: Exposition-Banner, 1987), 86.

150 Kurzman, *Left to Die*, 107.

151 ONI Narrative, Guadalcanal, 17

152 Hammel, *Guadalcanal*, 2332.

153 Ibid., 2332.

154 Ibid., 2332.

155 McCandless, "San Francisco."

156 Hammel, *Guadalcanal*, 2332–68.

157 Ibid., 2368.

158 Ibid., 2368.

159 Ibid., 2368.

160 Ibid., 2368; ONI Narrative, Guadalcanal, Appendix I.

161 Hammel, *Guadalcanal*, 2368; ONI Narrative, Guadalcanal, 17, Appendix I.

162 ONI Narrative, Guadalcanal, 17; Hammel, *Guadalcanal*, 2368.

163 Hammel, *Guadalcanal*, 2368; ONI Narrative, Guadalcanal, 17, Appendix I.

164 Hornfischer, *Neptune's Inferno*, 268.

165 Ibid., 268.

166 Hammel, *Guadalcanal*, 2368.

167 Hornfischer, *Neptune's Inferno*, 269.

168 Kurzman, *Left to Die*, 116–7.

169 Hornfischer, *Neptune's Inferno*, 269; ONI Narrative, Guadalcanal, Appendix I.

170 Hammel, *Guadalcanal*, 2379; ONI Narrative, Guadalcanal, Appendix I. Hornfischer (*Neptune's Inferno*, 269) says Admiral Callaghan denied permission. However, the voice radio logs of the *Helena* and the *Portland* as reproduced in Appendix I of the ONI Narrative of the action show that he actually granted permission at 1:43.

171 Hammel, *Guadalcanal*, 2424.

172 Ibid., 2466.

173 Calhoun, *Tin Can Sailor*, 1638.

174 Hara, Saito, and Pineau, *Destroyer Captain*, 130.

175 Ibid., 132.

176 Hara, Saito, and Pineau, *Destroyer Captain*, 130.

177 Frank, *Guadalcanal*, 440.

178 Grace, *Night Action*, 56; Howarth, *Fighting Ships*, 313.

179 Hara, Saito, and Pineau, *Destroyer Captain*, 130.

180 Grace, *Night Action*, 56.

181 Hara, Saito, and Pineau, *Destroyer Captain*, 130.

182 Ibid., 131. In recent years there has been some questioning of the accuracy of Commander Hara's account. Frank (*Guadalcanal*, 729 note to page 438) brings up multiple criticisms which may be summarized as follows: 1. Hara's account is technically problematic as to the decks of both battleships being littered with the Type 3 bombardment shells, each of which weighed in excess of 1,000lb; 2. Hara says the ammunition was switched over to Type 1 armor-piercing ammunition when the battle revealed the switch had not taken place; and 3. Hara is reporting the events on the *Hiei* and *Kirishima* secondhand, as he was not present on either ship and had no direct knowledge. While not directly joining Frank in his criticism of Hara, Grace (*Night Action*, 56), whose primary source for the events on the bridge of the *Hiei* was Admiral Abe's operations officer Commander Chihaya, who actually was present on the bridge of the *Hiei*, says Abe ordered the changeover to be made after five salvos and makes no mention of any panicked, chaotic changeover of ammunition that Hara alleges. These are valid criticisms that deserve to be addressed. Hara (136) got his information on "how the flagship fought" from communications officer Commander Sekino Hideo. Prados (*Islands of Destiny*, 175) concludes that Sekino was indeed the source for the story of the chaotic changeover. Prados also cites Lieutenant Yunoki Shigeru, who was the fire-control director on the *Hiei*. Hara's account is not entirely inconsistent with Chihaya's account as given by Grace. It was possible for the chaotic ammunition changeover to involve merely making the armor-piercing shells, buried deep in the magazines, accessible for the time when the first five salvos of incendiaries had been expended. There is also some evidence that an ammunition changeover of some sort did take place. The first is the period of some 6–9 minutes between the time the *Yudachi* reported the enemy contact and the *Hiei* turning on her searchlights. If the Japanese battleships were not changing their ammunition during that time period, why was there such a long delay between the *Yudachi*'s report and the *Hiei* snapping on her searchlights? Second, the destroyer *Laffey* was hit by at least one 14-inch shell from the battleship *Kirishima* that passed completely through her superstructure without detonating, suggesting the shell was armor-piercing. Finally, as reported by Hara, the board of inquiry into the loss of the *Hiei* censured Abe specifically because he did not turn the battleships around while he changed ammunition. For these reasons, Hara's account, as modified by the information in Grace, is accepted here to be true. But readers should be aware of the criticisms and decide for themselves.

183 Murphy, *Fighting Admiral*, 191.

184 Kurzman, *Left to Die*, 118.

185 Frank, *Guadalcanal*, 438.

186 Hammel, *Guadalcanal*, 2477.

187 McCandless, "San Francisco."

188 Murphy, *Fighting Admiral*, 192. ONI Narrative, Guadalcanal, Appendix I.

189 Hornfischer, *Neptune's Inferno*, 269; Hammel, *Guadalcanal*, 2434.

190 Hammel, *Guadalcanal*, 2477.

191 Ibid., 2477.

192 Calhoun, *Tin Can Sailor*, 1672.

193 Hammel, *Guadalcanal*, 2477.

194 Ibid., 3468.

195 McCandless, "San Francisco."

196 Hammel, *Guadalcanal*, 3045.

197 Kurzman, *Left to Die*, 118.

198 Hornfischer, *Neptune's Inferno*, 273.

199 Hammel, *Guadalcanal*, 2859.

200 Grace, *Night Action*, 59.

Chapter 2

1   Vincent P. O'Hara, *The US Navy Against the Axis: Surface Combat 1941–1945* (Annapolis: Naval Institute Press, 2007), Kindle edition.
2   Grace, *Night Action*, 56–7.
3   Frank, *Guadalcanal*, 437.
4   Hammel, *Guadalcanal*, 2514.
5   Hornfischer, *Neptune's Inferno*, 273.
6   Ibid., 274.
7   Ibid., 273–4.
8   Hammel, *Guadalcanal*, 2892.
9   Ibid., 3081.
10 Hara, Saito, and Pineau, *Destroyer Captain*, 133.
11 Grace, *Night Action*, 58; McCandless, "San Francisco."
12 Hornfischer, *Neptune's Inferno*, 274.
13 Grace, *Night Action*, 93–4.
14 Ibid., 94.
15 Ibid., 95, 125.
16 Hornfischer, *Neptune's Inferno*, 286.
17 Grace, *Night Action*, 69. There is a long-standing dispute as to when and by whom Admiral Scott and members of his staff were killed. It is generally acknowledged that at the time of his death Scott was standing on the starboard wing of the bridge. One side of this dispute believes Scott was killed by a Japanese shell very early in the battle. The other side holds that Scott was killed later, after the *Atlanta* had been disabled, by 8-inch armor-piercing shells from the *San Francisco* that passed through the bridge without exploding but spread flying debris.

One reason the dispute is not settled is the seemingly inconsistent statements made by Captain Jenkins after the battle. In a newspaper story titled "Bridge Blown to Pieces in Battle In Which Admiral Scott Died; Graphic Account by Captain of Lost Cruiser of Engagement Off Solomon Islands Early This Month" (*St. Louis Post-Dispatch*, November 30, 1942, 5C), Jenkins, who is not identified by name, says Scott was killed before the torpedo hit the *Atlanta*. However, Jenkins apparently told Fletcher Pratt for his book *The Navy's War* (New York; London: Harper, 1944) (267) that *after* the torpedo hit, one of the "nineteen big shells" killed Scott.

Nor does Captain Jenkins' After Action Report shed any light on the question. The narrative is light on discussion of the hits, aside from his belief that some of them came from a US ship. Enclosure (B) of the After Action Report, titled "List of Hits Received," itemizes all 49 known hits, with their locations, the specific damage received, and the probable type of shell used, but is curiously silent on when any of these hits were received.

The After Action Report does not address this possibility, suggested by Grace, that at least some of the hits classified as "5.5-inch" were actually 14-inch incendiary shells from the *Hiei*, but Jenkins specifically mentions that the 5.5-inch hits may have come from "special ammunition for shore bombardment of Guadalcanal" because they exploded on impact with almost no armor penetration. If that possibility is accepted, then at least two hits are of interest in Enclosure (B), quoted in relevant part:

2.   Thirteen 5.5 inch H.C. hits were counted, as follows:
[…]
(c.) Superstructure forward, immediately below bridge; set fire in "Senior Staff Officer's Cabin"; fragments ignited 20mm ammunition at gun 2 and in forward 20mm loading room. This fire spread, from explosion of ammunition penetrating decks, to two decks below in the wardroom.
(d.) Bridge splinter shield at port torpedo director; damaged director, killed torpedo control personnel and many signalmen, blew up port flag bags and fired debris.

Hit 2(d) would have been the hit that drew Jenkins from the starboard wing of the bridge while the *Atlanta* was still operational. Hit 2(c) was "immediately below (the) bridge." It was this hit and the resulting detonations of 20mm ammunition that started the major fire forward of the bridge. With Admiral Scott and most of his staff on the starboard wing of the bridge – that is, outside and exposed, with little protection – watching the action to the north, a position that suggests the *Atlanta* was still operational at the time, if this was an incendiary shell – and the fact that it started a major fire forward suggests it was – the concussion or the shrapnel could have killed the admiral and his staff.

If events on the *Atlanta* occurred as Captain Jenkins explained it in the *St. Louis Post-Dispatch* story, then it would seem that Admiral Scott and his staff were killed by a 14-inch incendiary shell from the *Hiei* that hit just below the bridge and started a major fire. Readers are left to decide this question for themselves. There is no conclusive evidence either way. When and by whom Admiral Scott and his staff were killed will likely always remain a mystery.

18 Hammel, *Guadalcanal*, 2889.

19 Grace, *Night Action*, 70.

20 O'Hara, *US Navy*, 2384.

21 Hornfischer, *Neptune's Inferno*, 284.

22 Ibid., 285.

23 Ibid., 285.

24 Hammel, *Guadalcanal*, 3004.

25 Morison, *Struggle*, 244; Howarth, *Fighting Ships*, 313; Calhoun, *Tin Can Sailor*, 1686.

26 Samuel Eliot Morison (*Struggle*, 244) said, "It is impossible to reconstruct their tracks; we can only relate what happened to each (American ship)." James Grace may take issue with Morison, having painstakingly reconstructed each ship's track and action for his seminal work *The Naval Battle of Guadalcanal: Night Action 13 November 1942*, in the process producing maps detailing the tracks that look like plates of black spaghetti.

27 Hornfischer, *Neptune's Inferno*, 275.

28 *Nagara* TROM.

29 Hammel, *Guadalcanal*, 2703.

30 Grace, *Night Action*, 60.

31 Frank, *Guadalcanal*, 443.

32 Calhoun, *Tin Can Sailor*, 1672. Later in this action, the *Sterett* nearly collided with the *Aaron Ward*. Calhoun may have garbled a recollection of that later event and confused it with the *O'Bannon* passing.

33 Hammel, *Guadalcanal*, 2597.

34 Grace, *Night Action*, 85; Hornfischer, *Neptune's Inferno*, 276.

35 Grace, *Night Action*, 84.

36 Ibid., 84.

37 Ibid., 84–5.

38 Hammel, *Guadalcanal*, 2525.

39 Hornfischer, *Neptune's Inferno*, 275.

40 Ibid., 275.

41 Calhoun, *Tin Can Sailor*, 1674.

42 Howarth, *Fighting Ships*, 313.

43 Grace, *Night Action*, 88.

44 Hornfischer, *Neptune's Inferno*, 276.

45 Hammel, *Guadalcanal*, 2560.

46 Ibid., 2631.

47 Calhoun, *Tin Can Sailor*, 1686.

48 Hammel, *Guadalcanal*, 2674.

49 Ibid., 2674.

50 Ibid., 2635. Some histories of the battle record the *Hiei*'s pagoda as actually collapsing on the Number 2 turret. Aside from Jenkins' statement, there is no evidence the *Hiei*'s pagoda collapsed. Though Japanese accounts discuss the damage to and fires in the pagoda, they do not mention the pagoda actually collapsing. Turret 2 continued to operate throughout the battle, indicative of no serious damage as a result of a pagoda collapse. US pilots who attacked the *Hiei* the next morning observed heavy damage to the *Hiei*'s topsides, but none mention the lack of a pagoda. Finally, photographs of the *Hiei* from those attacks do not show any damage consistent with a collapsed pagoda.

51 Hammel, *Guadalcanal*, 2677.

52 Grace, *Night Action*, 85–6; Hammel, *Guadalcanal*, 2635; Howarth, *Fighting Ships*, 313–4. The timing of the raking of the *Hiei*'s bridge with gunfire comes from Hara, Saito, and Pineau, *Destroyer Captain*, 136.

53 Grace, *Night Action*, 109–10.

54 Frank, *Guadalcanal*, 450; Hara, Saito, and Pineau, *Destroyer Captain*, 131; O'Hara, *US Navy*, 2426.

55 Hara, Saito, and Pineau, *Destroyer Captain*, 131.

56 Ibid., 133.

57 Grace, *Night Action*, 61.

58 Hammel, *Guadalcanal*, 3116.

59 Ibid., 3353.

60 Ibid., 3095.

61 Ibid., 3116.

62 *Hiei* TROM.

63 Grace, *Night Action*, 123.

64 *Hiei* TROM; Tony Tully, "Death of Battleship HIEI: Sunk by Gunfire or Air Attack?" *Imperial Japanese Navy Page* (www.combinedfleet.com).

65 Grace, *Night Action*, 108–9; O'Hara, *US Navy*, 2406–26; Howarth, *Fighting Ships*, 315.

66 Grace, *Night Action*, 109.

67 Appendix I TBS Logs of *Helena* and *Portland*. The message is sometimes reported as "Cease firing, own ships." See, e.g, Kilpatrick, *Night Battles*, 91. It may seem like a curious wording, as if Admiral Callaghan wanted to specify he was ordering "our" ships to cease fire, but not "their" ships. He seems to have been trying to say that "our" ships were being hit by friendly fire.

68 Kilpatrick, *Night Battles*, 91.

69 O'Hara, *US Navy*, 2426–47.

70 Engagement with Japanese surface forces off Guadalcanal night of 12–13 November 1942, and Loss of U.S.S. ATLANTA ("*Atlanta* Report"), Enclosure (B) – List Of Hits Received.

71 Hornfischer, *Neptune's Inferno*, 5400.

72 Hammel, *Guadalcanal*, 5110.

73 Hornfischer, *Neptune's Inferno*, 5397.

74 See, e.g., Hammel, *Guadalcanal*, 3119.

75 Hammel, *Guadalcanal*, 4026.

76 Grace, *Night Action*, 96.

77 Ibid., 67.

78 Hammel, *Guadalcanal*, 2555.

79 Ibid., 2553.

80 Ibid., 2595.

81 Hara, Saito, and Pineau, *Destroyer Captain*, 136.

82 Ibid., 136.

83 Grace, *Night Action*, 99.

84 Ibid., 99.

85 Ibid., 99.

86 Kurzman, *Left to Die*, 125.

87 Report of U.S.S. JUNEAU activity from November 11–13, 1942, inclusive ("*Juneau* Report").

88 Grace, *Night Action*, 99–101.

89 *Juneau* Report.

90 Kurzman, *Left to Die*, 128.

91 Hammel, *Guadalcanal*, 3702.

92 Grace, *Night Action*, 102.

93 Hornfischer, *Neptune's Inferno*, 277.

94 Hammel, *Guadalcanal*, 3702.

95 Hornfischer, *Neptune's Inferno*, 277.

96 Grace, *Night Action*, 102.

97 Ibid., 102; Hammel, *Guadalcanal*, 3787.

98 Grace (*Night Action*, 103) says the torpedo "possibly" came from the *Asagumo*. Frank (*Guadalcanal*, 442) believes the torpedo was "probably from *Teruzuki*." Hammel (*Guadalcanal*, 3817) says "destroyer *Teruzuki*'s claim of hitting *Laffey* with a going-away shot is more credible" than the idea that the *Laffey* was a victim of friendly fire.

99 Hornfischer, *Neptune's Inferno*, 5236.

100 Hammel, *Guadalcanal*, 3752.

101 Ibid., 3752.

102 Ibid., 3823.

103 Ibid., 3781–822.

104 Ibid., 3817.

105 Ibid., 3822.

106 Ibid., 4264.

107 Ibid., 4264–72.

108 Grace, *Night Action*, 97–8.

109 Hammel, *Guadalcanal*, 4358.

110 Ibid., 2762.

111 Grace, *Night Action*, 124–5. Multiple American and Japanese witnesses were so surprised by the slow speed of the *Hiei* – the *Sterett* and *O'Bannon* both even thought she was dead in the water – that they mentioned it in their accounts. Precisely why the *Hiei* was moving so slowly this early in the night engagement has not gotten a lot of attention. There was no tactical reason for her to slow down and every reason to maintain at least a reasonable fighting speed. Admiral Abe or Captain Nishida could have been attempting to avoid collision with the US destroyers in front of the *Hiei* but there is little evidence of this.

The *Hiei*'s slow speed appears to be related to the early 8-inch hit she took from the *San Francisco* that due to the close range had penetrated the battleship's hull near the stern and started flooding in her steering compartment. *Hiei*'s TROM states the following in relevant part:

> 0154: [...] HIEI is only able to get off two salvos before she is hit by two 8-inch shells, most probably from SAN FRANCISCO. One shell is a dud, but the other penetrates HIEI's hull on the starboard quarter and the resultant flooding disables HIEI's steering gear.

While the *San Francisco* was exchanging fire with the *Hiei*, she could see glimpses of the battleship's duel with the *Laffey*, who does not seem to have noticed the *Hiei* moving at a slow speed. Read in the context of the *Hiei*'s TROM, it appears the battleship took the hit to the steering compartment during her duel with the *Laffey*, and by the time the *Sterett* and *O'Bannon* were in front of her, she had slowed to about 5 knots. That is likely not a coincidence.

Grace says that the *Hiei*'s engineering spaces were fully functional at this point and for some time afterward, and mentions no cut in speed at this time. He also states that after the surface battle, Captain Nishida took damage reports in and ordered a cut in speed to try to slow down flooding in the steering compartment. Yet this leaves no explanation for eyewitnesses on the *Sterett*, *O'Bannon*, and *Amatsukaze* (Commander Hara) all insisting that the *Hiei* slowed down during, not after, the battle. Nor do Japanese accounts mention an order for the *Hiei* to slow down at this time.

In an attempt to harmonize these conflicting accounts, this account believes that after the hit to the steering compartment, Captain Nishida immediately ordered steering by engine, which often causes a reduction in speed, and an actual cut in speed to try to slow down the flooding, an order he affirmed after the engagement. The combination of these two reductions in speed slowed the *Hiei* to a crawl.

112 Calhoun, *Tin Can Sailor*, 1711.

113 Hammel, *Guadalcanal*, 2805.

114 Grace, *Night Action*, 87.

115 Hammel, *Guadalcanal*, 2805.

116 Grace, *Night Action*, 86

117 Ibid., 86–7.

118 Hammel, *Guadalcanal*, 2850; Grace, *Night Action*, 87.

119 Grace, *Night Action*, 87.

120 McCandless, "San Francisco."

121 ONI Narrative, 24.

122 Hammel, *Guadalcanal*, 3159; Grace, *Night Action*, 73, 75.

123 Hammel, *Guadalcanal*, 3153.

124 Ibid., 3177.

125 McCandless, "San Francisco"; *San Francisco* Gunfire Damage Report. The idea that the shell came from the *Kirishima* is a deduction based on Kilpatrick (*Night Battles*, 96). Grace (*Night Action*, 76) says it was from the *Kirishima*.

126 McCandless, "San Francisco"; Hammel, *Guadalcanal*, 3203.

127 McCandless, "San Francisco"; Hammel, *Guadalcanal*, 3241.

128 Hornfischer, *Neptune's Inferno*, 5528, 5774.

129 McCandless, "San Francisco."

130 Ibid.

131 Hara, Saito, and Pineau, *Destroyer Captain*, 137. Where Commander Hara got the idea that the *San Francisco* now had no turrets is a mystery. All three of the *San Francisco*'s 8-inch turrets were operational at this time. Photographs from the cruiser's entry at Espiritu Santo a few days later showed all three turrets in place.

132 Hara, Saito, and Pinea, *Destroyer Captain*, 137.

133 Ibid., 137. For some reason, Hara says the *Amatsukaze* had six 4-inch guns.

134 Hara, Saito, and Pineau, *Destroyer Captain*, 137.

135 Ibid., 137.

136 Ibid., 137.

137 Ibid., 137.

138 McCandless, "San Francisco."

139 Hara, Saito, and Pineau, *Destroyer Captain*, 137.

140 Ibid., 137.

141 Ibid., 137.

142 Ibid., 139.

143 Ibid., 139.

144 Griffith, *Guadalcanal*, 231.

145 Hammel, *Guadalcanal*, 3273–80; Grace, *Night Action*, 76.

146 Generous, *Sweet Pea*, 85–6.

147 Ibid., 86, 88.

148 Generous, *Sweet Pea*, 87–8; Hammel, *Guadalcanal*, 3397–402.

149 Generous (*Sweet Pea*, 88) tells the story of Radioman Henry Hight, who had been thrown around the radio room by the explosion of the torpedo. Hight was uninjured, or so he said. Hight would later insist the *Portland* had turned to port all night long. Generous comments, "He may have been smacked worse than he thought."

150 Generous, *Sweet Pea*, 88.

151 Grace, *Night Action*, 104.

152 Generous, *Sweet Pea*, 90–1.

153 Ibid., 91 (citing War Damage Report #35).

154 Hammel, *Guadalcanal*, 3438–445; Generous, *Sweet Pea*, 91.

155 Grace, *Night Action*, 81.

156 ONI Narrative, 33.

157 Hammel, *Guadalcanal*, 3290–5.

158 Ibid., 3295–301.

159 Ibid., 4682–94.

160 Hammel, *Guadalcanal*, 4702.

161 Grace, *Night Action*, 83.

162 O'Hara, *US Navy*, 2544.

163 Grace, *Night Action*, 110.

164 Hammel, *Guadalcanal*, 4948–55.

165 Grace, *Night Action*, 91; Hammel, *Guadalcanal*, 4969.

166 Hammel, *Guadalcanal*, 4969.

167 Grace, *Night Action*, 91; O'Hara, *US Navy*, 2508.

168 Calhoun, *Tin Can Sailor*, 1720–5; Grace, *Night Action*, 107; O'Hara, *US Navy*, 2508.

169 Calhoun, *Tin Can Sailor*, 1720.

170 Ibid., 1730.

171 Grace, *Night Action*, 111.

172 Hammel, *Guadalcanal*, 4911–18.; Grace, *Night Action*, 212–3.

173 Hammel, *Guadalcanal*, 5003–10.

174 Ibid., 5023.

175 *Aaron Ward* damage report.

176 Hammel, *Guadalcanal*, 5040–6.

177 Ibid., 5059.

178 Ibid., 3590.

179 Ibid., 3822.

180 Ibid., 3859–96.

181 Ibid., 3896.

182 Frank, *Guadalcanal*, 452.

183 Grace, *Night Action*, 140.

Chapter 3

1   Hornfischer, *Neptune's Inferno*, 6457.
2   David Byron Kimball, *Henry Stewart: An American Life* (unpublished, 2006), 21.
3   Commander Edward P. Stafford, USN, *The Big "E"* (New York: Ballantine, 1962), 199–200.
4   Halsey, *Admiral Halsey's Story*, 2610–29.
5   Prados, *Islands of Destiny*, 149–50.
6   Ibid., 150.
7   Stafford, *The Big "E"*, 198–9.
8   Hughes, *Admiral Bill Halsey*, 3447.
9   Lundstrom, *First Team*, 12454.
10 Stafford, *The Big "E"*, 198–9.
11 Joel Shepherd, "... And then there was one patched-up carrier," *USS ENTERPRISE CV-6, The Most Decorated Ship Of The Second World War* (http://www.cv6.org).
12 Frank, *Guadalcanal*, 432–3.
13 Lundstrom, *First Team*, 12473.
14 Prados, *Islands of Destiny*, 168.
15 Grace, *Night Action*, 138.
16 Miller, *Cactus*, 186–7.
17 Grace, *Night Action*, 138.
18 Lundstrom, *First Team*, 12692; Grace, *Night Action*, 149.
19 Lundstrom, *First Team*, 12678; VMSB-132 War Diary 11/13/1942. Except where otherwise noted, the account of Major Sailer's encounter with the *Hiei* comes from Alexander S. White, *Dauntless Marine: Joseph Sailer Jr., Dive-Bombing Ace of Guadalcanal* (Pacifica, CA: Pacifica Press, 1996), 92–3.
20 Hammel, *Guadalcanal*, 5881.
21 Grace (*Night Action*, 138, 149, citing MAAG 11 War Diary, 11/13/1942), Hammel (*Guadalcanal*, 5869–75); and Miller (*Cactus*, 187) mention this dawn attack on the *Hiei* by the lone SBD scout. Grace and Hammel even give specifics as to what the pilot and his gunner did, but none identifies the pilot or the gunner. Lundstrom (*First Team*, 12706–11, citing VMSB-132 War Diary) mentions the scouts but neither he nor White (*Dauntless Marine*, 93) mentions the dawn attack, and both indicate Major Sailer discovered the *Hiei*. White also gives a very specific description of Sailer's activities in doing so, based in part on accounts from witness Lieutenant Hap Simpson.

    It appears that the dawn attack on the *Hiei* is based on a misreading of the VMSB-132 War Diary, which for November 13 reads in relevant part as follows: "Lt. Herlihy and StffSgt. Wallof reported the Jap battleship while on a sector search ... Lt. Eck and Lt. Skinner, while on a sector search, reported a Japanese destroyer believed to be of the *Hatsuharu* class. Both pilots dove and missed with their bombs ..." The diary entry for Marine Air Group 23 reads in relevant part as follows: "Isabel [Santa Ysabel] search saw Jap BB [battleship] accompanied by four DD [destroyers], course 280 degrees, speed 30 knots. Fox search saw Jap DD at 265 degrees from Cactus, 80 miles out. Both planes attacked but missed." While the wording of the VMSB-23 diary entry is not the most transparent, the statements "Both pilots dove and missed with their bombs" and "Both planes attacked but missed" seem to refer to the attack on the destroyer. There is no specific reference to an attack on the *Hiei* at this time.
22 VMSB-132 War Diary; White, *Dauntless Marine*, 93.
23 Miller, *Cactus*, 187; Foss, *Flying Marine*, 1654; Hammel, *Guadalcanal*, 5877.
24 Hammel, *Guadalcanal*, 5877; Lundstrom, *First Team*, 12707.
25 Lundstrom, *First Team*, 12696.
26 Grace, *Night Action*, 114.
27 Ibid., 132.
28 Hornfischer, *Neptune's Inferno*, 3726–42.
29 Ibid., 5920.
30 Grace, *Night Action*, 114.
31 McCandless, "San Francisco."
32 Hornfischer, *Neptune's Inferno*, 314.
33 McCandless, "San Francisco."
34 Grace, *Night Action*, 111–3, 135.
35 Ibid., 133.

36   Ibid., 121–2.
37   Ibid., 122.
38   Ibid., 122.
39   Ibid., 118–9.
40   Hammel, *Guadalcanal*, 5262–9, 5281.
41   Ibid., 5266–84.
42   Ibid., 5287–94.
43   Generous, *Sweet Pea*, 92.
44   Hammel, *Guadalcanal*, 5320.
45   Hornfischer, *Neptune's Inferno*, 322.
46   Ibid., 322.
47   Ibid., 322.
48   *Atlanta* Report.
49   Hammel, *Guadalcanal*, 5220.
50   *Atlanta* Report, Enclosure (C).
51   Ibid.
52   Hammel, *Guadalcanal*, 5404.
53   Hornfischer, *Neptune's Inferno*, 332.
54   *Atlanta* Report.
55   *Atlanta* Report, Second Endorsement, 2.
56   Grace, *Night Action*, 147.
57   Hornfischer, *Neptune's Inferno*, 332.
58   Ibid., 332–3.
59   Generous, *Sweet Pea*, 98; Grace, *Night Action*, 147.
60   Grace, *Night Action*, 147–8; Hornfischer, *Neptune's Inferno*, 333.
61   Hornfischer, *Neptune's Inferno*, 333–4.
62   Submarine Torpedo Attack on Task Unit and Sinking of U.S.S. JUNEAU, Report of., 1
63   Grace, *Night Action*, 165.
64   Calhoun, *Tin Can Sailor*, 1876, 2014.
65   Hornfischer, *Neptune's Inferno*, 328.
66   Ibid., 328; McCandless, "San Francisco."
67   Hammel, *Guadalcanal*, 5662.
68   Hornfischer, *Neptune's Inferno*, 328.
69   Hammel, *Guadalcanal*, 5662.
70   McCandless, "San Francisco"; *San Francisco* Report.
71   Kurzman, *Left to Die*, 137.
72   Ibid., 137; Grace, *Night Action*, 165.
73   Hammel, *Guadalcanal*, 5704.
74   Kurzman, *Left to Die*, 137; Grace, *Night Action*, 165.
75   Hammel, *Guadalcanal*, 5690; Grace, *Night Action*, 165.
76   Grace, *Night Action*, 165.
77   Kurzman, *Left to Die*, 144.
78   Ibid., 1.
79   Hornfischer, *Neptune's Inferno*, 328.
80   Kurzman, *Left to Die*, 145.
81   Ibid., 145.
82   Hornfischer, *Neptune's Inferno*, 329.
83   McCandless, "San Francisco."
84   Calhoun, *Tin Can Sailor*, 2018.
85   *Juneau* Report.
86   Hornfischer, *Neptune's Inferno*, 329.
87   McCandless, "San Francisco."
88   Hornfischer, *Neptune's Inferno*, 329–30.
89   Calhoun, *Tin Can Sailor*, 2018.
90   Kurzman, *Left to Die*, 145; Grace, *Naval Battle*, 166.
91   McCandless, "San Francisco."

92   Kurzman, *Left to Die*, 155.
93   Ibid., 2.
94   Ibid., 2.
95   Ibid., 158.
96   Ibid., 242.
97   Hornfischer, *Neptune's Inferno*, 277.
98   "Night Battle: The Barroom Brawl Off Guadalcanal" – David Alan Johnson, Warfare History Network February 1, 2016.
99   Lundstrom, *First Team*, 12662.
100 Grace, *Night Action*, 110.
101 The ONI Narrative, 36, states, "Japanese use of searchlights was outstanding. Often one ship would illuminate while others joined in firing at the target." With the proviso "[T]he reports indicated that our ships concentrated on and immediately destroyed three of the enemy vessels which first illuminated."
102 Precisely what the *Hiei* was doing in the hours between the time the battleship disengaged at around 2:30 am and Major Sailer found her north-northwest of Savo Island just after dawn remains somewhat murky and has not gotten a lot of attention, with most histories just fast forwarding to her appearance when Sailer spotted her. What is presented here is based on deduction and an amalgamation of bits and pieces of information from various sources. The most complete source of information here is Grace, but even with his fine work, there remain numerous uncertainties and outright holes in the record of the *Hiei*'s activities during this time period. These issues include:

1.   Exactly when and from whom did the *Hiei* receive the hit to the steering compartment?
2.   Exactly when and why did the *Hiei* slow down?
3.   When and why did the *Hiei* turn to the west instead of following the other Japanese ships northward? It appears that no one has addressed this issue. At the end of her duel with the *San Francisco*, the *Hiei* was observed turning to port, that is, toward the north. Tully's account, quoted in relevant part, is ambiguous:

> With fires lighting her pagoda like lamps and flames rising higher than the stacks, HIEI completed her nearly 180 degree turn and began to head northward at reduced speed, leaving the battlefield astern where Japanese and American ships still dueled with one another.
> At 0200 as a result of the damage to his flagship and possibly distracted by his wound and the sheer ferocity of the American gunfire, Admiral Abe quickly lost heart and canceled the bombardment.
> Convinced he was facing a superior force he ordered a general withdrawal to the north of Savo. The HIEI continued to steer with her engines making about 10 knots while damage reports were assessed. While it is arguable that sister battleship KIRISHIMA should have stayed close by to lend assistance and cover, she did no such thing. Instead, despite having received only one 8 inch shell on the quarter-deck, KIRISHIMA was ordered north by Abe out of the battle zone at high speed. She proceeded north, passing east of Savo, while HIEI crawled around to the west of Savo. HIEI would have to cope with her damage as best she could with the assistance of light cruiser NAGARA which remained close-by.
> [...]
> For four hours the HIEI continued to bulldoze painfully north, but at 0600 as sunrise lighted the battlefield the steady flooding forced the stubborn men to abandon the manual-steering compartment.

Tully's account says the *Hiei* "crawled around to the west of Savo," but the only movement he mentions on the part of the *Hiei* is toward the north. It is known that during and immediately after the battle, the *Hiei* was southeast of Savo, so she must have turned west at some point. Grace references "steering difficulties," which would include the disabling of the steering motor, the necessity of physically holding the rudder centered, and steering by varying the relative speeds of the propellers. But that only addresses the what and not the why. Grace does not mention a turn to the west, either, but does say that the navigation officer Commander Shiwa Takeshi was communicating from the conning tower with the engine room through a voice tube. Grace states, "Because of the rudder problems, there seemed to be some confusion about the course to be steered." Almost all of the *Hiei*'s internal communications were down as a result of battle damage. That would make steering by engine extremely difficult, as the engine room could not very well see the course of the ship and had to get that information from the bridge. Further complicating matters was that the *Hiei*'s bridge had been smashed by the US destroyers and temporarily abandoned due to the fires in the pagoda. During this time, Captain Nishida was apparently walking the main deck, encouraging the firefighters. In such circumstances of a useless rudder, steering by engine, poor communications, and a smashed bridge with a disorganized command staff, it is not hard to see how the *Hiei* could have ended up badly off course. In fact, it appears the turn to the west occurred when the above difficulties were at their worst and thus may not have been entirely intentional. However, there could be a simpler explanation. Kilpatrick (*Night Battles*, 100) says that at dawn "*Hiei* was drifting with the current north of Savo Island [...]" There is a possibility that Captain Nishida turned west to take advantage of the prevailing currents or because heading up the east side of Savo Island put the slowed battleship against the current. However, it seems more likely that, for the reasons mentioned above, the *Hiei's* turn west was not fully intended. After the turn, she was struggling just to avoid running aground on Savo until the bridge could be reoccupied and thus communications from the bridge to the engine rooms reestablished.

What steps were taken to mitigate the flooding in the *Hiei's* steering compartment and when? This is another question that seems not to have been addressed. The only damage control measure mentioned during this period is the battleship slowing down on Captain Nishida's order to try to slow the inrush of water into the steering room. It is not until after dawn, after the steering room has been completely flooded and consequently abandoned by Petty Officer Kurabawa's crew, and after, as a result of the abandonment, the rudder swung hard to starboard and jammed, rendering the *Hiei* unnavigable, that any other steps are taken to try to stop or even minimize the flooding. That this was not attempted during combat is understandable, but there were some three hours after the battle during which it could have been attempted. Yet it seems that it was only tried once the rudder had jammed and the *Hiei* could only steam in circles; at that point, the Japanese sent "divers" over the side to try to stuff the hole with rolled-up blankets. Why did they not try to stop or at least slow down the flooding of this vital compartment earlier? What was more important than maintaining the navigability of the ship as it tries to escape promised air attacks? There really is no explanation for not trying to even slow down the flooding in the steering compartment earlier.

103 Grace, *Night Action*, 123.
104 Ibid., 123.
105 Ibid., 124.
106 Kilpatrick, *Night Battles*, 97.
107 Grace, *Night Action*, 123.
108 Ibid., 124.
109 Hara, Saito, and Pineau, *Destroyer Captain*, 151; Grace, *Night Action*, 125. As a reminder, times shown in Japanese reports are Tokyo time, which is two hours behind Guadalcanal.
110 Grace, *Night Action*, 149.
111 Ibid., 150.
112 Hara, Saito, and Pineau, *Night Action*, 142–3.
113 Lundstrom, *First Team*, 12717–24.
114 Grace, *Night Action*, 150; Tully, "Death of Battleship HIEI."
115 Grace, *Night Action*, 142–3; Hammel, *Guadalcanal*, 5306–14.
116 Grace, *Night Action*, 142–3; Hammel, *Guadalcanal*, 5306–14.
117 Hammel, *Guadalcanal*, 5306–14.
118 Grace, *Night Action*, 149.
119 Ibid., 143; Hammel, *Guadalcanal*, 5314–22; Lundstrom, *First Team*, 12711.
120 Hammel, *Guadalcanal*, 5894–902.
121 Lundstrom, *First Team*, 12736–42; Hammel, *Guadalcanal*, 5924.
122 Grace, *Night Action*, 150.
123 Time is from Grace (*Night Action*, 150) and Tully ("Death of Battleship HIEI"). Reconciling the times and composition of the various Japanese attempts to provide support to the *Hiei* has proven extremely difficult. Among the disparities:

The arrival of the *Yukikaze*. Grace (*Night Action*, 150) has it after the attack by the scout but before any other air attacks. Lundstrom (*First Team*, 12711) has it before any air attacks. Tully ("Death of Battleship HIEI") has it after Captain Dooley's and Major Sailer's attacks. Hammel (*Guadalcanal*, 5869, 5887) has *Yukikaze* arriving before the scout's attack but leaving before Captain Dooley's and Major Sailer's attacks.

The departure of the *Nagara*. Tully has it just after the arrival of the *Yukikaze* at 6:20. Grace (151) has it at around 7:00 after the arrival of the *Teruzuki* and 27th Destroyer Division. Lundstrom has the *Nagara* not there at all.

Arrival of the *Teruzuki*. Grace (151) has it arriving with 27th Destroyer Division at about 7:00. Tully says the same thing, but says it was at about 8:00 am. Hammel indicates the *Teruzuki* never arrived at all. Lundstrom does not give a time for the arrival of the *Teruzuki* but indicates it was with 27th Destroyer Division before 9:15.
124 Lundstrom, *First Team*, 12743–50.
125 The formal Japanese naval term is *3 Shiki tsujodan* or "Type 3 common shell." Eric Lacroix and Linton Wells II, *Japanese Cruisers of the Pacific War* (Annapolis: Naval Institute Press, 1997), 761.

126 And it did count for something. Lacroix and Wells (*Japanese Cruisers*, 761) say, "The Japanese considered these (Type 3) shells to be very effective against aircraft, at least when fired above the target, since the steel tubes fell as they burned. [...] The US Navy, however, found these rounds more spectacular than effective."

127 Grace, *Night Action*, 150; Hammel, *Guadalcanal*, 5955–61; Lundstrom, *First Team*, 12769–81.

128 Grace, *Night Action*, 150–1. This torpedo attack is being treated here as VMSB-1 (Captain Dooley's) first torpedo attack.

129 Grace, *Night Action*, 151. Tully ("Death of Battleship HIEI") says Abe transferred at 8:15.

130 Lundstrom, *First Team*, 12790.

131 Grace, *Night Action*, 151; Ugaki, Goldstein, and Dillon, *Fading Victory*, 266. Tully ("Death of Battleship HIEI") says the submarine hit the *Kirishima* with two dud torpedoes.

132 Ugaki, Goldstein, and Dillon (*Fading Victory*, 266) says the *Kirishima* aborted the mission and turned back north "on orders of the advance force," which was Admiral Kondo.

133 Grace, *Night Action*, 151.

134 Ibid., 155.

135 Lundstrom (*First Team*, 12790) says the F4Fs were led by Captain Robert B. Fraser of VMF-112.

136 Grace, *Night Action*, 152.

137 Lundstrom, *First Team*, 12790.

138 Hammel, *Guadalcanal*, 5970; Foss, *Flying Marine*, 1663. Foss goes into detail about the turn but omits the finger. Given that his book was first published in 1943 and Foss apparently had political aspirations – he was later governor of South Dakota, president of the National Rifle Association, and the first commissioner of the American Football League – this is not surprising.

139 Lundstrom, *First Team*, 12723.

140 Ibid., 12804.

141 Strafford, *The Big "E"*, 201–2.

142 Grace, *Night Action*, 153.

143 Lundstrom, *First Team*, 12811.

144 Ibid., 12811.

145 Hammel, *Guadalcanal*, 6026.

146 Lundstrom, *First Team*, 12829.

147 Grace, *Night Action*, 156 (citing *Senkan Hiei*, 45).

148 Lundstrom, *First Team*, 12829.

149 Grace, *Night Action*, 153; Lundstrom, *First Team*, 12829.

150 Grace, *Night Action*, 154.

151 Lundstrom, *First Team*, 12829.

152 Ibid., 12847.

153 Grace, *Night Action*, 158.

154 Ibid., 156.

155 Tully, "Death of Battleship HIEI."

156 Lundstrom, *First Team*, 12843.

157 Grace, *Night Action*, 156.

158 Lundstrom, *First Team*, 12845–63; Grace, *Night Action*, 154; Tully, "Death of Battleship HIEI." Grace (*Night Action*, 156), apparently relying on Japanese sources, says the torpedo that hit the starboard engine room was actually a dud and that the damage there was caused by a bomb from a B-17 that struck "between Turret III and the catapult, directly above the torpedo's point of impact," at roughly the same time as the torpedo. This cannot be correct. There was no B-17 attack at this time. There was the dive-bombing attack by eight Marine SBDs under 2nd Lieutenant McEniry, but they claimed no hits to the *Hiei* because the increasing low clouds ruined their approach. Ugaki (*Fading Victory*, 266) says the *Hiei* was hit by two torpedoes "and she listed." Ugaki does not specify where the torpedoes hit, but specifying that she listed suggests they were both on the starboard side. Lieutenant Commander S. Yunoki, the *Hiei*'s main battery fire control director, stated in his postwar interrogation, "We were hit by a number of aircraft torpedoes, but only three exploded" (Interrogation Nav No. 46, USSBS No. 195).

159 Grace, *Night Action*, 156–7.

160 Howarth, *Fighting Ships*, 314.

161 Grace, *Night Action*, 159.

162 Ibid., 160.

163 Grace, *Night Action*, 160; Howarth, *Fighting Ships*, 314–5.

164 Howarth, *Fighting Ships*, 314–5.
165 Ugaki, Goldstein, and Dillon, *Fading Victory*, 266.
166 Ibid., 267.
167 Ibid., 267.
168 O'Hara, *US Navy*, 114.
169 Halsey, *Story*, 2703.
170 Text of messages come from Halsey, *Story*, 2706–35.
171 Morison, *Struggle*, 261.
172 Halsey, *Story*, 2764.
173 Hornfischer, *Neptune's Inferno*, 337.
174 Morison (*Struggle*, 262 n. 40) notes that a northerly wind is a rarity in the Coral Sea during that time of the year.
175 Halsey, *Story*, 2767.
176 Hornfischer, *Neptune's Inferno*, 336–7.
177 Ibid., 337.
178 Lundstrom, *First Team*, 12996.
179 Ibid., 12996.

Chapter 4

1 Lieutenant Novak's experience comes from Hammel, *Guadalcanal*, 6127–46.
2 Frank, *Guadalcanal*, 463; Lawrence J. Hickey, *Ken's Men Against the Empire: The Illustrated History of the 43rd Bombardment Group During World War II, Volume I: Prewar to October 1943 The B-17 Era* (Boulder, CO: International Historical Research Associates, 2016), 78; *Michishio* TROM.
3 Lundstrom, *First Team*, 13026.
4 The story of Lieutenant Novak and his tentmates comes from Hammel, *Guadalcanal*, 6137–61.
5 Hammel, *Guadalcanal*, 6161–71.
6 Ibid., 6177–82.
7 Hornfischer, *Neptune's Inferno*, 6333–7.
8 Ibid., 6337.
9 Halsey, *Story*, 2764.
10 Hornfischer, *Neptune's Inferno*, 6337–42.
11 Hammel, *Guadalcanal*, 6200–5; Captain Robert J. Bulkley, Jr., USNR (Ret.), *At Close Quarters: PT Boats in the United States Navy* (Washington: Naval History Division, 1962), 92–3.
12 Lacroix and Wells, *Japanese Cruisers*, 311.
13 In January 1942 off Balikpapan, Admiral Nishimura allowed four old American destroyers to rampage through the transports he was guarding because he was convinced he was being attacked by a submarine.
14 In action in the Surigao Strait in 1944, Admiral Nishimura failed to notice that the battleship immediately behind his own in his column of heavy ships had been torpedoed, dropped out of formation, and sunk.
15 Lundstrom, *First Team*, 13033.
16 Ibid., 12997.
17 Ibid., 13049.
18 Lundstrom, *First Team*, 13064.
19 Ibid., 13286.
20 Stephen L. Moore, *The Battle for Hell's Island: How a Small Band of Carrier Dive Bombers Helped Save Guadalcanal* (New York: New American Library, 2015), Kindle edition, 355.
21 Frank, *Guadalcanal*, 464.
22 Miller, *Cactus*, 195.
23 Lundstrom, *First Team*, 13090.
24 Ibid., 13099.
25 Lundstrom, *First Team*, 13099; *Kinugasa* TROM.
26 Hammel, *Guadalcanal*, 6286; ONI Narrative, 50.
27 Hammel, *Guadalcanal*, 6286.
28 Ibid., 6303.
29 ONI Narrative, 50; Lundstrom, *First Team*, 13127.
30 Lundstrom, *First Team*, 13117–34.
31 Ibid., 13131.

32 Barrett Tillman, *Enterprise: America's Fightingest Ship and the Men Who Helped Win World War II* (New York: Simon & Schuster, 2012), 138.

33 Moore, *Hell's Island*, 361.

34 Lacroix and Wells, *Japanese Cruisers*, 311.

35 Hammel, *Guadalcanal*, 6338; Lundstrom, *First Team*, 13131–52.

36 Lacroix and Wells, *Japanese Cruisers*, 311; Lundstrom, *First Team*, 13131.

37 Lundstrom, *First Team*, 13169.

38 Ibid., 13169; Lacroix and Wells, *Japanese Cruisers*, 311.

39 *Isuzu* TROM

40 ONI Narrative, 51; Hammel, *Guadalcanal*, 6401.

41 Lundstrom, *First Team*, 13167–98.

42 Ibid., 13301–20.

43 Ibid., 13200.

44 Ibid., 13180–207.

45 According to the ONI Narrative (52), "Analysis of captured Japanese documents later enabled COMSOPAC's Combat Intelligence center to estimate that most of these ships were carrying supplies. Two battalions of the Japanese 229th Infantry Regiment and 2 battalions of the 230th Infantry Regiment (4,600 men all told) were aboard, as well as the 229th Regiment Artillery, the 230th Regiment Artillery, and the 38th Division Engineer Battalion."

46 Three of the transports, the *Sado Maru*, *Arizona Maru*, and *Hirokawa Maru*, were given the grandiose title of "antiaircraft transports" because they were equipped with six 13mm antiaircraft machine guns. The other transports had 13mm antiaircraft machine guns, but they were not "antiaircraft transports." Lundstrom, *First Team*, 13207.

47 Frank, *Guadalcanal*, 465.

48 Ibid.

49 Lundstrom, *First Team*, 13207.

50 Ibid., 13217.

51 Ibid., 13217.

52 Ibid., 13217.

53 ONI Narrative, 53.

54 Lundstrom, *First Team*, 13203, 13248; David C. Evans, (ed.) *The Japanese Navy in World War II in the Words of Former Japanese Naval Officers* (2nd ed.) (Annapolis: Naval Institute Press, 1986), 191. Lundstrom cites Major Sailer describing the convoy as "three groups of transports (four or five to a group) accompanied by two [light cruisers] and eight or nine [destroyers]." White (*Dauntless Marine*, 97) corroborates with this description of the transports as "arranged in three groups of transports, four or five to a group." The narrative here goes with Lundstrom over Admiral Tanaka himself, who says there were four columns, because Tanaka admits (Evans, *Japanese Navy*, 192) his memory of some of the details of this operation was vague by the time of his writing, although Miller (*Cactus*, 198) also says it was four columns.

55 Evans, *Japanese Navy*, 190.

56 Hammel, *Guadalcanal*, 6478.

57 Lundstrom, *First Team*, 13249.

58 Ibid., 13249.

59 Also known as the *Sato Maru*.

60 Lundstrom, *First Team*, 13249.

61 ONI Narrative, 53.

62 Lundstrom, *First Team*, 13249–77.

63 Ibid., 13277.

64 Hammel, *Guadalcanal*, 6495, 6274.

65 Evans, *Japanese Navy*, 191.

66 Lundstrom, *First Team*, 13277; *Sado Maru* TROM. She was sunk on November 18 by US Army Air Force B-17s and P-38s.

67 Lundstrom, *First Team*, 13298.

68 Ibid., 13298.

69 Ibid., 13298.

70 Moore, *Hell's Island*, 363–5. The photographers on the *Enterprise* were eager to develop the film on Gunner John Liska's camera, since he had been the only gunner with a camera who had photographed the attack on the convoy and returned. When they opened the camera, they found he had put the film in wrong.

71 Moore, *Hell's Island*, 373.
72 Lundstrom, *First Team*, 13305.
73 Moore, *Hell's Island*, 373.
74 Ibid., 373.
75 Ibid., 373.
76 Lundstrom, *First Team*, 13305.
77 Ibid., 13342.
78 White, *Dauntless Marine*, 97.
79 Moore, *Hell's Island*, 374.
80 Lundstrom, *First Team*, 13331.
81 Ibid., 13331.
82 Ibid., 13324.
83 *Brisbane Maru* TROM; Lundstrom, *First Team*, 13360.
84 Moore, *Hell's Island*, 376; ONI Narrative, 55.
85 Lundstrom, *First Team*, 13342.
86 Ibid., 13386.
87 Ibid., 13386.
88 Moore, *Hell's Island*, 381.
89 Lundstrom, *First Team*, 13398.
90 Evans, *Japanese Navy*, 191; *Shinanogawa Maru* TROM.
91 Evans, *Japanese Navy*, 192.
92 Lundstrom, *First Team*, 13421.
93 White, *Dauntless Marine*, 99.
94 Lundstrom, *First Team*, 13427.
95 Ibid., 13427.
96 Moore, *Hell's Island*, 384.
97 Lundstrom, *First Team*, 13479.
98 Moore, *Hell's Island*, 391; Lundstrom, *First Team*, 13481–94.
99 Moore, *Hell's Island*, 387; Lundstrom, *First Team*, 13463–87.
100 Moore, *Hell's Island*, 387–8; Lundstrom, *First Team*, 13487.
101 Given that the two other Japanese pilots who attacked, Chief Petty Officer Morishima Hideo and Petty Officer 2nd Class Nishimori Kikuo, who claimed three carrier bombers between them, fired a total of 40 20mm shells, all by Nishimori, the belief that Lieutenant Suganami shot down Lieutenants Welch and Wakeham is probably accurate. Lundstrom, *First Team*, 13487.
102 Lundstrom, *First Team*, 13518.
103 Ibid., 13532.
104 Lundstrom, *First Team*, 13533; Evans, *Japanese Navy*, 191–2.
105 Lundstrom, *First Team*, 13563.
106 Ibid., 13563–93.
107 Hammel, *Guadalcanal*, 6750.
108 Lundstrom, *First Team*, 13563.
109 Evans, *Japanese Navy*, 192.
110 Ibid., 193.
111 Frank, *Guadalcanal*, 469.
112 Kilpatrick, *Night Battles*, 110.
113 Time is from Frank, *Guadalcanal*, 469, who misidentifies the submarine as the *Flying Fish*; *Kirishima* TROM.
114 Robert Lundgren, "The Battleship Action 14–15 November 1942," *NavWeaps: Naval Weapons, Naval Technology and Naval Reunions* (www.navweaps.com), 3. Many thanks to Robert Lundgren for graciously granting permission for the use of his reports here.
115 Frank, *Guadalcanal*, 470.
116 Lundgren, "Battleship Action," 3.
117 Kilpatrick, *Night Battles*, 112.
118 Lundgren, "Battleship Action," 3.
119 Frank, *Guadalcanal*, 469.
120 Ibid., 470.

121 In Goldstein and Dillon (*Pacific War Papers*, 315), Admiral Kondo says, "[T]here were three enemy groups in the area south of *Guadalcanal*," and then proceeds to describe only two of them.

122 Kilpatrick, *Night Battles*, 112.

123 Ibid., 113.

124 Hornfischer, *Neptune's Inferno*, 6487.

125 Hammel, *Guadalcanal*, 6902; Lundgren, "Battleship Action," 4.

126 Hammel, *Guadalcanal*, 6939–60.

127 Ibid., 6291.

128 Hornfischer, *Neptune's Inferno*, 6458.

129 Hammel, *Guadalcanal*, 6976.

130 Kilpatrick, *Night Battles*, 114.

131 Ibid., 114.

132 Frank, *Guadalcanal*, 473; Hammel, *Guadalcanal*, 6839; Morison, *Struggle*, 273 and n. 55. Morison says there are five or six versions of this story, the most notable being the answer to the PT boats that Admiral Lee allegedly gave in rhyme: "This is 'Chung Ching' Lee. You mustn't fire 'fish' at me." At least one other version has one of the PTs, not knowing who Lee is, advocating torpedoing the battleships with "Let's slip the bum a 'pickle.'"

133 Frank, *Guadalcanal*, 472.

134 Lundgren, "Battleship Action," 3.

135 Of Admiral Kondo's deployment, Morison (*Struggle*, 274) said, "Kondo's plan could be considered the ultimate in the Japanese pattern of tactical dispersion. Fourteen ships were split four ways in a ten-mile-square area which had to be shared with the antagonist." In a similar vein, Frank (*Guadalcanal*, 477) said, "Kondo had achieved the ultimate in dispersion tactics: his fourteen ships were divided four ways within a square barely 12 miles on each side that they shared with their adversaries and Savo Island."

136 Kilpatrick, *Night Battles*, 114.

137 Hornfischer, *Neptune's Inferno*, 6560.

138 Hammel, *Guadalcanal*, 7039; Kilpatrick, *Night Battles*, 115.

139 Kilpatrick, *Night Battles*, 116.

140 Ibid., 116.

141 Frank, *Guadalcanal*, 475; time is from Kilpatrick, *Night Battles*, 115.

142 Frank, *Guadalcanal*, 473.

143 O'Hara, *US Navy*, 120

144 Hammel, *Guadalcanal*, 7033; Kilpatrick, *Night Battles*, 116.

145 Kilpatrick, *Night Battles*, 116.

146 Hornfischer, *Neptune's Inferno*, 6578; O'Hara, *US Navy*, 121.

147 Hammel, *Guadalcanal*, 7040–76; ONI Narrative, 65.

148 O'Hara, *US Navy*, 121.

149 Kilpatrick, *Night Battles*, 117.

150 O'Hara, *US Navy*, 122.

151 Ibid., 122.

152 O'Hara, *US Navy*, 122. Lundgren ("Battleship Action," 5 n. 3) notes the flashless powder intended to hide the Japanese from the enemy did not flash but did produce a red flame, "which through the smoke screen may have appeared *Shikinami* was on fire."

153 USS *South Dakota* Action Report, night engagement November 14–15, 1942, with Japanese naval units, off Savo Island ("*South Dakota* Report"), 2.

154 Kilpatrick, *Night Battles*, 117.

155 O'Hara, *US Navy*, 122.

156 Kilpatrick, *Night Battles*, 117.

157 Lundgren, "Battleship Action," 8.

158 ONI Narrative, 66; Lundgren, "Battleship Action," 8.

159 Lundgren, "Battleship Action," 7.

160 Kilpatrick, *Night Battles*, 120. The ONI Narrative (67) says, "The *Benham* also opened fire on it, using radar ranges and gun flashes as points of aim." The *Benham* had no radar.

161 Hammel, *Guadalcanal*, 7076. But it did leave a red flame.

162 Kilpatrick, *Night Battles*, 118.

163 Lundgren, "Battleship Action," 6.

164 Hammel, *Guadalcanal*, 7106.

165 Ibid., 7143.

166 Hammel, *Guadalcanal*, 7144; ONI Narrative, 67.

167 Kilpatrick, *Night Battles*, 118.

168 E. Andrew Wilde, *The USS* Preston *(DD-379) in World War II: Documents, Recollections and Photographs* (Needham, MA: self-published, 2001), 4.

169 Hammel, *Guadalcanal*, 7178.

170 Hammel, *Guadalcanal*, 7188. O'Hara (*US Navy*, 122) says, "At [11:32 pm] a large explosion rocked the *Preston*, as her own torpedoes cooked off in the conflagration." Kilpatrick (*Night Battles*, 119) says that at 11:34 pm, "*Preston* exploded 300 yards ahead of *Gwin*." If the times are to be believed, these were before the order to abandon ship was given. These were one or more torpedo hits from the *Ayanami*.

171 Lundgren, "Battleship Action," 7.

172 Kilpatrick, *Night Battles*, 118; Lundgren, "Battleship Action," 7.

173 ONI Narrative, 67.

174 Kilpatrick, *Night Battles*, 119.

175 David Byron Kimball, "Henry Stewart: An American Life" (unpublished, 2006).

176 Ibid.

177 Hammel, *Guadalcanal*, 7251.

178 Ibid., 7251.

179 Commander John Walsh (Ret.), "A Terrible Night for the USS Walke DD-416," *Guadalcanal Echoes* (January 1992), in Wilde, *The USS* Walke, 85.

180 Hammel, *Guadalcanal*, 7280.

181 Ibid., 7280.

182 Ibid., 7312.

183 Lundgren, "Battleship Action," 8.

184 Hammel, *Guadalcanal*, 7280.

185 Hammel, *Guadalcanal*, 7354; ONI Narrative, 68.

186 Kilpatrick (*Night Battles*, 120) quotes Lieutenant Commander Taylor as reporting, "Comparing the height and volume of water thrown up by the torpedo which hit *Benham* with the water thrown up by a premature explosion of our mark 15 torpedoes, I estimate the Japanese warhead carried a larger warhead than our MK 15." Of this statement, Kilpatrick opines with his customary rapier wit, "This is the greatest understatement of the battle."

187 ONI Narrative, 68.

188 Hammel, *Guadalcanal*, 7354; Lundgren, "Battleship Action," 9.

189 Kilpatrick, *Night Battles*, 120.

190 Lundgren, "Battleship Action," 7. One gun on the *Ayanami*'s Mount 3 was blown off.

191 Hammel, *Guadalcanal*, 7416.

192 Ibid., 7416.

193 Ibid., 7416.

194 Lundgren, "Battleship Action," 10.

195 Ibid., 7.

196 Ibid., 7, 10.

197 Hornfischer, *Neptune's Inferno*, 6668.

198 O'Hara, *US Navy*, 123.

199 Short description of the failure is from Frank, *Guadalcanal*, 477; Prados, *Islands of Destiny*, 3329; and Hornfischer, *Neptune's Inferno*, 6638–68. "*South Dakota* Report," 5–6, gives a more technical description of the *South Dakota*'s electrical failure:

> Lost all power, gyros and all electric fire control equipment out. Circuit breakers on No. 4 switch board tripped out. Load shifted to No. 3 switchboard. Bus transfer panel for No. 6 and 8 5" mounts shifted to alternate source on No. 3 board, causing No. 6 generator to trip out. Feeder circuit breaker also tripped. Regained power in plotting room then lost it again almost immediately.

200 O'Hara, *US Navy*, 123.

201 Hammel, *Guadalcanal*, 7476.

202 Kilpatrick, *Night Battles*, 122; USS *Gwin* "Report of Night Action November 14–15, 1942" ("*Gwin* Guadalcanal Report"), 3; "Report of Night Action Task Force 64 – November 14–15, 1942" ("Lee Report"), 3; USS *Washington* "Action Report, Night of November 14–15, 1942" ("*Washington* Report") misidentifies the *Gwin* as the *Benham*.

203 Kilpatrick, *Night Battles*, 122.

204 Lundgren, "Battleship Action," 10.

205 ONI Narrative, 73.

206 ONI Narrative, 73, which adds, "The comparative experience of the two ships in the next few minutes was dramatic evidence of the wisdom of remaining beyond effective searchlight illumination in order to capitalize on the advantage afforded by our fire-control radar."

207 Lundgren, "Battleship Action," 12.

208 Lundgren, "Battleship Action," 12. The ONI Narrative (73) says, "There were four lights in pairs, two over two."

209 Lundgren, "Battleship Action," 12; Hammel, *Guadalcanal*, 7476–515.

210 Robert Lundgren, "*South Dakota* Damage Analysis," *NavWeaps: Naval Weapons, Naval Technology and Naval Reunions* (www.navweaps.com), 47.

211 Hammel, *Guadalcanal*, 7515.

212 Ibid., 7515.

213 Lundgren, "*South Dakota* Damage Analysis," 48–9.

214 Ibid., 62–6.

215 Lundgren, "Battleship Action," 15.

216 Ibid., 15.

217 Kilpatrick, *Night Battles*, 122.

218 Lundgren, "Battleship Action," 15.

219 Lundgren, "South Dakota Damage Analysis," 67–77.

220 Lundgren, "Battleship Action," 20.

221 Ibid., 15.

222 Frank, *Guadalcanal*, 479.

223 Goldstein and Dillon, *Pacific War Papers*, 315. Admiral Kondo wrote, "[T]he sudden appearance of battleships in that area [off *Guadalcanal*] was utterly beyond my consideration."

224 Lundgren, "Battleship Action," 18 and n. 22, in which he explains, "*South Dakota*'s hull is painted with dark blue waves and a dark grey hull with sky grey superstructure. The dark paint on her hull makes it impossible to determine where her waterline is so determining her direction becomes extremely difficult." The effect of camouflage has generally been overrated in naval vessels, but this was one definite instance in which it paid off.

225 Lundgren, "Battleship Action," 19 and n. 31.

226 Lundgren, "Battleship Action," 18, 23, in which he explains, "*Washington* is sporting measure 12 camouflages making her appear awash and down by the bow. She is painted dark blue hull and a sky grey superstructure with just the tip of her bow sky grey." Details of the *Kirishima*'s damage comes from Robert Lundgren, "*Kirishima* Damage Analysis," *NavWeaps: Naval Weapons, Naval Technology and Naval Reunions* (www.navweaps.com), 8–23.

227 Lundgren, "Battleship Action," 20.

228 Ibid., 23.

229 O'Hara, *US Navy*, 125.

230 Hornfischer, *Neptune's Inferno*, 6731.

231 Interrogation of: Lieutenant Commander Tokuno Horishi, Assistant Gunnery Officer of *Kirishima*; Interrogation Nav No. 33, USSBS No. 138.

232 Kilpatrick, *Night Battles*, 124.

233 Lundgren, "Battleship Action," 21.

234 In the opinion of the ONI Narrative (75, n. 83), "The 5½ minutes of 16-inch shell fire required to destroy the battleship *Kirishima* contrasts significantly with the extraordinary aerial and torpedo pounding absorbed by her sister ship, the [*Hiei*], 2 days before."

235 *Washington* Report, 10; Lundgren, "Battleship Action," 19.

236 Lundgren, "Battleship Action," 18. Soy sauce was highly flammable in 1942, but not before or since.

237 Ibid., 18.

238 Ibid., 18.

239 *Washington* Report, 10.

240 Frank, *Guadalcanal*, 482; Lee Report, 4.

241 Lundgren, "Battleship Action," 121–56.

242 Hornfischer, *Neptune's Inferno*, 6680–711.

243 Lundgren, "Battleship Action," 20.

244 Frank, *Guadalcanal*, 481.

245 Ibid., 482.

246 *Washington* Report, 10.

247 Kilpatrick, *Night Battles*, 124–5.
248 Ibid., 124–5.
249 Ibid., 125.
250 Frank, *Guadalcanal*, 482.
251 Kilpatrick, *Night Battles*, 125.
252 Hornfischer, *Neptune's Inferno*, 6785.
253 O'Hara, *US Navy*, 127.
254 Ibid., 127.
255 Frank, *Guadalcanal*, 483.
256 Ibid., 483.
257 Frank, *Guadalcanal*, 484; Kilpatrick, *Night Battles*, 125.
258 Kilpatrick, *Night Battles*, 125.
259 Frank, *Guadalcanal*, 484.
260 Ugaki, Goldstein, and Dillon, *Fading Victory*, 276.
261 Ibid., 276.
262 Counting Captain Iwabuchi's plan with the *Kirishima* and Captain Nishida's plan with the *Hiei*, the Japanese would plan or even attempt to beach their battleships a grand total of six times, the four other times being: Battle of the Philippine Sea (*Fuso* and *Yamashiro*); Battle of Leyte Gulf (*Fuso* and *Yamashiro*, again); Battle of Leyte Gulf (*Musashi*); and Battle of Okinawa (*Yamato*).
263 Ugaki, Goldstein, and Dillon, *Fading Victory*, 271.
264 Ibid., 276.
265 Lundgren, "Battleship Action," 24.
266 Robert Lundgren's conclusion that the *Kirishima* capsized and was sunk by the flooding resulting from gunfire is accepted here as true, and the postwar testimony of Lieutenant Commander Tokuno Horishi, assistant gunnery officer of *Kirishima* (Interrogation Nav No. 33, USSBS No. 138) that the *Kirishima* was scuttled is not accepted per se. It seems probable that Tokuno had a garbled recollection of a report of the intentional flooding of the port-side engine room, which may have involved opening the Kingston valves.
267 Frank, *Guadalcanal*, 484.
268 Hammel, *Guadalcanal*, 7619.
269 Lundgren, *Kirishima Damage Analysis*, 27.
270 Hammel, *Guadalcanal*, 7654.
271 Lundstrom, *First Team*, 13704.
272 Ibid., 13704.
273 Hammel, *Guadalcanal*, 7654; ONI Narrative, 80.
274 Hammel, *Guadalcanal*, 7654.
275 Lundstrom, *First Team*, 13704.
276 Ibid., 13683.
277 Kilpatrick, *Night Battles*, 126.
278 Evans, *Japanese Navy*, 195.
279 Ibid., 195.
280 Frank, *Guadalcanal*, 487.
281 Evans, *Japanese Navy*, 195.
282 Ugaki, Goldstein, and Dillon, *Fading Victory*, 270.
283 Kilpatrick, *Night Battles*, 126.
284 Lundstrom, *First Team*, 13704.
285 Frank, *Guadalcanal*, 488; Lundstrom, *First Team*, 13702.
286 ONI Narrative, 80.
287 Lundstrom, *First Team*, 13704–34.
288 Moore, *Hell's Island*, 396; Lundstrom, *First Team*, 13704–34; ONI Narrative, 80.
289 Hammel, *Guadalcanal*, 7654.
290 Ibid., 7654.
291 Moore, *Hell's Island*, 396.
292 Lundstrom, *First Team*, 13734.
293 Ibid., 13734.
294 ONI Narrative, 80.
295 Frank, *Guadalcanal*, 488.

296 Lundstrom, *First Team*, 13752.

297 Moore, *Hell's Island*, 398; Lundstrom, *First Team*, 13752.

298 Lundstrom, *First Team*, 13752.

299 Ibid., 13753.

300 Ibid., 13753.

301 ONI Narrative, 83.

302 Moore, *Hell's Island*, 398.

303 Hammel, *Guadalcanal*, 7684.

304 Moore, *Hell's Island*, 398–9.

305 ONI Narrative, 82.

306 Hammel, *Guadalcanal*, 7716; Lundstrom, *First Team*, 13742.

307 Hammel, *Guadalcanal*, 7716; Lundstrom, *First Team*, 13830.

308 Lundstrom, *First Team*, 13792–850.

309 Ugaki, Goldstein, and Dillon, *Fading Victory*, 276.

310 Evans, *Japanese Navy*, 196.

311 Ugaki, Goldstein, and Dillon, *Fading Victory*, 278.

312 Hara, Saito, and Pineau, *Destroyer Captain*, 126.

313 Ibid., 145.

314 Ibid., 129.

315 Generous, *Sweet Pea*, 107–8.

316 Ibid., 108–9.

317 Kilpatrick, *Night Battles*, 126.

318 ONI Narrative, 70, n. 77.

319 Kilpatrick, *Night Battles*, 126; ONI Narrative, 70, n. 77.

320 ONI Narrative, 70, n. 77.

321 Kilpatrick, *Night Battles*, 126; Frank, *Guadalcanal*, 484.

322 Hammel, *Guadalcanal*, 7599.

323 Frank, *Guadalcanal*, 484–5.

324 Kilpatrick, *Night Battles*, 127.

325 Kilpatrick, *Night Battles*, 127; Frank, *Guadalcanal*, 485; ONI Narrative, 68, n. 73.

326 Frank, *Guadalcanal*, 485; ONI Narrative, 68, n. 73.

327 Hornfischer, *Neptune's Inferno*, 6839.

328 ONI Narrative, 76–7.

329 Ibid., 77.

330 Ibid., 77.

331 Ibid., 77.

332 Hornfischer, *Neptune's Inferno*, 6839.

333 Ibid., 6926.

334 Ibid., 6296.

335 McCandless, "San Francisco."

336 Kurzman, *Left to Die*, 180–1.

337 Ibid., 181.

338 Hammel, *Guadalcanal*, 5818.

339 Hornfischer, *Neptune's Inferno*, 7076; Hammel, *Guadalcanal*, 5809.

340 Halsey, *Story*, 2891.

Chapter 5

1 Frank, *Guadalcanal*, 499.

2 Toland, *Rising Sun*, 9312.

3 Ugaki, Goldstein, and Dillon, *Fading Victory*, 280.

4 Frank, *Guadalcanal*, 498.

5 Frank, *Guadalcanal*, 525; Ronnie Day, *New Georgia: The Second Battle for the Solomons* (Bloomington, IN: Indiana University Press, 2016), Kindle edition, 318. Roger Letourneau and Dennis Letourneau (*Operation KE: The Cactus Air Force and the Japanese Withdrawal From Guadalcanal* (Annapolis: Naval Institute Press, 2012), Kindle edition, 57, have the *Hakaze* landing on November 11.

6   Ugaki, Goldstein, and Dillon, *Fading Victory*, 281.

7   Day, *New Georgia*, 346; "Ballale Airfield," *Pacific Wrecks* (www.pacificwrecks.com).

8   Frank, *Guadalcanal*, 498.

9   Dean, Peter J. *MacArthur's Coalition: US and Australian Operations in the Southwest Pacific Area, 1942–1945.*
     Lawrence: University of Kansas Press, 2018. Kindle edition, 2439, 1844–64.

10   Quote is from Dean, *MacArthur's Coalition*, 2095; Rems, Alan. *South Pacific Cauldron: World War II's Great
     Forgotten Battlegrounds.* (Annapolis: Naval Institute Press, 2014.) Kindle edition, 550–4.

11   Hammel, *Air War*, 2151.

12   Ibid., 2151–71.

13   Dean, *MacArthur's Coalition*, 2565.

14   Ibid., 2118.

15   Ibid., 2118; Paul M. Edwards, *Between the Lines of World War II: Twenty-One Remarkable People and Events*
     (Jefferson, NC: McFarland, 2010), Kindle edition, 2113.

16   Edwards, *Between the Lines*, 2101–13.

17   Rems, *South Pacific Cauldron*, 613–37.

18   Dean, *MacArthur's Coalition*, 2118.

19   Rems, *South Pacific Cauldron*, 637.

20   Ed Drea, "World War II: Buna Mission," *HistoryNet* (www.historynet.com); Edwards, *Between the Lines*, 2124.

21   Rems, *South Pacific Cauldron*, 646–8.

22   Ibid., 637.

23   Ibid., 637.

24   Eichelberger, Robert L. *Our Jungle Road to Tokyo* (New York: Viking Press, 1950), Kindle edition, 36.

25   Rems, *South Pacific Cauldron*, 637.

26   Ugaki, Goldstein, and Dillon, *Fading Victory*, 277.

27   Ibid., 287.

28   Toland, *Rising Sun*, 9312.

29   Ibid., 9312–31.

30   Ibid., 9231.

31   Ugaki, Goldstein, and Dillon, *Fading Victory*, 284; Prados, *Islands of Destiny*, 206.

32   Ugaki, Goldstein, and Dillon, *Fading Victory*, 284.

33   Frank, *Guadalcanal*, 499–500.

34   Ugaki, Goldstein, and Dillon, *Fading Victory*, 305.

35   Prados, *Islands of Destiny*, 198.

36   Ibid., 201.

37   Frank, *Guadalcanal*, 500.

38   Prados, *Islands of Destiny*, 201.

39   Day, *New Georgia*, 410.

40   Letourneau and Letourneau, *Operation KE*, 65–6.

41   Frank, *Guadalcanal*, 501–2; Day, *New Georgia*, 426.

42   Frank, *Guadalcanal*, 501–2; Day, *New Georgia*, 426; Ugaki, Goldstein, and Dillon, *Fading Victory*, 316;
     Letourneau and Letourneau, *Operation KE*, 69–70. The *Imperial Japanese Navy Page* has TROMs for a *Kiku
     Maru* and *Azusa Maru*, but these are different ships than the two sunk off Wickham. There seems to be some
     confusion as to the date of the sinkings, with both Cressman, *Official Chronology*, and Frank claiming they
     occurred in November. While not mentioning the sea trucks by name, Admiral Ugaki is specific enough as to
     their cargo to indicate both were sunk December 28–29, not November 28–29.

43   Tanaka, "Struggle for Guadalcanal," 198–9.

44   Frank, *Guadalcanal*, 502–3.

45   Russell Sydnor Crenshaw, Jr., *The Battle of Tassafaronga* (Annapolis: Naval Institute Press, 1995), Kindle
     edition, 99.

46   Tanaka, "Struggle for Guadalcanal," 199.

47   Frank, *Guadalcanal*, 507.

48   Crenshaw, *Tassafaronga*, 101.

49   Ibid., 106.

50   Kilpatrick, *Night Battles*, 140.

51   Tanaka, "Struggle for Guadalcanal," 200.

52   Ibid., 200.

53 ONI, *United States Navy Combat Narrative: Battle of Tassafaronga, 30 November 1942 and Japanese Evacuation of Guadalcanal, 29 January–8 February 1943* (Washington, DC: Publications Branch, Office of Naval Intelligence, United States Navy, 1944), 2.

54 Frank, *Guadalcanal*, 503.

55 Ibid., 501–2.

56 Frank, *Guadalcanal*, 503; Morison, *Struggle*, 290; ONI Narrative, 2.

57 Morison, *Struggle*, 290.

58 Ibid., 290.

59 ONI Narrative, 2.

60 Ibid., 2.

61 Morison, *Struggle*, 294; Frank, *Guadalcanal*, 503.

62 Frank, *Guadalcanal*, 504.

63 Kilpatrick, *Night Battles*, 139.

64 Ibid., 139.

65 Ibid., 139.

66 Ibid., 140.

67 Ibid., 140.

68 Ibid., 141.

69 Ibid., 140.

70 Morison, *Struggle*, 295.

71 Kilpatrick, *Night Battles*, 141.

72 Ibid., 140–2.

73 ONI Narrative, 6.

74 Kilpatrick, *Night Battles*, 141.

75 Hornfischer, *Neptune's Inferno*, 7226.

76 Kilpatrick, *Night Battles*, 141–2.

77 ONI Narrative, 6.

78 Ibid., 6.

79 Kilpatrick, *Night Battles*, 141.

80 ONI Narrative, 6–7 n. 11. Morison (*Struggle*, 296) described Commander Abercrombie as "somewhat bewildered" by his orders from Admiral Halsey and lack of the same from Admiral Wright.

81 O'Hara, *US Navy*, 130.

82 Kilpatrick, *Night Battles*, 142.

83 ONI Narrative, 7.

84 Ibid., 7.

85 Ibid., 7.

86 Ibid., 7.

87 Ibid., 7; Kilpatrick, *Night Battles*, 143.

88 Kilpatrick, *Night Battles*, 143.

89 Crenshaw, *Tassafaronga*, 35.

90 Hornfischer, *Neptune's Inferno*, 7226; Crenshaw, *Tassafaronga*, 35; Kilpatrick, *Night Battles*, 144.

91 Hornfischer, *Neptune's Inferno*, 7226.

92 Crenshaw, *Tassafaronga*, 35.

93 Kilpatrick, *Night Battles*, 144.

94 Crenshaw, *Tassafaronga*, 33.

95 Ibid., 33.

96 Ibid., 54.

97 Ibid., 35.

98 Ibid., 36; ONI Narrative, 9.

99 Crenshaw, *Tassafaronga*, 36.

100 Kilpatrick, *Night Battles*, 145.

101 Crenshaw, *Tassafaronga*, 36; ONI Narrative, 8–9.

102 Crenshaw, *Tassafaronga*, 37; ONI Narrative, 9.

103 ONI Narrative, 9–10.

104 Ibid., 10.

105 Ibid., 10.

106 Ibid., 10.

107 Crenshaw, *Tassafaronga*, 144.

108 ONI Narrative, 12.

109 Kilpatrick, *Night Battles*, 143–4.

110 Crenshaw, *Tassafaronga*, 35–6.

111 Ibid., 106.

112 Tanaka, "Struggle for Guadalcanal," 200.

113 Ibid., 200.

114 INTERROGATION NAV NO. 60, USSBS NO. 252, Interrogation of: Captain Toyama Yasumi, 1 November 1945.

115 Evans, *Japanese Navy*, 3132.

116 Crenshaw, *Tassafaronga*, 36–7.

117 Ibid., 136.

118 Hara, Saito, and Pineau, *Destroyer Captain*, 152.

119 Crenshaw, *Tassafaronga*, 44.

120 ONI Narrative, 17.

121 Morison, *Struggle*, 305.

122 Ibid., 305.

123 Ibid., 305.

124 Crenshaw, *Tassafaronga*, 38–9.

125 Ibid., 39, 139; ONI Narrative, 15. The ONI says the *Pensacola* used her search radar to locate the target at a range of 4,000 yards, but the only search radar she had was the CXAM radar which was better at spotting aircraft. Crenshaw says she used her fire control radar at a range of 6,000 yards, which sounds more plausible.

126 Crenshaw, *Tassafaronga*, 139.

127 Ibid., 39.

128 Ibid., 39–40.

129 Ibid., 40.

130 Ibid., 107–8.

131 Ibid., 136.

132 Ibid., 136; *Suzukaze* TROM. Frank (*Guadalcanal*, 509) and Morison (*Struggle*, 302) state that the *Suzukaze* did in fact launch as many as eight torpedoes near the start of the battle; Frank even states they were launched from a "favorable firing position." Crenshaw is used here because his painstaking reconstruction of the battle represents the most recent scholarship. The *Suzukaze* TROM is in agreement with Crenshaw. O'Hara (*US Navy*, 133–4) follows Crenshaw (*Tassafaronga*) and the *Suzukaze* TROM.

133 Frank, *Guadalcanal*, 509.

134 *Makinami* TROM; Crenshaw, *Tassafaronga*, 135.

135 Radar was and is a helpful device, but it did have its bugs, which were especially noticeable when those new to it were using it. Search radar gives warning and approximate location of targets, and fire control radar, which in a pinch can serve as search radar, can lock onto a target and give more specific information. "Lock on" is shorthand, however. What really happens is the radar transmitter stays focused on the target bearing, so that nothing on either side of the target is detected, while the range for the radar is limited so that only the selected target would appear, not anything in front of it or behind it. This range limitation is known as a range-gate. The result is an area of detection for the fire control radar that in shape resembles a slice of pizza with the end cut off. Only one target should be within that slice of pizza. But the fire control radar could detect anything within that slice. So if two ships were there, the fire control would often average the range and, especially, the deflection, so that when a salvo is fired using the information provided by the fire control radar, neither ship is hit. The radar could and often did detect shell splashes within that slice of pizza, so what would end up happening is fire control would average the range and deflection between the target and the shell splash. The result here was that not only would the salvo miss the target, but any correction would miss the target as well because the shell splash would end up fouling the range and deflection. In short, instead of gunfire chasing the target, the gunfire would chase its own shell splashes. It was determined that this was a major reason why the US gunfire, especially that of the *Honolulu*, was off in deflection. See Crenshaw, *Tassafaronga*, 125–6.

136 Crenshaw, *Tassafaronga*, 40.

137 Ibid., 67–8; O'Hara, *US Navy*, 135.

138 ONI Narrative, 22.

139 Crenshaw, *Tassafaronga*, 144.

140 Frank, *Guadalcanal*, 512–3.
141 Crenshaw, *Tassafaronga*, 45.
142 Ibid., 143; *Oyashio* TROM.
143 O'Hara, *US Navy*, 136.
144 Crenshaw, *Tassafaronga*, 143.
145 Kilpatrick, *Night Battles*, 151.
146 Crenshaw, *Tassafaronga*, 145.
147 Ibid., 144–5. The *Minneapolis*'s report suggests the near-collision came well after this time, after the flagship had turned toward Tulagi. See, e.g. Crenshaw, *Tassafaronga*, 44. Crenshaw's analysis makes clear that the near collision happened much earlier, while the *Minneapolis* was still headed toward Lunga.
148 Kilpatrick, *Night Battles*, 152.
149 Ibid., 152.
150 Ibid., 152.
151 Ibid., 152.
152 Crenshaw, *Tassafaronga*, 43–44. Messages come from Kilpatrick, *Night Battles*, 153. Crenshaw says Admiral Tisdale ordered the floatplanes to "'secure' and return to Tulagi."
153 Kilpatrick, *Night Battles*, 152.
154 Ibid., 153.
155 Ibid., 152.
156 Crenshaw, *Tassafaronga*, 46.
157 Ibid., 143.
158 Tanaka, "Struggle for Guadalcanal," 202.
159 O'Hara, *US Navy*, 133.
160 Tanaka, "Struggle for Guadalcanal," 202–3.
161 Hara, Saito, and Pineau, *Destroyer Captain*, 154.
162 Ibid., 153.
163 Crenshaw, *Tassafaronga*, 46.
164 Ibid., 47.
165 Ibid., 44–5.
166 Ibid., 45.
167 Frank, *Guadalcanal*, 514.
168 Ibid., 514.
169 Crenshaw, *Tassafaronga*, 45; Frank, *Guadalcanal*, 514.
170 Crenshaw, *Tassafaronga*, 46; ONI Narrative, 22.
171 ONI Narrative, 14 n. 18.
172 Frank, *Guadalcanal*, 515.
173 Crenshaw, *Tassafaronga*, 47.
174 ONI Narrative, 18.
175 Crenshaw, *Tassafaronga*, 62.
176 Morison, *Struggle*, 313 n. 26.
177 Ibid., 313.
178 Frank, *Guadalcanal*, 516.
179 Crenshaw, *Tassafaronga*, 61.
180 Morison, *Struggle*, 314.
181 Crenshaw, *Tassafaronga*, 76.
182 See, e.g., Frank, *Guadalcanal*, 517; Morison, *Struggle*, 314.
183 Crenshaw, *Tassafaronga*, 75–6.
184 O'Hara (*US Navy*, 136) opines, "Tassafaronga proved to be the most deadly Japanese torpedo action of the war, not counting *Mogami*'s blow against friendly transports at Sunda Strait." A rather important proviso. In action against the Allied cruisers *Perth* and *Houston* off the Soenda Strait in 1942, the Japanese heavy cruiser *Mogami* launched a salvo of torpedoes at the cruisers. The torpedoes missed and sped on into an anchorage full of Japanese transports landing troops on Java, sinking four transports and a minesweeper. The *Mogami* later collided with her sister ship *Mikuma*, contributing to the latter's sinking. The *Mogami* was repaired and later collided with the heavy cruiser *Nachi*, contributing to the latter's sinking. The *Mogami* ended her fighting career having sunk more of her own ships than those of the enemy.
185 Hara, Saito, and Pineau, *Destroyer Captain*, 154.

186 Ibid., 154.

187 Tanaka, "Struggle for Guadalcanal," 203

188 Ibid., 203.

189 Ibid., 204; Frank, *Guadalcanal*, 520.

190 Tanaka, "Struggle for Guadalcanal," 204.

191 *Teruzuki* TROM.

192 "Tokyo Express," *PT King* (http://pt-king.gdinc.com/PT109-5.html).

193 White, *Dauntless Marine*, 102–4.

194 White, *Dauntless Marine*, 105.

195 Ibid., 105.

196 Frank, *Guadalcanal*, 520; Morison, *Struggle*, 318.

197 White, *Dauntless Marine*, 106.

198 Ibid., 106.

199 Ibid., 106.

200 Frank, *Guadalcanal*, 520.

201 White, *Dauntless Marine*, 108.

202 Frank, *Guadalcanal*, 520.

203 Morison, *Struggle*, 318.

204 Bulkley, *At Close Quarters*, 95–6.

205 Morison, *Struggle*, 319.

206 Ibid., 319.

207 "Tokyo Express," U.S. Navy PT Boats of World War II (http://pt-king.gdinc.com/index2.html).

208 Tanaka, "Struggle for Guadalcanal," 205.

209 Ibid., 205.

210 Frank, *Guadalcanal*, 523; Bulkley, *At Close Quarters*, 96; "Tokyo Express."

211 Tanaka, "Struggle for Guadalcanal," 206. Admiral Tanaka gives a number of destroyers from specific destroyer divisions, but does not identify the particular destroyers. To add to the confusion Tanaka's recollection appears to have been flawed here inasmuch as he has substituted the *Yugure* for the *Naganami*, which like the *Ariake* and *Arashi* is not a member of the mentioned 15th, 17th, or 24th destroyer divisions – a curious omission since the *Naganami* had been Tanaka's flagship and would be so again as a result of this action. But some confusion may be understandable because *Yugure* was in Shortland when Tanaka's force departed, having just returned from a supply run to Guadalcanal. See *Yugure* TROM.

212 Frank, *Guadalcanal*, 523.

213 Tanaka, "Struggle for Guadalcanal," 206; Frank, *Guadalcanal*, 523; Morison, *Struggle*, 319.

214 Jonathan Parshall, "Akizuki class," *Imperial Japanese Navy Page* (www.combinedfleet..com).

215 Allyn Nevitt, "*Akizuki* class notes." From the *Imperial Japanese Navy Page* (www.combinedfleet.com).

216 Ibid.

217 Tanaka, "Struggle for Guadalcanal," 206.

218 Ibid., 206–7.

219 Prados, *Islands of Destiny*, 207.

220 "Tokyo Express." The identity of the *Teruzuki*'s assailant is usually not mentioned, nor is there agreement on the boats involved. Bulkley (*At Close Quarters*, 96) only says, "Les Gamble, Stilly Taylor, and Lt. (jg.) Williams E. Kreiner 3d, USNR, all claimed torpedo hits. It is known that the PT's sank the destroyer [*Teruzuki*]." Morison (*Struggle*, 319) only says it was three boats under Lieutenant Gamble. Frank (*Guadalcanal*, 523) identifies the boats as *PT-37*, *PT-40*, and *PT-48*. The *Teruzuki* TROM lists only two boats, *PT-37* and *PT-40*.

221 Bulkley, *At Close Quarters*, 97. There is agreement that one of the boats was *PT-44*, but little on the identity of the other boat. Bulkley identified it as *PT-110* under Lieutenant Charles Tilden. Frank (*Guadalcanal*, 524) says the other boat was *PT-114*. "Tokyo Express" says the boat with *PT-44* was *PT-61* under Lieutenant Charles Tilden but the boat that charged in was *PT-109* under group senior officer Lieutenant John Searles.

222 Bulkley, *At Close Quarters*, 98–9; "Tokyo Express."

223 Morison, *Struggle*, 320; *Teruzuki* TROM.

224 Hara, Saito, and Pineau, *Destroyer Captain*, 154.

225 Tanaka, "Struggle for Guadalcanal," 206–7.

226 Ibid., 207.

227 Hara, Saito, and Pineau, *Destroyer Captain*, 154; Letourneau and Letourneau, *Operation KE*, 8–9.

Chapter 6

1   Prados, *Islands of Destiny*, 213.

2   Ibid., 213–4.

3   Rems, *South Pacific Cauldron*, 633.

4   Louis Morton, *United States Army in World War II The War in the Pacific Strategy and Command: The First Two Years* (Washington: Center of Military History, United States Army; 1962), 370.

5   Ibid., 370.

6   Ibid., 370.

7   Ibid., 370–1.

8   Ibid., 370–1.

9   Ibid., 370–1.

10 Ibid., 370–1.

11 Ibid., 372.

12 Ibid., 361–2.

13 Ibid., 362.

14 Hough, Ludwig, and Shaw, *Pearl Harbor to Guadalcanal*, 359.

15 Twining, *No Bended Knee*, 205.

16 Major John L. Zimmerman, *The Guadalcanal Campaign: Marines in World War II Historical Monograph* (Washington, DC: Historical Section, Division of Public Information, Headquarters, U.S. Marine Corps, 1949), 153.

17 Hough, Ludwig, and Shaw, *Pearl Harbor to Guadalcanal*, 359.

18 Ibid., 359.

19 T. Grady Gallant, *On Valor's Side: A Marine's Own Story of Parris Island and Guadalcanal* (New York: Doubleday, 1963), 5935.

20 Gallant, *On Valor's Side*, 5922.

21 Morison, *Struggle*, 334.

22 Leckie, *Challenge*, 6368.

23 Gallant, *On Valor's Side*, 5949.

24 Hough, Ludwig, and Shaw, *Pearl Harbor to Guadalcanal*, 359.

25 Ibid., 359.

26 Stanley Coleman Jersey, *Hell's Islands: The Untold Story of Guadalcanal* (College Station, TX: Texas A&M University Press, 2008), 4793–797.

27 "We made a plaque for Bill's grave today." Jim Donahue, Jr., "Journal entries by Pfc. James A. Donahue (1921–1998)," *Guadalcanal Journal* (https://web.archive.org/web/20131031231832/http://www.guadalcanaljournal.com/The-Journal.html) (Archived from original).

28 Morison, *Struggle*, x.

29 Hough, Ludwig, and Shaw, *Pearl Harbor to Guadalcanal*, 364.

30 Jersey, *Hell's Islands*, 4802–16; Lt. Col. John B. George, *Shots Fired in Anger* (Buford, GA: Canton Street, 2012), Kindle edition, 46–7.

31 George, *Shots Fired*, 46–7.

32 Ibid., 46.

33 Jersey, *Hell's Islands*, 4802–16.

34 Miller, *Guadalcanal*, 238–9.

35 Morison, *Struggle*, 336.

36 Frank, *Guadalcanal*, 531; George, *Shots Fired*, 321–4. Gifu Prefecture, whose capital is Gifu, is located on Honshu in roughly the center of the Home Islands. One of the few landlocked prefectures, Gifu's central position has earned it the historical if unofficial title of The Crossroads of Japan. In the 1500s, the century before the ascendance of the Tokugawa shogunate, people would say, "When you control Gifu, you control Japan." Jersey (*Hell's Islands*, 4744) says the position was named by men of the 230th Regiment, none of whom were defending Gifu at this time.

37 George, *Shots Fired*, 315–7.

38 Ibid., 321.

39 Griffith, *Guadalcanal*, 266; Miller, *Guadalcanal*, 249. There is some disagreement as well as to when Lieutenant Colonel George took over. Jersey (*Hell's Islands*, 4911) says December 28, 1942, but Miller (*Guadalcanal*, 249) says January 1, 1943. Jersey is used here because the December 30 order from 132nd Infantry headquarters

reads in relevant part, "Upon capture of Hill 27 a perimeter defense will be established and will be defended at all costs." This language matches the language Lieutenant Colonel George used in his pep talk to his regiment concerning how their mission must be accomplished "regardless of the price."

40   Jersey, *Hell's Islands*, 4927–41.

41   Ibid., 4941.

42   Miller, *Guadalcanal*, 249.

43   Ibid., 250–1.

44   Frank, *Guadalcanal*, 533.

45   Ibid., 544; Hammel, *Air War*, 4066.

46   Rear Admiral Richard H. O'Kane, USN, *Wahoo: The Patrols of America's Most Famous WWII Submarine* (New York: Presidio, 1987), Kindle edition, 87–8.

47   O'Kane, *Wahoo*, 89; Blair, *Silent Victory*, 333.

48   Blair, *Silent Victory*, 333. Curiously, O'Kane does not mention this incident in his book about the *Wahoo*.

49   USS *Wahoo* Report of Second War Patrol, 6.

50   *I-2* TROM.

51   There has been uncertainty about the target of the *Wahoo*'s attack and the target's fate. The *I-2* definitely survived this attack, and served until April 7, 1944, when she was sunk off New Hanover by the destroyer USS *Saufley*. Vernon Miller (*Japanese Submarine Losses*, 122–43) says the *I-2* was not in the area at the time, but this has been contradicted by the *I-2* TROM. Miller speculates that the poor visibility may have caused Lieutenant Commander Miller to misidentify the *I-22*. The last message received from the *I-22* was on October 4, more than two months before the *Wahoo*'s December 14 attack. Going more than two months without a message is highly unusual unless something has happened to the submarine. Indeed, the *I-22* TROM credits an attack by a PBY-5A Catalina flying boat for dropping four depth charges on a submarine in the *I-22*'s area, after which "Quantities of oil and bubbles appear and the submarine is considered sunk." However, the *I-22*'s TROM notes, "After the war, the Joint Army-Navy Assessment Committee (JANAC) officially credited the torpedo boat *PT-122* with the sinking of *I-22* off the Kumusi River on the night of December 23–24, 1942. How exactly JANAC reached this conclusion is unclear; newer research has discredited that claim." Lieutenant Commander Hashimoto Mochitsura (*Sunk*, 2838) goes with this explanation. Nevertheless, the same issue regarding the lack of communication since October 4 would seem to discredit this potential solution as well, especially in light of the October 6 attack. Miller says, "It seems feasible to assume that *Wahoo* witnessed a premature explosion or perhaps a low detonation explosion that damaged, but did not sink, the target. The commanding officer of *Wahoo* considered the attack successful, an opinion in which the [Joint Army-Navy] Assessment Committee did not concur." The events recited here are a combination of Miller and the *I-2* TROM (Vernon J. Miller, *Japanese Submarine Losses to Allied Submarines in World War 2* (Bennington, VT: Merriam, 1988), Kindle edition; Lieutenant Commander Mochitsura Hashimoto, *Sunk: The Story of the Japanese Submarine Fleet 1941–1945* (Pickle Partners Publishing, 2015), Kindle edition.

52   *Tenryu* and *Gokoku Maru* TROMs; Ugaki, Goldstein, and Dillon, *Fading Victory*, 308.

53   Ugaki, Goldstein, and Dillon, *Fading Victory*, 314.

54   Cressman, *Official Chronology*; Day, *New Georgia*, 367; *Bandoeng Maru* TROM, which reveals that the *Bandoeng Maru* had originally been called the *Kinno Maru* or the *Kinoo Maru*. It was also called the *Badoeng Maru* or the *Bandon Maru*. Day, *New Georgia*.

55   Hammel, *Air War*, 3947; *Mochizuki* TROM; Cressman, *Official Chronology*.

56   Frank, *Guadalcanal*, 500.

57   *I-4* TROM.

58   Ugaki, Goldstein, and Dillon, *Fading Victory*, 313.

59   Morison, *Struggle*, 323.

60   Hammel, *Air War*, 4012.

61   *Ariake*, *Urakaze*, and *Nankai Maru* TROMs; Morison, *Struggle*, 323; Ugaki, Goldstein, and Dillon, *Fading Victory*, 313; Day, *New Georgia*, 410.

62   Ugaki, Goldstein, and Dillon, *Fading Victory*, 313.

63   *Tachikaze* TROM; Hammel, *Air War*, 4012; Cressman, *Official Chronology*.

64   Hammel, *Air War*, 4018.

65   Frank, *Guadalcanal*, 545.

66   Ibid., 545.

67   *Naganami*, *Kawakaze*, *Suzukaze*, *Makinami*, *Isonami*, *Inazumi*, *Kuroshio*, *Kagero*, *Oyashio*, and *Arashio* TROMs; Frank, *Guadalcanal*, 547.

68 Frank, *Guadalcanal*, 547; *Inazumi* TROM.

69 "Tokyo Express."

70 Frank, *Guadalcanal*, 548.

71 Eichelberger, *Jungle Road*, 64.

72 William Manchester, *American Caesar: Douglas MacArthur, 1880–1964* (New York: Back Bay Books, 1978, 327.

73 Rems, *South Pacific Cauldron*, 680; Manchester, *American Caesar*, 327.

74 Manchester, *American Caesar*, 326.

75 Rems, *South Pacific Cauldron*, 719–23.

76 Louis B. Dorny, *US Navy PBY Catalina Units of the Pacific War* (Oxford: Osprey, 2013), 1482.

77 Dorny, *PBY Catalina Units*, 1482–508. The radio altimeter became so critical that if it failed during a night mission the aircraft immediately returned to base.

78 Morison, *Struggle*, 331.

79 Letourneau and Letourneau, *Operation KE*, 101–2; "Tokyo Express."

80 Morison, *Struggle*, 339; *Hatsukaze* TROM.

81 Letourneau and Letourneau, *Operation KE*, 102.

82 "Tokyo Express."

83 Letourneau and Letourneau, *Operation KE*, 102.

84 Ibid., 102.

85 Ibid., 101; *Hatsukaze* and *Tokitsukaze* TROMs.

86 Letourneau and Letourneau, *Operation KE*, 102.

87 Ibid., 103.

88 Ibid., 103.

89 Ibid., 104.

90 Ibid., 104–5. Flying a defensive circle over a target you are trying to protect was very common, but forming a defensive circle for mutual protection while in combat, as was done here, was not. This type of defensive circle is known as a Lufbury (or Lufberry or Lufbery or Luffberry) Circle (or Wheel). It is named after World War I French fighter ace Gervais Raoul Lufbery, who neither invented the Lufbery Circle nor used it.

91 Letourneau and Letourneau, *Operation KE*, 105–6.

92 Colonel Joe Foss, USMC (Ret.), *Joe Foss: Flying Marine* (Pickle Partners Publishing, 2013), 1871.

93 Letourneau and Letourneau, *Operation KE*, 107.

94 Ibid., 107.

95 Ibid., 107–8; *Urakaze* TROM.

96 "Tokyo Express."

97 Letourneau and Letourneau, *Operation KE*, 111; Foss, *Flying Marine*, 1875–94.

98 Letourneau and Letourneau, *Operation KE*, 110–111.

99 Ibid., 110–111.

100 Ibid., 113.

101 *Tanikaze* TROM.

102 Letourneau and Letourneau, *Operation KE*, 115–6.

103 Ibid., 116–7.

104 Frank, *Guadalcanal*, 545–6.

105 Ibid., 546.

106 *Ch-11* and *Kimposan Maru* TROMs.

107 *Senzan Maru* TROM.

108 *Kenkon Maru* TROM.

109 Ibid.

110 The *Nautilus*, who had been repeatedly detected within the screen of *Kido Butai*, attacked a battleship, later identified as the *Kirishima*, with one Mark 14 torpedo that missed and one that misfired and never launched. The *Kirishima* fired her secondary battery at the *Nautilus*'s periscope, but also missed. The destroyer *Arashi* was directed to sink the *Nautilus* or at least keep her down while *Kido Butai* escaped the area. Unable to sink the submarine, the *Arashi* raced to rejoin the carriers. As she did so, Commander C. Wade McCluskey, Jr., leading the Dauntlesses from the carrier *Enterprise*, spotted the *Arashi*'s wake and followed it to *Kido Butai* to begin his attack.

111 Cressman, *Official Chronology*.

112 *Akizuki* TROM.

113 *Myoho Maru* TROM.

114 *Kenkon Maru* TROM.

115 *Surabaya Maru*, *Kenkon Maru*, and *Ch-11* TROMs.

116 *Surabaya Maru*, *Kenkon Maru*, and *Ch-11* TROMs.

117 *Nichiun Maru* TROM.

118 Letourneau and Letourneau, *Operation KE*, 122–3.

119 Ibid., 123.

120 Foss, *Flying Marine*, 1975–93.

121 Ibid., 1993.

122 Letourneau and Letourneau, *Operation KE*, 123–4.

123 Foss, *Flying Marine*, 1993.

124 Letourneau and Letourneau, *Operation KE*, 126.

125 Ibid., 126–7.

126 Letourneau and Letourneau, *Operation KE*, 130.

127 Ibid., 129–30.

128 Ibid., 138–9.

129 Letourneau and Letourneau, *Operation KE*, 141–2. It was not uncommon for one name to be used for multiple Japanese transports, freighters, tankers, and cargo ships. Hence, *Mikage Maru No. 20.*

130 Day, *New Georgia*, 523.

131 Frank, *Guadalcanal*, 582.

132 Letourneau specifically identifies the submarine chaser as *Ch-17*. The *Ch-17* TROM does not specifically show this escort mission, but there is enough ambiguity in the TROM that the mission could have been carried out. Moreover, The *Imperial Japanese Navy Page* is very specific in its disclaimers that the TROMs for the smaller combatants such as subchasers are not always complete.

133 Letourneau and Letourneau, *Operation KE*, 145–6.

134 Ibid., 144–5.

135 Frank, *Guadalcanal*, 574.

136 Frank (*Guadalcanal*, 577) calls the signal "caustic[.]" Morison (*Struggle*, 352 n. 2) says King sent Nimitz and Halsey "a rather sharp dispatch about the relief of the 2nd Marine Division suggesting that 'wait, delay, and linger' had become the watchwords of the Guadalcanal campaign."

137 List of destroyers comes from *Lardner* War Diary, January 27, 1943.

138 Morison, *Struggle*, 353.

139 Frank, *Guadalcanal*, 578.

140 John J. Domagalski, *Lost at Guadalcanal: The Final Battles of the* Astoria *and* Chicago *as Described by Survivors and in Official Reports* (Jefferson, NC; London: MacFarland, 2010), 2974.

141 Kilpatrick, *Night Battles*, 161.

142 Morison, *Struggle*, 352.

143 Action Report – Task Force Eighteen, January 29–30, 1943 ("Rennell Island Report"), 2.

144 ONI Narrative.

145 John Wukovits, "Battle of Rennell Island: Setback in the Solomons," *World War II* magazine (March 2000), 1–2.

146 Morison, *Struggle*, 358.

147 In relating his experience during the Battle of Rennell Island working in the radio intelligence section of Guadalcanal, Lieutenant Commander Philip H. Jacobsen opined, "The scheduled daylight foray up the Slot on January 30 to catch the KE destroyers emerging from their sanctuaries in the Shortlands still could have been accomplished by a later arrival at Cape Hunter so it was not necessary to detach the jeep carriers to be ready for their ultimate operational task." Lieutenant Commander Philip H. Jacobsen, USN, "The Battle of Rennell Island," *The Thunder of the Guns: Battles of the Pacific War* (http://www.microworks.net/PACIFIC/battles/index.htm).

148 Rennell Island Report, 2–3.

149 Ibid., 2–3.

150 Domagalski, *Lost*, 3003.

151 ONI Narrative.

152 Action Report – USS *La Vallette* ("*La Vallette* Rennell Island Report"), 2.

153 Domagalski, *Lost*, 3022.

154 Rennell Island Report, 5.

155 Russell Sydnor Crenshaw, Jr., *South Pacific Destroyer: The Battle for the Solomons from Savo Island to Vella Gulf* (Annapolis: Naval Institute Press, 1998), Kindle edition, 1241.

156 Domagalski, *Lost*, 3024.

157 Morison, *Struggle*, 354; Kilpatrick, *Night Battles*, 163.

158 Translating *chutai* as "squadron."

159 Letourneau and Letourneau, *Operation KE*, 148.

160 Ibid., 148.

161 Jacobsen, "The Battle of Rennell Island."

162 Prados, *Islands of Destiny*, 224.

163 Osamu Tagaya and Mark Styling, *Mitsubishi Type 1 Rikko "Betty" Units of World War 2*. (Oxford: Osprey, 2001), Kindle edition, 50.

164 Domagalski, *Lost*, 3030.

165 USS *Wichita* Action Report – Torpedo Plane Attack, Night of 29 January, 1943 ("*Wichita* Rennell Island Report"), 1.

166 USS *Louisville* Report of Japanese Air Attack of January 29, 1943 ("*Louisville* Rennell Island Report"), 2.

167 Ibid.

168 Domagalski, *Lost*, 3040.

169 *La Vallette* Rennell Island Report, 3.

170 *Louisville* Rennell Island Report, 2.

171 Kilpatrick, *Night Battles*, 165.

172 Domagalski, *Lost*, 3041.

173 Ibid., 3047.

174 John Domagalski, "Battle of Rennell Island: A Fiery End for the USS Chicago," *Warfare History Network*, September 7, 2016 (http://warfarehistorynetwork.com/daily/wwii/battle-of-rennell-island-a-fiery-end-for-the-uss-chicago).

175 "USS CHICAGO (CA29) Loss in Action 29–30 January, 1943 Guadalcanal Island" (hereinafter *Chicago* Damage Report), 3.

176 Domagalski, "Rennell Island."

177 *Chicago* Damage Report, 3.

178 *Wichita* Rennell Island Report, 2; Domagalski, *Lost*, 3050.

179 Domagalski, *Lost*, 3046–56.

180 In his report on the damage to the *Chicago* (2), Captain Davis wrote:

> Cruisers of 10,000 tons and larger standard displacement, including CA's and CL's, are of such size and design that a single torpedo hit should never result in their sinking. Up to the time of preparation of this report, ten have suffered single torpedo hits and all have survived. Their chances of surviving two hits are good, provided the hits are reasonably spaced and provided liquid ballasting is followed.
>
> The trick is to convince the attacking torpedo planes to be "reasonable" in placement of torpedo hits.

181 *Chicago* Damage Report, 3–4.

182 Kilpatrick, *Night Battles*, 165.

183 *Columbia* War Diary, January 29, 1943.

184 USS *Conway* War Diary, January 29, 1943.

185 Kilpatrick, *Night Battles*, 166.

186 *Wichita* Rennell Island Report, 3; Kilpatrick, *Night Battles*, 166.

187 Kilpatrick, *Night Battles*, 166.

188 Ibid., 166.

189 Ibid., 166.

190 Domagalski, "Rennell Island."

191 Domagalski, *Lost*, 3129.

192 Ibid., 3129.

193 Domagalski, "Rennell Island"; Morison, *Struggle*, 358–9.

194 Kilpatrick, *Night Battles*, 167; Domagalski, "Rennell Island."

195 *Chicago* Rennell Island Damage Report, 3.

196 Morison, *Struggle*, 359.

197 Domagalski, "Rennell Island."

198 Domagalski, *Lost*, 3152.

199 Ibid., 3161.

200 Stafford, *The Big "E"*, 234–5.

201 Ibid., 234–5.

202 *Conway* War Diary, January 30, 1943.

203 ONI Narrative.

204 Domagalski, *Lost*, 3152.

205 USS *Enterprise* Action against Japanese Air Forces Attaching Task Force Eighteen off Rennel (sic) Island ("*Enterprise* Rennell Island Report"), 2; Domagalski, *Lost*, 3170–5; Stafford, *The Big "E"*, 235.

206 Jacobsen, "The Battle of Rennell Island."

207 Prados, *Islands of Destiny*, 225.

208 *Enterprise* Rennell Island Report, 2. The story behind this contact is not clear. The *Enterprise*'s report says:

> At [12:35 pm] January 30, 1943, search radar picked up a bogey bearing 230 degrees, distance 40 miles. Fighters were vectored out but in a forty mile (sic) chase to the NE, the bogey opened out on the VF. Estimated speed of bogey 200–220 knots. This bogey circled Task Force 18 and was tracked until [2:00 pm] when it faded from the screen.

> The issue here is that if the bogey was detected by the *Enterprise*'s radar 40 miles to the southwest, and the fighters pursued it 40 miles to the northeast, that would put it over the *Enterprise*. Based on the bogey ending the chase by circling the *Chicago* group, the report must mean the bogey was detected 40 miles southwest of the *Chicago*. What happened to this aircraft is unclear. It was not reported shot down, so why it would "fade" from radar is uncertain.

209 Morison, *Struggle*, 359.

210 Stafford, *The Big "E"*, 236.

211 Ibid., 236–7.

212 Ibid., 237.

213 Ibid., 239.

214 Tagaya and Styling, *Rikko Betty*, 1189.

215 Domagalski, "Rennell Island."

216 See, e.g., *Enterprise* Rennell Island Report, 4.

217 Domagalski, *Lost*, 3173.

218 Domagalski, "Rennell Island."

219 Stafford, *The Big "E"*, 239.

220 *Chicago* Damage Report, 4; ONI Narrative; Domagalski, *Lost*, 3182.

221 Morison, *Struggle*, 361.

222 Domagalski, *Lost*, 3211.

223 Ibid., 3211.

224 Ibid., 3192.

225 Frank, *Guadalcanal*, 580–1.

226 Chuck Witten, "The Battle of Rennell Island," *Destroyer History Foundation*, (www.destroyerhistory.org).

227 Action Report – *USS La Vallette* (for January 30, 1943), 4.

228 Witten, "Rennell Island"; *Tollberg* DANFS (Dictionary of American Naval Fighting Ships).

229 Frank, *Guadalcanal*, 581.

230 *Chicago* Damage Report, 1.

231 Ibid., 4; Domagalski, *Lost*, 3195.

232 Domagalski, *Lost*, 3233.

233 *Chicago* Rennell Island Damage Report, 1.

234 ONI Narrative.

235 Ibid.

236 Ibid.

237 Halsey, *Story*, 3142.

238 Wukovits, "Battle of Rennell Island," 3.

239 Frank, *Guadalcanal*, 581.

240 First Endorsement to Action Report – Task Force Eighteen, January 29–30, 1943 (March 10, 1942), 2–6.

241 Frank, *Guadalcanal*, 581.

242 Morison, *Struggle*, 349.

243 Frank, *Guadalcanal*, 574–5.

244 Morison, *Struggle*, 349; John Winton, *Ultra in the Pacific: How Breaking Japanese Codes & Ciphers Affected Naval Operations Against Japan* (London: Leo Cooper, 1993), 97.

245 Frank, *Guadalcanal*, 575.

246 Winton, *Ultra*, 97.

247 Morison, *Struggle*, 350.

248 *I-1* TROM; Prados, *Combined Fleet*, 400.

249 Prados, *Combined Fleet*, 400.

250 *Operational History of Japanese Naval Communications, December 1941–1945*, 85–6. Winton (*Ultra*, 102–4) was evidently misled by the word "comprised," which appears to be a typo, to conclude that *I-1* was carrying at least 200,000 code books. If the word "comprised" is replaced with "compromised," the figure of 200,000 code books makes much more sense.

251 Winton, *Ultra*, 98.

252 *I-1* TROM; *Operational History of Japanese Naval Communications, December 1941–1945*, 1. Technically, it was the 10th Section within the 4th Bureau of the Naval General Staff. The 4th Bureau was responsible for communications.

253 *I-1* TROM.

254 Ibid.

255 Ibid.

256 Winton, *Ultra*, 100–1.

257 *I-1* TROM.

258 Prados, *Islands of Destiny*, 224.

259 Ibid., 226.

260 Ibid., 222–3.

261 Ibid., 225–6.

Chapter 7

1 Buell, *Master of Seapower*, 265.

2 Ibid., 265–6.

3 Ibid., 265.

4 Ibid., 269.

5 Toland, *Rising Sun*, 9646.

6 Maurice Matloff and Edward M. Snell, *United States Army in World War II: The War Department, Volume III: Strategic Planning for Coalition Warfare 1941–1942* (Washington: Office of the Chief of Military History, Department of the Army, 1953), 31–2.

7 Morton, *First Two Years*, 382.

8 Ibid., 382.

9 Buell, *Master of Seapower*, 269.

10 Ibid., 271.

11 Ibid., 271–2.

12 Ibid., 271.

13 Matloff and Snell, *Strategic Planning*, 32–3.

14 Ibid., 33.

15 Buell, *Master of Seapower*, 272.

16 Ibid., 272–3.

17 Morton, *First Two Years*, 381.

18 Toland, *Rising Sun*, 9665.

19 Memorandum by the Combined Chiefs of Staff 155/1 "Conduct of the War in 1943" (January 19, 1943); "Foreign Relations of the United States, The Conferences at Washington, 1941–1942, and Casablanca, 1943 Document 408"; *Office of the Historian, United States Department of State* (https://history.state.gov/historicaldocuments/frus1941-43/d408).

20 Toland, *Rising Sun*, 9665.

21 Griffith, *Guadalcanal*, 267.

22 Hough, Ludwig, and Shaw, *Pearl Harbor to Guadalcanal*, 360.

23 Prados, *Islands of Destiny*, 220; Miller, *Guadalcanal*, 212.

24 Halsey, *Story*, 2986–3010.

25 Miller, *Guadalcanal*, 254. The commander of the 2nd Marine Division was Major General John Marston. Marston was senior in rank to Major General Patch, but since the US Army now provided most of the troops

on Guadalcanal, it was decided that a US Army general had to be in command. Marston remained in New Zealand so Patch and thus the US Army would have the command.

26 Miller, *Guadalcanal*, 253.

27 Frank, *Guadalcanal*, 550; Miller, *Guadalcanal*, Appendix B, 360–1.

28 Frank, *Guadalcanal*, 550.

29 Ibid., 552.

30 Morison, *Struggle*, 341.

31 Frank, *Guadalcanal*, 553.

32 Ibid., 553.

33 Miller, *Guadalcanal*, 286.

34 Frank, *Guadalcanal*, 553.

35 Miller, *Guadalcanal*, 273–4.

36 Ibid., 275–6.

37 Morison, *Struggle*, 341.

38 Mark E. Stille, *The Naval Battles for Guadalcanal 1942: Clash for Supremacy in the Pacific* (Oxford: Osprey, 2013), 84.

39 Miller, *Guadalcanal*, 303.

40 Ibid., 296.

41 Ibid., 303–4.

42 Foster Hailey, "Jap Dive-Bombing Attack" (excerpt from his book *Pacific Battle Line* (New York: MacMillan, 1944)), *USS DeHaven Sailors Association* (www.ussdehaven.org).

43 Hailey, "Jap Dive-Bombing Attack."

44 Ibid.

45 Letourneau and Letourneau, *Operation KE*, 196.

46 Ibid., 194.

47 Letourneau and Letourneau (*Operation KE*, 194) called the 47-to-3 odds "[D]esperate but not yet hopeless."

48 Letourneau and Letourneau, *KE*, 196.

49 Eric M. Bergerud, *Fire in the Sky: The Air War in the South Pacific* (Boulder, CO: Westview Press, 2000), 3484–88.

50 Letourneau and Letourneau, *KE*, 177.

51 Letourneau and Letourneau, *Operation KE*, 177.

52 Ibid., 179.

53 Frank, *Guadalcanal*, 583; Letourneau and Letourneau, *Operation KE*, 182.

54 Ibid., 181.

55 Hailey, "Jap Dive-Bombing Attack."

56 Ibid.

57 Ibid.

58 Letourneau and Letourneau, *Operation KE*, 181–2.

59 Hailey, "Jap Dive-Bombing Attack."

60 Ibid.

61 Frank, *Guadalcanal*, 585.

62 Ibid., 585.

63 Ibid., 585.

64 Ibid., 582.

65 Letourneau and Letourneau, *Operation KE*, 200.

66 Ibid., 200.

67 Ibid., 197.

68 Frank, *Guadalcanal*, 586; Letourneau and Letourneau, *Operation KE*, 197.

69 Letourneau and Letourneau, *Operation KE*, 184.

70 Ibid., 186.

71 W.R. Stevenson, "Three Bombs and Hell," *USS DeHaven Sailors Association* (www.ussdehaven.org).

72 Albert L. Breining, "Bye-Bye DD," *USS DeHaven Sailors Association* (www.ussdehaven.org).

73 Letourneau and Letourneau, *Operation KE*, 186; Stevenson, "Three Bombs and Hell."

74 Stevenson, "Three Bombs and Hell."

75 Letourneau and Letourneau, *Operation KE*, 186.

76 Leonard Elam, "Leonard Elam-469 Survivor," *USS DeHaven Sailors Association* (www.ussdehaven.org).

77 Letourneau and Letourneau, *Operation KE*, 186–8.

78   Ibid., 188.
79   Stevenson, "Three Bombs and Hell."
80   Breining, "Bye-Bye DD."
81   Ibid.
82   Letourneau and Letourneau, *Operation KE*, 183–4.
83   Ibid., 90.
84   Breining, "Bye-Bye DD."
85   Hailey, "Jap Dive-Bombing Attack."
86   Herr, "The Last Days of the USS DeHaven DD-469," *USS DeHaven Sailors Association* (www.ussdehaven.org); Hailey, "Jap Dive-Bombing Attack."
87   Herr, "The Last Days of the USS DeHaven DD-469."
88   Hailey, "Jap Dive-Bombing Attack."
89   Herr, "The Last Days of the USS DeHaven DD-469."
90   Letourneau and Letourneau, *Operation KE*, 198.
91   Ibid., 200; *Makinami* TROM.
92   Letourneau and Letourneau, *Operation KE*, 200–1.
93   Donald A. Davis, *Lightning Strike: The Secret Mission to Kill Admiral Yamamoto and Avenge Pearl Harbor* (New York: St. Martin's, 2005), Kindle edition, 144.
94   Letourneau and Letourneau, *Operation KE*, 202.
95   Ibid., 204.
96   Ibid., 207.
97   Letourneau and Letourneau, *Operation KE*, 208.
98   Bulkley, *At Close Quarters*, 103. Bulkley says the two boats "were ineffectually strafed and bombed by a large monoplane." But only the biplane F1M floatplanes were up that night.
99   Bulkley, *At Close Quarters*, 104; Kirkland, "The Tokyo Express," *PT King* (http://pt-king.gdinc.com); Letourneau and Letourneau, *Operation KE*, 209; Frank, *Guadalcanal*, 587.
100   Bulkley, *At Close Quarters*, 103–4; Letourneau and Letourneau, *Operation KE*, 209.
101   Bulkley, *At Close Quarters*, 104; Kirkland, "The Tokyo Express"; Letourneau and Letourneau, *Operation KE*, 209–10; Frank, *Guadalcanal*, 587.
102   Bulkley, *At Close Quarters*, 104–5; Kirkland, "The Tokyo Express"; Frank, *Guadalcanal*, 588; Letourneau and Letourneau, *Operation KE*, 210.
103   Letourneau and Letourneau, *Operation KE*, 207–8; *Makigumo* TROM, 104–5; Frank, *Guadalcanal*, 588.
104   Bulkley, *At Close Quarters*, 105.
105   Letourneau and Letourneau, *Operation KE*, 211–2.
106   *Makigumo* TROM.
107   Letourneau and Letourneau, *Operation KE*, 212.
108   Ibid., 212–3.
109   Ibid., 213–4.
110   Ibid., 213–4.
111   Ibid., 214–5.
112   Ibid., 216; Frank, *Guadalcanal*, 588.
113   Frank, *Guadalcanal*, 571.
114   Ibid., 571.
115   Ibid., 572.
116   Prados, *Islands of Destiny*, 228–9.
117   Frank, *Guadalcanal*, 591.
118   Letourneau and Letourneau, *Operation KE*, 229.
119   Ibid., 228–9.
120   Ibid., 230.
121   Ibid., 235–6; *Maikaze* TROM.
122   Letourneau and Letourneau, *Operation KE*, 236.
123   Ibid., 236–7.
124   Ibid., 240.
125   Ibid., 239; *Kuroshio* TROM.
126   Letourneau and Letourneau, *Operation KE*, 239.
127   Ibid., 239.

128 Frank (*Guadalcanal*, 591) has one Zero "failed to return," a second "force-landed," and three others were "damaged." Hammel (*Air War*, 4498–521) has 20 shot down, breaking it down as:

> VGS-11 F4F pilots down seven A6Ms and a VGS-11 TBF crew downs one A6M off New Georgia at 1530 hours; 347th Fighter Group P-39 pilots down two A6Ms near Kolombangara at 1610 hours; VF-72 F4F pilots down seven A6Ms off New Georgia at 1630 hours; and 347th Fighter Group P-40 pilots down three A6Ms near New Georgia at 1730 hours.

> Letourneau and Letourneau (*Operation KE*, 241), say "Acknowledged *Zuikaku* losses for the entire day's aerial combat totaled two Zeros shot down [...] Two more *Zuikaku* Zeros were damaged."

129 Letourneau and Letourneau, *Operation KE*, 241–2.
130 Ibid., 241.
131 Ibid., 241–2.
132 Ibid., 242–3.
133 Ibid., 242–3.
134 Ibid., 242–3.
135 Ibid., 245. Letourneau and Letourneau say that Admiral Hashimoto led the Reinforcement Unit south from Cape Esperance. This cannot be correct. The Black Cat PBY was monitoring Hashimoto's destroyers when they left Guadalcanal and would have reported such a move. Hashimoto's turn to the south to get outside The Slot had to be after the PBY had lost contact.
136 Prados, *Islands of Destiny*, 229.
137 Ibid., 229.
138 Morison, *Struggle*, 369–70.
139 Frank, *Guadalcanal*, 593.
140 Morison, *Guadalcanal*, 370.
141 Prados, *Islands of Destiny*, 230.
142 Frank, *Guadalcanal*, 521.
143 Ibid., 521, 746.
144 Ibid., 524.
145 Ibid., 525; Day, *New Georgia*, 318.
146 *Chihaya* and *Yamashimo Maru* TROMS.
147 Day, *New Georgia*, 358–76.
148 Ibid., 367.
149 Morison, *Struggle*, 322.
150 Hammel, *Air War*, 3860–90.
151 Morison, *Struggle*, 322.
152 Day, *New Georgia*, 381.
153 Ibid., 376.
154 Frank, *Guadalcanal*, 524–5; Ugaki, Goldstein, and Dillon, *Fading Victory*, 317.
155 Letourneau and Letourneau, *Operation KE*, 46–7.
156 Frank, *Guadalcanal*, 521.
157 Toland, *Rising Sun*, 9382.
158 Frank, *Guadalcanal*, 534.
159 Toland, *Rising Sun*, 9382.
160 Ibid., 9382.
161 Ibid., 9382.
162 Ibid., 9382.
163 Ibid., 9382–98.
164 Ibid., 9398.
165 Prados, *Islands of Destiny*, 209.
166 Ibid., 209.
167 Frank, *Guadalcanal*, 535.
168 Hara, *Japanese Destroyer Captain*, 161; Toland, *Rising Sun*, 13160; Bullard (trans.)/www.awm.gov.au, *Japanese Army Operations in the South Pacific Area: New Britain and Papua Campaigns, 1942–43* (Steven Bullard, trans.) (Canberra: Australian War Memorial, 2007), vi.
169 Toland, *Rising Sun*, 9393.

170 Frank, *Guadalcanal*, 535.
171 Except where otherwise specified, the account of the discussions between the Army General Staff and the War Ministry come from Toland, *Rising Sun*, 9399–432.
172 Frank, *Guadalcanal*, 536.
173 Ibid., 536-7.
174 The account of the Christmas Day negotiations and results comes from Toland, *Rising Sun*, 9457–87.
175 Prados, *Islands of Destiny*, 5.
176 Toland, *Rising Sun*, 9491.
177 Ibid., 9491.
178 Ibid., 9491.
179 Frank, *Guadalcanal*, 534–5.
180 Ibid., 536.
181 Ibid., 538.
182 Toland, *Rising Sun*, 9497.
183 Ibid., 9497.
184 Morison, *Struggle*, 317.
185 Frank, *Guadalcanal*, 539.
186 Prados, *Islands of Destiny*, 211.
187 Toland, *Rising Sun*, 9497.
188 Ugaki, Goldstein, and Dillon, *Fading Victory*, 319.
189 Prados, *Islands of Destiny*, 211–2.
190 Ibid., 211.
191 Ibid., 222.
192 Ibid., 222.
193 Miller, *Guadalcanal*, 338; Frank, *Guadalcanal*, 541.
194 Frank, *Guadalcanal*, 541.
195 Letourneau and Letourneau, *Operation KE*, 107.
196 Gordon L. Rottman, *Japanese Army in World War II: The South Pacific and New Guinea, 1942–43* (Oxford and New York: Osprey, 2005), 1382.
197 The account of Colonel Imoto's visit to Guadalcanal are an amalgamation of Griffith (*Guadalcanal*, 279–81); and Toland (*Rising Sun*, 9527–47).
198 Frank, *Guadalcanal*, 588.
199 Hiroyuki Agawa, *The Reluctant Admiral: Yamamoto and the Imperial Navy* (Tokyo; New York: Kodansha, 1979), 338.
200 Letourneau and Letourneau, *Operation KE*, 247; Frank, *Guadalcanal*, 590; Tagaya and Styling, *Rikko "Betty,"* 1214.
201 Letourneau and Letourneau, *Operation KE*, 247–8.
202 Frank, *Guadalcanal*, 590.
203 Toland, *Rising Sun*, 9587.
204 Frank, *Guadalcanal*, 594.
205 Letourneau and Letourneau, *Operation KE*, 248.
206 Ibid., 250.
207 Ibid., 250. The 17th was classified as a "light" photographic squadron, as opposed to a "heavy" photographic squadron.
208 Ibid., 250.
209 Ibid., 250–1; Hammel, *Air War*, 4521.
210 Letourneau and Letourneau, *Operation KE*, 251–2.
211 Ibid., 251.
212 Ibid., 254.
213 Frank, *Guadalcanal*, 594–5; Ikuhiko Hata, Yasuho Izawa, and Christopher Shores, *Japanese Naval Air Force Fighter Units and Their Aces* (London: Grub Street, 2011), 1194.
214 Letourneau and Letourneau, *Operation KE*, 252–3; *Hamakaze* TROM.
215 Jersey, *Hell's Islands*, 5470–2.
216 *Isokaze* and *Kawakaze* TROMs; Frank, *Guadalcanal*, 594. Letourneau and Letourneau (*Operation KE*, 253) say the *Isokaze* was hit by at least one bomb on the stern. Letourneau also insists the *Urakaze* was damaged by near misses, but the *Urakaze* TROM disagrees.

217 Letourneau and Letourneau, *Operation KE*, 254–5.

218 Frank, *Guadalcanal*, 595.

219 Letourneau and Letourneau, *Operation KE*, 256.

220 Frank, *Guadalcanal*, 595.

221 Jersey, *Hell's Islands*, 5521–522.

222 Frank, *Guadalcanal*, 595.

223 Prados, *Islands of Destiny*, 229.

Chapter 8

1 George, *Shots Fired*, 144–5.

2 Ibid., 146.

3 George (*Shots Fired*, 147) says that the 2nd Battalion was camped overlooking Beaufort Bay the night of February 8–9 and helplessly watching Japanese troops boarding a destroyer. The Army History (Miller, *Guadalcanal*, 345–6) has the 2nd Battalion leaving Marovovo the morning of February 8, which was northwest of Beaufort Bay.

4 George, *Shots Fired*, 147–8; Jersey, *Hell's Islands*, 5440.

5 Miller, *Guadalcanal*, 348.

6 Ibid., 348.

7 Halsey, *Story*, 3161.

8 Prados, *Islands of Destiny*, 231–2.

9 Ibid., 230.

10 Ibid., 231.

11 Dean, *MacArthur's Coalition*, 4291.

12 *Maikaze* and *Isokaze* TROMs.

13 General George C. Kenney, *General Kenney Reports: A Personal History of the Pacific War* (New York: Duell, Sloan and Pearce, 1949 [Reprint 1997]), 175–6; Gamble, *Fortress Rabaul*, 278.

14 Matthew K. Rodman, *War of Their Own* (Air University Press, 2005), 57.

15 Burton, John, *Fortnight of Infamy: The Collapse of Allied Airpower West of Pearl Harbor*. Annapolis: Naval Institute Press, 2006, 79.

16 Watson, Richard L., Jr. *The Fifth Air Force in the Huon Peninsula Campaign January to October 1943* (AAFRH-13). Washington: AAF Historical Offices, Headquarters, Army Air Forces, 1946, 84.

17 Rodman, *War of Their Own*, 28.

18 Ibid., 29.

19 Ibid., 29.

20 Ibid., 30.

21 Kenney, *Reports*, 143.

22 Lawrence J. Hickey, *Ken's Men Against the Empire: The Illustrated History of the 43rd Bombardment Group During World War II, Volume I: Prewar to October 1943 The B-17 Era* (Boulder, CO: International Historical Research Associates, 2016), 102; Lex McAulay, *The Battle of the Bismarck Sea 3 March 1943* (Maryborough, Qld: Banner Books, 2008), Kindle edition, 461; Gamble, *Fortress Rabaul*, 279.

23 Gamble, *Fortress Rabaul*, 279.

24 Ibid., 279.

25 Hickey, *Ken's Men*, 102, 104; Gamble, *Fortress Rabaul*, 280.

26 Martha Byrd, *Kenneth N. Walker: Airpower's Untempered Crusader* (Maxwell Air Force Base, AL: Air University Press, 1997), 113; "Whitehead, Ennis Clement (1895–1964)"; *Pacific War Online Encyclopedia* (http://pwencycl.kgbudge.com); Hickey, *Ken's Men*, 102, 104; Gamble, *Fortress Rabaul*, 280–1. Gamble says Major Lindbergh was flying the plane; Hickey says the plane was normally Captain Daniels' but on this day it was being piloted by Bleasdale. Both Hickey and Gamble list Bleasdale as a major, but casualty records list him as a lieutenant colonel.

27 Gamble, *Fortress Rabaul*, 279–80; Hickey, *Ken's Men*, 105–7.

28 W.F. Craven and J.L. Cate, (eds), *Army Air Forces in World War II*, Vol. IV: *The Pacific: Guadalcanal to Saipan August 1942 to July 1944* (Washington, DC: Office of Air Force History, 1983), 138.

29 *Keifuku* and *Kagu Maru* TROMs.

30 Gamble, *Fortress Rabaul*, 282.

31 Ibid., 282.

32 Hickey, *Ken's Men*, 105.

33   Ibid., 107.

34   Gamble, *Fortress Rabaul*, 284.

35   Kenney, *Reports*, 175–6.

36   McAulay, *Bismarck Sea*, 1544.

37   Hickey, *Ken's Men*, 109–10; Douglas Gillison, *Australia in the War of 1939–1945: Series Three (Air) Volume I – Royal Australian Air Force, 1939–1942* (Canberra: Australian War Memorial, 1962), 674.

38   Cressman, *Official Chronology*; Craven and Cate, *Army Air Forces*, 136; *Maikaze* and *Isokaze* TROMs.

39   Cressman, *Official Chronology*.

40   Multiple sources report that it was a Japanese seaplane that found and attacked the submarine. However, Cressman (*Official Chronology*) is very specific that the aircraft came from the 582 Air Group. The re-designated 2nd Air Group, the 582 was a mixed group of both Zero fighters and Aichi Type 99 (Val) carrier bombers. If the aircraft came from the 582, it was most likely a Type 99 carrier bomber and not a seaplane.

41   "The Loss of USS Argonaut (SS-166)," *On Eternal Patrol* (http://www.oneternalpatrol.com/uss-argonaut-166-loss.html).

42   Clay Blair, Jr., *Silent Victory: The US Submarine War Against Japan* (Annapolis: Naval Institute Press, 1975), 372. The loss of the *Argonaut* sparked controversy and questions as to why this boat, incapable of combat, had been vectored to intercept the heavily escorted, empty convoy as it headed back toward Rabaul.

43   Rear Admiral Richard H. O'Kane, USN (Ret.), *Wahoo: The Patrols of America's Most Famous WWII Submarine* (New York: Presidio, 1987), Kindle edition, 116.

44   Dean, *MacArthur's Coalition*, 4305.

45   Gillison, *Royal Australian Air Force*, 679–80.

46   Craven and Cate, Army Air Forces, 136.

47   McAulay, *Bismarck Sea*, 406; Craven and Cate, *Army Air Forces*, 137.

48   Samuel Eliot Morison, *History of United States Naval Operations in World War II, Vol VI: Breaking the Bismarcks Barrier 22 July 1942–1 May 1944* (Edison, NJ: Castle, 1950), 52.

49   Ibid., 55.

50   McAulay, *Bismarck Sea*, 942.

51   Ibid., 986–1008.

52   Phillip Bradley, *To Salamaua* (Cambridge: Cambridge University Press, 2010). Kindle edition, 356.

53   Hickey, *Ken's Men*, 133.

54   Hickey, *Ken's Men*, 133; McAulay, *Bismarck Sea*, 1087. The Japanese Army Air Force and Naval Air Force were organized in such fashions that were not directly analogous to Western air forces, or, in fact, to each other, and trying to present their activities, particularly those of the Army Air Force, in a readable fashion for the English-speaking reader can be a challenge. The Japanese Army Air Force tried to use terminology consistent with the land army, with only limited success. During the time period of the Java Sea Campaign, the basic unit was the *shotai* (flight or section) of three aircraft. Three or four shotai formed a *chutai* (squadron or company). Two or more chutai formed a *sentai*, usually translated as "air group" (the precise Japanese meaning is "combat group"), which was the basic operating unit of the Japanese Army Air Force. Two or more sentai formed a *hikodan* (wing, flying brigade, or flying battalion; hiko meaning "flying"), two or more hikodan would form a *hikoshudan* (flying corps) or, later, a *hikoshidan* (flying division), and two or more hikoshidan would form a *kokogun* (air force). The land-based elements of the Japanese Naval Air Force similarly used shotai and chutai, but multiple chutai comprised a *kokutai*, (sometimes shortened to "*ku*"), which is usually translated as "air group" or "air corps." Multiple kokutai would form an air flotilla. The kokutai was the basic unit of the land-based elements of the Japanese Naval Air Force. As such, their closest analogue in the Japanese Army Air Force was the sentai, but the navy kokutai were actually somewhat larger than the army sentai. To avoid overwhelming the reader with Japanese terminology, the term "air group" will be used for both the army sentai and the navy kokutai, with the caveat that they are not quite the same unit. Christopher Shores, Brian Cull, and Yasuho Izawa, *Bloody Shambles, Vol. 2: From the Defence of Sumatra to the fall of Burma* (London: Grub Street, 1993), 11–12; Mark Kaiser, "Unit Structure of IJA Air Force," *Japanese Aviation*, (www.markkaiser.com/japaneseaviation/jaafstructure.html). At the start of the Pacific War, the Japanese Naval Air Force's kokutai often operated using the name of their home base. Thus, the home base of the Takao Air Group was at Takao, on Formosa, and the home base of the Tainan Air Group was at Tainan, also on Formosa. However, starting on October 1, 1942 and finishing on November 1, 1942, the Japanese Naval Air Force's kokutai designations were changed completely into a numeric code. There is a long-standing disagreement as to how that redesignation of the Japanese Naval Air Force units should be translated. It is instinct among Westerners, to use the example here of the 751 (the former Kanoya) Air Group, to reference it as the "751st Air Group." However, to consider

these designations as ordinals appears to be inaccurate inasmuch as each digit in the new designation referred to a particular characteristic of the unit. To use the "751" example again, the "7" meant a land attack plane unit, the "5" meant its home base was in the Sasebo Naval District, and the "1" meant the unit was formerly a named unit. Since the Kanoya had been a mixed air group, the fighter component was spun off on November 1, 1942 as part of the 253 Air Group, the "2" denoting "single-engine carrier fighter" unit, the "5" again the Sasebo district, and the "3" again formerly a named unit (Mark Peattie, *Sunburst: The Rise of Japanese Naval Air Power, 1909–1941* (Annapolis: Naval Institute Press, 2013), 256). In short, the new numeric designation was not an ordinal but a code.

55 McAulay, *Bismarck Sea*, 964.

56 Morison, *Bismarcks Barrier*, 55–6; McAulay, *Bismarck Sea*, 1054.

57 McAulay, *Bismarck Sea*, 1028. The figure normally given for troops carried on the transports is 5,954, but McAulay explains that the *Kembu Maru*, ostensibly carrying only fuel, actually had 50 men on board from the 51st Division and 221st Airfield Battalion, which brings the traditionally held total up from 5,954 to 6,004. McAulay also brings up the possibility of other troops from assorted units being transported on the *Kembu Maru* as well, but any such passengers were never reported and their numbers are unknown.

58 Morison, *Bismarcks Barrier*, 56; Gamble, *Fortress Rabaul*, 303; Nevitt, "Battle of the Bismarck Sea," *Imperial Japanese Navy Page* (www.combinedfleet.com). The Imperial Navy ship *Nojima* involved in Operation *81* is often confused with the 7,190-ton *Nojima Maru*. The mistake is understandable inasmuch as the vast majority of Japanese transport and cargo ships are *Marus* and all of the other transports in Operation *81* were *Marus* as well. And both were Imperial Navy transports. Nevertheless, the *Nojima* and the *Nojima Maru* were separate ships. The *Nojima* was a member of the two-ship *Murota* class dating back to 1917, and, like the *Murota*, was originally a collier. (*Nojima* TROM; "Kyuryokan: Stories of the IJN's Supply and Special Service Ships," *Imperial Japanese Navy Page* (www.combinedfleet.com)). The *Nojima Maru* was launched in 1934 and had an eight-year career, but was beached a total loss before Operation *81*. The *Nojima Maru* was heavily damaged in a bombing raid in Kiska Harbor on September 16, 1942 and rendered unnavigable. She was towed from Kiska Harbor and beached on the anchoring shoal to Trout Lagoon to prevent her sinking, but was deemed a total loss and abandoned. (*Nojima Maru* TROM). It should also be noted that there were at least two *Teiyo Marus*. The *Teiyo Maru* involved in Operation *81* was the former German steamship *Saarland*. The other *Teiyo Maru* was a tanker.

59 McAulay, *Bismarck Sea*, 1114.

60 Ibid., 1028.

61 Morison, *Bismarcks Barrier*, 55.

62 McAulay, *Bismarck Sea*, 1147–69; Gamble, *Fortress Rabaul*, 303–4. As Gamble explains:

Kyokusei Maru, a merchant ship originally built in Canada in 1920, was by no means large, yet an estimated 1,200 soldiers were crammed aboard. The 5,943-ton vessel, which had been used at least once to transport POWs from Sumatra to Burma, had been modified to carry humans by fitting the box-shaped cargo holds with multiple levels of wooden decks, each containing row upon row of narrow sleeping platforms.

The other transports in Operation *81* were no different. As early as 1905, the Japanese had adapted a method called the *tsubo* system for calculating the minimum amount of space an individual needed aboard a transport ship. By 1941, the original meager allowance had been cut by a third. Packed into the troopships like sardines, soldiers were expected to withstand days or even weeks of excessive heat and unsanitary conditions without complaining. They called it *chomansai*, "extreme overload," and shrugged it off as part of military life.

63 Prados, *Islands of Destiny*, 252.

64 McAulay, *Bismarck Sea*, 1087–114.

65 Ibid., 1008.

66 Ibid., 1147.

67 Ibid., 1114; *Kyokusei Maru* TROM.

68 McAulay, *Bismarck Sea*, 1114; *Kyokusei Maru* TROM.

69 Kenney, *Reports*, 202; Hammel, *Air War*, 4773.

70 McAulay, *Bismarck Sea*, 1263.

71 Hickey, *Ken's Men*, 133.

72 McAulay, *Bismarck Sea*, 1240.

73 Ibid., 1263, 3588.

74 Ibid., 1263.

75 Ibid., 1285.

76 Bradley, *To Salamaua*, 460.

77 The Port Moresby Airfield Complex contained seven airfields (or "airdromes") which, though they had proper names, Americans referenced by what they thought was the airfield's distance from Port Moresby. In addition to Jackson Field/7-Mile (which later became Port Moresby's international airport), there was Kila (3-Mile Drome), Wards (5-Mile), Berry (12-Mile), Schwimmer (14-Mile), Durand (17-Mile), and Rogers (30-Mile).

78 James T. Murphy and A.B. Feuer, *Skip Bombing* (Praeger Publishing, Westport, NY, 1993), 107.

79 McAulay, *Bismarck Sea*, 1285; Hickey, *Ken's Men*, 133.

80 Maj. H.T. Hastings and George L. Moorad, "No Survivors," *Saturday Evening Post*, May 22, 1943, 18.

81 Murphy and Feuer, *Skip Bombing*, 107; Gene Salecker, *Fortress Against the Sun: The B-17 Flying Fortress in the Pacific* (Conshocken, PA: Combined Publishing, 2001), 5560–69; McAulay, *Bismarck Sea*, 1285; Hastings and Moorad, "No Survivors," 18.

82 Gillison, *Royal Australian Air Force*, 691; McAulay, *Bismarck Sea*, 1285; Phil H. Listemann, *The Douglas Boston & Havoc: the Australians. (Squadrons No. 22)* (Philedition, 2017), Kindle edition, 185.

83 Adjusted from Japan Standard Time to local time. Salecker, *Fortress*, 5564–69; Hata, Izawa, and Shores, *Japanese Naval Air Force*, 1226.

84 McAulay, *Bismarck Sea*, 1285; Kenney, *Reports*, 202. There seem to be two schools of thought on when the 320th Squadron B-24 Liberator found the Japanese convoy and in so doing kicked off the day's events. One expressed by Kenney, McAulay, and others is that the Liberator found the convoy at 8:15 am and radioed it in as seven warships and seven merchantmen at 05.05 degrees South, 148.30 degrees East. The other, expressed by Watson (*Fifth Air Force*, 88; Craven and Cate, *Army Air Forces*, 143), is that the Liberator found the convoy "midmorning." The Watson version, as expressed by Gillison (*Royal Australian Air Force*, 691), holds "[S]earching Liberator crews were flying through poor weather until, about 10 am, one crew again found the convoy, reporting it to consist of a light cruiser, five destroyers and eight transports (the "cruiser" proving to be a large destroyer)." Gillison continues, "A formation of 8 Flying Fortresses, followed an hour later by a second of 20, took off to attack." Obviously, the two schools are completely incompatible as far as timeline is concerned. The version here is the Kenney version, as the Watson version is vague on times, and when a time is mentioned ("shortly before 1000 [the eight B-17s] carried out their attack from 6,500 feet against a convoy which they reported as containing a light cruiser, five destroyers and eight merchant vessels," Watson, *Fifth Air Force*, 88) it is not consistent with discovering the convoy at "midmorning" or 10:00 am. The Watson version appears to be a conflation of the B-24's arrival and the B-17s' attack and contact report.

85 Martin Caidin, *Fork-Tailed Devil: The P38* (Dering Harbor, NY: iBooks, 2011), 3714; McAulay, *Bismarck Sea*, 1285.

86 Caidin, *Fork-Tailed Devil*, 3714.

87 McAulay, *Bismarck Sea*, 1285–1305. McAulay says that 18th Army records confirm that three Imperial Navy planes were shot down during the day, but does not specify when. Captain King (Caidin, *Fork-Tailed Devil*, 3714) remembered only two. Stanaway (*P-38*, 611) says Japanese records confirm only two.

88 John Stanaway, *P-38 Lightning Aces of the Pacific and CBI* (Oxford: Osprey, 1997), Kindle edition, 611–23.

89 McAulay, *Bismarck Sea*, 1305; Salecker, *Fortress*, 5569–77.

90 Hickey, *Ken's Men*, 134; Salecker, *Fortress*, 5569; McAulay, *Bismarck Sea*, 1305.

91 Salecker, *Fortress*, 5569–77; McAulay, *Bismarck Sea*, 1305.

92 Hickey, *Ken's Men*, 134.

93 McAulay, *Bismarck Sea*, 1305–28; Watson, *Fifth Air Force*, 88–9; 63rd Bombardment Squadron (H), 43rd Bombardment Group (H), Office of the Intelligence Officer, "Narrative Report and Sketches of Attacks on Lae Convoy, March 2, 1943."

94 McAulay, *Bismarck Sea*, 1305; Salecker, *Fortress*, 5569–77.

95 McAulay, *Bismarck Sea*, 1328–51; Bradley, *To Salamaua*, 339; *Kyokusei Maru* TROM.

96 Hickey, *Ken's Men*, 134–5.

97 McAulay, *Bismarck Sea*, 1328–51

98 Murphy and Feuer, *Skip Bombing*, 109–10; Salecker, *Fortress*, 5581–85.

99 Salecker, *Fortress*, 5585–6; McAulay, *Bismarck Sea*, 1351.

100 McAulay, *Bismarck Sea*, 1351.

101 Ibid., 1351.

102 McAulay, *Bismarck Sea*, 1351–78; Salecker, *Fortress*, 5586–91.

103 Watson, *Fifth Air Force*, 88–9.

104 McAulay, *Bismarck Sea*, 1376.

105 Salecker, *Fortress*, 5591–2.

106 McAulay, *Bismarck Sea*, 1398.

107 Salecker, *Fortress*, 5593–95.

108 McAulay, *Bismarck Sea*, 1420; Gilbert, *Bismarck Sea*, 36–7.

109 Hata, Izawa, and Shores, *Japanese Naval Air Force*, 1226.

110 Watson, *Fifth Air Force*, 89; Craven and Cate, *Army Air Force*, 143; McAulay, *Bismarck Sea*, 1420.

111 Watson, *Fifth Air Force*, 88–9; Craven and Cate, *Army Air Force*, 143.

112 Craven and Cate, *Army Air Force*, 143.

113 McAulay, *Bismarck Sea*, 1328–51.

114 Ibid., 1328. The *Kyokusei Maru* gives the time of her sinking as 11:26.

115 McAulay, *Bismarck Sea*, 1444; *Kyokusei Maru* TROM.

116 Kane Yoshihara and Doris Heath (trans.), *Southern Cross* (Canberra: Australia-Japan Research Project, Australian War Memorial, 1955).

117 McAulay, *Bismarck Sea*, 1444.

118 Ibid., 1420.

119 Craven and Cate, *Army Air Force*, 143.

120 Gillison, *Royal Australian Air Force*, 696; McAulay, *Bismarck Sea*, 1493–516.

121 Craven and Cate, *Army Air Force*, 143.

122 McAulay, *Bismarck Sea*, 1444.

123 The numbers of B-17s involved in this attack are disputed. The "typical" figure given is 11, based on Watson (who authored the Craven and Cate account), *Fifth Air Force*, 90; (see, e.g., Craven and Cate, *Army Air Forces*, 143). That figure is used by, among others, Gillison (*Royal Australian Air Force*, 691) and Bradley (*To Salamaua*, 481–95). But no breakdown of this figure is given. Gamble (*Fortress*, 305) says 18 Fortresses from the 64th and 65th attacked, damaging the *Teiyo Maru*, but does not discuss the second morning attack, suggesting he conflated that attack with the late afternoon attack that did damage the *Teiyo Maru*. Salecker (*Fortress*, 5599–600) identifies the aircraft as five from the 64th and three from the 403rd. Hickey (*Ken's Men*, 135) just says, "The 43rd dispatched nine more aircraft" but gives no breakdown. He adds that at 6:20 pm, the formation "dispersed into three elements of three. The smaller elements again claimed hits or near misses." It's not clear which of the three elements of three would be smaller. McAulay (*Bismarck Sea*, 1444) is the most specific of the historians, saying the attack was by nine B-17s of the 64th and 403rd Squadrons and identifying all the pilots: "Major McCullar, Captains Giddings and Holsey, and Lieutenants Humrichouse, Schultz and McMullen of the 64th and from the 403rd Captains Smith and Brecht, with Lieutenant Gowdy." McAulay is also the only historian who references the solo attack by the B-17 from the 403rd, and he does not identify the pilot.

124 McAulay, *Bismarck Sea*, 1444–68; Watson, *Fifth Air Force*, 90; Craven and Cate, *Army Air Forces*, 143.

125 The narrative of Captain Holsey's B-17 comes from Murphy and Feuer, *Skip Bombing*, 113–4; Hickey, *Ken's Men*, 135–6; Salecker, *Fortress*, 5602–8; McAulay, *Bismarck Sea*, 1444–68; Hastings and Moorad, "No Survivors," 89; and "B-17E 'Frank Buck' Serial Number 41-2659," *Pacific Wrecks*, (https://www.pacificwrecks.com/aircraft/b-17/41-2659.html).

126 McAulay, *Bismarck Sea*, 1468.

127 Ibid., 1468; Hickey, *Ken's Men*, 137.

128 Unless specified otherwise, the story of the 11 Squadron RAAF Catalina comes from McAulay, *Bismarck Sea*, 1516–82.

129 Squadron Leader Coventry seems to have been very inexperienced. McAulay (*Bismarck Sea*, 1520–40) related a story Flight Lieutenant Duigan had told him:

It does not seem as if Coventry had flown to Milne Bay before; Duigan recalled a joke played on new arrivals. When approaching Milne Bay from the south, the mountains appear as a continuous line, but just west of the head of the bay, at Mullins Harbour the coast makes a little "zig-zag," allowing low-level entry into the anchorage. The usual thick weather disguised this short cut, but the old hands knew it, and used it to watch the effect on new co-pilots. With solid cloud down to 400 feet, to the uninitiated, the coast seemed to be a wall of mountains.

At the correct moment, Duigan turned the big "Cat" and flew at the coast. To Coventry, it seemed they were flying straight into the hillside. "As we approached eternity," recalled Duigan, "from the corner of my eye I could see white knuckles gripping his wheel, perhaps contemplating a Caine Mutiny. Then we slid through a saddle and popped into the clear, floats down, throttles back, and alighted, to drop off the step just short of our mooring buoy."

130 It was only after this mission, when they reported the almost instantaneous ignition of the flare, that it was presumed defective aerial flares caused the loss of three other Catalinas which had signaled to base "on fire!" but were not heard of again (McAulay, *Bismarck Sea*, 1560). The Americans had also had problems with premature ignition of flares. It should be remembered that immediately before the Battle of Cape Esperance off Guadalcanal in October 1942, a premature ignition of a flare caused an American cruiser floatplane to crash and burn on the water.

131 Salecker, *Fortress*, 5609–11.

132 McAulay, *Bismarck Sea*, 1582.

133 Watson (*Fifth Air Force*, 90) and Craven and Cate (*Army Air Forces*, 143) have Lieutenant Trigg taking over for Flight Lieutenant Duigan at 5:45 am. The Australian histories are clear and specific in that Duigan left at 2:40 am for the purposes of avoiding potential daylight combat.

134 Prados, *Islands of Destiny*, 253.

135 Yoshihara and Heath, *Southern Cross*.

136 The arrangement of the convoy is from McAulay (*Bismarck Sea*, 1821), but he posits a significant caveat:

> The following diagram of the convoy formation at 10 a.m. 3 March 1943 is compiled from captured Japanese documents, prisoner interrogations from Allied sources and Japanese reports after the battle. None agrees entirely with any other, but a * after the name of a ship indicates its position has been given as such by two or more sources. For example, DD Uranami* shows that the ship is referred to in at least two documents as being in the right flank leading position.

The only ship in the diagram that does not have an asterisk is the *Kembu Maru*.

137 Adjusted from Japan Standard Time to local time. Hata, Izawa, and Shores, *Japanese Naval Air Force*, 1246; Gamble, *Fortress Rabaul*, 308; Hata, Shores, and Izawa say "18 of the *Zuiho* aircraft from Kavieng arrived at 0805" [9:05 local time]. Gamble says that the *Zuiho*'s Zeros had staged into Kavieng the previous day. McAulay (*Bismarck Sea*, 1846) says the *Zuiho*'s fighters were based at Lae. It makes no sense for fighters based in Kavieng to fly down to escort a convoy near Lae, which has its own airfields. The bigger issue with the *Zuiho*'s fighters basing at Lae is that Lae was attacked by Australian A-20 Bostons and US B-25 Mitchells the morning of March 3, after which Allied fighters patrolled over Lae that morning to keep the Japanese fighters down. The *Zuiho*'s fighters could not have taken off on March 3 if they had been based at Lae. What may have happened here is the *Zuiho*'s fighters took off from Kavieng, patrolled over the convoy, then landed at Lae. In too many instances fighters were coming from Rabaul to cover the convoy in, say, the Vitiaz Strait. It makes no sense, unless they were switching between Rabaul and Lae with each patrol. And even then it's highly questionable.

138 Yoshihara and Heath, *Southern Cross*.

139 McAulay, *Bismarck Sea*, 1798.

140 Except where specified otherwise, the account of events on the *Oigawa Maru* comes from McAulay, *Bismarck Sea*, 1846. And before you ask, McAulay calls it "a scene … one could imagine included in a wartime Hollywood film, but one which actually happened." Such scenes occur more often than one might think. In this case, two witnesses in Privates Machida and Yamada have attested to it.

141 Unless you were Colonel Tsuji.

142 McAulay, *Bismarck Sea*, 1054, 1846.

143 Yoshihara and Heath, *Southern Cross*.

144 McAulay, *Bismarck Sea*, 1868.

145 Major Timothy D. Gann, *Fifth Air Force Light and Medium Bomber Operations During 1942 and 1943: Building Doctrine and Forces that Triumphed in the World War II Battle of the Bismarck Sea and the Wewak Raid* (Maxwell AFB, AL: Air University, 1992), 19–20.

146 *Magic* was mainly a secret of naval intelligence, which caused some friction with their counterparts in the Army. The Navy radio intelligence chief in Melbourne, Lieutenant Commander Rudolph Fabian, had a policy of relating the information in the *Magic* decrypts but not letting anyone see the actual decrypted messages except the top commander, General MacArthur. It was a policy that brought clashes with MacArthur's incompetent intelligence officer, General Willoughby. On one occasion, when Willoughby demanded to see a dispatch, Fabian carried a copy to Willoughby's office, took out his cigarette lighter, and burned it in front of the enraged general. Prados, *Islands of Destiny*, 239.

147 Gann, *Fifth Air Force*, 19–20.

148 Prados, *Islands of Destiny*, 251.

149 Kenney, *Reports*, 198.

150 Ibid., 197–8.

151 Major Benn had gone out on January 18 to scout out possible locations for a new airfield near Bona. He issued no reports after takeoff and did not return. A search mission on January 20 failed to find any sign of Benn, his crew, or his aircraft. The crash site was finally located in August 1956 by a Patrol Officer from Tapini. Two bodies were recovered from the site. It was concluded that the pilot flew blind into a valley and crashed into the mountains.

In January 1956, a Royal Australian Air Force team visited the site and examined the wreckage, which was in the upper Bubu Valley near Mount Strong. They found bullet holes in the aircraft. They also found the starboard engine controls were set to "full rich" mixture and the propeller for the port engine had been "feathered" – the blades turned parallel to the airflow to reduce drag. They concluded the Japanese had fired at Benn's plane, disabling the port engine, without which the B-25 may not have been able to exit the valley. In short, Benn's B-25 was shot down. Six sets of remains were recovered, of which ultimately five were identified through their dog tags. "B-25C 'Algernon IV' Serial Number 41-12485," *Pacific Wrecks* (www.pacificwrecks.com).

152 Watson, *Fifth Air Force*, 36.

153 Rodman, *War of Their Own*, 60.

154 Gann, *Fifth Air Force*, 15.

155 General George C. Kenney, *The Saga of Pappy Gunn* (Sapere Books, 2017), Kindle edition, 39.

156 Ibid., 41.

157 Ibid., 41.

158 Ibid., 43.

159 Ibid., 45.

160 Ibid., 46.

161 Ibid., 47.

162 Rodman, *War of Their Own*, 59.

163 Ibid., 59.

164 Kenney, *Reports*, 168–9, 173; Gamble, *Fortress Rabaul*, 300–1.

165 Gamble, *Fortress Rabaul*, 300.

166 Watson, *Fifth Air Force*, 84; McAulay, *Bismarck Sea*, 690.

167 Kenney, *Reports*, 201.

168 Gamble, *Fortress Rabaul*, 300–1.

169 McAulay, *Bismarck Sea*, 711.

170 Kenney, *Reports*, 199.

171 McAulay, *Bismarck Sea*, 1252.

172 Kenney, *Reports*, 201.

173 Nathaniel Gunn, *Pappy Gunn* (Bloomington, IN: AuthorHouse, 2004), 235.

174 Ibid., 235.

175 Rodman, *War of Their Own*, 64.

176 Gann, *Fifth Air Force*, 23

177 Rodman, *War of Their Own*, 64; Gillison, *Royal Australian Air Force*, 692; William Wolf, *The 5th Fighter Command in World War II: Vol.1: Pearl Harbor to the Reduction of Rabaul* (Atglen, PA: Schiffer, 2011), 248, 253.

178 Rodman, *War of Their Own*, 65–6.

179 McAulay, *Bismarck Sea*, 1680.

180 Ibid., 1680.

181 Ibid., 1723.

182 McAulay, *Bismarck Sea*, 1767–89; Wolf, *5th Fighter Command*, 248; Gillison, *Royal Australian Air Force*, 692.

183 Caidin, *Fork-Tailed Devil*, 3727.

184 Ibid., 3727–35.

185 Murphy and Feuer, *Skip Bombing*, 114–5.

186 McAulay, *Bismarck Sea*, 1789.

187 Ibid., 1835. From this point forward in the timeline, there is little agreement among sources over who attacked what and when. Even official sources, (i.e. Craven and Cate, *Army Air Forces*; and Gillison, *Royal Australian Air Force*) tend to be very general in describing the attack. Basically the bible of the Battle of the Bismarck Sea is McAulay's appropriately titled *Battle of the Bismarck Sea*, in which he presents a detailed reconstruction of the

battle, including who attacked what and when, a result of what must have been painstaking research and organization. The version of events presented here will largely track with McAulay, with supporting details provided by Bradley, *To Salamaua*; Hata, Izawa, and Shores, *Japanese Naval Air Force*, Gamble, *Fortress Rabaul*; Rodman, *A War of Their Own*; Hickey, *Ken's Men*; Murphy and Feuer, *Skip Bombing*; and Wolf, *5th Fighter Command*.

188 McAulay, *Bismarck Sea*, 1857.
189 Hata, Izawa, and Shores, *Japanese Naval Air Force*, 1244.
190 Ibid., 1244.
191 Ibid., 1244.
192 Hickey, *Ken's Men*, 139–40.
193 Hata, Izawa, and Shores, *Japanese Naval Air Force*, 1244; Hickey, *Ken's Men*, 139–40; Salecker, *Fortress*, 5640–45; Gamble, *Fortress Rabaul*, 309.
194 McAulay, *Bismarck Sea*, 1883.
195 Ibid., 1883.
196 Jim Turner, "March 3, 1943 The Battle Of The Bismarck Sea," *Beaufighter – 30 Squadron RAAF* (http://www.beaufighter30squadronraaf.com.au).
197 McAulay, *Bismarck Sea*, 1922.
198 Gillison, *Royal Australian Air Force*, 693.
199 McAulay, *Bismarck Sea*, 1944.
200 Gamble, *Fortress Rabaul*, 306.
201 Ibid., 306; Bradley, *To Salamaua*, 578.
202 Gamble, *Fortress Rabaul*, 306; Bradley, *To Salamaua*, 578, 596, 608; *Shirayuki* TROM.
203 Rodman, *War of Their Own*, 67.
204 Ibid., 68.
205 McAulay, *Bismarck Sea*, 1987.
206 Ibid., 1987–2012.
207 Ibid., 2033.
208 McAulay, *Bismarck Sea*, 793. McAulay says, "The RAAF supplied men to almost every US bomber and transport unit, from early 1942 to mid-1943. Their contribution to the war effort has been largely ignored in official histories and publications." It is mentioned here specifically to call attention to that contribution and to express this author's appreciation and thanks for that contribution.
209 McAulay, *Bismarck Sea*, 2033.
210 Ibid., 2033; Bradley, *To Salamaua*, 653; *Teiyo Maru* TROM.
211 Haruko Taya Cook and Theodore F. Cook, *Japan at War: An Oral History* (New York: The New Press, 1992), 301.
212 McAulay, *Bismarck Sea*, 2125.
213 Cook and Cook, *Japan at War*, 301.
214 McAulay, *Bismarck Sea*, 2168.
215 Ibid., 2192.
216 Ibid., 2192.
217 Ibid., 2012, 2261; Bradley, *To Salamaua*, 633–53.
218 McAulay, *Bismarck Sea*, 2268.
219 Bradley, *To Salamaua*, 633.
220 McAulay, *Bismarck Sea*, 2007, 2425–46, 2466.
221 Ibid., 2413.
222 Ibid., 2146.
223 Except where specified otherwise, the account of General Yoshihara's experience on the *Tokitsukaze* comes from Yoshihara and Heath, *Southern Cross*.
224 *Tokitsukaze* TROM; McAulay, *Bismarck Sea*, 2092, 2282.
225 McAulay, *Bismarck Sea*, 2758.
226 Cook and Cook, *Japan at War*, 301.
227 Rodman, *War of Their Own*, 69.
228 Gamble, *Fortress Rabaul*, 310.
229 McAulay, *Bismarck Sea*, 2872.
230 Hickey, *Ken's Men*, 140.
231 Murphy, *Skip Bombing*, 116–7.
232 Ibid., 116–7.

233 McAulay, *Bismarck Sea*, 2912–39.

234 Ibid., 2960.

235 Ibid., 2960.

236 Ibid., 2978.

237 Hickey, *Ken's Men*, 140–3.

238 Ibid., 143.

239 *Asashio* TROM.

240 McAulay, *Bismarck Sea*, 3031; Hickey, *Ken's Men*, 145; *Asashio* TROM.

241 McAulay, *Bismarck Sea*, 3031; Hickey, *Ken's Men*, 145.

242 McAulay, *Bismarck Sea*, 3031; Hickey, *Ken's Men*, 145.

243 Bradley, *To Salamaua*, 675.

244 McAulay, *Bismarck Sea*, 3031–55.

245 *Asashio* TROM; McAulay, *Bismarck Sea*, 3055.

246 McAulay, *Bismarck Sea*, 3081.

247 Cook and Cook, *Japan at War*, 302.

248 Gamble, *Fortress Rabaul*, 313.

249 Ibid., 311–2.

250 McAulay, *Bismarck Sea*, 3098–3121.

251 Ibid., 3341.

252 Gunn, *Pappy Gunn*, 237.

253 McAulay, *Bismarck Sea*, 3333–55.

254 Cook and Cook, *Japan at War*, 302.

255 *Tokitsukaze* TROM.

256 Hickey, *Ken's Men*, 147.

257 *Tokitsukaze* TROM; Hickey, *Ken's Men*, 147.

258 *Tokitsukaze* TROM; McAulay, *Bismarck Sea*, 3459.

259 *Tokitsukaze* TROM.

260 David Dexter, *The New Guinea Offensives. Australia in the War of 1939–1945. Series 1 – Army. Volume 6* (Canberra: Australian War Memorial, 1961), 10–11.

261 Gunn, *Pappy Gunn*, 237.

262 Kenney, *Reports*, 205–6.

263 Prados, *Islands of Destiny*, 255.

264 Gamble, *Fortress Rabaul*, 316.

265 Bradley, *To Salamaua*, 758.

Epilogue

1 Sherrod, *History*, 134–5; Tillman, *Fighter Squadrons*, 40.

2 Gerald Astor, *Semper Fi in the Sky: The Marine Air Battles of World War II* (New York: Presidio, 2007), 2578.

3 Barrett Tillman, *Corsair: The F4U in World War II and Korea* (Annapolis: Naval Institute Press, 1979), Kindle edition, 580; Louis B. Dorny, *US Navy PBY Catalina Units of the Pacific War* (Oxford: Osprey, 2013), 1712; Morison, *Struggle*, 332–3.

4 Day, *New Georgia*, 1098.

5 Ibid., 1098–115; Sherrod, *History*, 134–5.

6 *Hitachi Maru* TROM. *Hitachi* is sometimes rendered as *Hitati*.

7 Day, *New Georgia*, 1098–1115; Hata, Izawa, and Shores, *Japanese Naval Air Force*, 1263.

8 Tillman, *Fighter Squadrons*, 40; Day, *New Georgia*, 1098–1115; Hata, Izawa, and Shores, *Japanese Naval Air Force*, 1263.

9 Tillman, *Fighter Squadrons*, 40; Day, *New Georgia*, 1098–1115; Hata, Izawa, and Shores, *Japanese Naval Air Force*, 1263. Day says the *Hitachi Maru* was hit by four bombs from high altitude. The *Hitachi Maru* TROM says only two hits.

10 Sherrod, *History*, 135.

11 Tillman, *Corsair*, 601.

12 Ibid., 601; Day, *New Georgia*, 1115.

13 Hammel, *Air War*, 4618–38.

14   William Wolf, *13th Fighter Command in World War II: Air Combat Over Guadalcanal and the Solomons* (Atglen, PA: Schiffer, 2004), 100–1.

15   Morison, *Bismarcks Barrier*, 89.

16   Wolf, *13th Fighter Command*, 119; Eric Hammel, *Coral and Blood* (Pacifica, CA: Pacifica Military History, 2009). Kindle edition, 1749.

17   Letourneau and Letourneau, *Operation KE*, 61.

18   Ibid., 61–2.

19   Day, *New Georgia*, 384; Letourneau and Letourneau, *Operation KE*, 62–3.

20   Day, *New Georgia*, 384.

21   Prados, *Islands of Destiny*, 219.

22   "Ainsworth, Walden Lee (1886–1960)," *Pacific War Online Encyclopedia* (http://www.pwencycl.kgbudge.com.

23   Day, *New Georgia*, 478; Letourneau and Letourneau, *Operation KE*, 78.

24   Letourneau and Letourneau, *Operation KE*, 78.

25   Ibid., 80. The records of the 956 Air Group for January 1943 are not available.

26   Ibid., 80.

27   Day, *New Georgia*, 396.

28   Ibid., 396.

29   Ibid., 396.

30   Letourneau and Letourneau, *Operation KE*, 91; *Mochizuki* TROM; "*Seia Maru*-Class Auxiliary Transport," *Imperial Japanese Navy Page* (www.combinedfleet.com).

31   Letourneau and Letourneau, *Operation KE*, 91; *Yamashimo Maru*, TROM.

32   Letourneau and Letourneau, *Operation KE*, 91.

33   Ibid., 91–2; Morison, *Struggle*, 345.

34   Morison, *Struggle*, 345; Letourneau and Letourneau, *Operation KE*, 92–3.

35   *Toa Maru No. 2 Go* TROM; Letourneau and Letourneau, *Operation KE*, 93.

36   Letourneau and Letourneau, *Operation KE*, 92–4.

37   Ibid., 95–6.

38   Ibid., 98; *Ch-26* TROM.

39   Letourneau and Letourneau, *Operation KE*, 98–9.

40   *Toa Maru No. 2 Go*, TROM; Letourneau and Letourneau, *Operation KE*, 165.

41   *Toa Maru No. 2 Go*, TROM.

42   Letourneau and Letourneau, *Operation KE*, 165.

43   Ibid., 165.

44   Day, *New Georgia*, 520; Letourneau and Letourneau, *Operation KE*, 165; Walter Lord, *Lonely Vigil: Coastwatchers of the Solomons* (New York: Open Road, 1977), Kindle edition, 143.

45   Day, *New Georgia*, 520.

46   *Toa Maru No. 2 Go* TROM; Letourneau and Letourneau, *Operation KE*, 165.

47   Letourneau and Letourneau, *Operation KE*, 166–7. Letourneau and Letourneau identify the subchaser that escorted the *Toa Maru No. 2* as *Ch-30*, coming out from Shortland with the transport on January 30, citing the *Ch-30*'s TROM as a source. The TROMs of both *Ch-23* and *Toa Maru No. 2* make clear that the *Ch-23* was with the transport beginning with her departure from Rabaul on January 28 all the way to her demise on January 30. The *Toa Maru No. 2*'s TROM suggests she didn't even stop in the Shortlands, which would be a bit unusual. The *Ch-30*'s TROM makes no reference to escorting the *Toa Maru No. 2* at this time. And while the *Ch-30*'s TROM has enough uncertainty to leave room for her to have joined the *Toa Maru No. 2*'s convoy as Letourneau and Letourneau allege, the accounts of sightings of and attacks on the convoy reference only two escorts.

48   Ibid., 168–71.

49   Iwabuchi Sanji would be heard from again, but, arguably, his sanity died with the *Kirishima*. Promoted to Rear Admiral in 1943, Iwabuchi Sanji would eventually command 31st Naval Special Base Force in Manila, consisting of some 15,000 naval troops and 4,000 army troops. After the American invasion of Luzon, in an effort to consolidate his forces and to avoid civilian casualties, the Japanese commander in the Philippines, Lieutenant General Yamashita Tomoyuki (who had commanded the conquest of Malaya and Singapore in 1942), gave Iwabuchi a direct order to evacuate Manila without a fight. Iwabuchi refused on multiple occasions, citing his shame at having lost the *Kirishima* and his belief he could redeem himself only by holding his position to the death. Iwabuchi had his units entrench in the old walled portion of Manila called Intramuros, especially Fort Santiago. During lulls in the brutal urban combat, Iwabuchi's troops committed violent mutilations, rapes, and murders against the civilian population in what has become known as the

"Manila Massacre." Estimates of civilian deaths range from 100,000 to 500,000. Almost all of Iwabuchi's troops were killed in the combat. Iwabuchi himself is believed to have committed suicide on February 25, 1945, but his body was never recovered.

50 *Toa Maru No. 2* TROM; Letourneau and Letourneau, *Operation KE*, 172–3; "Toa Maru No. 2 Go (Toa Maru)," *Pacific Wrecks* (www.pacificwrecks.com). Subsequent dives on the wreck of the *Toa Maru No. 2* revealed evidence of only one bomb hit on the transport, that on the port side amidships.

51 Letourneau and Letourneau, *Operation KE*, 172–3; Lord, *Lonely Vigil*, 143; "Toa Maru No. 2 Go (Toa Maru)." Even now, the *Toa Maru No. 2*'s luck has not completely abandoned her. Her wreck is a very popular diving site and in 2011 was named as one of the top 20 wreck dives in the world by *Diver Magazine*. Kaj Metz, "Shipwreck 'Toa Maru No.2,'" *Traces of War* (www.tracesofwar.com).

52 Day, *New Georgia*, 905–25.

53 Ibid., 944; *Kirikawa Maru* TROM.

54 *Kirikawa Maru* TROM.

55 Ibid.

56 *W-22* TROM. *W-22* seems to have been slightly east or southeast of the position of the air attack, suggesting she was left behind. *Ch-26* is not mentioned in connection with this submarine attack.

57 *W-22* TROM.

58 Day, *New Georgia*, 947.

59 Ibid., 962.

60 Morison, *Bismarcks Barrier*, 107.

61 Ibid., 107; O'Hara, *US Navy*, 3689.

62 Ed Howard, "The Oil Slick In Blackett Strait," *U.S. Submarines Lost In WWII* (www.subsowespac.org).

63 Ibid.

64 Day, *New Georgia*, 1006.

65 16.15 seconds, to be exact, with 6-inch guns elevated 6 degrees 39 minutes. Kilpatrick, *Night Battles*, 176.

66 O'Hara, *US Navy*, 3705.

67 Kilpatrick, *Night Battles*, 174.

68 Ibid., 175.

69 O'Hara, *US Navy*, 3689.

70 Kilpatrick, *Night Battles*, 175.

71 Ibid., 175.

72 O'Hara, *US Navy*, 3703.

73 Ibid., 3689–705.

74 Kilpatrick, *Night Battles*, 176.

75 *Waller* DANFS.

76 Kilpatrick, *Night Battles*, 176. The idea of the torpedo hitting the aft magazine is a deduction from the large number of survivors from the area of the *Murasame*'s bridge, including Captain Tachibana, Lieutenant Commander Tanegashima, and Lieutenant Kayama, of only 53 survivors. The bridge is close to the forward 5-inch mount beneath which is the magazine or "handling room." Though much further away than on some US destroyers, the bridge would have suffered significant casualties if the forward magazine had detonated. There were two 5-inch mounts near the stern, one single and the other dual. The *Murasame* took 128 down with her. By comparison, the *Minegumo* lost 46, including skipper Lieutenant Commander Uesugi, and, despite being further out to sea, had 124 survivors, two of whom were captured. *Murasame* and *Minegumo* TROMs.

77 Day, *New Georgia*, 996–1013.

78 USSBS Interrogation of Lieutenant Commander Tokuno Hiroshi.

79 Day, *New Georgia*, 1013.

80 Prados, *Islands of Destiny*, 243.

81 O'Hara, *US Navy*, 3723.

82 Ibid., 3723.

83 USSBS Interrogation of Lieutenant Commander Tokuno Hiroshi.

84 *Murasame* and *Minegumo* TROMs.

85 Task Force 63 War Diary.

86 Hara, *Japanese Destroyer Captain*, 164.

87 O'Hara, *US Navy*, 3731.

BIBLIOGRAPHY

Books and articles

Agawa, Hiroyuki, *The Reluctant Admiral: Yamamoto and the Imperial Navy* (Tokyo; New York: Kodansha, 1979)

Bergerud, Eric M., *Fire in The Sky: The Air War in the South Pacific* (Boulder, CO: Westview Press, 2000 – Kindle edition)

Blair, Clay, Jr., *Silent Victory: The US Submarine War Against Japan* (Annapolis: Naval Institute Press, 1975)

Borneman, Walter R., *The Admirals: Nimitz, Halsey, Leahy, and King – The Five-Star Admirals Who Won the War at Sea* (New York; Boston; London: Little, Brown, and Company, 2012)

Bradley, Phillip, *To Salamaua* (Cambridge: Cambridge University Press, 2010 – Kindle edition)

Buell, Thomas B., *Master of Seapower: A Biography of Fleet Admiral Ernest J. King* (Annapolis: Naval Institute Press, 1980 – Kindle edition)

Bulkley, Captain Robert J., Jr., USNR (Ret.), *At Close Quarters: PT Boats in the United States Navy* (Washington: Naval History Division, 1962)

Burton, John, *Fortnight of Infamy: The Collapse of Allied Airpower West of Pearl Harbor* (Annapolis: Naval Institute Press, 2006)

Byrd, Martha, *Kenneth N. Walker: Airpower's Untempered Crusader* (Maxwell Air Force Base, AL: Air University Press, 1997)

Caidin, Martin, *Fork-Tailed Devil: The P-38* (Dering Harbor, NY: iBooks, 2001 – Kindle edition)

Calhoun, C. Raymond, *Tin Can Sailor: Life Aboard the USS Sterett, 1939–1945* (Annapolis: Naval Institute Press, 1993 – Kindle edition)

Clemens, Martin, *Alone on Guadalcanal: A Coastwatcher's Story* (Annapolis: Naval Institute Press, 1998 – Kindle edition)

Cook, Haruko Taya, and Theodore F. Cook, *Japan at War: An Oral History* (New York: The New Press, 1992)

Craven, W.F., and J.L. Cate, (editors), *Army Air Forces in World War II*, Vol. IV: *The Pacific: Guadalcanal to Saipan August 1942 to July 1944* (Washington, DC: Office of Air Force History, 1983)

Crenshaw, Russell Sydnor, Jr., *South Pacific Destroyer: The Battle for the Solomons from Savo Island to Vella Gulf* (Annapolis: Naval Institute Press, 1998 – Kindle edition)

Crenshaw, Russell Sydnor, Jr., *The Battle of Tassafaronga* (Annapolis: Naval Institute Press, 1995 – Kindle edition)

Cressman, Robert J., *The Official Chronology of the U.S. Navy in World War II* (Washington, DC: Contemporary History Branch, Naval Historical Center, 1999)

Davis, Donald A., *Lightning Strike: The Secret Mission to Kill Admiral Yamamoto and Avenge Pearl Harbor* (New York: St. Martin's, 2005 – Kindle edition)

Day, Ronnie, *New Georgia: The Second Battle for the Solomons* (Bloomington, IN: Indiana University Press, 2016 – Kindle edition)

Dean, Peter J., *MacArthur's Coalition: US and Australian Operations in the Southwest Pacific Area, 1942–1945* (Lawrence: University of Kansas Press, 2018 – Kindle edition)

Dexter, David, *The New Guinea Offensives. Australia in the War of 1939–1945. Series 1 – Army. Volume 6* (Canberra: Australian War Memorial, 1961)

Domagalski, John J., *Lost at Guadalcanal: The Final Battles of the Astoria and Chicago as Described by Survivors and in Official Reports* (Jefferson, NC; London: MacFarland, 2010 – Kindle edition)

Dorny, Louis B., *US Navy PBY Catalina Units of the Pacific War* (Oxford: Osprey, 2013 – Kindle edition)

Dyer, Vice Admiral George Carroll, USN (Ret.), *The Amphibians Came to Conquer: The Story of Admiral Richmond Kelly Turner* (Washington, DC: US Government Printing Office, 1971)

Edwards, Paul M., *Between the Lines of World War II: Twenty-One Remarkable People and Events* (Jefferson, NC: McFarland, 2010 – Kindle edition)

Evans, David C. (ed.), *The Japanese Navy in World War II in the Words of Former Japanese Naval Officers* (Annapolis: Naval Institute Press, 1986, 2nd [Kindle] edition)

Foss, Col. Joe, USMC (Ret.), *Joe Foss: Flying Marine* (Pickle Partners Publishing, 2013 – Kindle edition)

Frank, Richard B., *Guadalcanal: The Definitive Account of the Landmark Battle* (New York: Penguin, 1992)

Gallant, T. Grady, *On Valor's Side: A Marine's Own Story of Parris Island and Guadalcanal* (New York: Doubleday, 1963 – Kindle edition)

Gamble, Bruce, *Fortress Rabaul: The Battle for the Southwest Pacific, January 1942–April 1943* (Zenith Press, 2013 – Kindle edition)

Gann, Maj. Timothy, USAF, *Fifth Air Force Light and Medium Bomber Operations During 1942 and 1943: Building Doctrine and Forces that Triumphed in the Battle of the Bismarck Sea and the Wewak Raid* (Maxwell AFB, AL: Air University Press, 1992)

Generous, William Thomas, Jr., *Sweet Pea at War: A History of USS Portland* (Lexington, KY: University Press of Kentucky, 2003)

George, Lt. Col. John B., *Shots Fired in Anger* (Buford, GA: Canton Street, 2012 – Kindle edition)

Gilbert, Gregory P., *The Battle of the Bismarck Sea, March 1943* (Canberra: The Air Power Development Centre, 2013)

Gillison, Douglas, *Australia in the War of 1939–1945: Series Three (Air) Volume I – Royal Australian Air Force, 1939–1942* (Canberra: Australian War Memorial, 1962)

Grace, James W., *The Naval Battle of Guadalcanal: Night Action 13 November 1942* (Annapolis: Naval Institute Press, 1999)

Griffith, Brigadier General Samuel B., USMC (Ret.), *The Battle for Guadalcanal* (Toronto; New York; London; Sydney: Bantam, 1980)

Gunn, Nathaniel, *Pappy Gunn* (Bloomington, IN: AuthorHouse, 2004)

Halsey, Fleet Admiral William F., USN, *Admiral Halsey's Story* (Pickle Partners Publishing, 2013 – Kindle edition)

Hammel, Eric, *Air War Pacific Chronology: America's Air War Against Japan in East Asia and the Pacific 1941–1945* (Pacifica, CA: Pacifica Military History, 1998 – Kindle edition)

Hammel, Eric, *Carrier Strike: The Battle of the Santa Cruz Islands October 1942* (Pacifica, CA: Pacifica Military History, 1999 – Kindle edition)

Hammel, Eric, *Coral and Blood* (Pacifica, CA: Pacifica Military History, 2009 – Kindle edition)

Hammel, Eric, *Guadalcanal: Decision at Sea: The Naval Battle of Guadalcanal November 13–15, 1942* (Pacifica, CA: Pacifica Military History, 1988 – Kindle edition)

Hammel, Eric, *Guadalcanal: Starvation Island* (Pacifica, CA: Pacifica Military History, 1987 – Kindle edition)

Hara, Tameichi, Fred Saito, and Roger Pineau, *Japanese Destroyer Captain: Pearl Harbor, Guadalcanal, Midway – The Great Naval Battles as Seen Through Japanese Eyes* (Annapolis: Naval Institute Press, 1967 – Kindle edition)

Hashimoto, Lieutenant Commander Mochitsura, *Sunk: The Story of the Japanese Submarine Fleet 1941–1945* (Pickle Partners Publishing, 2015 – Kindle edition)

Hata, Ikuhiko, Yasuho Izawa, and Christopher Shores, *Japanese Naval Air Force Fighter Units and Their Aces* (London: Grub Street, 2011 – Kindle edition)

Hickey, Lawrence J., *Ken's Men Against the Empire: The Illustrated History of the 43rd Bombardment Group During World War II, Volume I: Prewar to October 1943 The B-17 Era* (Boulder, CO: International Historical Research Associates, 2016)

Hornfischer, James D., *Neptune's Inferno: The US Navy at Guadalcanal* (New York: Bantam, 2011 – Kindle edition)

Hough, Lieutenant Colonel Frank O., USMCR, Major Verle E. Ludwig, USMC, and Henry I. Shaw, Jr., *History of U.S. Marine Corps Operations in World War II, Volume I: Pearl Harbor to Guadalcanal* (Washington, DC: Historical Branch, G-3 Division, Headquarters, US Marine Corps, 1958)

Howarth, Stephen, *The Fighting Ships of the Rising Sun: The Drama of the Imperial Japanese Navy 1895–1945* (New York: Atheneum, 1983)

Hoyt, Edwin P., *How They Won the War in the Pacific: Nimitz and His Admirals* (Guilford, CN: Lyons Press, 2012 – Kindle edition)

Hughes, Thomas Alexander, *Admiral Bill Halsey: A Naval Life* (Cambridge, MA: Harvard University Press, 2016)

Intelligence Office of Assistant Chief of Air Staff, *Wings At War Commemorative Edition Pacific Counterblow: The 11th Bombardment Group and The 67th Fighter Squadron in the Battle For Guadalcanal* (Washington, DC: Center for Air Force History, 1992)

Jersey, Stanley Coleman, *Hell's Islands: The Untold Story of Guadalcanal* (College Station, TX: Texas A&M University Press, 2008 – Kindle edition)

Johnson, William Bruce, *The Pacific Campaign in World War II: From Pearl Harbor to Guadalcanal* (London; New York: Routledge, 2006 – Kindle edition)

Kenney, General George C., *General Kenney Reports: A Personal History of the Pacific War* (New York: Duell, Sloan and Pearce, 1949 [Reprint 1997])

Kenney, General George C., *The Saga of Pappy Gunn* (Sapere Books, 2017 – Kindle edition)

Kilpatrick, C.W., *The Night Naval Battles in the Solomons* (Pompano Beach, FL: Exposition-Banner, 1987)

Kurzman, Dan, *Left to Die: The Tragedy of the USS* Juneau (New York: Pocket Books, 1994)

Lacroix, Eric, and Linton Wells II, *Japanese Cruisers of the Pacific War* (Annapolis: Naval Institute Press, 1997)

Leckie, Robert, *Challenge for the Pacific – Guadalcanal: The Turning Point of the War* (New York: Bantam, 1965 – Kindle edition)

Letorneau, Roger, and Dennis Letorneau, *Operation KE: The Cactus Air Force and the Japanese Withdrawal from Guadalcanal* (Annapolis: Naval Institute Press, 2012 – Kindle edition)

Listemann, Phil H., *The Douglas Boston & Havoc: the Australians. (Squadrons No. 22)* (Philedition, 2017 – Kindle edition)

Lord, Walter, *Lonely Vigil: Coastwatchers of the Solomons* (New York: Open Road, 1977 – Kindle edition)

Lundstrom, John B., *Black Shoe Carrier Admiral: Frank Jack Fletcher at Coral Sea, Midway, and Guadalcanal* (Annapolis: Naval Institute Press, 2006)

Lundstrom, John B., *The First Team and the Guadalcanal Campaign: Naval Fighter Combat from August to November 1942* (Annapolis: Naval Institute Press, 1994 – Kindle edition)

Manchester, William, *American Caesar: Douglas MacArthur1880–1964* (New York: Back Bay Books, 1978 – Kindle edition)

Manchester, William, *Goodbye, Darkness: A Memoir of the Pacific War* (New York: Back Bay Books, 1979 – Kindle edition)

Matloff, Maurice, and Edwin M. Snell, *United States Army in World War II: The War Department, Volume III: Strategic Planning for Coalition Warfare 1941–1942* (Washington: Office of the Chief of Military History, Department of the Army, 1953)

McAulay, Lex, *The Battle of the Bismarck Sea 3 March 1943* (Maryborough, Qld: Banner Books, 2008 – Kindle edition)

Miller, Thomas G., *The Cactus Air Force* (New York: Bantam, 1981)

Miller, Vernon J., *Japanese Submarine Losses to Allied Submarines in World War 2* (Bennington, VT: Merriam, 1988 – Kindle edition)

Moore, Stephen L., *The Battle for Hell's Island: How a Small Band of Carrier Dive Bombers Helped Save Guadalcanal* (New York: New American Library, 2015 – Kindle edition)

Morison, Samuel Eliot, *History of United States Naval Operations in World War II, Vol V: The Struggle for Guadalcanal August 1942–February 1943* (Edison, NJ: Castle, 1949)

Morison, Samuel Eliot, *History of United States Naval Operations in World War II, Vol VI: Breaking the Bismarcks Barrier 22 July 1942–1 May 1944* (Edison, NJ: Castle, 1950)

Morison, Samuel Eliot, *The Two-Ocean War: A Short History of the United States Navy in the Second World War* (Boston; Toronto; London: Little, Brown, and Company, 1963)

Morris, Lieutenant C.G., USNR, and Hugh B. Cave, *The Fightin'est Ship: The Story of the Cruiser Helena* (Holicong, PA: Wildside Press, 1944)

Morton, Louis, *United States Army in World War II The War in the Pacific Strategy and Command: The First Two Years* (Washington: Center of Military History, United States Army, 1962)

Murphy, Francis X., *Fighting Admiral: The Story of Dan Callaghan* (New York: Vantage Press, 1952)

Murphy, James T., and A.B. Feuer, *Skip Bombing* (Westport, CN: Praeger, 1993)

Murray, Williamson, and Allan R. Millett, *A War to be Won: Fighting the Second World War* (Cambridge, MA; London: Belknap Press of Harvard University Press, 2000 – Kindle edition)

Newpower, Anthony, *Iron Men and Tin Fish: The Race to Build a Better Torpedo During World War II* (Annapolis: Naval Institute Press, 2006)

O'Hara, Vincent P., *The US Navy Against the Axis: Surface Combat 1941–1945* (Annapolis: Naval Institute Press, 2007 – Kindle edition)

O'Kane, Rear Admiral Richard H., USN (Ret.), *Clear the Bridge!: The War Patrols of the USS Tang* (New York: Ballantine, 1977 – Kindle edition)

O'Kane, Rear Admiral Richard H., USN (Ret.), *Wahoo: The Patrols of America's Most Famous WWII Submarine* (New York: Presidio, 1987 – Kindle edition)

Office of Naval Intelligence ("ONI"), *United States Navy Combat Narrative: Battle of Tassafaronga, 30 November 1942 and Japanese Evacuation of Guadalcanal, 29 January–8 February 1943* (Washington, DC: Publications Branch, Office of Naval Intelligence, United States Navy, 1944)

Okumiya, Masatake, Jiro Horikoshi, and Martin Caidin, *Zero!* (Pickle Partners Publishing, 2014 – Kindle edition)

Peattie, Mark, *Sunburst: The Rise of Japanese Naval Air Power, 1909–1941* (Annapolis: Naval Institute Press, 2013)

Poor, Henry V., Henry A. Mustin, and Colin G. Jameson, *United States Navy Combat Narrative: The Battles of Cape Esperance, 11 October 1942 and Santa Cruz Islands, 26 October 1942* (Washington, DC: Publications Branch, Office of Naval Intelligence, United States Navy, 1943)

Potter, E.B., *Nimitz* (Annapolis: Naval Institute Press, 1976 – Kindle edition)

Prados, John, *Combined Fleet Decoded: The Secret History of American Intelligence and the Japanese Navy in World War II* (Annapolis: Naval Institute Press, 1995)

Prados, John, *Islands of Destiny: The Solomons Campaign and the Eclipse of the Rising Sun* (New York: NAL Caliber, 2012 – Kindle edition)

Prange, Gordon, *At Dawn We Slept: The Untold Story of Pearl Harbor* (New York: Penguin, 1981)

Pratt, Fletcher, *The Navy's War* (New York; London: Harper, 1944)

Rems, Alan, *South Pacific Cauldron: World War II's Great Forgotten Battlegrounds* (Annapolis: Naval Institute Press, 2014 – Kindle edition)

Rodman, Capt. Matthew K., *A War of Their Own: Bombers over the Southwest Pacific* (Maxwell AFB, AL: Air University Press, 2005)

Rose, Lisle A., *The Ship That Held the Line: The USS* Hornet *and the First Year of the Pacific War* (Annapolis: Naval Institute Press, 1995 – Kindle edition)

Ross, J.M.S., *Official History of New Zealand in the Second World War 1939–45: Royal New Zealand Air Force* (Wellington: War History Branch, Department of Internal Affairs, 1955)

Rottman, Gordon L., *Japanese Army in World War II: The South Pacific and New Guinea, 1942–43* (Oxford and New York: Osprey, 2005)

Salecker, Gene Eric, *Fortress Against The Sun: The B-17 Flying Fortress in the Pacific* (Conshocken, PA: Combined Publishing, 2001 – Kindle edition)

Sherrod, Robert, *History of Marine Corps Aviation in World War II* (Washington, DC: Combat Forces Press, 1952)

Shores, Christopher, Brian Cull, and Yasuho Izawa, *Bloody Shambles, Vol. 2: From the Defence of Sumatra to the Fall of Burma* (London: Grub Street, 1993)

Smith, George W., *The Do-Or-Die Men: The 1st Marine Raider Battalion at Guadalcanal* (New York: Pocket Books, 2003 – Kindle edition)

Smith, Michael S., *Bloody Ridge: The Battle That Saved Guadalcanal* (Novato, CA: Presidio, 2000 – Kindle edition)

Stafford, Commander Edward P., USN, *The Big "E"* (New York: Ballantine, 1962)

Stanaway, John, *P-38 Lightning Aces of the Pacific and CBI* (Oxford: Osprey, 1997 – Kindle edition)

Stille, Mark, *The Naval Battles for Guadalcanal 1942: Clash for Supremacy in the Pacific* (Oxford: Osprey, 2013)

Tagaya, Osamu, and Mark Styling, *Mitsubishi Type 1 Rikko "Betty" Units of World War 2* (Oxford: Osprey, 2001 – Kindle edition)

Tillman, Barrett, *Corsair: The F4U in World War II and Korea* (Annapolis: Naval Institute Press, 1979 – Kindle edition)

Tillman, Barrett, *Enterprise: America's Fightingest Ship and the Men Who Helped Win World War II* (New York: Simon & Schuster, 2012)

Tillman, Barrett, *US Marine Corps Fighter Squadrons of World War II* (Oxford, Osprey, 2014 – Kindle edition)

Toland, John, *The Rising Sun: The Decline and Fall of the Japanese Empire 1936–1945* (New York: Random House, 1970 – Kindle edition)

Tuohy, William, *America's Fighting Admirals: Winning the War at Sea in World War II* (St. Paul, MN: Zenith Press, 2007 – Kindle edition)

Twining, Lieutenant General Merrill B., USMC (Ret.), *No Bended Knee: The Battle for Guadalcanal* (New York: Presidio, 1996 – Kindle edition)

Ugaki, Matome, Donald M. Goldstein, and Katherine V. Dillon, (ed.), *Fading Victory: The Diary of Admiral Matome Ugaki* (Pittsburgh: University of Pittsburgh Press, 1991)

Vandegrift, General Alexander A., USMC, and Robert B. Asprey, *Once A Marine: The Memoirs of General A.A. Vandegrift, USMC* (New York: W.W. Norton & Co., 1964)

Watson, Richard L., Jr. *The Fifth Air Force in the Huon Peninsula Campaign January to October 1943* (AAFRH-13) (Washington: AAF Historical Offices, Headquarters, Army Air Forces, 1946)

White, Alexander S., *Dauntless Marine: Joseph Sailer Jr., Dive-Bombing Ace of Guadalcanal* (Pacifica, CA: Pacifica Press, 1996)

Winton, John, *Ultra in the Pacific: How Breaking Japanese Codes & Ciphers Affected Naval Operations Against Japan* (London: Leo Cooper, 1993)

Wolf, William, *The 5th Fighter Command in World War II: Vol.1: Pearl Harbor to the Reduction of Rabaul* (Atglen, PA: Schiffer, 2011)

Wukovits, John, *Admiral "Bull" Halsey: The Life and Wars of the Navy's Most Controversial Commander* (New York: St. Martin's Press; 2010 – Kindle edition)

Yoshihara, Kane, and Doris Heath (trans.), *Southern Cross* (Canberra: Australia-Japan Research Project, Australian War Memorial, 1955)

Zimmerman, Major John L., USMCR, *The Guadalcanal Campaign: Marines in World War II Historical Monograph* (Washington, DC: Historical Section, Division of Public Information, Headquarters, US Marine Corps, 1949)

Primary sources

Baldwin, Hanson W., "US Hold in Solomons Bolstered," *New York Times*, 11/3/1942, 4

Bates, Richard W. (1950) "The Battle of Savo Island, August 9, 1942. Strategical and Tactical Analysis. Part I" (PDF). Naval War College. Archived (PDF) from the original on August 24, 2006. Retrieved August 11, 2006

Bureau of Ships, Navy Department, "Catalogue of Naval Electronic Equipment," NavShips 900, 116 (April 1946) (available from *The Historic Naval Ships Association* [www.hnsa.org])

McCandless, Rear Admiral Bruce, "The San Francisco Story," *Proceedings*, Vol. 84/11/669 (Nov. 1958)

INTERROGATION NAV NO. 13, USSBS NO. 96, Interrogation of: Captain Watanabe Yasuji, 15 October 1945

INTERROGATION NAV NO. 60, USSBS NO. 252, Interrogation of: Captain Toyama Yasumi, 1 November 1945

St. Louis Post-Dispatch, "Bridge Blown to Pieces in Battle In Which Admiral Scott Died; Graphic Account by Captain of Lost Cruiser of Engagement Off Solomon Islands Early This Month," November 30, 1942, p. 5C

"U.S.S. CHICAGO (CA29) Loss in Action 29–30 January, 1943 Guadalcanal Island" (*Chicago* Loss Report)

Online sources

Camp, Dick, "Star-Crossed Translator," Leatherneck, Military.com (www.historynet.com/star-crossed-translator), retrieved February 14, 2017

Czarnecki, Joseph, "Turboelectric Drive in American Capital Ships," *NavWeaps* (www.navweaps.com/index_tech/tech-038), retrieved March 3, 2017

Del Gasche, "While Some Complained About Rationing … Our Hearts Bled for Them!" *Fighting 69th Infantry Division Association, Inc. Bulletin,* Vol. 53, No. 3 (May–August 2000) 18–23, 19 (Original in *Farmland News* (9/7/1999)) www.69th-infantry-division.com/pdf/USArmy69InfDiv_Vol53_No3_MayAug2000

Domagalski, John, "Battle of Rennell Island: A Fiery End for the USS Chicago," Warfare History Network September 7, 2016, www.warfarehistorynetwork.com/daily/wwii/battle-of-rennell-island-a-fiery-end-for-the-uss-chicago

Geddes, Eric, "Sole Survivor of WWII RAAF Aircrew Wins Fight to Erase Historic Slur Over Savo Island Bloodbath" – ABC News (Australian Broadcasting Corporation) by Adam Harvey, October 28, 2014 09:18:21 *Pacific War of WW2* The Battle of Savo Island – August 9, 1942 (www.ww2pacific.com/hudsonrep.html), retrieved February 21, 2017

Gregory, Mackenzie J., "H.M.A.S. Canberra and the Battle of Savo Island" Ahoy – Mac's Web Log – Naval, Maritime, Australian History and more (http://www.ahoy.tk-jk.net/Savo/Savo11HepburnsConclusions.html), retrieved January 19, 2016

Jersey, Stan, "The Mysterious Mr. Moto on Guadalcanal," *Pacific Wrecks* (http://www.pacificwrecks.com/people/veterans/ishimoto/index.html), retrieved February 13, 2017

Lundgren, Robert, "The Battleship Action 14–15 November 1942," *NavWeaps* (http://navweaps.com/index_lundgren/Battleship_Action_Guadalcanal.pdf), retrieved March 5, 2010

Lundgren, Robert, "*Kirishima* Damage Analysis," *NavWeaps* (http://navweaps.com/index_lundgren/kirishimaDamageAnalysis.php), retrieved September 28, 2010

Lundgren, Robert, "Internal Diagrams of Battleship *Kirishima*," *NavWeaps* (http://www.navweaps.com/index_lundgren/Kirishima_Internal_Diagrams.pdf), retrieved 2009

Lundgren, Robert, "*USS South Dakota* Damage Analysis," *NavWeaps* (www.navweaps.com/index_lundgren/South_Dakota_Damage_Analysis.php), retrieved October 3, 2010

New Zealand History, Royal NZ Navy's Bird-class ships. Page 4 – Moa and Kiwi bag a sub, www.nzhistory.govt.nz/war/bird-class-minesweepers/moa-and-kiwi-bag-a-sub

New Zealand Electronic Text Collection, The Pacific: I: The Navy in the Solomons, http://nzetc.victoria.ac.nz/tm/scholarly/tei-WH2Paci-_N85673.html

Warships Associated with World War II in the Pacific – USS *North Carolina* (https://www.nps.gov/parkhistory/online_books/butowsky1/northcarolina.html), retrieved February 27, 2017

Periodicals

Blee, Ben W., Capt USN, "Whodunnit?" *Proceedings of the US Naval Institute*, July 1982, 108 (7/953)

Hone, Thomas C., "The Similarity of Past and Present Standoff Threats," *Proceedings of the U.S. Naval Institute*, Annapolis, Maryland (Vol. 107, No. 9, September 1981), pp. 113–116

Rogers, Keith, "WWII Memories Remain Vivid for Navy Veteran, 91," *Las Vegas Review-Journal*, December 7, 2012

Smedberg, William R. III, VADM USN (Ret.), "As I Recall ... Sink the Wasp!" *Proceedings of the US Naval Institute*, July 1982.108 (7/953)

Wukovits, John, "Battle of Rennell Island: Setback in the Solomons," *World War II* magazine (March 2000), p. 2

Tabular Records of Movement ("TROMs") for Japanese ships mentioned in the text come from *the Imperial Japanese Navy Page*, www.combinedfleet.com, edited by Jonathan Parshall, Tony Tully, Bob Hackett, Allyn D.Nevitt, Sander Kingsepp, Peter Cundall, and Gilbert Casse

INDEX

Page numbers in **bold** refer to maps.